1915 1920 1925

1932
International Telecommunication
Convention becomes charter for
the merging International
Telegraph Union and the
Radiotelegraph Union.

1927
Radio Act of 1927 is passed.
Forms the five-member Federal
Radio Commission (FRC).

1927
Whitehurst v. *Grimes*
Federal control takes precendent
over state or local control of
license.

1933
Pote (Station WLOE) v. *FRC.*
FRC upheld in denial of license
transfer.

1922
First National Radio Conference
examines regulation and breakdown
of 1912 law.

1926
U.S. v. *Zenith Radio Corporation.*
1912 law is interpreted as
permitting stations to operate at
other frequencies beyond
restrictions of license.

1932
Trinity Methodist Church, South
v. *FRC.* Reverend Doctor Shuler's
ministry of the air ceases as
appeals court upholds FCC
denial of license.

1914
Amateur Radio Operators from
the American Radio Relay League
(A.R.R.L.). Later becomes active
in lobbying efforts against
government ownership of
broadcasting.

1924
Third National Radio Conference
convenes. Addresses the issue of
A.T.&T. involvement in
broadcasting and development
of networks.

1931
Court of Appeals rules in the
Brinkley case. *KFKB* v. *FCC.*
Dr. John Brinkley's over-the-air
prescriptions cease.

1925
Fourth National Radio Conference
convenes. Recommends system of
station classifications. Admonishes
Congress to pass legislation.

1923
Second National Radio Conference
convenes. Reaffirms problems of
interference and recommends
discretion in frequency allocations.

1931
Westinghouse v. *FRC.*
Public hearing required before
action can be taken against a
station. FRC checked in
regulatory powers.

1934
Communications Act of 1934 is
passed. Forms seven-member
Federal Communications
Commission (FCC).

1923
Hoover v. *Intercity Radio Co. Inc.*
Interprets 1912 law as requiring
Secretary of Commerce to issue
license to Intercity despite
crowded spectrum.

1931
Reading Broadcasting v. *FRC.*
Journal Co. v. *FRC.*
Broadcasters gain protection
against arbitrary action affecting
change of frequency, reduced
power, operating times.

1922–1923
National Association of
Broadcasters (NAB) is formed.

1929
NAB "Code of Ethics" and
"Commerical Standards" passed.

1933
FRC v. *Nelson Bros. Bond and
Mortgage Co.* Public interest
standard upheld by
U.S. Supreme Court.

1915 1920 1925 1930 1935

Broadcast Law and Regulation

John R. Bittner
The University of North Carolina at Chapel Hill

PRENTICE-HALL INC. Englewood Cliffs, New Jersey 07632

Library of Congress Cataloging in Publication Data

Bittner, John R.
  Broadcast law and regulation.

  Includes bibliographies and index.
  1. Broadcasting—Law and legislation—United States.
  2. Radio—Law and legislation—United States.
  3. Television—Law and legislation—United States.
  I. Title.
  KF2805.B58   343.73′0994   81-8701
  ISBN 0-13-083592-7   347.303994   AACR2

Editorial Production/Supervision
  and Interior Design: Barbara Kelly
Cover Design: Frederick Charles Ltd.
Manufacturing Buyer: Edmund W. Leone

© 1982 by Prentice-Hall, Inc., Englewood Cliffs, N.J. 07632

Printed in the United States of America

10 9 8 7 6 5 4 3

ISBN 0-13-083592-7

Prentice-Hall International, Inc., *London*
Prentice-Hall of Australia Pty. Limited, *Sydney*
Prentice-Hall of Canada, Ltd., *Toronto*
Prentice-Hall of India Private Limited, *New Delhi*
Prentice-Hall of Japan, Inc., *Tokyo*
Prentice-Hall of Southeast Asia Pte. Ltd., *Singapore*
Whitehall Books Limited, *Wellington, New Zealand*

for John Charles Bittner

a very special son

Contents

II programming and policy 109

CHAPTER 4 REGULATING ENTERTAINMENT AND POLITICAL PROGRAMMING 111

CHAPTER 5 THE FAIRNESS DOCTRINE 146

CHAPTER 6 THE BROADCAST PRESS 184

III   broadcast and cable operations   255

CHAPTER 8   THE STATION   257

CHAPTER 9 CABLE 290

IV citizens, self-regulation, and legislation 313 ⸻

CHAPTER 10 THE CITIZENS' MOVEMENT 315

CHAPTER 11 SELF-REGULATION AND ETHICS 352

Preface

Readers studying broadcast law outside the law school curriculum face the need for two perspectives: (1) that of the academician and legal scholar viewing the broader and vitally important policy issues and cases which are part of broadcast law, and (2) that of the broadcasting industry itself, which views broadcast regulation from the day-to-day operation of a broadcasting station. The purpose of this book is to provide a balance between these two perspectives; a balance which hopefully recognizes and respects the importance of each.

When used as a text, the classroom instructor retains the freedom to alter the balance in favor of one or the other approach through supplementary materials, class lectures, and discussions. At the same time, however, the student is assured of leaving the course with a comfortable awareness of both points of view.

The book is composed of five parts: (I) The Regulatory Framework; (II) Programming and Policy; (III) Broadcast and Cable Operations; (IV) Citizens, Self-Regulation, and Legislation; and (V) The Legal System and Legal Research.

Cases are the very foundation of the American system of jurisprudence, *stare decisis,* where judicial decisions become the core of interpreting the law. As a result, this book includes a number of important cases. For the most part, they appear at the end of each chapter, following a general discussion on the area of the law to which the decisions apply. Chapter end material is also complemented with FCC decisions, selected provisions of the Communications Act, FCC Rules, and, in some instances, policy positions.

Within this book, the reader will also find the various "forms" or samples of the "paper work" used in the broadcasting industry—forms which are an integral part of broadcast regulation. In some instances, the form itself is an excellent guide to understanding a specific law, rule, FCC decision, or case.

If papers are to be assigned, or if there is a major research emphasis in the course, the instructor may want to introduce chapter 13, "Understanding the Legal System and Legal Research," at a point earlier in the course, when students begin their research. Chapters 1 through 12 also contain sections titled "Questions for Discussion and Further Research," which serve to direct the reader's attention to important areas of inquiry.

At the end of each chapter are "Additional Resources," including books, articles, and, where appropriate, cases the reader can seek out to acquire a deeper understanding of the subject matter contained in the chapter.

Although this is a book on the subject of broadcast law and regulation, the important decisions that deal with the print media, and consequently affect broadcasting, are also an important part of the book.

A word of caution is due. Laws and regulations change rapidly. Moreover, no text can deal with every situation, every rule, or every law governing an industry. If the reader becomes involved in specific issues, he or she should always seek counsel skilled in communications law.

Finally, I hope that through this book the reader will acquire a familiarity that breeds respect for the legal system and an appreciation for the many fascinating realms of broadcast law. Knowing about broadcast law and regulation sharpens our expertise and better equips us to relate intelligently to the roles that radio and television play in our lives, no matter whether we are an aspiring industry professional, a future communications attorney, or a responsible consumer of broadcast communication in society.

J. R. B.
Chapel Hill, North Carolina

Acknowledgments

This book would not have been possible without the cooperation and understanding of the author's family, who provided undaunting support and encouragement, even though it was given, to a great extent, in the middle of their summer vacations.

As author, I am deeply indebted to the students in my courses at The University of North Carolina at Chapel Hill, and De Pauw University, and equally to the staff I had when serving as general manager of a broadcasting station and, prior to that, as a radio news director and television journalist. These acknowledgments can only begin to express my gratitude to those who have helped during the four years this book has been in preparation.

In addition, my colleagues, who have made suggestions and offered critiques and encouragement, have my warmest and sincere gratitude.

Professional associates in the broadcast industry and communication law have played a part in the book's development. Also, the people at the FCC were always generous with their time and information. At The University of North Carolina at Chapel Hill many people continue to add friendship and support. They include: Robert Allen, Ed Bliss, Elizabeth Czech, A. Richard Elam, Robert Gwyn, William Hardy, Hap Kindem, Paul Nickell, Kenneth Pauwels, Richard Settle, and Loy Singleton. At the heartbeat of an organization are the office and technical staffs and include Dot Stolle, Janet Edwards, Jan Carroll, Leslie Meeds, David Haynes, Ron Smith, Jim McCulloch, and Landon Whitt.

ACKNOWLEDGMENTS

A special acknowledgment is made to attorney Grainger R. Barrett of the Institute of Government at The University of North Carolina at Chapel Hill for providing important material on local ordinances for cable television.

In addition, deserving special mention are Beverly Whitaker-Long, Bill Chamberlin, and Tommi Jones.

Professional associations, such as the Broadcast Education Association; National Association of Broadcasters; National Cable Television Association; Radio-Television News Directors Association; American Women in Radio and Television; Women in Communications, Inc.; Speech Communication Association; Association for Education in Journalism; American Bar Association; International Communication Association; and the Society of Professional Journalists, Sigma Delta Chi; have all helped immeasurably through both their personnel, their publications, and in some cases, their legal staffs.

Few authors have the support and professional association of an organization of the caliber of Prentice-Hall, Inc. Especially important are Barbara Kelly, Steven Dalphin, Bruce Kennan, Bobbie Christenberry, Stan Wakefield, Ed Stanford, Robert S. Haltiwanger, Charles T. Briqueleur, Bill Wagstaff, and Michele Pattwell.

No one deserves more credit than Denise.
... and Stormy.

Introduction

The legal forces which have helped mold broadcast communication range from basic constitutional documents to obscure local ordinances. They range from major international treaties affecting satellite communication and multi-national networks, to agreements which guard against "electronic" border disputes.

The Limited Resource

Today, despite burgeoning technology, the control of broadcasting still centers around supply and demand. We know that if there is a great demand for a product and a shortage of that product, certain rules will evolve to avoid chaos. Imagine a group of children all wanting a piece of candy, with only half as many pieces of candy available as there are children. Who gets the candy? Perhaps the children who have perfect behavior records will get the candy. Perhaps only those who agree to share their candy with others will get candy. Perhaps those who eat responsibly and do not gobble the candy will be rewarded. Or perhaps only those who can afford to buy the candy will get some. Our example illustrates the need for controls, both to regulate the allocation of the product and to maintain order.

Now transpose our example to the allocation of frequencies on the electromagnetic spectrum. The spectrum has only so much space upon which people can operate radio and television stations. Consequently, this limitation has historically been the rationale behind much of broadcast regulation.

Mass Influence

The second important rationale has been broadcasting's influence on a large number of people. The citizens' band radio that sends out a 5-watt signal to a passing motorist has little impact on a "mass" audience. If the operator decides to sing songs into the microphone, tell a joke, or provide "smokey" reports, the chances are that the FCC will not be overly concerned. On the other hand, if a local television station decides to forego all its regular programming for a steady diet of test patterns, then the station will have a difficult time justifying its privilege to operate. The fact that broadcasting sends messages to the masses makes its impact on society considerable.

Proscriptive Versus Prescriptive Control

At this point you may say: "Fine, we set up certain rules, people follow the rules, and the system functions." Unfortunately, it's not that simple. Everyone from FCC commissioners to citizens' groups to broadcasters argue the legitimacy of the regulatory process. Part of the discussion centers around the legal philosophy upon which our society operates. Law in America, with its roots in much of seventeenth and eighteenth century Europe, places its faith in man's ability to reason as the safest basis for government.[1] The practical application of this philosophy is negative, or proscriptive, as opposed to positive, or prescriptive.[2] In other words, we forbid behavior which might harm us but do not necessarily require behavior that society determines is beneficial. We do not require the best behavior we are capable of or, to some degree, that is even socially desirable. By prohibiting antisocial behavior, we provide the widest latitude for personal choice, for individual liberty, and for freedom.[3]

From the standpoint of broadcasting, we can see the head of regulatory conflict beginning to protrude. Although we must control the allocation of frequencies on the electromagnetic spectrum, to control programming on those frequencies goes against traditional American legal philosophy.

The arguments run between two extremes. One point of view suggests a total lack of control. Herein supporters point out that the First Amendment assures free press and free speech. Some legal scholars suggest one freedom embodies the other.[4] Those arguing for total control make the assumptions that in broadcasting, a reliable basis exists for determining program quality, that we can determine the public interest of a single broadcast independent of all others, and that quality programs are available and will continue to be available if the government commands it.[5]

Compounding these issues is the fact we live at a time when new technology is expanding at such a rapid rate that the judicial system may not be able to cope with it. In a recent conversation among colleagues at a national meeting, we speculated on how our use of home computers interfaced with larger regional and national computers will make our use of "mass" media a self-determined "processing" experience, as opposed to a receive-only entertainment or information experience, typical of standard broadcast programming. We are rapidly moving into a telecommunication age, and it is incorporating our traditional view of broadcasting.

Whether these new "processing experiences" will be commonplace in the immediate future or will await more rational development over a period of several years is open to speculation. What is *not* open to speculation is the need to predict how law and policy will meet the future, whatever it may bring. Thus, while we will approach our study of broadcast regulation from such traditional perspectives as the limited resource of the electromagnetic spectrum and the mass influence that broadcasting enjoys, we should continue to keep alert to the new developments taking place beyond the pages of this book. Upon learning of new applications of technology—from two-way cable public opinion polling to the electronic newspapers of viewdata and teletext—we should ponder how future regulatory frameworks might be molded.

It is difficult to imagine what, if any, different language our forefathers would have written into the U.S. Constitution if they had known that slightly more than a hundred years later, a new technology would encompass the globe. Thus, legal scholars continue to argue about the influence that the Constitution has on the electromagnetic spectrum. It is in this context of guarding against censorship while trying to assure responsible use of the electromagnetic spectrum that we begin our discussion of broadcast law and regulation.

I

The Regulatory Framework

1

History *and* *Development*

For America in the late 1800s, thoughts of government regulation of communication centered around the telegraph. With a network of wires running across the United States, and the Atlantic Cable connecting North America with Europe, the attention was focused on the prosperity of the industrial revolution. But all this would soon change. Ushered in with the news that an Italian working with the support of the British government had sent wireless signals across the Atlantic, the twentieth century would prove to be an age of communication technology. Guglielmo Marconi, flying an antenna kite in December 1901, heard the crackle of the letter "S" resounding in his earphones at Signal Hill, Newfoundland. As he received the signals from the English coast, magazines and newspapers heralded the feat, and Marconi's name flashed across the same telegraph wires that his own accomplishments would someday make obsolete.

For Marconi, the experimental broadcast across the Atlantic was only the beginning. He was as much a businessman as an inventor, and as his empire began to stretch worldwide, it became a dominant force in the growing application of wireless to ship-to-shore communication.

In the United States and elsewhere, government attention turned to regulating wireless when the Marconi companies started to prohibit ships and shore stations from communicating with each other unless they were equipped with Marconi equipment. Germany was especially affected by Marconi's strategy, since it housed a competing Slaby-Arco wireless system. Finally the Germans took the initiative and in 1903 called a conference in Berlin, where a protocol

3

agreement was reached for international cooperation in wireless communication. Three years later, Berlin hosted the first International Radiotelegraph Convention, out of which an agreement was signed by twenty-seven nations. In the United States, the stage was now set for domestic legislation, which would embody the spirit of the Berlin agreement and foster safety and cooperation among American shipping interests.

The Wireless Ship Act of 1910

The year 1910 held few visions of commercial broadcasting stations as we know them today. Transatlantic experiments were less than a decade old, and Congress was only now thinking about safety applications of the new medium, especially for ships at sea. Some ships, but by no means all, had installed wireless apparatus. It was in this atmosphere that the Wireless Ship Act of 1910 was passed. Encompassing only four paragraphs, it set the stage for maritime communication:

> Be it enacted by the Senate and House of Representatives of the United States of America in Congress assembled, That from and after the first day of July, nineteen hundred and eleven, it shall be unlawful for any ocean-going steamer of the United States, or of any foreign country, carrying passengers and carrying fifty or more persons, including passengers and crew, to leave or attempt to leave any port of the United States unless such steamer shall be equipped with an efficient apparatus for radio-communication, in good working order, in charge of a person skilled in the use of such apparatus, which apparatus shall be capable of transmitting and receiving messages over a distance of at least one hundred miles, night or day: Provided, That the provisions of this act shall not apply to steamers plying only between ports less than two hundred miles apart.
>
> Sec. 2. That for the purpose of this act apparatus for radio-communication shall not be deemed to be efficient unless the company installing it shall contract in writing to exchange, and shall, in fact, exchange, as far as may be physically practicable, to be determined by the master of the vessel, messages with shore or ship stations using other systems of radio-communication.
>
> Sec. 3. That the master or other person being in charge of any such vessel which leaves or attempts to leave any port of the United States in violation of any of the provisions of this act shall, upon conviction, be fined in a sum not more than five thousand dollars, and any such fine shall be a lien upon such vessel, and such vessel may be libeled therefor in any district court of the United States within the jurisdiction of which such vessel shall arrive or depart, and the leaving or attempting to leave each and every port of the United States shall constitute a separate offense.
>
> Sec. 4. That the Secretary of Commerce and Labor shall make such regulations as may be necessary to secure the proper execution of this act by collectors of customs and other officers of the Government.[1]

The United States had its first instrument of broadcast regulation. It made no mention of anything resembling the pioneer stations, such as KDKA, WHA, or WWJ, that would follow ten years later. It also made no mention of the licenses, the definition of radio communication, or the wavelengths that would follow just two years later.

The Radio Act of 1912

By 1912, wireless had achieved international recognition and cooperation. Yet, the United States had been lax in these agreements, partially because wireless was not totally under government control as it was in some other countries. That all changed on an April night in 1912, when an iceberg took the ship *Titanic* to the bottom of the North Atlantic. The days and months to follow were filled with news of the sinking and of the role of wireless in the event. Reports centered on everything from the way wireless shipboard operators might have prevented the sinking to the brilliant role the medium played in relaying news of survivors.

One of the more famous figures of the day was a telegraph operator for the American Marconi Company. David Sarnoff had been assigned to the American Marconi shore station atop the John Wanamaker Department Store in New York City. When the luxury liner went down, the government-cleared airwaves were filled with communication of the rescue efforts, and David Sarnoff stayed at his post coordinating many of the efforts and collecting lists of survivors. He later became commerical manager of American Marconi. When American Marconi became part of RCA, David Sarnoff started up the executive ranks and eventually became President and Chairman of the Board of RCA.

Uncannily, four months before the tragedy, the provisions of the 1906 Berlin treaty had been taken out of congressional mothballs for discussion by committees of the Senate. Those discussions, spurred on by the sinking of the *Titanic,* prompted the August passage of the Radio Act of 1912. It read in part:

> Be it enacted by the Senate and House of Representatives of the United States of America in Congress assembled, That a person, company, or corporation within the jurisdiction of the United States shall not use or operate any apparatus for radio communication as a means of commercial intercourse among the several States, or with foreign nations, or upon any vessel of the United States engaged in interstate or foreign commerce, or for the transmission of radiograms or signals the effect of which extends beyond the jurisdiction of the State or Territory in which the same are made, or where interference would be caused thereby with the receipt of messages or signals from beyond the jurisdiction of the said State or Territory, except under and in accordance with a license, revocable for cause, in that behalf granted by the Secretary of Commerce and Labor upon application therefor; but nothing in this Act shall be construed to apply to the transmission and exchange of radiograms or signals between points situated in the same State: Provided, That the effect thereof shall not extend beyond the jurisdiction of the said State or interfere with the reception of radiograms or signals from beyond said jurisdiction; and a license shall not be required for the transmission or exchange of radiograms or signals by or on behalf of the Government of the United States, but every Government station on land or sea shall have special call letters designated and published in the list of radio stations of the United States by the Department of Commerce and Labor. Any person, company, or corporation that shall use or operate any apparatus for radio communication in violation of this section, or knowingly aid or abet another person, company, or corporation in so doing, shall be deemed guilty of a misdemeanor, and on conviction thereof shall be punished by a fine not exceeding five hundred dollars, and the apparatus or device so unlawfully used and operated may be adjudged forfeited to the United States.
>
> Sec. 2. That every such license shall be in such form as the Secretary of Commerce and Labor shall determine and shall contain the restrictions, pursuant to this Act, on and

5

subject to which the license is granted; that every such license shall be issued only to citizens of the United States or Puerto Rico or to a company incorporated under the laws of some State or Territory or of the United States or Puerto Rico, and shall specify the ownership and location of the station in which said apparatus shall be used and other particulars for its identification and to enable its range to be estimated; shall state the purpose of the station, and, in case of a station in actual operation at the date of passage of this Act, shall contain the statement that satisfactory proof has been furnished that it was actually operating on the above-mentioned date; shall state the wave length or the wave lengths authorized for use by the station for the prevention of interference and the hours for which the station is licensed for work; and shall not be construed to authorize the use of any apparatus for radio communication in any other station than that specified. Every such license shall be subject to the regulations contained herein, and such regulations as may be established from time to time by authority of this act or subsequent acts and treaties of the United States. Every such license shall provide that the President of the United States in time of war or public peril or disaster may cause the closing of any station for radio communication and the removal therefrom of all radio apparatus, or may authorize the use or control of any such station or apparatus by any department of the Government, upon just compensation to the owners.

Sec. 3. That every such apparatus shall at all times while in use and operation as aforesaid be in charge or under the supervision of a person or persons licensed for that purpose by the Secretary of Commerce and Labor. Every person so licensed who in the operation of any radio apparatus shall fail to observe and obey regulations contained in or made pursuant to this act or subsequent acts or treaties of the United States, or any one of them, or who shall fail to enforce obedience thereto by an unlicensed person while serving under his supervision, in addition to the punishments and penalties herein prescribed, may suffer the suspension of the said license for a period to be fixed by the Secretary of Commerce and Labor not exceeding one year. It shall be unlawful to employ any unlicensed person or for any unlicensed person to serve in charge or in supervision of the use and operation of such apparatus, and any person violating this provision shall be guilty of a misdemeanor, and on conviction thereof shall be punished by a fine of not more than one hundred dollars or imprisonment for not more than two months; or both, in the discretion of the court, for each and every such offense: Provided, That in case of emergency the Secretary of Commerce and Labor may authorize a collector of customs to issue a temporary permit, in lieu of a license, to the operator on a vessel subject to the radio ship act of June twenty-fourth, nineteen hundred and ten.

Sec. 4. That for the purpose of preventing or minimizing interference with communication between stations in which such apparatus is operated, to facilitate radio communication, and to further the prompt receipt of distress signals, said private and commercial stations shall be subject to the regulations of this section. These regulations shall be enforced by the Secretary of Commerce and Labor through the collectors of customs and other officers of the Government as other regulations herein provided for.

The Secretary of Commerce and Labor may, in his discretion, waive the provisions of any or all of these regulations when no interference of the character above mentioned can ensue.

The Secretary of Commerce and Labor may grant special temporary licenses to stations actually engaged in conducting experiments for the development of the science of radio communication, or the apparatus pertaining thereto, to carry on special tests, using any amount of power or any wave lengths, at such hours and under such conditions as will insure the least interference with the sending or receipt of commercial or Government radiograms, of distress signals and radiograms, or with the work of other stations.

In these regulations the naval and military stations shall be understood to be stations on land.²

Much more encompassing than the 1910 legislation, the 1912 Act provided for definitions of authority between federal and state governments and established call letters for government stations. Along with providing clauses for revoking a license and fines for violators, it also established the assignment of frequencies, stating that the license of the station would "state the wave length or the wave lengths authorized for use by the station for the prevention of interference and the hours for which the station is licensed to work;..." But in addition to these specified wave lengths, stations could still use "other sending wave lengths." The 1912 Act recognized the famous S-O-S distress signal, allowing it to be broadcast with a maximum of interference to override other stations. For the first time, the Act defined *radio communication* as: "any system of electrical communication by telegraphy or telephony without the aid of any wire connecting the points from and at which the radiograms, signals, or other communications are sent or received." Other provisions of the Act covered secrecy-of-messages restrictions to protect government stations' signals, rules for ship-to-shore communication, and a ban on stations refusing to receive messages from those which were not equipped with apparatus manufactured by a certain company.

Despite being particularly reactionary to the sinking of the *Titanic*, the 1912 Act was a valiant effort to control wireless communication. But few legislators could foresee the exploding growth that wireless would take, and, even if they had, the legislative processes could not begin to keep up with the new technology. It was not long before the regulatory framework began to crumble.

The National Radio Conferences: The 1912 Law in Trouble

Before long, the United States and radio were involved in World War I. For the U.S. Navy, it meant hurriedly constructed wireless towers on warships. Taking over the country's radio stations, the government put a lid on radio's development for anything but wartime service. But when the war ended, it was like uncapping a bottle. All the pent up enthusiasm was released, and new experimenters eagerly flocked to their equipment. Although the Radio Act of 1912 had survived the World War, it was headed for trouble in an exploding radio industry. By the 1920s, the chaos on the spectrum had mushroomed out of proportion. In 1922 alone, receiving set sales climbed 1,200 percent. The airwaves were flooded with everything from marine military operations to thousands of amateur radio experimenters. Added to this flood was the advent of commercial radio and its powerful stations booming onto the air. On February 27, 1922, groups of government officials, amateur radio operators, and commercial radio representatives met in Washington, D.C., for the First National Radio Conference.³ The Conference was addressed by representatives of all opposing factions. Amateur radio operators were afraid that their privileges were going to be trimmed under the influence of such large commercial firms as General Electric and Westinghouse; whereas the large commercial firms were afraid that their privileges were going to be relegated to the military. After the rhetoric subsided, the Conference split into three committees: amateur, technical, and legislative. Since interference was still the biggest problem, it was not surprising that the technical committee's recommendations received the most attention. Based on that report, legislation was introduced in Congress in 1923, but it never emerged from a Senate Committee.

The Second Conference began on March 20, 1923. This one reaffirmed the problems of interference and recommended discretion in frequency allocations. Taking into account the commercial interests of the new medium, the Conference suggested that allowing more stations on the air would only fragment an already shaky financial condition. By today's standards of competition among almost 8,000 stations, the proposal seems inappropriate. Realizing that different geographical areas had different problems, the Second Conference suggested splitting up the country into zones, with each zone tackling its individual problems on a local basis. As he had done with the First Conference, Representative Wallace White of Maine introduced legislation, which again did not budge out of congressional committees.

The deafening interference continued straight into the convening of the Third National Radio Conference, on October 6, 1924. Two major developments captured the attention of these delegates. Network broadcasting had become a reality. AT&T's wire system and Westinghouse's short-wave system were proving that interstation connection was not only possible but also cautiously successful. Almost simultaneously, David Sarnoff announced that RCA was going to experiment with the concept of superpower stations crisscrossing the country. It is little wonder the Third Conference recommended resolutions opposing monopoly and even encouraged government intervention. Nevertheless, the Conference supported the development of network broadcasting, and although agreeing to let the superpower experiments proceed, warned that they "should only be permitted under strict government scrutiny."[4] On a request from Secretary of Commerce Herbert Hoover, Representative White refrained from introducing legislation. A third defeat would have been bad politically, and the decision was made to wait until still another Conference was called.

Convening on November 11, 1925, the Fourth National Radio Conference resulted in proposals which later became the foundation of the Radio Act of 1927. This Conference suggested a system of station classifications and admonished Congress to pass some workable broadcasting legislation. The delegates recommended preventing monopoly, installing five-year terms for licenses, requiring stations to operate in the public interest, providing for licenses to be revoked, and giving the Secretary of Commerce the power to enforce regulations. Its participants tried to guard against government censorship of programming, provide for due process of law, give the President control of stations in wartime, and see to it that broadcasting not be thought of as a public utility. But their good intentions were too late.

Judicial Setbacks for the Radio Act of 1912

Despite the radio conferences' valiant efforts to make the 1912 law workable, two law suits and an opinion from the United States Attorney General soon made it clear that the law was in serious trouble. Highlighting the problem, in 1923, was

Hoover v. *Intercity Radio Co., Inc.*[5] Intercity had been engaged in telegraph communication between New York and other points under a license issued by the Secretary of Commerce and Labor. Upon expiration, Intercity applied for and was denied a renewal, because there was not enough space available on the spectrum for a frequency assignment that would not interfere with government and private stations.

The issue went to court, where the judges ruled that the Secretary had overstepped his bounds in refusing to renew Intercity's license. Cited as justification was a statement made by the chairman of the Committee on Commerce when the bill was passed to the effect that "it is compulsory with the Secretary of Commerce and Labor that upon application, these licenses shall be issued."

The interpretation meant that the Secretary of Commerce and Labor, although having the power to place restrictions on licenses and to prevent interference, could not refuse to issue a license as a means of curtailing that interference. The court stated: "In the present case, the duty of naming a wavelength is mandatory upon the Secretary. The only discretionary act is in selecting a wavelength within the limitations prescribed in the statute, which, in his judgment, will result in the least possible interference." The court went on to define the relationship between the restrictions and a license, stating: "The issuing of a license is not dependent upon the fixing of a wavelength. It is a restriction entering into the license. The wavelength named by the Secretary merely measures the extent of the privilege granted to the Licensee."

For the Secretary of Commerce and Labor, the ruling was extremely frustrating. Broadcasting was way beyond the experimental and military stages. The Secretary was faced with regulating a limited resource, and the court was telling him that he had to give some to everyone who wanted it. The Act had charged the Secretary with broad responsibilities, but the provisions of the Act did not give him the power to carry them out.

This was only the first of the Secretary's setbacks. Three years later came *United States* v. *Zenith Radio Corporation* et al.[6] Zenith had received a license which authorized it to operate on a wavelength of 332.4 meters on Thursday night from 10 to 12 P.M., "when the use of this period is not desired by the General Electric Company's Denver Station." Zenith clashed with the Secretary when it operated at other times and on another, unauthorized, frequency. Yet the court ruled in favor of Zenith. The legal catch: a section of the 1912 law reading: "In addition to normal sending wave length, all stations . . . may use other sending wave lengths: . . ."

The crowning blow came when Acting Secretary of Commerce Stephen Davis answered a request from the Chicago Federation of Labor.[7] The application itself had not even reached Washington before Davis wrote the Federation, telling them that all the wave lengths were in use, and that if the Federation constructed a station, there would be no license forthcoming. Davis put the blame on the Fourth National Radio Conference, where it certainly did not belong, since the Conference did not have the power to dictate policy. Some politicians began to be concerned, and as the situation grew worse and the stations continued to interfere with each other, the Office of the Secretary of Commerce sought an opinion from the Attorney General.

In a letter of June 4, 1926, the Secretary asked the Attorney General for a definition of power. The questions posed in the letter, as interpreted by the Attorney General were:

(1) Does the 1912 Act require broadcasting stations to obtain licenses, and is the operation of such a station without a license an offense under that Act?

(2) Has the Secretary of Commerce authority under the 1912 Act to assign wave lengths and times of operation and limit the power of stations?

(3) Has a station, whose license stipulates a wave length for its use, the right to use any other wave length, and if it does operate on a different wave length, is it in violation of the law and does it become subject to the penalties of the Act?

(4) If a station, whose license stipulates a period during which only the station may operate and limits its power, transmits at different times, or with excessive power, is it in violation of the Act, and does it become subject to the penalties of the Act?

(5) Has the Secretary of Commerce power to fix the duration of the licenses which he issues or should they be indeterminate, continuing in effect until revoked or until Congress otherwise provides?[8]

The Attorney General's answers made it clear that the problems were going to grow worse, not better. The answer to the first question was affirmative. The Act definitely provided for stations to be licensed, and stations operating without a license were clearly in violation. As to the second question, the Attorney General said that the Secretary had the right to assign a wave length to each station under one provision of the Act, but that, for the most part, the stations could use whatever other frequency they so desired, whenever they wanted. With the exception of two minor provisions, the Attorney General also stated that the Secretary had no power to designate hours of operation. Also lost was the argument over limiting power. The Act stated that stations should use the "minimum amount of energy necessary to carry out any communication desired." The Attorney General said: "It does not appear that the Secretary is given the power to determine in advance what this minimum amount should be for every case; and I therefore conclude that you have no authority to insert such a determination as a part of any license."

The third answer was obvious. Stations could use any other wavelength they desired. The Act and the courts had affirmed that point. That also answered the fourth question. Since the Secretary could not limit power or operating times beyond the actual license, stations were free to use other wavelengths with different power outputs and at different times than the license stated. The Attorney General said in answer to the fifth question that he could "find no authority in the Act for the issuance of licenses of limited duration."

Clearly, a law which only a decade earlier had seemed in firm control of the new medium was now almost worthless. Four months later, on December 7, 1926, President Coolidge sent a message to Congress. He called for legislation to remedy the chaotic situation that threatened to destroy radio broadcasting:

The Department of Commerce has for some years urgently presented the necessity for further legislation in order to protect radio listeners from interference between broadcasting stations and to carry out other regulatory functions. Both branches of Congress at the last session passed enactments intended to effect such regulation, but the two bills yet remain to be brought into agreement and final passage.

Due to decisions of the courts, the authority of the department under the law of 1912 has broken down; many more stations have been operating than can be accommodated within the limited number of wave lengths available; further stations are in course of construction; many stations have departed from the scheme of allocation set down by the department, and the whole service of this most important public function has drifted into such chaos as seems likely, if not remedied, to destroy its great value. I most urgently recommend that this legislation should be speedily enacted.

I do not believe it is desirable to set up further independent agencies in the Government. Rather I believe it advisable to entrust the important functions of deciding who shall exercise the privilege of radio transmission and under what conditions, the assigning of wave lengths and determination of power, to a board to be assembed whenever action on such questions becomes necessary. There should be right of appeal to the courts from the decisions of such board. The administration of the decisions of the board and the other features of regulation and promotion of radio in the public interest, together with scientific research, should remain in the Department of Commerce. Such an arrangement makes for more expert, more efficient, and more economical administration than an independent agency or board, whose duties, after initial stages, require but little attention, in which administrative functions are confused with semijudicial functions and from which of necessity there must be greatly increased personnel and expenditure.[9]

The next day, he signed a joint resolution of Congress stopping the further licensing of broadcasting stations until specific legislation could be passed.

The Radio Act of 1927

Congress had been working on the Radio Act of 1927 before Coolidge's message. The Act passed both houses of Congress and received the President's signature on February 23, 1927. The Radio Act of 1927 was administered by the Secretary of Commerce, and it provided for the formation of a Federal Radio Commission (FRC) to oversee broadcasting. The Act was intended to remain in force for only a year, but it was subsequently extended until 1934. With court decisions as guides, Congress did an admirable job of plugging the holes left by the 1912 law.

forming the federal radio commission

The most important provision of the 1927 Act was the formation of a Federal Radio Commission "composed of five commissioners appointed by the President, by and with the advice and consent of the Senate, and one of whom the President shall designate as chairman. . . ."[10] (Figure 1-1). The law specified that each commissioner must be a citizen of the United States and that each would receive compensation of $10,000 for the first year of service. The commissioner system, as well as many other provisions of the 1927 legislation, became part of the Communications Act of 1934.

The Federal Radio Commission was organized into a series of divisions and sections, a close examination of which provides us with an intriguing insight into the first real administrative effort to regulate radio broadcasting. At the head of the Federal Radio Commission were the Commissioners themselves, who were directly over the three divisions listed below.

FEDERAL RADIO COMMISSION

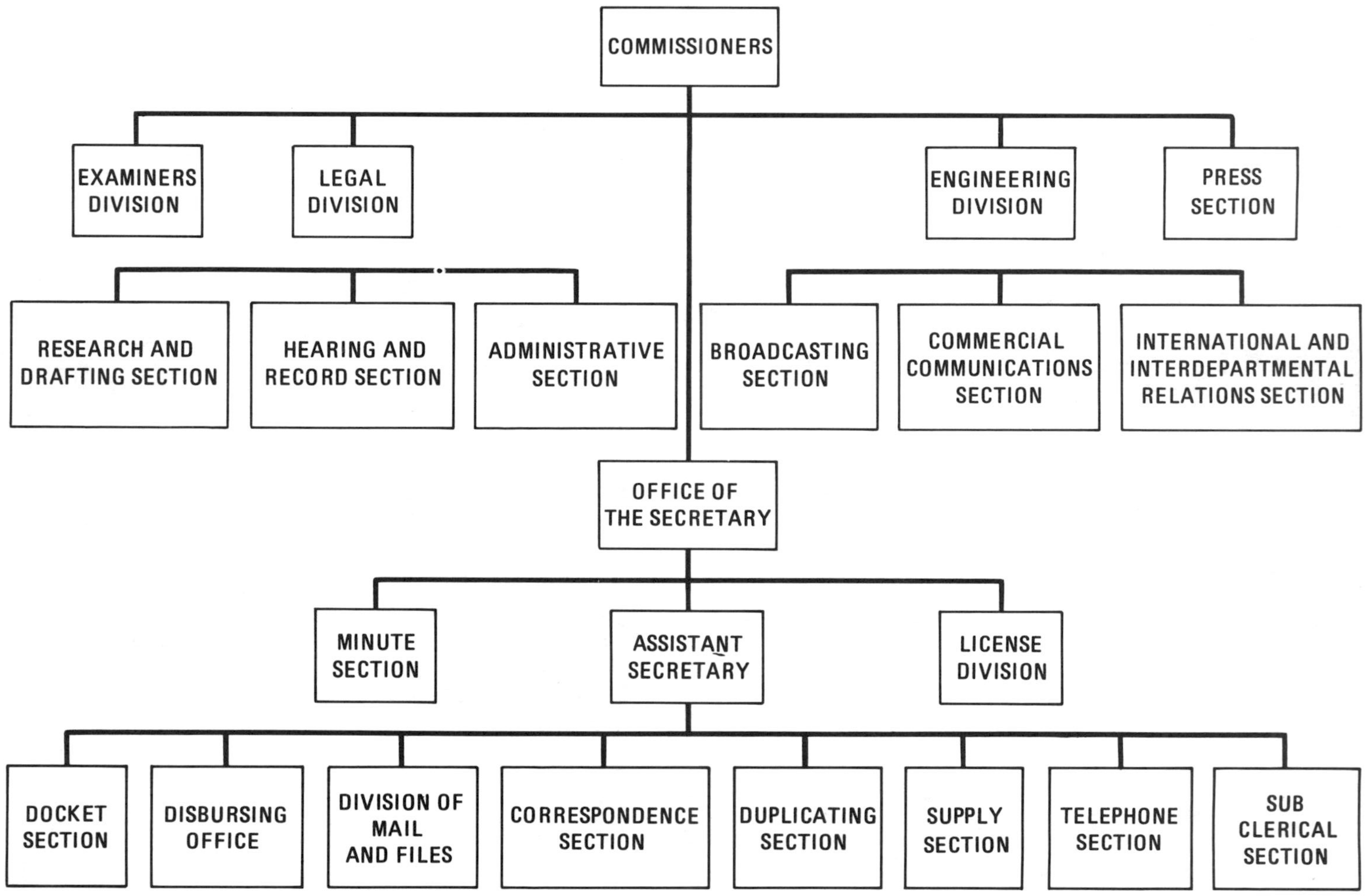

Figure 1-1

Examiners Division. The Examiners Division was supervised by a Chief Examiner. It was charged with the duties of hearing applicants on the applications for radio facilities that had been designated by the Commission for a hearing and of submitting written reports and recommendations thereon to the Commission.

Legal Division. The General Counsel was the chief legal adviser to the Commission and the head of the Legal Division.

Engineering Division. The Chief Engineer was the chief technical adviser of the Commission and head of the Engineering Division.

Press Section. The Press Section was responsible for the preparation and release of all press releases and for the distribution to the press of Commission orders, publications, etc. The head of the Section acted as the contact with the members of the press.

Research and Drafting Section. The Research and Drafting Section was supervised by an Assistant General Counsel and was responsible for the preparation for trial and the trial of cases in which the Commission was a party arising under the Radio Act of 1927, as amended; and for the drafting of decisions, orders, and rules; and for advising the Commission concerning legal phrases of international treaties and agreements.

Hearing and Record Section. The Hearing and Record Section was supervised by an Assistant General Counsel and was charged with the duty of representing the Commission at all formal hearings.

Administrative Section. The Administrative Section was supervised by an Assistant General Counsel and was responsible for the legal examination of all legal phrases relating to all applications for radio facilities; for the preparation of recommendations thereon to the Commission; and for investigating complaints of alleged violations of the Radio Act of 1927, as amended, and/or the rules and orders made thereunder.

Broadcasting Section. The Broadcasting Section was supervised by an Assistant Chief Engineer and was responsible for the technical examination of all matters relating to applications for radio broadcasting facilities (550 to 1500 kc); the preparation and presentation of expert testimony at formal hearings; the study and preparation of technical regulations; and the study and research needed to determine ways and means of making better use of the facilities available.

International and Interdepartmental Relations Section. The International and Interdepartmental Relations Section was supervised by an engineer and was charged with the duty of coordinating the international and interdepartmental relations of the Commission; making plans for United States participation in the organized preparatory work for international radio conferences and technical meetings; and advising the Commission concerning the technical and engineering phases of international treaties, agreements, etc.

Office of the Secretary. The Secretary was the Chief Administrative Officer of the Commission. Pursuant to Section 214 of the Act approved June 10, 1921,

(U.S.C. Title 31, Sec. 22), the Secretary was designated the Budget Officer of the Commission.

Minute Section.   The Minute Section was charged with the preparation and preservation of the minutes of Commission meetings.

Assistant Secretary.   The Assistant Secretary was charged with the immediate supervision and direction of the work in the Divisions and Sections here indicated and with acting for the Secretary in the latter's absence.

License Division.   The License Division was charged with the receipt of all applications for radio facilities, the administrative examination thereof, the maintenance of records showing Commission action thereon, and the issuance of licenses and orders in conformity therewith.

Docket Section.   The Docket Section was charged with the preparation of the Hearing Calendar, the publication of reports of Examiners, and the preparation of the dockets for Commission action.

Disbursing Office.   The Disbursing Office was charged with the disbursement of all moneys appropriated for use by the Commission and with the maintenance of fiscal control records.

Division of Mail and Files.   The Division of Mail and Files was the depository of all the files of the Commission (except technical files) and was charged with the receipt, recording, indexing, and classifying of all mail received by or sent out of the Commission.

Correspondence Section.   The Correspondence Section was charged with the receipt of all correspondence of a general character and with the preparation of replies thereto.

Duplicating Section.   The Duplicating Section was charged with the mimeograph, multigraph, and addressograph work of the Commission and with the preparation of such material for mailing.

Supply Section.   The Supply Section was charged with the procurement, storage, and issue of all supplies.

Telephone Section.   The Telephone Section was charged with the operation of the telephone switchboard and with the examination and audit of vouchers for telephone service.

Subclerical Section.   The Subclerical Section was charged with performance of miscellaneous custodial work.

provisions of the radio act of 1927

Other provisions in the 1927 Act included dividing the United States into zones represented by the individual commissioners. No more than one commissioner could be appointed from any one zone. Zone One encompassed New England and the upper tip of the Middle Atlantic states, including the District of Columbia, Puerto Rico, and the Virgin Islands. The second zone included the upper

Middle Atlantic states west to Michigan and Kentucky. The third zone encompassed the South, and the fourth and fifth zones the Great Plains and the West, respectively.

The Act provided for the licensing of stations, but only for a specified time, and gave the government considerable control over the electromagnetic spectrum. The Act also set out to define states' rights. Keep in mind that federal regulation over intrastate commerce, for which wireless was used, was not popular. So it was not surprising that the Radio Act of 1927 tried to avoid direct control of intrastate communication, while at the same time retaining control of communication across state borders. The Act stated that the law's jurisdiction would extend "within any State when the effects of such use extend beyond the borders of said State. . . ." The most quoted provision came from Section 4, with its statement that stations should operate "as public convenience, interest, or necessity requires. . . ."

Section 4 also prescribed the "nature of the service to be rendered by each class of licensed station and each station within any class." Control over frequency, power, and times of operation were covered by the Act, giving the FRC power to: "Assign bands or frequencies or wave lengths to the various classes of stations, and assign frequencies or wave lengths for each individual station and determine the power which each station shall use and the time during which it may operate." Coverage areas for stations were to be fixed by the FRC, and the Commission was to have power over "chain" or network broadcasting. Stations were also required to keep operating logs.

In addition to regulating the industry, the 1927 Act gave the Commission quasi-judicial powers, with the "authority to hold hearings, summon witnesses, administer oaths, compel the production of books, documents, and papers and to make such investigations as may be necessary in the performance of its duties." The Secretary of Commerce was empowered to "prescribe the qualifications of station operators, to classify them according to the duties to be performed, to fix the forms of such licenses, and to issue them to such persons as he finds qualified." The Secretary was also empowered to issue call letters to all stations and to "publish" the call letters. But, before issuing a license, the government made certain that the prospective licensee gave up all rights to the frequency. The applicant had to sign a "waiver of any claim to the use of any particular frequency or wave length. . . ." Once granted, station licenses were limited to a three-year duration.

Closing the wave length loophole of the 1912 legislation, the 1927 law stated that: "The station license shall not vest in the licensee any right to operate the station nor any right in the use of the frequencies or wave length designated in the license beyond the term thereof nor in any other manner than authorized therein." The Act also discouraged monopolies and prohibited the transfer of licenses without Commission approval. It also gave the Commission power to revoke licenses for "issuing false statements or failing to operate substantially as set forth in the license."

The wording for the famous Section 315 of the Communications Act of 1934 came from the 1927 legislation, with: "If any licensee shall permit any person who is a legally qualified candidate for any public office to use a broadcasting station, he shall afford equal opportunities to all other such candidates for that office. . . ." And commercial broadcasting gained instant recognition and regulation by the requirement that paid commercials were to be announced as paid or furnished by the sponsor.

Putting a station on the air was another important provision of the Act. As we'll see later in this chapter, this issue also arose in the appeals process. Specifically, the Act stated: "No license shall be issued under the authority of this Act for the operation of any station, the construction of which is begun or is continued after this Act takes effect, unless a permit for its construction has been granted by the licensing authority upon written application thereof." The law acknowledged that construction permits for stations would specify the "earliest and latest dates between which the actual operation of such station is expected to begin, and shall provide that said permit will be automatically forfeited if the station is not ready for operation within the time specified. . . ."

The anticensorship provision, later to become incorporated into Section 326 of the Communications Act of 1934, was also included. Ironically, that provision was immediately followed with: "No person within the jurisdiction of the United States shall utter any obscene, indecent, or profane language by means of radio communication."

We can immediately see the conflicts that could develop, not only between these two provisions but also in the "convenience, interest, and necessity" clause. And indeed, it was not very long before the broadcasters and the government were arguing. Yet, keep in mind that the 1927 law is the very foundation of contemporary broadcast regulation. It was simple and straightforward, and the courts gave it strong support.

Court Challenges to the Radio Act of 1927

It was only natural that the Radio Act of 1927 would be challenged with much the same ferocity, although not the same success, as the 1912 legislation. Don R. Le Duc and Thomas A. McCain examined the judicial processes that took place before the 1934 law went into effect. They concluded that the "federal judiciary, during the period in which it considered appeals from Federal Radio Commission decisions, generally supported the regulatory authority of the agency, and by providing such support, enhanced its ability to supervise the broadcasting industry."[11] Supervision of the industry was no small task. Because of the leniency of the 1912 legislation, it was necessary to trim the wings of some of the stations already on the air in order to return a semblance of stability to the industry.

The seriousness of each decision was embodied in the fact that federal judges had to distinguish between regulations on broadcasting stations serving the public and the traditional common carrier regulations that were more appropriate to public utilities. As Le Duc and McCain point out, unless a judge "could distinguish broadcast regulation from other types of government control, affirmance of the standard used by the FRC would allow all federal agencies much broader latitude in their regulatory functions."[12]

The authority of the FRC to refuse a license was first tested in the case of

Technical Radio Laboratory v. *FRC*.[13] Technical Radio Laboratory operated station WTRL in Midland Park, New Jersey, but was denied a license renewal by the FRC, since there simply were not enough frequencies available for every station that wanted on the air. The court affirmed the FRC's decision. Further legal support for this power was affirmed in the case of *Carrell* v. *FRC*, when the FRC was upheld in its decision not to renew the licenses of stations WKBG, WIBJ, and WHBM, all operated by Carrell.[14] The "public interest" concept of the 1927 law was to come under scrutiny by the courts in the case of *FRC* v. *Nelson Brothers Bond and Mortgage Co*.[15] The FRC had approved the application of station WJKS in Gary, Indiana, causing the termination of licenses for station WIBO, owned by Nelson Brothers, and station WPCC in Chicago. It is little wonder that the case went to court. The Circuit Court of Appeals overturned the FRC's decision, but the Supreme Court agreed to review the decision of the Appeals Court and ruled in favor of the FRC. The FRC gained more clout in the case of *Pote (Station WLOE)* v. *FRC*, when the FRC denied the transfer of the license for station WLOE from Boston Broadcasting to William Pote.[16]

One of the most sensitive areas of the new law was the concept of federal jurisdiction over intrastate commerce. The Radio Act of 1912 was weak in this regard, and although the Radio Act of 1927 tried to enact stronger measures, states' rights were nothing to tamper with. For this reason, the broadcasters found themselves confronted with licenses both at the federal and at the municipal levels. Brought to the court's attention in *Whitehurst* v. *Grimes, Chief of Police,* et al.[17] the case arose when amateur radio station 9ALM was charged a local license tax by the city of Lexington, Kentucky. The tax came under a city ordinance, but a judge ruled that 9ALM's *federal* license preempted local control, due to the station's effect on interstate communication.

The law was further broadened in the case of *United States* v. *Gregg* et al.,[18] when the court said that "even an *unlicensed* party whose signal was admittedly only intrastate in range would come within the purview of federal control because . . . any signal on a channel within the spectrum of frequencies requiring federal licensing would have an 'effect' upon interstate communication."[19] The decision stopped an unlicensed Houston, Texas station, "The Voice of Labor," from operating without a license.

Although the FRC did receive its share of support, unleashed federal power could and would not go unchecked. A series of decisions trimmed the ability of the FRC to act without regard to the rights and due process of the people involved. When the FRC limited the broadcasting rights of Westinghouse, the case went to court in *Westinghouse Electric and Manufacturing Co.* v. *FRC*.[20] The FRC was held in error for not permitting Westinghouse a hearing before taking action against it. Nevertheless, the FRC still had the "public convenience, interest, and necessity" clause up its sleeve as a basis for waiving a *public* hearing whenever it deemed appropriate.[21]

As we mentioned earlier, broadcasters gained support in cases affecting the construction of new stations. The FRC was taken to court by a Richmond, Virginia firm that had applied to construct a station in Roanoke. In the case of *Richmond Development* v. *FRC,* the court recognized the right of the construction permit holder to challenge the FRC when the Commission refused to extend the time of the permit.[22] The court noted that the FRC knew that Richmond Development might not be able to complete construction when the permit was issued.

Additional support for the broadcaster came in the cases of *Reading Broadcasting* v. *FRC* and *Journal Co.* v. *FRC*.[23] Each of these cases protected the broadcaster against arbitrary action affecting a change of frequency, reduction in power, or limitations in hours of operation when the stations could show that, over an extended period of time, they had operated in the public interest.

the brinkley and schuler cases

Just as the FRC was restrained from arbitrarily imposing restrictions on stations that could show good performance records, it was supported in refusing renewals to licensees who did not meet the "public convenience, interest, and necessity." Such power was of concern, since, theoretically, to deny a license for material used on the station could be construed as an infringement of First Amendment rights of free speech. In the case of *KFKB Broadcasting* v. *FRC,* the FRC denied the renewal of station KFKB.[24] Among other items, the station had broadcast programs by Dr. John R. Brinkley, during which Dr. Brinkley prescribed medicine for patients who wrote him or the station about their problems. The prescriptions were listed by number, and the patients were advised to obtain the prescriptions from the Brinkley Pharmaceutical Association. Two such broadcasts the court found as typical were as follows:

> Here's one from Tillie. She says she had an operation, had some trouble 10 years ago. I think the operation was unnecessary, and it isn't very good sense to have an ovary removed with the expectation of motherhood resulting therefrom. My advice to you is to use Women's Tonic No. 50, 67, and 61. This combination will do for you what you desire if any combination will, after three months' persistent use.
>
> Sunflower State, from Dresden, Kansas. Probably he has gall stones. No, I don't mean that, I mean kidney stones. My advice to you is to put him on Prescription No. 80 and 50 for men, also 64. I think that he will be a whole lot better. Also drink a lot of water.[25]

It is little wonder that Dr. Brinkley's prescriptions did not impress the court. Dr. Brinkley claimed that refusal to renew the license was a case of censorship. The court indicated that nothing had been prohibited from being aired prior to the broadcast, and that the FRC was assuming that the renewal of the license would encourage the same type of programming that was indicative of the station's past performance. The court stated: "In considering the question whether the public interest, convenience, or necessity will be served by a renewal of appellant's license, the Commission has merely exercised its undoubted right to take note of appellant's past conduct, which is not censorship."[26]

In a similar case, *Trinity Methodist Church, South* v. *FRC,* the right to refuse renewal of a license was further affirmed.[27] In this case, the Reverend Doctor Schuler was alleged to have used a radio station to attack the Roman Catholic Church. Trinity claimed that the refusal to renew the license violated the right of free speech, that it deprived Dr. Schuler "of his property without due process of law," and that the FRC decision violated the Radio Act of 1927, because there was not sufficient evidence to deny the renewal. It argued, therefore, that the FRC's decision was "arbitrary and capricious."[28] The evidence against Dr. Schuler included a contempt of court citation under appeal to the Supreme Court of California. The Court criticized Schuler, stating:

> Appellant, not satisfied with attacking the judges of the courts in cases then pending before them, attacked the bar association for its activities in recommending judges, charging it with ulterior and sinister purposes. With no more justification, he charged particular judges with sundry immoral acts. He made defamatory statements against the board of health. He charged that the labor temple in Los Angeles was a bootlegging and gambling joint.[29]

In affirming the FRC's decision to deny Trinity's license renewal, the court seriously damaged arguments that such denials were in violation of either a licensee's right of free speech or of rights of due process. Keep in mind that the denial occurred after, not before, Dr. Schuler had aired his comments; thus it was not a form of prior restraint.

defining limits of authority: cases and the act of july 1, 1930

When Congress passed the Radio Act of 1927, it provided in Section 16 that the Court of Appeals of the District of Columbia had the right to hear appeals to FRC decisions. So, if a broadcaster felt that an FRC decision was indeed "arbitrary and capricious," he still had another forum in which to argue. But if the broadcaster was not satisfied with the appeals court's decision, could the case go all the way to the Supreme Court? The first case to test this question was *FRC* v. *General Electric Company.* In this case, as Le Duc and McCain point out, the Court held that "by allowing a federal court to engage in fact finding, Congress had made it an administrative agency whose decisions could not be subjected to review by the Supreme Court within the Judiciary Act of 1789."

Congress amended Section 16 on July 1, 1930. The 1930 legislation, which was also cited by the appeals court in the Brinkley case and used as a basis of appeal in the Schuler case, stated that the "review by the court shall be limited to questions of law and that findings of fact by the Commission, if supported by substantial evidence, shall be conclusive unless it shall clearly appear that the findings of the Commission are arbitrary or capricious."[30] In other words, if the FRC did its homework prior to delivering an opinion, the facts would stand as originally presented, and the appeals process would consist of arguments about the law.

From 1927 to 1934, the Radio Act of 1927 withstood challenges from all sides. It achieved the ability to regulate effectively the expanding medium of "wireless," which now encompassed the nation with entertainment and new programming envisioned by few of the 1910 pioneer regulators. It is hardly suprising that the 1927 law was liberally quoted in the Communications Act of 1934, the law governing contemporary broadcasting. This was the law that took broadcasting out of the Department of Commerce entirely and gave it separate status as an independent agency of government.

The Communications Act of 1934

It was becoming clear that broadcasting needed a new more comprehensive regulatory agency. The FRC was still limited in its scope, having to share responsibilities with the U.S. Department of Commerce. And although the Commerce Department had at one time been an appropriate home, the predominant trend was toward the public consumption of radio, overshadowing its commercial uses. Although commercial stations would still far outnumber those directing their signals to the public, guarding the public's convenience, interest, and necessity was no small task. After a number of proposals to coordinate regulation had been examined, President Franklin D. Roosevelt sent to Congress on February 26, 1934, a proposal to create a separate agency, known as the Federal Communications Commission. Roosevelt's message said that the FCC should have the authority "now lying in the Federal Radio Commission and with such authority over communications as now lies with the Interstate Commerce Commission— the services affected to be all of those which rely on wires, cables, or radio as a medium of transmission."[31]

The change to a separate independent agency also resolved the dilemma that had plagued regulation under the FRC, in that an agency of "Commerce" had been charged with administering issues which were inherently part of the free speech–free press clause of the First Amendment to the Constitution. It would be interesting to speculate what would have occurred to the future of legislation and the media of radio and television had the air waves continued to be viewed as instruments of "commerce."

Congress responded to Roosevelt's proposal by passing the Communications Act of 1934. And with it came the Federal Communications Commission, which in the next forty-five years was to see its domain increase over everything from citizens' band (CB) radio to satellite communication, from intrastate to international communication. Although it took only five months for Roosevelt's message to become law, the scope of the FCC had already been hammered out in court challenges to the 1927 law. In fact, much of the 1927 law was left intact, including the guiding phrase, "public convenience, interest, or necessity," which was retained as a nebulous but very powerful component of the 1934 legislation.[32] A few minor changes dealt with the actual wording of the law. "Wave length" was changed to "frequency," and whereas the 1927 law was concerned with "wireless communication," the FCC was charged with governing both wire and wireless.

As is the case with most laws, the 1934 legislation has been amended many times. It would take many volumes to discuss *all* the decisions and cases that have molded today's version, but this book will examine some of the specific provisions and amendments of the 1934 Act that have a direct effect on current broadcasting.

summary

Chapter 1 traces the government's role in early broadcasting. An outgrowth of the Berlin meetings of 1903 and 1906, the Wireless Ship Act of 1910 provided an early safeguard for ships at sea. It required them to be equipped with radio apparatus which could communicate with other ships and shore stations. Violations meant possible fines and court proceedings. Two years later, the Radio Act of 1912 expanded on the 1910 legislation but could not even begin to deal with radio's exploding growth during the 1920s. Four National Radio Conferences convened and discussed how to bring the new medium under government control that was acceptable to the industry yet permitted the orderly use of the spectrum. The combination of these four Conferences and the two landmark court cases that threatened the legality of the 1912 legislation generated enough support in Congress to pass the Radio Act of 1927. The Act created the Federal Radio Commission, which was renewed on a year-to-year basis while it fought a series of court battles to affirm its control over radio. Seven years later, the Communications Act of 1934 passed Congress and established the Federal Communications Commission, a separate, independent, government agency.

material for analysis

Throughout this text, we will encounter various provisions of the Communications Act of 1934. To prime us for Chapter 2, which deals with the Federal Communications Commission, we will first examine the main provisions concerning the creation and functioning of that Commission. Although the Act has remained a fairly flexible document throughout the years and has been amended with various pieces of legislation, major congressional discussions began in 1976 to overhaul it completely. We will discuss these proposals in more detail in later chapters of the text. Much of the Act is a continuation of the policies first established in the Radio Act of 1927. The broadest foundation of the Act, as noted earlier, is the "public interest, convenience, and necessity" clause, which gives the FCC extremely wide powers to regulate broadcasting and to establish and enforce communication policy.

The Communications Act of 1934 – Selected Provisions

CREATING THE FCC

Sec. 1. For the purpose of regulating interstate and foreign commerce in communication by wire and radio so as to make available, so far as possible, to all the people of the United States a rapid, efficient, Nation-wide, and world-wide wire and radio communication service with adequate facilities at reasonable charges, for the purpose of the national defense, for the purpose of promoting safety of life and property through the use of wire and radio communication, and for the purpose of securing a more effective execution of this policy by centralizing authority heretofore granted by law to several agencies and by granting additional authority with respect to interstate and foreign commerce in wire and radio communication, there is hereby created a commission to be known as the "Federal Communications Commission," which shall be constituted as hereinafter provided, and which shall execute and enforce the provisions of this Act.

APPLYING THE PROVISIONS OF THE ACT

Sec. 2. (a) The provisions of this Act shall apply to all interstate and foreign communication by wire or radio and all interstate and foreign transmission of energy by radio, which originates and/or is received within the United States, and to all persons engaged within the United States in such communication or such transmission of energy by radio, and to the licensing and regulating of all radio stations as hereinafter provided; but it shall not apply to persons engaged in wire or radio communication or transmission in the Canal Zone, or to wire or radio communication or transmission wholly within the Canal Zone.

(b) Subject to the provisions of section 301, nothing in this Act shall be construed to apply or to give the Commission jurisdiction with respect to (1) charges, classifications, practices, services, facilities, or regulations for or in connection with intrastate communication service by wire or radio of any carrier, or (2) any carrier engaged in interstate or foreign communication solely through physical connection with the facilities of another carrier not directly or indirectly controlling or controlled by, or under direct or indirect common control with such carrier, or (3) any carrier engaged in interstate or foreign communication solely through connection by radio, or by wire and radio, with facilities, located in an adjoining State or in Canada or Mexico (where they adjoin the State in which the carrier is doing business), of another carrier not directly or indirectly controlling or controlled by, or under direct or indirect common control with such carrier, or (4) any carrier to which clause (2) or clause (3) would be applicable except for furnishing interstate mobile radio communication service or radio communication service to mobile stations on land vehicles in Canada or Mexico; except that sections 201 through 205 of this Act, both inclusive, shall, except as otherwise provided therein, apply to carriers described in clauses (2), (3), and (4).

DEFINITIONS

Sec. 3. For the purposes of this Act, unless the context otherwise requires—

(a) "Wire communication" or "communication by wire" means the transmission of writing, signs, signals, pictures, and sounds of all kinds by aid of wire, cable, or other like connection between the points of origin and reception of such transmission, including all instrumentalities, facilities, apparatus, and services (among other things, the receipt, forwarding, and delivery of communications) incidental to such transmission.

(b) "Radio communication" or "communication by radio" means the transmission by radio of writing, signs, signals, pictures, and sounds of all kinds, including all instrumentalities, facilities, apparatus, and services (among other things, the receipt, forwarding, and delivery of communications) incidental to such transmission.

(c) "Licensee" means the holder of a radio station license granted or continued in force under authority of this Act.

(d) "Transmission of energy by radio" or "radio transmission of energy" includes both such transmission and all intrumentalities, facilities, and services incidental to such transmission.

(e) "Interstate communication" or "interstate transmission" means communication or transmission (1) from any State, Territory, or possession of the United States (other than the Canal Zone), or the District of Columbia, to any other State, Territory, or possession of the United States (other than the Canal Zone), or the District of Columbia, (2) from or to the United States to or from the Canal Zone, insofar as such communication of transmission takes place within the United States, or (3) between points within the United States but through a foreign country; but shall not, with respect to the provisions of title II of this Act (other than section 223 thereof), include wire or radio communication between points in the same State, Territory, or possession of the United States, or the District of Columbia, through any place outside thereof, if such communication is regulated by a State commission.

(f) "Foreign communication" or "foreign transmission" means communication or transmission from or to any place in the United States to or from a foreign country, or between a station in the United States and a mobile station located outside the United States.

(g) "United States" means the several States and Territories, the District of Columbia, and the possessions of the United States, but does not include the Canal Zone.

(h) "Common carrier" or "carrier" means any person engaged as a common carrier for hire, in interstate or foreign communication by wire or radio or in interstate or foreign radio transmission of energy, except where reference is made to common carriers not subject to this Act; but a person engaged in radio broadcasting shall not, insofar as such person is so engaged, be deemed a common carrier.

(i) "Person" includes an individual, partnership, association, joint-stock company, trust, or corporation.

(j) "Corporation" includes any corporation, joint-stock company, or association.

(k) "Radio station" or "station" means a station equipped to engage in radio communication or radio transmission of energy.

(l) "Mobile station" means a radio-communication station capable of being moved and which ordinarily does move.

(m) "Land station" meant a station, other than a mobile station, used for radio communication with mobile stations.

(n) "Mobile service" means the radio-communication service carried on between mobile stations and land stations, and by mobile stations communicating among themselves.

(o) "Broadcasting" means the dissemination of radio communications intended to be received by the public, directly or by the intermediary of relay stations.

(p) "Chain broadcasting" means simultaneous broadcasting of an identical program by two or more connected stations.

(q) "Amateur station" means a radio station operated by a duly authorized person interested in radio technique solely with a personal aim and without pecuniary interest. . . .

(cc) "Station license," "radio station license," or "license" means that instrument of authorization required by this Act or the rules and regulations of the Commission made pursuant to this Act, for the use or operation of apparatus for transmission of energy, or communications, or signals by radio by whatever name the instrument may be designated by the Commission.

(dd) "Broadcast station," "broadcasting station," or "radio broadcast station" means a radio station equipped to engage in broadcasting as herein defined.

(ee) "Construction permit" or "permit for construction" means that instrument of authorization required by this Act or the rules and regulations of the Commission made pursuant to this Act for the construction of a station, or the installation of apparatus, for the transmission of energy, or communications, or signals by radio, by whatever name the instrument may be designated by the Commission. . . .

COMPOSITION OF THE COMMISSION

Sec. 4. (a) The Federal Communications Commission (in this Act referred to as the "Commission") shall be composed of seven commissioners appointed by the President, by and with the advice and consent of the

Senate, one of whom the President shall designate as chairman.

(b) Each member of the Commission shall be a citizen of the United States. No member of the Commission or person in its employ shall be financially interested in the manufacture or sale of radio apparatus or of apparatus for wire or radio communication; in communication by wire or radio or in radio transmission of energy; in any company furnishing services or such apparatus to any company engaged in communication by wire or radio or to any company manufacturing or selling apparatus used for communication by wire or radio; or in any company owning stocks, bonds, or other securities of any such company; nor be in the employ of or hold any official relation to any person subject to any of the provisions of this Act, nor own stocks, bonds, or other securities of any corporation subject to any of the provisions of this Act. Such commissioners shall not engage in any other business, vocation, profession, or employment. Any such commissioner serving as such after one year from the date of enactment of the Communications Act Amendments, 1952, shall not for a period of one year following the termination of his service as a commissioner represent any person before the Commission in a professional capacity, except that this restriction shall not apply to any commissioner who has served the full term for which he was appointed. Not more than four members of the Commission shall be members of the same political party.

(c) The Commissioners first appointed under this Act shall continue in office for the terms of one, two, three, four, five, six, and seven years, respectively, from the date of the taking effect of this Act, the term of each to be designated by the President, but their successors shall be appointed for terms of seven years and until their successors are appointed and have qualified, except that they shall not continue to serve beyond the expiration of the next session of Congress subsequent to the expiration of said fixed term of office; except that any person chosen to fill a vacancy shall be appointed only for the unexpired term of the Commissioner whom he succeeds. No vacancy in the Commission shall impair the right of the remaining commissioners to exercise all the powers of the Commission.

(d) Each commissioner shall receive an annual salary ... payable in monthly installments, and the chairman during the period of his service as chairman, shall receive an annual salary. ...

(e) The principal office of the Commission shall be in the District of Columbia, where its general sessions shall be held; but whenever the convenience of the public or of the parties may be promoted or delay or expense prevented thereby, the Commission may hold special sessions in any part of the United States.

(f) (1) The Commission shall have authority, subject to the provisions of the civil-service laws and the Classifications Act of 1949, as amended, to appoint such officers, engineers, accountants, attorneys, inspectors, examiners, and other employees as are necessary in the exercise of its functions.

(2) Without regard to the civil-service laws, but subject to the Classification Act of 1949, each commissioner may appoint a legal assistant, an engineering assistant, and a secretary, each of whom shall perform such duties as such commissioner shall direct. In addition, the chairman of the Commission may appoint, without regard to the civil-service laws, but subject to the Classification Act of 1949, an administrative assistant who shall perform such duties as the chairman shall direct. ...

(h) Four members of the Commission shall constitute a quorum thereof. The Commission shall have an official seal which shall be judicially noticed.

(i) The Commission may perform any

and all acts, make such rules and regulations, and issue such orders, not inconsistent with this Act, as may be necessary in the execution of its functions. . . .

ORGANIZATION AND FUNCTIONS OF THE FCC

Sec. 5. (a) The member of the Commission designated by the President as chairman shall be the chief executive officer of the Commission. It shall be his duty to preside at all meetings and sessions of the Commission, to represent the Commission in all matters relating to legislation and legislative reports, except that any commissioner may present his own or minority views or supplemental reports, to represent the Commission in all matters requiring conferences or communications with other governmental officers, departments or agencies, and generally to coordinate and organize the work of the Commission in such manner as to promote prompt and efficient disposition of all matters within the jurisdiction of the Commission. In the case of a vacancy in the office of the chairman of the Commission, or the absence or inability of the chairman to serve, the Commission may temporarily designate one of its members to act as chairman until the cause or circumstance requiring such designation shall have been eliminated or corrected. . . .

(d) (1) When necessary to the proper functioning of the Commission and the prompt and orderly conduct of its business, the Commission may, by published rule or by order, delegate any of its functions (except functions granted to the Commission by this paragraph and by paragraphs (4), (5), and (6) of this subsection) to a panel of commissioners, an individual commissioner, an employee board, or an individual employee, including functions with respect to hearing, determining, ordering, certifying, reporting, or otherwise acting as to any work, business, or matter; except that in delegating review functions to employees in cases of adjudication (as defined in the Administrative Procedure Act), the delegation in any such case may be made only to an employee board consisting of three or more employees referred to in paragraph (8). Any such rule or order may be adopted, amended, or rescinded only by a vote of a majority of the members of the Commission then holding office. Nothing in this paragraph shall authorize the Commission to provide for the conduct, by any person or persons other than persons referred to in clauses (2) and (3) of section 7(a) of the Administrative Procedure Act, of any hearing to which such section 7(a) applies. . . .

(e) Meetings of the Commission shall be held at regular intervals, not less frequently than once each calendar month, at which times the functioning of the Commission and the handling of its work load shall be reviewed and such orders shall be entered and other action taken as may be necessary or appropriate to expedite the prompt and orderly conduct of the business of the Commission with the objective of rendering a final decision (1) within three months from the date of filing in all original application, renewal, and transfer cases in which it will not be necessary to hold a hearing, and (2) within six months from the final date of the hearing in all hearing cases; and the Commission shall promptly report to the Congress each such case which has been pending before it more than such three- or six-month period, respectively, stating the reasons therefor.

questions for discussion and further research _____

1. Although only two years separated the Wireless Ship Act of 1910 and the Radio Act of 1912, fifteen years separated the 1912 law and the Radio Act of 1927. Why,

as broadcasting began to develop in the late teens and early twenties, didn't Congress act to shore up the seemingly ineffectual legislation?

2. Experimental voice broadcasting arrived a full six years before the passage of the Radio Act of 1912. Why, then, didn't the law address the probable effects of this new development in wireless?

3. Although the sinking of the *Titanic* rallied popular support for new regulations governing wireless, did it also create a certain "rush to judgment," resulting in a law inadequate for the years immediately following the passage of the Radio Act of 1912?

4. What would have been the impact on future legislation and the broadcasting industry had the court ruled differently in *United States* v. *Zenith*?

5. What would have happened if the court ruled differently in *Hoover* v. *Intercity Radio Co., Inc.*?

6. Had the amateur radio operators' lobbying efforts been weaker when the National Radio Conferences were taking place, would the structure of American broadcasting have evolved differently?

7. Were the National Radio Conferences effective, or did they just prolong the badly needed revisions in the Radio Act of 1912?

8. If the legislative process in the early 1920s was too slow to patch up the Radio Act of 1912, how can today's political bureaucracy handle legislation governing such things as satellite communication?

9. Why, with so much attention paid to radio's exploding popularity, did it take so long from the time the first major stations signed on the air, about 1920, to the time the Radio Act of 1927 materialized?

10. Consider the five questions posed to the Attorney General by the Secretary of Commerce in his letter of June 4, 1926. What might have happened to the structure of American broadcasting if the Attorney General's answers had been different? Was any one of the Secretary's questions more critical than the others?

11. The Radio Act of 1927 proved a rather solid document when challenged in court between 1927 and 1934. What would have been the long-term effects on broadcasting if the document had proved weak and ineffectual?

12. What cases challenging the Radio Act of 1927 were the most important in establishing the structure of broadcast regulation?

13. Are there any advantages to the type of five-member commission that operated with the Federal Radio Commission as opposed to the seven-member commission operating the FCC?

14. The Communications Act of 1934 placed broadcasting under the Federal Communications Commission. How might our broadcasting system of today have evolved differently if broadcasting had remained in the Department of Commerce?

additional resources

books

Bartlett, J., ed., *The First Amendment in a Free Society,* New York: H. W. Wilson, 1979.

Berns, W., *The First Amendment and the Future of American Democracy,* New York: Basic Books, 1976.

Clark, M. J., ed., *Politics and the Media: Film and Television for the Political Scientist and Historian,* Oxford and New York: Pergamon Press, 1979.

Dennis, E. E., D. M. Gillmor, and D. L. Grey,

eds., *Justice Hugo Black and the First Amendment,* Ames: Iowa State University Press, 1978.

Devol, K. S., ed., *Mass Media and the Supreme Court: The Legacy of the Warren Years,* New York: Hastings House, 1976.

Kurland, P. B., ed., *Free Speech and Association: The Supreme Court and the First Amendment,* Chicago: University of Chicago Press, 1976.

Owen, B. M., *Economics and Freedom of Expres-*

sion: Media Structure and the First Amendment, Cambridge, Mass.: Ballinger Publishing Co., 1975.

Seiden, M. H., *Who Controls the Mass Media?* New York: Basic Books, 1975.

articles

Bensman, M. R., "Regulation of Broadcasting by the Department of Commerce, 1921–1927," in *American Broadcasting: A Source Book on the History of Radio and Television,* eds. L. W. Lichty and M. C. Topping, New York: Hastings House, 1975, p. 60.

Berman, M. K., "Regulation of Radio Broadcasting," 13 *Boston University Law Review* 60 (1933).

Brown, T. H., "State Regulation of Radio," 2 *Journal of Air Law* 35 (1931).

Caldwell, L. G., "Appeals from Decisions of the Federal Radio Commission," 1 *Journal of Air Law* 274 (1930).

Caldwell, L. G., "Practice and Procedure before the Federal Radio Commission," 1 *Journal of Air Law* 144 (1930).

Chamberlain, J. P., "The Radio Act of 1927," 13 *American Bar Association Journal* 343 (1927).

Chapman, L. R., "The Power of the Federal Radio Commission to Regulate or Censor Radio Broadcasts," 1 *George Washington Law Review* 380 (1933).

Dyer, R. J., "Radio Interference as a Tort," 17 *St. Louis Law Review* 125 (1932).

Elliott, S. D., "Radio and Rate Regulation," 2 *Journal of Radio Law* 272 (1932).

Felix, E. H., "FRC—Equalization of Broadcasting Facilities Among Zones—General Order No. 102," 2 *Air Law Review* 260 (1931).

Godfrey, D. G., "Senator Dill and the 1927 Radio Act," 23 *Journal of Broadcasting,* 477 (1979).

Jameson, G., "The Federal Radio Commission and the Public Service Responsibility of Broadcast Licensees," 11 *Federal Communications Bar Journal* 5 (1950).

Le Duc, D. R., and T. A. McCain, "The Federal Radio Commission in Federal Court: Origins of Broadcast Regulatory Doctrines," 14 *Journal of Broadcasting* 393 (1970).

Lovett, E. C., "The Antitrust Provisions of the Radio Act," 2 *Journal of Radio Law* 1 (1932).

Masters, K., "Construction of the Equality Clause in the Davis Amendment," 1 *Journal of Radio Law* 1 (1931).

Miller, J., "Principles of Law Limiting Radio Broadcasting," 9 *Federal Rules and Decisions* 217 (1939).

Miller, N., "Legal Aspects of the Chain Broadcasting Regulations," 12 *Air Law Review* 293 (1941).

Minasian, J. R., "Political Economy of Broadcasting in the 1920s," 12 *Journal of Law and Economics* 391 (1969).

Nordhaus, R. J., "Judicial Control of the Federal Radio Commission," 2 *Journal of Radio Law* 447 (1932).

O'Shea, C. F., "Radio—Federal Jurisdiction and Regulatory Power over Radio Communication," 17 *Georgetown Law Journal* 339 (1929).

Patrick, D. M., "The Regulation of Radio and Some of Its Legal Problems," 10 *Michigan State Bar Journal* 233 (1931).

Penstone, G. H., "Meaning of the Term 'Public Interest, Convenience, or Necessity' under the Communications Act of 1934," 9 *George Washington Law Review* 873 (1941).

Porter, J. A., "Radio Act of 1927—Constitutionality of Davis Amendment—Validity of Enforcing Regulations," 4 *Air Law Review* 182 (1933).

Sarno, E. F., Jr., "The National Radio Conferences," 13 *Journal of Broadcasting* 189 (1969).

Scharfeld, A. W., "Statements of Grounds for Decision by Federal Radio Commission," 1 *Journal of Radio Law* 101 (1931).

Seidman, B. S., "The Communications Act of 1934," 5 *Air Law Review* 299 (1934).

Shelby, M. E., "John R. Brinkley and the 'Kansas City Star'," 22 *Journal of Broadcasting* 33 (1978).

Siegel, S. N., "A Realistic Approach to the Law of Communications," 8 *Air Law Review* 81 (1937).

Sturtevant, R. D., "The Law of Radio Broadcasting," 3 *Dakota Law Review* 67 (1930).

Warner, H. P., "Monopoly and Monopolistic Practice and the Communications Act of

1934," 6 *Federal Communications Bar Journal* 26, 55 (1941).

Webster, B. M., Jr., "The Power of the Court of Appeals, D.C., to Review Decisions of the Federal Radio Commission," 1 *Air Law Review* 416 (1930).

Zollman, C., "Recent Federal Legislation: Radio Act of 1927," 11 *Marquette Law Review* 121 (1927).

cases

American Bond and Mortgage v. *United States,* 52 F.2d 318 (C.C.A. Ill.), opinion affirmed (1931).

Ansley v. *F.R.C.,* 46 F.2d 600 (1931).

Beebe v. *F.R.C.,* 61 F.2d 914 (1932).

Boston Broadcasting Co. (Station WLOE) v. *F.R.C.* (New England Broadcasting Co., intervenor), 67 F.2d 505 (1933).

Brahy v. *F.R.C.,* 59 F.2d 879 (1932).

Carrell v. *F.R.C.,* 36 F.2d 117 (1929).

Chicago Federation of Labor v. *F.R.C.* (Atlass Co., Inc., intervenor), 41 F.2d 422 (1929).

City of New York v. *F.R.C.,* 36 F.2d 115 (1929).

City of New York v. *F.R.C.,* 64 F.2d 719 (1933).

Davidson v. *F.R.C.,* 61 F.2d 401 (1932).

Durham Life Insurance Co. v. *F.R.C.,* 55 F.2d 537 (1932).

F.R.C. v. *General Electric,* 281 U.S. 464 (1929).

F.R.C. v. *Nelson Bros. Bond & Mortgage Co. (Station WICO),* 289 U.S. 266 (1933).

General Broadcasting v. *Bridgeport Broadcasting,* 53 F.2d 664 (1931).

Goss v. *F.R.C.,* 67 F.2d 507 (1934).

Great Lakes Broadcasting Co. et al. v. *F.R.C.,* 37 F.2d 933 (1929).

Havens & Martin v. *F.R.C.,* 45 F.2d 295 (1931).

Hoover v. *Intercity Radio Co., Inc.,* 286 F. 1003 (1923).

In re *Great Lakes Broadcasting* v. *F.R.C.,* 3 F.R.C. Ann. Rep. 32 (1929), 37 F.2d 993 (1930).

Journal Co. v. *F.R.C.,* 48 F.2d 461 (1931).

KFKB Broadcasting v. *F.R.C.,* 47 F.2d 670 (1931).

Pacific Development Radio Co. (Station KECA) v. *F.R.C.,* 55 F.2d 540 (1932).

Pote (Station WLOE) v. *F.R.C.,* 67 F.2d 509 (1933).

Radio Investment Company, Inc. v. *F.R.C.* (New Jersey Broadcasting Corp., intervenor), 62 F.2d 381 (1932).

Reading Broadcasting v. *F.R.C.,* 48 F.2d 458 (1931).

Richmond Development v. *F.R.C.,* 35 F.2d 883 (1930).

Riker (Station KFQU) v. *F.R.C.,* 55 F.2d 535 (1932).

Sproul v. *F.R.C.,* 54 F.2d 444 (1932).

Strawbridge and Clothier (WFI Radio) v. *F.R.C.,* 57 F.2d 434 (1932).

Symons Broadcasting Co. v. *F.R.C.* (Radio Service Corp., intervenor), 64 F.2d 381 (1932).

Technical Radio Laboratory v. *F.R.C.,* 36 F.2d 111 (1929).

Telegraph Herald Co. v. *F.R.C.* (Sanders Brothers, intervenor), 66 F.2d 220 (1933).

Trinity Methodist Church, South v. *F.R.C.,* 62 F.2d 650 (1932).

United States v. *Gregg* et al., 5 F.Supp. 848 (1933).

United States v. *Zenith Radio Corp.,* 12 F.2d 616 (1926).

Unity School of Christianity v. *F.R.C.* et al., 64 F.2d 550 (1933).

Universal Service Wireless Inc. v. *F.R.C.,* 41 F2d 933 (1929).

Westinghouse Electric and Manufacturing Co. v. *F.R.C.,* 47 F.2d 415 (1931).

WGN v. *F.R.C.,* 68 F.2d 432 (1934).

WHB Broadcasting Co. v. *F.R.C.,* 56 F.2d 311 (1932).

White v. *F.R.C.,* 29 F.2d 113 (1928).

White v. *Johnson* et al., 282 U.S. 367 (1931).

Whitehurst v. *Grimes, Chief of Police,* et al., 21 F.2d 787 (1927).

WREC, Inc. v. *F.R.C.* (Waterloo Broadcasting, intervenor), 67 F.2d 578 (1934).

2

The Federal
Communications
Commission

Although in different forms with varying amounts of independence, federal agencies have been in some control of broadcasting since the passage of the Wireless Ship Act of 1910. While the Department of Commerce yielded to the Federal Radio Commission in 1927, it still set the stage for a government agency at the federal level to govern the development of radio and television. As we learned in Chapter 1, the Federal Communications Commission was formed in 1934. Seven commissioners (five as of July 1, 1983) head the FCC. Directly responsible to Congress, the FCC's structure has withstood almost a half-century of challenges from United States Presidents and attempts by Congress to replace it or significantly change its makeup.

In this chapter we'll examine the Federal Communications Commission—including its functions and jurisdiction—and see how the FCC conducts business, with a look at a typical FCC agenda, the organization of the FCC, its powers of enforcement, FCC inspections and investigations, consumer complaints to the FCC, input to FCC rulemaking, the FCC's notice of inquiry, and criticism of the FCC. In Chapter 3, we'll examine allied regulatory agencies, including the Federal Trade Commission (FTC), the National Telecommunications and Information Administration (NTIA), and the International Telecommunication Union (ITU) of the United Nations. We'll be examining how these regulatory agencies directly and indirectly affect the broadcasting industry. As a responsible consumer of broadcast communication, or perhaps as a practicing professional, you will in some way have your life touched by the actions of one of these many agencies, and it is important to know how the regulatory process works.

Powers of the Commission

The FCC's general powers are spelled out in Sec. 303 of the Communications Act of 1934:[1]

Sec. 303.   Except as otherwise provided in this Act, the Commission from time to time, as public convenience, interest, or necessity requires, shall—

(a)   Classify radio stations;

(b)   Prescribe the nature of the service to be rendered by each class of licensed stations and each station within any class;

(c)   Assign bands of frequencies to the various classes of stations, and assign frequencies for each individual station and determine the power which each station shall use and the time during which it may operate;

(d)   Determine the location of classes of stations or individual stations;

(e)   Regulate the kind of apparatus to be used with respect to its external effects and the purity and sharpness of the emissions from each station and from the apparatus therein;

(f)   Make such regulations not inconsistent with law as it may deem necessary to prevent interference between stations and to carry out the provisions of this Act: *Provided, however,* that changes in the frequencies, authorized power, or in the times of operation of any station, shall not be made without the consent of the station licensee unless, after a public hearing, the Commission shall determine that such changes will promote public convenience or interest or will serve public necessity, or the provisions of this Act will be more fully complied with;

(g)   Study new uses for radio, provide for experimental uses of frequencies, and generally encourage the larger and more effective use of radio in the public interest;

(h)   Have authority to establish areas or zones to be served by any station;

(i)   Have authority to make special regulations applicable to radio stations engaged in chain broadcasting;

(j)   Have authority to make general rules and regulations requiring stations to keep such records of programs, transmissions of energy, communications, or signals as it may deem desirable;

(k)   Have authority to exclude from the requirements of any regulations in whole or in part any radio station upon railroad rolling stock, or to modify such regulations in its discretion;

(l)   (1)   Have authority to prescribe the qualifications of station operators, to classify them according to the duties to be performed, to fix the forms of such licenses, and to issue them to such citizens or nationals of the United States, or citizens of the Trust Territory of the Pacific Islands presenting valid identity certificates issued by the high Commissioner of such Territory, as the Commission finds qualified, except that in issuing licenses for the operation of radio stations on aircraft the Commission may, if it finds that the public interest will be served thereby, waive the requirement of citizenship in the case of persons holding United States pilot certificates or in the case of persons holding foreign aircraft pilot certificates which are valid in the United States on the basis of reciprocal agreements entered into with foreign governments. . . .

(m)   (1)   Have authority to suspend the license of any operator upon proof sufficient to satisfy the Commission that the licensee—

(A)   Has violated any provision of any Act, treaty, or convention binding on the United States, which the Commission is authorized to administer, or any regulation made by the Commission under any such Act, treaty, or convention; or

(B) Has failed to carry out a lawful order of the master or person lawfully in charge of the ship or aircraft on which he is employed; or

(C) Has willfully damaged or permitted radio apparatus or installations to be damaged; or

(D) Has transmitted superfluous radio communications or signals or communications containing profane or obscene words, language, or meaning, or has knowingly transmitted—

(1) False or deceptive signals or communications, or

(2) A call signal or letter which has not been assigned by proper authority to the station he is operating; or

(E) Has willfully or maliciously interfered with any other radio communications or signals; or

(F) Has obtained or attempted to obtain, or has assisted another to obtain or attempt to obtain, an operator's license by fraudulent means. . . .

(n) Have authority to inspect all radio installations associated with stations required to be licensed by any Act or which are subject to the provisions of any Act, treaty, or convention binding on the United States, to ascertain whether in construction, installation, and operation they conform to the requirements of the rules and regulations of the Commission, the provisions of any Act, the terms of any treaty or convention binding on the United States, and the conditions of the license or other instrument of authorization under which they are constructed, installed, or operated.

(o) Have authority to designate call letters of all stations;

(p) Have authority to cause to be published such call letters and such other announcements and data as in the judgment of the Commission may be required for the efficient operation of radio stations subject to the jurisdiction of the United States and for the proper enforcement of this Act;

(q) Have authority to require the painting and/or illumination of radio towers if and when in its judgment such towers constitute, or there is a reasonable possibility that they may constitute, a menace to air navigation. The permittee or licensee shall maintain the painting and/or illumination of the tower as prescribed by the Commission pursuant to this section. In the event that the tower ceases to be licensed by the Commission for the transmission of radio energy, the owner of the tower shall maintain the prescribed painting and/or illumination of such tower until it is dismantled, and the Commission may require the owner to dismantle and remove the tower when the Administrator of the Federal Aviation Agency determines that there is a reasonable possibility that it may constitute a menace to air navigation.

(r) Make such rules and regulations and prescribe such restrictions and conditions, not inconsistent with law, as may be necessary to carry out the provisions of this Act, or any international radio or wire communications treaty or convention, or regulations annexed thereto, including any treaty or convention insofar as it relates to the use of radio, to which the United States is or may hereafter become a party.

(s) Have authority to require that apparatus designed to receive television pictures broadcast simultaneously with sound be capable of adequately receiving all frequencies allocated by the Commission to television broadcasting when such apparatus is shipped in interstate commerce, or is imported from any foreign country into the United States, for sale or resale to the public.

The television station in a major market or the CB radio in the middle of Wyoming are all part of the FCC's domain, a domain stretching beyond the fifty states into Guam, Puerto Rico, and the Virgin Islands.

What the FCC Does Not Control

Equally important is to know over which activities the FCC *does not* have jurisdiction.[2] Many people perceive the FCC as having broad powers of regulation. Consumers feel this way, especially when unhappy about something they have seen or heard on local radio or television. But we've already learned that the Commission has very little control over the *content* of broadcast messages. With the exception of obscene and indecent programming—and with even that area being somewhat nebulous—lotteries and deceptive advertising are about the only areas the FCC can regulate without infringing on the First Amendment. Even when it does act in these areas, a court battle is bound to arise over that very Amendment.

By the same token, the FCC cannot tell a station when to air a program. Nor can it tell a station when to run commercials or public service announcements. The FCC will not substitute its judgment for that of the local broadcaster in those areas. Although some network contracts prohibit editing of certain programs, that is solely between the network and the station, not the FCC. And despite the "no-editing" clauses, the licensee retains control over local programming, with the right to delete the network's entire offering if it feels it would not be in the local public interest to air it.

Although lotteries are forbidden, the FCC has little jurisdiction over the conduct of legitimate contests, especially the awarding of prizes. If a station runs a contest, and you win a prize which, for some reason, does not satisfy you, the best recourse would be to deal directly with the station or the manufacturer of the prize. The FCC would not have the authority to tell the manufacturer to give you a different prize or to help you obtain repairs for a defective item. Similarly, although stations broadcast a variety of sporting events, the FCC has no jurisdiction over the promoters or organizers of those sporting events. If your favorite boxer unexpectedly fails to appear on the local televised "Golden Gloves" championship, you are free to write the Boxing Commission, but the FCC won't be able to help you.

Similarly, the Commission does not have any jurisdiction over countries whose radio or television signals cross into the United States. Although reciprocal international agreements oversee the use of the electromagnetic spectrum, the consumer in Michigan who complains to the FCC about a Canadian radio station would receive little satisfaction. A listener in Southern California complaining to the FCC about a station in Mexico would experience similar frustration. An exception would be if the Canadian or Mexican station were operating off frequency and interfering with American stations, although even in these cases, the FCC would have to go through the respective regulatory agencies in Canada and Mexico to solve the problem.

The FCC also has no jurisdiction over news gathering organizations, either local or national.[3] Press associations, such as United Press International, Associated Press, and Reuters, are independent of the broadcast stations they serve and are not regulated by the FCC. To the extent that such organizations use radio frequencies or satellites to transmit information, the FCC does have jurisdiction, but only in the technical sense. Similarly, the Commission does not directly control the networks, but does control network-owned broadcasting stations. The musical rights organizations, although directly involved in serving stations and collecting royalties from them for airing performers' works, are also not under the jurisdiction of the FCC. Firms such as ASCAP, BMI, and SESAC are independent organizations and are not involved in the activities that the Commission controls. In addition, audience measurement firms, such as Nielsen and Arbitron, are independent of the FCC, although a station's fraudulent use of audience ratings reflects on the licensee's commitment to serve the public interest.

The Commission has instituted rules affecting the duplication ("simulcasting") of programs on commonly owned AM and FM stations, but the FCC has no jurisdiction to tell a radio station that it must broadcast in stereo or quadraphonic sound nor the authority to tell a television station it should broadcast a program in color. And although the FCC *can act* in the *public interest* to question over-commercialization of radio and television, the *direct* authority to tell a station that it must air so many commercials per hour is nonexistent. Similarly, the Commission views the amount of public service programming as a condition for license renewal, but has no authority to tell a station what public service programming to air. If the local licensee chooses to air public service announcements for the Red Cross instead of the American Cancer Society, that is the station's prerogative. The exception to this rule would be if the public service announcements discussed a controversial issue. Then, because of the Fairness Doctrine, the Commission would want to make sure that the station aired a balanced presentation of the issue through whatever type of programming the station chose.

Libel and slander during radio and television broadcasts is another area over which the FCC has no jurisdiction. If you feel that you have been libeled or slandered (both terms sometimes apply to "broadcast" speech which is "published"), your best recourse would be to consult an attorney, not the FCC. Even in the instances of license renewal, the FCC shies away from becoming involved in these matters. In fact, when defamation did become an issue in a license renewal, the FCC stated in part:

> It is the judgment of the Commission, as it has been the judgment of those who drafted our Constitution and of the overwhelming majority of our legislators and judges over the years, that the public interest is best served by permitting the expression of any views that do not involve, quoting from Supreme Court decisions, "a clear and present danger of serious substantive evil that rises far above public inconvenience, annoyance or unrest." . . . this principle insures that the most diverse and opposing opinions will be expressed, many of which may be even highly offensive to those officials who thus protect the rights of others to free speech. If there is to be free speech, it must be free for speech that we abhor and hate as well as for speech that we find tolerable or congenial.[4]

Once again, we see the First Amendment arising to protect free speech, even when that free speech is unpopular. In the same vein, program content which contains derogatory comments about sex, race, or religious beliefs also enjoys the protection of the First Amendment, although we'll see later how the Fairness Doctrine can apply when an individual or group is verbally attacked on the air. Ethnic humor on such shows as *Sanford and Son* and *All in the Family* may naturally offend some people, but any attempt to control this area of programming would, for the most part, be outside the FCC's jurisdiction.

Conducting FCC Business

At the top of the Commission hierarchy are seven FCC Commissioners, headed by a chairman. Appointed by the President of the United States and confirmed by the Senate, Commissioners are prohibited from having a financial interest in any of the industries they regulate. This includes industries which are only partially in FCC-regulated businesses. No more than four Commissioners can be from the same political party, and their terms, lasting seven years, are staggered so that one position opens up each year. Appointees who fill the unexpired term of a Commissioner may or may not be reappointed when that term expires. The Commissioners hold weekly meetings and executive sessions to oversee Commission activities. Their meetings are open to the public, a procedure started in 1977 under mandate by Congress. But closed meetings can be called by a majority vote of the entire Commission. These meetings normally concern matters of national defense, manufacturers' trade secrets, criminal matters, or when the parties concerned with the FCC decision specifically request the meeting be closed.[5]

fcc agenda

A typical FCC agenda is grouped in a manner that reflects the nature of the FCC's organization.[6] Our discussion here will be in *general terms* and the actual titles used to describe a particular agenda item may vary depending on the issue or order of business and a particular policy or procedure in effect at any given time.

In order of business, the categories can include: Hearing, General, Safety and Special, Common Carrier, Personnel, Classified, CATV (Cable Television), Assignment and Transfer, Renewals, Aural, Television, Broadcast, and Complaints and Compliance. The Commission usually deals with these agenda items after they have received a series of briefings by the respective FCC bureaus and offices. In a *Hearing*, the FCC acts as the final tribunal in an appellate process involving decisions previously made by the FCC Administrative Law Judge and, in some cases, the FCC Review Board. The *General* is a catch-all, consisting of items not found in the other categories. For example, a representative from another federal agency may discuss FCC compliance with that agency's rules. *Safety and Special* deals with the application of broadcast communication to such areas as fire department, taxicab, and police department radios. Other industrial applications handled might be the business use of mobile radios, citizens band radio, and amateurs' (hams') services. The next matter of business, *Common Carrier,* deals with the FCC's regulation of telephone and telegraph systems. Here, the Commission acts in a quasi-public utility fashion over issues concerning microwave and satellite systems, among others. Next comes *Personnel:* FCC staffing matters and promotion and appointments come under this agenda category. Promotions are basically routine, though, since three other

FCC officers—Bureau Chief, Personnel Chief, and Executive Director—have usually approved the promotions before they reach the seven Commissioners.[7]

If national security, manufacturers' trade secrets, or other "classified" matters need to be discussed, they would be in the *Classified* category. *Cable Television* is next on the agenda. Approval of a new linkup between two cable systems, mergers of cable companies, consideration of new cable systems beginning operation, and matters concerning a public-access channel can be resolved here. If you should buy or sell a radio station, the transaction would be approved or rejected during the next order of business: *Assignment and Transfer*. The Commission's deliberations may dwell upon previous inquiries about the transactions, such as a hearing or recommendations by an Administrative Law Judge. If a group of stations is seeking to acquire more broadcasting properties, the discussion might center around the possible powerful influence of a single owner of multiple broadcast properties and on whether the public interest would be served by approving such a sale.[8] A controversy surrounding the sale of a station or the transfer of its license would be discussed during this order of business.[9] If you already own a station and it comes up for license renewal, the renewal might be acted upon during the next agenda category, *Renewal*. Most of the renewals reaching the Commissioner level are contested renewals, however. Uncontested renewals are usually approved at the staff level.

If you are applying for permission to start a new radio or television station, a decision will be made on your application during either *Aural* or *Television*, respectively. Altering the service your station is already licensed to provide will also be acted upon at this time. If your station is already on the air and for some reason wishes to seek a waiver of FCC rules, your request will be dealt with during the next item on the Commission's Agenda, *Broadcast*. For example, a network may request a waiver of the prime-time access rule to offer a special sports program. Or a station operating in an area where one network affiliate already exists may request permission to affiliate with the same network.[10] Rule violations are considered during *Complaints and Compliance*. A station that has seriously violated FCC rules, complaints about the Fairness Doctrine, or fraudulent operating practices would all receive action at this time. It goes without saying that every single violation is not dealt with by the entire Commission. However, when a violator feels that a legitimate injustice has been rendered, then the case can reach this level.

commissioner influence

Individual Commissioners can help in shaping regulatory policy. Researchers Lawrence Lichty[11] and Wenmouth Williams, Jr.,[12] studied the impact of this influence on FCC decisions. It is not surprising that during the early years of the Federal Radio Commission, the Commissioners, four of whom were trained in law, were comfortable in the atmosphere of frequent court challenges that surrounded these early decisions. The fact that the FRC added a legal division one year after it was formed is evidence of the importance the Commissioners placed on not only fighting but also winning those court challenges.

The FCC carried on this tradition in 1939 when it began its six-year "trust-busting" era, breaking up networks and setting up rules for chain broadcasting. Two FCC chairmen, Frank R. McNich and James L. Fly, led the fight and weathered the appeals that tried to claim that the regulations were unconstitutional. McNich was a lawyer who had served on the Federal Power Commission; Fly had headed the legal department of the Tennessee Valley Authority and had been in charge of judicial proceedings defending TVA's constitutionality.

Researcher Williams found President Kennedy's era characterized by a Commission oriented toward strict regulation. Newton Minow set the pace with his "vast wasteland" speech and was joined by liberal FCC democrats E. William Henry and Kenneth Cox. During the Kennedy administration, the FCC passed nonduplication rules governing simulcasting on AM and FM and also brought cable under the regulatory umbrella. President Nixon's appointment of Benjamin Hooks emphasized the role of the minority in broadcasting. The Chairmanship of Richard Wiley, under Presidents Nixon, Ford, and Carter, was characterized by attempts, many successful, to streamline FCC decision-making. Chairman Charles Ferris tended to support deregulation of radio while being critical of children's television programming. Ferris relinquished his responsibilities at the Commission in February 1981, and veteran commissioner Robert E. Lee filled in as an interim "acting" chairman until an official appointment was made by the Reagan administration. Lee was replaced as chairman by Washington, D.C. communications attorney Mark Fowler.

Organization

Let us now examine the organization of the FCC (Figure 2-1).

offices

Directly under the Commissioners are the Office of Plans and Policy, the Office of Opinions and Review. the Office of Administrative Law Judges, the Review Board, the Office of General Counsel, the Office of Science and Technology, and the Office of the Executive Director.[13]

Office of Plans and Policy.   The Office of Plans and Policy is responsible for developing the long-range policy decisions for industries coming under FCC jurisdiction. It also is responsible for assessing the policy implications of FCC decisions, providing policy analyses and recommendations to the Commission staff, and coordinating policy research. The Chief of the Office of Plans and Policy recommends budgets and priorities for the Commission policy research program and functions as the central account manager for all contractual research studies funded by the FCC.

Office of Opinions and Review.   When the FCC issues a major decision, the document outlining that decision is written in consultation with and with the assistance of the Office of Opinions and Review. This office serves as the Commission's legal staff, advising it on procedural matters, researching judicial precedent, and overseeing hearings ordered by the Commission. The Office then

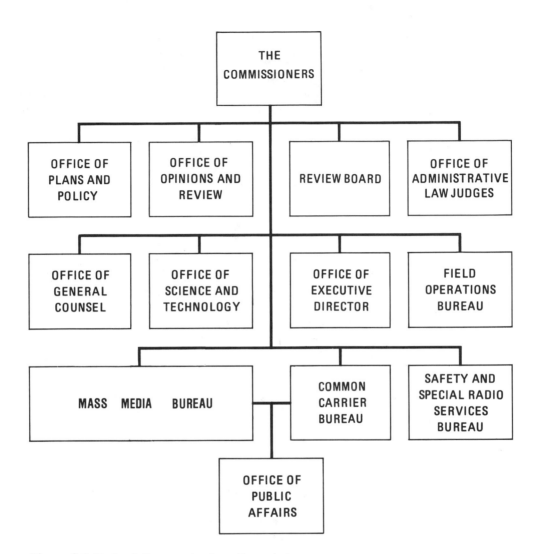

Figure 2-1 Federal Communications Commission

recommends action to the Commission, based on the evidence presented by the parties involved.

Office of Administrative Law Judges. This office is the first rung of the ladder in the appeals process. The Administrative Law Judges preside over hearings and render initial decisions, but it is not unusual for their decisions to be appealed. When two applicants for a broadcast license appear at a hearing, both have a major investment at stake, and a ruling in favor of one party will usually prompt the other to continue the appeals process.

Review Board.   The Review Board is the second step in the FCC appellate process, between the Administrative Law Judges and the Commissioners. In some cases, the decisions of the Administrative Law Judges are reversed by the Review Board and then reversed again by the seven Commissioners. This is not so much a reflection on the ability of the Judges to adhere to judicial procedure as it is an indication of the desire of the offended to exhaust every administrative remedy.

In special cases, initial decisions can be reviewed directly by the Commissioners. If, for example, a renewal decision goes against a licensee, the licensee can appeal to the Review Board, which consists of senior-level employees of the Commission. Individual FCC bureaus can also appeal to the Review Board. If, for instance, a bureau rules against a licensee, and an Administrative Law Judge rules in the licensee's favor, then the bureau can appeal to the Review Board. If the ruling still goes against the bureau—or against the licensee, for that matter—the party can appeal that ruling to the Commissioners, who, as a body, choose which cases to accept for review. The seven Commissioners are the last appeals step before the matter goes into the Federal Court of Appeals.

Office of the General Counsel.   The Office of the General Counsel is the Commission's attorney, representing it before the courts. The Office also aids in preparation of legislative programs fostered by the Commission and works closely with the Attorney General and the Justice Department in cases which involve prosecution or jurisdiction across agency boundaries. An example of this cooperation might be the prosecution of violations of the Criminal Code or of other violations that are associated with wrongdoings beyond those under the jurisdiction of the FCC. If a person steals radio equipment and then uses it to broadcast illegally, both the Justice Department and the FCC would become jointly involved in this matter. The Office of the General Counsel also works closely with the Office of Opinions and Review, since the decisions that the latter writes may be the basis for the former's defense of the Commission in court.

Office of Science and Technology.   This office is the top "technical" office at the Commission. The responsibilities of administering the electromagnetic spectrum and all of the policies associated with this implementation are developed by the Office of Science and Technology. About half of the staff are engineers, and they deal with such matters as determining the number of stations in a given market, equipment testing and certification, frequency allocations and modifications, and requests for increases in power output. The Office of Science and Technology also operates a Laboratory Division near Laurel, Maryland. Here, new equipment is tested to see whether it meets FCC specifications. For example, manufacturers of radio and television transmitters must first receive authorization before they can sell them for broadcast use. The Commission normally uses the technical data submitted by the manufacturer to base its authorization, but on occasion it spot-checks equipment to verify the test data. Citizens' band radios, for example, are tested at the Laurel, Maryland facility.[14] With the help of this testing, the FCC issues approximately one thousand authorizations per year over a wide range of equipment. The Office also works with other organizations involved in testing new equipment and its applicability to broadcasting.

Office of the Executive Director.   Despite the role of the Commissioners as the highest ranking officers of the FCC, the FCC's Executive Director coordinates the overall operation of the Commission. The position is somewhat analogous to a city manager running a municipality even though the city council is the highest level in the administrative hierarchy. The Executive Director coordinates the activities of the different staff units, including the personnel division; internal review and security division; financial management division; and the public information officer.[15]

bureaus

If it can be said that the decisions are made at the level of the FCC Offices, then the FCC Bureaus are where those decisions are carried out. Here, the day-to-day administrative services are performed that control the thousands of broadcast stations and licenses. The Commission is divided into five bureaus: Broadcast, Safety and Special Radio Services, Cable Television, Field Operations, and Common Carrier. Those dealing *most directly* with broadcasting are the Broadcast Bureau, the Cable Television Bureau, and the Field Operations Bureau.

The *Broadcast Bureau* handles matters concerning commercial and non-commercial broadcasting stations. License renewals, for example, are handled by the Bureau's Renewal and Transfer Division. Other divisions within the Bureau include the Office of Network Study, the Broadcast Facilities Division, the Complaints and Compliance Division, the Hearing Division, the Policy and Rules Division, and the License Division.[16]

The *Cable Television Bureau,* as the name implies, is responsible for overseeing the day-to-day operations of the cable television industry. Within the bureau are five divisions: the Compliance Division, the Special Relief and Microwave Division, the Policy Review and Development Division, the Research Division, and the Records and Systems Management Division.

The prime enforcement arm of the FCC is the *Field Operations Bureau,* which maintains a number of field offices in the larger cities across the United States, as well as mobile monitoring stations in specially-equipped vans. Certain members of the field staff are assigned to make on-location inspections of stations, and a separate unit concentrates on CB radio violators. The field offices are also contact points for the public, where people can obtain information about the FCC and the communications industry. In addition, this Bureau is responsible for administering FCC license examinations.

The Field Operations Bureau maintains sophisticated equipment, which can monitor a station's signal and pinpoint its location. It can thus nab illegal CB transmitters, violating amateur stations, and even "pirate" broadcasting stations operating on frequencies assigned to commercial AM and FM radio stations. For someone caught operating an illegal station, it means a "raid" by the FCC and U.S. Marshals, with equipment being seized as evidence. The organization of the Field Operations Bureau consists of four divisions: (1) The Enforcement Division, which directs the field enforcement programs, including monitoring, inspections, and investigations; (2) The Regional Services Division, which directs the public service programs, including radio operator licensing and marking and lighting of antenna towers; (3) The Violations Division, which receives and processes enforcement reports, such as violation files and investigations; and (4) The Engineering Division, which provides engineering support and equipment specifications and construction for the field facilities.[17]

In addition to the Field Operations, Cable, and Broadcast Bureaus, the Commission also includes the *Common Carrier Bureau* and the *Safety and Special Radio Services Bureau*. The Common Carrier Bureau handles common carrier matters, such as telephone and telegraph, and the Safety and Special Radio Services Bureau deals with such areas as aviation and marine radio. An *Office of Public Affairs* assumes responsibility for public information and public liaison with the Commission. Especially helpful for those wanting to obtain information from and about the Commission is the Consumer Assistance Division, which operates out of the Office of Public Affairs.

Powers of Enforcement

The Communications Act specifies that violators of its provisions will be penalized, and the Commission has at its disposal a number of enforcement measures to keep the industry in tow. Depending on the type of violation, the Commission can impose penalties ranging from a simple letter of reprimand, a cease-and-desist order, a forfeiture (fine), short-term license renewal, and license revocation or denial of renewal.

letters

Letters are usually employed in less serious matters or in those in which the FCC accepts amends instead of imposing a forfeiture. Letters can be used to reprimand stations for incomplete community needs and ascertainment surveys, lack of programming to meet Fairness Doctrine requirements, or improper submission or lack of submission of required FCC documents—such as employment reports—or for missing exhibits from a license renewal application. The letters are not always reprimands, but in case of a license renewal, for example, they can state that the license renewal is being withheld pending receipt of the required exhibit and that after a certain date the license will be forfeited.

cease-and-desist orders

Cease-and-desist orders are rare, partially because of the effectiveness of the Commission's forfeitures and other sanctions. Professors Donald M. Gillmor and Jerome A. Barron cite one case of a minister asking the FCC to issue a cease-and-desist order prohibiting a religious program from being dropped by a station. The FCC declined to issue the order under the anticensorship provision of the Communications Act, although it reaffirmed that it did have the authority to issue the order.[18] The cease-and-desist order was employed, on the other hand, by the Commission to prevent an AM station from broadcasting off-color remarks.[19]

forfeitures

The most common sanction placed upon a station is a forfeiture, usually imposed because of a technical rule violation or the more serious offense of fraudulent billing, although the latter can set the stage for a license revocation. The amount of forfeitures vary and may be based not only on the violation but on the ability of the station to pay. They can range up to $10,000 for serious violations of major market stations. Typical of forfeiture notices for alleged violations is the following partial list of apparent liabilities announced during a single week of Commission activity:

-Broadcast Bureau ordered licensee to forfeit $250 for failing to calibrate remote ammeters to indicate within 2 percent of regular meter.
-Broadcast Bureau ordered licensee to forfeit $1,000 for failing to maintain actual antenna input power as near as practical to authorized power.
-Broadcast Bureau ordered licensee to forfeit $500 for failing to keep proper log as required.
-Broadcast Bureau ordered licensee to forfeit $500 for operating with antenna input power greater than 105 percent of authorized power during daytime operation.
-Broadcast Bureau notified licensee that it had incurred apparent liability for $1,300 for failing to maintain receiver capable of receiving Emergency Broadcast System tests or emergency action notifications and terminations at nighttime control point.
-Broadcast Bureau ordered licensee to forfeit $2,000 for operating with modes of power other than those specified in basic instrument of authorization.[20]

Notice that with the exception of logging violations and failure to have equipment to monitor the Emergency Broadcast System, these alleged violations consisted of infractions of technical rules. Now consider the following list of more sizable apparent liabilities:

-$10,000 for logging violations and for fraudulent billing practices.
-$5,000 for failure to make time available to political candidates at the lowest unit charge, charging different rates for political announcements of the same class and duration to legally qualified candidates for the same office, and failure to comply with logging requirements.
-$8,000 for failure to comply with logging requirements (program-length commercial.)
-$10,000 for falsification of operating logs.
-$10,000 for fraudulent billing practices.
-$8,000 for broadcasting information concerning a lottery.[21]

Notice the increased seriousness with which the Commission regards alleged violations of commercial matter. This is one area wherein a maximum fine is not uncommon, and even stations in small communities can incur substantial liabilities associated with these violations. Figure 2-2 explains some of the other considerations that the Commission may use to determine the amount of a fine. The left-hand side of Figure 2-2 represents the conditions that can result in a minimum sanction or even in avoiding a sanction altogether. On the right are

FORFEITURE MULTIPLIER CHART

| Violation | (willful or repeated) |

Response to Notice of Violation

Quick	Delayed answer
Complete	Incomplete
Honest	Problem not fixed
Problem fixed	Misrepresentation
System of prevention prior to violation (which failed)	No system of prevention
System of prevention after violation (a must)	

Multiply Potential Fine By:

Less   More

No
Fine

Licensee Circumstance

Small Market	Experienced Broadcaster
New Broadcaster,	Group owned
Limited experience	Strong financial position
Weak financial posture	Should have known better

Multiply Potential Fine By:

Less   More

Licensee Record

Few violations in file	Number of past violations
Little renewal questions	Letters of admonishment
Record of good public service	Conditional renewals
	Minimum public service

Multiply Potential Fine By:

Less   More

Figure 2-2 (National Association of Broadcasters)

conditions which can result in increased penalties. Remember, the listings here do not necessarily denote guilt on the part of the stations, only that forfeiture notices were served.

The Commission issued its first letter of apparent liability in March 1961, one month after it outlined its policy and procedures regarding forfeitures. Authority to issue forfeitures had been granted in September 1960.[22] Researchers Charles Clift, III; Fredric A. Weiss, and John D. Abel studied the pattern of FCC forfeitures over the decade immediately following enactment of the law and found that the highest percentage (87.1 percent) of forfeitures occurred because of failure to observe a provision of the Act or a rule or regulation of the Commission.[23] Included in this category were such infractions as logging violations, fraudulent billing, unlicensed or underlicensed operators, improper station identifications, and failure to conduct equipment performance measurements. The second highest category (8.0 percent) of forfeiture notices arose over failure to operate the station as set forth in the license. Violations of broadcasting hours, power, and presunrise authorization were some of the abuses here, bringing in 3.4 percent of all forfeiture notices, including violations of sponsorship identifications and "rigged" contests. The fourth category— violations of lottery, fraud, or obscene language sections of Title 18 of the United States Code—accounted for 1.4 percent of the forfeiture notices. The researchers found no forfeiture notices germinating from failure to observe a Commission cease-and-desist order.

short-term renewals

Next to forfeitures, the most severe sanction placed upon a station is a short-term license renewal. Typical short-term renewal can range from six months to two years. The purpose of such a renewal is to give the Commission an early opportunity to review alleged past deficiencies.[24] Typical of short-term license renewals are those issued for the following infractions:

1. Station's equal employment.
2. Utilization of broadcast facility to gain competitive advantage in nonbroadcast business activities; fraudulent billing.
3. Fraudulent billing; inadvertent misrepresentations to the Commission, falsification of logs; violation of logging rules; nonfulfillment of prior proposals concerning public service announcements; lack of supervision and control over station operations.
4. Broadcast of false, misleading, or deceptive advertising in connection with the promotion of a contest.
5. Predetermining the outcome of a contest.
6. Fraudulent billing.
7. Conducting contests during audience survey periods ("hypoing").[25]

Notice, again, that alleged violations centering around commercial matters were responsible for most of these short-term renewals, indicating the seriousness that the FCC places upon such actions.

One study, by Maurice E. Shelby, investigated 156 short-term license renewals granted by the Commission in the decade immediately following the passage of the statute.[26] It showed that 113 stations (72 percent) received one-year renewals, 29 stations (19 percent) received renewals for more than one year (but less than three); and 14 (9 percent) were licensed for less than a year. Three main reasons accounted for the majority of short-term renewals: (1) improper control over station operation, which generally meant that the owner was not adequately supervising employees; (2) repeated rule violations, both technical and programming; and (3) performance vs. promise, or, in other words, that the licensee was not living up to the promises made in the previous license renewal.[27] Research has yet to tell us whether any of these trends has changed in the second decade of their issuance, but a perusal of current short-term renewals finds that the same reasons are still justifying FCC action.

renewal denials and revocation

The most serious penalty the FCC can impose against a licensee is to deny it the right to operate, either through revoking its license or denying renewal of its license. The FCC has leveled such sanctions against noncommercial as well as commercial broadcasters. In a sweeping action, the FCC lifted the licenses of an entire state's educational television commission. It was a precedent-setting example, designed to show that the Commission was not going to tolerate what it considered lack of service to an audience, in this case, to the black audience.

FCC Inspections

Any broadcast station is subject to an FCC inspection. When an inspector arrives at the station or monitors the station from a remote location, such as a field truck, violation of a technical rule can result in an official communiqué from the Commission. For minor violations, the station may receive an *Advisory Notice,* which is somewhat analogous to a warning citation for a traffic violation. It is the least severe of the various official sanctions that can be placed upon an operator or, in this case, a station. The Advisory Notice tells the violator to correct any unsatisfactory condition. No written reply is required, but a copy is placed on file with the FCC.

More serious is the *Official Notice of Violation,* to which a written reply is required within ten days, which must be sent to the FCC office from which the violation notice originated. The written answer is critical and can determine what further action might be taken by the FCC. Stations are warned that one of the most, if not *the* most, serious rule violation is to lie or misrepresent something to the Commission. In some cases, the Commission may have accumulated considerably more evidence against a station than the notice itself details. Information from FCC remote monitoring may already be on file, and such information can quickly contradict an attempt by a licensee to gloss over a problem in a written reply.

Figure 2-3 shows the "routing" of an FCC violation notice. The notice to which the broadcaster must reply originates from an individual inspector, monitoring station, or field truck. The reply, along with the FCC violation notice, is reviewed by the FCC and then forwarded to the Field Operations

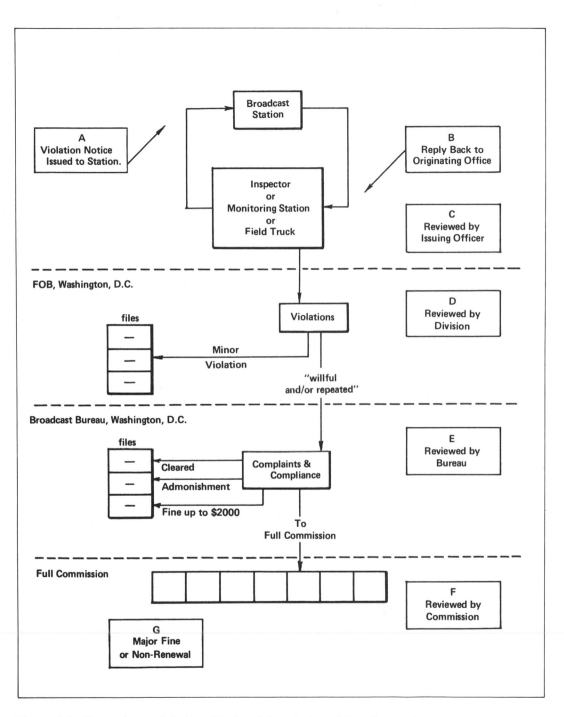

Figure 2-3 Processing a violation. (National Association of Broadcasters)

Bureau's (FOB) Violations Division in Washington. It can stop there, or, if serious enough, it can go on to the Broadcast Bureau's Complaints Division, where a fine can be issued. In very serious circumstances, the matter may come before the full Commission.

FCC Investigations

Up to now, we have been using the term "inspection" to describe monitoring or a visit by the FCC. In most cases, such an "inspection" is concerned with the routine operation of the station and its technical, logging, public file, or operator functions. Not all visits by the FCC, however, are inspections per se. In some cases, the action is serious enough for a full-scale *investigation* to take place. The station may have garnered a series of violations or such serious and frequent complaints from the public or other sources that its ability to continue to operate in the public interest is questioned. What happens in an FCC investigation can be the beginning of the procedures that determine whether the licensee remains in business. How does a broadcaster handle these more serious FCC visits? The answer is critical and can have a direct influence on the outcome of the investigation.

Advice to station management was offered by attorney Mark Fowler when serving as a member of the Washington, D.C., law firm of Fowler and Myers:

I. Investigators will inform station management and affected employees of the subject matter of the investigation upon their arrival, or prior to their arrival if the investigator believes that advance arrangements will not compromise the investigation's effectiveness. You should insist that the investigator describe his mission as clearly as possible. Then, you should immediately contact your communications attorney to get his guidance and advice.

II. When an investigator asks to see specific documents which would be relevant to the subject matter being investigated, the FCC expects the licensee to produce those papers unless those documents have nothing to do with the subject matter. It is my opinion, however, that you can refuse to give the documents to the investigator immediately so that you may consult with your attorney, provided that you indicate that the papers will be turned over in a reasonably short period of time. You cannot, however, flatly refuse to provide these documents, unless you want to insure that you are jeopardizing your license. When you furnish documents, the investigator must give you a receipt describing each document provided. You are wise to make copies of everything which you provide, because once the documents are in the hands of the FCC, these documents will not be returned. Having made a copy, you will be able to provide these documents to your attorney, so that he knows what has been produced. This could be important in determining your future defense strategy.

III. Unless the investigator advises the licensee that the alleged violation may result in criminal prosecution, the licensee is expected to cooperate with the investigation without demand for a subpoena.

IV. If there is a reason to believe that the investigation will lead to criminal prosecution, the investigator will advise the person under investigation of his rights, including the rights to counsel and to refuse to answer questions, whether the person is an owner or employee of the licensee. A broadcast owner has a right to counsel when statements are taken from him by the investigator, but he cannot insist on this right for his employees. If an employee or other third party states that he would like to consult with counsel or have his lawyer present, the investigator will not discourage him from such consultation. The FCC expects, however, that any person interviewed would consult with counsel by telephone if possible, to arrange for the presence of counsel at the earliest time possible, and to cooperate with the investigator in the meantime on aspects of the investigation which do not involve his interview.

V. When an owner is asked by an investigator to sign a statement prepared by the investigator, I insist that my clients tell the investigator that before signing, it is desired to send the statement to FCC counsel for review. Your attorney may wish to make corrections, consistent with the truth, to avoid your saying something which you did not intend because it was made in the heat of the moment.

VI. You cannot prevent your employees from giving statements and you cannot require them to provide you with a copy of any statement given. You can, however, ask your employees to provide you with a copy of the statement because the Commission has no right to prevent your employees from doing so. But, the FCC will not give you copies of such statements. If you ask an employee for a copy of such a statement, make sure you do it in a noncoercive manner. When you ask, it is a good idea to have a friendly witness present to establish that your request was noncoercive.

VII. The degree of cooperation of a station with an investigation is not a factor in determining the sanction which the Commission might impose. It is a mitigating factor, however, if a licensee reports its own violation to the Commission before an investigation begins and before the licensee learns that an investigation of the matter is pending. Licensees are expected to cooperate and to be candid with the investigators.

VIII. Interviews with owners and employees are usually conducted in the business offices of the licensee during normal business hours, but they may be conducted elsewhere if the owner requests, especially in the case where the investigation might be unduly disruptive of normal station operations. Try to work out an accommodation with the investigators on this.

IX. If an investigator prepares a statement for signature by an owner or employee, the interviewee may object to signing the statement, and the investigator will not persist.

X. Any questions or complaints about the conduct of an investigator should immediately be communicated to the Chief of Complaints and Compliance at the FCC or to the Chief of the FCC's Broadcast Bureau, and to your Washington attorney.

XI. Above all, always tell the truth; make sure your employees are instructed to do so. No matter how bad the situation may seem, if the owner lies or encourages his employees to lie, and he is caught, he will invariably lose his license because he has made a deliberate misrepresentation to the FCC. If you find out that an employee has lied, immediately inform the FCC. And, always consult with your FCC counsel. This is one time not to attempt to save legal fees.

An investigation of your station is always an ordeal, presenting many anxious moments to both owners and employees. If you follow the guidelines set forth above, you will be better prepared to deal with it.

Attorney Fowler's advice underscores the importance both of the FCC investigation and of the actions of the broadcaster involved.

Many responsible broadcasters operate for years without a visit from the FCC. Such broadcasters are in the majority, and their records are usually without blemish. They fully understand the importance of operating as a regulated industry and also the importance that the Commission places on serving the public interest. On occasion, however, unscrupulous individuals may, at the expense of the public interest, fail to take seriously the power or purpose of the Commission. In such cases, it is usually only a matter of time until a meeting between the broadcaster and the Commission occurs and results in the loss of the station's license.

Consumer Complaints to the FCC

Although even the FCC recommends that an individual try first to iron out a complaint or difference with a local station, when this process becomes difficult or when communication breaks down, another avenue open to the individual is to communicate directly with the Commission. Complaints from the public are directed to the FCC's Complaint Division, which handles upward of 54,000 letters a year about broadcast stations, approximately half of which are complaints. From these figures, it is clear a letter to a local broadcaster stands a much greater chance of receiving personal attention than a letter to the FCC. If, however, you are not satisfied with the local response and decide to pursue the matter to the FCC, you are advised to follow some guidelines, similar to those which apply to writing a local broadcaster. The guidelines are outlined in the manual titled *The Public Broadcasting—A Procedure Manual,* issued by the FCC. Let us summarize its contents.

filing a complaint

The most important point about your letter is to include only those items over which the FCC has jurisdiction. Many people are under the misconception that the FCC totally controls local broadcasters. Such is not the case. True, the FCC enforces many rules and regulations, but many of these concern the engineering practices of the station and have no relationship to programming and other operations. In the *Procedure Manual,* the FCC points out that it: "cannot direct that a particular program be put on or taken off the air, nor are we arbiters of taste." The FCC's concern is with the total community, "rather than with the personal preferences or grievances of the individuals."

If you have complained first to the station involved ("far preferable to complaining initially to the Commission"), then include a copy of that correspondence with your letter to the Commission. (The exception to this procedure would be if, for some reason, you do not want your identity disclosed to the station and prefer to request the FCC to keep it confidential. However, keep in mind our earlier comment about the volume of FCC complaints.) As with writing the local broadcaster, complain promptly. Include your full name and address, the call letters of the station, and a "statement of what the station has done or failed to do which causes you to file a complaint. Be as specific as possible. Furnish names, dates, places, and other details." The organization of your letter is also important. The *Procedure Manual* suggests that you be brief and to the point: "state the facts fully and at the beginning." It goes on to state: "If the facts are self-explanatory, avoid argument, let the facts speak for themselves. Avoid repetition or exaggeration. If you think a specific law or regulation has been violated, tell us what it is. If possible, use a typewriter, but if you do write by hand, take special pains to write legibly." Assuming that you do write the FCC, let's now examine what happens to your complaint.

processing a complaint

First, if you have not followed the guidelines specified in the above paragraphs, or if your complaint "does not allege a substantial violation or statute of Commission rule or policy," then you'll probably receive a form letter in the mail explaining that this is the case. If, on the other hand, the information is complete and there appears to be an alleged violation, your complaint will be investigated, most likely by a letter to the station or, in rare instances, by a personal visit from an FCC official. Such visits are called *field inquiries* and are infrequent because of the Commission's small investigatory staff. If the FCC staff feels that the station has violated one of the FCC rules, it can do one of three things. The *Procedure Manual* states that it "may recommend to the Commission that sanctions be imposed on the station; it may direct remedial action (such as equal opportunities for a candidate for public office); or, where extenuating circumstances are present (as where the violation follows from an honest mistake or misjudgment or where the station otherwise has a good record), it may note the violation but not recommend a sanction."

Input to FCC Rulemaking

Keep in mind that FCC rules and regulations are designed to keep the broadcaster operating according to the "public interest, convenience, and necessity." But there are some practical limitations as to how far the Commission can go. Some rules would simply be too costly to be practical. Others would not be feasible on a wide scale. And, despite the fact that the FCC has the power to enact rules, the broadcaster must still be able to implement the Commission's decisions. As a result, the Commission is careful to take every opportunity to seek feedback on any proposed action from as many people as possible and from as many varying viewpoints as possible. A multistep process (Figure 2-4) is used in formulating FCC regulations, and attention is given at every step to feedback from both broadcasters and the public.

petitioning for rulemaking

FCC decision-making can begin two ways. First, the Commission can make a motion to consider a *petition for rulemaking*. Second, any citizen or broadcaster can contact the Commission and submit a petition for rulemaking. The FCC staff will then examine the petition and determine whether it has merits.

As a *highly abbreviated* example, let's assume that you have made a persuasive

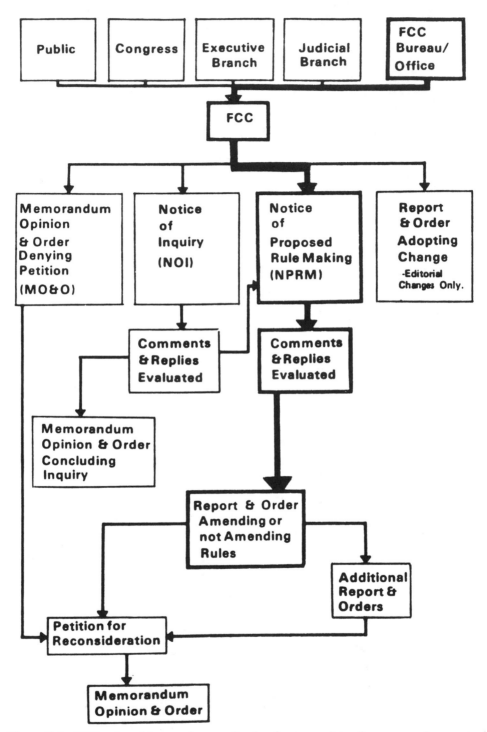

Figure 2-4 FCC rulemaking can be seen flowing from a variety of sources to the eventual issuance of a Memorandum Opinion and Order. The heavy arrows represent the most common route. Lighter arrows represent optional routes. (Source: *FCC Communicator,* September, 1975)

argument for rulemaking, that it is legally and technically sound, and that the FCC decides it wants to investigate the matter further. The Commission now issues a *file number*. The file number opens the door for broadcasters and members of the public alike to *comment* on your proposal. As an example, we'll assume that you have petitioned the Commission that all cable companies in markets of less than 3,500 subscribers should have full-color studios to permit the elderly to produce their own television programs.

Perhaps certain consumer groups feel that your proposal has merit, and they file comments with the FCC. They argue that the facilities would permit the elderly to form their own television production companies and produce programs for national syndication. At the same time, the cable companies respond to your petition. They argue that the expense of a full-scale color television studio would cost a minimum of $200,000, which is more money than a cable company grosses in five years.

With all of this information, the Commission now takes the matter under advisement. We'll assume that they feel the petition still has some merit, but that they need more information. If, after evaluating the public responses, the Commission felt that the proposal did not have merit, they could dispose of it then and there by issuing a *Memorandum Opinion and Order*.

The Commission's next step, if it feels that a petition has considerable merit, is to issue a *Notice of Proposed Rulemaking* and to give it a *Docket Number*. It then accepts both *comments* and *reply comments* to the Notice. These are essentially written forms of discussion and debate. One group of elderly people might think that the idea of production facilities is great and file a comment. Then along comes a national association of cable operators, which files a reply comment to the statement made by the elderly group.

issuing the final decision

With all of these comments and reply comments available, the Commission must now make a decision on the proposed rulemaking. It issues a *Report and Order,* in which it discusses all of the pro and con arguments for the proposed rule and states why it has arrived at its decision. The Report and Order is the Commission's official notification of its final decision. If the proposal is complex, the Commission may issue more than one Report and Order.

The FCC's Notice of Inquiry

At any point in the rulemaking process or while the Commission is considering a rulemaking petition, it may issue a *Notice of Inquiry,* asking for more information on an issue. This is the FCC's way of saying: "We want opinions before we proceed." Although broadcasters and the public can respond at any time, the Notice of Inquiry usually shifts the input process into high gear. Especially important to the FCC are comments from people who have had experience related to the proposed rulemaking or who would be directly affected by it. In our example of the senior citizen cable television programs, a comment from a senior volunteer organization or a cable company would be more important than comments from someone who would not be affected by the FCC's decision. In recent years, the FCC has become more and more concerned about the general

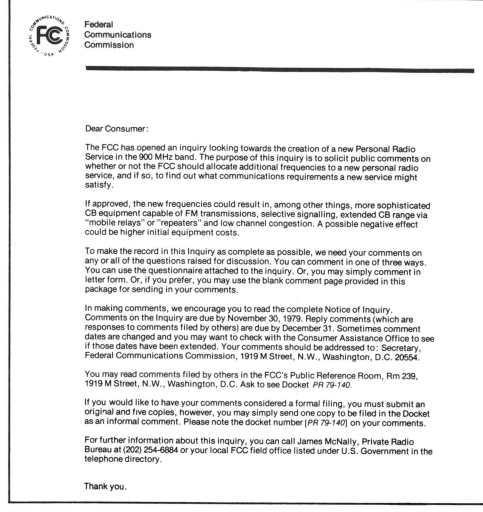

Federal
Communications
Commission

Dear Consumer:

The FCC has opened an inquiry looking towards the creation of a new Personal Radio Service in the 900 MHz band. The purpose of this inquiry is to solicit public comments on whether or not the FCC should allocate additional frequencies to a new personal radio service, and if so, to find out what communications requirements a new service might satisfy.

If approved, the new frequencies could result in, among other things, more sophisticated CB equipment capable of FM transmissions, selective signalling, extended CB range via "mobile relays" or "repeaters" and low channel congestion. A possible negative effect could be higher initial equipment costs.

To make the record in this Inquiry as complete as possible, we need your comments on any or all of the questions raised for discussion. You can comment in one of three ways. You can use the questionnaire attached to the inquiry. Or, you may simply comment in letter form. Or, if you prefer, you may use the blank comment page provided in this package for sending in your comments.

In making comments, we encourage you to read the complete Notice of Inquiry. Comments on the Inquiry are due by November 30, 1979. Reply comments (which are responses to comments filed by others) are due by December 31. Sometimes comment dates are changed and you may want to check with the Consumer Assistance Office to see if those dates have been extended. Your comments should be addressed to: Secretary, Federal Communications Commission, 1919 M Street, N.W., Washington, D.C. 20554.

You may read comments filed by others in the FCC's Public Reference Room, Rm 239, 1919 M Street, N.W., Washington, D.C. Ask to see Docket *PR 79-140.*

If you would like to have your comments considered a formal filing, you must submit an original and five copies, however, you may simply send one copy to be filed in the Docket as an informal comment. Please note the docket number [*PR 79-140*] on your comments.

For further information about this inquiry, you can call James McNally, Private Radio Bureau at (202) 254-6884 or your local FCC field office listed under U.S. Government in the telephone directory.

Thank you.

Figure 2-5

public's input into FCC rulemaking. As a result, with considerable help from the Consumer Assistance Office, a Notice of Inquiry may be directed toward the general public. One example is seen in Figure 2-5, an introductory letter on a Notice of Inquiry about a new Personal Radio Service. Following this letter came the Notice of Inquiry itself. To encourage still further response, the Notice of Inquiry included a forty-six-item, multiple-choice questionnaire. The first two pages of the questionnaire are illustrated in Figure 2-6.

content of a broadcaster's response

What type of response would a broadcaster write? Let's look at an example by R. Lyell Bremser, Vice President and General Manager of KFAB-AM in Omaha,

Nebraska. Mr. Bremser responded to an FCC proposal that would have required stations to retain for public inspection a transcript, tape, or disc of all programs except entertainment and sports.

> The proposal to require all stations to retain for public inspection a transcript, tape or disc of all programs except entertainment and sports, is counter to the Commission's deregulation program. In an assessment of our own operation, the following is a breakdown of the costs and chaos involved:
>
> 1. 47 hours of programming other than entertainment and sports would have to be taped, weekly. Tape is the only viable method.
> 2. Tape requirements would be sixteen 12-inch reels per week. Cost per reel is $8.00. Out of pocket tape cost would be $128.00 per week.
> 3. Special recorder for full-time use, approximately $3,500.00.
> 4. Special equipment for activating tape recorder, cost unknown.
> 5. File space would require a minimum of special tape cabinets to hold 52 weeks of tapes. The cost involved approximately $1,500.00.
> 6. It is impossible to estimate the cost of man-hours involved in all of the above, but it would be substantial.
>
> The proposal to require radio stations to make program logs available for public inspection . . . is unnecessary. To my knowledge, we have never had a listener ask to see our program logs. The proposal to require radio stations to make items in the Public File available for copying by members of the general public also runs counter to the deregulation program. Many stations are not equipped to provide such service. Also, there seems to be no evidence of need for such a requirement. Radio stations should not be required to continue a Public File retention of letters from the general public. We have been maintaining such a file since the rule was instituted. It has been another time-consuming burden. In the entire period, there has never been a request from a listener to inspect our Public File. It is obvious that keeping such a file serves no purpose and is a complete waste of time.

Notice that the letter first stated the specific issue being discussed. Immediately following, it succinctly stated the thrust of the opposing argument, that it was "counter to the Commission's deregulation program." The letter then methodically listed the specific points upon which the argument was based. Finally, it explained the writer's own experience with similar FCC rules, stating that the station has never had a request from anyone to inspect the public file. Mr. Bremser's letter is a good example of the form and organization of content to follow in writing to the FCC. But keep in mind that you don't have to be a broadcaster to respond to FCC decision-making. As a responsible consumer of broadcast messages, your input is vital.

encouraging public response

In August 1975, the FCC instituted a publication called *FCC Actions Alert,* which summarizes the Commission's rulemaking activities for the week. In December

I. instructions

Read the Notice of Inquiry on the "Creation of an Additional Personal Radio Service" (Docket No. 79-140, adopted June 7, 1979). It explains everything mentioned in this questionnaire.

All the questions are multiple-choice. Choose the one or more answers that best reflect your opinion, and print the letters of your choices on the numbered line to the right of each question. If you choose more than one answer to a question, print the letters of all your choices on the same line. For example, in answering question 3 below, if you were licensed in the Citizens Band, Amateur, and General Mobile radio services, you would print your answers like this: 3. A, B, C.

If you wish, you may write additional comments for each question either in the space below it or on a separate piece of paper. Be sure to number your written comments if they are separate from the questions.

Answer as many questions as you can, but feel free to ignore any questions you don't care to answer. If you're confused by any question, refer to the Notice of Inquiry to find a discussion of the subject of that question. When you've finished the questionnaire, send it to:

Secretary
Federal Communications Commission
1919 M Street, N.W.
Washington, DC 20554

II. information about person filing these comments

1. Who are you filing these comments for?

   A. yourself as individual
   B. club or association
   C. wholesaler or retailer
   D. local government entity
      (specify in 2 below)

   E. component manufacturer
   F. equipment manufacturer
   G. common carrier (wire)
   H. radio common carrier
   I. other (specify below) 1._____

2.

your name PLEASE PRINT	your title (if any)
Name of group you represent (if any)	
Address	
City and State	Zip Code

3. In what radio service(s) are you a licensee or an authorized user?

   A. Citizens Band
   B. Amateur
   C. General Mobile
   D. Radio Control
   E. Business
   F. other Industrial

   G. Public Safety
   H. Land Transportation
   I. Special Emergency
   J. Domestic Public
   K. other
   L. none 3._____

III. general questions

4. Are you A. for, B. against, C. undecided about, the creation of a new Personal Radio Service?

    4._____

5. Do you think the 27 MHz Citizens Band (CB) Radio Service is adequate as is for your 2-way radio communications needs?

    A. Yes B. Undecided C. No

    5._____

6. Do you think the General Mobile Radio Service (GMRS) at 460 MHz is an adequate alternative to CB for personal radio communications?

    A. Yes B. Undecided C. No

    6._____

7. CB and GMRS would be adequate for you if:
    A. The FCC allocated some 27 MHz frequencies for SSB-only use.
    B. The FCC did more to enforce its rules.
    C. "Skip" and other sources of interference were not so bad.
    D. If SSB was made mandatory on all of the present 40 CB channels.
    F. If 460 MHz Band General Mobile Radio Service equipment was less expensive.
    G. If "Business" users were not allowed in the General Mobile Radio Service.
    H. Other.

    7._____

8. What interests you most about personal radio?
    A. Home to vehicle communications.
    B. Base-to-base communications of a largely social nature.
    C. Skip-working.
    D. Car-to-car communications about the location of radar traps, directions, and emergency radio assistance.
    E. Communications of a technical nature which serve as an alternative to operation in the Amateur Radio Service.
    F. Other.

    8._____

9. If the only advantages of 900 MHz operation were freedom from skip, no ignition noise and higher quality communications, would you seriously consider buying 900 MHz equipment?

    A. Yes B. No C. Undecided

    9._____

IV. equipment features

10. If the FCC creates a new Personal Radio Service at 900 MHz, should manufacturers make radios that could be used for both 27 MHz and 900 MHz operation, so the user could switch back and forth?

    A. Yes B. No C. I don't know

    10._____

Figure 2-6

55

1976, the FCC published the first in a series of "Special Feedback Editions" of the *FCC Actions Alert*. Designed to increase public input into the FCC's decisions, these Special Editions are written in layman's language. They are sent to as many public interest groups as can be identified, and they list the name, address, and telephone number of the specific FCC office that can answer questions about the proposed rules. The public is urged to file either an "informal comment" or a "formal filing," the latter of which requires five copies instead of the former's one copy. The content of the Feedback Editions can and does find its way into the newsletters of various consumer groups and service organizations.

Criticism of the FCC

Perhaps because it is regulating a very "visible" industry, and perhaps, too, because that industry directly affects all of us on a daily basis, the FCC has come under serious criticism from the public, the Congress, and even from the Commissioners within its ranks. Issuing rulings in conflict with judicial precedent is one criticism. Nicholas Johnson and John Dystel cite a case in which the FCC issued permission for AT&T to build a 350-foot tower near a residential area in Maryland.[28] Despite opposition from citizens' groups, the Commission granted the request, partly because AT&T had already conducted an environmental impact study and found that the tower would not harm the environment. Johnson and Dystel note that the tower was approved despite the fact that the courts have ruled that federal agencies cannot rely on interested parties' environmental impact statements.[29]

The relationship of the FCC's middle staff to the Commissioners is another bone of contention among critics. Erwin Krasnow and Lawrence Longley, in their book, *The Politics of Broadcast Regulation,* point out that the middle staff exerts influence over the Commissioners by controlling the channels of internal communication at the FCC.[30] Thus, when the Commissioners need to choose among alternative policies, they must rely on the information that their staff feels is relevant and significant. The authors also state that since hundreds of decisions are made every day, implementation of policy must be delegated to middle staff personnel.[31]

Furthermore, not everyone feels that the way in which the FCC allocates frequencies on the electromagnetic spectrum is in the best interest of the public. For example, the designation of certain frequencies for marine use means that there are wide areas of the country where these frequencies go unused, simply because there is no demand for marine communication.[32] Moreover, this policy has perpetuated itself for years, and trying to change it now would involve major capital expenditures for the industries affected.

The Commission's local station concept, allocating certain frequencies for lower-powered stations serving small communities, also has disadvantages in that it ties up a sizable portion of the spectrum for local station use. This is especially true since one means of lessening crowding on the spectrum is to switch to regional allocations. The result of such a switch would be fewer but higher-powered stations, serving larger regions. Some would contend, however, that the idea, although technologically sound, becomes somewhat impractical when we think of the "local" service that would be lost.[33] A regional station in Chicago serving a small town in Illinois would be hard pressed to include the Illinois community's local news on its regional program fare.

Two other areas of criticism have landed squarely on the FCC's Equal Employment Opportunity (EEO) policies and on the role of citizens' groups in FCC decision-making. A report by the Citizens' Communications Center claims that the criteria for stations' compliance with the FCC's EEO requirements are vague and can be met by broadcasters who still discriminate.[34] The report also asserts that the Commission requires an unrealistically high standard of proof of discrimination practices before designating a hearing in a renewal case. Another report critical of the Commission's EEO policies has been issued by the U.S. Commission on Civil Rights.[35] Yet, this report suggests that the FCC should improve the image of women and minorities in television programming, an area, many would argue, that is clearly outside the Commission's jurisdiction, any action in which would fly in the face of the First Amendment. A report prepared by the Rand Corporation suggests that the Commission should do more to encourage citizen participation, one such effort being to support legislation that would provide financial assistance to citizens' groups involved in Commission proceedings.[36] High on the list of recommendations would also be to give citizens' groups access to any evidence that might support their causes. Under current judicial processes, a person or group can gain access to information, called the "right of discovery," only after proceedings have begun in the courts or, in the case of the FCC, after a hearing has been designated.

One of the most serious criticisms of the FCC is that it is sluggish in making important decisions. Krasnow and Longley remark that the FCC is "incapable of policy planning, of disposing within a reasonable period of time the business before it, of fashioning procedures that are effective to deal with its problems."[37] The classic case is that of the proceedings affecting the assignment of WHDH-TV in Boston. The case started in 1947, when WHDH filed an application for a license to operate Channel 5. This channel allocation was the subject of competing applications and FCC decrees for twenty-five years. It was one of the longest proceedings ever to transpire before the FCC. Professors Robert Smith and Paul Prince reviewed the chronology of the WHDH-TV case[38] and concluded that there was no clear winner in the proceedings, but the public was a significant loser. Sterling Quinlan, writing a book about the case, quotes a former Commissioner as saying, "Let's face it. This was the 'Whorehouse Era' of the Commission. When matters were arranged, not adjudicated."[39]

The Commission has, on occasion, been called to task for potential conflict of interest because its staff owned stocks of corporations regulated by the FCC. A staff report of the House Oversight and Investigations Subcommittee criticized members for transferring shares of stock in communication-related industries to immediate members of their own families (although the law, as it now stands, does not prohibit that practice). Some of the stock ownership reported by the Subcommittee included shares of General Electric owned by the spouse of a staff member in the Office of the Chief Engineer, shares of AT&T owned by the spouse of a staff member in the Common Carrier Bureau, and shares of AT&T owned by the spouse of an engineer in charge of an FCC field office.[40]

Johnson and Dystel summarized and divided their own critique of the FCC into seven areas. They contend that: (1) The FCC delves into areas beyond its expertise and issues beyond its ken. (2) It takes years to resolve important cases. (3) The FCC is manipulated by its own staff and the industries it is supposed to regulate, and that such manipulations result in precedents that return to "haunt" the Commission. (4) Principled decision-making does not exist, because the FCC no longer approves of its own rules and precedents, but ignores them instead— either by waiving them or evading them. (5) The Commission ignores its own administrative principles and those established by the judiciary. (6) The Commissioners decide cases they don't understand. (7) The FCC has yet to develop "rational" policies for governing its day-to-day decisions.[41]

Criticism of the Commission will undoubtedly continue, regardless of what changes the future may hold. However, some critics feel that it is time for an in-depth evaluation of the entire Commission. It is operating under procedures established in 1934, at a time when cable, satellites, microwaves, and fiber optics were only a dream. As things stand today, the prospect that the communications industry may become completely unmanageable is far from remote. The Commission has established various bureaus that are responsible for specific areas of the industry, but because so much is at stake when two competing corporations seek allocations or permission to develop new technology, a ruling against one corporation sends the matter through an appeals process that eventually reaches all seven Commissioners. And those seven may very well be forced into making a decision that they are not qualified to make. As a result, the numerous reversals of decisions made by the Administrative Law Judges and the Courts play havoc with anything that even resembles judicial precedent.

summary

The Federal Communications Commission is the main regulatory agency concerned with radio and television. Formed by the Communications Act of 1934, it evolved from the former Federal Radio Commission, which controlled broadcasting between 1927 and 1934.

The FCC sees itself as having thirteen functions, which, among others, include overseeing the orderly development, operation, and regulation of all broadcast services—commercial and educational AM, FM, and TV. While the FCC can regulate the day-to-day operation of a broadcast station and see that it operates in accordance with the public interest, convenience, and necessity, it has limited control over radio and television programming.

FCC business is based on an agenda that reflects the agency's different offices and bureaus. A typical FCC meeting may consist of the following agenda: hearing, general, safety and special, common carrier, personnel, classified, cable television, assignment and transfer, renewal, aural, television, broadcast, and complaints and compliance. The FCC offices consist of the Office of Plans and Policy, Office of Opinions and Review, Office of Administrative Law Judges, Review Board, Office of the General Counsel, Office of Chief Scientist, and the Office of the Executive Director. The three bureaus of the FCC that most directly deal with broadcasting are the Broadcast Bureau, the Cable Television Bureau, and the Field Operations Bureau.

The FCC's powers of enforcement include letters, cease-and-desist orders, forfeitures, short-term renewals, renewal denials, and revocation. The public can complain directly to the FCC, although it is recommended that communication first take place with the local broadcaster involved. Along with writing letters to the FCC, consumers can also participate in rulemaking decisions.

Over the years, the FCC has, like most agencies of government, received its share of criticism. This has ranged from charges that the FCC has not allocated frequencies in the public interest to the charge that Commissioners make judgments based on evidence from the middle-line staff, which controls the channels of communication to the Commissioners.

material for analysis

Although the FCC attempts to follow established procedures in carrying out its charge under the Communications Act, it frequently finds itself in court as a defendant in litigation that challenges such procedures. In excerpts from case examples, we'll move from the general to the specific in examining two challenges. The first concerns the FCC's rulemaking procedures, in a decision not to impose regulations on children's television advertising as proposed by the citizens' group, Action for Children's Television (ACT). The case, *Action for Children's Television* v. *FCC and United States of America,* especially the "Procedural Complaint" portion, provides a discussion of the FCC rulemaking function and the delicate relationship that exists between the FCC and the industry it regulates.

In *Pleasant Broadcasting Company* v. *FCC* (consolidated for decision with *WIYN Radio, Inc.* v. *FCC*) the issue is whether the district or appeals court has jurisdiction, in the first instance, to review FCC forfeiture (fines) orders. We see how the activities of the Commission spill over into the federal court system, where the layers of judicial review can prove frustrating for broadcasters.

Finally, from Sections 401 and 402 of the Communications Act of 1934, we will examine the precise wording of regulations affecting the administrative procedures involved in FCC enforcement functions.

Action for Children's Television v. *F.C.C.**

UNITED STATES COURT OF APPEALS, DISTRICT OF COLUMBIA CIRCUIT, 1977
2 Med.L. Rptr. 2110

Tamm, *Circuit Judge:* This appeal comes to us upon a petition for review of a decision by the Federal Communications Commission (Commission or FCC) not to adopt certain rules proposed by a public-interest organization to improve children's television. We affirm the Commission because we find that it substantially complied

---

*To aid in the comprehension of the main arguments surrounding an issue, some material appearing in the cases in this book has been deleted where indicated. Some citations and notes have been deleted without indication. Readers wishing the complete opinion with citations and notes should consult the original opinion of the court involved.

with the applicable procedures, provided a reasoned analysis for its action, did not depart from established policies, and did not otherwise abuse its discretion.

I. BACKGROUND

a. the rulemaking proceedings

In February, 1970, Action for Children's Television (ACT), a Massachusetts nonprofit corporation, submitted several proposals to the Commission to improve children's television fare, principally by eliminating all sponsorship and commercial content from such programming and by requiring all licensees to provide a minimum amount of age-specific programming for children. Specifically, ACT urged the adoption of the following rules:

(a) There shall be no sponsorship and no commercials on children's programs;

(b) No performer shall be permitted to use or mention products, services or stores by brand names during children's programs, nor shall such names be included in any way during children's programs;

(c) Each station shall provide programming for children and in no case shall this be less than 14 hours a week, as a part of its public service requirement. Provision shall be made for programming in each of the age groups specified below, and during the time periods specified:

  (i) Pre-school; 7 am–6 pm daily
      ages 2–5 7 am–6 pm weekends
  (ii) primary; 4 pm–8 pm daily
      ages 6–9 8 am–8 pm weekends
  (iii) elementary; 5 pm–9 pm daily
      ages 10–12 9 am–9 pm weekends

... The Commission accepted ACT's submission as a petition for rulemaking and invited public comments on the proposals. ...

By its own description, response to the Commission's *Notice* was "overwhelming." More than 100,000 comments were filed, filling 63 docket volumes, licensees and networks submitted extensive formal pleadings and programming data and, during 1972 and 1973, the Commission hosted three days of panel discussions and three days of oral argument during which representatives of the industry and members of the general public were afforded an opportunity to express their views regarding the full spectrum of children's television practices.

In the wake of such manifestly widespread public support for ACT's proposed rules, and, perhaps, in apprehensive anticipation of possible agency adoption of those rules, the broadcast industry undertook limited self-regulation. In 1971, the self-regulatory Code of the National Association of Broadcasters (NAB) was reinterpreted to prohibit the use of certain possibly deceptive advertising techniques. A year later, the Code was amended to limit the proportion of time devoted to publicizing premium offers within any commercial to 50 percent, and the NAB Code authority voted to reduce, from 16 to 12 minutes per hour, the time which could be devoted to non-program material during children's programming. Subsequently, the NAB began to require that advertisements for breakfast cereals emphasize the importance of a balanced diet, that no advertisement encourage children to ingest immoderate amounts of candy and snack foods, and that children not be directly encouraged to pressure their parents into buying advertised products.

These salutary reforms in the broadcast industry reached their climax when, in June, 1974, after NAB officials had met privately with the Commission Chairman, the NAB Television Code adopted the following restrictions:

(1) Beginning in January, 1975, the Code would permit 10 minutes of

non-program material per hour on Saturday and Sunday children's programs and 14 minutes during the week; by January, 1976, the amount would be further reduced to 9½ and 12 minutes, respectively;

(2) commercials for vitamins or drugs would be prohibited during children's programs;

(3) host or hero selling was to be restricted;

(4) program and advertising content was to be clearly separated by an "appropriate device", and

(5) products advertised were to comport with generally accepted safety standards.

Soon thereafter, the Association of Independent Television Stations (INTV) followed suit and recommended that member-stations reduce the non-program content of children's programs to 9½ minutes per hour by January 1, 1976.

These manifestations of industry willingness to improve the quality of children's television by self-regulation satisfied the Commission for the time being, and in October, 1974, it issued a *Children's Television Report and Policy Statement* (the *Report*), which identified areas where improvement was necessary in children's television and which explained the Commission's decision not to adopt specific rules governing children's television practices at that time.

II. PROCEDURAL COMPLIANCE

ACT claims at the outset that the manner in which the Commission concluded these rulemaking proceedings "epitomizes abuse of the administrative process" by its failure to solicit public comment on the industry proposals for self-regulation negotiated "behind the closed doors of Chairman Wiley's office in a private meeting with NAB officials ... [in which] the industry was clearly coerced into action under the threat of FCC regulation." ACT contends

that such action undermines the administrative process since it denies public participation at *every* stage of the regulatory process when issues of critical public importance are considered, frustrates effective judicial review, and renders the extensive comment-gathering stage "little more than a sop. . . ."

In response the Commission argues preliminarily that ACT's procedural objections are not reviewable because neither ACT nor any other party raised them before the Commission through a petition for reconsideration. The literal language of section 405 of the Communications Act certainly supports this contention:

The filing of a petition for rehearing shall not be a condition precedent to judicial review of any such order, decision, report, or action, except where the party seeking such review ... relies on questions of fact or law upon which the Commission, or designated authority within the Commission, has been afforded no opportunity to pass.

The purpose of section 405 is to afford the Commission the initial opportunity of correcting any errors, considering any newly discovered evidence, and generally passing upon all matters prior to their presentation to a reviewing court. The courts have generally given effect to this sound policy by holding that section 405 does preclude a review of objections not first raised before the Commission through a petition for rehearing. This exhaustion requirement is not an inflexible or arbitrary one, however; "it leaves room for the operation of sound judicial discretion to determine whether and to what extent judicial review of questions not raised before the agency should be denied." Nonetheless, we have insisted that the policy of administrative rules embodied in section 405 be departed from only "upon a showing of particular cause and sufficient justification in the public interest."

ACT offers no justification for its failure to raise the issue, of "closed door bargaining" in its petition for rehearing beyond unsupported conclusory assertions that it is "most unlikely" that the Commission would have attempted to cure its "error" had ACT in fact raised the issue in time for the Commission to do so. Such an assertion would be uncompelling in the absence of any concrete indication that reconsideration would have been futile, and, in other circumstances, we would be constrained from entertaining the objection. That objection, however, essentially alleging a denial of administrative due process, raises neither a novel factual issue for which an initial Commission determination is quite clearly both necessary and appropriate, nor a legal issue on which the Commission, *see, e.g., Rules Governing Ex Parte Communications,* 1 F.C.C. 2d 49 (1964), and even this court, *see Courtaulds (Alabama) Inc.* v. *Dixon,* 294 F.2d 899 (D.C. Cir. 1961); *see generally, Sangamon Valley Television Corp.* v. *United States,* 269 F.2d 221 (D.C. Cir. 1959), has not already made known it general views to the contrary. Thus, we believe that a thorough airing of the merits of ACT's procedural challenge would not be inappropriate in this case, especially in light of the agency's tentative conclusion of these informal rulemaking proceedings shortly after ex parte discussions with regulatee representatives.

ACT's characterization of the Commission's action as an abuse of the administrative process misconceives the agency's role in, and the flexibility of, the informal rulemaking proceeding through which the Commission explored the issues raised by ACT's petition. In informal rulemaking, an agency must publish notice in the *Federal Register* of the proposed proceeding, including "either the terms or substance of the proposed rule or a description of the subjects and issues involved." 5 U.S.C. §553(b)(3)(1970). Since the public is generally entitled to submit their views and relevant data on any proposals, the notice "must be sufficient to fairly apprise interested parties of the issues involved...,"

S. Doc. No. 248, 79th Cong., 2d Sess. 258 (1946), but it need not specify "every precise proposal which [the agency] may ultimately adopt as a rule." *California Citizens Band Ass'n* v. *United States,* 375, F.2d 43, 48 (9th Cir.), *cert. denied,* 389 U.S. 844 (1967). *See also Logansport Broadcasting Corp.* v. *United States,* 210 F.2d 24, 28 (D.C. Cir. 1954). The notice publicizing the proceedings on the issues raised by ACT was sufficiently specific, in light of the result, to meet these requirements. The possibility of Commission reliance on industry self-regulation could not have first suggested itself to ACT only when the Commission finally issued its *Report.* The Commission has traditionally relied upon self-regulation when it comes to programming matters. Moreover, the *Notice of Inquiry and Proposed Rulemaking* in Docket 19142 specifically requested comments on the "provisions of the NAB Television Code and its guidelines" concerning restrictions on commercials, 28 F.C.C.2d at 372, J.A. 120, and the industry urged from the outset of these proceedings, in public comments available to ACT, that self-regulation was the only appropriate avenue for corrective action. *See, e.g.,* J.A. 196–219 (comments of NAB).

In addition to notice, an agency must permit meaningful public participation by giving "interested parties an opportunity to participate in the rule making through a submission of written data, views, arguments with or without opportunity for oral presentation." 5 U.S.C. §553(c) (Supp. V 1975). The procedures available to satisfy this requirement are correspondingly diverse, though less so than formerly. No hearing is usually required, and generally no procedural uniformity is imposed. 1 K Davis, Adminstrative Law Treatise §6.01, at 360–61 (1958). The more limited procedural safeguards in informal rulemaking are justified by its more wideranging functional emphasis on questions of law, policy and legislatively-conferred discretion rather than on the contested facts of an individual case. *See* 1 Davis, *supra* at 413. The issues facing the Commission in the proceeding *sub judice* were clearly of a legislative nature, policy considerations predominated, and any rules ultimately adopted would have affected the television and advertising industries, and a significant proportion of television programming.

Under section 553, then, ACT and other interested members of the public, including industry representatives, were entitled to a reasonable opportunity to comment and submit data in support of, or in opposition to, the rules proposed. The Commission substantially met this requirement by permitting a lengthy period for the submission of written comments and by holding six days of informal panel discussions and formal oral arguments. The information gathered by the Commission during this informal rulemaking process, along with any information put forth by the agency itself, represent the factual basis on which the agency must necessarily proceed in making its final determination. This factual predicate must be limited in this way in order to give interested parties proper notice of the reasoning behind the agency's actions and to give meaning to the right to submit comments on the proposed rule. While the agency must consider, analyze and rely on these factual materials which are in the public domain, the agency may draw upon its own expertise in interpreting the facts or upon broader policy considerations not present in the record. We believe that the Commission operated within this framework in this case.

We do not consider that ACT's lack of opportunity to respond directly to NAB's specific self-regulatory proposals vitiated the Commission's decision to accept tentatively those proposals, as *indicia* that self-regulation could prove effective, in lieu of adopting specific rules. On balance, the procedures used by the Commission constitute substantial compliance with the APA's mandate of limited, yet meaningful, public participation. *See Texaco, Inc.* v. *FEA*, 531 F.2d 1071, 1081–82 (T.E.C.A.), *cert. denied*, 426 U.S. 941 (1976).

The Commission's treatment of the various issues and its extended explanation for the action taken detailed in the *Report* show that ACT's participation in these proceedings was not just *pro forma,* and that its submissions were not simply ignored. We have long recognized that any judicial review of administrative action cannot be meaningfully conducted unless the court is fully informed of the basis for that action. *See, e.g., P.A.M. New Corp.* v. *Hardin,* 440 F.2d 255, 259 n.6 (D.C. Cir. 1971). Such review is facilitated by section 553's requirement that an agency incorporate in any rules adopted a statement of their basis and purpose, "[a]fter consideration of the relevant matter presented. . . ." 5 U.S.C. §553(c) (Supp. V, 1975). In *Rodway* v. *United States Dept. of Agriculture,* 514 F.2d 809 (D.C. Cir. 1975), we once again explained the full import of this particular statutory requirement in cautioning that

> [t]he basis and purpose statement is not intended to be an abstract explanation addressed to imaginary complaints. Rather, its purpose is, at least in part, to respond in a reasoned manner to the comments received, to explain how the agency resolved any significant problems raised by the comments, and to show how that resolution led the agency to the ultimate rule.

Here, notwithstanding that no rule was adopted into which the Commission might "incorporate" its basis and purpose, the Commission did explain the reason for its decision to rely for the time being on self-regulation rather than specific rules. This explanation is contained in the record now before us, and it furnishes a basis for effective judicial review.

In holding that ACT's position was not prejudiced by the manner in which the Commission pursued the temporary resolution of these proceedings, we wish to emphasize that we are not insensitive to ACT's disenchantment with what it considered to be the agency's undue deference to the interests of those it was created to regulate. Meaningful public participation is always to be encouraged, since, at the very least, it "[p]ermits administrative agencies to inform themselves and to afford adequate safeguards to private interests." *Final Report of the Attorney General's Committee on Administrative Practice* 103 (1941), *quoted in S. Doc. No.* 248, 79th Cong., 2d Sess. 19–20 (1946). *See* Bonfield, *Public Participation in Federal Rulemaking Relating to Public Property, Loans, Grants, Benefits, or Contracts,* 118 U. Pa. L. Rev. 540, 540–49 (1970). We previously have warned that "when Congress creates a procedure that gives the public a role in deciding important questions of public policy, that procedure may not lightly be sidestepped by administrators." *Environmental Defense Fund, Inc.* v. *Ruckelshaus,* 439 F.2d 584, 594 (D.C. Cir. 1971), *see, e.g., Office of Communication of the United Church of Christ* v. *FCC,* 359 F.2d 994 (D.C. Cir. 1966); *id.,* 465 F.2d 543 (D.C. Cir. 1969) (reversing agency's decision on remand). Nevertheless, while it may have been impolitic for the Commission not to invite further comment on the NAB's proposals, especially in view of the fact that there was no necessity for deciding these difficult issues quickly, we still cannot say that the Commission abused its discretion in deciding not to; *but see Consolidated Rail Corp.* v. *United States,* No. 75-2089, slip op. at 38–39 n.66 (D.C. Cir. Apr. 1, 1977) Wright, J., dissenting), nor are we persuaded that ACT's interests in these proceedings were inadequately protected, much less subverted, by the Commission's action. . . .

IV. CONCLUSION

We might occasionally wish that judges were imbued with legislative powers as well, but we know that under our constitutional system of government we are not. Our authority is limited, both constitutionally and by statute, and this is no less true when we sit in review of the orders of administrative agencies. The Commission, as the expert agency entrusted by Congress with the administration and regulation of the crucial, dynamic, communications field, requires and deserves some latitude in carrying out its substantial responsibilities. It may not be the sole guardian of the public's interest in broadcasting—licensees, the courts and the general public in varying ways share responsibility with it for defining and advancing that interest—but, in the formulation of broadcast policy, the Commission nevertheless must continue to play a leading role.

If our relationship with the Commission and other federal agencies is to remain a partnership, we may not succumb to the temptation of casting ourselves in the unsuited role of *primus inter pares.* Rather, our function in passing upon these particular proceedings must come to an end once we have concluded that the Commission's action was a reasoned exercise of its discretion. Having so concluded upon a careful review of the record before us, the order of the Commission challenged by ACT here is

Affirmed.

Pleasant Broadcasting Company v. *FCC*

UNITED STATES COURT OF APPEALS, DISTRICT OF COLUMBIA CIRCUIT, 1977
2 Med.L.Rptr. 2277

McGowan, *Circuit Judge:* These cases, although argued separately, raise the same threshold issue: whether the court of appeals has jurisdiction to entertain petitions for review of Federal Communications Commission orders imposing monetary forfeitures on broadcast licensees. By an order entered today, the cases have been consolidated for decision. On the basis of the reasons set forth below, we hold that section 504 of the Communications Act of 1934, *as amended,* 47 U.S.C. §504 (1970), vests exclusive jurisdiction in the district courts to review, in the first instance, licensee challenges to forfeiture orders, and accordingly dismisses the petitions for review filed herein.

I

Section 503(b) of the Communications Act, 47 U.S.C. §503(b) (1970), added by the Communications Act Amendments of 1960, Pub. L. 86–752, §7(a), 74 Stat. 894–95, provides the FCC with authority to assess forfeitures of up to $1,000 per violation against any broadcast licensee who "willfully or repeatedly fails to observe any of the provisions of [the Communications] Act or of any rule or regulation of the Commission prescribed under authority of [the] Act. . . ." 47 U.S.C. §503(b)(1)(B). Assessment of a forfeiture must be preceded by written "notice of apparent liability," setting forth the nature of the alleged violation, and by an opportunity for the licensee to show in writing why he should not be held liable. 47 U.S.C. §503(b)(2).[1]

Under section 504(a) of the Act, forfeitures imposed by the Commission are recoverable, absent voluntary payment, only in civil proceedings brought by United States Attorneys in the district courts. *See* 47 U.S.C. §504(a) (1970). *See also* 28 U.S.C.

§1355 (1970). The 1960 Amendments, while expanding the Commission's powers through enactment of section 503(b), inserted language into section 504(a) specifying that in such suits for recovery the Commission's findings and conclusions shall be subject to trial *de novo.* Communications Act Amendments of 1960, *supra,* §7(b), 74 Stat. 895.[2] The Amendments also added a new subsection to section 504 providing that "[i]n any case where the Commission issues a notice of apparent liability looking toward the imposition of a forfeiture . . ., that fact shall not be used, in any other

---

[1] Section 503(b) provides in full: (b)(1) Any licensee or permittee of a broadcast station who—

(A) willfully or repeatedly fails to operate such station substantially as set forth in his license or permit,

(B) willfully or repeatedly fails to observe any of the provisions of this chapter or of any rule or regulation of the Commission prescribed under authority of this chapter or under authority of any treaty ratified by the United States,

(C) fails to observe any final cease and desist order issued by the Commission,

(D) violates section 317(c) or section 509(a)(4) of this title, or

(E) violates section 1304, 1343, or 1464 of Title 18, shall forfeit to the United States a sum not to exceed $1,000. Each day during which such violation occurs shall constitute a separate offense. Such forfeiture shall be in addition to any other penalty provided by this chapter.

(2) No forfeiture liability under paragraph (1) of this subsection (b) shall attach unless a written notice of apparent liability shall have been issued by the Commission and such notice has been received by the licensee or permittee or the Commission shall have sent such notice by registered or certified mail to the last known address of the licensee or permittee. A licensee or permittee so notified shall be granted an opportunity to show in writing, within such reasonable period as the Commission shall by regulations prescribe, why he should not be held liable. A notice issued under this paragraph shall not be valid unless it sets forth the date, facts, and nature of the act or omission with which the licensee or permittee is charged and specifically identifies the particular provision or provisions of the law, rule, or regulation or the license, permit, or cease and desist order involved.

(3) No forfeiture liability under paragraph (1) of this subsection (b) shall attach for any violation occurring more than one year prior to the date of issuance of the notice of apparent liability and in no event shall the forfeiture imposed for the acts or omissions set forth in any notice of apparent liability exceed $10,000.

[2] As amended, section 504(a) provides in relevant part:

(a) The forfeitures provided for in this chapter shall be payable into the Treasury of the United States, and shall be recoverable in a civil suit in the name of the United States brought in the district where the person or carrier has its principal operating office or in any district through which the line or system of the carrier runs; *Provided,* That any suit for the recovery of a forfeiture imposed pursuant to the provisions of this chapter shall be a trial de novo. . . . Such forfeitures shall be in addition to any other general or specific penalties provided in this chapter. It shall be the duty of the various United States attorneys, under the direction of the Attorney General of the United States, to prosecute for the recovery of forfeitures under this chapter. . . .

proceeding before the Commission, to the prejudice of the person to whom such notice was issued, unless (i) the forfeiture has been paid, or (ii) a court of competent jurisdiction has ordered payment of such forfeiture, and such order has become final." *Id.,* §7(d), *now codified at* 47 U.S.C. §504(c) (1970).

Petitioners in the instant cases are two broadcast licensees who are requesting that the respective forfeiture orders entered against them by the Commission under section 503(b) be set aside. As of this date, the forfeitures in question have neither been paid nor made the subject of collection proceedings in the district court. Each petitioner seeks review in this court on the basis of the administrative record compiled before the Commission; and each has represented that, if we uphold the order against it; it will pay the forfeiture without pressing its right to a trial *de novo* in the district court under section 504. . . .

Certainly it is unlikely that Congress intended for persons in the position of petitioners to have two bites at the apple— that is, to be able to challenge the forfeiture order in a court of appeals on the basis of the administrative record and, if unsuccessful, to litigate all issues *de novo* in the district court, with a right of appeal to the court of appeals. Although petitioners have represented that, if we were to rule against them on the merits, they would pay the fines without forcing a collection proceeding in the district court, the enforceability of these representations is open to question. To be sure, it might be possible to devise a workable system for guaranteeing that broadcast licensees who choose to come to a court of appeals would be foreclosed from pursuing the matter further in the district court.[6] But, again, we would be

reluctant to give litigants a choice of forums for review, without some support in the language or history of the forfeiture statute, or some showing that the special procedure enacted by Congress is unavailable or inadequate. . . .

As to the availability and adequacy of district court review, petitioners' main contention appears to be that broadcast licensees wishing to challenge forfeiture orders should not be compelled to endure the burden of an "additional layer" of review, before legal issues are resolved by the court of appeals. Although this consideration conceivably might argue in favor of legislation giving licensees the option of going directly to the court of appeals when they are willing to settle for review on the basis of the administrative record in lieu of trial *de novo, see* note 6 *supra,* we do not think it is a sufficient ground for overriding the review mechanism written into law by Congress. If a licensee does not wish to raise any factual issues with respect to the proposed forfeiture, he may stipulate to the facts and thereby obtain an expedited decision on his legal claims by the district court.[9]

---

[6]For example, petitioners could be required, as a precondition of filing a petition for review, to pay the amount of the proposed forfeiture into the registry of the court of appeals, with the stipulation that the

court would return the money in the event of a successful challenge to the Commission's order, but pay the sum over to the United States Treasury if the order is upheld. This system would have the advantage of eliminating the "double-layer" of review in cases in which the person subjected to the forfeiture order is willing, in effect, to waive his right to a trial *de novo* in the district court. On the other hand, the review function would be split between two courts, with some danger of forum-shopping and of challenges being brought in the court of appeals in cases in which review cannot in fact take place on the basis of the administrative record.

[9]Although this is not a case where the parties are endeavoring to confer jurisdiction on this court by consent, since the respondent Commission is actively asserting that this court lacks jurisdiction, it is well to remember throughout this discussion that jurisdiction founded upon the consent of the parties is not recognized in the federal system. Moreover, in considering the immediate contention about the desirability of avoiding successive consideration of purely legal issues by two different courts, it is to be remem-

The fact that section 504(a) does not expressly provide for initiation of review by aggrieved licensees in no way renders the district court an inadequate forum. If . . . a licensee is suffering from demonstrably adverse consequences from government delay in initiating the collection proceeding, we assume that the licensee could bring a declaratory judgment action against the United States in the district court, and that all issues of fact and law presented by the licensee would be subject to the trial *de novo* procedure set forth in section 504(a).

The Communications Act of 1934 – Selected Provisions

JURISDICTIONS

Sec.401. (a) The district courts of the United States shall have jurisdiction, upon application of the Attorney General of the United States at the request of the Commission, alleging a failure to comply with or a violation of any of the provisions of this Act by any person, to issue a writ or writs of mandamus commanding such person to comply with the provisions of this Act.

(b) If any person fails or neglects to obey any order of the Commission other than for the payment of money, while the same is in effect, the Commission or any party injured thereby, or the United States, by its Attorney General, may apply to the appropriate district court of the United States for the enforcement of such order. If, after hearing, that court determines that the order was regularly made and duly served, and that the person is in disobedience of the same, the court shall enforce obedience to such order by a writ of injunction or other proper process, mandatory or otherwise, to restrain such person or the officers, agents, or representatives of such person, from further disobedience of such order, or to enjoin upon it or them obedience to the same.

(c) Upon the request of the Commission it shall be the duty of any United States attorney to whom the Commission may apply to institute in the proper court and to prosecute under the direction of the Attorney General of the United States all necessary proceedings for the enforcement of the provisions of this Act and for the punishment of all violations thereof, and the costs and expenses of such prosecutions shall be paid out of the appropriations for the expenses of the courts of the United States.

APPEALING COMMISSION DECISIONS

Sec. 402. (a) Any proceeding to enjoin, set aside, annul, or suspend any order of the Commission under this Act (except those appealable under subsection (b) of this section) shall be brought as provided by and in the manner prescribed in Public Law 901, Eighty-first Congress, approved December 29, 1950.

(b) Appeals may be taken from decisions and orders of the Commission to the United States Court of Appeals for the District of Columbia in any of the following cases:

(1) By any applicant for a construction permit or station license, whose application is denied by the Commission.

(2) By any applicant for the renewal or modification of any such instrument of authorization whose application is denied by the Commission.

(3) By any party to an application for authority to transfer, assign, or dis-

---

bered that in ordinary civil litigation parties must go to the District Court even if they wish only to litigate "purely legal" questions, and even if both parties agree that they would prefer to go to the appellate court in the first instance.

pose of any such instrument of authorization, or any rights thereunder, whose application is denied by the Commission.

(4) By any applicant for the permit required by section 325 of this Act whose application has been denied by the Commission, or by any permittee under said section whose permit has been revoked by the Commission.

(5) By the holder of any construction permit or station license which has been modified or revoked by the Commission.

(6) By any other person who is aggrieved or whose interests are adversely affected by any order of the Commission granting or denying any application described in paragraphs (1), (2), (3), and (4) hereof.

(7) By any person upon whom an order to cease and desist has been served under section 312 of this Act.

(8) By any radio operator whose license has been suspended by the Commission.

(c) Such appeal shall be taken by filing a notice of appeal with the court within thirty days from the date upon which public notice is given of the decision or order complained of. Such notice of appeal shall contain a concise statement of the nature of the proceedings as to which the appeal is taken; a concise statement of the reasons on which the applicant intends to rely, separately stated and numbered; and proof of service of a true copy of said notice and statement upon the Commission. Upon filing of such notice, the court shall have jurisdiction of the proceedings and of the questions determined therein and shall have power, by order, directed to the Commission or any other party to the appeal, to grant such temporary relief as it may deem just and proper. Orders granting temporary relief may be either affirmative or negative in their scope and application so as to permit either the maintenance of the status quo in the matter in which the appeal is taken or the restoration of a position or status terminated or adversely affected by the order appealed from and shall, unless otherwise ordered by the court, be effective pending hearing and determination of said appeal and compliance by the Commission with the final judgment of the court rendered in said appeal.

(d) Upon the filing of any such notice of appeal the Commission shall, not later than five days after the date of service upon it, notify each person shown by the records of the Commission to be interested in said appeal of the filing and pendency of the same and shall thereafter permit any such person to inspect and make copies of said notice and statement of reasons therefor at the office of the Commission in the city of Washington. Within thirty days after the filing of an appeal, the Commission shall file with the court the record upon which the order complained of was entered, as provided in Section 2112 of Title 28, United States Code.

(e) Within thirty days after the filing of any such appeal any interested person may intervene and participate in the proceedings had upon said appeal by filing with the court a notice of intention to intervene and a verified statement showing the nature of the interest of such party, together with proof of service of true copies of said notice and statement, both upon appellant and upon the Commission. Any person who would be aggrieved or whose interest would be adversely affected by a reversal or modification of the order of the Commission complained of shall be considered an interested party.

(f) The record and briefs upon which any such appeal shall be heard and determined by the court shall contain such information and material, and shall be prepared within such time and in such manner as the court may by rule prescribe.

(g) At the earliest convenient time the court shall hear and determine the appeal upon the record before it in the manner prescribed by section 10(e) of the Administrative Procedure Act.

(h) In the event that the court shall render a decision and enter an order reversing the order of the Commission, it shall remand the case to the Commission to carry out the judgment of the court and it shall be the duty of the Commission, in the absence of the proceedings to review such judgment, to forthwith give effect thereto, and unless otherwise ordered by the court, to do so upon the basis of the proceedings already had and the record upon which said appeal was heard and determined.

(i) The court may, in its discretion, enter judgment for costs in favor of or against an appellant, or other interested parties intervening in said appeal, but not against the Commission, depending upon the nature of the issues involved upon said appeal and the outcome thereof.

(j) The court's judgment shall be final, subject, however, to review by the Supreme Court of the United States upon writ of certiorari on petition therefor under section 1254 of title 28 of the United States Code, by the appellant, by the Commission, or by any interested party intervening in the appeal, or by certification by the court pursuant to the provisions of that section.

questions for discussion and further research

1. The FCC issues some of its stiffest penalties for violations of rules affecting commercial programming (fraudulent billing, etc.). Why are the penalties so strict in this area of programming?

2. Although critics would be quick to point out any unnecessary growth in the federal bureaucracy, might there be justification for splitting off the common carrier and safety services (telephone, telegraph) functions of the FCC into a separate regulatory agency and permit the FCC to concentrate its efforts more on radio and television broadcast stations?

3. We have discussed specific areas over which the FCC *does not* have jurisdiction. Should some of these areas come under FCC jurisdiction, such as the times when a station runs commercials, the control of legitimate giveaways or contests, news gathering organizations, stereo or quadraphonic broadcasting, libel and slander?

4. Why does the FCC consider one of the most serious violations to be willful misrepresentation?

5. Should the Field Operations Bureau of the FCC have the authority to levy fines without having the violation reviewed by the Broadcast Bureau?

6. Should any fine, regardless of the amount, be brought before the seven FCC commissioners?

7. In its "Notice of Inquiry on a Personal Radio Service," the FCC employed a questionnaire as one method of soliciting reactions from the public. Do you feel that such procedures to collect information are useful?

8. If the criticism is justified that middle staff members exert influence over individual Commissioners by controlling the channels of internal communication at the FCC, is there any solution to the problem?

9. In any regulatory agency, commissioners or the relatives of commissioners owning stock in industries regulated by the agency opens up the potential for charges of conflict of interest. Should specific rules be enacted prohibiting such relatives from owning stock in those industries, and, if so, how distant from a commissioner would a relative have to be to come under the prohibition?

10. Consider Judge Tamm's concluding statement in *Action for Children's Television* v.

FCC and United States: "The Commission, as the expert agency entrusted by Congress with the administration and regulation of the crucial, dynamic, communications field, requires and deserves some latitude in carrying out its substantial responsibilities." What is the meaning of the words "expert agency" in this context, and how much "latitude" does the FCC actually deserve?

11. Is the communications field any more "crucial" and "dynamic" than other industries regulated by government, such as the airlines or railroads?

12. Is industry self-regulation a satisfactory alternative to government control of broadcast programming?

13. What are the advantages and disadvantages to the many layers of review, both within the FCC and the court system, that a broadcaster faces when challenging an FCC decision. (See *Pleasant Broadcasting* v. *FCC*)

14. Should or could the layers of review be reduced?

15. In *Pleasant Broadcasting Company* v. *FCC* (see footnote 6) the court offered the opinion that:

> petitioners could be required, as a precondition of filing a petition for review, to pay the amount of the proposed forfeiture into the registry of the court of appeals, with the stipulation that the court would return the money in the event of a successful challenge to the Commission's order, but pay the sum over to the United States Treasury if the order is upheld. This system would have the advantage of eliminating the "double-layer" of review in cases in which the person subjected to the forfeiture order is willing, in effect, to waive his right to a trial *de novo* in the district court.

Although the court offers the opinion that such an arrangement might result in "forum shopping," do you feel that the proposal as a whole has merit?

additional resources

books

Dordick, H. S., ed., *Proceedings of the Sixth Annual Telecommunications Policy Research Conference,* Lexington, Mass.: Lexington Books/Health, 1979.

Levin, H. J., *Fact and Fancy in Television Regulation,* New York: Russel Sage Foundation, 1980.

Magnant, R. S., *Domestic Satellite: An FCC Giant Step—Toward Competitive Telecommunications Policy,* Boulder, Colo.: Westview Press, 1977.

Mosco, V., *The Regulation of Innovations in the Broadcasting Market,* Cambridge, Mass.: Harvard Program on Information Technologies and Public Policy, 1975.

Owen, B. M., and R. Braeutigam, *The Regulation Game: Strategic Use of the Administrative Process,* Cambridge, Mass.: Ballinger Publishing Co., 1978.

Phillips, C. F., Jr., ed., *Competition and Monopoly in the Domestic Telecommunications Industry,* Lexington, Va.: Department of Economics, Washington and Lee University, 1974.

Phillips, C. F., Jr., ed., *Expanding Economic Concepts of Regulation in Health, Postal, and Telecommunications Services,* Lexington, Va.: Department of Economics, Washington and Lee University, 1977.

Phillips, C. F., Jr., ed., *Telecommunications, Regulation, and Public Choice,* Lexington, Va.: Department of Economics, Washington and Lee University, 1975.

Shepherd, W. G., and T. G. Gies, *Regulation in Further Perspective: The Little Engine That Might,* Cambridge, Mass.: Ballinger Publishing Co., 1974.

Smith, A., *The Politics of Information: Problems of Policy in Modern Media,* London: Macmillan/Atlantic Highlands, N.J.: Humanities Press, 1978.

Steinberg, C. S., *The Information Establishment:*

Our Government and the Media, New York: Hastings House, 1980.

Welborn, D. M., *Governance of Federal Regulatory Agencies,* Knoxville: University of Tennessee Press, 1977.

articles

Adams, A. A., "Broadcasters' Attitudes Toward Public Responsibility: An Ohio Case Study," 16 *Journal of Broadcasting* 407(1972).

Baker, J., "Free Speech and Federal Control: The U.S. Approach to Broadcasting Regulation," 39 *Modern Law Review* 147 (1976).

Bennett, R. W., "Media Concentration and the FCC: Focusing with a Section Seven Lens," 66 *Northwestern University Law Review* 159 (1971).

Brotman, S. N., "Informal Rulemaking Procedures at the Federal Communications Commission: Judicial, Administrative, and Legislative Reform," 1 *Communications and thd Law* 3 (1979).

Brotman, S. N., "Judicial Review of the FCC: The Developing Legacy of Greater Boston," 30 *Journal of Communication* 31 (1980).

Busby, L. J., "Broadcast Regulatory Policy: The Managerial View," 23 *Journal of Broadcasting* 331 (1979).

Busterna, J. C., "Diversity of Ownership as a Criterion in FCC Licensing Since 1965," 20 *Journal of Broadcasting* 101 (1976).

Campbell, D. C., and J. B. Campbell, "Public Television as a Public Good," 28 *Journal of Communication* 52 (1978).

Chamberlin, B. F., "The Impact of Public Affairs Programming Regulation: A Study of the FCC's Effectiveness," 23 *Journal of Broadcasting* 197 (1979).

Chisman, F. P., "Public Interest and FCC Policy Making," 27 *Journal of Communication* 77 (1977).

Clift, C. III, J. D. Abel, and R. Garay, "Forfeitures and the Federal Communications Commission: An Update," 24 *Journal of Broadcasting* 301 (1980).

Colon, F. T., "The Court and the Commissions: *Ex Parte* Contacts and the Sangamon Valley Case," 19 *Federal Communications Bar Journal* 367 (1964-65).

Comay, S. D., "Television Programming, Communication Research, and the FCC," 23 *University of Pittsburgh Law Review* 993 (1962).

Danna, S. R., "The Six-Year Fight to Save WEFM," 22 *Journal of Broadcasting* 425 (1978).

Doyle, S. E., "Do We Really Need a Federal Department of Telecommunications?" 21 *Federal Communications Bar Journal* 3 (1967).

Dugan, T. E., "FCC—Constitutional Right to Free Speech—Limp Libidinal Language," 61 *Marquette Law Review* 534 (1978).

Ford, F. W., "The Impact of Judicial Review on the Federal Communications Commission," 63 *West Virginia Law Review* 25 (1960).

Ford, F. W., "Some Current Problems in Broadcast Regulation," 17 *Federal Communications Bar Journal* 76 (1960).

Garay, R., "The FCC and the U.S. Court of Appeals: Telecommunications Policy by Judicial Decree?," 23 *Journal of Broadcasting* 301 (1979).

Geller, H., and G. Young, "Family Viewing: An FCC Tumble from the Tightrope?" 27 *Journal of Communication* 193 (1977).

Glick, E. L., "WBAP/WFAA—570/820: Till Money Did Them Part," 21 *Journal of Broadcasting* 473 (1977), 473–86.

Kahn, F. J., "The Quasi-Utility Basis for Broadcast Regulation," 18 *Journal of Broadcasting* 259 (1974), 259–76.

Krasnow, E. G., and S. H. Robb, "Telecommunications and the 94th Congress: An Overview of Major Congressional Actions," 29 *Federal Communications Bar Journal* 117 (1976).

Krugman, D. M., "FCC Commissioner, Legal Assistant and Staff Perceptions of Cable TV," 56 *Journalism Quarterly* 3 (1979).

Krugman, D. M., and L. N. Reid, "The 'Public Interest' as Defined by FCC Policy Makers," 24 *Journal of Broadcasting* 301 (1980).

LeDuc, D. R., "Transforming Principles into Policy," 30 *Journal of Communication* 196 (1980).

Litman, B. R., "Public Interest Programming and the Carroll Doctrine: A Reexamination," 23 *Journal of Broadcasting* 51 (1979).

Loevinger, L., "Is There Intelligent Life in Washington?" 29 *Federal Communications Bar Journal* 189 (1976).

Pember, D. R., "Broadcaster and the Public Interest: A Proposal to Replace an Unfaithful Servant," 4 *Loyola of Los Angeles Law Review* 83 (1971).

Pennypacker, J. H., "Comparative Renewal Hearings: Another Dialogue Between Commission and Court," 24 *Journal of Broadcasting* 527 (1980).

Prisuta, R. H., "Broadcast Economics and Public Interest Programming," 54 *Journalism Quarterly* 782 (1977).

Puntigam, C. A., "Television and the Congress: Preserving the Balance," 26 *Federal Communications Bar Journal* 209 (1973).

Robinson, G. O., "FCC and the First Amendment: Observations on 40 Years of Radio and Television Regulation," 52 *Minnesota Law Review* 67 (1967).

Robinson, G. O., "Federal Communications Commission: An Essay on Regulatory Watchdogs," 64 *Virginia Law Review* 169 (1978).

Rosenblum, V. G., "Low Visibility Decision-Making by Administrative Agencies: The Problem of Radio Spectrum Allocation," 18 *Administrative Law Review* 19 (1965).

Rosenfeld, M., "Jurisprudence of Fairness: Freedom through Regulation in the Marketplace of Ideas," 44 *Fordham Law Review* 877 (1976).

Smith, E. C., "Practice and Procedure before the FCC as Viewed by a Hearing Examiner," 7 *Oklahoma Law Review* 276 (1934).

Smith, R. R., and P. T. Prince, "WHDH: The Unconscionable Delay," 18 *Journal of Broadcasting* 85 (1973–74).

Stambler, A., "The Declaratory Order at the Federal Communications Commission," 21 *Federal Communications Bar Journal* 123 (1967).

Stukas, W. B., "Federal Communications Commission and Program Regulation—Violation of the First Amendment?" 41 *Nebraska Law Review* 826 (1962).

Sweeney, W. H., "Regulation of Television Program Content by the Federal Communications Commission," 8 *University of Richmond Law Review* 233 (1974).

Thomas, L. S., Jr., "Federal Communications Commission: Control of 'Deceptive Programming'," 108 *University of Pennsylvania Law Review* 868 (1960).

Warner, H. P., "Subjective Judicial Review of the Federal Communications Commission," 38 *Michigan Law Review* 632 (1940).

Williams, W., Jr., "Impact of Commissioner Background on FCC Decisions: 1962–1975," 20 *Journal of Broadcasting* 239 (1976).

Wollert, J. A., and M. O. Wirth, "UHF Television Program Performance: Continuing Questions on Spectrum Use," 56 *Journalism Quarterly* 346 (1979).

cases

Action for Children's Television v. *F.C.C.,* 2 Med.L.Reptr. 2120 (D.C.Cir. 1977).

Communications System v. *F.C.C.,* 4 Med.L.Rptr. 2003 (D.C.Cir. 1978).

Faulkner Radio v. *F.C.C.,* 2 Med.L.Rptr. 1994 (D.C.Cir. 1977).

The reader will find that while the cases listed above deal with examples of specific "procedures" employed in F.C.C. decision-making, cases found elsewhere in the text, while dealing with broader policy issues, also address issues in Commission procedure.

Allied Agencies

While the Federal Communications Commission is the primary federal agency responsible for regulating broadcasting, other agencies also play important roles. Domestically, the Federal Trade Commission (FTC) has become increasingly concerned with the quality of broadcast advertising. In addition to the FTC, the executive branch of government has been actively involved in regulatory policy affecting radio and television for almost a decade, especially with the creation of the National Telecommunications and Information Administration (NTIA).

In recent years, the U.S. Department of Justice has been increasingly involved in activities concerning broadcasting. We will also examine this agency and see how its efforts integrate with those of the FCC.

In addition, we'll touch briefly on the Office of Technology Assessment (OTA), which supports Congress by providing information for policy decisions on the effects of technology on our society. And on the international scene, we'll examine how the International Telecommunication Union (ITU) works to coordinate the responsible use of the electromagnetic spectrum among countries.

Federal Trade Commission (FTC)

Where broadcasting is concerned, the FTC integrates many of its functions with those of the FCC. In such areas as station promotions, complaints are forwarded to the FTC. The FTC also frequently enters the arena of broadcast advertising, especially when commercial claims are allegedly unwarranted. Because of the increased consumer attention to broadcast advertising, the FTC is acquiring clout, and it is important that we gain a basic understanding of its functions.[1]

The Federal Trade Commission was formed in 1914 by enactment of the FTC Act. The Act's purpose was succinctly stated in its phrase: "unfair methods of competition in commerce are hereby declared unlawful." Closely related to the FTC Act was the Clayton Act, also passed in 1914, which guarded against corporate mergers that would lessen competition. Since 1914, the FTC Act has been amended many times. Some of the most familiar pieces of legislation are the 1966 Fair Packaging and Labeling Act and the 1969 Truth in Lending Act, which requres full disclosure of credit terms. The FTC has five Commissioners, who are appointed, like those of the FCC, by the President with the advice and consent of the Senate for seven-year staggered terms. No more than three Commissioners can be from the same political party. The President designates one of them as chairperson.

FTC organization

The organization of the FTC revolves around the Commissioners and the various departments within the FTC. The *Office of Public Information* acts as a liaison between the FTC and the public and is charged with three primary functions: (1) informing the public about the enforcement activities of the FTC; (2) keeping the Commission advised on public information policy; and (3) coordinating the public information programs of the FTC regional offices.[2] Working under the direction of the FTC chairman, the *Executive Director* is the chief administrative officer of the FTC. The *Administrative Law Judges* conduct trials in cases in which the FTC has issued a complaint. They serve as the initial fact-finders and have tenure much like Federal Judges.[3] Advising the FTC in questions of law and policy is the *General Counsel* who acts as the FTC's chief law officer. The General Counsel represents the Commission in federal courts. The *Secretary* is responsible for keeping the minutes of FTC proceedings and also acts as the custodian of the FTC's records. The signature of the Secretary appears on all FTC orders. This person also handles requests from the public for information via the Freedom of Information and Privacy Acts. Planning the activities of the FTC is the *Office of Policy Planning and Evaluation.* This Office has three functions: (1) to evaluate the Commission's programs every six months and suggest new ones for it to undertake; (2) to develop questions to elicit the information needed by the Commission to assess where the public's interest lies in a given matter; and (3) to determine the effect of previous FTC decisions on the public.[4]

Three key bureaus handle most of the tasks that affect both consumers and practitioners of broadcast advertising. They are the *Bureau of Competition,* responsible for enforcing the antitrust laws; the *Bureau of Economics,* advising the Commission on the economic impact of its decisions; and the *Bureau of Consumer Protection,* charged with investigating trade practices alleged to be unfair to consumers.

The Bureau of Consumer Protection is one of the closest allies of the public, helping to guard it against deceptive advertising. Formed in 1971, the Bureau brought together under one roof all of the various consumer related activities that had been performed by the FTC.[5] The following divisions help to carry out the Bureau's activities:

The Compliance Division is responsible for obtaining and maintaining compliance with Trade Regulation Rules and all cease-and-desist orders prohibiting false and deceptive trade practices under Sections 5 and 12 of the FTC Act, the Wool Products Labeling Act, the Fur Products Labeling Act, the Textile Fiber Products Identification Act, and other statutes for which the FTC has enforcement responsibilities. Regional offices handle the compliance aspects of the cases initiated in their offices.

The Marketing Practices Division is responsible for enforcement of the FTC Act with respect to deceptive or unfair marketing practices which are national in scope.

The National Advertising Division is responsible for enforcing those provisions of the FTC Act which forbid misrepresentation and unfairness in national advertising, particularly food, drug, and cosmetic advertising. . . .

The Special Projects Division has primary responsibility for developing and implementing the "unfairness" doctrine announced in 1972 by the Supreme Court in the Sperry and Hutchinson decision to combat a broad spectrum of abusive practices.

The Special Statutes Division undertakes special non-litigative assignments from the Commission or the Director of the Bureau of Consumer Protection. The Division also enforces the Fair Packaging and Labeling Act, the Truth in Lending Act, and the Fair Credit Reporting Act. Additionally, the Division has enforcement responsibility for the Wool Products Labeling Act, the Textile Fiber Products Identification Act, the Fur Products Labeling Act, and all other special legislation within the Commission's jurisdiction. It has specific responsibility for developing rules relating to warranties.

The Evaluation Division is responsible for advising the Bureau Director and the Commission on how resources should be allocated to most effectively remedy consumer losses. . . .[6]

enforcement functions: investigations

The real power of the FTC lies in its enforcement functions. We'll first review these, then look at a hypothetical case review by the Commission. At the root of the enforcement function is the investigatory process.[7] Here, the FTC can initiate an investigation on its own initiative or at the request of another party, which may issue an official complaint against an advertising claim or other trade practice. During the investigation, the Commission can issue subpoenas or orders requiring persons to testify as well as produce documents. Anyone who is subpoenaed can file an opposition to the order or subpoena within ten days. The FTC can also hold investigational hearings and can order depositions to be taken.

enforcement functions: remedies

The Commission has at its disposal various remedies to correct what it may consider fraudulent trade practices. They include:

Assurance of Voluntary Compliance (Non-Adjudicative). If the Commission believes the public interest will be fully safeguarded, it may dispose of a matter under investigation by accepting a promise that the questioned practice will be discontinued. A number of factors are considered by the Commission in the rare cases in which it accepts such a promise, including (1) the nature and gravity of the practice in question, and (2) the prior record and good faith of the party.

Consent Order. Instead of litigating a complaint, a respondent may execute an appropriate agreement containing an order for consideration by the Commission. If the agreement is accepted by the Commission, the order is placed on the public record for sixty (60) days during which time comments or views concerning the order may be filed by any interested persons. Upon receipt of such comments or views, the Commission may withdraw its acceptance and set the matter down for a formal proceeding, issue the complaint and order in accordance with the agreement, or take such action as it may consider appropriate. Respondents in consent orders do not admit violations of the law, but such orders have the same force and effect as adjudicative orders.

Adjudicative Order. An adjudicative order is based on evidence of record obtained during an adjudicative proceeding that starts when a complaint is issued. The proceeding is conducted before an Administrative Law Judge who serves as the initial trier of facts. After the hearings the judge within 90 days issues his initial decision, which is subject to review by the Commission on the motion of either party or on the Commission's own motion. Appeals from a final Commission decision and order may be made to any proper Court of Appeals and ultimately to the Supreme Court.

Preliminary Injunctions. The Federal Trade Commission has statutory authority to seek preliminary injunctive relief in Federal district court against anyone who is violating or about to violate any provision of law enforced by the FTC.[8]

processing an FTC complaint

To better understand the FTC's enforcement process, let's imagine that you have received a complaint from the FTC, alleging that you are airing false and deceptive commercials (see Figure 3-1).[9] The first notice you would probably receive from the FTC would be a letter. You would then have the opportunity to reply to that letter and explain your position. The FTC at this point may decide that your arguments have merit and simply decide not to pursue. But if the FTC is not satisfied with your arguments, it may proceed to subpoena all pertinent records, such as the details of any product testing you may have undertaken.

Examining the records takes us to step 3 in the review process. If the records clearly show your claims not to be deceptive, then the FTC may consider your case closed. If, on the other hand, it is not content with your test results and still feels the advertising to be deceptive, enter step 4, the beginning of negotiation. Two developments will normally take place during this phase. First, you may offer a consent order, stating that you will agree to remedy the problem, perhaps by taking your commercials off the air. The FTC then has an opportunity either to accept or to reject your consent agreement. If the Commission accepts your agreement, it will be placed on the public record for sixty days. During that time, other parties can file pro or con comments on the agreement. And if the evidence builds up against you, the FTC can actually withdraw from the consent agreement and begin formal proceedings.[10] Second, if the consent order is signed, that usually ends the matter at step 5.

Let us assume that the evidence built up against you during the sixty-day period was substantial, and that the FTC decides to proceed to step 6 and issue a complaint. Moving to step 7, an Administrative Law Judge rules on that complaint. In step 8, the Law Judge issues a decision, which is then reviewed by the

THE FTC ADVERTISING REVIEW PROCESS

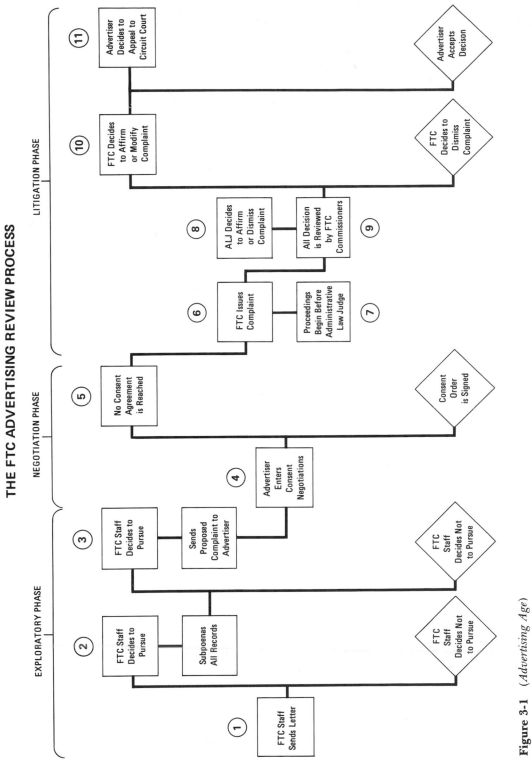

Figure 3-1 (*Advertising Age*)

77

FTC Commissioners in step 9. Once again, you have two options. In step 10, the FTC can decide either (1) to affirm or modify the decision of the Law Judge or (2) to dismiss the complaint. We'll assume that it was not your lucky day, and that the FTC decided to uphold the decision of the Administrative Law Judge, which was to prohibit you from using the commercials in any future advertising. Once again, you have two choices awaiting you in step 11. You can either accept the FTC decision and tell your ad agency to move on some new commercials, or you can tell your lawyers to appeal the FTC decision to the Circuit Court.

Regardless of which decision you make at step 11, one thing is certain: the road to the Court has been both long and rough. You undoubtedly spent large sums of money fighting the case through the Commission, and you will now face additional expense in the appeals process. Keep in mind that although you may feel as though you have been overwhelmed by the power of a high federal agency, the FTC would contend that such safeguards are for the benefit of the public. For the Commission, enforcement powers are a stern warning to advertisers to see that their advertising meets the standards of truth and accuracy. A broadcasting station hyping a rating, misrepresenting a coverage map, or participating in unfair competition faces not only the wrath of the FCC but an equally arduous battle at the Federal Trade Commission.

a note on the FTC's future

While the FTC has been one of the most powerful government agencies, its role and authority may be challenged by the budget cuts proposed by the White House economic program. Recommendations by the Office of Management and Budget would eliminate the FTC's regional offices and trim its budget by 1982 from approximately $74 down to $69 million. More noticeable than the budget cuts would be personnel cuts from a staff of 1780 down to a staff of 1467.

National Telecommunications and Information Administration (NTIA)

In the sphere of regulatory influence, the distinction between the different media and the carriers of communication is becoming increasingly blurred. Network programs travel over telephone company facilities or satellite systems linking domestic and international carriers of communication. Computers whirl forth all kinds of decisions—from election night returns to cost analysis figures to wire service feeds. And trying to project cost analysis for a new cable system becomes more complex when we see the cable system being used for so much more than merely relaying television programs. When the electromagnetic spectrum is being shared by many different countries, all competing for their allotment of available frequencies, how does the United States determine international communications policy? Who looks out for the interests of government in its competition with private industry for use of the spectrum?

These questions force us to look beyond the term *broadcasting* to a new term, which is being used more frequently to label the entire realm of communication services, from broadcasting to computer technology. The term is *telecommunications*,[11] and it encompasses all of the components of our new age of "information technology." This new age includes not only the evening network news but also electronic funds transfers, where a computer does everything from depositing your paycheck to paying your electric bill.

With this new growth of the telecommunications industry, much of which is already under the FCC's jurisdiction, it is not surprising that other political entities have taken an active interest in it. The newest agency to directly concern itself with telecommunications, including radio and television, is the National Telecommunications and Information Administration. Formed under President Jimmy Carter's reorganization plan, the NTIA consolidated the functions of the former Office of Telecommunications Policy (OTP) in the Office of the President and the Office of Telecommunication (OT) in the Department of Commerce. The NTIA, also in the Department of Commerce, has its roots in the Nixon era, which is where we'll begin our discussion.

historical background: the role of the white house and the OTP

The first efforts to elevate telecommunications in importance took place in 1970 under President Richard Nixon, when he established the Office of Telecommunications Policy in the Executive Office of the President. The OTP was formed by an Executive Order, which was part of Nixon's Reorganization Plan. No. 1. Section 2 of the Executive Order spelled out the charge to the new OTP.

> Subject to the authority and control of the President and the Director of the Office of Telecommunications Policy . . . among other things, OTP's charge was to:
>
> (1) Serve as the President's principal advisor on telecommunications; (2) assure that the executive branch views are effectively presented to the Congress and the Federal Communications Commission on telecommunications policy matters; (3) review telecommunications research and development, system improvement and expansion programs, and programs for the testing, operation, and use of telecommunications systems by Federal agencies, and (4) develop, in cooperation with the Federal Communications Commission, a comprehensive long-range plan for improved management of all electromagnetic spectrum resources.[12]

The Director and the Deputy Director of the OTP were appointed by the President with the advice and consent of the Senate. Both were prohibited from holding any other jobs while serving in their respective capacities. With OTP taking control of the duties of the Office of Emergency Preparedness, that office was abolished.[13]

The idea of the White House jumping feet first into communication regulation was not surprising to many political observers, but it was not to the liking of many people either. After all, it was Vice President Spiro Agnew who had leveled strong criticism against the television networks in his famous Des Moines, Iowa speech of 1969. And although the OTP was sounding in theory like a "coordinating" and "advising" agency, the broadcasting industry was still wary. The Executive Order did state it would not "impair any existing authority or jurisdiction of the Federal Communications Commission,"[14] but with the President already able to appoint at least one FCC Commissioner per year, the added influence of this White House directive seemed less than subtle.

Caution was replaced by outright concern in 1972, when OTP Director Clay Whitehead used an Indianapolis, Indiana luncheon of the Society of Professional Journalists, Sigma Delta Chi, to level an Agnew-type critique of the networks. The forum was appropriate for the Nixon administration. Indiana had been a big supporter of Nixon, and a luncheon of journalists is an optimum forum for publicity, even when the speaker is not always newsworthy. Whitehead's speech made news all right—national news. He said: "It's been easy for broadcasters to give lip service to the uniquely American principle of placing broadcasting power and responsibility at the local level." It's been too easy "for broadcasters to turn around and sell their responsibility along with their audience to a network at the going rate for affiliate compensation.... When affiliates consistently pass the buck to the networks, they're frustrating the fundamental purposes of the First Amendment free press provision." Then came the cake. Whitehead announced the administration's intention to sponsor legislation which would rescue local broadcasters from the FCC's "trap door" by extending from three to five years the time for license renewal.

But there was a price to pay. Whitehead proposed that *local* broadcasters would need to meet the needs of their local communities, regardless of where the programs originated. Second, broadcasters would need to show that they "afforded reasonable, realistic, and practical opportunities for the presentation and discussion of conflicting views on controversial issues." Neither idea was new, but Whitehead's statement did catapult them to the public's attention, and it gave the newspaper reporters, who didn't really understand much about broadcast regulation, something to write about. Not forgetting the networks, Whitehead suggested that the plan "should be applied with particular force ... " to the "15 stations owned by the TV networks and the stations that are owned by other large groups." The bombshell was yet to come, however. A longer license renewal for doing what was already being expected of broadcasters, although not universally practiced, was not an equal exchange. There had to be more, ... and there was.

The problem had been how to gain some control over news coverage, coverage with which the Nixon administration had long been dissatisfied. Dipping into a local or network news department was not something for which reporters or the First Amendment would stand still, but if anyone could control the broadcast journalists, it was their bosses, the people who signed the paychecks—*management*. Whitehead went right for the jugular vein. He noted that when a disc jockey lined his pockets with payola money, management would take decisive action. "But men also stress or suppress information in accordance with their beliefs. Will station licenses or network executives also take action against this ideological plugola?" He suggested that "insulating station and network news departments from management oversight and supervision has *never* been responsible and never will be."

"Who else but management ... can assure that the audience is being served by journalists dedicated to the highest professional standards? Who else but management can or should correct so-called professionals who confuse sensationalism with sense and who dispense elitist gossip in the guise of news analysis?"[15] The offer was now clear. If broadcast management would clean up local and network news bias, as perceived by the Nixon administration, the reward would be a five-year license renewal. It was clear that this OTP was a force with which to be reckoned.

The OTP survived the early 1970s intact and continued to be involved in policy making. Finding an ally among cable operators, the OTP proposed the deregulation of cable, so that it could prosper in a free, competitive atmosphere. Since the cable companies had not been making any great strides with the FCC and the Communications Act interpretations, the OTP was a breath of fresh air. The OTP stated that the "framework for the present regulation of cable communications is premised on a law that addresses only limited-signal technologies and that does not, therefore, recognize the potential for this new medium."[16] It also encouraged commercial development to replace the government-supported benefits of the ATS-6 and NASA satellites, which had beamed educational television programming domestically and internationally, and it represented the United States in international treaty negotiations involving INTELSAT and the International Telecommunication Union (ITU), a United Nations organization involved in seeking cooperative international efforts in the development of telecommunication.

Yet whatever accomplishments the OTP did manage to achieve, it did so under a handicap. The Nixon administration's antinetwork views, as reflected in the Agnew and Whitehead speeches, placed a taint on the office from the very beginning. From a broadcaster's viewpoint, having another political appointee from the White House in addition to the FCC Commissioners left much to be desired. And the Office could also very quickly turn into a political liability. Its pro-cable stance didn't thrill the commercial broadcasters; research contracted by the office, regardless of how objective, was susceptible to charges of favoring administration policies; and unlike the FCC, where blame could be spread over seven Commissioners, OTP critics could center theirs directly on the White House.

When Jimmy Carter was elected President, the OTP, which had continued to function under President Gerald Ford, became one of the targets of Carter's own reorganization efforts. Carter appointed an "acting director" of the OTP and sent to Congress a proposal to move the OTP's functions out of the White House and into the Department of Commerce. The Office of Telecommunications was already in the Commerce Department, and it was already doing a large share of the OTP's work.

historical background: the department of commerce and the OT

In response to the Executive Order issued under President Nixon, the Department of Commerce formed the Office of Telecommunications. Section 13 of the Executive Order stated that the OT would, among other things, "(1) conduct technical and economical research . . . ; and (2) conduct research and analysis on radio propagation, radio systems' characteristics, and operating techniques affecting the utilization of the radio spectrum. . . ."[17]

It is easier to understand the rationale for transferring the functions of the NTIA to the Department of Commerce when we see that prior to the recommendation for transfer, fully 41 percent of the Office of Telecommunications budget came from jobs done for the OTP.[18] The OT's organization provided four major units—the Institute for Telecommunication Sciences, the Policy Research Division, the Analytical Support Division, and the Spectrum Management Support Division.

The *Institute for Telecommunication Sciences* was located at Boulder, Colorado, and provided the engineering, technical, and scientific competence for research on electromagnetic wave transmission. It also supported research, engineering, and analyses in telecommunication science for state and local governments, as well as for federal agencies. The three divisions comprising the Institute were the Applied Electromagnetic Science Division, the Spectrum Utilization Division, and the Systems Technology and Standards Division.

The *Policy Research Division* was also located in Boulder. Together with the *Analytical Support Division,* located in Washington, D.C., it conducted the background research and analysis for the areas that came under the auspices of the OTP. The Analytical Support Division concentrated on international and federal communications, while the Policy Research Division concentrated on long-range national communication issues.

The *Spectrum Management Support Division* also addressed the services that were delegated to the OTP. Its functions included conducting engineering analysis, developing computer software, and processing data. Additional functions included coordinating frequency assignments, expanding the electromagnetic spectrum's usable space, and studying radio interference. It also housed the Secretariat of the Interdepartment Radio Advisory Committee (IRAC), which was charged with advising the FCC and the Department of Commerce on frequency assignments and spectrum management policy.

Out of the efforts of these four OT units came various research and policy directions. The OT's *applied research program* analyses, for example, the effectiveness of transmission and receiver systems for the United States Information Agency's Voice of America.[19] The research program developed formulas which helped predict the "electronic" effectiveness of VOA transmissions months in advance, across a wide range of frequencies. Conducting research on the application of fiber optic technology, the OT formed the Task Force on Optical Communications, comprised of representatives from business, government, and education. The Task Force met to discuss new developments and applications of this technology.

Research in *public safety* examined such areas as early warning systems for natural disasters, which would not only aid in predicting a potential disaster caused by natural phenomena but also beam radio and television warning signals directly to home receivers.[20]

In the area of *international telecommunications,* the OT worked closely with the International Telecommunication Union (ITU) in planning international conferences and negotiations. In fact, policy initiatives for the 1979 World Administrative Radio Conference (WARC) resulted from OT research and planning. Two committees of ITU—the International Radio Consultive Committee (CCIR) and the International Telephone and Telegraph Consultive Committee (CCITT) —sponsor study groups that deal with technical problems of common interest to member nations.[21] The OT served in various capacities on these committees, representing the interests of the United States and offering technical knowledge. In cooperation with the ITU, the OT conducted a series of fellowship programs to help educate specialists in ITU member countries. It also initiated a series of broadcast engineering consultancies for foreign countries.[22] OT found itself surveying the radio and television needs of the Ministry of *information exchange*. OT also conducted seminars for other Federal employees and maintained a public information program for nongovernment organizations.[23]

the NTIA is formed

President Carter's reorganization plan creating the NTIA specifically provided for five actions:

1. It transferred all functions of the Office of Telecommunications Policy to the Department of Commerce.
2. It abolished the Office of Telecommunications Policy.
3. It abolished the Office of Telecommunications.
4. It established an Assistant Secretary for Communications and Information in the Department of Commerce.
5. It formed the National Telecommunications and Information Administration, with the Assistant Secretary for Communications and Information as the NTIA Director.

President Carter appointed Henry Geller as the first head of the agency. Geller had been a former Deputy General Counsel and General Counsel of the FCC under two Presidents and had served a stint with the Rand Corporation and later the Aspen Institute Program on Communications and Society.

Although the NTIA's charge is still one of advising the President, and although it is still an Executive Branch agency, its removal from the Office of the President has at least presented the appearance of detachment and created the potential for better cooperation with other agencies of government. How effective that cooperation will be remains to be seen.

Similar in many ways to the old Office of Telecommunications, the NTIA sees itself as having four primary functions, or *program elements*, as the NTIA calls them. The first is *Policy Analysis and Development*, which includes analyzing the issues surrounding common carrier industries, such as telephone communication, developing options for deregulating cable and broadcasting, analyzing issues in international telecommunication, and assessing the issue of protecting privacy in data communications. A second program element is *Telecommunications Applications*, under which are found such concerns as improving telecommunication in rural areas; stimulating minority ownership in broadcasting and cable TV stations; local and state coordination of telecommunication policy; and working on user-industry cooperation in developing satellite systems for public service activities. A third program element is *Federal Systems Spectrum Management*. Under this element falls assessing the Federal use of the electromagnetic spectrum and evaluating the procurement plans of other federal agencies. The fourth program element is *Telecommunication Sciences*, the research arm of NTIA. Studying climatic effects on radio waves, the study of various direct-broadcast systems for public service use, and developing user-oriented standards for federal data communication systems are functions of the Telecommunications Sciences element.

The program elements we have been discussing are just *some* of those perceived by NTIA at its inception as being appropriate functions of the agency. Only the future will determine what road the new agency will take, how much it will become involved in politics, and how effective it will be in formulating policy and dealing with other federal agencies.

U.S. Department of Justice

Sometimes called the largest law office in the world, the U.S. Department of Justice (Figure 3-2) encompasses nine offices, six divisions, seven bureaus, and two boards. The employees of the Department, including all aspects from the Attorney General to the federal prison system, number about 55,000. About 3,600 of this total are engaged as full-time lawyers.[24]

relationship to the FCC

Since 1968, the U.S. Department of Justice, through the Antitrust Division's Special Regulated Industries Section, has participated as a party in both adjudicatory and rulemaking proceedings at the FCC. The reason for its participation is that the United States is a statutory respondent in almost all appeals on FCC decisions. This means that a case would be titled, as a hypothetical example, *WAAA* v. *FCC and the United States*. The Attorney General, who represents the United States, has delegated responsibility in these cases to the Antitrust Division, where it is discharged by the Appellate Section.

Of all the issues confronting the U.S. Department of Justice and the Federal Communications Commission, perhaps none has involved the two agencies more deeply than crossownership. Moreover, that involvement has not always been amicable. Professor Linda Cobb-Reiley of The University of Tulsa has detailed the interaction of the two agencies over crossownership during the 1960s and 1970s. In this excerpt from a paper presented to the Law Division of the Association for Education in Journalism, she writes:

antitrust division and FCC interactions

The first significant dispute between the Antitrust Division and the FCC centered on the proposed merger between the ABC network and International Telephone and Telegraph in 1966. This conglomerate merger required the transfer of ABC's broadcast licenses to ITT. Thus, the merger proposal was submitted to the FCC, which routinely approved it, as is their practice with most license transfers.[25] After a long delay, the Division intervened and asked the FCC for a re-hearing on the matter, charging that the merger would have anti-competitive effects and involved conflicts of interest. Under pressure from the Division, the FCC reconsidered the proposed merger, but again gave its approval. The Antitrust Division promptly filed suit and the case was docketed under the unusual title of *United States* v. *FCC*. Before litigation could proceed, however, the merger plans were dropped by ABC and ITT.[26]

This case demonstrated the Division's reluctance to act even when it has clear jurisdic-

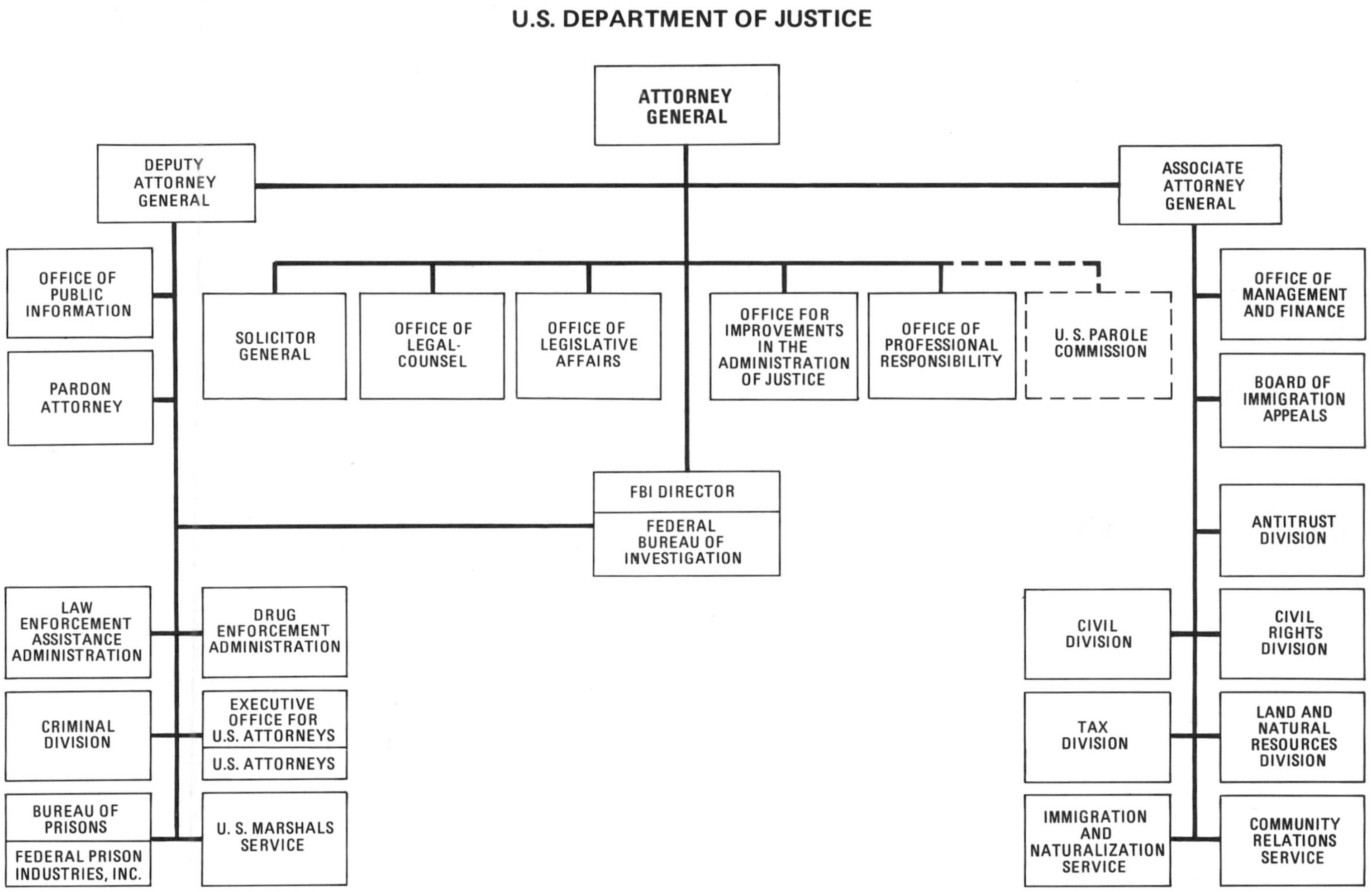
U.S. DEPARTMENT OF JUSTICE
ATTORNEY GENERAL
DEPUTY ATTORNEY GENERAL
ASSOCIATE ATTORNEY GENERAL
OFFICE OF PUBLIC INFORMATION
PARDON ATTORNEY
SOLICITOR GENERAL
OFFICE OF LEGAL-COUNSEL
OFFICE OF LEGISLATIVE AFFAIRS
OFFICE FOR IMPROVEMENTS IN THE ADMINISTRATION OF JUSTICE
OFFICE OF PROFESSIONAL RESPONSIBILITY
U. S. PAROLE COMMISSION
OFFICE OF MANAGEMENT AND FINANCE
BOARD OF IMMIGRATION APPEALS
FBI DIRECTOR
FEDERAL BUREAU OF INVESTIGATION
ANTITRUST DIVISION
LAW ENFORCEMENT ASSISTANCE ADMINISTRATION
DRUG ENFORCEMENT ADMINISTRATION
CRIMINAL DIVISION
EXECUTIVE OFFICE FOR U.S. ATTORNEYS
U.S. ATTORNEYS
BUREAU OF PRISONS
FEDERAL PRISON INDUSTRIES, INC.
U. S. MARSHALS SERVICE
CIVIL DIVISION
CIVIL RIGHTS DIVISION
TAX DIVISION
LAND AND NATURAL RESOURCES DIVISION
IMMIGRATION AND NATURALIZATION SERVICE
COMMUNITY RELATIONS SERVICE

Figure 3-2

tion over a possible antitrust violation as well as its practice of working through the regulating agencies. More importantly, the case signaled the beginning of the Division's attempts to force the FCC to give more attention to the anti-competitive problems emerging in the broadcast industry. Shortly after the ABC-ITT merger was dropped, the Division submitted formal comments and suggestions in the Commission's rulemaking proceedings on cable television and multiple ownership, advocating the adoption of a strong diversification of ownership policy and suggesting that the FCC look into the anti-competitive effects of cross-media ownership.[27]

The Division took even more direct action during this same period by intervening in FCC licensing proceedings. In 1968, it opposed the transfer of a television license in Beaumont, Texas to the owner of the town's only newspaper on grounds that Section 7 of the Clayton Act would be violated.[28]

The next year, the Division requested a full hearing on the license renewal of the only television station in Cheyenne, Wyoming which was operated by the owner of the only newpaper in that market.[29] After the Division's intervention, the Beaumont transfer request was withdrawn and the Cheyenne newspaper owner sold the television station. In a related action, which did not directly involve the FCC but which indicates the Division's concern with cross-ownership, a civil antitrust complaint was filed against the Gannett Company under Section 7 of the Clayton Act. Gannett owned the only newspapers as well as a television station in Rockford, Illinois. The case was eventually settled by a consent decree and Gannett sold the television station.[30]

When the FCC announced its proposed rulemaking on cross-media ownership in 1970, it justified the proposal on the basis of "promoting competition among the mass media involved, and maximizing diversification of service sources and viewpoints. . . ." The proposal also acknowledged the Division's suggestion that the problem of newspaper-broadcasting combinations be pursued.[31] While the Commission's proposal lay dormant for almost three years, the Division increased its intervention in Commission activities. In 1973, the Division filed comments in opposition to the renewal of three Milwaukee broadcast licenses held by the Journal Company, which published morning and evening newspapers in that city. No antitrust violations were alleged, but the Division pointed out the possible anti-competitive effects of this cross-ownership.[32] Then, in 1974, the Division filed petitions to deny television license renewals in seven cities where the stations were owned by newspaper interests.[33] In all of the petitions, the Division argued that local advertising was monopolized by the cross-ownerships in possible violation of Section 7 of the Clayton Act.[34]

Antitrust Division Officials give at least three reasons to explain their 1973–74 license renewal challenges. First, the Division believed that in all of the markets involved in the challenges, an anti-competitive situation existed which violated the antitrust laws.[35] Second, the Division had urged for some time that the FCC ought to deal with cross-ownership monopoly problems on a general rulemaking basis rather than on a case-by-case basis.[36] Finally, the Division was clearly impatient with the FCC's three-year delay in terminating Docket No. 18110. As Assistant Attorney General Thomas Kauper argued before a Senate hearing:

> . . . the practical reasons for filing (the license renewal challenges) reflect, I think, first the fact that the FCC is already considering such issues in docket 18110, which is the rulemaking proceeding addressing these matters. That proceeding is virtually dormant, or was prior to the time we filed these particular petitions. Indeed, part of our reason for filing was to stimulate activity in docket 18110.[37]

The FCC's reaction to the Antitrust Division's concentrated assault on cross-media ownership was predictably routine. Commission Chairman Richard F. Wiley said the petitions would be reviewed by the staff and, if there was any "substance" to the filings, hearings would be held. He also said a decision on the petitions might take several years.[38] However, almost immediately after the petitions were filed, the FCC decided to hold hearings on Docket 18110. According to one FCC legal expert, the Antitrust Division's strategy worked because: "Once enough cases are brought against the FCC resulting in a danger to it of content analysis of individual cases, the Commissioners prefer a rulemaking proceeding which raises less sensitive problems."[39] Division attorneys insisted that the petitions to deny licenses were brought in good faith because they were necessary, but added that "if the petitions have the collateral effect of forcing the FCC into general rulemaking, that result will be long overdue."[40]

Even though the Antitrust Division is not a broadcast regulatory agency like the FCC, it has remained sensitive to public concern over broadcasting. Public interest groups, the industry, and lobbying organizations are familiar with Justice Department procedures and personnel, and each makes an active attempt to be informed on matters in which the Justice Department may play a part.

Office of Technology Assessment (OTA)

Created in 1972, the Office of Technology Assessment (OTA) provides Congress with forecasts on the impact of technology in society. The issues tackled by the OTA range from technology on water supplies to solar-powered satellites. Specifically, the OTA is charged with bringing "a long-term global and comprehensive perspective to bear and to provide Congress with independent, authoritative, evenhanded assessments."[41] For Congress, the OTA is a ready source of digestible information on long-range goals, separate from the more narrow issues that confront the daily pattern of lawmaking. Projects for the OTA are initiated after the approval of a Technology Assessment Board, composed of six senators and six congressmen. Initial requests for studies by the OTA can originate from the OTA Director, the members of the Board, or from the chairpersons of congressional committees.[42]

An example of an OTA technology assessment study is one that was proposed to study the new uses and allocations of the electromagnetic spectrum emerging from the 1979 World Administrative Radio Conference (WARC). Another study deals with education. The OTA sees the potential of new technology moving education away from the local level to a global level.[43] Communication satellites distributing television courses anywhere in the world open up tremendous new policy issues, associated not only with technology but with the future of education as well. The role of the OTA in assessing this future perspective would include:

Technology as a means of improving the quality and availability of education in the formal and informal education systems.

The implications of global educational technology for U.S. educational and foreign policy.

The cost-benefit calculus for technological innovation in education.

The role of institutional factors in the successful introduction of new educational technologies.

The effect of new technologies of education on students' ability to acquire basic skills (e.g., reading) and personality traits (e.g., persistence).[44]

A broad-based issue assessment of new technology in society took place in 1978 and 1979 under OTA auspices. Over 5,000 people responded to a request for priorities for the OTA to examine. From a list of items selected from individuals and publications, the OTA is now focusing its efforts on these high priority items.

Defense Communications Agency (DCA)

As our worldwide communication systems become increasingly integrated, and as satellite communication becomes widespread and important, more agencies of government are becoming deeply involved in using these channels of communication that are made possible by the electromagnetic spectrum. Consequently, the communication roles that these agencies, services, and bureaus play are taking on critical new dimensions. As broadcasting in the traditional sense integrates with the wider realm of telecommunications, the services that are performed and how they are coordinated and controlled demand our attention. It means new demands on new channels of communication. In many cases, these channels carry computer data. In others, they carry voice networks for issuing directives or commanding remote outposts.

Coordinating much of this activity in government-controlled systems is an agency within the Department of Defense, the Defense Communications Agency (DCA). Established in 1960 as a Department of Defense Management Organization (Figure 3-3), the DCA provides central management functions to certain communications-related activities of the Army, Navy, and Air Force.[45] The DCA's primary responsibility is the management and direction of the Defense Communications System (DCS), which includes all long-haul, point-to-point communication systems of the Army, Navy, and Air Force. Included under the DCS umbrella are supervision of circuitry by radio, wire, submarine cable, and satellites. Not included are the Navy's fleet broadcast and ship-to-shore circuits, ground-to-air and air-to-air communications of the Air Force, and the Army's tactical communications between field units where mobile equipment is employed.

Operating as part of a worldwide communication network, the DCS has an operation control center located in Washington, D.C. Area centers operate in the Pacific and Europe; and regional centers, which report to the area centers, are located in Japan and the Phillipines (Figure 3-4). Both area and regional centers are in constant contact with each other by telephone or teletype. The DCS is also the "architect" of satellite communication related to defense. In this role, it plans the engineering requirements as well as the integration of Army, Navy, and Air Force use of satellite communication.

Along with the responsibilities for hardware and communication components of the DCS, the Director of the agency oversees a Vice Director, Deputy Director for Plans and Programs, Deputy Director for Operations, Deputy Director for Command and Control, Deputy Director for Systems Engineering,

DEFENSE DEPARTMENT MANAGEMENT AGENCIES

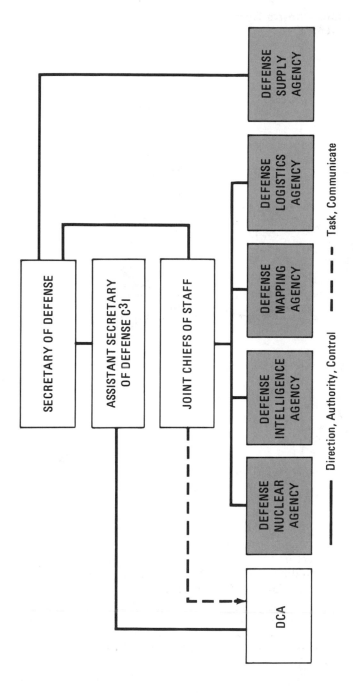

Direction, Authority, Control

Task, Communicate

DCA Operations Control Complex
(DOCC)

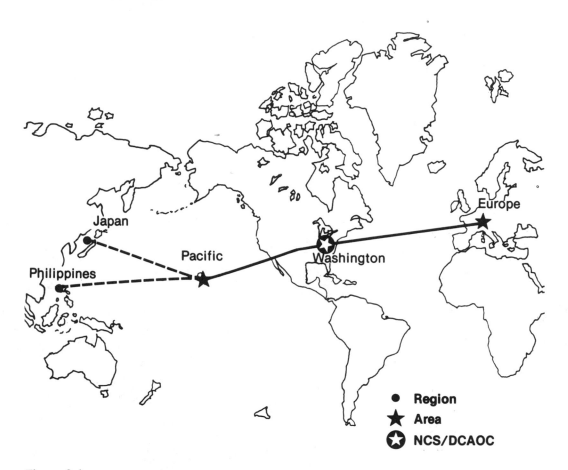

Figure 3-4

Deputy Director for Military Satellite Communications, a Comptroller, and about 1,500 military and 1,500 civilian support personnel.[46] The Director is also Manager of the National Communications System (NCS), which incorporates the major communication networks of the Department of State, Federal Aviation Administration, General Services Administration, National Aeronautics and Space Administration, Department of Energy, Central Intelligence Agency, Department of the Interior, Department of Commerce, and International Communications Agency.[47]

In an age of advanced technology and big government, communication systems are vital. We need to keep alert as to how these systems function and what impact they will have on the global communication needs of the future.

The International Telecommunication Union (ITU)

The International Telecommunication Union is a United Nations organization responsible for coordinating the use of telecommunications among nations.[48] It does not have the enforcement powers of the Federal Communications Commission or of the Radio and Television Commission in Canada. Rather, it is a collective body of sovereign states and is only as strong as the willingness of the sovereign states to abide by its treaties. In other words, if a country violates an ITU agreement, no "field office" will revoke licenses or impose forfeitures. ITU's sovereign states view it not so much as an independent agency but as an arena in which to negotiate the uses of telecommunications.[49] And as that arena, it has been effective.

background and functions

The history of the International Telecommunication Union (ITU) dates back to 1849, when the impact of the telegraph was dawning on Europe. In that year, Austria and Prussia signed a treaty to join their telegraph lines. By 1865, the treaties that had been signed and the new technology prompted twenty European states to meet in Paris to approve an international agreement, entitled the *International Telegraph Convention*. Included in that agreement (convention) were a set of Telegraph Regulations. A series of Telegraph Conferences grew out of the Paris agreement, and at the Vienna Conference in 1868, the International Bureau of Telegraph Administrations was formed. Located in Berne, Switzerland, it became known as the "Berne Bureau," and it was charged with a variety of administrative functions. It was staffed and funded mostly by the Swiss. The 1865 Convention, the periodic conferences, and the Berne Bureau collectively became known in 1875 as the International Telegraph Union, with the International Telegraph Convention as its charter. By 1885, the International Telegraph Union was involved with telephone as well as with telegraph.

At this same time, Marconi was tinkering with the new technology that would soon revolutionize the world's concepts of communication. The rapid corporate development of the British Marconi Wireless Company created a worldwide monopoly. This irritated the German government to the point that it convened a conference in 1903 to resolve some of the problems resulting from the monopoly, specifically the failure of ships equipped with Marconi apparatus to communicate with ships equipped with apparatus manufactured by other companies. Six of the eight sovereign states in attendance signed an agreement, which, although mostly protocol, became the foundation for international radio regulations. The agreement called for wireless stations to "operate, as far as possible, in such a manner as not to interfere with the working of other stations."[50] Further international cooperation emerged from the first International Radio-Telegraph Conference in 1906. There, twenty-seven nations adopted the Radio-Telegraph Convention and specific Radiotelegraph Regulations. Realizing that radio was a rapidly changing technology, the nations also made provisions to meet at periodic administrative conferences. The Berne Bureau, already serving the telegraph and telephone interests, was designated to handle the administrative duties of the radio organization.

Gradually the Radio-telegraph Convention (agreements) and the periodic conferences together came to be called the Radio-telegraph Union. Except for the fact that they shared the Berne Bureau, the two organizations—the International Telegraph Union and the Radio-telegraph Union—operated independently in 1932. It was in that year that the two agreements were combined. The International Telegraph Convention and the Radio-telegraph Convention merged into a unified agreement called the International Telecommunication Convention.

Both organizations also combined. The International Telegraph Union and the Radio-telegraph Union became the International Telecommunication Union, with the Convention as its charter. The respective radio, telegraph, and telephone regulations of the previous organizations were welded into three sets of international regulations—radio, telegraph, and telephone—and annexed to the International Telecommunication Convention. The primary functions of the ITU include:

(1) Effective allocations of the radio frequency spectrum and registration of radio frequency assignments;

(2) Coordinating efforts to eliminate harmful interference between radio stations of different countries and to improve the use made of the radio frequency spectrum;

(3) Fostering collaboration with respect to the establishment of the lowest possible rates;

(4) Fostering the creation, development, and improvement of telecommunication equipment and networks in new or developing countries by every means at its disposal, especially its participation in the appropriate programs of the United Nations;

(5) Promoting the adoption of measures for ensuring the safety of life through the cooperation of telecommunication services;

(6) Undertaking studies, making regulations, adopting resolutions, formulating recommendations and opinions, and collecting and publishing information concerning telecommunications matters benefiting all Members and Associate Members.[51]

organization

Let's examine typical ITU activities. At any given time, the ITU may send cooperative teams of experts to help developing nations establish modern communications systems. On an annual basis, upward of 300 experts are out on field missions, and 400 people are undergoing training in telecommunication services. ITU's technical cooperation activity continues to center on "(1) promoting the development of regional telecommunication networks in Africa, Asia, and Latin America; (2) strengthening the telecommunication technical and administrative services in developing countries; and (3) developing the human resources required for telecommunications."[52] The ITU also sponsors numerous feasibility studies for new systems of communication. In addition, it is directly involved in negotiations to secure funding sources for new telecommunication systems. Some of these sources include the International Bank for Reconstruction and Development, the African Development Bank, the Asian Development Bank, and regional banks.

The machinery to carry out the functions of ITU is housed in six areas, which have evolved out of various conferences and mergers over the years. The six are:[53]

Plenipotentiary Conference. The Plenipotentiary Conference is the supreme body of the ITU. It is composed of all of the ITU member nations, and it meets approximately every seven years to revise the International Telecommunication Convention. It differs somewhat from other UN conferences in that it tackles a complete, not a partial, revision of the Convention, and, compared to other conferences, it meets rather infrequently.

Administrative Council. The Administrative Council is composed of twenty-nine members elected on a regional basis. The Council meets for about a month each year to conduct business between the Plenipotentiary Conferences.

Administrative Conferences. Administrative Conferences are called periodically to revise the regulations annexed to the Convention. The Radio Conferences, called World Administrative Radio Conferences (WARC), examine such issues as international allocation of the electromagnetic spectrum.

International Consultative Committee. We learned earlier that the two International Consultative Committees are the International Radio Consultative Committee (CCIR) and the International Telephone and Telegraph Consultative Committee (CCITT). Both the CCIR and the CCITT consist of plenary assemblies that meet every three to five years, periodically convened Study Groups, and full-time specialized Secretariats. The Committees make recommendations on such developments as technical specifications for equipment. The origin of the CCIT dates back to a 1955 merger of two separate Committees, the CCIF, which dealt with telephone, and the CCIT, representing telegraph interests. The CCIT and CCIF were originally formed at the 1926 Paris Conference of the International Telegraph Union. The CCIR traces its founding to the 1927 Washington Radio-Telegraph Conference.

International Frequency Registration Board (IFRB). The IFRB is composed of five elected members—reduced from nine in 1965 as a compromise with those who wanted it abolished altogether. The Board is responsible for adopting international telecommunication technical standards, and it maintains a Master Register of international frequency use. When a country desires to use a certain frequency, it notifies the IFRB, which then determines if the use will meet the regulations of the ITU and not interfere with other registrants.

General Secretariat. The General Secretariat carries out the administrative duties of the ITU. It consists of an elected Secretary General and Deputy Secretary General. The General Secretariat does not have the authority to establish policy.

world administrative radio conferences (WARC)

The World Administrative Radio Conferences (WARC) that are called by the ITU leave an indelible impression on international radio regulation. These conferences meet periodically to consider either limited or general topics of importance to member nations and the world use of communications. An example of a limited WARC was held in 1977 to deal with satellite communication. After five weeks of negotiations, a treaty emerged, which provided for direct-to-home and conventional satellite communications in the 11.7 to 12.2 Ghz area of the electromagnetic spectrum. A more general conference, WARC 1979, was held in Geneva, Switzerland. WARC reviewed the entire international use of the electromagnetic spectrum and established policy for that use for much of the remainder of the twentieth century. Since each country has one vote, the superpowers do not necessarily control policy the way they do in other international negotiations. The Conference examines frequency use based on different regions of the world, with a common goal of permitting the greatest latitude of spectrum use without interference.

The planning for the 1979 WARC began long before the meeting date, for policy first had to be formulated on a national basis and then presented to the international conference. A number of government agencies were involved in this policy formation in the United States, including the FCC, the OTP, and the OT in the Commerce Department. The FCC issued Notices of Inquiries, seeking response from broadcasters on various topics of importance to WARC 1979. Special editions of *FCC Actions Alert* called the WARC meeting to the attention of the public and citizens' groups. At the same time, the Commission established a series of FCC Service Working Groups to deal with specific types of communication needs. These groups developed recommendations for such topics as aeronautical mobile, amateur radio, aural AM broadcasting, aural FM broadcasting, auxiliary broadcast services, broadcasting-satellite, domestic land mobile radio, fixed-satellite, international broadcasting, land mobile radio, maritime mobile, private microwave, radio astronomy, radio relay, and television broadcasting. Armed with this feedback, the FCC then developed, in cooperation with the other agencies, policies to reflect the needs of each of those areas represented. The United States Department of State took over at that point, officially representing America at the International Conference. Whenever a treaty is agreed upon at a conference such as WARC, the State Department presents the treaty for ratification by the President with the advice and consent of the Senate. Once signed, the treaty becomes international law.

As with any organization of international magnitude, the ITU has many critics, and continuing measures are undertaken to reorganize it and change or redistribute its policy and administrative functions. Sovereign states are very much concerned with autonomy where their communication systems are concerned. And this attitude has caused resistance to any increase in power for the ITU beyond its current registry and coordinating functions. The relationship with the United Nations still remains somewhat of a stumbling block, since nations that are not UN members cannot be members of the ITU. In fact, one recommendation for changing the ITU is to open its membership to all countries of the world.[54] It has been recommended that the ITU should have the ability to arbitrate conflicts between its members and also have some enforcement powers over its Conventions, since a Convention or regulation, once ratified and accepted by the member countries, becomes international law. Both of these courses would require the establishment of full-scale judicial machinery, although this would bring with it the problem of enforcement. Other suggestions for improving the ITU include establishing an international communication research center to supplement the work now being done at the domestic level and expanding technical assistance.

summary

Along with the FCC, other regulatory agencies involved in broadcasting are the Federal Trade Commission (FTC), the National Telecommunications and Information Administration (NTIA), and the International Telecommunication Union (ITU).

The FTC is organized much like its communication counterpart, the FCC. The Executive Director is the chief administrator, Administrative Law Judges conduct trials in complaint cases, the General Counsel is the FTC's attorney, and the Secretary keeps minutes in FTC meetings and keeps the FTC's records. An Office of Policy Planning and Evaluation is charged with evaluating programs, developing questions to elicit information, and determining the effects of FTC decisions on the public. The three FTC bureaus most directly concerned with broadcasting are the Bureau of Competition, the Bureau of Economics, and the Bureau of Consumer Protection.

The newest federal agency responsible for telecommunication policy is the National Telecommunications and Information Administration. The NTIA's history dates back to the Nixon administration's reorganization plan, which formed the Office of Telecommunications Policy (OTP) in the Office of the President and the Office of Telecommunication (OT) in the Department of Commerce. The OTP was beset with numerous political issues, which limited its effectiveness. President Carter reduced the Executive Branch's involvement in telecommunications policy by abolishing the OTP and the OT and creating the NTIA in the Department of Commerce. In recent years, the U.S. Department of Justice has become more involved in broadcast regulation, principally as a party in crossownership issues. Giving support to Congress on policy matters is the Office of Technology Assessment (OTA), which issues even-handed reports on the probable effects of new technology on society. With more and more government agencies using communication, and with the traditional media of radio and television becoming more and more integrated with data communication, agencies such as the Defense Communications Agency (DCA) will play increasingly important roles in coordinating government's needs for space on the electromagnetic spectrum.

At the international level, the International Telecommunication Union (ITU) works to establish and administer agreements between countries on the use of the electromagnetic spectrum. A United Nations agency, the ITU is an outgrowth of the telegraph era of the mid-1800s. It has gradually evolved through a series of telegraph and radiotelegraph agreements (conventions) into its current role as a coordinator of telecommunication policies and applications throughout the world.

material for analysis

The Federal Trade Commission has taken an active and well-publicized role in controlling advertising content. Moreover, the courts have ruled somewhat favorably toward the FTC, giving it broad authority in many recent and significant cases. One well-publicized and precedent-setting case involved Listerine Antiseptic mouthwash and the affirmation by the United States Court of Ap-

95

peals for the District of Columbia that Listerine would be required to engage in corrective advertising. In addition to raising the issue of freedom of speech, the Warner-Lambert Company, as the makers of Listerine, challenged the power of the FTC to issue corrective advertising orders. By reading the Appeals Court's position on FTC power, we can gain a deeper understanding of how the FTC operates and the role it can play over the content of advertising in both broadcast and print media. This case in particular provides some important issues to which we should be alert. When reading the decision, we can compare the power of the Federal Trade Commission to that of the Federal Communications Commission. Then we should ask ourselves if the First Amendment takes a back seat to the important guarantee of truth in advertising.

We will also examine the UNESCO Declaration concerning the mass media's role in strengthening understanding. Notice the breadth of the resolution. Notice also that enforcement of such a document is predicated on the good faith efforts of the member nations. Such a Declaration can become both the justification and the supporting evidence for responsible use of the mass media in international forums. Could it be considered a statement of international "public interest, convenience, and necessity?"

Warner-Lambert Company v. *Federal Trade Commission*

UNITED STATES COURT OF APPEALS, DISTRICT OF COLUMBIA, 1977

562 F.2d 749, 183 U.S.App.D.C. 230 2 Med.L.Rptr. 2303

Wright Circuit Judge: The Warner-Lambert Company petitions for review of an order of the Federal Trade Commission requiring it to cease and desist from advertising that its product, Listerine Antiseptic mouthwash, prevents, cures, or alleviates the common cold. The FTC order further requires Warner-Lambert to disclose in future Listerine Advertisements that: "Contrary to prior advertising, Listerine will not help prevent colds or sore throats or lessen their severity."[1] We affirm but modify the order to delete from the required disclosure the phrase "Contrary to prior advertising."

I. BACKGROUND

The order under review represents the culmination of a proceeding begun in 1972,

when the FTC issued a complaint charging petitioner with violation of Section 5 (a) (1) of the Federal Trade Commission Act[2] by misrepresenting the efficacy of Listerine against the common cold.

Listerine has been on the market since 1879. Its formula has never changed. Ever since its introduction it has been represented as being beneficial in certain respects for colds, cold symptoms, and sore throats. Direct advertising to the consumer, including the cold claims as well as others, began in 1921.

Following the 1972 complaint, hearings were held before an administrative law judge (ALJ). The hearings consumed over four months and produced an evidentiary

---

[1]This requirement terminates when petitioner has expended on Listerine advertising a sum equal to the average annual Listerine advertising budget for the period of April 1962 to March 1972, approximately ten million dollars.

[2]15 U.S.C. §45(a)(1) (1970). At the time the complaint issued, §5(a)(1) stated that "[u]nfair methods of competition in commerce, and unfair or deceptive acts or practices in commerce, are hereby declared unlawful." This was amended in 1975 to substitute "in or affecting commerce" for the phrase "in commerce." *See* 15 U.S.C. §45(a)(1) (Supp. V 1975).

record consisting of approximately 4,000 pages of documentary exhibits and the testimony of 46 witnesses. In 1974 the ALJ issued an initial decision sustaining the allegations of the complaint. Petitioner appealed this decision to the Commission. On December 9, 1975, the Commission issued its decision essentially affirming the ALJ's findings. It concluded that petitioner had made the challenged representations that Listerine will ameliorate, prevent, and cure colds and sore throats, and that these representations were false. Therefore the Commission ordered petitioner to:

(1) cease and desist from representing that Listerine will cure colds or sore throats, prevent colds or sore throats, or that users of Listerine will have fewer colds than nonusers;[3]

(2) cease and desist from representing that Listerine is a treatment for, or will lessen the severity of, colds or sore throats; that it will have any significant beneficial effect on the symptoms of sore throats or any beneficial effect on symptoms of colds; or that the ability of Listerine to kill germs is of medical significance in the treatment of colds or sore throats or their symptoms;

(3) cease and desist from disseminating any advertisement for Listerine unless it is clearly and conspicuously disclosed in each such advertisement, in the exact language below, that: "Contrary to prior advertising, Listerine will not help prevent colds or sore throats or lessen their severity." This requirement extends only to the next ten million dollars of Listerine advertising.[4]

Petitioner seeks review of this order. The American Advertising Federation and the Association of National Advertisers have filed briefs as *amici curiae*....

[3]Petitioner does not contest this part of the order on appeal.
[4]*See* note 1 *supra*.

III. THE COMMISSION'S POWER

Petitioner contends that even if its advertising claims in the past were false, the portion of the Commission's order requiring "corrective advertising" exceeds the Commission's statutory power. The argument is based upon a literal reading of Section 5 of the Federal Trade Commission Act, which authorizes the Commission to issue "cease and desist" orders against violators and does not expressly mention any other remedies. The Commission's position, on the other hand, is that the affirmative disclosure that Listerine will not prevent colds or lessen their severity is absolutely necessary to give effect to the prospective cease and desist order; a hundred years of false cold claims have built up a large reservoir of erroneous consumer belief which would persist, unless corrected, long after petitioner ceased making the claims.

The need for the corrective advertising remedy and its appropriateness in this case are important issues which we will explore *infra*. But the threshold question is whether the Commission has the authority to issue such an order. We hold that it does.

Petitioner's narrow reading of Section 5 was at one time shared by the Supreme Court. In *FTC* v. *Eastman Kodak Co.* the Court held that the Commission's authority did not exceed that expressly conferred by statute. The Commission has not, the Court said, "been delegated the authority of a court of equity."

But the modern view is very different. In 1963 the Court ruled that the Civil Aeronautics Board has authority to order divestiture in addition to ordering cessation of unfair methods of competition by air carriers. The CAB statute, like Section 5, spoke only of the authority to issue cease and desist orders, but the Court said, "We do not read the Act so restrictively.... [W]here the problem lies within the purview of the Board, ... Congress must have intended to give it authority that was ample to deal with the evil at hand." The Court continued, "Authority to mold administrative decrees is indeed like the authority of courts to frame injunctive decrees. . . . [The] power to order divestiture need not be explicitly included in the powers of an administrative agency to be part of its arsenal of authority. . . .

Later, in *FTC* v. *Dean Foods Co.,* the Court applied *Pan American* to the Federal Trade Commission. In upholding the Commission's power to seek a preliminary injunction against a proposed merger, the Court held that it was not necessary to find express statutory authority for the power. Rather, the Court concluded, "It would stultify congressional purpose to say that the Commission did not have the . . . power . . . . Such ancillary powers have always been treated as essential to the effective discharge of the Commission's responsibilities."

Thus it is clear that the Commission has the power to shape remedies which go beyond the simple cease and desist order. Our next inquiry must be whether a corrective advertising order is for any reason outside the range of permissible remedies. Petitioner and *amici curiae* argue that it is because (1) legislative history precludes it, (2) it impinges on the First Amendment, and (3) it has never been approved by any court.

a. legislative history

Petitioner relies on the legislative history of the 1914 Federal Trade Commission Act and the Wheeler-Lea amendments to it in 1938 for the proposition that corrective advertising was not contemplated. In 1914 and in 1938 Congress chose not to authorize such remedies as criminal penalties, treble damages, or civil penalties, but that fact does not dispose of the question of corrective advertising.[33]

Petitioner's reliance on the legislative history of the 1975 amendments to the Act is also misplaced. The amendments added a new Section 19 to the Act authorizing the Commission to bring suits in federal District Court to redress injury to consumers resulting from a deceptive practice. The section authorizes the court to grant such relief as it "finds necessary to redress injury to consumers or other persons, partnerships, and corporations resulting from the rule violation or the unfair or deceptive act or practice," including, but not limited to,

> rescission or reformation of contracts, the refund of money or return of property, the payment of damages, and public notification respecting the rule violation or the unfair or deceptive act or practice. . . .

Petitioner and *amici* contend that this congressional grant *to a court* of power to order public notification of a violation establishes that the Commission by itself does not have that power.

We note first that "public notification" is not synonymous with corrective advertising; public notification is a much broader term and may take any one of many forms.[36] Second, the "public notification" contemplated by the amendment is directed at *past* consumers of the product ("to redress injury"), whereas the type of

---

[33]It is true that one Court of Appeals has relied on this history in concluding that the Commission does not have power to order restitution of ill-gotten monies to the injured consumers. *Heater* v. *FTC*, 503 F.2d 321 (9th Cir. 1974). But restitution is not corrective advertising. Ordering refunds to *past* consumers is very different from ordering affirmative disclosure to correct misconceptions which *future* consumers may hold. Moreover, the *Heater* court itself recognized this distinction and expressly distinguished corrective advertising, which it said the Commission is authorized to order, from restitution. 503 F.2d at 323 n.7 and 325 n.13.

[36]For example, it might encompass requiring the defendant to run special advertisements reporting the FTC finding, advertisements advising consumers of the availability of a refund, or the posting of notices in the defendant's place of business.

corrective advertising currently before us is directed at *future* consumers. Third, petitioner's construction of the section runs directly contrary to the congressional intent as expressed in a later subsection: "Nothing in this section shall be construed to affect any authority of the Commission under any other provision of law." Moreover, this intent is amplified by the conference committee's report:

> The section . . . is not intended to modify or limit any existing power the Commission may have to itself issue orders designed to remedying [*sic*] violations of the law. That issue is now before the courts. It is not the intent of the Conferees to influence the outcome in any way.

We conclude that this legislative history cannot be said to remove corrective advertising from the class of permissible remedies.

b.   the first amendment

[1] Petitioner and *amici* further contend that corrective advertising is not a permissible remedy because it trenches on the First Amendment. Petitioner is correct that this triggers a special responsibility on the Commission to order corrective advertising only if the restriction inherent in its order is no greater than necessary to serve the interest involved. But this goes to the appropriateness of the order in this case, an issue we reach in Part IV of this opinion. *Amici curiae* go further, arguing that, since the Supreme Court has recently extended First Amendment protection to commercial advertising, mandatory corrective advertising is unconstitutional.

A careful reading of *Virginia State Board of Pharmacy* v. *Virginia Citizens Consumer Council* compels rejection of this argument. For the Supreme Court expressly noted that the First Amendment presents "no obstacle" to government regulation of false or misleading advertising. The First Amendment, the Court said,

as we construe it today, does not prohibit the State from insuring that the stream of commercial information flow[s] cleanly as well as freely.

In a footnote the Court went on to delineate several differences between commercial speech and other forms which may suggest "that a different degree of protection is necessary. . . ." For example, the Court said, they may

make it appropriate to require that a commercial message appear in such a form, or include such additional information, warnings, and disclaimers, as are necessary to prevent its being deceptive.

The Supreme Court clearly foresaw the very question before us, and its statement is dispositive of *amici's* contention.

c.   precedents

According to petitioner, "The first reference to corrective advertising in Commission decisions occurred in 1970, nearly fifty years and untold numbers of false advertising cases after passage of the Act." In petitioner's view, the late emergence of this "newly discovered" remedy is itself evidence that it is beyond the Commission's authority. This argument fails on two counts. First the fact that an agency has not asserted a power over a period of years is not proof that the agency lacks such power. Second, and more importantly, we are not convinced that the corrective advertising remedy is really such an innovation. The label may be newly coined, but the concept is well established. It is simply that under certain circumstances an advertiser may be required to make affirmative disclosure of unfavorable facts.

One such circumstance is when an advertisement that did not contain the disclosure would be misleading. For example, the Commission has ordered the sellers of treatments for baldness to disclose that the vast majority of cases of thinning hair and baldness are attributable to heredity, age, and endocrine balance (so-called "male pattern baldness") and that their treatment would have no effect whatever on this type of baldness. It has ordered the promoters of a device for stopping bedwetting to disclose that the device would not be of value in cases caused by organic defects or diseases. And it has ordered the makers of Geritol, an iron supplement, to disclose that Geritol will relieve symptoms of tiredness only in persons who suffer from iron deficiency anemia, and that the vast majority of people who experience such symptoms do not have such a deficiency.

Each of these orders was approved on appeal over objections that it exceeded the Commission's statutory authority. The decisions reflect a recognition that, as the Supreme Court has stated,

> If the Commission is to attain the objectives Congress envisioned, it cannot be required to confine its road block to the narrow lane the transgressor has traveled; it must be allowed effectively to close all roads to the prohibited goal, so that its order may not be by-passed with impunity.

Affirmative disclosure has also been required when an advertisement, although not misleading if taken alone, becomes misleading considered in light of past advertisements. For example, for 60 years Royal Baking Powder Company had stressed in its advertising that its product was superior because it was made with cream of tartar, not phosphate. But, faced with rising costs of cream of tartar, the time came when it changed its ingredients and became a phosphate baking powder. It carefully removed from all labels and advertisements any reference to cream of tartar and corrected the list of ingredients. But the new labels used the familiar arrangement of lettering, coloration, and design, so that they looked exactly like the old ones. A new advertising campaign stressed the new low cost of the product and dropped all reference to cream of tartar. But the advertisements were also silent on the subject of phosphate and did not disclose the change in the product.

The Commission held, and the Second Circuit agreed, that the new advertisements were deceptive, since they did not advise consumers that their reasons for buying the powder in the past no longer applied. The court held that it was proper to require the company to take affirmative steps to advise the public. To continue to sell the new powder on the strength of the reputation attained through 60 years of its manufacture and sale and wide advertising of its superior powder, under an impression induced by its advertisements that the product purchased was the same in kind and as superior as that which had been so long manufactured by it, was unfair alike to the public and to the competitors in the baking powder business.

In another case the Waltham Watch Company of Massachusetts had become renowned for the manufacture of fine clocks since 1849. Soon after it stopped manufacturing clocks in the 1950's, it transferred its trademarks, good will, and the trade name "Waltham" to a successor corporation, which began importing clocks from Europe for resale in the United States. The imported clocks were advertised as "product of Waltham Watch Company since 1850," "a famous 150-year-old company."

The Commission found that the advertisements caused consumers to believe they were buying the same fine Massachusetts clocks of which they had heard for many years. To correct this impression the Commission ordered the company to disclose in all advertisements and on the product that the clock was not made by the old Waltham company and that it was imported. The Seventh Circuit affirmed, relying on "the well-established general principle that the Commission may require affirmative disclosure for the purpose of preventing future deception."

It appears to us that the orders in *Royal* and *Waltham* were the same kind of remedy the Commission has ordered here. Like Royal and Waltham, Listerine has built up over a period of many years a widespread reputation. When it was ascertained that that reputation no longer applied to the product, it was necessary to take action to correct it. Here, as in *Royal* and *Waltham,* it is the accumulated impact of *past* advertising that necessitates disclosure in *future* advertising. To allow consumers to continue to buy the product on the strength of the impression built up by prior advertising—an impression which is now known to be false—would be unfair and deceptive.

Robb, Circuit Judge, dissenting in part: I agree with the majority that there is substantial evidence in the record to support an order requiring Warner-Lambert to cease and desist from advertising Listerine as a remedy for colds and sore throats. I therefore agree that Parts I, II, IV and V of the Commission's order must be affirmed.

I dissent from the affirmance of Section III of the order which (1) forbids Warner-Lambert to disseminate any advertisement for Listerine unless accompanied by a corrective statement relating to past advertising, and (2) provides that this

"duty to disclose the corrective statement shall continue until respondent has expended on Listerine advertising a sum equal to the average annual Listerine advertising budget for the period of April 1962 to March 1972."—a sum of approximately ten million dollars. In my judgment this requirement of corrective advertising is beyond the statutory authority of the Federal Trade Commission. The Commission's authority to enter cease and desist orders is prospective in nature; the purpose of cease and desist orders is "to prevent illegal practices in the future", *FTC* v. *Ruberoid Co.,* 343 U.S. 470, 473 (1952), not "to punish or to fasten liability on respondents for past conduct". *FTC* v. *Cement Institute,* 333 U.S. 683, 706 (1948). The cases that have construed the Commission's remedial power, *e.g., FTC* v. *Sperry & Hutchinson Co.,* 405 U.S. 233, 244 (1972); *FTC* v. *Mandel Brothers, Inc.,* 359 U.S. 385, 392–93 (1959); *FTC* v. *Ruberoid Co., supra; FTC* v. *National Lead Co.,* 352 U.S. 419, 428–29 (1957); *Jacob Siegel Co.* v. *FTC,* 327 U.S. 608, 610–12 (1946), stand only for the proposition that the Commission has broad discretion in determining what conduct of a respondent shall be forbidden prospectively. I think this authority does not encompass the power to employ the retrospective remedy of corrective advertising; and I find no other basis for that asserted power.

The Declaration of Fundamental Principles Concerning the Contribution of the Mass Media to Strengthening Peace and International Understanding, the Promotion of Human Rights and to Countering Racialism, Apartheid and Incitement to War.

FOLLOWING IS THE TEXT OF THE ARTICLES ADOPTED ON NOVEMBER 22, 1978, BY THE UNESCO GENERAL CONFERENCE.

ARTICLE I

The strengthening of peace and international understanding, the promotion of human rights and the countering of racialism, apartheid and incitement to war demand a free flow and a wider and better balanced dissemination of information. To this end, the mass media have a leading contribution to make. This contribution will be the more effective to the extent that the information reflects the different aspects of the subject dealt with.

ARTICLE II

1. The exercise of freedom of opinion, expression and information, recognized as an integral part of human rights and fundamental freedoms, is a vital factor in the strengthening of peace and international understanding.

2. Access by the public to information should be guaranteed by the diversity of the sources and means of information available to it, thus enabling each individual to check the accuracy of facts and to appraise events objectively. To this end, journalists must have freedom to report and the fullest possible facilities of access to information. Similarly, it is important that the mass media be responsive to concerns of peoples and individuals, thus promoting the participation of the public in the elaboration of information.

3. With a view to the strengthening of peace and international understanding, to promoting human rights and to countering racialism, apartheid and incitement to war, the mass media throughout the world, by reason of their role, contribute effectively to promoting human rights in particular by giving expression to oppressed peoples who struggle against colonialism, neo-colonialism, foreign occupation and all forms of racial discrimination and oppression and who are unable to make their voices heard within their own territories.

4. If the mass media are to be in a position to promote the principles of this declaration in their activities, it is essential that journalists and other agents of the mass media, in their own country or abroad, be assured of protection guaranteeing them the best conditions for the exercise of their profession.

ARTICLE III

1. The mass media have an important contribution to make to the strengthening of peace and international understanding and in countering racialism, apartheid and incitement to war.

2. In countering aggressive war, racialism, apartheid and other violations of human rights which are inter alia spawned by prejudice and ignorance, the mass media, by disseminating information on the aims, aspirations, cultures and needs of all people, contribute to eliminate ignorance and misunderstanding between peoples, to make nationals of a country sensitive to the needs and desires of others, to ensure the respect of the rights and dignity of all nations, all peoples and all individuals without distinction of race, sex, language, religion or nationality and to draw attention to the great evils which afflict humanity, such as poverty, malnutrition and diseases, thereby promoting the formulation by states of policies best able to promote the reduction of international tension and the peaceful and the equitable settlement of international disputes.

ARTICLE IV

The mass media have an essential part to play in the education of young people in a spirit of peace, justice, freedom, mutual respect and understanding, in order to promote human rights, equality of rights as between all human beings and all nations, and economic and social progress. Equally they have an important role to play in making known the views and aspirations of the younger generation.

ARTICLE V

In order to respect freedom of opinion, expression and information and in order that information may reflect all points of view, it is important that the points of view presented by those who consider that the information published or disseminated about them has seriously prejudiced their effort to strengthen peace and international understanding, to promote human rights or to counter racialism, apartheid and incitement to war be disseminated.

ARTICLE VI

For the establishment of a new equilibrium and great reciprocity in the flow of information, which will be conducive to the institution of a just and lasting peace and to the economic and political independence of the developing countries, it is necessary to correct the inequalities in the flow of information to and from developing countries, and between those countries. To this end, it is essential that their mass media should have conditions and resources enabling them to gain strength and expand, and to cooperate both among themselves and with the mass media in developed countries.

ARTICLE VII

By disseminating more widely all of the information concerning the objectives and principles universally accepted which are the bases of the resolutions adopted by the different organs of the United Nations, the mass media contribute effectively to the strengthening of peace and international understanding, to the promotion of human rights, as well as to the establishment of a more just and equitable international economic order.

ARTICLE VIII

Professional organizations, and people who participate in the professional training of journalists and other agents of the mass media and who assist them in performing their functions in a responsible manner should attach special importance to the principles of this declaration when drawing up and ensuring application of their code of ethics.

ARTICLE IX

In the spirit of this declaration, it is for the international community to contribute to the creation of the conditions for a free flow and wider and more balanced dissemination of information, and the conditions for the protection, in the exercise of their functions, of journalists and other agents of the mass media. UNESCO is well placed to make a valuable contribution in this respect.

ARTICLE X

1. With due respect for constitutional provisions designed to guarantee freedom of information and for the applicable international instruments and agreements, it is indispensable to create and maintain throughout the world the conditions which make it possible for the organizations and persons professionally involved in the dissemination of information to achieve the objectives of this declaration.

2. It is important that a free flow and wider and better balanced dissemination of information be encouraged.

3. To this end, it is necessary that states should facilitate the procurement, by the mass media in the developing countries, of adequate conditions and resources enabling them to gain strength and expand, and that they should support cooperation by the latter both among themselves and with the mass media in developed countries.

4. Similarly, on a basis of equality of rights, mutual advantage, and respect for the diversity of cultures which go to make up the common heritage of mankind, it is essential that bilateral and multilateral exchanges of information among all states, and in particular between those which have different economic and social systems be encouraged and developed.

ARTICLE XI

For this declaration to be fully effective it is necessary, with due respect for the legislative and administrative provisions and the other obligations of member states, to guarantee the existence of favorable conditions for the operation of the mass media, in conformity with the provisions of the Universal Declaration of Human Rights and with the corresponding principles proclaimed in the International Covenant on Civil and Political Rights adopted by the General Assembly of the United Nations in 1966.

questions for discussion and further research ───────────

1. In what areas could regulatory conflicts develop between the Federal Communications Commission and the Federal Trade Commission?

2. In what areas could regulatory conflicts develop between the Federal Communications Commission and the National Telecommunications and Information Agency?

3. Are there ways in which you feel the advertising review process of the Federal Trade Commission could be improved?

4. Does an advertiser have an equal chance in the advertising review process against the FTC?

5. What are the advantages or disadvantages of the NTIA as opposed to the existence in the early 1970s of the OT in the Department of Commerce and the OTP in the White House?

6. What potential exists for the executive branch of government to influence broadcast policy through regulatory agencies?

7. Why couldn't the work performed by the Office of Technology Assessment be performed by the Office of Plans and Policy of the Federal Communications Commission?

8. If we consider the FCC as the "expert" agency involved in broadcast regulations, why is the U.S. Department of Justice so deeply involved in issues such as cross-ownership of newspapers and the broadcast media?

9. What is the purpose of having the Director of the Defense Communications Agency also manage the National Communications System?

10. Given the ITU's posture in influencing international regulation of telecommunication policy, what position is the United States in, by working through the United Nations and the U.S. Department of State, to influence policy through the ITU?

11. As a result of satellite technology, the flow of broadcast programming across national boundaries and the sharing of spectrum space with other nations is becoming increasingly important as a topic of policy making. What role will the U.S. Department of State play in the future of such policy, and how will the Department integrate that role with other domestic regulatory agencies?

12. Are World Administrative Radio Conferences an efficient means of establishing policy for the global uses of the electromagnetic spectrum?

13. Would regional, WARC-type conferences be more beneficial than global policy sessions?

14. In *Warner-Lambert* v. *FTC,* do you agree with the dissenting opinion of Judge Robb?

15. What function or purpose does the *UNESCO Declaration of Fundamental Principles* have on the global communication policy?

additional resources ──────────────────

books

Hochman, S., and S. Wong, *Satellite Spies: The Frightening Impact of a New Technology,* Indianapolis: Bobbs-Merrill, 1976.

Kinsley, M. E., *Outer Space and Inner Sanctums: Government, Business, and Satellite Communication,* New York: Wiley-Interscience, 1976.

Leive, D. M., *International Telecommunications and International Law: The Regulation of the Radio Spectrum,* Dobbs Ferry, N.Y.: A. W. Sijthoff, Leyden, and Oceana Publications, 1971.

Lent, J. A., *Third World Mass Communications: Rural and Developmental Journalism, Cultural Imperialism, Research and Education,* Hong Kong: Asian Research Service, 1979.

Markle Foundation and the Twentieth Century Fund, eds., *Global Communications in the Space Age: Toward a New ITU,* New York: Markle Foundation and the Twentieth Century Fund, 1972.

Pelton, J. N., *Global Communications Satellite Policy: INTELSAT, Politics and Functionalism,* Mt. Airy, Md.: Lomond Systems, 1974.

Pelton, J. N., and M. S. Snow, eds., *Economic and Policy Problems in Satellite Communications,* New York: Praeger Special Studies, 1977.

Rohrer, D. M., *Freedom of Speech and Human Rights: An International Perspective,* Dubuque, Iowa: Kendall/Hunt Publishing Co., 1979.

Signitzer, B., *Regulation of Direct Broadcasting from Satellites: The U.N. Involvement,* New York: Praeger Publishers, 1976.

Van Trees, H. L., ed., *Satellite Communications,* New York: IEEE/John Wiley, 1979.

Will, T. E., *Telecommunications Structure and Management in the Executive Branch of Government, 1900–1970,* Boulder, Colo.: Westview Press, 1978.

articles

Acheson, D. C., "Competition Problems in International Communications," 13 *Antitrust Bulletin* 963 (1968).

Beelar, D. C., "Cables in the Sky and the Struggle for Their Control," 21 *Federal Communications Bar Journal* 26 (1967).

Boskey, B., "Monopoly and Antitrust Aspects of Communications Satellite Operations," 58 *Northwestern University Law Review* 266 (1963).

Chayes, A., "Current Issues in International Telecommunications Policy," 6 *Indiana Law Review* 182 (1972).

Colino, R. R., "INTELSAT: Doing Business in Outer Space," 6 *Columbia Journal of Transnational Law* 17 (1967).

Colino, R. R., "International Satellite Telecommunications and Developing Countries," 3 *Journal of Law & Economic Development* 8 (1968).

Dalfen, C. M., "International Legislative Process: Direct Broadcasting and Remote Earth Sensing by Satellite Compared," 10 *Canadian Yearbook of International Law* 186 (1972).

Dingell, J. D., "The Role of Spectrum Allocation in Monopoly or Competition in Communications," 13 *Antitrust Bulletin* 937 (1968).

Dizard, W. P., "The U.S. Position: DBS and Free Flow," 30 *Journal of Communication* 157 (1980).

Elrod, L. D., "Federal Trade Commission: Deceptive Advertising and the Colgate–Palmolive Company," 12 *Washburn Law Journal* 133 (1973).

Estep, S. D., "International Lawmakers in a Technological World: Space Communications and Nuclear Energy," 33 *George Washington Law Review* 162 (1964).

Estep, S. D., "Some International Aspects of Communications Satellite Systems," 58 *Northwestern University Law Review* 237 (1963).

Estep, S. D., and A. L. Kearse, "Space Communications and the Law: Adequate International Control after 1963?" 60 *Michigan Law Review* 873 (1962).

Evensen, J., "Aspects of International Law Relating to Modern Radio Communications," 115 *Academie* 477 (1965).

Gatling, D. B., "Radio Advertising and the Federal Trade Commission," 9 *Federal Communications Bar Journal* 74 (1948).

Geller, H., "Competition and Monopoly Policies in Domestic Satellite Communications," 13 *Antitrust Bulletin* 953 (1968).

Grad, F. P., and D. C. Goldfarb, "Government Regulation of International Telecommunications," 15 *Columbia Journal of Transnational Law* 384 (1976).

Grandi, R., and G. Richeri, "Western Europe: The Development of DBS Systems," 30 *Journal of Communication* 169 (1980).

Haley, A. G., "Law of Outer Space—Practical Legal Rules for Human Conduct," 16 *Federal Communications Bar Journal* 163 (1959).

Howkins, J., "What is the World Administrative

Radio Conference?" 29 *Journal of Communication* 144 (1979).

Jasentuliyana, N., "Regulatory Functions of I.T.U. in the Field of Space Telecommunications," 34 *Journal of Air Law & Commerce* 62 (1968).

Johnson, J. A., "International Cooperation in Satellite Communications Systems," 61 *American Society of International Law Proceedings* 24 (1967).

Johnson, J. A., "Satellite Communications: The Challenge and the Opportunity for International Cooperation," 19 *Federal Communications Bar Journal* 88 (1964-65).

Mansbach, B. T., "'The Authorized Entity'— 'Authorized User' Question in the Communications Satellite Act of 1962," 20 *Federal Communications Bar Journal* 117 (1966).

Marks, L. R., "Domestic Communication Satellites and International Co-operation," 61 *American Society of International Law Proceedings* 36 (1967).

McDaniel, D., and L. A. Day, "INTELSAT and Communist Nations' Policy on Communications Satellites," 18 *Journal of Broadcasting* 311 (1974).

Mosco, V., "Who Makes U.S. Government Policy in World Communication?" 29 *Journal of Communication* 158 (1979).

Nielsen, R. P., and A. B. Nielsen, "Canadian TV Content Regulation and U.S. Cultural 'Overflow'," 20 *Journal of Broadcasting* 461 (1976).

Ploman, E. W., "Western Europe: International Ambiguity," 30 *Journal of Communication* 178 (1980).

Powell, J. T., "Direct Broadcast Satellites: The Conceptual Convergence of the Free Flow of Information and National Sovereignty," 6 *California Western International Law Journal* 1 (1975).

Ruddy, F. S., "American Constitutional Law and Restrictions on the Content of Private International Broadcasting," 5 *The International Lawyer* 102 (1971).

Schiller, H. I., "Freedom from the 'Free Flow'," 24 *Journal of Communication* 110 (1974).

Schwartz, H., "Comsat, the Carriers, and the Earth Stations: Some Problems with 'Melding Variegated Interests'," 76 *Yale Law Journal* 441 (1967).

Snow, M. S., "INTELSAT: An International Example," 30 *Journal of Communication* 147 (1980).

Thain, G., "Suffer the Hucksters to Come Unto the Little Children? Possible Restrictions of Television Advertising to Children under Section 5 of the Federal Trade Commission Act," 56 *Boston University Law Review* 651 (1976).

Trooboff, P. D., "INTELSAT: Approaches to the Renegotiation," 9 *Harvard International Law Journal* 1 (1968).

Varis, T., "Global Traffic in Television," 24 *Journal of Communication* 102 (1974).

Wigand, R. T., "The Direct Satellite Connection: Definitions and Prospects," 30 *Journal of Communication* 140 (1980).

Woetzel, R. K., "International Cooperation in Telecommunication for Educational and Cultural Purposes," 61 *American Society of International Law Proceedings* 29 (1967).

Wozencraft, F. M., "INTELSAT Arbitration Agreement—A Pattern for the Future?" 3 *The International Lawyer* 759 (1969).

cases

Beneficial Corp. v. *F.T.C.*, 542 F.2d 611 (1976), certiorari denied.

Carlay v. *F.T.C.*, 153 F.2d 493 (7th Cir. 1946).

F.T.C. v. *Colgate-Palmolive Co.*, 85 S.Ct. 1035, 380 U.S. 374, 13 L.Ed.2d 904 (1965).

F.T.C. v. *Mary Carter Paint Co.*, 86 S.Ct. 219, 382 U.S. 46, 15 L.Ed.2d 128 (1965).

F.T.C. v. *National Commission on Egg Nutrition*, 517 F.2d 485, certiorari denied; 96 S.Ct. 2623, 426 U.S. 919, 49 L.Ed.2d 372, appeal after remand 570 F.2d 157 (1975).

F.T.C. v. *Raladam Co.*, 283 U.S. 643 (1931).

F.T.C. v. *Rhodes Pharmacal Co.*, 191 F.2d 744 (7th Cir. 1951).

F.T.C. v. *Simeon Management Corp.*, 391 F.Supp. 697, affirmed 532 F.2d 708 (1975).

F.T.C. v. *Simeon Management Corp.*, 532 F.2d 708 (1976).

F.T.C. v. *Standard Educational Society*, 302 U.S. 112 (1937).

F.T.C. v. *Sterling Drug, Inc.*, 317 F.2d 669 (1963).

F.T.C. v. *The Sperry & Hutchinson Co.*, 405 U.S. 233 (1972).

F.T.C. v. *Winsted Hosiery Co.*, 258 U.S. 483 (1922).

Keele Hair & Scalp Specialist, Inc. v. *F.T.C.*, 275 F.2d 18 (5th Cir. 1960).

Libbey-Owens-Ford Glass Co. v. *F.T.C.*, 352 F.2d 415 (1965).

Warner-Lambert Co. v. *F.T.C.*, 562 F.2d 749, 183 U.S.App.D.C. 230, certiorari denied; 98 S.Ct. 1575, two cases, 435 U.S. 950, 55, L.Ed.2d 800 (1977).

II

Programming
and
Policy

4

Regulating Entertainment and Political Programming

Although the free press clause of the U.S. Constitution is used as a basis for prohibiting government's intrusion into media content, and even though Section 326 of the Communications Act of 1934 prohibits censorship of radio and television programming, both the courts and the government have given the FCC the power to become involved in programming when the public interest warrants. In some areas, such as obscenity, the FCC has exercised this authority. In others, such as determining station formats, the Commission has attempted, although unsuccessfully, to steer clear of involvement. Chapter 4 examines the areas of control over entertainment programming that most directly affect consumers of broadcasting. We'll discuss obscene, indecent, and profane material. We'll also examine the FCC's position on station formats, prime-time access, and Section 315 of the Communications Act of 1934, which regulates political programming. The Section 315 material should be read not only for its applicability to political programming but also for its close integration with the Fairness Doctrine, which we will examine in Chapter 5.

Obscene, Indecent, and Profane Material

One of the most complex areas of broadcast regulation is obscene and indecent programming. The statutes governing such programming have evolved from both the Radio Act of 1927 and the Communications Act of 1934. The Radio Act of 1927 provided for penalties of up to $5,000 and imprisonment for five years for anyone convicted of violating the Act, including its obscenity provisions. The Communications Act of 1934 changed this to $10,000 and two years in jail, stating that the violator's license could be suspended for up to two years. In 1937, the penal provisions covering obscenity were amended to include license suspension for those transmitting communications containing profane or obscene "words, language, or meaning. . . ." The license suspension was no longer limited to two years, and the word "meaning" became even more appropriate as television increased in popularity.[1]

In 1948, Congress lifted the obscenity provisions out of the Communications Act of 1934 and placed them into the United States Code. Thus, U.S. Criminal Code Section 1464 states: "Whoever utters any obscene, indecent, or profane language by means of radio communication shall be fined not more than $10,000 or imprisoned not more than two years or both."[2] "Radio communication" includes television. Both the Department of Justice and the FCC have the power to enforce Section 1464. Penalties include forfeiture of a license or construction permit and fines of $1,000 for each day the offense occurs, not to exceed a total of $10,000. The Justice Department can also prosecute under Section 1464 and send a licensee to jail.

Although paving the way for enforcing the Code, the FCC still finds itself clashing not only with the First Amendment but also with the anticensorship provision of the Communications Act, which states in Section 326 that: "Nothing in this chapter shall be understood or construed to give the Commission the power of censorship over the radio communications or signals transmitted by any radio station, and no regulation or condition shall be promulgated or fixed by the Commission which shall interfere with the right of free speech by means of radio communication." The difficulty in enforcing the obscenity statute lies in a number of judicial conflicts that have developed since the 1948 codification. These have included not only the First Amendment dilemma stated above but also different meanings for "indecency," "profanity" and "obscenity"; varied applications between print and broadcast media; and the application of different standards to different communities.

definitions, application, and enforcement

Tracing the development of obscenity legislation takes us on a road leading back to English common law and libel law. Our road starts in England in 1868, with the case of *Regina* v. *Hicklin*. In an appeal to the Court of Queens Bench, the Court defined a test of obscenity as "whether the tendency of the matter charged as obscenity is to deprave and corrupt those whose minds are open to such immoral influences. . . ."[3] The definition cited in the Hicklin case was used as a basis for obscenity statutes in both the United States and England all the way into the twentieth century. Its primary thrust was that the publication had to be judged on its potential to reach the most susceptible of the audience. A series of cases upheld the Hicklin definition even into the 1930s.[4] Although the definition began to crumble, a Portland, Oregon, case brought broadcasting into the obscenity picture for the first time and found the Hicklin definition sufficient to warrant conviction.[5] In that case, Robert Gordon Duncan was charged with violating the obscenity statute of the Radio Act of 1927, and in 1931 was convicted in the case *Duncan* v. *United States.*[6] The main issue in the case was whether the language used by Duncan was obscene, indecent, or profane under the statute. The court based its decision on a definition similar to the one in the Hicklin case:

> In construing the word "obscene" as used therein, it has been uniformly held that, if the matter complained of were of such a nature as would tend to corrupt the morals of those whose minds are open to such influences by arousing or implanting in such minds lewd or lascivious thoughts or desires, it is within the prohibition of the statute....[7]

Within the Duncan decision can also be found reference to both indecency and profanity. The court stated that indecent language, like obscenity, is language that has a "tendency to excite libidinous thoughts on the part of the hearers... and is calculated to arouse ... sexual passions and desires." The court considered the words spoken by Duncan also to be profane in his references to an individual being damned and using the term "By God" irreverently.[8] Important to the Duncan decision as well as to decisions preceding it was the fact that the courts viewed a broadcast (or a publication) as obscene without examining the context of the remarks or the specific audience to whom it was directed. In 1936, the courts had had enough of the Hicklin definition and, in the case of *United States* v. *Levine,* although not dealing with broadcasting, established that a publication (a book in this case) should be considered in its entirety and by the effect it might have on the audience it would most likely reach.[9]

A landmark obscenity decision occurred in 1957, with the case of *Roth* v. *United States.*[10] In the Roth case, a legal test of obscenity was based on "whether to the average person, applying contemporary community standards, the dominant theme of the material taken as a whole appeals to prurient interests." The Court also believed that some obscenity statutes were unconstitutional when they punished, "incitation to impure sexual thoughts, not shown to be related to an overt anti-social conduct...." *Separating sex from obscenity,* the Court said: "sex and obscenity are not synonymous. Obscene material is material which deals with sex in a manner appealing to prurient interest."

Still another important obscenity ruling occurred in 1968, in the case of *Ginsberg* v. *State of New York.*[11] Sam Ginsberg operated a store on Long Island and was prosecuted under a New York law which made it a misdemeanor to sell a magazine to a minor under seventeen years of age when the magazine showed female buttocks or breasts with less than "full opaque covering." After selling two "girlie" magazines to a sixteen-year-old, Ginsberg was found guilty under the statute. In its decision, the Supreme Court established what has become known as the "variable obscenity" concept. In other words, what may be obscene for children, may not be for adults. We'll see shortly how both the Roth and the Ginsberg decisions became intertwined with subsequent broadcast rulings on obscenity.

As the print media continued to battle obscenity, broadcasting was developing some precedents of its own. In *United States* v. *Walker,* disc jockey Charlie Walker was found guilty by a jury of broadcasting offensive language on a radio station in Kingstree, South Carolina, from January to April, 1960.[12] The statute used to convict Walker was the Criminal Code. As if that was not enough, when WDKD's license came up for renewal, the FCC denied it, and the case went to court in *Robinson* v. *Federal Communications Commission*.[13] Although the main issue in the license renewal was an alleged attempt to mislead the FCC with false evidence, the court also made reference to Charlie Walker's broadcasts as "vulgar," "indecent," and "filth." Left unclear in both cases was a true test of the obscenity issue, since the Walker case did not go beyond the district court, and the Robinson case was indirectly related to obscenity.

Although the Criminal Code prohibits "obscene, indecent, or profane language," the FCC attempted to stick with the actionable term of "indecent" and avoid "obscenity," which had substantial precedent for defense in the First Amendment. In 1970, the Commission fined noncommercial WUHY-FM $100, because an interview guest had supposedly expressed his view on current topics by "frequently interspersing" words which are slang for sexual intercourse and removal of bodily waste. Again, the fine was based on a charge of "indecency," not "obscenity." The Commission went so far as to *define* indecency by stating: "we believe that the statutory term, 'indecent' should be applicable, and that in the broadcast field, the standard for its applicability should be that the material broadcast is (a) patently offensive by contemporary community standards, and (b) utterly without social value."[14]

topless radio and George Carlin's four-letter words

Finally, in 1973, the FCC found itself squarely in the obscenity arena with a case involving a station in Oak Parks, Illinois. The topic for the call-in program on February 23d was oral sex, and female listeners called moderator Morgan Moore with graphic descriptions of their experiences. The format, also employed at other stations, was known as "topless radio." But female listeners were not the only ones to contact the station. The FCC notified them of their apparent liability of $2,000 for violating *both* the indecency and obscenity clauses of the Criminal Code.[15] Sounding much like the court in *Roth* v. *United States,* the FCC quickly pointed out that it was not saying that sex was forbidden on the broadcast medium:

> We are emphatically *not* saying that *sex per se* is a forbidden subject on the broadcast medium. We are well aware that sex is a vital human relationship which has concerned humanity over the centuries, and that sex and obscenity are not the same thing. In this area as well as others, we recognize the licensee's right to present provocative or unpopular programming which may offend some listeners....

Echoing the court in *Ginsberg* v. *State of New York,* the FCC noted that children were in the audience:

> There are significant numbers of children in the audience during these afternoon hours—and not all of a pre-school age. Thus, there is always a significant percentage of school age children out of school on any given day. Many listen to radio; indeed it is almost the constant companion of the teenager. In this very instance, the station received the following call complaining about the oral sex discussion....

Female Listener: Yes, hello, what I wanted to know about your show was how can you people be so frank about things like this out in the open—I was always taught to believe that what the husband and wife do is for their bedroom only and between themselves—now my daughter happens to be home and she's 13 and she accidently listened to this show, I mean, don't you think about children that are home from school?

*Announcer:*Certainly, that's why we don't allow anyone on the air under the age of 18. There is evidence that this program is not intended solely for adults. On the February 16, 1973, program on "Do you always achieve orgasm?" the announcer moved from a discussion of orgasm to a comment aimed in large part at the 16–20 year-old audience....

The FCC's action on the Oak Park station arose from still a third case of the annals of obscenity law, *Ginzburg* v. *United States.* In the Ginzburg case (spelled differently, and not to be confused with Ginsberg) a sharply divided Supreme Court upheld a fine and prison term for publisher Ralph Ginzburg on the charge that he was guilty of "commercial exploitation of erotica" in connection with alleged "pandering" of material which was supposedly "titillating" and appealed to "prurient interests." The dissenting justices were vehement in their disagreement with Justice Stewart, stating that although Ginzburg's conviction was upheld on the above grounds, he was not even charged with "commercial exploitation," "pandering," or "titillation!" Justice Stewart affirmed that he knew of no federal statute under which those three activities were a criminal offense. This, however, did not stop the FCC. It stated: "There is here commercial exploitation, an effort at pandering. Formats like Femme Forum, aptly called topless radio, are designed to garner larger audiences through titillating sexual discussions. The announcer actively solicits the titillating response...."

Two groups, the Illinois Citizens' Committee for Broadcasting and the Illinois Division of the American Civil Liberties Union, asked the FCC to reconsider the ruling. When the Commission declined, the Illinois Citizens' Committee for Broadcasting appealed in *Illinois Citizens' Committee for Broadcasting* v. *Federal Communications Commission.* The court upheld the FCC's action and in effect ruled that the Commission was not acting unconstitutionally. Left untouched was an interpretation of "indecent."

On the afternoon of October 30, 1973, WBAI-FM warned its listeners that the broadcast that would follow included sensitive language, which might be offensive to some. What followed was a recording by comedian George Carlin from his album *George Carlin: Occupation Foole.* Carlin's monologue was a satire on seven four-letter words which could not be used on radio or television because they depict sexual or excretory organs and activities. A month later, the FCC received a complaint from a man who said he was driving with his son and had heard the broadcast. It was the only complaint received about the broadcast, which had been aired as part of a discussion on contemporary societies' attitudes about language.

The FCC issued a declatory ruling against WBAI-FM, and this time went back to *indecent* as the actionable term. Clarifying its definition of indecent language, the FCC stated that such language: "... describes, in terms patently offensive as measured by contemporary community standards for the broadcast medium, sexual or excretory activities and organs, at times of the day where there is a reasonable risk that children may be in the audience."[16]

In issuing its definition, the Commission drew on both the Roth and the WUHY-FM decisions when referring to community standards and also applied the variable obscenity standard of the Ginsberg case. Yet this standard was not used to prohibit speech, but rather to "channel" it to a time when children weren't present. Still moving cautiously on obscenity, however, the FCC said that the language in the Carlin recording was not so much obscene as it was indecent. It defined indecent as distinguishable from obscene in that indecent language "(1) lacks the element of appeal to the prurient interest. . . . and (2) when children may be in the audience, it cannot be redeemed by a claim that it has literary, artistic, political, or scientific value." The Commission did suggest that such material might be broadcast at night if it could be considered to have serious literary, artistic, political, or scientific value.

The Commission also rationalized that broadcast media should be treated differently than print media for the purposes of regulating indecent material, because broadcast media are intrusive, based on four considerations:

> (1) children have access to radio and in some cases are unsupervised by parents; (2) radio receivers are in the home, a place where people's privacy interest is entitled to extra deference; (3) unconsenting adults may tune in a station without any warning that offensive language is being or will be broadcast; and (4) there is a scarcity of spectrum space, the use of which the government must therefore license in the public interest.[17]

The Commission reiterated that it was not in the business of censorship but that it did have a statutory obligation to enforce those provisions of the Criminal Code that regulated obscene, indecent, or profane language.

Whatever good intentions the Commission had in issuing its declaratory order, the U.S. Court of Appeals for the District of Columbia did not agree with the FCC's rationale, and did little to uphold it. Striking down most of the Commission's major arguments, the court gave the FCC a judicial setback that caused considerable embarrassment. It first found that the Commission's order was in direct violation of Section 326 of the Communications Act of 1934, which prohibits the FCC from censoring programming. Although the FCC clearly stated that it was not censoring, the appeals court felt that it was doing just that, simply by issuing the order.

The court also criticized the Commission for failing to place the responsibility of programming content on the licensee, something which it had done in previous decisions but apparently had ignored in the WBAI case. The court pointed out that in another decision, a broadcaster had aired the record "Murder at Kent State," and although it was agreed that the recording contained material that could, under normal circumstances, have been considered obscene, it was not considered so this time. The FCC held that the Kent State broadcast was not for shock or sensationalism ". . . but rather for the purpose of presenting a vivid, accurate account of a disastrous incident in our recent history." So what had been a compliment in one incident was condemnation in another.

Even the Commission's suggestion that late-night programming was all right for such material was refuted by the court when it cited a study claiming that

"...large numbers of children are in the broadcast audience until 1:30 A.M.," and even that "...the number of children watching television does not fall below one million until 1:00 A.M."[18] Moreover, the court saw no reason to distinguish between "obscene" and "indecent," pointing out that the primary issue in this case was the anticensorship provision of the Communications Act.

In one of its most biting comments, the court indicated that the Commission's order would prohibit the broadcast of Shakespeare's *The Tempest* or *Two Gentlemen of Verona,* as well as parts of the Bible. The court also added a footnote, declaring that the order would prohibit "works of Auden, Becket, Lord Byron, Chaucer, Fielding, Greene, Hemingway, Joyce, Knowles, Lawrence, Orwell, Scott, Swift, and the Nixon tapes...."[19]

The court also made reference to *Miller* v. *California*.[20] The *Miller* case is famous for returning to local communities the responsibility for determining what is obscene. The *Miller* standard is:

(a) whether the average person, applying contemporary community standards, would find that the work, taken as a whole, appeals to the prurient interest;
(b) whether the work depicts or describes in a patently offensive way, sexual conduct specifically defined by the applicable state law;
(c) whether the work, taken as whole, lacks serious literary, artistic, political, or scientific value.

The appeals court said that: "applying the *Miller* standard to the language used in the Carlin monologue, it is clear that although the language is crude and vulgar by most standards it is not obscene." The court went on to indicate that the words "quite possibly could have literary, political, or artisitic value. Therefore, this non-obscene speech is entitled to First Amendment protection."

Why did the Commission proceed with such vigor in the case? Why did it choose a single complaint about this album aired at this time upon which to base a declaratory ruling? This ruling supposedly clarified the FCC's official position on indecent programming. Was it because complaints to the FCC about sexually-oriented programming had jumped from 2,000 per year in 1972 to 25,000 in 1974?[21] If the Commissioners had accepted the right of the licensee to air "Murder at Kent State," why did they act against WBAI? If a professor of semantics had used the same four-letter words in the same discussion of language in society, would the Commission have taken action?

All of these questions became moot in 1978, when the Supreme Court had the chance to hear the FCC's case against WBAI. Indicative of the varying interpretations of obscenity law, the Supreme Court ruled in favor of the FCC, saying that the Commission *did* have the authority to regulate the kind of language contained in the Carlin album when children might be present in the audience. The text of the *Pacifica* case is found at the end of this chapter.

Controlling Radio Station Formats

While the FCC has valiantly tried to regulate offensive language, it has not tried to dictate radio formats. In fact, the courts have tried to force regulatory power over this area on the Commission; regulatory power it does not want, feels to be unconstitutional, and believes to be contrary to the intended purpose of the Communications Act.

precedent for format control

Traditionally, the decision of what format a radio station provides for its audience has been the sole prerogative of the licensee. And over the years, stations have shifted formats to meet the pace of competition, not only from other radio stations but also from television. As television grew in popularity, radio decided to compete by incorporating specialized formats. The rock-and-roll of the 1950s thus became soft-rock, top-40 rock, progressive rock, oldie rock, and country rock. The diversity succeeded as radio stations were able to capture a specialized audience and attract advertisers wanting to reach that audience. But the marketplace dictated the diversity, not the FCC.

Then, 1970 placed government intervention on the doorsteps of the broadcasting industry.[22] It started in Georgia with the Citizens' Committee to Preserve the Voice of the Arts in Atlanta. In a U.S. Court of Appeals case, the group successfully preserved a classical music format on a local radio station. But the case that set the Commission back on its heels involved station WEFM-FM in Chicago. Owned by the Zenith Radio Corporation and having programmed classical music since 1940, the station went up for sale. The prospective buyer, GCC Communications of Chicago, announced that it would change WEFM-FM's format to contemporary music. Citizen uproar abounded, but the FCC stood firm and approved the sale of the station. It rationalized that the Communications Act prohibited it from making decisions based on formats—in a sense from prohibiting the licensee from having the freedom to operate in the public interest. But the decision was appealed, and the Washington, D.C. District Court said that the FCC erred and should have held a hearing prior to making a decision on the sale.

At this point, the FCC decided to take a closer look at its role in deciding station formats. It asked for opinions on the issue, and broadcasters responded, aided by powerful lobbying from the National Association of Broadcasters. After considering the evidence, the FCC took an unprecedented stance in direct opposition to the court and said that it saw no reason to become involved in determining station formats.[23]

the licensee's right to choose a format: FCC support

The FCC's first argument defending its stance was that it was unconstitutional for it to become involved in such decisions, and that opening up hearings every time a citizens' group complained about a change in format would create an administrative nightmare. Furthermore, the FCC felt that the marketplace was the arena in which formats should be decided. Audiences and advertisers could determine what best served the public interest. After all, broadcasting was still a business.

Another argument centered on the format itself. How could the FCC determine when format changes actually took place? The difference between classical and rock music was one thing, but differentiating between different types of rock music could be extremely difficult, let alone inappropriate, for a government agency. Furthermore, if the FCC were to rule on one format, to be equitable, it should examine every format of every station in every market. The Commission would soon be telling each community what format was best and what radio station should program what format.

Nevertheless, to completely wash its hands of any further consideration of format selection did not seem appropriate. There was still the matter of making sure that stations served the public interest. FCC Commissioner Benjamin Hooks believed that the FCC should still " . . . take an extra hard look at the reasonableness of any proposal which would deprive a community of its only source of a particular type of programming."[24] Commissioner Hooks also felt that minorities should be serviced with programming, even if the marketplace did not inherently provide it. Those sentiments were echoed by citizens' groups. Among others, the Action Alliance of Senior Citizens of Greater Philadelphia protested that broadcasters direct their programming to groups whom the advertisers pay the most to reach, thus discriminating against senior citizens. Spanish-American groups also felt that Spanish-culture formats might be eliminated without any recourse for the Spanish-American audience.

The arguments supporting the holding of hearings on formats during licensing proceedings again came to the forefront in the summer of 1979, when the U.S. Court of Appeals reaffirmed its position, criticizing the Commission for being lax in its responsibility to "carry out its legal duties as interpreted by the court."

The U.S. Supreme Court agreed to hear the case and in 1981 ruled in favor of the FCC. After a decade of wrestling with the issue of who could have final control over a format, the FCC's position that the licensee would determine the format gained the High Court's approval. Specifically, the marketplace would become the regulator. Although the Supreme Court's decision would not stop a challenge to a format change, it did give the local broadcaster strong protection against such challenges.

format control in syndicated programming

With the increase in both the number of automated stations and the reliance on syndicated musical programming, the issue of format control is also important to the field of syndicated programming. It is important to keep in mind the fact that the FCC still feels the licensee should be responsible for its format in order to serve public interest. As a result of some rather binding contracts offered to broadcasters by syndication companies, the FCC adopted guidelines for broadcasters to follow when agreeing to carry syndicated programming. The Commission suggests that stations should not enter into contracts which:

1. Fix the number of broadcast hours;
2. Prohibit AM-FM duplication;
3. Prohibit sub-carrier authorizations;
4. Require the exclusive use of any music format service, or prohibit other sources;
5. Fix the amount of format service company music broadcast; [sic.]
6. Prohibit any announcement by the station;
7. Fix the number of commercials broadcast;
8. Limit the content or source of any non-musical programming;

9. Fix the amount of air time for news, music, or other programming;
10. Prohibit automatic gain control of company-supplied material; or
11. Allow termination in the event of program format changes by a licensee exercising his responsibility for the public interest.[25]

The key to the contracts is to retain flexibility. This is especially important in dealing with long-term contracts. The FCC does not want the licensee obligated to the degree that programming "in the public interest" might not air because of restrictions placed upon the station by the syndicator.

Syndication contracts have also received close scrutiny because of recent changes in rules affecting simulcasting. Prior to 1977, an FM station owned together with an AM station could not duplicate the programming of the AM station more than 50 percent of the time in markets over 100,000 in population. In 1977, the rule was changed to 25 percent duplication in markets over 100,000, and in 1979, the 25 percent duplication rule became effective for stations in markets over 25,000. Additional syndicated programming was thus often instituted to meet these nonduplication requirements.

Prime-Time Access

Concern over the dominance of network programming prompted the FCC in 1971 to take measures assuring that alternative programming would also be aired during the evening hours. Out of these measures came the prime-time access rules. The latest, the 1975 Prime Time Access Rule III (PTAR III), charges stations in the top fifty markets which are either network-affiliated or network-owned to clear an hour from network prime-time programming, which is 7:00 P.M. to 11:00 P.M. in Eastern and Pacific time zones and 6:00 P.M. to 10:00 P.M. in Central and Mountain time zones.[26] PTAR III was "refined" by order of the United States Second Circuit Court of Appeals in the case *National Association of Independent Television Producers and Distributors et al.* v. *FCC.*[27] The rule is designed to (1) give independent producers and syndicators a market for their programming and (2) encourage local stations to develop creative programming. By applying the rule to the top fifty markets, the FCC has successfully covered the nation. Yet the rule has been more successful in providing time for syndicated programming than in stimulating local creativity. The result has been a plethora of quiz and game shows in the 6:00 to 8:00 P.M. time periods across the country.

PTAR III still allows a series of exemptions. Stations *can* broadcast network or off-network documentaries, public affairs, and children's programming. Public affairs programming is defined in the same terms as it is in the FCC logging rules, as " . . . talks, commentaries, discussions, speeches, editorials, political programs, documentaries, forums, panels, roundtables, and similar programs primarily concerning local, national, and international public affairs." Feature films can also be broadcast, as can network news programming of the fast-breaking variety of interest to the viewing audience. In other words, if a network provides its affiliates with coverage of a major news event, such as an assassination or a natural disaster, the local affiliates can carry the program and have it count as prime-time access. If a television station produces an hour of local news that immediately precedes the prime-time access hour—for example local news from 6:00 to 7:00 P.M.—then the station can carry network news programming up to one-half hour into the access period, or until 7:30 P.M.

Sports programming is also exempted. If a sports event is scheduled to end at the beginning of prime-time access but lasts longer, stations are permitted to continue their sports coverage. Major sports events for which all of prime-time is devoted to their coverage, such as New Year's Day football games or the Olympic games, receive the same exemption. Under continued scrutiny is the antiblack-out law (Public Law 93-107), which permits the telecast of a home football game during prime time, but only if the game is sold out seventy-two hours before kickoff.

Copyright

In 1976, Congress passed a new copyright law, completely overhauling copyright legislation for the first time since 1909. Sections of interest to broadcasters included the length of copyright works, provisions covering cable television, and reproduction of programming for educational purposes.

Most of the content of broadcast programming can be copyrighted. A local commercial, for example, that was prepared by an ad agency or by someone at the station can fall under copyright.[28] Even a disc jockey's afternoon radio show can be copyrighted.[29] The original script of a television drama, the local or network evening news, and a sports documentary can all be copyrighted. Copyright law is designed to protect all of these from infringement by other parties who may want to use the material for personal gain.

We think most often of copyrighted material as being books, magazine articles, or pictures. But these only scratch the copyright surface. Even an idea can be copyrighted if it can be recorded aurally or visually and retained as evidence of the idea's origin. Network news programs have been copyrighted for years as a protection against someone recording them and selling them as either entertainment or source material. And we are all familiar with the careful protection that copyright gives to musical recordings in an industry where pirated tapes and records are a constant concern.

length of copyright

Under the 1976 copyright law, the length of copyright was extended from a maximum of fifty-six years (two twenty-eight year terms) to the length of the author's life plus fifty years. Especially meaningful to heirs, the extended term permits the "estate of the deceased to benefit from profits obtained from the copyrighted work."[30]

reproduction for educational purposes

The fair use provisions of the law provide for certain reproduction of broadcast programs by teachers and libraries. However, this area of the law is nebulous, and "fair use" is a very flexible term, applicable in different ways under different conditions. No one can unlawfully record a program without incurring the possibility of copyright infringement. Most "home recordings" of television programs are not considered a copyright infringement, however, and if programs are legally recorded, such as local or network news programs recorded by libraries or archives, the recordings can be used for research purposes.[31] Teachers can use certain programs in classroom teaching situations if, again, they have been legally reproduced. But even the fact that a library can legally record a program does not mean that the program automatically can be used for teaching purposes.

As the new copyright law undergoes court tests, its exact interpretation will become clearer. In the meantime, the best protection against using a copyrighted work is to get written permission from the copyright holder. Questions about specific legal matters should be referred to counsel.

Cable television systems are affected by copyright law, and we will learn more about those provisions later on in the text.

Section 315 of the Communications Act

Of all of the provisions of the Communications Act of 1934, few have received as much attention or notoriety as Section 315, regulating political broadcasting. The provision instructs the broadcaster and the candidate on how the electronic media are to be used as part of our political system. It, along with the Fairness Doctrine, has an effect on how we, the consumers of broadcast communication, are informed about our electoral process.

The most prominent wording of Section 315 is its "equal-time" provision which states:

> If any licensee shall permit any person who is a legally qualified candidate for public office to use a broadcasting station, he shall afford equal opportunities to all other such candidates for that office in the use of such broadcasting station.

It is the equal-time provision that has received major criticism from both broadcasters and politicians. Archibald Cox remarked that: "If we truly mean to restore openness and a sense of honor to our national life, we should acknowledge that equal time is dead and that broadcasters are as free as newspapers to determine what coverage to give candidates and their speeches."[32] Because of the equal-time provision the press has backed away from coverage of candidate appearances precisely including White House requests for news coverage when a President is a legally declared candidate for public office.[33]

definitions guiding equal-time provisions

The Communications Act defines a legally qualified candidate as:

> any person who has publicly announced that he is a candidate for nomination by a convention of a political party or for nomination or election in a primary, special, or general election, municipal, county, state or national, and who meets the qualifications prescribed by the applicable laws to hold the office for which he is a candidate, so that

he may be voted for by the electorate directly or by means of delegates or electors, and who:

(1) has qualified for a place on the ballot or

(2) is eligible under the applicable law to be voted for by sticker, by writing in his name on the ballot, or by other method, and

    (i) has been duly nominated by a political party which is commonly known and regarded as such, or

    (ii) makes a substantial showing that he is a bona fide candidate for nomination or office, as the case may be.[34]

In addition to this definition, there are hundreds of state and local statutes further clarifying political eligibility. Yet broadcasters are prohibited from exercising their own judgment as to who may be considered legally qualified. And it makes little difference if the candidate has a chance of winning. If the law says that the candidate is qualified, and if the candidate has publicly announced his or her candidacy, then the equal-time provisions apply. Those provisions also apply to cable television systems. Section 315 specifically defines a *broadcasting station* to include a "community antenna television system."

anticensorship provisions

As a further safeguard against unfair treatment to political candidates, Section 315 expressly prohibits the broadcaster from censoring the content of any political message. The law succinctly states that the licensee "shall have no power of censorship over the material broadcast under provisions of this section."

Up until 1959, broadcasters were in a quandry over the noncensorship rule, fearing it was only a matter of time until some candidate blatantly libeled an opponent, and the station would be sued for damages. The dreaded event happened that year in North Dakota, when U.S. senatorial candidate A. C. Townley charged on the air that the North Dakota Farmers' Union was Communist-controlled. The Farmers' Union sued the station and Townley for $100,000.[35] But the North Dakota Supreme Court ruled that the station was not liable and that the suit should have been brought against Townley alone. Undoubtedly, the Farmers' Union had thought about that, but knew that since Townley made only $98.50 a month, the prospect for recovering damages was not rosy.

The Farmers' Union appealed to the Supreme Court. Justice Black, in delivering the opinion of the Court, stated: "Quite possibly, if a station were held responsible for the broadcast of libelous material, all remarks even faintly objectionable would be excluded out of an excess of caution . . . . if any censorship were permissible, a station so inclined could intentionally inhibit a candidate's legitimate presentation under the guise of lawful censorship of libelous matter."[36]

An AM/FM station in Connecticut was fined $10,000 by the FCC for allegedly violating Section 315 after censoring the scripts of the Democratic and Fusion Party candidates because they were supposedly in bad taste. The two candidates for mayor affected by the censorship action filed suit for damages. A circuit court judge ruled that because the stations were the only ones in Stamford, the government had delegated control over the air waves to them, and therefore the censorship was actually federal action. This new twist in legal posture exemplifies the complex regulatory philosophy that can encompass Section 315. Although the decision was open to appeal, the legal interpretation of radio stations being instruments of the government opened up a whole new frontier of arguments dealing with the very basis of broadcast regulation. The Radio-Television News Directors' Association joined with ABC, NBC, CBS, NAB, and PBS in filing an amicus curiae (friend of the court) brief on behalf of WSTC, arguing that broadcast licensees should not be considered instruments of government.[37]

exemptions to the equal-time provision

Exempt from the equal-time provisions are appearances by candidates on the following types of news programming:

(1) bona fide newscast,
(2) bona fide news interview,
(3) bona fide news documentary (if the appearance of the candidate is incidental to the presentation of the subject or subjects covered by the news documentary), or
(4) on-the-spot coverage of bona fide news events (including but not limited to political conventions and activities incidental thereto). . . .

In 1975, the FCC added political debates and news conferences to the exemption list, if they were broadcast *in their entirety,* and if the broadcaster made a good-faith judgment that they constituted a *bona fide news event.* In 1976, a three-judge panel of the U.S. Court of Appeals in Washington, D.C., upheld the FCC's right to include the added exemption.[38] The court split in a 2–1 decision, and in offering the verdict, noted that it took comfort in the fact that Congress could correct the FCC if it in fact had overstepped its authority in the added exemption.[39]

The exemption itself is a hot political issue, since party loyalty as well as Congressional autonomy tend to surface during election years. The argument is not that minority candidates should not be given the right to be heard, but that the economic and time constraints placed on stations and networks in election years were overburdening. In fact, the FCC found it necessary to increase the acceptable level of broadcasting's "commercial minutes" during election time, partly because of the equal-time demands placed upon stations.[40]

The bona fide news event category has been expanded to include delayed broadcasts up to twenty-four hours after the event occurred. This expansion occurred when station WILM in Wilmington, Delaware asked the FCC for permission to delay a broadcast of a political debate until later in the evening, yet still receive exemption under Section 315. The FCC Broadcast Bureau denied the request. Not satisfied, WILM, along with RTNDA and NAB, asked the FCC to review its Broadcast Bureau's decision. It did so, and reversed the decision, permitting an exemption of a twenty-four-hour delayed broadcast from the equal-time provision when the broadcast is of a bona fide news event.[41] The RTNDA filed a brief in support of the FCC's decision, but said that the coverage should "not be limited solely to events broadcast in their entirety and within 24 hours of their on-the-spot coverage." RTNDA argued that such limitations constituted "an unlawful chilling effect upon the broadcasters' press function."[42] The FCC's ruling was upheld on appeal.

Despite the explicit wording of the law, candidates have not stopped trying to challenge it. When the three commercial television networks carried the year-end interview with President Lyndon Johnson in 1967, Senator Eugene J. McCarthy requested equal time. McCarthy had just announced his candidacy for President and claimed that Johnson was also a legally qualified candidate. The interview series was not new. The networks had started it in 1962 with President John F. Kennedy.

The FCC denied Senator McCarthy's request. It based its decision on the grounds that the interview was exempt because Johnson was not an announced candidate for office. McCarthy appealed to the circuit court, and the court affirmed the Commission's decision not to grant equal time. The court noted that since Congress had delegated the power to enforce Section 315 to the FCC, all the court could do was simply determine if the law was contrary to what Congress meant it to be, or was simply unreasonable. They found it to be neither and affirmed the FCC. The case did answer the question of when an incumbent President actually becomes a legally qualified candidate—whether it is when he or she announces his or her candidacy for re-election or at the time of the convention nomination.[43]

Although exemptions are rarely contested when part of a bona fide newscast, a station cannot simply log a program as a newscast and claim exemption. Allowing such an arbitrary application of Section 315 would make it easy for an unscrupulous broadcaster to bestow candidacy favoritism. To guard against this, the FCC looks at how long the program has been logged as news to determine whether it is bona fide. If a station has aired a 6:00 P.M. television newscast for five years and schedules in an appearance of a candidate, an opponent would have little grounds to demand equal time. On the other hand, if a candidate appears on an 8:00 P.M. program which is logged for the very first time as news, an opponent would have a legitimate request for equal time. Such requests must be made within seven days after the broadcast. The NAB's *Political Broadcast Catechism* lists seven elements in determining a bona fide program: "The following considerations among others, may be pertinent: (1) the format, nature and content of the program; (2) whether the format, nature and content of the program has changed since its inception and, if so, in what respects; (3) who initiates the program; (4) who produces and controls the program; (5) when was the program initiated; (6) is the program regularly scheduled; and (7) if the program is regularly scheduled, the time and day of the week when it is broadcast."[44]

selling time: the lowest unit charge

In addition to granting equal time to candidates, Section 315 also spells out how much they are to be charged for the use of broadcast facilities:

(b)   The charges made for the use of any broadcasting station by any person who is a legally qualified candidate for any public office in connection with his campaign for nomination for election, or election, to such office shall not exceed:

    (1)   during the forty-five days preceding the date of a primary or primary runoff election and during the sixty days preceding the date of a general or special election in which such person is a candidate, the lowest unit charge of the station for the same class and amount of time for the same period, and

    (2)   at any time, the charges made for comparable use of such station by other users thereof.

The above is known as the "lowest unit charge" rule. To understand it more clearly, assume that you are the sales manager for a television station. The station's rate card charges an advertiser $1,000 to buy a single one-minute commercial in prime time. An advertiser purchasing two commercials receives a discount and is charged only $850 per commercial. We'll assume that the rate card permits an advertiser purchasing twenty-five commercials to receive an even bigger discount, whereby each commercial costs $500. Along comes candidate John Doe, who is running for senator. Doe wants to buy just one commercial to remind his friends that he's running for office. He wants to run it in prime time. What will you charge him for the cost of his one commercial? You'll charge him $500. Even though he is buying only one commercial, the law states that you must charge him the "lowest unit charge." If he wanted to purchase a commercial in a fringe-time period, in which the rates are lower, then you would charge him the "lowest unit charge" for that time period.

It is easy to see why Section 315 is not the darling of many broadcasters. For example, station WGN in Chicago had a long-standing rule that candidates could purchase only a minimum block of five minutes of commercial time. In the 1976 Illinois Presidential primary, the committee to elect Gerald Ford wanted to buy sixty-second and thirty-second commercials promoting the candidate. These shorter commercials are often favored by candidates, since longer ones make some viewers change channels. When WGN said no, the committee petitioned the FCC, and the Commission overruled WGN's five-minute policy, requiring it to sell the shorter commercials. To make matters more confusing, a year later, a Chicago mayoral candidate claimed that he could not buy program-length commercials on two Chicago stations.[45] The stations offered commercials of up to five minutes, and this time the FCC upheld the stations' right, not the candidate's. The decision clouded the decision issued a year earlier concerning WGN. The Commission was quoted as saying that, the "law giving a political candidate the same standing as commercial advertisers meant *only* that the candidate must be charged the lowest commercial rate for air time."[46] Some Commissioners did not support the decision of the FCC giving the station control over the length of the commercial message. Commissioner Benjamin Hooks was quoted as saying that the ruling would make it more difficult for candidates to gain access to broadcasting outlets.[47] Commissioners Robert E. Lee and Abbott Washburn joined Hooks in dissent of the 4–3 decision.

Many stations and account executives dealing with local politicians use an agreement form (Figure 4-1) executed between the station and the candidate. One form offered by the NAB provides space to list the length of the broadcast, the hours, dates, times per week, total number of weeks, and rates for the commer-

Station and Location _____ 19___

I, _____ (being)
(on behalf of)_____

_____

a legally qualified candidate of the_____

political party for the office of_____

_____

in the _____ election to be held on _____,
do hereby request station time as follows:

Length of Broadcast   Times Per Week

Hour   Total No. Weeks

Days   Rate

Date of First Broadcast

Date of Last Broadcast

Total Charges: _____

The broadcast time will be used by _____
I represent that the advance payment for the above-described broadcast time has been
furnished by _____

_____

and you are authorized to so describe that sponsor in your log and to announce the program as
paid for by such person or entity. The entity furnishing the payment, if other than an individual person, is: ( ) a corporation; ( ) a committee; ( ) an association; or ( ) other un-
incorporated group. The names and offices of the chief executive officers of the entity are:

_____

It is my understanding that: If the time is to be used by the candidate himself within 45 days of
a primary or primary runoff election, or within 60 days of a general or special election, the
above charges represent the lowest unit charge of the station for the same class and amount of
time for the same period; where the use is by a person or entity other than the candidate or is by
the candidate but outside the aforementioned 45 or 60 day periods, the above charges do not

Figure 4-1 (National Association of Broadcasters)

exceed the charges made for comparable use of such station by other users.

It is agreed that use of the station for the above-stated purposes will be governed by the Communications Act of 1934, as amended, and the FCC's rules and regulations, particularly those provisions reprinted on the back hereof, which I have read and understand. I further agree to indemnify and hold harmless the station for any damages or liability that may ensue from the performance of the above-stated broadcasts. For the above-stated broadcasts I also agree to prepare a script or transcription, which will be delivered to the station at least _____ before the time of the scheduled broadcasts; (*note:* the two preceding sentences are not applicable if the candidate is personally using the time).

Date: _____

_____
(Candidate, Supporter or Agent)

Accepted
Rejected   by _____

Title _____

This application, whether accepted or rejected, will be available for public inspection for a period of two years in accordance with FCC regulations (AM, Section 73.120; FM, Section 73,290; TV, Section 73.657).

Figure 4-1 continued.

cial schedule used by the candidate. Total charges are included along with the dates of the first and last broadcast, as well as an explanation of the lowest unit charge, the fact the information will be kept in the public file, and the agreement on the part of the candidate to hold the station harmless for any damages or liability that could occur as a result of the broadcast.

Access: The Relationship of Section 312 to Section 315

Our discussion of Section 315 would not be complete without mention of another section of the Communication Act of 1934, Section 312, and of how it relates to Section 315. Section 312 is actually a prerequisite to 315, since 312 clearly states that the station must not deny access to any candidate for federal office, regardless of what form that access takes. Section 312 cautions the broadcaster that a station license may be revoked: "for willful or repeated failure to allow reasonable access to or to permit purchase of reasonable amounts of time for the use of a broadcasting station by a legally qualified candidate for Federal elective office on behalf of his candidacy."

candidates for "federal" office

Notice that the law reads "Federal elective office." This clause has been a bone of some contention and confusion in interpretations of Section 315, especially when candidates at other than the federal level are involved. Some stations have used Section 312 as grounds for refusing to sell commercial time to candidates other than those running for federal offices. The advantage in such a policy is primarily economic. First of all, federal candidates number fewer than local candidates, translating into fewer political commercials. You may ask: "But isn't the station in business to sell commercials?" Yes, but remember that lowest unit charge. If a department store is paying a nondiscounted rate for commercials but cannot get on the air because of the plethora of political commercials sold at the lowest unit charge, then the station is losing money. Second, federal candidates often place their advertising through advertising agencies. Although the station must still give a discount to the agency, the number of commercials purchased is usually more than what candidates would purchase on their own. Thus, the overall dollar spent is closer to the actual profit made from typical business advertising. Third, the commercials from the agency are usually prerecorded, which eliminates the need for the local station to tie up its staff and facilities in helping a candidate to produce a commercial which may only run one time at the lowest unit charge.

By inserting the term "Federal," then, Section 312 left no definition of "reasonable access" for candidates running for state and local offices. Historically, the station has had some latitude for flexibility in such cases. In its *Guidelines* to political candidates, the Commission says: "The licensee in its own good-faith judgment in serving the public interest may determine which political races are of greatest interest and significance to its service area, and therefore may refuse to sell time to candidates for less important offices, provided it treats all candidates for such offices equally."[48]

state vs. federal access

A station refusing equal opportunities to purchase time is still on shaky ground if it refuses some privileges to candidates running for non-federal elective office, while providing privileges to candidates for federal elective office. For example, one station refused to offer run-of-station commercials, which are the least expensive because they are purchased in bulk and aired at the station's discretion, to a candidate for state office. Instead, the station offered fixed-position commercials which were more expensive. The FCC sided with the station. But in an appeal to the U.S. Court of Appeals in Washington, the candidate won.[48a]

Even commercial networks have been found not to be exempt from the provisions of Section 312. The U.S. Court of Appeals upheld an FCC ruling that ABC, NBC, and CBS had violated Section 312 by refusing to sell the Carter-Mondale presidential committee a half-hour of time to run a documentary kicking off President Carter's campaign for re-election.[48b]

access to noncommercial stations

Not even noncommercial stations are exempt from Section 312. That ruling came in 1976, when New York Senator James Buckley complained that he had not received reasonable access to five public broadcasting stations in upstate New York.[49] Buckley claimed that the stations would not air a five-minute program that he had provided them. But the stations felt that they had met the reasonable access requirement by carrying a debate between Buckley and his opponent, Daniel Moynihan. The FCC, in a 6–0 decision, agreed with Buckley, although indicating that each situation should be considered on an individual basis. They were not making policy for every noncommercial broadcasting station in the country.

Noncommercial educational stations which are not selling commercials but which operate on unreserved channels and whose charters or articles of incorporation permit them to charge for air time can charge for political commercials.[50] They must, however, notify the FCC of the change in operating procedures. Since they probably do not have rate cards upon which to judge the lowest unit charge, these stations are usually safe in setting rates which are in line with other commerical stations in the same broadcast market.

print vs. broadcast

Before concluding our discussion of political broadcasting, we should remind ourselves that the regulations we have been discussing apply only to the broadcast media and not to the print media. Under the rationale that the electromagnetic spectrum is a limited resource, the FCC has the authority under the Communications Act to institute such rules as it deems in the public interest. Section 315 and Section 312 are good examples. In print media enterprises, the editor or publisher has total discretion on who gains access to the paper and what is said about that person. With new technologies increasing the number of electronic communication channels, the future may see a relaxation of rules governing political broadcasting.

Even when the most precise language possible is used in court cases, FCC decisions, and amended rules and regulations, Section 315 is and will continue to be in a state of flux. With thousands of broadcasting stations and many more times the number of candidates, the law will continue to be challenged. As a responsible consumer of broadcast communication, you should try to remain alert to the individual issues in your own community which may arise from a dispute between a candidate and a station over the meaning of Section 315.

summary

Obscene, indecent, and profane material is one of the most complex areas of law and regulation. Part of the complexity results from the many different definitions of exactly what obscenity, indecency, and profanity are, plus the questions of which definition applies to any given example of material and what role the FCC and the courts should play in controlling this type of programming.

The broadcasting of obscene, indecent and profane material is controlled by the U.S. Criminal Code, and the FCC has the authority to enforce the Code as it applies to radio and television.

The FCC has stayed away as much as possible from controlling radio station formats, although not without pressure from citizens' groups to take an active hand in such control. Court precedent for preserving a classical music format in Georgia and a reprimand from a court in Chicago prodded the FCC to examine its role in determining station formats. The examination concluded that the licensee should retain the right to choose the format and that, if there should be any major questions over the wisdom of that choice, it should be weighed against the public interest clause of the Communications Act of 1934. Citizens' groups are appealing the FCC's conclusions, however. If they succeed, the Supreme Court may decide how much involvement the FCC should have in deciding formats.

The FCC has stepped in to give local stations more opportunity to air local programming. Its prime-time rules require local television stations to clear an hour of network programming for locally originated programs.

Section 315 of the Communications Act of 1934 controls political programming on radio and television. Providing equal time for candidates and charging them the lowest unit charge are just two areas encompassed by Section 315.

Section 312 guarantees access to stations by candidates for federal and in some cases state offices.

materials for analysis

Two laws which seemingly clash head on are Sec. 1464 of the United States Criminal Code and Sec. 326 of the Communications Act of 1934. One states the penalties for uttering obscene, indecent, or profane language on the air, and the other prohibits censorship of broadcast communication. In *Federal Communications Commission* v. *Pacifica Foundation,* the United States Supreme Court offers us an unusually detailed debate of the two provisions and their relationship to the First Amendment. The case occupies center stage in obscenity law interpretation and is unique in its application to the broadcast media.

Section 315 becomes the issue in *Office of Communication of the United Church of Christ* v. *FCC.* When the FCC ruled that television political debates delayed up to twenty-four hours were exempt from Sec. 315's equal-time provision, the United Church of Christ's Office of Communication intervened. The decision provides a forum for discussion of the relationship of the "journalistic process" to this specific area of communications law.

United States Criminal Code: Sec. 1464

Whoever utters any obscene, indecent, or profane language by means of radio communication shall be fined not more than $10,000 or imprisoned not more than two years, or both.

Sec. 326: Communications Act of 1934

Nothing in this Act shall be understood or construed to give the Commission the power of censorship over the radio communications or signals transmitted by any radio station, and no regulation or condition shall be promulgated or fixed by the Commission which shall interfere with the right of free speech by means or radio communication.

Federal Communications Commission v. Pacifica Foundation

UNITED STATES SUPREME COURT, 1978
438 U.S. 726, 98 S.Ct. 3026, 57 L.Ed.2d 1073, 3 Med.L.Rptr. 2553

Mr. Justice STEVENS delivered the opinion of the Court:

The relevant statutory questions are whether the Commission's action is forbidden "censorship" within the meaning of 47 U.S.C. §326 and whether speech that concededly is not obscene may be restricted as "indecent" under the authority of 18 U.S.C. §1464. The questions are not unrelated, for the two statutory provisions have a common origin. Nevertheless, we analyze them separately....

The prohibition against censorship unequivocally denies the Commission any power to edit proposed broadcasts in advance and to excise material considered inappropriate for the airwaves. The prohibition, however, has never been construed to deny the Commission the power to review the content of completed broadcasts in the performance of its regulatory duties....

Not only did the Federal Radio Commission so construe the statute prior to 1934; its successor, the Federal Communications Commission, has consistently interpreted the provision in the same way ever since....

Entirely apart from the fact that the subsequent review of program content is not the sort of censorship at which the statute was directed, its history makes it perfectly clear that it was not intended to limit the Commission's power to regulate the broadcast of obscene, indecent, or profane language. A single section of the 1927 Act is the source of both the anticensorship provision and the Commission's authority to impose sanctions for the broadcast of indecent or obscene language. Quite plainly, Congress intended to give meaning to both provisions. Respect for that intent requires that the censorship language be read as inapplicable to the prohibition on broadcasting obscene, indecent, or profane language....

We conclude, therefore, that §326 does not limit the Commission's authority to impose sanctions on licensees who engage in obscene, indecent, or profane broadcasting.

The only other statutory question presented by this case is whether the afternoon broadcast of the "Filthy Words" monologue was indecent within the meaning of §1464.[13] Even that question is nar-

---

[13]In addition to §1464, the Commission also relied on its power to regulate in the public interest under 47 U.S.C. §303(g). We do not need to consider whether §303 may have independent significance in a case such as this. The statutes authorizing civil penalties incorporate §1464, a criminal statute. See 47 U.S.C. §§312(a)(6). 312(b)(2), and 503(b)(1)(E). But the validity of the civil sanctions is not linked to the validity of the criminal penalty. The legislative history of the provisions establishes their independence. As enacted in 1927 and 1934, the prohibition on indecent speech was separate from the provisions imposing civil and criminal penalties for violating the prohibition. Radio Act of 1927 §§14.29 and 23.44 Stat. 1168 and 1173; Communications Act of 1934 §§312,326, and 501, 48 Stat. 1086, 1091, and 1100, 47 U.S.C. §§312,326, and

rowly confined by the arguments of the parties.

The Commission identified several words that referred to excretory or sexual activities or organs, stated that the repetitive, deliberate use of those words in an afternoon broadcast when children are in the audience was patently offensive, and held that the broadcast was indecent. Pacifica takes issue with the Commission's definition of indecency, but does not dispute the Commission's preliminary determination that each of the components of its definition was present. Specifically, Pacifica does not quarrel with the conclusion that this afternoon broadcast was patently offensive. Pacifica's claim that the broadcast was not indecent within the meaning of the statute rests entirely on the absence of prurient appeal.

The plain language of the statute does not support Pacifica's argument. The words "obscene, indecent, or profane" are written in the disjunctive, implying that each has a separate meaning. Prurient appeal is an element of the obscene, but the normal definition of "indecent" merely refers to nonconformance with accepted standards of morality. . . .

Because neither our prior decisions nor the language or history of §1464 supports the conclusion that prurient appeal is an essential component of indecent language, we reject Pacifica's construction of the statute. When that construction is put to one side, there is no basis for disagreeing

with the Commission's conclusion that indecent language was used in this broadcast.

Pacifica makes two constitutional attacks on the Commission's order. First, it argues that the Commission's construction of the statutory language broadly encompasses so much constitutionally protected speech that reversal is required even if Pacifica's broadcast of the "Filthy Words" monologue is not itself protected by the First Amendment. Second, Pacifica argues that inasmuch as the recording is not obscene, the Constitution forbids any abridgment of the right to broadcast it on the radio.

The first argument fails because our review is limited to the question whether the Commission has the authority to proscribe this particular broadcast. As the Commission itself emphasized, its order was "issued in a specific factual context." . . . It is true that the Commission's order may lead some broadcasters to censor themselves. At most, however, the Commission's definition of indecency will deter only the broadcasting of patently offensive references to excretory and sexual organs and activities. While some of these references may be protected, they surely lie at the periphery of First Amendment concern. The danger dismissed so summarily in *Red Lion,* in contrast, was that broadcasters would respond to the vagueness of the regulations by refusing to present programs dealing with important social and political controversies. Invalidating any rule on the basis of its hypothetical application to situations not before the Court is "strong medicine" to be applied "sparingly and only as a last resort." We decline to administer that medicine to preserve the vigor of patently offensive sexual and excretory speech.

When the issue is narrowed to the facts of this case, the question is whether the First Amendment denies government any power to restrict the public broadcast of indecent language in any circumstances. For if the government has any such power,

---

501. The 1927 and 1934 Acts indicated in the strongest possible language that any invalid provision was separable from the rest of the Act. Radio Act of 1927 §38, 44 Stat. 1175; Communications Act of 1934 §608, 48 Stat. 1105, 47 U.S.C. §608. Although the 1948 codification of the criminal laws and the addition of new civil penalties changed the statutory structure, no substantive change was apparently intended. Cf. *Tidewater Oil Co.* v. *United States, Supra,* at 162. Accordingly, we need not consider any question relating to the possible application of §1464 as a criminal statute.

this was an appropriate occasion for its exercise.

The words of the Carlin monologue are unquestionably "speech" within the meaning of the First Amendment. It is equally clear that the Commission's objections to the broadcast were based in part on its content. The order must therefore fall if, as Pacifica argues, the First Amendment prohibits all governmental regulation that depends on the content of speech. Our past cases demonstrate, however, that no such absolute rule is mandated by the Constitution.

The classic exposition of the proposition that both the content and the context of speech are critical elements of First Amendment analysis is Mr. Justice Holmes' statement for the Court in *Schenk* v. *United States:*

> "We admit that in many places and in ordinary times the defendants in saying all that was said in the circular would have been within their constitutional rights. But the character of every act depends upon the circumstances in which it is done. . . . The most stringent protection of free speech would not protect a man in falsely shouting fire in a theatre and causing a panic. It does not even protect a man from an injunction against uttering words that may have all the effect of force. . . . The question in every case is whether the words used are used in such circumstances and are of such a nature as to create a clear and present danger that they will bring about the substantive evils that Congress has a right to prevent." 249 U.S. 47, 52. . . .

In this case it is undisputed that the content of Pacifica's broadcast was "vulgar," "offensive," and "shocking." Because content of that character is not entitled to absolute constitutional protection under all circumstances, we must consider its context in order to determine whether the Commission's action was constitutionally permissible.

We have long recognized that each medium of expression presents special First Amendment problems. And of all forms of communication, it is broadcasting that has received the most limited First Amendment protection. Thus, although other speakers cannot be licensed except under laws that carefully define and narrow official discretion, a broadcaster may be deprived of his license and his forum if the Commission decides that such an action would serve "the public interest, convenience, and necessity." Similarly, although the First Amendment protects newspaper publishers from being required to print the replies of those whom they criticize, it affords no such protection to broadcasters; on the contrary, they must give free time to the victims of their criticism.

The reasons for these distinctions are complex, but two have relevance to the present case. First, the broadcast media have established a uniquely pervasive presence in the lives of all Americans. Patently offensive, indecent material presented over the airwaves confronts the citizen, not only in public, but also in the privacy of the home, where the individual's right to be let alone plainly outweighs the First Amendment rights of an intruder. Because the broadcast audience is constantly tuning in and out, prior warnings cannot completely protect the listener or viewer from unexpected program content. To say that one may avoid further offense by turning off the radio when he hears indecent language is like saying that the remedy for an assault is to run away after the first blow. One may hang up on an indecent phone call, but that option does not give the caller a constitutional immunity or avoid a harm that has already taken place.

Second, broadcasting is uniquely accessible to children, even those too young to read. . . .

Pacifica's broadcast could have enlarged a child's vocabulary in an instant. Other forms of offensive expression may be withheld from the young without restricting the expression at its source. Bookstores and motion picture theaters, for example, may be prohibited from making indecent material available to children. We held in *Ginsberg* v. *New York*, 390 U.S. 629, that the government's interest in the "well being of its youth" and in supporting "parents' claim to authority in their own household" justified the regulation of otherwise protected expression. *Id.*, at 640 and 639. The ease with which children may obtain access to broadcast material, coupled with the concerns recognized in *Ginsberg*, amply justify special treatment of indecent broadcasting.

It is appropriate, in conclusion, to emphasize the narrowness of our holding. This case does not involve a two-way radio conversation between a cab driver and a dispatcher, or a telecast of an Elizabethan comedy. We have not decided that an occasional expletive in either setting would justify any sanction or, indeed, that this broadcast would justify a criminal prosecution. The Commission's decision rested entirely on a nuisance rationale under which context is all-important. The concept requires consideration of a host of variables. The time of day was emphasized by the Commission. The content of the program in which the language is used will also affect the composition of the audience, and differences between radio, television, and perhaps closed-circuit transmissions, may also be relevant. As Mr. Justice Sutherland wrote, a "nuisance may be merely a right thing in the wrong place—like a pig in the parlor instead of the barnyard." *Euclid* v. *Ambler Realty Co.* 272 U.S. 365, 388. We simply hold that when the Commission finds that a pig has entered the parlor, the exercise of its regulatory power does not depend on proof that the pig is obscene.

The judgment of the Court of Appeals is reversed. . . .

Mr. Justice POWELL, with whom Mr. Justice BLACKMUN joins, concurring:
. . . The Court today reviews only the Commission's holding that Carlin's monologue was indecent "as broadcast" at two o'clock in the afternoon, and not the broad sweep of the Commission's opinion. In addition to being consistent with our settled practice of not deciding constitutional issues unnecessarily, this narrow focus also is conducive to the orderly development of this relatively new and difficult area of law, in the first instance by the Commission, and then by the reviewing courts.

The Commission's primary concern was to prevent the broadcast from reaching the ears of unsupervised children who were likely to be in the audience at that hour. In essence, the Commission sought to "channel" the monologue to hours when the fewest unsupervised children would be exposed to it. In my view, this consideration provides strong support for the Commission's holding. . . .

In most instances, the dissemination of this kind of speech to children may be limited without also limiting willing adults' access to it. Sellers of printed and recorded matter and exhibitors of motion pictures and live performances may be required to shut their doors to children, but such a requirement has no effect on adults' access. The difficulty is that such a physical separation of the audience cannot be accomplished in the broadcast media. During most of the broadcast hours, both adults and unsupervised children are likely to be in the broadcast audience, and the broadcaster cannot reach willing adults without also reaching children. This, as the Court emphasizes, is one of the distinctions between the broadcast and other media to which we often have adverted as justifying a different treatment of the broadcast media for First Amendment purposes. . . .

In my view, the Commission was entitled to give substantial weight to this difference in reaching its decision in this case.

A second difference, not without relevance, is that broadcasting—unlike most other forms of communication—comes directly into the home, the one place where people ordinarily have the right not to be assaulted by uninvited and offensive sights and sounds. . . .

Although the First Amendment may require unwilling adults to absorb the first blow of offensive but protected speech when they are in public before they turn away. . . .

a different order or values obtains in the home. The Commission also was entitled to give this factor appropriate weight in the circumstances of the instant case. This is not to say, however, that the Commission has an unrestricted license to decide what speech, protected in other media, may be banned from the airwaves in order to protect unwilling adults from momentary exposure to it in their homes. Making the sensitive judgments required in these cases in not easy. But this responsibility has been reposed initially in the Commission, and its judgment is entitled to respect.

It is argued that despite society's right to protect its children from this kind of speech, and despite everyone's interest in not being assaulted by offensive speech in the home, the Commission's holding in this case is impermissible because it prevents willing adults from listening to Carlin's monologue over the radio in the early afternoon hours. It is said that this ruling will have the effect of "reduc[ing] the adult population . . . to [hearing] only what is fit for children." *Butler* v. *Michigan*, 352 U.S. 380, 383 (1957). This argument is not without force. The Commission certainly should consider it as it develops standards in this area. But it is not sufficiently strong to leave the Commission powerless to act in circumstances such as those in this case.

The Commission's holding does not prevent willing adults from purchasing Carlin's record, from attending his performances, or, indeed, from reading the transcript reprinted as an appendix to the Court's opinion. On its face, it does not prevent respondent from broadcasting the monologue during late evening hours when fewer children are likely to be in the audience, nor from broadcasting discussions of the contemporary use of language at any time during the day. The Commission's holding, and certainly the Court's holding today, does not speak to cases involving the isolated use of a potentially offensive word in the course of a radio broadcast, as distinguished from the verbal shock treatment administered by respondent here. In short, I agree that on the facts of this case, the Commission's order did not violate respondent's First Amendments rights. . . .

Mr. Justice BRENNAN, with whom Mr. Justice MARSHALL joins, dissenting:

. . . For the second time in two years, the Court refuses to embrace the notion, completely antithetical to basic First Amendment values, that the degree of protection the First Amendment affords protected speech varies with the social value ascribed to that speech by five Members of this Court. Moreover, as do all parties, all Members of the Court agree that the Carlin monologue aired by Station WBAI does not fall within one of the categories of speech, such as "fighting words," *Chaplinsky* v. *New Hampshire*, 315 U.S. 568 (1942), or obscenity, *Roth* v. *United States*, 354 U.S. 476 (1957), that is totally without First Amendment protection. This conclusion, of course, is compelled by our cases expressly holding that communications containing some of the words found condemnable here are fully protected by the First Amendment in other contexts. . . .

Yet despite the Court's refusal to create a sliding scale of First Amendment protection calibrated to this Court's perception of the worth of a communication's content, and despite our unanimous agreement that the Carlin monologue is protected speech, a majority of the Court nevertheless finds that, on the facts of this case, the FCC is not constitutionally barred from imposing sanctions on Pacifica for its airing of the Carlin monologue. This majority apparently believes that the FCC's disapproval of Pacifica's afternoon broadcast of Carlin's "Dirty Words"' recording is a permissible time, place, and manner regulation. . . .

Without question, the privacy interests of an individual in his home are substantial and deserving of significant protection. In finding these interests sufficient to justify the content regulation of protected speech, however, the Court commits two errors. First, it misconceives the nature of the privacy interests involved where an individual voluntarily chooses to admit radio communications into his home. Second, it ignores the constitutionally protected interests of both those who wish to transmit and those who desire to receive broadcasts that many—including the FCC and this Court—might find offensive.

"The ability of government, consonant with the Constitution, to shut off discourse solely to protect others from hearing it is . . . dependent upon a showing that substantial privacy interests are being invaded in an essentially intolerable manner. Any broader view of this authority would effectively empower a majority to silence dissidents simply as a matter of personal predilections" . . . .

However, I believe that an individual's actions in switching on and listening to communications transmitted over the public airways and directed to the public at-large do not implicate fundamental privacy interests, even when engaged in within the home. Instead, because the radio is undeniably a public medium, these actions are more properly viewed as a decision to take part, if only as a listener, in an ongoing public discourse. Although an individual's decision to allow public radio communications into his home undoubtedly does not abrogate all of his privacy interests, the residual privacy interests he retains vis-à-vis the communication he voluntarily admits into his home are surely no greater than those of the people present in the corridor of the Los Angeles courthouse in *Cohen* who bore witness to the words "Fuck the Draft" emblazoned across Cohen's jacket. Their privacy interests were held insufficient to justify punishing Cohen for his offensive communication.

Even if an individual who voluntarily opens his home to radio communications retains privacy interests of sufficient moment to justify a ban on protected speech if those interests are "invaded in an essentially intolerable manner," the very fact that those interests are threatened only by a radio broadcast precludes any intolerable invasion of privacy; for unlike other intrusive modes of communication, such as sound trucks, "[t]he radio can be turned off,"—and with a minimum of effort. As Judge Bazelon aptly observed below, "having elected to receive public airwaves, the scanner who stumbles onto an offensive program is in the same position as the unsuspected passers-by in *Cohen* and *Erznoznik* [v. *City of Jacksonville*, 422 U.S. 205 (1975)]; he can avert his attention by changing channels or turning off the set." *Pacifica Foundation* v. *FCC*, U.S. App. D.C. . . . , 556 F.2d9, 26 (1977). Whatever the minimal discomfort suffered by a listener who inadvertently tunes into a program he finds offensive during the brief interval before he can simply extend his arm and switch stations or flick the "off" button, it is surely worth the candle to preserve the broadcaster's right to send, and the right of those interested to receive, a message entitled to full First Amendment protection. To reach a contrary balance, as does the Court, is clearly, to follow Mr. Justice STEVENS' reliance on animal metaphors, "to burn the house to roast the pig." . . .

Most parents will undoubtedly find understandable as well as commendable the Court's sympathy with the FCC's desire to prevent offensive broadcasts from reaching the ears of unsupervised children. Unfortunately, the facial appeal of this justification for radio censorship masks its constitutional insufficiency. Although the government unquestionably has a special interest in the well-being of children and consequently "can adopt more stringent controls on communicative materials available to youths than on those available to adults," the Court has accounted for this social interest by adopting a "variable obscenity" standard that permits the prurient appeal of material available to children to be assessed in terms of the sexual interests of minors. . . .

Because the Carlin monologue is obviously not an erotic appeal to the prurient interests of children, the Court, for the first time, allows the government to prevent minors from gaining access to materials that are not obscene, and are therefore protected, as to them. It thus ignores our recent admonition that "[s]peech that is neither obscene as to youths nor subject to some other legitimate proscription cannot be suppressed solely to protect the young from ideas or images that a legislative body thinks unsuitable for them." The Court's refusal to follow its own pronouncements is especially lamentable since it has the anomalous subsidiary effect, at least in the radio context at issue here, of making completely unavailable to adults material which may not constitutionally be kept even from children. . . .

In concluding that the presence of children in the listening audience provides an adequate basis for the FCC to impose sanctions for Pacifica's broadcast of the Carlin monologue, the opinions of my Brother POWELL, *ante,* at 3, and my Brother STEVENS, *ante,* at 21, both stress the time-honored right of a parent to raise his child as he sees fit—a right this Court has consistently been vigilant to protect. Yet this principle supports a result directly contrary to that reached by the Court. *Yoder* and *Pierce* hold that parents, not the government, have the right to make certain decisions regarding the upbringing of their children. As surprising as it may be to individual Members of this Court, some parents may actually find Mr. Carlin's unabashed attitude towards the seven "dirty words" healthy, and deem it desirable to expose their children to the manner in which Mr. Carlin defuses the taboo surrounding the words. Such parents may constitute a minority of the American public, but the absence of great numbers willing to exercise the right to raise their children in this fashion does not alter the right's nature or its existence. Only the Court's regrettable decision does that. . . .

My Brother STEVENS also finds relevant to his First Amendment analysis the fact that "[a]dults who feel the need may purchase tapes and records or go to theatres and nightclubs to hear [the tabooed] words." My Brother POWELL agrees: "The Commission's holding does not prevent willing adults from purchasing Carlin's record, from attending his performances, or. indeed, from reading the transcript reprinted as an appendix to the Court's opinion." The opinions of my Brethren display both a sad insensitivity to the fact that these alternatives involve the expenditure of money, time, and effort that many of those wishing to hear Mr. Carlin's message may not be able to afford, and a naive innocence of the reality that in many cases, the medium may well be the message. . . .

Moreover, it is doubtful that even those frustrated listeners in a position to follow my Brother POWELL's gratuitous advice and attend one of Carlin's performances or purchase one of his records would receive precisely the same message Pacifica's radio station sent its audience. The airways are capable not only of carrying a message, but also of transforming it. A satirist's monologue may be most potent when delivered to a live audience; yet the choice whether this will in fact be the manner in which the message is delivered and received is one the First Amendment prohibits the government from making.

It is quite evident that I find the Court's attempt to unstitch the warp and woof of First Amendment law in an effort to reshape its fabric to cover the patently wrong result the Court reaches in this case dangerous as well as lamentable. Yet there runs throughout the opinions of my Brothers POWELL and STEVENS another vein I find equally disturbing: a depressing inability to appreciate that in our land of cultural pluralism, there are many who think, act, and talk differently from the Members of this Court, and who do not share their fragile sensibilities. It is only an acute ethnocentric myopia that enables the Court to approve the censorship of communications solely because of the words they contain. . . .

Today's decision will thus have its greatest impact on broadcasters desiring to reach, and listening audiences comprised of persons who do not share the Court's view as to which words or expressions are acceptable and who, for a variety of reasons, including a conscious desire to flout majoritarian conventions, express themselves using words that may be regarded as offensive by those from different socioeconomic backgrounds. In this context, the Court's decision may be seen for what, in the broader perspective, it really is: another of the dominant culture's inevitable efforts to force those groups who do not share its mores to conform to its way of thinking, acting, and speaking. . . .

Mr. Justice STEWART, with whom Mr. Justice BRENNAN, Mr. Justice WHITE, and Mr. Justice MARSHALL join, dissenting: . . . The statute pursuant to which the Commission acted, 18 U.S.C. §1464, makes it a federal offense to utter "any obscene, indecent, or profane language by means of radio communication." The Commission held, and the Court today agrees, that "indecent" is a broader concept than "obscene" as the latter term was defined in *Miller* v. *California,* 413 U.S. 15, because language can be "indecent" although it has social, political or artistic value and lacks prurient appeal. 56 F.C.C. 2d, at 97-98. But this construction of §1464, while perhaps plausible, is by no means compelled. To the contrary, I think that "indecent" should properly be read as meaning no more than "obscene." Since the Carlin monologue concededly was not "obscene," I believe that the Commission lacked statutory authority to ban it. Under this construction of the statute, it is unnecessary to address the difficult and important issue of the Commission's constitutional power to prohibit speech that would be constitutionally protected outside the context of electronic broadcasting.

This Court has recently decided the meaning of the term "indecent" in a closely related statutory context. In *Hamling* v. *United States,* 418 U.S. 87, the petitioner was convicted of violating 18 U.S.C. §1461, which prohibits the mailing of "[e]very obscene, lewd, lascivious, indecent, filthy or vile article." The Court "construe[d] the generic terms in [§1461] to be limited to the sort of 'patently offensive representations or descriptions of that specific "hard core" sexual conduct given as examples in *Miller* v. *California.*'" Thus, the clear holding of *Hamling* is that "indecent" as used in §1461 has the same meaning as "obscene" as that term was defined in the *Miller* case.

Nothing requires the conclusion that the word "indecent" has any meaning in §1464 other than that ascribed to the same word in §1461. Indeed, although the legislative history is largely silent such indications as there are support the view that §§1461 and 1464 should be construed similarly. The view that "indecent" means no more than "obscene" in §1461 and similar statutes long antedated *Hamling*. And although §§1461 and 1464 were originally enacted separately, they were codified together in the Criminal Code of 1948 as part of a chapter entitled "Obscenity." There is nothing in the legislative history to suggest that Congress intended that the same word in two closely related sections should have different meanings. See H. R. Rep. No. 304, 80th Cong., 1st Sess., A104-A106 (1947).

I would hold, therefore, that Congress intended, by using the word "indecent" in §1464, to prohibit nothing more than obscene speech. Under that reading of the statue, the Commission's order in this case was not authorized, and on that basis I would affirm the judgment of the Court of Appeals.

Office of Communication of the United Church of Christ v. Federal Communications Commission

UNITED STATES COURT OF APPEALS, DISTRICT OF COLUMBIA CIRCUIT, 1978

4 Med.L.Rptr. 1410

BAZELON, Circuit Judge: ... Section 315(a) establishes four exemptions to the equal opportunities requirement, determined according to type of news coverage: (1) regularly scheduled newscasts, (2) news interview shows, (3) news documentaries, and (4) on-the-spot coverage of news events. By modifying all four categories with the phrase "bona fide," Congress plainly emphasized its reliance on newsworthiness as the basis for an exemption.

Section 315(a) (4) exempts a broadcast licensee from an equal time obligation if any candidates appear in "on-the-spot coverage of bona fide news events (including but not limited to political conventions and activities incidental thereto)." 47 U.S.C. §315(a) (4) (1970). The central ambiguity in the provision is the meaning of the phrase "on-the-spot." Petitioner insists that the term refers to events broadcast "as they happen, i.e., on the spot." Reply Brief of Petitioner, at 9. Respondents, citing submissions by intervenors from the broadcast industry contend that the phrase is a "term of art" in the industry that refers "primarily to the location of the news coverage rather than to the time it was broadcast." ...

Some light is shed on the meaning of the phrase "on-the-spot coverage" by the statute's use of political conventions as a paradigm for such coverage, and by the shared characteristics of the parallel exemptions granted in §315(a).

The exemption in question developed in some measure from a congressional desire to protect news coverage of national political conventions from the equal time doctrine. That Congress included the exemption to reach more broadly, however, is clear from its inclusion of news events other than conventions. Although much convention coverage is ordinarily presented live, the use of taped or filmed segments on such broadcasts is common, suggesting that on-the-spot coverage is not necessarily limited to live broadcast.

In addition, the other exempt news shows—regular newscasts, documentaries, and news interviews—make liberal use of previously recorded material. Admittedly, the term "on-the-spot" connotes an element of timeliness or newsworthiness. Nevertheless, it seems most unlikely that, in the absence of more specific language, Congress would have singled out on-the-spot coverage for a complete prohibition on the use of taped material. . . .

Under the 1959 Amendments, the equal opportunities doctrine was tempered by the conviction that broadcasters should have greater freedom to perform their professional function of informing the public on current issues.

> Thus, it is necessary, in the public interest, to achieve a balance between substantial equality of opportunity of political candidates on the one hand, and the need, on the other hand, of broadcasters to be free from unreasonable restraints in the exercise of their news judgment insofar as the appearance of political candidates is concerned.

H.P. Rep. No. 802 86th Cong., 1st Sess. 4-5 (1959). The automatic equal time provision was supplanted by a legislative directive to balance the competing interests of equal treatment of candidates and full coverage of political questions. Congress recognized that striking a proper balance would be difficult, but insisted that "[t]he difficulties which lie in the path of achieving such a balance should not be magnified to an extent where either of these principles is lost sight of." . . .

The Commission also noted that some flexibility in broadcast time is warranted to accommodate scheduling problems, particularly when a news event is broadcast across several time zones, and to deal with special concerns such as captioning for deaf viewers and delayed transmission for broadcasters with daytime-only licenses.

Nor can we agree that the Commission overstepped its legal powers in dealing with this difficult problem. By revising its interpretation of §315(a)(4), the FCC attempted to reconcile the arguably con-

tradictory currents within the statute. The concern in the original provision for fairness to candidates confronts the congressional desire, expressed in the 1959 Amendments, to encourage coverage of political campaigns by broadcast licensees. When such important interests must be balanced, there can be no simple, clear resolution of the matter. The range of interpretations of the on-the-spot coverage provision—amply illustrated by the FCC's shifting view of it—reflects the tensions within the statute. Although that range is not unlimited, we cannot find that the Commission has exceeded its delegated authority.

ADJUDICATION V. RULE-MAKING

In *Chisholm* v. *FCC, supra,* this court rejected the contention that the Commission improperly used an adjudicative proceeding to expand its interpretation of §315(a)(4). The ruling in *Chisholm,* which involved a more drastic shift of FCC policy than that before us in this case, was based on the proposition that, absent a demonstration of abuse of discretion, an agency can reasonably determine whether to proceed by rulemaking or adjudication. 358 F.2d at 364-65.

In ratifying the use of an adjudicative proceeding, the *Chisholm* court stressed that the Commission provided a reasoned opinion explaining its action, and that interested groups who were not parties to the proceeding had an opportunity to comment on the matter before the agency. 538 F.2d at 365. Both criteria are satisfied in this case. As discussed above, the FCC's opinion presented a sound analysis of the issues involved, satisfying the requirement of the Administrative Procedure Act that agency action not be arbitrary or capricious. 5 U.S.C. §706(2)(A) (Supp. VI 1976). In addition, there were seven intervenors, including petitioner, in the Commission's proceeding, providing some assurance that there was an extensive discussion of the issues before the Commission. Indeed, the instant case may present an even stronger basis for acting through adjudication since, unlike *Chisholm,* the Commission here reviewed specific facts involving an attempt to provide on-the-spot news coverage. As the FCC's earlier rulings did not reach the question of delayed broadcasts under the on-the-spot exemption adjudication of that issue was appropriate.

According, the Commission's order is *Affirmed.*

questions for discussion and further research

1. If the prime-time access period has become proliferated with shows, should new regulations be instituted to encourage increasing the amount of locally produced public affairs programming used in this time period?

2. Are contractual areas prohibited by the FCC's station-syndication agreements too restrictive? How is the broadcast audience affected by such agreements?

3. In the *Pacifica* decision, the Court stated: "The plain language of the statute (Sec. 1464) does not support Pacifica's argument. The words 'obscene, indecent, or profane' are written in the disjunctive, implying that each has a separate meaning." From your knowledge of the meaning of these words or their common use in society, would you agree with the Supreme Court's interpretation?

4. The *Pacifica* decision was limited to material broadcast during a discussion program about language in society. What would happen if a station reported the Pacifica decision in a regularly scheduled newscast and, in doing so, repeated the filthy words used in the Carlin monologue?

5. In *Pacifica,* the Supreme Court stated: "It is true that the Commission's order may lead some broadcasters to censor themselves." Could this "threat" of reprisal from the FCC or the courts be considered censorship in the traditional sense of prior restraint against a message? If it is, is it justified?

6. Mr. JUSTICE POWELL and Mr. JUSTICE BLACKMUN concurred in the *Pacifica* decision. The concurring opinion stated: "The Commission's primary concern was to prevent the broadcast from reaching the ears of unsupervised children who were likely to be in the audience at that hour. In essence, the Commission sought to 'channel' the monologue to hours when the fewest unsupervised children would be exposed to it." Is there any time of day, based on this interpretation of FCC action, when it would be suitable to air the Carlin monologue? The concurring opinion also stated: "On its face, it does not prevent respondent from broadcasting the monologue during late evening hours when fewer children are likely to be in the audience. . . ." Would this opinion give broadcasters a blanket go-ahead to broadcast the monologue during "late evening hours"? What are "late evening hours"? What if the monologue were broadcast nationally on a network radio?

7. In the concurring opinion of Mr. JUSTICE POWELL, with whom Mr. JUSTICE BLACKMUN concurred, reference was made to the " . . . orderly development of this relatively new and difficult area of law. . . ." What issues do you see developing in the future if more cases similar to *Pacifica* occur?

8. Is the fact that a person can shut off a radio or turn to another television channel reason enough not to place certain real or implied restrictions against broadcast speech?

9. In his dissenting opinion, Mr. JUSTICE BRENNAN, with whom Mr. JUSTICE MARSHALL joined, stated: "The opinions of my Brethren display both a sad insensitivity to the fact that these alternatives [purchasing the album or attending a live performance] involve the expenditure of money, time, and effort that many of those wishing to hear Mr. Carlin's message may not be able to afford, and a naive innocence of the reality that in many cases, the

medium may well be the message." What do you feel is meant by the statement "the medium may well be the message"?

10. Based on the Miller decision, do you feel that a community could enact an enforceable ordinance prohibiting the sale of the Carlin album in that community?

11. Do you agree with Mr. JUSTICE BRENNAN's statement that: " . . . the Court's decision may be seen for what, in the broader perspective, it really is: another of the dominant culture's inevitable efforts to force those groups who do not share its mores to conform to its way of thinking, acting, and speaking"?

12. Is twenty-four hours a reasonable time frame to delay broadcasting a political debate and have it exempt from the equal-time provision of Sec. 315?

13. What happens if a political debate takes place at 11:00 P.M. on Saturday night, and a radio station has no regularly scheduled newscast on Sunday? Should the debate aired on Monday morning still be exempt from the equal-time provision? Would it be exempt?

14. Given the relatively large number of radio stations existing in major markets, is Section 315 really necessary in these locales?

15. Is the lowest unit charge an equitable way of assuring some degree of access to candidates with small campaign budgets?

additional resources

books

Asher, T. R., and J. V. Hahn, *Broadcast Media Guide for Candidates,* Washington, D.C.: Media Access Project, 1974.

Lewis, F. F., *Literature, Obscenity, and Law,* Carbondale: Southern Illinois University Press, 1976.

Mielke, K., R. Johnson, and B. Cole, *The Federal Role in Children's Television Programming,* Washington, D.C.: National Association of Educational Broadcasters, 1975.

Saldich, A. R., *Electronic Democracy: Television's Impact on the American Political Process,* New York: Praeger Special Studies, 1979.

Taubman, J., *Performing Arts Management and Law: Forms Books,* New York: Law-Arts Publishers, 1974.

articles

Abrams, B. A., and R. F. Settle, "Broadcasting and the Political Campaign Spending 'Arms Race'", 21 *Journal of Broadcasting* 153 (1977).

Adams, W. C., and P. H. Ferber, "Television Interview Shows: The Politics of Visibility," 21 *Journal of Broadcasting* 141 (1977).

Aisenberg, M. A., "Political Speech and the Electronic Soap Box: Citizen Access to Media in Post-Broadcasting America," 21 *St. Louis University Law Journal* 76 (1977).

Barrow, R. L., "Presidential Debates of 1976: Toward a Two-Party Political System," 46 *University of Cincinnati Law Review* 123 (1977).

Barton, R. L., "The Lingering Legacy of *Pacifica:* Broadcasters' Freedom of Silence," 53 *Journalism Quarterly* 429 (1976).

Bragg, D. E., "Regulation of Program Content to Protect Children after *Pacifica,*" 32 *Vanderbilt Law Review* 1377 (1979).

Carroll, R. L., "Economic Influences on Commercial Network Television Documentary Scheduling," 23 *Journal of Broadcasting* 411 (1979).

Day, L. A., "A Copyright Dilemma: The TV Format," 22 *Journal of Broadcasting* 249 (1978).

Erbst, L. A., "Equal Time for Candidates: Fairness or Frustration?" 34 *Southern California Law Review* 190 (1961).

Feldman, D., and S. Tickton, "Obscene/Indecent Programming: Regulation of Ambiguity," 20 *Journal of Broadcasting* 273 (1976).

Fisher, R., "Lawyers, Television, and Public Affairs," 53 *Chicago Bar Record* 250 (1972).

George, B. J., Jr., "Obscenity Litigation: An Overview of Current Legal Controversies," 3

National Journal of Criminal Defense 189 (1977).

Golomb, J., "Regulation of Indecency in Political Broadcasting," 13 *University of Michigan Journal of Law Reform No. 1.* (1979).

Hanks, W., and P. Longini, "Television Access: A Pittsburgh Experiment," 18 *Journal of Broadcasting* 289 (1974).

Hochberg, P. R., "Congress Kicks a Field Goal: The Legislative Attack in the 93d Congress on Sports Broadcasting Practices," 27 *Federal Communications Bar Journal* 27 (1974).

Hochberg, P. R., "Congress Tackles Sports and Broadcasting," 3 *Western State University Law Review* 223 (1976).

Hofstetter, C. R., and C. Zukin, "TV Network Political News and Advertising in the Nixon and McGovern Campaigns," 56 *Journalism Quarterly* 106 (1979).

Killenberg, G. M., "Free Expression Implications of New Federal Election Law," 50 *Journalism Quarterly* 527 (1973).

Litman, B. R., "The Television Networks, Competition and Program Diversity," 23 *Journal of Broadcasting* 393 (1979).

Loevinger, L., "The Issues in Program Regulation," 20 *Federal Communications Bar Journal* 3 (1966).

Maltz, E. M., and L. L. Hogue, "On Keeping Pigs out of the Parlor: Speech as Public Nuisance after *FCC v. Pacifica Foundation,*" 31 *South Carolina Law Review* 337 (1980).

McGranery, R. C., "Exemptions from the Section 315 Equal Time Standard: A Proposal for Presidential Elections," 24 *Federal Communications Bar Journal* 177 (1970–71).

Osborn, J. W., P. Driscoll, and R. C. Johnson, "Prime Time Network Television Programming Preemptions," 23 *Journal of Broadcasting* 427 (1979).

Ostroff, D. H., "Equal Time: Origins of Section 18 of the Radio Act of 1927," 24 *Journal of Broadcasting* 367 (1980).

Owen, B. M., "Regulating Diversity: The Case of Radio Fromats," 21 *Journal of Broadcasting* 305 (1977).

Pennybacker, J. H., "The Format Change Issue: FCC vs. U.S. Court of Appeals," 22 *Journal of Broadcasting* 411 (1978).

Sadowski, R. P., "Broadcasting and State Statutory Laws," 18 *Journal of Broadcasting* 433 (1974).

Saliba, M. T., "Television Programming and the Public Interest: Subscription TV versus Public Ownership," 6 *Antitrust Law & Economics Review* 109 (1973).

Schauer, F., "Speech and 'Speech'—Obscenity and 'Obscenity': An Exercise in the Interpretation of Constitutional Language," 67 *Georgetown Law Journal* 899 (1979).

Schmidt, B. C., Jr., "Access to the Broadcast Media: The Legislative Precedents," 28 *Journal of Communication* 60 (1978).

Shooshan, H. M., III, "Confrontation with Congress: Professional Sports and the Television Antiblackout Law," 25 *Syracuse Law Review* 713 (1974).

Smith, F. L., "The Charlie Walker Case," 23 *Journal of Broadcasting* 137 (1979).

Stevens, G. E., "Media Incitement: The 'Born Innocent' Case," 56 *Journalism Quarterly* 622 (1979).

Tannenwald, P., and A. Auckenthaler,"Changes in Radio Entertainment Formats," 21 *St. Louis University Law Journal* 358 (1977).

Thain, G. J., "The 'Seven Dirty Words' Decision: A Potential Scrubbrush for Commercials on Children's Television?" 67 *Kentucky Law Journal* 947 (1978–79).

Tickton, S. D., "Obscene/Indecent Programming: The FCC and WBAL," 1 *Communications and the Law* 15 (1979).

Turow, J., "Non-Fiction on Commercial Children's Television: Trends and Policy Implications," 24 *Journal of Broadcasting* 437 (1980).

Waters, K., "*Pacifica* and the Broadcast of Indecency," 16 *Houston Law Review* 551 (1979).

Wiley, R. E., "Family Viewing: A Balancing of Interests," 27 *Journal of Communication* 188 (1977).

Wirth, M. O., and J. A. Wollert, "Public Interest Programming: Taxation by Regulation," 23 *Journal of Broadcasting* 319 (1979).

cases: obscenity

A Book Etc. (Memoirs) v. Attorney General of Com. Mass., 383 U.S. 413, 86 S.Ct. 975, 16 L.Ed.2d 1, 1 Med.L.Rptr. 1390 (1966).

Duncan v. *United States,* 48 F.2d 128 (9th Cir. 1931), certiorari denied.

Erznoznik v. *City of Jacksonville,* 442 U.S. 205, 1 Med.L.Rptr. 1508 (1975).

F.C.C. v. *Pacifica Foundation,* 438 U.S. 726, 98 S.Ct. 3026, 57 L.Ed.2d 1073 (1978).

Freedman v. *State of Maryland,* 380 U.S. 51, 85 S.Ct. 734, 13 L.Ed.2d 649 (1965).

Ginsberg v. *State of New York,* 390 U.S. 629, 1 Med.L.Rptr. 1424 (1968).

Ginzburg v. *United States,* 383 U.S. 463, 86 S.Ct. 942, 16 L.Ed.2d 31, 1 Med.L.Rptr. 1409 (1966).

Hamling v. *United States,* 418 U.S. 87, 1 Med.L.Rptr. 1479 (1974).

Illinois Citizens' Committee for Broadcasting v. *F.C.C.,* 515 F.2d 397 (D.C.Cir. 1975).

Jenkins v. *Georgia,* 418 U.S. 153, 1 Med.L.Rptr. 1504 (1974).

Joseph Burstyn, Inc. v. *Wilson,* 343 U.S. 495, 1 Med.L.Rptr. 1357 (1952).

McKinney v. *Alabama,* 424 U.S. 669, 1 Med.L. Rptr. 1516 (1975).

Miller v. *State of California,* 413 U.S. 15, 93 S.Ct. 2607, 37 L.Ed.2d 419, 1 Med.L.Rptr. 1441 (1973).

National Association of Independent Television Producers and Distributors v. *F.C.C.,* 516 F.2d 526 (2dCir. 1975).

Paris Adult Theatre I v. *Slaton,* 413 U.S. 49, 93 S.Ct. 2628, 37 L.Ed.2d 446, 1 Med.L.Rptr. 1454 (1973).

Regina v. *Hicklin,* L. R. 3 Q.B. 360 (1868).

Robinson v. *F.C.C.,* 334 F.2d 534 (D.C. Cir. 1964).

Roth v. *United States,* 354 U.S. 476, 77 S.Ct. 1304, 1 L.Ed.2d 1498, 1 Med.L.Rptr. 1375 (1957).

Times Film Corp. v. *City of Chicago,* 365 U.S. 43 (1961).

U.S. v. *Levine,* 83 F.2d 156 (2d Cir. 1936).

U.S. v. *One Book Called "Ulysses,"* 5 F.Supp. 182 (S.D.N.Y. 1933).

Young v. *American Mini Theatres, Inc.,* 427 U.S. 50 (1976).

cases: equal-time, sec. 315

Aspen Institute, 55 F.C.C.2d 697 (1975).

Chisholm v. *F.C.C.,* 538 F.2d 349 (D.C. Cir. 1976) certiorari denied.

Flory v. *F.C.C.,* 528 F.2d 124 (7th Cir. 1975).

Graham v. *Clusen,* 2 Med.L.Rptr.1543 (D.C.D.C. 1977).

Kay v. *F.C.C.,* 443 F.2d 638 (D.C. Cir. 1970).

Martin-Trigona, 40 R.R.2d 1189 (1977).

McCarthy v. *F.C.C.,* 390 F.2d 471 (D.C. Cir. 1968).

Nicholas Zapple, 23 F.C.C.2d 707, 19 R.R.2d 421 (1970).

Office of Communication of the United Church of Christ v. *F.C.C.,* 4 Med.L.Rptr. 1410 (1978).

5

The Fairness Doctrine

Closely related to Section 315, which we discussed in Chapter 4, is the *Fairness Doctrine*. First issued in 1949, the Fairness Doctrine concerns itself with assuring the fair treatment of controversial issues of public importance.[1] Its current status is an outgrowth of both court cases and FCC inquiries dating back to 1941 with the famous *Mayflower* decision. The FCC re-examined the Doctrine in 1964, 1974, and 1976.

Early Policies on Fairness

The Federal Radio Commission, in discussing the limited spectrum space, noted that if issues "are of sufficient importance to the listening public, the microphone will undoubtedly be available. If not, a well-founded complaint will receive the careful consideration of the commission."[2] Concern over this fairness issue crystalized in 1941 with the *Mayflower* decision, involving station WAAB in Boston.[3] The Mayflower Broadcasting Corporation petitioned the FCC to give Mayflower the facilities of WAAB. Although the FCC ruled in favor of WAAB, the station was strongly criticized by the Commission for its practice of "editorializing." The FCC stated that it is " . . . clear that with the limitations in frequencies inherent in the nature of radio, the public interest can never be served by a dedication of any broadcast facility to the support of his own partisan ends."[4] The FCC offered the opinion that: "A truly free radio cannot be used to advocate the causes of the licensee. . . . In brief, the broadcaster cannot be an advocate."[5] It is difficult to determine how many stations were editorializing in 1941. But the *Mayflower* decision successfully discouraged others from jumping on the editorial bandwagon.

While the *Mayflower* decision was stifling editorials, the Code of the National Association of Broadcasters was stifling discussion of controversial issues by prohibiting the purchase of commercials to air those issues. It wasn't long before one station was caught in a triangular conflict among the FCC, the NAB Code, and the First Amendment. Station WHKC in Columbus, Ohio, believing that it was operating in the public interest, adhered to the NAB Code and promptly found itself in a dispute with a labor union. The union claimed that the station had refused to sell it time and had censored the scripts it had submitted.

The union filed a petition against WHKC's license renewal. The FCC held a hearing on the matter in August, 1944 and heard the argument about the NAB Code. By October, the union and the station had agreed to a compromise. The agreement broke with the Code and prohibited any further censorship of scripts, dropping the station's policy that banned selling time for controversial issues. The agreement stated: "With respect to public issues of a controversial nature, the station's policy will be one of open-mindedness and impartiality."[6] It went on to state that the station would "make time available . . . on a commercial basis, for the full and free discussion of issues of public importance, including controversial issues. . . ." The FCC, in accepting the agreement, recognized that the radio spectrum was limited and not available to everyone who desired access. But it added that:

> These facts, however, in no way impinge upon the duty of each station licensee to be sensitive to the problems of public concern in the community and to make sufficient time available on a nondiscriminatory basis, for full discussion thereof, without any type of censorship which would undertake to impose the views of the licensee upon the material to be broadcast.

Further support for airing controversial issues occurred in 1946, when Robert Harold Scott of Palo Alto, California filed a petition asking the FCC to revoke the licenses of radio stations KQW, KPO, and KFRC. Scott claimed that he wanted time to expound his views about atheism, providing a balance for the station's "direct statements and arguments against atheism as well as for indirect arguments, such as church services, prayers, Bible reading, and other kinds of religious programs."[7] Scott's petition did not result in the stations' license revocations, but the FCC did reaffirm in its decision its views on access and fairness by referring to the freedom of speech clause of the First Amendment to the Constitution:

> Underlying the conception of freedom of speech is not only the recognition of the importance of the free flow of ideas and the information to the effective functioning of democratic forms of government and ways of life, but also belief that immunity from criticism is dangerous. . . . Sound and vital ideas and institutions become strong and develop with criticism so long as they themselves have full opportunity for expression; it is dangerous that the unsound be permitted to flourish for want of criticism.

The Commission also stated that the mere fact of an issue being unpopular did not alleviate the broadcaster's responsibility to air it:

The fact that a licensee's duty to make time available for the presentation of opposing views on current controversial issues of public importance may not extend to all possible differences of opinion within the ambit of human contemplation cannot serve as the basis for any rigid policy that time shall be denied for the presentation of views which may have a high degree of unpopularity.

With the Scott and the WHKC decisions, the FCC made it clear that it expected stations to be responsive to issues which were controversial and of public importance and not to avoid them simply because they were unpopular. Still left unclear, however, was the whole subject of the *Mayflower* decision discouraging editorializing. The issue had its moot points since commentators had appeared for years and delivered statements on the air which could easily have been considered equivalent to editorializing.

Issuing the Fairness Doctrine

The Commission began to tackle the editorializing issue in March and April of 1948 when it held eight days of hearings on the subject. Other persons filed written motions. Out of these hearings came a statement issued by the FCC on June 1, 1949, under the heading: *In the Matter of Editorializing by Broadcast Licensees.* It was to become known as the *Fairness Doctrine.* In the Doctrine, the Commission reasserted its commitment to free expression of controversial issues of public importance, as stated in the WHKC and Scott decisions. It also *reversed* the *Mayflower* decision by supporting broadcast editorials. The Commission came "to the conclusion that overt licensee editorialization, within reasonable limits and subject to the general requirements of fairness . . . , is not contrary to the public interest."[8] At the same time, it cautioned broadcasters against abuse of the editorial:

> It should also be clearly indicated that the question of the relationship of broadcast editorialization, . . . to operation in the public interest, is not identical with the broader problem of assuring "fairness" in the presentation of news, comment or opinion, but is rather one specific facet of this larger problem. . . . In the absence of a duty to present all sides of controversial issues, overt editorialization by station licensees could conceivably result in serious abuse. But where, as we believe to be the case under the Communications Act, such a responsibility for a fair and balanced presentation of controversial public issues exists, we cannot see how the open espousal of one point of view by the licensee should necessarily prevent him from affording a fair opportunity for the presentation of contrary positions or make more difficult the enforcement of the statuory standard of fairness upon any licensee.

What had been, only one decade earlier, the ultimate discouragement was now unqualified support for broadcasters to air their subjective views.

Additional Support for Fairness

As expected, complaints were soon filed with the FCC alleging abuse of the Fairness Doctrine. In 1950, the FCC inquired about the practice of a station broadcasting a series of programs supporting the National Fair Employment

Practices Commission (NFEPC). The station replied that it had not presented the views of those opposing the NFEPC. The FCC informed the station that it had not acted properly. The NFEPC issue was of public importance simply because the station had broadcast so many programs on the subject. In short, it was a controversial issue of public importance, and the station had not been fair in presenting both sides.[9]

In another case, a station broadcast a series of programs about pay TV, much of the content opposing pay TV. In an FCC hearing, the question arose of whether or not the station had complied with the requirements of the Fairness Doctrine with these programs. The station argued that although the pay TV issue was a controversial issue nationally, it did not feel that it was controversial to the local area served by the station. Again, the station was advised that it had not acted properly. And the FCC again noted that because the station had broadcast considerable programming about pay TV, it had elevated the issue to local importance. Moreover, after presenting a network program with balanced views on the subject, the station pre-empted local programming to present the views of a Senator who was opposed to the issue "with the apparent design of neutralizing any possible public sympathy for pay TV which might have arisen from the preceding network forum."[10]

The Fairness Primer

In 1964, the FCC published its first set of guidelines since the Fairness Doctrine's inception in 1949. The 1964 document, commonly called the "Fairness Primer," brought together the representative FCC rulings that had transpired over those years.[11] It gave people an opportunity to study the FCC's decisions, as well as shedding light on other stations' practices and policies, showing where complaints might be warranted, and guiding stations on how to meet Fairness Doctrine requirements.

Still waiting, however, was a major legal test of the constitutionality of the Fairness Doctrine. This came in an appeals court case in 1967, which reached the Supreme Court in 1969. Called the *Red Lion* decision, it affirmed the constitutionality of the Fairness Doctrine.[12]

The *Red Lion* Decision

The *Red Lion* decision involved the Red Lion Broadcasting Company of Red Lion, Pennsylvania. In November 1964, the Reverend Billy James Hargis lashed out on Red Lion's radio station against the author of a book about Barry Goldwater. The author, Fred J. Cook, was held in low esteem by Hargis, who detailed what he felt to be the less favorable aspects of Cook's career as a writer. Cook contacted the station for a chance to reply to Hargis. But the station claimed that it did not have to offer free time to Cook unless he could prove that there was no commercial sponsorship available to present his views. Cook went to the FCC, which ruled in his favor, citing the Fairness Doctrine. In the case of *Red Lion Broadcasting Co.* v. *Federal Communications Commission,* the appeals court upheld the FCC's decision.

At that point, the Radio-Television News Directors' Association entered the picture and appealed the case once more, this time to the United States Court of Appeals for the Seventh Circuit in Chicago. In the case of *Radio-Televison News Directors' Association* v. *United States,* the court ruled that the Fairness Doctrine's personal attack and editorial rules would "contravene the first amendment."[13] But RTNDA's victory was short-lived. The FCC then took the case to the Supreme Court, which reviewed both the circuit and the appeals court decisions. The Supreme Court ruled: "In view of the prevalence of scarcity of broadcast frequencies, the Government's role in allocating those frequencies, and the legitimate claims of those unable without governmental assistance to gain access to those frequencies for expression of their views, we hold the regulations and ruling at issue here are both authorized by statute and constitutional."[14] With this, the Supreme Court upheld the FCC and reversed the decision in the RTNDA case. The Fairness Doctrine was now not only just a broadcast regulation issued by the FCC but one that had been reaffirmed by judicial precedent by the highest court in the land.

Personal Attack and Political Editorializing

One area of the Fairness Doctrine that remained somewhat nebulous concerned the broadcast of direct personal attacks against individuals or organizations. In an attempt to clarify the responsibilities of broadcasters in this area, the FCC issued an advisee in July, 1963 on how to handle personal attacks.[15] The advisee called upon broadcasters to transmit the text of the attack to the person or group attacked and to offer time for a reply. The same applied to editorials, and broadcasters were again reminded of their responsibilities for overall fairness.

But the advise was just that—advice. The FCC felt that it needed to strengthen this advice into a requirement. So when the *Red Lion* issue came to the attention of the FCC, it decided that this was the time for a ruling. Effective August 14, 1967, the FCC's rules regarding personal attack read:

> (a) When, during the presentation of views on a controversial issue of public importance, an attack is made upon the honesty, character, integrity or like personal qualities of an identified person or group, the licensee shall, within a reasonable time and in no event later than one week after the attack, transmit to the person or group attacked (1) notification of the date, time and identification of the broadcast; (2) a script or tape (or accurate summary if a script or tape is not available) of the attack; and (3) an offer of a responsible opportunity to respond over licensee's facilities. . . .[16]

The rules exempt foreign groups or foreign public figures, certain types of attacks made by political candidates during campaigns, and, with the same provisions as Section 315, various bona fide news events.

The FCC has extended the personal attack rule to cover comments made "in relation to" a given broadcast as well as on the broadcast itself. This extension occurred after a politician was called a "coward" by a talk show host two hours after a program on meat boycotts had been aired. The "coward" remark was in relation to the politician's participation on the boycott program. The FCC said that the station should have notified the politician about the charge, but the U.S.

Court of Appeals overruled the FCC, saying that the Commission had just extended the personal attack rule, and that the station could not have predicted the new interpretation. The court also said, however, that the rule *could* be extended in future incidents, and the FCC made it clear that this would become policy.[17]

At the same time that it spelled out the new personal attack policy, the FCC also spelled out new rules covering editorials:

> (c) Where a licensee in an editorial, (i) endorses or (ii) opposes a legally qualified candidate or candidates, the licensee shall, within 24 hours after the editorial, transmit to respectively (i) the other qualified candidate or candidates for the same office or (ii) the candidate opposed in the editorial (1) notification of the date and the time of the editorial; (2) a script or tape of the editorial; and (3) an offer of a reasonable opportunity for the candidate or a spokesman of the candidate to respond over the licensee's facilities: *Provided, however,* That where such editorials are broadcast within 72 hours prior to the day of the election, the licensee shall comply with the provisions of this paragraph sufficiently far in advance of the broadcast to enable the candidate or candidates to have a reasonable opportunity to prepare a response and to present it in a timely fashion.

With these 1967 rules, broadcasters know exactly what is expected of them when such incidents occur on their stations. They do, however, have the discretion to determine what constitutes a personal attack. Here, the FCC has permitted broadcast management to remain in charge of its local programming—if not carte blanche, at least somewhat uninhibited by a federal agency.

The Fairness Doctrine and Broadcast Advertising

The FCC's position on the fairness issue is that the *overall* programming of a station should reflect its commitment to fairness, not just a single program. Advertising's role in this programming became a contested issue when WCBS-TV was approached by New York lawyer, John W. Banzhaf, who requested equal time to reply to cigarette commercials. WCBS-TV refused to grant him time, but the FCC agreed with Banzhaf. The FCC's decision was upheld by the appeals court, which tried to confine the decision to cigarette advertising. But that was too much to hope for, and over the years, the Fairness Doctrine has been applied to many factions of advertising. Cigarette advertising was meanwhile banned on radio and television after 1971 by the Public Health Cigarette Smoking Act of 1969.

In another case, the Media Access Project, Inc. (MAP) contended that Georgia Power Company had sponsored ten commercials which lobbied for a rate increase pending before the Georgia Public Service Commission. MAP complained that two Augusta, Georgia stations had not met their obligations under the Fairness Doctrine by avoiding an effort to redress what MAP considered an imbalance of programming. The stations contended that the issue was not controversial, since the hearings on the rate increase were being held in Atlanta, not Augusta, which was the area served by the stations. They also suggested that the advertisements were "institutional" and thus not even covered under the Fairness Doctrine. Moreover, one of the stations had broadcast contrasting viewpoints on nine different occasions. The FCC, however, said that these programs were not enough to balance what it felt was a controversial issue. The Commission directed the stations to inform it of what programming they had broadcast or intended to broadcast to present contrasting viewpoints on the issue.[18]

In a sweeping FCC order, eight California stations were caught in a Fairness Doctrine controversy over programming about nuclear power plants. At a time when people in California were being asked to sign a petition for a referendum on nuclear power plants, the stations aired commercials sponsored by the Pacific Gas and Electric Company. The commercials promoted nuclear power and power plants. Citizens' action groups brought the matter to the FCC's attention and, in 1974, filed an action against thirteen stations. The Commission found that five stations had presented the issue fairly, with programming advancing the antinuclear stand. Eight others were required to show the FCC how they intended to comply with the Fairness Doctrine. The Commission felt that the issue was controversial and of public importance and it investigated "to the minute" the amount of time the stations had devoted to different sides of the issue.[19]

When Texaco sponsored commercials showing pieces of a puzzle being fitted together, "each representing a different phase of the oil industry, coming together into what is described as an efficient and economical company," the FCC said that it was a controversial issue and aired at a time when legislation was pending in Congress to break up the oil companies. The complaint was filed by the Media Access Project against NBC, ABC, and Washington, D.C. stations WRC-TV and WTOP-TV. The FCC ruled in favor of the two networks and WRC, but said that WTOP-TV had to present viewpoints of those who favored the breakup of the oil companies.

But not all of the complaints against broadcasters have ended up in favor of the complainants. For example, a resident of Poland Springs, Maine asked a local television station for equal time to present arguments against the use of snowmobiles. Snowmobiles had been advertised on the station as making winter "just one big fun-filled season."[20] The resident claimed that because the Maine legislature was considering a bill to regulate snowmobiles, and because the resident felt the machines to be dangerous to wildlife and vegetation, he should be able to present his views under the Fairness Doctrine. The FCC ruled that the commercials were standard product commercials, and that the resident was not entitled to air time. The appeals court upheld the FCC and said that the commercials were not directed toward the snowmobile controversy.

In another case, the Polish-American Congress, Inc. complained that the broadcasting of Polish jokes on ABC's "Dick Cavett Show" were actually attacks disguised as ethnic humor. The Broadcast Bureau of the FCC ruled that the jokes were not attacks on Polish-Americans, "since it had not been shown that there was any controversy in this country concerning the intelligence or other qualities of Polish-Americans."[21] The Polish-American Congress requested that the entire Commission review the ruling of its Broadcast Bureau. The request was denied, and the case went to the Court of Appeals. The court ruled that the jokes did not constitute a controversial issue and did not require the network to offer free time for a response. The Supreme Court refused to review the lower court's decision.

   Three stations in San Francisco and two in Los Angeles became involved in a Fairness Doctrine complaint after broadcasting commercials for Chevron F-310 gasoline. Alan F. Neckritz and Lawrence B. Ordower of Berkley, California contended that the commercials presented only one side of a controversial issue: whether or not Chevron F-310 helped to solve air pollution. The FCC ruled that the commercials did not deal with a controversial issue of public importance, but instead were statements of a claim of product efficiency. Neckritz appealed to the Washington, D.C. Circuit Court. In a decision on June 28, 1974, the appeals court ruled in favor of the FCC.[22]

   The FCC's decisions are not always upheld. When NBC broadcast its documentary, "Pensions: The Broken Promise," the FCC requested the network to indicate how it would meet its obligations under the Fairness Doctrine. NBC felt that it had been fair in presenting the documentary and should not be required to offer additional time on the matter. The network took the matter to court, and the court ruled in its favor. The appeals court "disagreed with the FCC's judgment that the documentary was unbalanced on the *broad issue* of overall pension plan performance for workers, and the network was reasonable in asserting that the documentary was on the *less controversial issue* of 'problems' with pensions."[23]

Penalties for Abuse: The WXUR Decision

Although the FCC has a variety of sanctions to impose upon broadcasters who violate its rules, the most stringent is to deny renewal of a broadcast license. This maximum penalty was imposed on station WXUR in Media, Pennsylvania after the FCC determined that the station had violated the Fairness Doctrine by openly criticizing groups and individuals, yet not informing them of their right to reply. The station had been operated by Brandywine Main Line Radio, Inc., which was wholly owned by the Faith Theological Seminary under the direction of fundamentalist preacher Carl McIntire. McIntire's group applied for ownership of the station in 1965, but the FCC approved the application only on the basis that the group would "provide the opportunity for the expression of opposing viewpoints on controversial public issues."[24] When renewal time arrived, citizens protested. The FCC revoked the station's license, finding that "Brandywine failed to establish any regular procedure for previewing, monitoring or reviewing its broadcasts, and thus did not regularly know what views were being presented on controversial issues of public importance."[25]

   The FCC decision was appealed in *Brandywine–Main Line Radio, Inc.* v. *Federal Communications Commission.* The court upheld the FCC, pointing out that almost immediately after the new owners took over, the station started airing a series of programs which were characterized as "The Hate Clubs of the Air." The Commission found the other evidence substantial and the public outcry considerable. One complaint was filed with the Media, Pennsylvania, Borough Council, and the Pennsylvania Legislature even passed a resolution condemning the programming practices of Carl McIntire.[26]

   Despite the fact that the case represented a precedent for Fairness Doctrine penalties, one of the more widely quoted aspects of the case came in a dissenting opinion from Chief Judge Bazelon of the Washington, D.C. Appeals Court, which heard the *Brandywine* litigation. Bazelon believed that the decision to revoke the license was a prima facie affront to free speech and press. He suggested that the time had come for "the Commission to draw back and consider whether time and technology have so eroded the necessity for governmental imposition of Fairness obligations that the Doctrine has come to defeat its purpose in a variety of circumstances. . . ."[27] Two years later, the FCC issued a "re-evaluation" of the Fairness Doctrine.

One of the most celebrated cases occurred in West Virginia in 1976, when station WHAR was hit by a Fairness Doctrine complaint from, among others, Representative Patsy Mink, who was supporting anti-strip-mining legislation in Congress. In the *Patsy Mink* case, the FCC ruled in favor of the complainants in one of the best examples of how the Commission could assert its authority and affirm a station's duty not only to air but to seek out issues of importance to a local community. In the *Patsy Mink* case, the FCC itself determined what was and was not an important issue in Clarksburg, West Virginia. It found that strip mining was important, and determined that the issue came under the Fairness Doctrine. The complete text of the FCC's *Patsy Mink* case is found at the end of this chapter.

The Fairness Report: 1974

Undoubtedly sensing the consternation of broadcasters, the public, and the courts over the Fairness Doctrine, the FCC filed a Notice of Inquiry in 1971, seeking opinions on the applicability and usefulness of the Doctrine as well as its interpretations.[28] Out of the inquiry came a statement by the FCC in 1974, commonly known as the "Fairness Report."[29] Broadcasters who thought the report might provide some relief from the Fairness Doctrine were disappointed. The Commission did, however, attempt to clarify some of the issues that had raised problems. And as it stands, the Report is the document currently guiding broadcasters in meeting their obligations under the Fairness Doctrine.

determining adequate time for opposing viewpoints

The Report reiterated that the licensee had an "affirmative responsibility" to provide a "reasonable" amount of time for the presentation of important issues. Although it was still up to the licensee to determine how much time to devote to presentations, the Report made it clear that the Commission believes that the "medium can make a great contribution to an informed public opinion." But it was "not prepared to allow this purpose to be frustrated by broadcasters who consistently ignore their public interest responsibilities." The Report regarded strict adherence to the Fairness Doctrine as the single most important requirement in the operation of a station and an essential element for license renewal.

The Report also cautioned broadcasters against falling back on their network to meet Fairness requirements. The responsibility could not be delegated to any other "person or group" or be "unduly fettered by contractual agreements. . . ." The FCC felt that "stations, in carrying out this responsibility, should be alert to the opportunity to complement network offerings with local programming on these issues, or with syndicated programming."

But how will these quasi-hands-off policies contribute to an informed public opinion? The Commission felt that even though it was *not* requiring that equal time be made available, the requirement that contrasting viewpoints be provided would "greatly increase the likelihood that individual members of the public will be exposed to varying points of view."

defining a controversial issue

One of the most difficult issues confronting the Commission and broadcasters alike is just what constitutes a controversial issue. If you were a broadcaster, how would you determine this? First you would check the 1974 "Fairness Report" guidelines. For example, the mere fact that an issue is newsworthy and receives attention in the press does not necessarily mean that the Fairness Doctrine is applicable to it.[30] However, the amount of media coverage *is* something to consider. So is the amount of attention the issue receives from government officials and "other community leaders." But even with these factors, the broadcaster is still faced with a "subjective evaluation of the impact that the issue is likely to have on the community at large." The Report specifies: "The licensee should be able to tell with a reasonable degree of objectivity, whether an issue is the subject of vigorous debate with substantial elements of the community in opposition to one another." Yet broadcasters and the public are cautioned that the "Fairness Doctrine was not designed for the purpose of providing a forum for private disputes of no consequence to the general public."

identifying the issue

Closely related to defining an issue is *identifying* it. That may seem quite simple, but often an issue is camouflaged by unrelated discussions. In recognizing this fact, the 1974 "Fairness Report" used the example of a community debate on a school bond issue:

> The broadcast presents a spokesman who forcefully asserts that new school construction is urgently needed and that there is also a need for substantial increases in teachers' salaries, both principal arguments advanced by proponents of the bond issue. The spokesman, however, does not explicitly mention or advocate passage of the bond issue. In this case, the licensee would be faced with a need to determine whether the spokesman had raised the issue of whether the school bonds should be authorized (which is controversial), or whether he had merely raised the question of whether present school facilities and teacher salaries are adequate (which might not be at all controversial).

How would you rule if you were managing a broadcasting station? According to the Report: "The licensee's inquiry should focus not on whether the statement bears some tangential relevance to the school bond question, but rather on whether the statement in the context of the ongoing community debate, is so obviously and substantially related to the School bond issue as to amount to advocacy of a position on that question."

If, for example, the program was logged as a discussion of the school bond issue, then there would be little question that the Fairness Doctrine would apply. If the spokesman was the chairperson of a committee actively supporting the bond issue, then this would be an instance to provide time to people opposing the issue. Regardless of the examples, the broadcaster has the final say, notwithstanding an FCC review, and every community and local issue presents its own set of problems.

providing opportunities for contrasting viewpoints

One of the hazy areas of the Report deals with the *way* broadcasters provide time for opposing viewpoints. Perhaps here more than in any other area, the FCC has adopted a hands-off policy, staying away from strict reprisal unless the licensee has acted in an "arbitrary and unreasonable fashion." For the Commission to interfere too heavily with this process would mean a head-on collision with the First Amendment, especially where news programming is concerned. Consequently, the Report indicates that although "The Licensee has a duty to play a conscious and positive role in encouraging the presentation of opposing viewpoints," the FCC does not believe that it is necessary to establish a "formula" in locating spokesmen. If, on the other hand, the licensee does not present opposing viewpoints, then the FCC expects the broadcaster to be "prepared to demonstrate that he has made a diligent, good-faith effort. . . ."

The Report also acknowledges that an issue may have more than two sides, and that the licensee has an obligation to present different opinions or "shades" of opinion. But the FCC reaffirms that "equal" time is not necessary: "we have long felt that the basic goal of creating an informed citizenry would be frustrated if for every controversial item or presentation on a newscast or other broadcast the licensee had to offer equal time to the other side." The Report does specify certain actions which clearly are abuses of the Fairness Doctrine. For example, if one side of an issue is presented in prime time and the other side after midnight, then a complaint might be justified. Or an imbalance "might be a reflection of the total amount of time afforded to each side, or the frequency with which each side is presented, . . . or of a combination of factors."

The Commission reiterates that it will not issue an equal time "formula" per se, but that in examining a Fairness complaint, it may examine the ratio of time made available to opposing viewpoints. This, too, can be difficult. Transcripts of programs may not be available, and relying on listener or management recollections can be shaky. Yet in dealing with commercials, the formula concept becomes easier to interpret, as in the case of the eight California stations caught in the nuclear power issue. The mere discussion of the Commission's time concepts in this case gave broadcasters their first "formula" to follow as a Fairness Doctrine guideline.

rethinking the decision on cigarette advertising

The 1974 Report also reconsidered advertising. The FCC admitted that its original decision, upheld in *Banzhaf* v. *Federal Communications Commission,* should not be viewed as current policy and that, in retrospect, "we believe that this mechanical approach to the Fairness Doctrine represented a serious departure from the Doctrine's central purpose. . . ." The Report reflected the Commission's opinion that "standard product commercials, such as the old cigarette ads, make no meaningful contribution toward informing the public on any side of any issue." Reflecting on all this, had the Public Health Cigarette Smoking Act not been passed in 1969, there might have been strong arguments to return "product" cigarette advertising to radio and television after the issuance of the 1974 Fairness Report.

Reconsideration of the Fairness Doctrine: 1976

In 1976, the FCC again examined the Fairness Doctrine.[31] Coming on the heels of the 1974 Report, the Commission's action was prompted by petitions filed by citizens' groups wanting more access. Overall, the FCC found the 1974 document to be in good health. It reaffirmed its decision to apply the Fairness Doctrine to advertisements that deal with public issues, not just the advertising that lauds the merits of a given product. It also agreed that editorials should come under the Doctrine's regulatory umbrella. The Commission ruled that a "tenuous" relationship to an issue would not trigger the Doctrine. In its 1976 *Memorandum Opinion and Order,* it reiterated that it would still let the broadcaster decide what was necessary to meet the Doctrine's requirement, and that if a broadcaster was found in error, the Commission would probably just direct the station to offer time to the opposing issue.

Relating the Fairness Doctrine to Section 315

Confusion frequently arises over the interpretations of the Fairness Doctrine and Section 315. Part of this confusion results from the imprecise use of the two concepts in everything from popular literature to the reports of uninformed broadcasters. Both documents are designed to afford "equal opportunities" if not "equal time" to opposing points of view. But remember, Section 315 deals with *political* broadcasting and candidates for public office, regardless of what they say.

Let us assume that an incumbent candidate for Congress talks about the construction of a flood control dam during a local radio program. The dam has been hotly contested in the station's community, and could easily be classified as a controversial issue of public importance. After the candidate's broadcast, his opponent requests and is granted the opportunity to appear on the program. But the opponent, instead of discussing the flood control dam on the program, talks about urban renewal. Has the broadcaster met the requirements of Section 315 and the Fairness Doctrine?

We could assume that with the appearance of both candidates, the requirements of Section 315 have been satisfied. But that is *not* necessarily the case as far as the Fairness Doctrine is concerned. Since the incumbent discussed a controversial issue of public importance, he triggered the Fairness Doctrine machinery. So the broadcaster, under the Fairness Doctrine, must still present an opposing view to the flood control project. If the opponent had discussed his opposition to the dam, then perhaps that would have fulfilled the requirement. But he didn't. Now along comes a spokesperson for the group opposing the dam. That person is also given the opportunity to appear on the station, this time to speak in opposition to the dam. But keep in mind that the broadcaster might not be *required* (although it is advisable) to give "equal time" for the spokesperson's viewpoints.

It is also important to remember that although Section 315 exempts most news programming, the Fairness Doctrine does not. The FCC is not going to dictate news content, but if controversial issues of public importance are heard on news programs, then in some way the broadcaster has the obligation to present opposing sides of those issues. And even Section 315 states that the news programming exemptions do not excuse broadcasters from "the obligation imposed upon them under this Act to operate in the public interest and to afford reasonable opportunity for the discussion of conflicting views on issues of public importance."

The Fairness Doctrine Under Attack: Issues and Criticism

In addition to being one of the most important pieces of broadcast regulation that exists, the Fairness Doctrine is also one of the most highly criticized. Those who cry out against its alleged injustices do so loudly; those who support it are equally intense. Supporters base their arguments on concepts we have already discussed in detail: limited spectrum space, the need to assure responsible use of the spectrum by providing all sides of opposing viewpoints, assuring open and unchecked views in a marketplace of ideas, fostering unbiased news reporting, and guaranteeing the presentation of programming devoted to issues of public importance. Critics feel that the Doctrine is at best an unnecessary restraint, at worst a blatant case of government intrusion, colliding head on with the First Amendment. Between these two extremes are a multitude of opinions, from an abundance of spokespersons.

General criticism has come from such industry sources as NBC's Julian Goodman, who remarked: "The Fairness Doctrine has discouraged the very type of discussion it purports to foster. It has done this by giving Government the right to intervene as a frequently partisan editor in the process of broadcast journalism.... The Fairness Doctrine has been a muzzle on broadcast journalism's pursuit of stories and issues the public should know about and it has enabled the Government to stand at the broadcaster's shoulder and ask him to justify or amend his journalistic effort."[32]

At the heart of the criticism is the "limited resource" of the electromagnetic spectrum. The right of government to establish regulations for broadcasting has traditionally been based on the fact that the spectrum has only so much room, and thus not everyone can operate a broadcasting station. Therefore, the rules that guide broadcasters in their "privilege" not "right" to operate a station are both legal and appropriate. It is under this "limited resource" concept that the Fairness Doctrine operates. Is this a legitimate justification for the Doctrine?

Back in 1964, Joseph L. Brechner, President and General Manager of an Orlando, Florida television station, spoke to the National Broadcast Editorial Conference. In his address, later published in the *Journal of Broadcasting*, he said: "in almost no area in this great country, with its vastly developed broadcasting system, is there a likelihood of a single viewpoint or political position, an area which could be said to be dominated or tyrannized by a broadcaster. On the contrary, broadcasting and broadcasters represent or offer the protection against single-newspaper editorial tyranny."[33] Echoing Brechner's sentiment, FCC Chairman Richard Wiley suggested, when the FCC was reconsidering the Fairness Doctrine in 1976, that the Commission suspend the Doctrine in some larger markets on an experimental basis. His suggestion remained just that—a suggestion.

Another analysis of the "limited resource" argument was posted by Herbert W. Hobler, President of the Nassau Broadcasting Company of Princeton, New Jersey. Addressing the 1975 New Jersey Broadcasters' Association, he said: "There are today, only 1,774 daily newspapers in this country—many of which are actually only six-day newspapers. There are some 7,640 weeklies, of all sizes and shapes. That's a total of 9,400 newspapers—and a total of 500 *less* papers than existed ten years ago. In 1973 alone, 169 went out of business and 78 merged. Another way to look at this is that there are close to 500 *less* editorial opinions available to the public. . . . There are some 7,737 commercial radio and TV stations in this country—and all of them are on seven days a week. And that's an INCREASE of 2,072 stations in the past ten years."[34]

Albeit the merits of the Fairness Doctrine, other critics disagree with the print-broadcast analysis. The Communications Law Committee of the American Bar Association contends:

> Critics of the Fairness Doctrine thus miss the point when they argue that there are thousands more radio broadcast licensees than daily newspapers. The matter is not a question of the scarcity of broadcast facilities as compared to daily newspapers. What-ever the economics of the daily newspaper field, it is technologically open to all. Radio is inherently not so open. The government must license or there will be a pattern of frequency interference. It chooses one licensee for a frequency and forecloses all others—a crucial difference from the print media.[35]

However, the Law Committee has some persuasive legal arguments against the Fairness Doctrine. It cites the case of the *Miami Herald Publishing Co.* v. *Tornillo,* which struck down a Florida statute requiring the right of reply to people attacked in newspaper editorials.[36] The U.S. Supreme Court concluded:

> The choice of material to go into a newspaper, and the decisions made as to limitations on the size and content of the paper, and treatment of public issues and public officials—whether fair or unfair—constitute the exercise of editorial control and judgment. It has yet to be demonstrated how governmental regulation of this crucial process can be exercised consistent with First Amendment guarantees of a free press. . . .

The Committee suggests that the right of reply statute "has the same commend-able purpose as the Commission's Fairness Doctrine . . ." but asks: "Why is the FCC's rule as to broadcast journalism consistent with the First Amendment and Florida's print statute inconsistent?"[37] The answer again lies in the "limited re-source" concept that gives the government the power to regulate broadcasting.

The Law Committee suggested the possibility of substituting access programming for what it termed "governmentally-regulated fairness."[38] How would access programming work? Instead of being concerned primarily with the *content* of programming, the broadcaster would provide ample opportunity for opposing viewpoints and the presentation of issues of public importance. Note that the emphasis is on providing the *opportunity,* as opposed to the current emphasis not only on opportunity but on the actual content of programming. At the same time, the Committee recommends that if the "regulated" approach is to remain, then there should still be "wide discretion in the licensee to make Fairness judgments," and the Fairness Doctrine scrutiny should come primarily at license renewal time, as opposed to the "ad-hoc" consideration of complaints whenever they occur.

Whereas many in the industry feel that the Fairness Doctrine is an outright violation of the First Amendment, the American Bar Committee is less emphatic on that stance. It can accept the constitutionality of the Fairness Doctrine, but only if government releases its hold on the programming functions of the licensee. The fact remains that the Fairness Doctrine, almost as much as the Communications Act itself, will undoubtedly remain at the forefront of public debate for some time.

summary

The Fairness Doctrine is designed to assure fair treatment of controversial issues of public importance. It grew out of the FCC's 1941 *Mayflower* decision, which ironically argued the opposite stand, that a truly free radio cannot be used to advocate the causes of the licensee. Yet the FCC changed its mind when it affirmed an Ohio station's agreement to accept commercials explaining both sides of a union dispute. In 1946, the *Scott* case further affirmed the spirit of the Fairness Doctrine, which was officially issued by the FCC in 1949.

In its 1964 Fairness Primer, the FCC issued its first set of guidelines to help broadcasters interpret the Doctrine's meaning. In the 1967 *Red Lion* decision, the courts affirmed the FCC's position. Since then, the Doctrine has been used to provide an assurance of equal reply when someone is verbally attacked on radio or television and when controversial issues are expressed in broadcast advertising.

The FCC filed a Notice of Inquiry in 1971 in order to take another look at the Doctrine. Out of this Inquiry arose the 1974 Fairness Report, which reiterated the affirmative responsibility of the licensee to provide time for controversial issues of public importance. At the prodding of citizens' groups, the FCC again stated its affirmation of the Doctrine in 1976, supporting the licensee's responsibility to uphold the spirit of fairness in broadcast programming.

material for analysis

Two issues that have been at the forefront of discussions about the Fairness Doctrine are (1) the constitutionality of the Doctrine and (2) the exact nature of the programming to which the Doctrine applies. In *Red Lion Broadcasting Co.,*

Inc. v. *Federal Communications Commission,* we can read in detail the rationale touched upon briefly earlier in this chapter. Keep in mind that the *Red Lion* decision has become the foundation for the constitutionality of the Fairness Doctrine. The decision has withstood the test of time, and although not everyone agrees with the Doctrine, *Red Lion* has provided a solid basis for the FCC to enforce its provisions. As you read the Doctrine, ask yourself what kind of political climate might have existed at the time *Red Lion* was rendered. In what way might this climate have contributed to the ruling? If the political climate had been different, might the Supreme Court and lower courts have ruled differently?

If an FCC decision can be described as a "classic," then so far as where the Fairness Doctrine is concerned, the *Patsy Mink* case (59 F.C.C. 2d 987) could be considered such a decision. The decision was issued after the Commission considered the complaint of the Media Access Project on behalf of Representative Patsy Mink, the Environmental Policy Center, and O. D. Hagedorn (a citizen of Clarksburg, West Virginia) against station WHAR in Clarksburg. The complaint charged that WHAR had violated the Fairness Doctrine by failing to sufficiently address the issue of strip mining. Representative Mink, a sponsor of anti-strip-mining legislation before Congress, wrote several stations, including WHAR, and asked them to broadcast an eleven-minute tape about her proposal, which she claimed would balance the opinion of a U.S. Chamber of Commerce program titled "What's the Issue (No. 684)" presenting a pro-strip-mining stance. WHAR refused, and after further inquiry, the complaint was filed. The *Patsy Mink* case is important because it stands as an example of the FCC's position of a station's affirmative responsibility to seek out and air programming about issues of local importance. While you are reading the decision, try to judge the strength of WHAR's case and the FCC's response.

Red Lion Broadcasting Co., Inc. v. Federal Communications Commission

UNITED STATES SUPREME COURT, 1969

395 U.S. 367, 89 S.Ct. 1794, 23 L.Ed.2d 371 1 Med.L.Rptr. 2053

Mr Justice WHITE delivered the opinion of the Court.

The Federal Communications Commission has for many years imposed on radio and television broadcasters the requirement that discussion of public issues be presented on broadcast stations, and that each side of those issues must be given fair coverage. This is known as the fairness doctrine, which originated very early in the history of broadcasting and has maintained its present outlines for some time. It is an obligation whose content has been defined in a long series of FCC rulings in particular cases, and which is distinct from the statutory requirement of § 315 of the Communications Act that equal time be allotted all qualified candidates for public office. Two aspects of the fairness doctrine, relating to personal attacks in the context of controversial public issues and to political editorializing, were codified more precisely in the form of FCC regulations in 1967. The two cases before us now, which were decided separately below, challenge the constitutional and statutory bases of the doctrine and component rules. *Red Lion* involves the application of the fairness doctrine to a particular broadcast, and *RTNDA** arises as an action to review the FCC's 1967 promulgation of the personal attack and political editorializing regulations, which were laid down after the *Red Lion* litigation had begun.

I.

a.

The Red Lion Broadcasting Company is licensed to operate a Pennsylvania radio station, WGCB. On November 27, 1964, WGCB carried a 15-minute broadcast by the Reverend Billy James Hargis as part of a "Christian Crusade" series. A book by Fred J. Cook entitled "Goldwater—Extremist on the Right" was discussed by Hargis, who said that Cook had been fired by a newspaper for making false charges against city officials; that Cook had then worked for a Communist-affiliated publication; that he had defended Alger Hiss and attacked J. Edgar Hoover and the Central Intelligence Agency; and that he had now written a "book to smear and destroy Barry Goldwater." When Cook heard of the broadcast he concluded that he had been personally attacked and demanded free reply time, which the station refused. After an exchange of letters among Cook, Red Lion, and the FCC, the FCC declared that the Hargis broadcast constituted a personal attack on Cook; that Red Lion had failed to meet its obligation under the fairness doctrine as expressed in *Times-Mirror Broadcasting Co.* to send a tape, transcript, or summary of the broadcast to Cook and offer him reply time; and that the station must provide reply time whether or not Cook would pay for it. On review in the Court of Appeals for the District of Columbia Circuit the FCC's position was upheld as constitutional and otherwise proper.

b.

Not long after the *Red Lion* litigation was begun, the FCC issued a Notice of Proposed Rule Making, with an eye to making the personal attack aspect of the fairness doctrine more precise and more readily enforceable, and to specifying its rules relating to political editorials. . . .

As they now stand amended, the regulations read as follows: "Personal attacks; political editorials.

"(a) When, during the presentation of views on a controversial issue of public importance, an attack is made upon the honesty, character, integrity or like personal qualities of an identified person or group, the licensee shall, within a reasonable time and in no event later than 1 week after the attack, transmit to the person or group attacked (1) notification of the date, time and identification of the broadcast; (2) a script or tape (or an accurate summary if a script or tape is not available) of the attack; and (3) an offer of a reasonable opportunity to respond over the licensee's facilities.

"(b) The provisions of paragrah (a) of this section shall not be applicable (1) to attacks on foreign groups or foreign public figures; (2) to personal attacks which are made by legally qualified candidates, their authorized spokesmen, or those associated with them in the campaign, on other such candidates, their authorized spokesmen, or persons associated with the candidates in the campaign; and (3) to bona fide newscasts, bona fide news interviews, and on-the-spot coverage of a bona fide news event (including commentary or analysis contained in the foregoing programs, but the provisions of paragraph (a) of this section shall be applicable to editorials of the licensee).

c.

Believing that the specific application of the fairness doctrine in *Red Lion,* and the promulgation of the regulations in *RTNDA,* are both authorized by Congress and enhance rather than abridge the freedoms of speech and press protected by the First Amendment, we hold them valid and constitutional, reversing the judgment below in *RTNDA* and affirming the judgment below in *Red Lion.*

II.

The history of the emergence of the fairness doctrine and of the related legislation shows that the Commission's action in the *Red Lion* case did not exceed its authority, and that in adopting the new regulations the Commission was implementing congressional policy rather than embarking on a frolic of its own. . . .

Without government control, the medium would be of little use because of the cacophony of competing voices, none of which could be clearly and predictably heard. Consequently, the Federal Radio Commission was established to allocate frequencies among competing applicants in a manner responsive to the public "convenience, interest, or necessity."

Very shortly thereafter the Commission expressed its view that the "public interest requires ample play for the free and fair competition of opposing views, and the commission believes that the principle applies . . . to all discussions of issues of importance to the public." . . .

There is a twofold duty laid down by the FCC's decisions and described by the 1949 Report on Editorializing by Broadcast Licensees. The broadcaster must give adequate coverage to public issues and coverage must be fair in that it accurately reflects the opposing views. This must be done at the broadcaster's own expense if sponsorship is unavailable. Moreover, the duty must be met by programming obtained at the licensee's own initiative if available from no other source. The Federal Radio Commission had imposed these two basic duties on broadcasters since the outset, and in particular respects the personal attack rules and regulations at issue here have spelled them out in greater detail.

When a personal attack has been made on a figure involved in a public issue, both the doctrine of cases such as *Red Lion* and *Times-Mirror Broadcasting Co.,* and also the 1967 regulations at issue in *RTNDA* require that the individual attacked himself be offered an opportunity to respond. Likewise, where one candidate is endorsed in a political editorial, the other candidates must themselves be offered reply time to use personally or through a spokesman. These obligations differ from the general fairness requirement that issues be presented, and presented with coverage of competing views, in that the broadcaster does not have the option of presenting the attacked party's side himself or choosing a third party to represent that side. But insofar as there is an obligation of the broadcaster to see that both sides are presented, and insofar as that is an affirmative obligation, the personal attack doctrine and regulations do not differ from the preceding fairness doctrine. The simple fact that the attacked men or unendorsed candidates may respond themselves or through agents is not a critical distinction, and indeed, it is not unreasonable for the FCC to conclude that the objective of adequate presentation of all sides may best be served by allowing those most closely affected to make the response, rather than leaving the response in the hands of the station which has attacked their candidacies, endorsed their opponents, or carried a personal attack upon them.

b.

The statutory authority of the FCC to promulgate these regulations derives from the mandate to the "Commission from time to time, as public convenience, interest, or necessity requires" to promulgate "such rules and regulations and prescribe such restrictions and conditions . . . as may be necessary to carry out the provisions of this chapter. . . ." This mandate to the FCC to assure that broadcasters operate in the public interest is a broad one.... It is broad enough to encompass these regulations.

The fairness doctrine finds specific recognition in statutory form, is in part modeled on explicit statutory provisions relating to political candidates, and is approvingly reflected in legislative history.

In 1959 the Congress amended the statuory requirement of § 315 that equal time be accorded each political candidate to except certain appearances on news programs, but added that this constituted no exception *"from the obligation imposed upon them under this Act to operate in the public interest and to afford reasonable opportunity for the discussion of conflicting views on issues of public importance."* This language makes it very plain that Congress, in 1959, announced that the phrase "public interest," which had been in the Act since 1927, imposed a duty on broadcasters to discuss both sides of controversial public issues. In other words, the amendment vindicated the FCC's general view that the fairness doctrine inhered in the public interest standard....

The objectives of §315 themselves could readily be circumvented but for the complementary fairness doctrine ratified by § 315. The section applies only to campaign appearances by candidates, and not by family, friends, campaign managers, or other supporters. Without the fairness doctrine, then, a licensee could ban all campaign appearances by candidates themselves from the air and proceed to deliver over his station entirely to the supporters of one slate of candidates, to the exclusion of all others. In this way the broadcaster could have a far greater impact on the favored candidacy than he could by simply allowing a spot appearance by the candidate himself. It is the fairness doctrine as an aspect of the obligation to operate in the public interest, rather than § 315, which

prohibits the broadcaster from taking such a step.

The legislative history reinforces this view of the effect of the 1959 amendment. Even before the language relevant here was added, the Senate report on amending § 315 noted that "broadcast frequencies are limited and, therefore, they have been necessarily considered a public trust. Every licensee who is fortunate in obtaining a license is mandated to operate in the public interest and has assumed the obligation of presenting important public questions fairly and without bias." ...

It is true that the personal attack aspect of the fairness doctrine was not actually adjudicated until after 1959, so that Congress then did not have those rules specifically before it. However, the obligation to offer time to reply to a personal attack was presaged by the FCC's 1949 Report on Editorializing, which the FCC views as the principal summary of its *ratio decidendi* in cases in this area:

"In determining whether to honor specific requests for time, the station will inevitably be confronted with such questions as ... whether there may not be other available groups or individuals who might be more appropriate spokesmen for the particular point of view than the person making the request. The latter's personal involvement in the controversy may also be a factor which must be considered, for elementary considerations of fairness may dictate that time be allocated to a person or group which have been specifically attacked over the station, where otherwise no such obligation would exist." 13 F.C.C., at 1251–1252.

When the Congress ratified the FCC's implication of a fairness doctrine in 1959 it did not, of course, approve every past decision or pronouncement by the Commission on this subject, or give it a completely free hand for the future. The statutory authority does not go so far. But we cannot say that when a station publishes personal attacks or endorses political candidates, it is a misconstruction of the public interest standard to require the station to offer time for a response rather than to leave the response entirely within the control of the station which has attacked either the candidacies or the men who wish to reply in their own defense. When a broadcaster grants time to a political candidate, Congress itself requires that equal time be offered to his opponents. It would exceed our competence to hold that the Commission is unauthorized by the statute to employ a similar device where personal attacks or political editorials are broadcast by a radio or television station.

In light of the fact that the "public interest" in broadcasting clearly encompasses the presentation of vigorous debate of controversial issues of importance and concern to the public; the fact that the FCC has rested upon that language from its very inception a doctrine that these issues must be discussed, and fairly; and the fact that Congress has acknowledged that the analogous provisions of § 315 are not preclusive in this area, and knowingly preserved the FCC's complementary efforts, we think the fairness doctrine and its component personal attack and political editorializing regulations are a legitimate exercise of congressionally delegated authority. The Communications Act is not notable for the precision of its substantive standards and in this respect the explicit provisions of § 315, and the doctrine and rules at issue here which are closely modeled upon that section, are far more explicit than the generalized "public interest" standard in which the Commission ordinarily finds its sole guidance, and which we have held a broad but adequate standard before. We cannot say that the FCC's declaratory ruling in *Red Lion,* or the regulations at issue in *RTNDA,* are beyond the scope of the congressionally conferred power to assure that stations are operated by those whose possession of a license serves "the public interest."

III.

The broadcasters challenge the fairness doctrine and its specific manifestations in the personal attack and political editorial rules on conventional First Amendment grounds, alleging that the rules abridge their freedom of speech and press. Their contention is that the First Amendment protects their desire to use their allotted frequencies continuously to broadcast whatever they choose, and to exclude whomever they choose from ever using that frequency. No man may be prevented from saying or publishing what he thinks, or from refusing in his speech or other utterances to give equal weight to the views of his opponents. This right, they say, applies equally to broadcasters.

a.

Although broadcasting is clearly a medium affected by a First Amendment interest, differences in the characteristics of new media justify differences in the First Amendment standards applied to them. For example, the ability of new technology to produce sounds more raucous than those of the human voice justifies restrictions on the sound level, and on the hours and places of use, of sound trucks so long as the restrictions are reasonable and applied without discrimination.

Just as the Government may limit the use of sound-amplifying equipment potentially so noisy that it drowns out civilized private speech, so may the Government limit the use of broadcast equipment. The right of free speech of a broadcaster, the user of a sound truck, or any other individual does not embrace a right to snuff out the free speech of others.

When two people converse face to face, both should not speak at once if either is to be clearly understood. But the range of the human voice is so limited that there could be meaningful communications if half the people in the United States were talking and the other half listening. Just as clearly, half the people might publish and the other half read. But the reach of radio signals is incomparably greater than the range of the human voice and the problem of interference is a massive reality. The lack of know-how and equipment may keep many from the air, but only a tiny fraction of those with resources and intelligence can hope to communicate by radio at the same time if intelligible communication is to be had, even if the entire radio spectrum is utilized in the present state of commercially acceptable technology.

It was this fact, and the chaos which ensued from permitting anyone to use any frequency at whatever power level he wished, which made necessary the enactment of the Radio Act of 1927 and the Communications Act of 1934, as the Court has noted at length before. It was this reality which at the very least necessitated first the division of the radio spectrum into portions reserved respectively for public broadcasting and for other important radio uses such as amateur operation, aircraft, police, defense, and navigation; and then the subdivision of each portion, and assignment of specific frequencies to individual users or groups of users. Beyond this, however, because the frequencies reserved for public broadcasting were limited in number, it was essential for the Government to tell some applicants that they could not broadcast at all because there was room for only a few.

Where there are substantially more individuals who want to broadcast than there are frequencies to allocate, it is idle to posit an unabridgeable First Amendment right to broadcast comparable to the right of every individual to speak, write, or publish. If 100 persons want broadcast licenses but there are only 10 frequencies to allocate, all of them may have the same "right" to a license; but if there is to be any effective communication by radio, only a few can be licensed and the rest must be barred from the airwaves. It would be strange if the First Amendment, aimed at protecting and furthering communications, prevented the Government from making radio communication possible by requiring licenses to broadcast and by limiting the number of licenses so as not to overcrowd the spectrum.

This has been the consistent view of the Court. Congress unquestionably has the power to grant and deny licenses and to eliminate existing stations. No one has a First Amendment right to a license or to monopolize a radio frequency; to deny a station license because "the public interest" requires it "is not a denial of free speech."

By the same token, as far as the First Amendment is concerned those who are licensed stand no better than those to whom licenses are refused. A license permits broadcasting, but the licensee has no constitutional right to be the one who holds the license or to monopolize a radio frequency to the exclusion of his fellow citizens. There is nothing in the First Amendment which prevents the Government from requiring a licensee to share his frequency with others and to conduct himself as a proxy or fiduciary with obligations to present those views and voices which are representative of his community and which would otherwise, by necessity, be barred from the airwaves.

This is not to say that the First Amendment is irrelevant to public broadcasting. On the contrary, it has a major role to play as the Congress itself recognized in § 326, which forbids FCC interference with "the right of free speech by means of radio communication." Because of the scarcity of radio frequencies, the Government is permitted to put restraints on licensees in favor of others whose views should be expressed on this unique medium. But the people as a whole retain their interest in free speech by radio and their collective right to have the medium function consistently with the ends and purposes of the First Amendment. It is the right of the viewers and listeners, not the right of the broadcasters, which is paramount. . . .

It is the purpose of the First Amendment to preserve an uninhibited marketplace of ideas in which truth will ultimately prevail, rather than to countenance monopolization of that market, whether it be by the Government itself or a private licensee. . . .

It is the right of the public to receive suitable access to social, political, esthetic, moral, and other ideas and experiences which is crucial here. That right may not constitutionally be abridged either by Congress or by the FCC. . . .

Nor can we say that it is inconsistent with the First Amendment goal of producing an informed public capable of conducting its own affairs to require a broadcaster to permit answers to personal attacks occurring in the course of discussing controversial issues, or to require that the political opponents of those endorsed by the station be given a chance to communicate with the public. Otherwise, station owners and a few networks would have unfettered power to make time available only to the highest bidders, to communicate only their own views on public issues, people and candidates, and to permit on the air only those with whom they agreed. There is no sanctuary in the First Amendment for unlimited private censorship operating in a medium not open to all. "Freedom of the press from governmental interference under the First Amendment does not sanc-

tion repression of that freedom by private interests."

c.

It is strenuously argued, however, that if political editorials or personal attacks will trigger an obligation in broadcasters to afford the opportunity for expression to speakers who need not pay for time and whose views are unpalatable to the licensees, then broadcasters will be irresitibly forced to self-censorship and their coverage of controversial public issues will be eliminated or at least rendered wholly ineffective. Such a result would indeed be a serious matter, for should licensees actually eliminate their coverage of controversial issues, the purposes of the doctrine would be stifled.

At this point, however, as the Federal Communications Commission has indicated, that possibility is at best speculative. The communications industry, and in particular the networks, have taken pains to present controversial issues in the past, and even now they do not assert that they intend to abandon their efforts in this regard. It would be better if the FCC's encouragement were never necessary to induce the broadcasters to meet their responsibility. And if experience with the administration of these doctrines indicates that they have the net effect of reducing rather than enhancing the volume and quality of coverage, there will be time enough to reconsider the constitutional implications. The fairness doctrine in the past has had no such overall effect.

That this will occur now seems unlikely, however, since if present licensees should suddenly prove timorous, the Commission is not powerless to insist that they give adequate and fair attention to public issues. It does not violate the First Amendment to treat licensees given the privilege of using scarce radio frequencies as proxies for the entire community, obligated to give suitable time and attention to matters of great public concern. To condition the granting or renewal of licenses on a willingness to present representative community views on controversial issues is consistent with the ends and purposes of those constitutional provisions forbidding the abridgment of freedom of speech and freedom of the press. Congress need not stand idly by and permit those with licenses to ignore the problems which beset the people or to exclude from the airways anything but their own views of fundamental questions. The statute, long administrative practice, and cases are to this effect....

e.

It is argued that even if at one time the lack of available frequencies for all who wished to use them justified the Government's choice of those who would best serve the public interest by acting as proxy for those who would present differing views, or by giving the latter access directly to broadcast facilities, this condition no longer prevails so that continuing control is not justified. To this there are several answers.

Scarcity is not entirely a thing of the past. Advances in technology, such as microwave transmission, have led to more efficient utilization of the frequency spectrum, but uses for that spectrum have also grown apace. Portions of the spectrum must be reserved for vital uses unconnected with human communication, such as radio-navigational aids used by aircraft and vessels....

Comparative hearings between competing applicants for broadcast spectrum space are by no means a thing of the past. The radio spectrum has become so congested that at times it has been necessary to suspend new applications. The very high frequency television spectrum is, in the country's major markets, almost entirely occupied, although space reserved for ultra high frequency television transmission, which is a relatively recent develop-

ment as a commercially viable alternative, has not yet been completely filled.

The rapidity with which technological advances succeed one another to create more efficient use of spectrum space on the one hand, and to create new uses for that space by ever growing numbers of people on the other, makes it unwise to speculate on the future allocation of that space. It is enough to say that the resource is one of considerable and growing importance whose scarcity impelled its regulation by an agency authorized by Congress. Nothing in this record, or in our own researches, convinces us that the resource is no longer one for which there are more immediate and potential uses than can be accommodated, and for which wise planning is essential. This does not mean, of course, that every possible wavelength must be occupied at every hour by some vital use in order to sustain the congressional judgment. The substantial capital investment required for many uses, in addition to the potentiality for confusion and interference inherent in any scheme for continuous kaleidoscopic reallocation of all available space may make this unfeasible. The allocation need not be made at such a breakneck pace that the objectives of the allocation are themselves imperiled.

Even where there are gaps in spectrum utilization, the fact remains that existing broadcasters have often attained their present position because of their initial government selection in competition with others before new technological advances opened new opportunities for further uses. Long experience in broadcasting, confirmed habits of listeners and viewers, network affiliation, and other advantages in program procurement give existing broadcasters a substantial advantage over new entrants, even where new entry is technologically possible. These advantages are the fruit of a preferred position conferred by the Government. Some present possibility for new entry by competing stations is not enough, in itself, to render unconstitutional the Goverment's effort to assure that a broadcaster's programming ranges widely enough to serve the public interest.

In view of the scarcity of broadcast frequencies, the Government's role in allocating those frequencies, and the legitimate claims of those unable without governmental assistance to gain access to those frequencies for expression of their views, we hold the regulations and ruling at issue here are both authorized by statute and constitutional.[28] The judgment of the Court of Appeals in *Red Lion* is affirmed and that in *RTNDA* reversed and the causes remanded for proceedings consistent with this opinion.

It is so ordered.

Not having heard oral argument in these cases, Mr. Justice Douglas took no part in the Court's decision.

Patsy Mink v. *WHAR*

BEFORE THE FEDERAL COMMUNICATIONS COMMISSION WASHINGTON, D.C. 20554

In Re Complaint of
Representative Patsy Mink, The
Environmental Policy Center and O.D.
Hagedorn against Radio Station
WHAR, Clarksburg, West Virginia

MEMORANDUM OPINION AND ORDER

(Adopted: June 8, 1976; Released: June 16, 1976)

BY THE COMMISSION:
COMMISSIONERS WILEY,
CHAIRMAN; AND QUELLO
CONCURRING IN THE RESULT;
COMMISSIONER ROBINSON
CONCURRING AND ISSUING
A STATEMENT.

1. The Commission received a fairness doctrine complaint dated September 25, 1974 against radio station WHAR, Clarksburg, West Virginia, filed by the Media Access Project on behalf of Representative Patsy Mink, the Environmental Policy Center and O. D. Hagedorn, a citizen of Clarksburg. The thrust of the complaint is that WHAR is in "violation of its affirmative obligations under the fairness doctrine to 'devote a reasonable percentage of [its] broadcast time to the coverage' of the national, state and local controversial issue of public importance of strip mining."

2. On July 8, 1974 Representative Mink, a sponsor of anti-strip mining legislation then before Congress, wrote to WHAR and numerous other broadcast stations requesting that they broadcast an 11-minute tape regarding her proposal which she claimed would contrast viewpoints presented during a U.S. Chamber of Commerce program entitled "What's the Issue (No. 684)," representing a pro-strip min-

---

[28]We need not deal with the argument that even if there is no longer a technological scarcity of frequencies limiting the number of broadcasters, there nevertheless is an economic scarcity in the sense that the Commission could or does limit entry to the broadcasting market on economic grounds and license no more stations than the market will support. Hence, it is said, the fairness doctrine or its equivalent is essential to satisfy the claims of those excluded and of the public generally. A related argument, which we also put aside, is that quite apart from scarcity of frequencies, technological or economic, Congress does not abridge freedom of speech or press by legislation directly or indirectly multiplying the voices and views presented to the public through time sharing, fairness doctrines, or other devices which limit or dissipate the power of those who sit astride the channels of communication with the general public. Cf. *Citizen Publishing Co.* v. *United States*, 394 U.S. 131 (1969).

ing position that had previously been broadcast by "hundreds of stations . . . including WHAR."

3. On July 10, 1974, WHAR responded to Representative Mink's request by returning the tape and stating that it was "not going to broadcast it," and that "furthermore . . . [the station is] well aware of . . . [its] responsibility to inform the public of all sides of a controversial issue." Complainants wrote the station on July 22 seeking a clarification of its action in order to "determine whether [the licensee] violated the fairness doctrine." On July 23 the licensee responded by stating:

"1. WHAR did not air What's the Issue program number 684.

2. WHAR has presented no programming on the Strip Mining controversy.

3. WHAR has aired no contrasting viewpoints on the Strip Mining Issue."

Thereafter complainants filed their complaint with the Commission alleging that "the licensee has failed for at least a four-month period when Congress was considering strip mining legislation to air *any* programming on the strip-mining controversy," (emphasis in original), and that this issue has continued to be "of extreme importance to the economy and environment of the area served by WHAR and, consequently, is of extraordinary controversiality and public importance to WHAR's listeners."

4. In support of its contention that the strip mining issue was at that time extremely controversial, complainants cited the "battle over strip mining . . . being waged in the halls of Congress," referring specifically to House Report No. 93–1072, at page 60, which lists the various organizations reacting in some fashion to such legislation. Complainants cited similar legislation introduced by West Virginia Congressman Ken Hechler, who they stated has "vociferously challenged" strip mining in that state. Moreover, the complainants

argued that the "failure to impose stringent controls on strip mining . . . is bound to hurt the deep-mining industry, still the backbone of the Appalachian economy," and referred to the coverage the issue has received in area newspapers such as the *Herald-Dispatch* in Huntington, and the *Gazette-Mail* in Charleston, national periodicals such as *Business Week,* May 11, 1974, as well as in the local *Clarksburg Telegram* which they claimed devoted nine front page stories from July 10 to July 21, 1974 to "the local and national debate about strip mining." Additionally, they stated that on September 9, 1971 a group of citizens from Clarksburg called "The Concerned Citizens" filed comments with the Commission in which they referred to the controversiality of this issue. Those comments are included in *In Re Handling of Public Issues Under the Fairness Doctrine and the Public Interest Standard of the Communications Act, Docket No. 19260.* Furthermore, complainants enclosed a report dated February 6, 1971 compiled by the Appalachian Research and Development Fund, Inc., of Charleston, West Virginia, entitled "Legal Duty of Broadcasters to Present Strip Mining Abolition Issue Adequately and Fairly—Strip Mining Abolition: A Controversial Issue of Public Importance," which the complainants claimed put all broadcasters in the area on notice of the importance of this issue. In that report, it was noted:

"That the abolition of strip mining of coal in West Virginia is a controversial issue of public importance, there can be no doubt. . . . Numerous public officials, high and low, have issued pronouncements on both sides of the subject. Private citizens throughout the state have aired their views in unprecedented fashion. Newspaper articles daily declare the urgency of that issue. Economic and biological reports have [been] issued and are in process of issuance from government, both state and federal, which document the environmental and economic havoc caused by strip mining. Most recently, the West Virginia Surface Mine Association has found this topic so menacing to its self-interest, as to justify purchase of broadcast time throughout the state."

5. The complainants argued that "by neglecting the strip mining controversy .... WHAR has totally failed to afford its listeners any programming on perhaps the most important controversial issue in the Clarksburg area, an issue which intimately affects the day-to-day economic and physical well-being of those listeners." They stated that "perhaps the most stinging indictment of the station's self-professed failure to cover the current strip mining controversy" is its statements in its 1972 license renewal application that "[t]he economy of [its] area is basically industrial. The major industry is glass, followed closely by Surface and Deep Mining." In addition, they asserted that WHAR, in its renewal application, cited "Development of new industry" and "Air and Water Pollution" as issues of great concern to its listeners.

6. The complainants requested that the Commission direct the station to "schedule substantial programming immediately on strip mining," claiming that the failure to require such programming would "make a mockery of not only the fairness doctrine, but of the Commission's *Primer on Ascertainment of Community Problems by Broadcast Applicants*, 20 FCC 2d 650 (1971)" which they asserted requires that community problems "receive suitable attention" during the licensee's programming as well as in its application for license.

7. Inasmuch as the Commission had no independent information regarding this complaint other than the licensee's statement that it had presented no programming on strip mining, we sent the licensee a letter of inquiry dated December 11, 1974 requesting that it comment on the complaint. In its response dated January 13, 1975, WHAR referred to this matter as "a misunderstanding of the facts," stating that "[w]here, in answer to [complainants'] letter, the licensee replied that it had 'presented no programming on the strip mining controversy' and 'aired no contrasting viewpoints on that issue,' it meant only that it had originated no local programming that dealt with, or presented contrasting views on the controversy. The licensee stated that it did not mean that it had refused to carry or failed to carry *any* information at all on this controversy, for that was not at all the case." The licensee claimed that to the contrary it broadcast "a significant amount of information concerning the [strip mining] controversy." To substantiate this claim, it cited its broadcast of the Associated Press news service which it asserted "carried continuous bombardment of stories [referred to as news summaries] relating to the strip mining issue, most of which were carried over WHAR." It declared that, in addition, it subscribes to ABC Contemporary Network's news and public affairs programs including the *Issues and Answers* program. It advised the Commission that it would submit further information concerning the extent of the coverage that the strip mining issue had received during these programs upon receipt of such data from ABC.

8. WHAR also argued that even if the Commission were to determine that the licensee had failed to "adequately cover" the strip mining controversy, it doubted "whether the licensee is answerable to the Commission for selection of those issues" to be broadcast and therefore whether it would be proper for the Commission to take any action in view of such apparent failure. It stated that *Red Lion Broadcasting Co.* v. *FCC*, 395 U.S. 367 (1969), which it characterized as the basis for the Commis-

sion's language in its *Fairness Report,* 48 FCC 2d 1 (1974), that the licensee has an obligation to present coverage of controversial issues, "does not say that each licensee must treat . . . [each critical issue], and it does not, in any way, imply that a broadcaster has no discretion to decide to handle some of those issues and leave others to be treated by other licensees." WHAR contends that there is presently no established precedent or rule requiring a particular licensee to cover any particular issue, and cited our ruling in *Gary Soucie,* 24 FCC 2d 743 (1969), which also was referred to in our *Fairness Report, supra,* as prescribing a general obligation for "broadcasting" as an industry rather than individual licensees to cover controversial issues. It argued that any attempt by the government to designate the issues which must be discussed by a licensee "enfleshes [the] . . . specter of censorship," and would interfere with the licensee's discretion under the fairness doctrine to determine the nature and amount of coverage to be given to particular subject matter.

9. In attacking the assertion that strip mining was a critical issue in Clarksburg, WHAR claimed that it found no problems relating to strip mining mentioned among principal needs and interests in its community as determined in two ascertainment surveys accompanying its 1970 renewal application and its 1974 application for a new FM license in Clarksburg. As to the assertion that wide coverage of the issue in the print media should require similar coverage by licensees, WHAR argues that this would deprive broadcasters of their own editorial discretion. In addition, it asserted that the complainants neither attempted to negotiate with the licensee nor filed a complaint with the station but rather went immediately to the Commission after receiving WHAR's July 10, 1974 response to their correspondence, and therefore cut off the possibility of addi-

tional programming devoted to the strip mining issue.

10. WHAR requested that the Commission retract the language in its *Fairness Report* which the licensee argues gives the Commission the power to determine "which are the 'critical' issues or whether and to what extent those issues have been covered." Furthermore, it stated that if the Commission "should affirm such a policy," WHAR should not be subject to sanction because the Commission would be establishing a "new guideline for all stations to follow."

11. The licensee attached the affidavit of James Fawcett, President and majority shareholder of WHAR who reiterated therein that WHAR never carried any of the United States Chamber of Commerce programs, and that "[a]lthough strip mining is, admittedly, a matter of importance to many of the inhabitants of the Clarksburg area, WHAR has never had any request whatsoever to produce or broadcast any programming on that issue other than the request from Representative Mink." Fawcett stated that WHAR had not ignored this issue, although he acknowledged that its programming thereon had been limited to what it had received from the ABC Network and syndicated wire services. Fawcett asserted that the Charleston Bureau of the Associated Press advised him that it had compiled 128 items on strip mining from March to June 1974 and 102 items from October to December 1974 and stated that "WHAR would probably have carried over 75% of these stories." He declared that WHAR broadcast other programs which dealt with environmental concerns, such as a weekly 15-minute program produced by the West Virginia Extension Service which discussed various ecological problems: "Outdoors Angles," a program on hunting and fishing which indirectly touches upon ecological concerns, and "Focus on the Issues," a call-in discussion program during

which listeners may discuss any issue they so desire.

12. Thereafter, the complainants, in a January 28, 1975 letter, informed the Commission that they intended to submit further comments upon receipt of information concerning the extent of network programming on strip mining broadcast by WHAR. As promised in its January 13, 1975 reply, WHAR, on February 4, 1975, submitted additional material to substantiate its claim that it presented numerous news items on strip mining, enclosing Associated Press tear sheet items broadcast between June 1 and July 30, 1974. The licensee also referred to seven *Issues and Answers* programs which it believed could possibly have involved strip mining. Additionally, on March 19, 1975, WHAR informed the Commission that on February 22 it had carried a five-minute tape on strip mining provided by Representative Ken Hechler of the 4th Congressional District of West Virginia.

13. In its April 7, 1975 response to the licensee's comments, the complainants asserted that "in view of the tremendous and permanent consequences which the congressionally-debated strip mining legislation would have on all aspects of the life styles of West Virginia and Harrison County citizens, it was *probably the single most important issue to arise in several decades* ... [and] in Clarksburg and Harrison County ... the most important issue during the time period within which the complaint is concerned." In support of this claim the complainants enclosed numerous news articles from various communities in West Virginia concerning the debate over strip mining. While most of the articles submitted by complainants were from outside of WHAR's service area, complainants maintained that taken as a whole they illustrated the concern over the strip mining controversy in communities similarly affected by the proposed legislation. In one such

article in *Vantage Point,* a publication of the Commission on Religion in Appalachia, 1973 edition, it was stated:

> Because of strip mining, mountain people are turned against one another. The mountaineers in the hollows facing a crumbling mountain are dead-set against other mountaineers who are manning the strippers' earth moving equipment. There is nothing more demeaning than a mountaineer being told by a strip mine operator that he must strip his neighbor's land if he wants to put bread on his family's table. . . .

Articles from the local press indicate the impact that strip mining has already had on residents of Clarksburg. In the June 15, 1974 *Clarksburg Telegram* it was stated that:

> "[R]esidents of Suan Terrace [in Clarksburg] are organized and ready to mobilize if the 'excavation' near their homes yields any coal."

The *Charleston Gazette,* October 22, 1974, reported:

> James Hawkins, a resident of Suan Terrace where the stripping was done, said a prospecting permit was granted to keep opponents from their right to protest. He said a petition with about 200 names was submitted to reclamation division A.

The complainants submitted a copy of statements given before Congress supporting the claim that the strip mining controversy is both economic and ecological, some of which are set forth below:

> The human suffering of those who live near strip mining sites is pitiful. The blasting and bulldozers have frequently set boulders onto the property and even into the homes of those on the fringes of strip mining ... *Statement of Honorable Ken Hechler, Representative from West Virginia.*

To me the most critical aspect of strip mining is what is happening to people in Appalachia, and to the quality of their lives. . . . The coming of strip mining has caused the most ruthless attack yet to be put on the people and their land. Central Appalachia, where strip mining prevails, has become a land that resembles the battlefields of war. Where the people are the victims and the land becomes a waste. . . . In 1971 the Legislature of West Virginia employed the Stanford Research Institute to do a study of the effects of strip mining in that State. One of their findings was that in the mountain region of Appalachia, for every acre of land stripped 3 to 5 adjoining acres were directly and adversely affected. *Statement of Rev. Baldwin Lloyd, Appalachia People's Service Organization.*

Surface mining in West Virginia has virtually outgrown its earlier status as an emotional issue because of proven reclamation success, increased energy fuel requirements, and rigid enforcement of stringent state regulations. . . . By any yardstick of reason, those who advocate elimination of surface mining for environmental protection could only be intepreted as ill-advised and unrealistic. It is unsound because it ignores the serious and damaging consequences to the economy of both West Virginia and the nation. At best it is an extremist solution of what is essentially an aesthetic problem. *Statement of James L. Wilkinson, President, West Virginia Surface Mining and Reclamation Associaton.*

The complainants enclosed the above referred to Stanford Research Institute study on the effects of strip mining in West Virginia. Included in this report was the determination that surface mining produces severe land erosion, that it will ultimately have an adverse effect on West Virginia's economy; that Harrison County

(which includes Clarksburg) leads all other counties in West Virginia with the most land disturbed; and that these disadvantageous effects will continue and become more pronounced in the future.

14. Complainants submit that such local environmental concerns uncovered in WHAR's ascertainment survey, such as air and water pollution and the lack of recreational facilities, arise to a large part as a result of the strip mining in and around Clarksburg; that, in contrast, the licensee's broadcast of Associated Press wire service items "reveals absolutely no substantive information on the environmental, economic, physical or other aspect of strip mining in Clarksburg or Harrison County, or even in West Virginia"; that there was no local perspective, genuine partisan voices or varying point of view; and that, therefore, WHAR failed to tailor its programming to the needs of the community.

15. The complainants assert that in regard to the *Issues and Answers* programs cited by WHAR, the transcripts of those programs disclose that at no time was strip mining discussed during any of the seven broadcasts; that WHAR read the Associated Press news items verbatim "letting AP decide what was best suited to meet the needs of WHAR's listeners," and that in so doing, it exercised no editorial judgment and thus represents "an impermissible delegation of licensee programming responsibility"; and that WHAR's failure to know precisely what was broadcast during the network programs over its facilities "further evidences total failure of WHAR to make a 'conscientious and positive effort' to meet its affirmative fairness doctrine obligations." In regard to WHAR's claim that complainants had not negotiated with it or notified it that a complaint was being filed, complainants state that they informed WHAR that if they had not received its response to complainants' inquiry to the station within seven days they were going to "file a formal complaint with the FCC."

Complainants also state that the "licensee's request to [the FCC to] reconsider a portion of the Commission's fairness doctrine regulation is appropriate only in a rule-making situation.

16. In additional correspondence dated May 28, 1975 complainants ask us not to consider the February 22 broadcast of the Hechler tape. They allege that this statement was devoted not to a discussion of strip mining but rather to mine safety in general. It was also maintained that the tape "was aired almost a year after the time period within which it is contended that WHAR failed to comply with the fairness doctrine in regard to the coverage of the 'burning issue' of strip mining as it affects the life and well being of persons in the Clarksburg area and in West Virginia generally—a time during which Congress was considering a strip mining bill which would have enormous effect on Clarksburg and West Virginia citizens."

17. On June 13, 1975 WHAR submitted a copy of the Hechler tape with transcript to support its contention that the Congressman's comments did touch upon strip mining. The transcript indicates that during the first part of his commentary Hechler attempted to rebut the argument that strip mining was safer than deep mining.

18. The complainants replied on June 18 to WHAR's response by arguing that the emphasis of the tape commentary was on mine safety and not on strip mining reclamation—the issue referred to in their complaint. They emphasize that Hechler "mentions strip mining tangentially in the context of the national problem of mine safety about which there is no controversy."

discussion

19. The Commission has previously notified broadcasters that it regards strict adherence to the fairness doctrine—including the affirmative obligation to provide coverage of issues of public importance—as the single most important

requirement of operation in the public interest. *Committee for the Fair Broadcasting of Controversial Issues,* 25 FCC 2d 283, 292 (1970). This obligation includes informing listeners of issues of particular concern to the communities which they are licensed to serve. As far back as our *Report on Editorializing by Broadcast Licensees,* 13 FCC 1246 (1949), we stated that:

> It is axiomatic that one of the most vital questions of mass communication in a democracy is the development of an informed public opinion through the public dissemination of news and ideas concerning the vital public issues of the day.... The Commission has consequently recognized the necessity for licensees to devote a reasonable percentage of their broadcast time to the presentation of news and programs devoted to the consideration and discussion of public issues of interest in the community served by the particular station. *Id.* at 1249.

20. The above-stated principles reflected the Supreme Court's observation in *Associated Press* v. *U.S.,* 326 U.S. 1, 20 (1945), that the purpose of the First Amendment was to provide "the widest possible dissemination of information from diverse and antagonistic sources." With this in mind, the fairness doctrine "imposes two affirmative responsibilities on the broadcaster: coverage of issues of public importance must be adequate and must fairly reflect differing viewpoints." *Columbia Broadcasting System* v. *Democratic National Committee,* 412 U.S. 94, 111 (1973). Without licensee compliance with the responsibility to cover adequately vital public issues, the obligation to present contrasting views would have little success as a means to inform the listening public. If the fairness doctrine is to have any meaningful impact, broadcasters must cover, at the very least, those topics which are of vital concern to their listeners. It was the view of

the Court of Appeals for the District of Columbia that "the essential basis of any fairness doctrine, no matter with what specificity the standards are defined, is that the American public must not be left uninformed." *Green* v. *FCC*, 447 F2d 323, 329 (1973).

21. The Commission, however, has no intention of intruding on licensees' day-to-day editorial decision-making. Rather, it has been our policy, in light of the prohibition against government censorship set forth in Section 326 of the Communications Act, to afford to licensees great leeway in their selection of program matter. As we stated in our *Report on Editorializing, supra:*

> The licensee will in each instance be called upon to exercise his best judgment and good sense in determining what subjects should be considered, the particular format of the program to be devoted to each subject, the different shades of opinion to be presented, and the spokesman for each point of view. *Id.* at 1251.

22. Consistent with this view, we have in the past stated that "the public's need to be informed can best be served through a system in which the individual broadcaster exercises wide journalistc discretion, and in which the government's role is limited to a determination of whether the licensee has acted reasonably and in good faith. *Fairness Doctrine Primer*, 40 FCC 598, 599 (1964). See *Citizens Communication Center*, 25 FCC 2d 701 (1970). While it is our policy to defer to licensees' journalistic discretion, we must emphasize that that discretion is not absolute, *Committee for the Fair Broadcasting of Controversial Issues, supra,* at 292, and we have previously advised licensees that "some issues are so critical or of such great public importance that it would be unreasonable for a licensee to ignore them completely." *Fairness Report, supra* at 10. While it would be an exceptional situa-

tion and would not counter our intention to stay out of decisions concerning the selection of specific programming matter, we believe that the unreasonable exercise of this licensee discretion, i.e., failure to adequately cover a "critical issue" in a particular community, would require appropriate remedial action on the part of the Commission. Such action in those rare instances was contemplated by the Supreme Court in *Red Lion* when it declared:

> ... if the present licensees should suddenly prove timorous, the Commission is not powerless to insist that they give adequate and fair attention to public issues. ... Congress need not stand idly by and permit those with licenses to ignore the problems which beset the people. *Red Lion* at 393.

These are rare instances, however, and licensees are not obligated to address each and every important issue which may be considered a controversial issue of public importance. *Public Communications Inc.*, 50 FCC 2d 395 (1974); *Fairness Report, supra* at 10.

23. The question of whether a licensee has presented significant coverage of vital issues of public importance, which has been found to be necessary to fully inform the public, has been the subject of previous Commission action: *Committee for the Fair Broadcasting of Controversial Issues, supra* (responsibility of adequate coverage of the Vietnam war); *WSNT, Inc.*, 27 FCC 2d 992 (1971) (failure to cover various events organized by local civil rights organizations in the community raised the question of whether the licensee had met the obligation to "serve the public by presenting important local news.") Particularly, in *Gary Soucie*, 24 FCC 2d 743 (1969), we emphasized that commercial broadcast facilities "must be used to inform," and in spite of the licensee's editorial discretion regarding the nature of its coverage of vital environmental issues, specifically the

automobile gasoline/air pollution issue, "broadcasters must discharge their public trust by contributing fairly and effectively to an informed electorate on these vital issues." 24 FCC 2d at 750.[1] We now turn to the facts before us.

24. In the present case the extensive amount of supporting material furnished by complainants sufficiently illustrates the fact that strip mining is of extreme importance to the people of Clarksburg. There is evidence from Congressional testimony, newspaper and magazine articles and research studies which illustrates the enormous impact strip mining has already had on the air and water quality and the immediate economic stability of the region. For example, Harrison County (Clarksburg and vicinity) has the highest percentage of strip mined land of any county in the State. This information also reveals that the long term environmental picture and countless future employment opportunities in deep and surface mining and other related industries would be altered significantly by the mandatory reclamation of strip mined land provisions included in the legislation debated in Congress. The licensee has itself stated that strip mining is "a matter of importance to many of the inhabitants of the Clarksburg area," Fawcett affidavit, page 1 (attached to WHAR response of January 13, 1975). Moreover, there is evidence of the highly controversial nature of the issue of strip mining, illustrated by citizen protests concerning strip mining in Clarksburg (see paragraph 13, *supra*), the nine "front page" stories in the *Clarksburg Telegram* over an eleven day period in July 1974,

and the lengthy debate in Congress concerning the strip mining bill followed on May 20, 1975 by the President's veto of the measure. We believe it would be unreasonable for WHAR to deny that the issue of strip mining is a critical controversial issue of public importance in Clarksburg. It would therefore appear that a total failure to cover an issue of such extreme importance to the particular community would raise serious questions concerning whether the licensee has acted reasonably in fulfilling its obligations under the fairness doctrine.

25. To support its claim that it had not ignored strip mining but rather had provided continuous news coverage, the licensee submitted copies of news items compiled for broadcast between June 1 and June 30, 1974 by the Associated Press, 25 of which were related to some degree to strip mining. Included among these 25 items are references to two Congressmen's characterization of the Nixon Administration's opposition to strip mining legislation as "unfair and unjustified" (June 7); a statement by a local strip mining abolitionist that in view of his opposition to the legislation Interior Secretary Morton is a traitor to Appalachia (June 9); estimates of money spent by surface mining industry to support candidates for public office in West Virginia (June 14); statistics indicating that 68% of the land used for coal mining between 1930 and 1971 has been reclaimed (June 23); and a statement by FEA Administrator John Sawhill that the legislation at issue will undermine efforts to revitalize the coal industry (June 30). Many related to statements by state officials outside West Virginia about matters which had no bearing on either the Clarksburg community or the federal legislation. Since the licensee stated only that it carried "well over" 75% of the items it submitted, it cannot be determined which of these items were actually broadcast.

26. As set forth above, WHAR sub-

---

[1] In *Soucie* we pointed out that:

Of course, the broadcast licensee retains the discretion as to issues, format, appropriate spokesmen, etc. Thus, a broadcaster located in an area with no air pollution issue but a severe water pollution one would clearly focus on the latter ... there remains wide access for judgment by the licensee based upon the facts of its particular area. 24 FCC 2d at 751.

sequently indicated that it had carried a five-minute tape furnished by Representative Ken Hechler which, according to the station's logs, concerned "strip mining/mine safety." However, while it is noted that Representative Hechler was a well-known proponent of the then pending strip mining legislation, neither that legislation nor the ecological or environmental impact of strip mining was mentioned during his statement.[2] Furthermore, we note that the licensee was unable to document its assertion that it presented other related programming furnished by the ABC Contemporary Network.

27. In *WHEC Inc.,* 52 FCC 2d 1079 (1975), we concluded that, concerning the issue of adequacy of programming on local issues, "[t]he key is the responsiveness to [community] needs and not necessarily the original source of broadcast matter." *Id* at 1085. We have on many occasions emphasized that licensees should be able to show that its programming is to some significant extent tailored to specific community needs. *In re City of Camden,* 13 FCC 2d 412 (1969). Although we believe that the nature of the coverage is for the station management to decide, we have stated that the licensee "should be alert to the opportunity to complement network offerings with local programming . . . or with syndi-

cated programming," to fully inform the community on issues of public importance. WHAR cannot rely on the fact that prior to this complaint it had not received any request for strip mining related programming, since it is the station's obligation to make an affirmative effort to program on issues of concern to its community. *Fairness Report* at 10. We do not believe that WHAR has shown what programming, if any, it broadcast which was devoted to a discussion of the local ramifications of strip mining and/or the proposed legislation. It neither originated such programming nor provided syndicated material aimed at informing its listeners in any depth of the nature of the issue cited in the instant complaint—that issue being the effects of strip mining in and around Clarksburg.

28. However, even more significant than the absence of locally originated programming on the issue of strip mining is the fact that WHAR cannot, with a reasonable degree of certainty, state what specific programming it has broadcast relating to this issue. We cannot accept the list of news items provided by the Associated Press and submitted by the licensee as evidence of compliance with the fairness doctrine when it is not all certain that they were aired by WHAR. Moreover, we cannot accept WHAR's statement to the effect that it may have presented ABC Contemporary program matter related to the strip mining controversy without references to specific programming broadcast over their facilities. We note that none of the *Issues and Answers* broadcasts cited by the licensee as having appeared on the station included a discussion of strip mining.[3] As we stated in the *Fairness Report, supra,* "we expect that licensees will be cognizant of the pro-

---

[2]We do not agree with the complainants' contention that the Hechler tape should not be considered in determining whether WHAR presented programming related to the issue of strip mining because the program, aired on February 22, 1975, did not fall within the March-June 1974 time frame set out in their complaint. It appears that the issue of reclamation of strip mined land has continued to be controversial up to the present date. Legislation providing reclamation standards was passed by Congress, subsequently vetoed by the President on May 20, 1975 and the veto was sustained on June 10. Presently new legislation similar in nature to the previous legislation was introduced by Representative John Mecher of Montana (HR 9725, introduced on September 19, 1975). We therefore believe that the Hechler tape is relevant to our present considerations.

---

[3]Also it has not been shown by WHAR that the other programming it cites as having concerned environmental matters such as its *Outdoor Angles,* did in fact include a discussion of topics even tangentially related to strip-mining.

gramming which has been presented on their stations, for it is difficult to see how a broadcaster who is ignorant of such matters could possibly be making a conscious and positive effort to meet his fairness obligations." *Id* at 20. Since the determination as to what programming will best meet the needs of a particular community served by the licensee cannot reasonably be delegated to others, *En Banc Programming Policy,* 44 FCC 2303, 2313–14 (1960), we are unable to sustain a licensee's judgment to defer to a non-broadcast entity editorial decision-making on whether to cover an issue of such extreme importance and impact on the station's listening audience. In this case, the licensee's total reliance on outside programming related to strip mining and its failure to know which of the material was presented clearly indicates that WHAR did delegate its programming responsibility and has not made a sufficiently diligent effort to inform its listeners. Under these circumstances, we are unable to conclude that WHAR has adequately covered the issue of strip mining.

29. It is our belief, as stated in the *Fairness Report, supra,* that the licensee could not reasonably fail to cover an issue which has tremendous impact within the local service area—that such failure would violate the fairness doctrine. We now reaffirm that principle. Where, as in the present case, an issue has significant and possibly unique impact on the licensee's service area, it will not be sufficient for the licensee as an indication of compliance with the fairness doctrine to show that it may have broadcast an unknown amount of news touching on a general topic related to the issue cited in a complaint. Rather it must be shown that there has been some attempt to inform the public of the nature of the controversy, not only that such a controversy exists. We must conclude, therefore, that WHAR has acted unreasonably in failing to cover the issue of strip mining, an issue which clearly may determine the quality of life in Clarksburg for decades to come.

30. Given these findings, we are of the opinion that the licensee of radio station WHAR is in violation of the fairness doctrine. Considering the continuing controversial nature of the issue of strip mining, the licensee is requested to inform the Commission within 20 days of the release date of this Order on how it intends to meet its fairness obligations with respect to adequate coverage of the aforementioned issue.

**Federal Communications Commission,
Vincent J. Mullins, Secretary.**

CONCURRING STATEMENT OF COMMISSIONER GLEN O. ROBINSON

This is the first time the Commission has ever found that a particular issue of public controversy was so important that a licensee was compelled, under the first part of the fairness doctrine, to offer at least some programming addressing it. I, for one, derive no satisfaction from participating in this precedent-setting case; it goes against my grain to so intrude in the programming discretion of a licensee. As I have made clear elsewhere, I am not a supporter of the fairness doctrine; measuring the uncertain benefits of this law against its probable adverse effects on free speech. I believe we would be better off without it, or with some substitute access rule. See my dissenting statement in *Fairness Doctrine Reconsideration,* —— FCC 2d —— ,FCC 76-265 (1976).

However, this general complaint is not pertinent here. As long as the fairness doctrine is established law, the Commission has the responsibility to enforce it in a fair and reasonable manner. We are here confronted with a case which fairly calls for enforcement and I see no basis for withholding my assent to the Commission's decision to take action. Indeed, if the first part of the fairness doctrine does not apply to this case, it would have to be concluded that it does not apply to this case, it would have to be concluded that it does not apply anywhere, and that a rule which purports to be binding is, in fact, merely precatory. I do not see how we could treat the first part of the fairness doctrine differently from the second in this respect—both purport to be integral parts of a legally binding rule.[1]

I cannot predict where this ruling will lead in the future. The Commission correctly emphasizes that the occasions for directing a station to air a particular issue to meet the first part of the fairness obligation are exceptional. Thus, not every issue of public importance or controversy whose presentation might trigger an obligation under part two of the fairness doctrine is

sufficient to create an affirmative obligation for coverage by the station under part one. The Commission uses the term "critical issues" to describe the occasion for the latter obligation; in *Gary Soucie,* 24 FCC 2d 743, 750 (1970), the Commission spoke of "burning issues." I suppose one question-begging adjective is as good as another in this foggy business of defining such ephemeral responsibilities. I would only add that it is not merely an issue which is "critical" or "burning," but one which all reasonable men must acknowledge to be such, that triggers this obligation. Strip mining in West Virginia is such an issue[2] and, on the facts presented here, the obligation has not been met.[3]

Nevertheless, much as we may stress the exceptional character of our enforcement of this requirement, we should not fool ourselves that the Commission will escape demands to enforce this requirement with greater zeal than has heretofore been demonstrated (or expected). I think we can say with certainty that many of such demands will prove unjustified. With equal certainty, however, we can predict that some—perhaps many—of the demands

---

[1]Concededly, enforcement of the first obligation constitutes a somewhat greater degree of government interference than enforcement of the second inasmuch as it is not triggered by the *licensee's* program choice. For this reason I agree with the Commission's caution that the first obligation of the fairness doctrine is limited to "exceptional" circumstances. However, the first and second obligations differ more in degree than in kind. Enforcement of either obligation requires us to scrutinize licensee judgment, overturn it where it is unreasonable, compelling a licensee to carry some program which it has chosen not to air. Even though in the former instance we can say it has "opened the door" by presenting one side of a controversial issue of public importance, the fact remains that it is our determination, not the licensee's, which ultimately decides whether this door has been opened. Thus, as a practical matter, there is relatively little difference between our telling a radio station in Eureka, California, that nuclear power generation is an issue of controversial public importance in Eureka for purposes of enforcing the second obligation of the fairness doctrine in *Public Media Center,* —FCC 3d—, FCC 76-453 (May 18, 1976), and our telling WHAR that strip mining is a "burning issue" in Clarksburg for purposes of the first part of the fairness doctrine.

I am not suggesting that it is not possible to have the second part of the fairness doctrine without the first. I am suggesting merely that once we have made all the necessary assumptions required to justify the second obligation—to provide balanced coverage of an important issue—we have made the requisite assumptions to justify the first obligation—to cover important issues.

[2]The fact that it was not revealed as such in WHAR's 1974 ascertainment (see letter of January 17, 1975, from WHAR's president to the Commission) reveals more about the ascertainment process than it does about the issue.

[3]In this regard, I do not think coverage necessarily requires locally originated programming. Nor do I understand the Commission's opinion to hold otherwise. While the Commission talks about licensees not being permitted to delegate to others their responsibility to cover critical issues, I understand this to mean merely that the obligation cannot be avoided by relying on coverage by other local media. This is inherent in the requirement since one crucial indication that an issue is of "critical importance" is that it is so treated by other media. However, while I accept this (insofar as I feel bound to accept the requirement itself), I do not interpret it to mean that the broadcaster cannot rely on nonlocal programming in carrying out its obligation. The problem here is that the licensee has not been able to show meaningful coverage by local or other programming.

will be indistinguishable from this case, and any attempt to artificially limit this case—as the Commission attempted to do with its famous cigarette ruling—must ultimately fail. *Friends of the Earth* v. *FCC*, 449 F.2d 1164 (D.C. Cir. 1971). In any event, I shall not be surprised if, as a consequence of our action today, the Commission soon finds itself involved more deeply in program judgments than it presently desires or even foresees.[4] If and when that happens, present distress about the fairness doctrine will almost certainly become more intense and more widespread— perhaps even to the point where the courts, if not Congress, direct the abolition of this mischievous doctrine. It is to be hoped; the best thing to be said of today's decision, other than that it conforms to the current law, is that it may bring us closer to the day when that law is changed.

questions for discussion and further research

1. Consider this statement from *Red Lion:*

   ... The ability of new technology to produce sounds more raucous than those of the human voice justifies restrictions on the sound level, and on the hours and places of use, of sound trucks so long as the restrictions are reasonable and applied without discrimination.... Just as the government may limit the use of sound-amplifying equipment potentially so noisy that it drowns out civilized private speech, so may the government limit the use of broadcast equipment....

   Question: Do you feel that the argument for limiting the use of sound trucks is grounds for government control of broadcasting?

2. New technology is rapidly changing the broadcasting industry. Fiber-optic technology can carry thousands of channels on a thin strand of glass. As this new technology continues to develop, and as the "limited spectrum" concept becomes less and less applicable to broadcasting, at least in theory, will the arguments for continuing the Fairness Doctrine remain sound?

3. Thousands more broadcasting stations than daily newspapers operate in the United States. Why, then, do we continue to hear the "limited resource" argument as a reason for enforcing the Fairness Doctrine?

4. Should the government enact a law establishing a "Fairness Doctrine" for newspapers? If such a law were enacted, would it survive a test of its constitutionality under the First Amendment?

5. In arguing for or against the constitutionality of a newspaper Fairness Doctrine, what arguments could support each position?

6. In footnote 28 of *Red Lion,* the Court stated: ... We need not deal with the argument that even if there is no longer a technological scarcity of frequencies limiting the number of broadcasters, there nevertheless is an economic scarcity in the sense that the Commission could or does limit entry to the broadcasting market on economic grounds and licenses no more stations than the market will support.
   Question: Is the "economic scarcity" argument a sound argument for applying the Fairness Doctrine to broadcasting?

7. Given that economic constraints limit the number of newspapers in a community, would the "economic scarcity" apply to the establishment of a newspaper Fairness Doctrine?

---

[4]I do not take much comfort in the well-rehearsed rubric that the licensee has large discretion in selecting the issues to be programmed. See *Soucie, supra; Public Communications, Inc.,* 50 FCC 2d 395 (1974). *Cf. Straus Communications, Inc.* v. *FCC,* 530 F.2d 1001 (D.C. Cir. 1976). As the Commission here recognizes, it is implicit in the existence of an enforceable obligation that the discretion is not unlimited. Moreover, if the vaguely defined "critical issues" concept leaves large room for licensee discretion it also leaves some room for Commission discretion as well, and it is that discretion which should be the cause for anxiety.

8. If you were managing a broadcasting station, do you feel that the presence of the Fairness Doctrine would enhance or stifle your station's treatment of controversial issues of public importance?

9. Consider the community where you live. What issues could be considered controversial issues of public importance that might surface on the broadcast media and invoke the Fairness Doctrine?

10. How did these issues become controversial and of local importance?

11. Since broadcasters have great discretion in determining what constitutes a controversial issue of public importance, ask yourself this question: What criteria are or should be used to make such determinations?

12. In the *Patsy Mink* case, the FCC, in building a case that strip mining was a local issue of importance, quotes various newspapers which covered the issue. Why couldn't the newspaper coverage of a local issue suffice to alert the public to the consequences of that issue, instead of having coverage of that issue by the electronic media be required by a federal agency?

13. Is the FCC on dangerous grounds in making a determination of what is and what is not a local issue of importance?

14. What other evidence could the FCC use when investigating a complaint to determine whether an issue is of such importance as to warrant treatment under the Fairness Doctrine?

15. In the *Patsy Mink* case, the FCC reiterated its position that the Fairness Doctrine can include the journalistic functions of a station. Consider the implications of a federal agency having indirect control over such programming. Does such control serve the public interest that the FCC is charged with protecting? Does the FCC really have any significant control, even though the Fairness Doctrine can be applied to news programming? Under highly charged political issues, could politics enter into the FCC's judgments about treatment of such issues under the Fairness Doctrine?

16. Why would a station want to avoid covering a controversial issue of local importance?

17. Clarksburg is in the mining country of West Virginia. What about other stations located in areas where ecology is an important concern? Should stations located in resort towns carry programming about the pros and cons of summer visitors? Of eroding beaches?

additional resources

books

Geller, H., *The Fairness Doctrine in Broadcasting: Problems and Suggested Courses of Action,* Santa Monica, Calif.: Rand Corp., 1973.

Simmons, S. J., *The Fairness Doctrine and the Media,* Berkeley: University of California Press, 1978.

articles

Barron, J. A., "In Defense of 'Fairness': A First Amendment Rationale for Broadcasting's 'Fairness' Doctrine," 37 *University of Colorado Law Review* 31 (1964).

Barron, J. A., "The Federal Communications Commission's Fairness Doctrine: An Evaluation," 30 *George Washington Law Review* 1 (1961).

Barrow, R. L., "Equal Opportunities and Fairness Doctrines in Broadcasting: Pillars in the Forum of Democracy," 37 *University of Cincinnati Law Review* 447 (1968).

Barrow, R. L., "Fairness Doctrine: A Double Standard for Electronic and Print Media," 26 *Hastings Law Jorunal* 659 (1975).

Buss, R. F., and G. D. Malaney, "How Broadcasters Feel about Fairness Doctrine," 55 *Journalism Quarterly* 793 (1978).

Cahill, R. V., "'Fairness' and the FCC," 21 *Federal Communications Bar Journal* 17 (1967).

Chamberlin, B. F., "The FCC and the First Principle of the Fairness Doctrine: A History of Neglect and Distortion," 31 *Federal Communications Law Journal* 361 (1979).

Cohn, D. S., "Access to Television to Rebut the

President of the United States: An Analysis and Proposal," 45 *Temple Law Quarterly* 141 (1972).

Hamburg, M. I., "Use of Broadcasting Facilities: A Matter of Fairness," 21 *New York Law Forum* 209 (1975).

Hanks, W. E., and M. Lazar, "Using the Fairness Doctrine: Case History of a Learning Project," 16 *Journal of Broadcasting* 475 (1972).

Hoffer, T. W., and G. A. Butterfield, "The Right to Reply: A Florida First Amendment Aberration," 53 *Journalism Quarterly* 111 (1976).

Houser, T. J., "Fairness Doctrine—An Historical Perspective," 47 *Notre Dame Lawyer* 550 (1972).

Jaffe, L. L., "Editorial Responsibility of the Broadcaster: Reflections on Fairness and Access," 85 *Harvard Law Review* 768 (1972).

Lange, D. L., "Role of the Access Doctrine in the Regulation of the Mass Media: A Critical Review and Assessment," 52 *North Carolina Law Review* 1 (1973).

Malone, D. M., "Broadcasting, the Reluctant Dragon: Will the First Amendment Right of Access End the Suppressing of Controversial Ideas?" 5 *University of Michigan Journal of Law Reform* 193 (1972).

Meeske, M. D., "Editorial Advertising and the First Amendment," 17 *Journal of Broadcasting* 417 (1973).

Meeske, M. D., and R. Handberg, Jr., "Attitudes of ETV Managers toward the Fairness Doctrine," 54 *Journalism Quarterly* 146 (1977).

Meeske, M. D., and R. Handberg, Jr., "News Directors' Attitudes toward the Fairness Doctrine," 53 *Journalism Quarterly* 126 (1976).

Schenkkan, P. M., "Power in the Marketplace of Ideas: The Fairness Doctrine and the First Amendment," 52 *Texas Law Review* 727 (1974).

Schiro, R., "Diversity in Television's Speech: Balancing Programs in the Eyes of the Viewer," 27 *Case Western Reserve Law Review* 336 (1976).

Simmons, S. J., "Fairness Doctrine and Cable TV," 11 *Harvard Journal on Legislation* 629 (1974).

Simmons, S. J., "Fairness Doctrine: The Early History," 29 *Federal Communications Bar Journal* 207 (1976).

Simmons, S. J., "FCC's Personal Attack and Political Editorial Rules Reconsidered," 125 *University of Pennsylvania Law Review* 990 (1977).

Simmons, S. J., "Problem of 'Issue' in the Administration of the Fairness Doctrine," 65 *California Law Review* 546 (1977).

Wilson, J. L., "Fairness Doctrine: Big Brother in the Newsroom," 61 *American Bar Association Journal* 1492 (1975).

cases

Banzhaf v. *F.C.C.*, 405 F.2d 1082, 132 U.S.App.D.C. 14, 1 Med.L.Rptr. 2037 (1968), certiorari denied.

Cullman Broadcasting Co., 40 F.C.C. 516 (1963).

Farmers Ed. and Co-Op. Union of America, North Dakota Division v. *WDAY, Inc.*, 79 S.Ct. 1302, 360 U.S. 525, 3 L.Ed.2d 1407 (1959).

Miami Herald Publishing Co. v. *Tornillo,* 418 U.S. 241 (1974).

National Citizens' Committee for Broadcasting and Friends of the Earth v. *F.C.C.*, 567 F.2d 1095, 3 Med.L.Rptr. 1273 (1977).

Public Interest Research Group v. *F.C.C.*, 522 F.2d 1060 (1975).

Public Media Center v. *F.C.C.*, 587 F.2d 1322, 190 U.S.App.D.C. 425, 4 Med.L.Rptr. 1644 (1978).

Red Lion Broadcasting Co. v. *F.C.C.*, 89 S.Ct. 1794, 395 U.S. 367, 23 S.Ed.2d 371, 1 Med.L.Rptr. 2053 (1969).

6

The Broadcast Press

Even though, as compared to other countries, the broadcast press in America enjoys considerable freedom, there are still certain controls which even a responsible press must face. Some of these are common to both print and broadcast journalism, such as reporters' shield laws and freedom of information laws. Others, such as the rules governing the use of television cameras in courtrooms, have become primarily the concern of broadcasting. In any case, these controls operate within the framework of the United States Constitution, helping to assure a free press.

One of the strongest and most lasting statements in support of freedom of the press came with the U.S. Supreme Court's decision in *Near* v. *Minnesota.* The case, decided in 1931, was brought to court when a Minnesota statute prohibiting publication of certain "malicious, scandalous, and defamatory" material was used to stop publication of a newspaper called the *Saturday Press*. The *Press* had set out to clean up so-called political corruption in Minneapolis and was found guilty of being a public nuisance by publishing defamatory remarks about the Jewish race, the *Minneapolis Tribune,* and the *Minneapolis Journal.* More specifically, the publication charged that a Jewish gangster was in control of gambling, bootlegging, and racketeering in Minneapolis, and that the law enforcement agencies were not energetically performing their duties. The chief of police came under scrutiny and was claimed to be having illicit relations with gangsters and participating in graft. The mayor was highlighted as being derelict in his duty, and a member of the grand jury was accused of being in sympathy with the gangsters. The county attorney, who was also out of favor with the newspaper, was incensed by the articles and brought action to stop them against the publishers, J. N. Near and H. Guilford. The case went to the Minnesota Supreme Court, where the public nuisance statute was upheld. Near next took the case to the U.S. Supreme Court. Guilford, meanwhile, had been shot by gangsters.

In issuing the majority opinion, Justice Hughes wrote in *Near* v. *Minnesota*:

> The fact that for approximately one hundred and fifty years there has been almost an entire absence of attempts to impose previous restraints upon publications relating to the malfeasance of public officers is significant of the deep-seated conviction that such restraints would violate constitutional rights. Public officers whose character and conduct remain open to debate and free discussion in the press, find their remedies for false accusations in actions under libel laws not proceedings to restrain the publication of newspapers and periodicals. . . .

The Role of the U.S. Constitution

The relationship of the broadcast press to the Constitution is most closely aligned with the First Amendment's phrase: "Congress shall make no law . . . abridging the freedom of speech, or of the press. . . ." To give some assurance that a state could not wholeheartedly negate the U.S. Constitution, the Fourteenth Amendment was passed, stating: "No State shall make or enforce any law which shall abridge the privileges or immunities of citizens of the United States; nor shall any state deprive any person of life, liberty, or property, without due process of law. . . ." The Fourteenth Amendment was not affirmed by the courts until 1925, in the case of *Gitlow* v. *New York*. In this case, the Supreme Court declared: "For present purposes, we may and do assume that freedom of speech and of the press—which are protected by the First Amendment from abridgement by Congress—are among the fundamental personal rights and liberties protected by the due process clause of the Fourteenth Amendment from impairment by the states."[1]

Although that declaration might seem to clearly state a basis for judicial and legislative precedent, such has not always been the case. The First Amendment has offered certain protections to the broadcast *press* but has been strained by such matters as equal time for political candidates, political advertising, and license renewals, to name a few.

affirmation or delimitation?

The Constitution has not stopped the states from passing countless laws affecting the confidentiality of sources, for both print and broadcast journalists; from passing laws affecting the right of access to public meetings or for cameras in the courtroom; nor from passing laws governing cable television. The twentieth-century concept of the electromagnetic spectrum as a limited resource has been used as a basis for more and more legislation and interpretation, although not without criticism. Former CBS commentator Eric Sevareid, addressing a meeting of the National Association of Broadcasters, remarked: "I could never understand why so basic a right as the First Amendment could be diluted or abridged simply because of technological change in the dissemination and reception of information and ideas."[2]

The broadcast press has continually had to fight for its rights as an equal partner with the print media under the First Amendment. This fight has included visible lobbying efforts by the NAB, such as its Declaration of Broadcast Freedoms, which was passed as a resolution by NAB's Board on June 17, 1976. In the Declaration, the broadcasters state that they: "will increase our vigilance in defending our rights to stand equal to the written press . . . and that we will use every proper means to defend, on behalf of those we serve, their inalienable rights to have a free electronic press." Spokespersons for the broadcasting industry have been equally vocal. CBS's William S. Paley remarked that the First Amendment freedom, "presupposes, in us as broadcasters, a greater sense of responsibility. If we fail to see the dimensions of that responsibility and to measure up to them, we are in for constant threats of restrictions and policing."[3]

broadcast versus print: equal status

Along with the rhetoric has come some judicial support for the First Amendment's application to broadcasting. In the case of *CBS* v. *the Democratic National Committee,* Justice William O. Douglas wrote: "My conclusion is that the TV and radio stand in the same protected position under the First Amendment as do newspapers and magazines. The philosophy of the First Amendment requires that result, for the fear that Madison and Jefferson had of government intrusion is perhaps even more relevant to TV and radio than it is to newspapers and other like publications."[4] A panel of five justices of the New York State Supreme Court affirmed the right of WABC-TV to show a documentary about conditions in a children's home.[5] Presiding Justice Harold A. Stevens wrote: "While the protection of freedom of the press is not absolute, the burden of demonstrating a condition which warrants a prior restraint is indeed a heavy one. Television broadcasting falls under the umbrella of protection afforded the press, for it too, in matters such as the subject under review, is engaged in the dissemination of information of public concern."[6] Ironically, while affirming the right to show the documentary, the court stopped the broadcast for five days to give the children's home time to appeal.

The spirit of the First Amendment is inherent in the Communications Act of 1934 and in its amendments.[7] Section 315, dealing with political advertising, states that licensees ". . . shall have no power of censorship over material broadcast under the provisions of this section." Section 326 of the Communications Act of 1934, also affirmed by the Radio Act of 1927, states: "Nothing in this Act shall be understood or construed to give the Commission the power of censorship over the radio communications or . . . shall interfere with the right of free speech by means of radio communication."

Although the U.S. Constitution remains the umbrella document under which legal theory functions in America, it is only a small part of the total regulatory scheme affecting the broadcast press.

Free Press versus Fair Trial

Three separate amendments to the U.S. Constitution interact to cause the conflict surrounding the free press–fair trial issue. Specifically, these are the First Amendment, which states:

Congress shall make no law . . . abridging the freedom of speech, or of the press. . . .

the Sixth Amendment:

In all criminal prosecutions, the accused shall enjoy the right to a speedy and public trial, by an impartial jury. . . .

and the Fourteenth Amendment:

. . . nor shall any State deprive any person of life, liberty, or property, without due process of law; nor deny to any person within its jurisdiction the equal protection of the laws.

During an amendment clash, the press claims its rights of a free press under the First Amendment and the "public trial" guarantees of the Sixth Amendment as a basis for permitting cameras in court. Lawyers and judges opposed to such access fall in behind the "impartial jury" guarantees of the Sixth Amendment and the "due process" guarantees of the Fourteenth. At the center of this argument is the legal issue of both pretrial and trial publicity.

lindbergh and the evolving canons of judicial ethics

The concern over cameras in the courtrooms actually began before television was an accepted part of the American scene. When Bruno Hauptmann was tried for the kidnapping of famed aviator Charles Lindbergh's son, the courtroom resembled more a county fair than a judicial proceeding. Reporters were falling over reporters, vendors were selling souvenirs, and when the judge barred cameras from the courtroom, an enterprising chap managed to sneak a camera into the balcony and snap a picture of the courtroom that bannered in papers across the country.

Since the Lindbergh trial, everyone from Supreme Court justices to bar associations have grappled with the difficult issues of how much publicity is too much and *how* and *whether* television cameras and recording equipment interfere with a fair trial. The American Bar Association approved its famous Canon 35 two years after the Lindbergh trial. Amended in 1963 to include television, Canon 35 forbade either the taking of photographs or the broadcasting of court proceedings. Individual states were quick to affirm Canon 35's principles and place it in statutes affecting court proceedings. The Federal Rules of Criminal Procedures, specifically Rule 53, carry the prohibition of cameras in Federal Courts. And a special committee of the Judicial Conference of the United States reaffirmed Canon 35 in 1968, calling for prohibition of ". . . radio or television broadcasting from the courtroom or its environs, during the progress of or in connection with judicial proceedings. . . ." In a further examination of the Canons in 1972, Canon 35 became Canon 3A(7). And with still no sympathy for the presence of television cameras, Canon 3A(7) reads:

> A judge should prohibit broadcasting, televising, recording, or taking photographs in the courtroom and areas immediately adjacent thereto during sessions of court or recesses between sessions, except that a judge may authorize:
> (a) the use of electronic or photographic means for the presentation of evidence, for the perpetuation of a record, or for other purposes of judicial administration;
> (b) the broadcasting, televising, recording, or photographing of investitive, ceremonial, or nationalization proceedings;
> (c) the photographic or electronic recording and reproduction of appropriate court proceedings under the following conditions:
>   (i) the means of recording will not distract participants or impair the dignity of the proceedings;
>   (ii) the parties have consented, and the consent to being depicted or recorded has been obtained from each witness appearing in the recording and reproduction;
>   (iii) the reproduction will not be exhibited until after the proceeding has been concluded and all direct appeals have been exhausted; and
>   (iv) the reproduction will be exhibited only for instructional purposes in education institutions.

Clearly from the standpoint of the courts and many lawyers, there is popular support for the free trial position.

rideau and estes

Such claims for constitutional priority are not founded merely in supposition or conjecture. The annals of case law are filled with overturned verdicts, appeals, and charges of biased juries, because of the fact that the news media have been less than restrained in their coverage. The cases that stand out as being of particular interest include *Rideau* v. *Louisiana.*[8] In this case, the suspect was interviewed by a county sheriff, and the interview was filmed and played on local television. The suspect's confessions made during the interview and the subsequent televising of those confessions prompted the defense attorney to request a change of venue. A denial and subsequent guilty verdict caused the United States Supreme Court to reverse the conviction and state that the jury should have been drawn from a community whose residents had not seen the televised interview.

The case of Texas businessman Billie Sol Estes added fuel to this constitutional fire. Estes was tried and convicted of swindling. An appeals court affirmed the conviction, but when the case reached the United States Supreme Court in 1965, in *Estes* v. *State of Texas,* the conviction was reversed.[9] Massive national publicity surrounded the trial, and when it first went to court, the trial judge permitted television coverage of portions of the trial. In fact, the initial hearings were carried live. The scene was described by Justice Clark:

> Indeed, at least 12 cameramen were engaged in the courtroom throughout the hearing taking motion and still pictures and televising the proceedings. Cables and wires

were snaked across the courtroom floor, three microphones were on the judges' bench, and others were beamed at the jury box and the counsel table. It is conceded that the activities of the television crews and news photographers led to considerable disruption of the hearings.

Justice Clark summarized four areas in which television could interfere with a trial: (1) Television can have an impact on the jury. The mere announcement of a televised trial can alert the community to "all the morbid details surrounding" the trial. "Every juror carries with him into the jury box, those solemn facts and thus increases the chance of prejudice that is present in every criminal case." (2) Television can impair the quality of testimony. "The impact upon a witness of the knowledge that he is being viewed by a vast audience is simply incalculable. Some may be demoralized and frightened, some cocky and given to overstatement; memories may falter. . . ." (3) Television places additional responsibilities on the trial judge. Along with other supervisory duties, the judge must also supervise television. The job of the judge "is to make certain that the accused receives a fair trial. This most difficult task requires his undivided attention." (4) On the defendant, television "is a form of mental if not physical harassment, resembling a police line-up or the third degree. The inevitable closeups of his gestures and expressions during the ordeal of his trial might well transgress his personal sensibilities, his dignity, and his ability to concentrate. . . ."

experimenting with cameras in court

Despite the High Court's decision, broadcasters continued their fight for courtroom access for the omnipresent television camera. In 1972, the American Bar Association's House of Delegates approved a Code of Professional Responsibility, permitting the use of television in the courtroom for such activities as presenting evidence. Another breakthrough came in 1974, when the Washington State Supreme Court instructed a County Superior Court to select a trial and to experiment, for "educational" purposes, with televising it. The experiment was generally successful.[10] In Las Vagas, Nevada, during the fall of 1976, KLAS-TV televised a criminal court trial in color. Sixty hours of courtroom activity, including interviews with the defendant, jury, and attorneys, were videotaped and edited for a three-part, prime-time special. Another publicized trial took place in Florida in 1977, when a teenager was accused of murder. Segments of the trial appeared regularly on network television, calling national attention to the camera–courtroom issue. A few weeks later, when the verdict was read in an Indiana kidnapping case, cameras were again present, and the courtroom once again made national television.

chandler ruling

Finally in 1981 a major breakthrough occurred when the U.S. Supreme Court again considered the issue of cameras in the courts. In the case of *Chandler* v. *Florida,* the Supreme Court ruled that Florida's own authorization of cameras (both television and still cameras), when subject to the control of the presiding judge and with guidelines which protected the criminal defendant's right to a fair trial, do not violate the U.S. Constitution. The ruling paved the way for states to adopt their own guidelines without fear of them being deemed unconstitutional. As we will now see, other states had proceeded to establish guidelines before the *Chandler* ruling.

court guidelines for cameras: two examples

Of the various states experimenting with television cameras in court, Alabama is credited with establishing a substantial precedent. With the cooperation of the news media in Mobile, Alabama, Judge Robert H. Hodnette, Jr., of the Thirteenth Circuit Court of Alabama, drew up plans for the broadcast coverage of trials. The Alabama Supreme Court approved his plans, which have become a model for other states to follow. They include the following provisions:

1. Proceedings of the Supreme Court held in the courtroom of the Judicial Building may be broadcast by television or radio, and may be recorded electronically or photographed, if in compliance with the provisions of this plan, and Canon 3A(7B) of the Canons of Judicial Ethics.
2. No broadcasting, recording or photographing should detract from the dignity of the court proceedings.
3. Persons desiring to broadcast, record or photograph official court proceedings must make a timely request to the Clerk of the Supreme Court prior to the hearing, trial or event, specifying the particular case, hearing or event for which coverage is desired.
4. Written consent from attorneys and parties, if present, shall be obtained on a form, copies of which are available in the Clerk's office.
5. Consent to cover a proceeding shall be granted pursuant to these rules without partiality or preference to any person, media outlet, or type of coverage. Consent may not be given, refused or withdrawn as to one type of coverage, or as to any particular media outlet, and given, refused or withdrawn to another type or another media outlet.
6. No more than four (4) still photographers and two (2) television cameras will be permitted in the courtroom for coverage at any time while a trial or hearing is in session. However, the Marshal shall allow all photographers and television stations to participate either by pooling, or by dividing the time so that all will be allowed to participate. The positioning and removal of cameras shall be done as quietly as possible and in no event shall disturb the proceedings of the court.
7. The court, upon request, will permit persons to obtain audio from the court's recording system on a first come, first served basis, if the systems are compatible. The Marshal, in his discretion, may allow microphones and wiring to be placed at the counsel's lectern and at no more than three locations on the bench. Microphones shall be placed in advance of the trial or hearing and shall be unobtrusive or hidden. All wiring shall be located on the floor next to the wall or along the bottom of the bench, where possible. Otherwise, the wires must be placed where they will not interfere with anyone or constitute a hazard. The Marshal shall inspect the location of any wires and microphones to see that they shall comply with the rules. Wiring cannot be removed while court is in session, except during recesses.
8. Overhead lights, when provided, shall be switched on and off by the Marshal. No other lights, flashbulbs, flashes or sudden light changes, may be used except with the express authorization of the Marshal or the court.

9. Every person desiring to cover a proceeding will furnish his own equipment.

10. All television cameras are restricted to the platform in the rear corners of the courtroom. Television cameras or still cameras which produce distracting noise or sound cannot be used.

11. During sessions of court, photographers using still cameras may sit anywhere in the courtroom designated for use by the public, and may take pictures, but the Marshal, upon request of a party, attorney, witness or justice, may require them to take photographs only while standing behind the back row of seats. If a photographer wants to take pictures while standing, he must take them from the area behind the back row of seats.

12. Television personnel shall be limited in their movements to the area behind the back row of seats.

13. The Marshal may allow wireless recording devices to be operated in the courtroom if they are not too bulky and if they do not make a disturbing sound. The operator may sit or stand. If he stands, he must keep the recording device with him.

14. All persons covering a hearing, event or trial will avoid activity which might distract, and will remain within the restricted areas designated by the court of the Marshal.

15. In a trial where testimony is taken, any party, witness, attorney or justice may request a cessation of coverage by notifying the court, in which event the court will require the coverage to cease.

16. Attorneys must observe Disciplinary Rule 7-107, Trial Publicity, Code of Professional Responsibility of the Alabama State Bar, which covers the conduct of all attorneys with respect to trial publicity.

17. This plan shall not preclude the coverage of a trial, event or hearing by a news reporter or other person who is not using a camera or electronic equipment, but is taking notes or making sketches.

18. All persons who request and are granted permission to cover a hearing, event or trial are subject to this plan and thereby agree to observe the rules and objectives set out in it.

19. In the event the court is in session at a place other than the courtroom in the Judicial Building, this plan shall be followed to the extent possible. Details regarding coverage of sessions held outside of Montgomery must be cleared with the Marshal, prior to the session.

20. The restrictions under this plan are not applicable to the coverage of investiture, ceremonial or non-judicial proceedings.

Under guideline 4, reference is made to obtaining written consent from attorneys as well as the parties involved in the case. In Alabama, this involves a request form (Figure 6-1) completed by the media representative desiring to cover the trial and a similar form completed by the attorney and parties involved (Figure 6-2). From that point on, the main responsibility of the court is to conduct a fair trial. And the main responsibility of the media is to report the trial, not to disrupt it.

Georgia is another state that has approved broadcast equipment in court. Television stations in Atlanta broke the ice in 1977 by televising proceedings of the Georgia Supreme Court, while Atlanta radio stations patched into the court's public address system.[11] As in similar cases, this action necessitated a revision of the State's code of judicial conduct. Georgia's revised code now authorizes the "broadcasting, televising, recording, filming and taking of photographs in its date _____

name of media _____

reporter or technician _____

type of coverage desired:

        RECORDING   _____

        TELEVISION   _____

        STILL CAMERA   _____

        RADIO   _____

        OTHER   _____

event to be covered _____

date of coverage _____

purpose of requested coverage:

    Instructional or Educational for the Following Use:

_____

_____

_____

    News: _____

I request permission to cover the above event under the Plan for Media Coverage of the Supreme Court of Alabama. I agree to abide by the provisions of the Plan, and I hereby certify that I will obtain all consents required by the Plan before I begin any photographing, recording or broadcasting.

_____
        Media Representative

Approved: _____ Date:_____
                    Clerk,
          Supreme Court of Alabama

    Note: The Clerk will notify the Marshal when a request is approved.

Figure 6-1

case number ______________________ **date** ______________

style of case ____

____

____

Consent is hereby given to broadcast, electronically record or photograph the proceedings in the above-styled case in the Supreme Court, pursuant to the Plan for Media Coverage adopted by the court.

____

Signature

Attorney ( )

Witness ( )

Party ( )

Figure 6-2

courtroom, or the courtroom of any other state court of Georgia, during any judicial hearing."[12] The guidelines under which the code functions necessitate that:

1. Both attorneys must give written approval before their oral arguments can be covered.
2. TV cameras are allowed only in the courtroom alcove.
3. The presence of more than three TV cameras requires a special court motion.
4. Still photographers are restricted to one area.
5. A permanent sound system had to be installed and 10 radio outlets provided under back-row seats.
6. A lighting system designed to cut down glare was required to be installed behind the bench.[13]

lawyers' opinions on cameras in court

While there is reason for broadcast journalists to be optimistic about the future of cameras and recording equipment in judicial proceedings, especially in view of recent gains made in numerous states, there is also room for a note of caution.[14] A poll published in the *American Bar Association Journal* showed that, overall, lawyers are a long way from being overly supportive of the idea.[15] In a telephone random sample of 600 attorneys, respondents leaned toward more control by a 68 to 24 percentage rather than less. There was a general feeling that cameras would distract witnesses, that lawyers and judges might grandstand, and that barring television from courtrooms did *not* discriminate against that news source.

the key factors: public access, responsible constraint

The future status of cameras in court hinges on two key factors: (1) the willingness of the courts to recognize the public's right of access to trials by permitting in the courtroom the apparatus necessary to capture the actual sounds and sights of the court in session, and (2) the willingness of the broadcast press to use restraint and the highest degree of professional attitude and activity while covering a trial. Certainly, not all of the courts across the country are going to open their doors to broadcasting overnight. The process will be slow and gradual, and many trials will remain closed at the request of the parties involved. Meanwhile, the talented courtroom artists who are employed by many of the networks and larger television stations will continue their craft of capturing on sketch pads the activity barred from the eyes of the television camera.

Covering Legislative Proceedings

Many critics argue that in government, the real news is in the legislature. Too many times, the sensational decisions of the judiciary and the ever-present charisma of the executive branch demand the media's attention at the expense of the real issues, which are being hashed out in the legislature. This situation holds true not only for the U.S. Congress but also for state legislatures as well. And just as the live television coverage of judicial proceedings has been of keen interest to broadcast journalists, so has television coverage of the legislative branch.

television and the u.s. house of representatives

Widespread attention to live coverage of the House of Representatives was attracted by the hearings conducted in 1974. But the issue itself is much older. As early as 1922, Representative Vincent Brennan introduced a joint resolution "providing for the installation and operation of radio–telephone transmitting apparatus for the purpose of transmitting the proceedings and debates of the Senate and the House of Representatives."[16] Between 1922 and 1974, the issue arose again many times. But in 1974, the previous proposals, which had been mostly stillborn, took on a new meaning when President Richard Nixon's involvement in a political scandal called Watergate brought impeachment discussions to the House Judiciary Committee, and television brought the live drama to the nation. The presence of television did not create all the liabilities critics said it would. And on top of public opinion polls showing a new lack of confidence in Congress, the time was ripe for serious discussions.

Hearings held in February and March of 1974 considered:

First. How can the role of Congress be more fully and accurately covered in the news media?

Second. How can spokesmen for Congress gain direct access more readily to the broadcast media to present congressional viewpoints on issues?

Third. What additional facilities, staff and other supporting services, if any, are required to provide Congress with more adequate institutional capability in the area of mass communications?[17]

The summary of positions resulting from the 1974 hearings provides a succinct statement of a general philosophy inherent in the issues surrounding the live coverage of legislative proceedings, not only in Congress but in state bodies as well. A case for the presence of television centers around three points:

1. Most Americans know less than they need to know about the workings of Congress and its constitutional role;
2. part of the blame for ineffective communication lies in Congress, in procedural constraints as well as in other aspects of its organization and operation which can— and should—be changed; and
3. declining public confidence in Congress—along with other democratic institutions— urgently demands corrective action, including provision for broadcast coverage of House and Senate floor proceedings.[18]

Equally important are points that have been made in *opposition* to live television coverage. Again, although applying primarily to the House, they are echoed in state legislatures as well. Opponents claim that television would:

1. Subject members to the pressures of performing before a mass audience, distracting them from concentration on complex issues, and inhibiting the necessary compromises that go into the making of legislative decisions.
2. Result in members having to spend more of their already too thinly divided time on the floor (to avoid being charged with 'absenteeism'), conflicting with committee work and other necessary duties elsewhere.
3. Limit or eliminate the use of revise-and-extend procedures, extending debate unnecessarily and requiring more floor time for consideration of legislation.
4. Place the less aggressive or articulate members at a disadvantage, providing at the same time a forum for a few to 'showboat' in an effort to appeal favorably to their constituents.
5. Require the installation of bright lights, bulky cameras, cumbersome cables, and the presence of technical personnel and commentators in the galleries, creating uncomfortable glare and other distractions in the chambers.
6. Present a distorted picture of the congressional process, focusing undue attention on the final stage of legislative activity, much of which is either too dull to be interesting or too complicated to be understandable to the average viewer or listener.[19]

The pros and cons had their judgment day in October 1977, when the House voted 342-44 to open its chambers to television. The critics lined up with their final shots, as proponents called it an "electronic age" whose time has come.[20] Others heralded it as bringing full First Amendment freedom to the House for both print and electronic journalism. Still another called it a "historic moment." Opponents also chimed in, with one representative suggesting that a new "theme song" would surely appear as a lead-in to each opening session.[21] Still another claimed the House would change from a forum to a theatre.

Amidst all of the rhetoric, there was a real concern over who would control the television feeds. The three commercial networks wanted unlimited control, and some representatives were in their corner. Others, like Representative James Cleveland, stated: "We are not going to turn this over to a monopoly of the big three TV networks."[22] One argument was that smaller radio and television stations would have to "pay through the nose" for feeds, while with House control, the feeds would be free.

In March 1979, the system went into full operation with the House in control and the news media shouting "Censorship!" House Speaker Tip O'Neill recognized the "chill" that existed between the House members and the broadcast press, but predicted that someday, when the House became comfortable with the presence of cameras, the press would be able to bring their own equipment into the chambers to televise proceedings.[23] Of particular objection to the news media was the practice of blacking out everything but the tally board during voting. Some felt that seeing the representatives actually voting was as important as seeing the vote totals. The RTNDA sent a letter of protest to Speaker O'Neill.[24] O'Neill denied any censorship, but the squabbles continue. In the meantime, the Cable Satellite Public Affairs Network has been carrying live coverage nationwide, and the public television stations have been more supportive of the concept than the commercial stations.

Six months into the operation of the House system, the network news chiefs still had complaints. Sid Davis of NBC said: "It's like covering a football game with cameras that never focus on the coaches or the players on the sidelines,"[25] and Ed Fouhy (CBS) complained: "We'd like to go in there and do what we do everywhere else, with professionals taking pictures wherever there is news."[26] Despite criticisms, however, there are indications that when a key legislative issue should emerge, the news teams will not hesitate to take advantage of the House's pooled coverage.

Another side of the legislature coverage issue, however, centers on the unknown results of unlimited television coverage in an atmosphere of competition. What would be the result if the networks had a free rein to cover and choose news on the "sidelines"? Would the demands of competitive journalism give the viewing audience television drama, rather than the issues of government? Moreover, with so much of the real decision-making going on in committees and hearings, is this where the real coverage issue lies, and not on the House floor?

coverage at the state level

In legislatures where live television cameras are not permitted, the same two factors continually snarl access: (1) the necessity to garner enough votes to pass a full-coverage measure, and (2) the inability to muster a plan for the coverage. Sticky points include whether or not cameras should show all of the chamber.

Can the gallery be seen? Do the cameras need to be in fixed positions? Who will determine what will and will not be televised? Will the charismatic representatives steal the show from their less "polished" counterparts? Will politicians play to the cameras, instead of doing their job?

Nevertheless, the broadcast press is making progress. After court pressure was brought by a Chicago station, the Illinois Commerce Commission opened up its sessions to television coverage in March 1977. Temporary guidelines were issued, and later permanent ones were adopted. Photo-journalists had similar restrictions placed upon them and were prohibited from using flash bulbs during the Conference.[27]

With the House of Representatives paving the way, and with bodies such as the Illinois Commerce Commission opening proceedings to live broadcast coverage, more and more state bodies should begin to follow suit. Moreover, legislatures do not wrestle with the classic Constitutional dilemma of free press versus fair trial, as the courts do. All of these factors should cause increased coverage, if responsible media activity prevails and is accompanied by a unified attempt to gain access.

Open Meeting Laws

Closely aligned with televised coverage of legislative proceedings are open meeting laws. Open meeting laws require the press and, in many cases, the public to be admitted to official, governmental decision-making bodies. Although that does not necessarily include the presence of television cameras or other recording equipment, it is a step in the right direction.

Laws differ from state to state. In a special report on the status of open meeting laws, John B. Adams of The University of North Carolina at Chapel Hill categorized open meeting laws in the fifty states.[28] In order to rank the different laws according to openness, eleven criteria were established. Meeting all eleven represented maximum openness. These included laws which:

> (1) Include a statement of public policy in support of openness; (2) provide for an open legislature; (3) provide for open legislative committees; (4) provide for open meetings of state agencies or bodies; (5) provide for open meetings of agencies and bodies of the political subdivisions of the state; (6) provide for open County Boards; (7) provide for open City Councils (or their equivalent); (8) forbid closed executive sessions; (9) provide legal recourse to halt secrecy; (10) declare actions taken in meetings which violate the law to be null and void; (11) provide for penalties for those who violate the law.[29]

Among the fifty states, Adams found open meeting laws ranged from nonexistent to very comprehensive.[30]

As a responsible consumer of broadcasting in society, you should try to keep aware of the open meeting laws in your state. What access does the press have in covering government? Are there distinctions between the print and the broadcast press? Do any open meeting laws specifically provide for the live broadcast coverage of proceedings?

Shield Laws

While you are researching open meeting laws, see if your state also has a reporters' shield law.

what shield laws protect

Shield laws protect the anonymity of reporters' sources, notes, outtakes, and other materials used in the reporting process. For example, assume you are filming a documentary about drug usage at a local high school. You conduct a series of interviews, carefully shielding the face of the interviewee from the cameras. The interviewee admits not only to using drugs but also to selling them illegally. You air the documentary on a local television station and later receive a summons to tell the county prosecutor whom you interviewed. The prosecutor wants to arrest your source for using and selling drugs. You refuse, are sentenced for contempt, and end up in jail. What recourse do you have, and what protection do you have against the prosecutor's inquiry?

The answer may lie in your state's shield law. Most comprehensive shield laws protect the confidentiality of reporters' sources as a natural outgrowth of freedom of the press, although some see them delimiting the First Amendment, not protecting it. The emphasis on shield laws surfaced in earnest in the early 1970s, when reporters kept finding themselves behind bars for refusing to divulge their sources of information.

a state shield law

Considerable national publicity over the jailings of such reporters resulted, pressuring many legislatures either to enact new shield laws or to update old ones. Indiana, for example, updated its shield law, which now reads:

> Any person connected with, or any person who has been so connected with or employed by a . . . newspaper or other periodical issued at regular intervals and having a general circulation or a recognized press association; a wire service as a bona fide owner, editorial or reportorial employee, who receives or has received his or her principal income from legitimate gathering, writing, editing and interpretation of news, and any person connected with a licensed radio or television station as owner, official, or as an editorial or reportorial employee who received or has received . . . income from. . . . announcing or broadcasting of news, shall not be compelled to disclose in any legal proceedings or elsewhere the source of any information procured or obtained in the course of his employment or representation of such newspaper, periodical, press association, radio station, or television station, or wire service, whether published or not published in the newspaper or periodical, or by the press association or wire service or broadcast or not broadcast by the radio station or television station by which he is employed.[31]

Some of the old laws passed years ago did not specifically protect the broadcast press, and broadcast reporters often found themselves spending time in jail until an appeals court freed them. Most laws now on the books encompass all

198

media. Some, such as Oregon's, even include cable television, wire services, and books. The specific statement in Oregon's statute defines a medium of communication as ".... any newspaper, magazine or other periodical, book, pamphlet, news service, wire service, news or feature syndicate, broadcast station or network, or cable television system."

Regardless of how complete your own state's shield law may be, there are certain areas in which courts still challenge a reporter's confidentiality. The weakest ground exists in the area of grand jury proceedings. Such proceedings are expected to be an arena for protection as well as prosecution. In *Branzburg* v. *Hayes,* the United States Supreme Court ruled that the press does not enjoy a separate privilege under the First Amendment, any more than any other citizen. Justice White, in delivering the Opinion of the Court in the *Branzburg* case, stated:

> The argument that the flow of news will be diminished by compelling reporters to aid the grand jury in a criminal investigation is not irrational, nor are the records before us silent on the matter. But we remain unclear how often and to what extent informers are actually deterred from furnishing information when newsmen are forced to testify before a grand jury. The available data indicates that some newsmen rely a great deal on confidential sources and that some informants are particularly sensitive to the threat of exposure and may be silenced if it is held by this Court that, ordinarily, newsmen must testify pursuant to subpoenas, but the evidence fails to demonstrate that there would be a significant construction of the flow of news to the public if this Court reaffirms the prior common law and constitutional rule regarding the testimonial obligations of newsmen. Estimates of the inhibiting effect of such subpoenas on the willingness of informants to make disclosures to newsmen are widely divergent and to a great extent speculative. It would be difficult to canvass the views of the informants themselves; surveys of reporters on this topic are chiefly opinions of predicted informant behavior and must be viewed in the light of the professional self-interest of the interviewees. Reliance by the press on confidential informants does not mean that all such sources will in fact dry up because of the later possible appearance of the newsman before a grand jury. The reporter may never be called and if he objects to testifying, the prosecution may not insist. Also, the relationship of many informants to the press is a symbiotic one which is unlikely to be greatly inhibited by the threat of subpoena: quite often, such informants are members of a minority political or cultural group which relies heavily on the media to propagate its views, publicize its aims, and magnify its exposure to the public. Moreover, grand juries characteristically conduct secret proceedings, and law enforcement officers are themselves experienced in dealing with informers and have their own methods for protecting them without interference with the effective administration of justice. There is little before us indicating that informants whose interest in avoiding exposure is that it may threaten job security, personal safety, or peace of mind, would in fact, be in a worse position, or would think they would be, if they risked placing their trust in public officials as well as reporters. We doubt if the informer who prefers anonymity but is sincerely interested in furnishing evidence of crime will always or very often be deterred by the prospect of dealing with those public authorities characteristically charged with the duty to protect the public interest as well as his.
>
> Accepting the fact, however, that an undetermined number of informants not themselves implicated in crime will nevertheless, for whatever reason, refuse to talk to newsmen if they fear identification by a reporter in an official investigation, we cannot accept the argument that the public interest in possible future news about crime from

undisclosed, unverified sources must take precedence over the public interest in pursuing and prosecuting those crimes reported to the press by informants and in thus deterring the commision of such crimes in the future.

Gag Orders

Another regulatory issue facing the broadcast press is raised directly by the judges. Place yourself, for a moment, behind a judicial bench at a preliminary hearing, determining whether an accused murderer will stand trial. It is your responsibility as a judge to conduct a trial which seeks the truth before a fair and impartial jury. If anything less than that occurs, you can expect your decision to be appealed to a higher court and risk having the verdict overturned or a new trial ordered. How do you protect the defendant's rights to a fair trial? You may decide to issue a gag order, muzzling the press and prohibiting it from reporting certain details of the case.[32]

Now return to being a reporter. You have an obligation as a reporter to inform the public. It is not your role to decide whether the community that watches the coverage of the crime may become so biased that a fair and impartial jury cannot be chosen. How do you handle the gag order? You can obey it. You can permit yourself to be muzzled and abide by the judge's decision. Many reporters would do just that. Others would be appalled at the thought. If you are, you could defy the court order and report the proceedings. That could also find you in the same cell with the reporter who refused to reveal his confidential source of information. You risk being found in contempt of court. Fortunately, history shows that in most cases gag orders have little chance of holding up in an appellate court. Nevertheless, judges continue to issue them, knowing they carry little weight but feeling that the fair trial that can ensue while the gag order is being appealed is more important than freedom of the press.

The next time you read about a judge issuing a gag order, follow carefully the outcome of the case as well as the outcome of the gag order. Does the press obey the gag order or defy it?

Access to Pretrial Proceedings

While seeming to win the battles for television cameras in courtrooms and against gag rules, the press was taking a beating from the Supreme Court in the 1979 decision limiting pretrial access for members of the press. In the case of *Gannett Company, Inc.* v. *DePasquale*[33] the Court held that the defendant, not the public or the press, is the key to the guarantee of a fair trial, and that judges have an affirmative duty to minimize the effects of pretrial publicity. And when all litigants—the judge, the defendant, and the prosecutor—agree to a closed hearing, then it is legal and appropriate. The majority opinion, written by Justice Stewart, stated:

> This court has recognized that adverse publicity can endanger the ability of a defendant to receive a fair trial. To safeguard the due process rights of the accused, a trial judge has an affirmative constitutional duty to minimize the effects of prejudicial pretrial publicity.

Among the guarantees that the Sixth Amendment provides to a person charged with the commission of a criminal offense, and to him alone, is the "right to a speedy and public trial, by an impartial jury." The Constitution nowhere mentions any right of access to a criminal trial on the part of the public; its guarantee, like the others enumerated, is personal to the accused.

We certainly do not disparage the general desirability of open judicial proceedings. But we are not asked here to declare whether open proceedings represent beneficial social policy, or whether there would be a constitutional barrier to a state law that imposed a stricter standard of closure than the one here employed by the New York courts. Rather, we are asked to hold that the Constitution itself gave the petitioner an affirmative right of access to this pretrial proceeding, even though all the participants in the litigation agreed that it should be closed to protect the fair trial rights of the defendants. . . .

We hold that the Constitution provides no such right. . . .

Justice Rehnquist concurred, writing in part:

The Court's discussion of the need to preserve the defendant's right to a fair trial should not be interpreted to mean that under the Sixth Amendment a trial court can close a pretrial hearing or trial only when there is a danger that prejudicial publicity will harm the defendant.

To the contrary, since the Court holds that the public does not have any Sixth Amendment right of access to such proceedings, it necessarily follows that if the parties agree on a closed proceeding, the trial court is not required by the Sixth Amendment to advance any reason whatsoever for declining to open a pretrial hearing or trial to the public.

Jack Landau of the Reporters' Committee for a Free Press predicted that the decision would "encourage federal and state trial judges all over the nation to convert our open court system into secret judicial forums."[34] Echoing Landau's comments was Paul Davis, speaking as president of the Radio Television News Directors' Association. He said: "in its zeal to protect a defendant's right to a fair trial, the Supreme Court has seriously crippled the concept of public scrutiny without which the integrity of the American judicial system cannot survive."[35] And while Chief Justice Warren E. Burger pointed out the issue was *pre*trial and not trial, Landau pointed out that fully 89 percent of all criminal cases are settled during pretrial proceedings.[36] Glimmerings of hope for future decisions to swing the pendulum away from closed sessions came from Justice Blackmun, who wrote: "Publicity is essential to the preservation of public confidence in the rule of law and in the operation of courts. Only in rare circumstances does this principle clash with the rights of the criminal defendant to a fair trial so as to justify exclusion."[37]

Access to Trials

While the Gannett decision left its mark, the United States Supreme Court took some of the bite out of the decision in 1980 in the case *Richmond Newspapers, Inc.* v. *Commonwealth of Virginia.* On appeal from the Supreme Court of Virginia, the *Richmond Newspapers* case established in a 7-1 decision the importance of the First

Amendment rights of journalists to attend criminal trials. In the majority opinion, Justice Burger stated: "We hold that the right to attend criminal trials is implicit in the guarantees of the First Amendment; without the freedom to attend such trials, which people have exercised for centuries, important aspects of freedom of speech and of the press could be eviscerated." In a concurring opinion, Justice Stevens said: "Until today the Court has accorded virtually absolute protection to the dissemination of information or ideas, but never before has it squarely held that the acquisition of newsworthy matter is entitled to any constitutional protection whatsoever." Justice Brennan went on to concur, saying:

> Secrecy is profoundly inimical to this demonstrative purpose of the trial process. Open trials assure the public that procedural rights are respected, and that justice is afforded equally. Closed trials breed suspicion of prejudice and arbitrariness, which in turn spawns disrespect for law. Public access is essential, therefore, if trial adjudication is to achieve the objective of maintaining public confidence in the administration of justice.
>
> But the trial is more a demonstrably just method of adjudicating disputes and protecting rights. It plays a pivotal role in the entire judicial process, and, by extension, in our form of government. Under our system, judges are not mere umpires, but, in their own sphere, lawmakers—a coordinate branch of government. While individual cases turn upon the controversies between parties, or involve particular prosecutions, court rulings impose official and practical consequences upon members of society at large. Moreover, judges bear responsibility for the vitally important task of construing and securing constitutional rights. Thus, so far as the trial is the mechanism for judicial factfinding, as well as the initial forum for legal decisionmaking, it is a genuine governmental proceeding.

The *Richmond Newspapers* case thus clarified the scope of *Gannett* and gave the press a sigh of relief that judges could not use *Gannett* to close a criminal trial under the same rationale as that used in pretrial proceedings.

Libel

Perhaps the strongest safeguards against an irresponsible press rest in libel law. Libel is a false statement about a person or institution that results in public hatred, contempt, or ridicule and one that can cause the person or institution harm. That harm is not necessarily physical harm. Being shunned by friends, losing business, or similar suffering can be construed as grounds for libel. In court, a libel suit brought against a reporter or station can cause substantial damages, running into the thousands or even millions of dollars. Irresponsible reporting is nothing to take lightly and can bring serious consequences. Even public figures, such as politicians or celebrities, can win libel suits if they can prove that a statement is false and malicious.

foundations of libel law

In 1964, the classic case of *New York Times Co.* v. *Sullivan* established the principle that only when deliberate knowledge of falsity or reckless disregard for the truth had been present could a public official collect damages for libel. Proving deliberate knowledge of falsity and reckless disregard for the truth was exceptionally difficult, and time and time again, the courts sided with the news media. In 1971, the case of *Curtis Publishing Co.* v. *Butts* expanded the rule used in the *New York Times* case to include public figures—in this instance, well-known college athletic officials. The *Curtis* case dealt a severe blow to the old *Saturday Evening Post,* which saw itself liable for punitive and actual damages close to three-quarters of a million dollars.

Since the *Curtis* case, the courts have continued to define libel law—specifically what is and what is not a public figure, and what is required for damages. The 1974 case of *Gertz* v. *Robert Welch, Inc.* saw a prominent Chicago lawyer win a libel suit when he was falsely characterized by a right-wing magazine as being a Communist and having a criminal record. Despite the fact that the lawyer was representing a client in a newsworthy proceeding, the court said that this action was not enough to place him in the category of a public figure. A further refining of the definition of a public figure occurred in the 1976 case of *Time, Inc.* v. *Firestone,* when the well-known socialite, Mary Alice Firestone, was involved in a widely publicized divorce suit. The court found that she deserved some protection as a private person, instead of being labeled a public figure in the traditional categories previously mentioned. This case signaled an end to the no-holds-barred attitude that the press had assumed at the time of the *New York Times* decision.

causes of libel

If you were prosecuting a libel case, you would be responsible for proving certain facts. First, the statement prompting the libel action would have to be *proved false.* That may not be difficult, however, since the simple lack of the defendant's ability to prove that the statement is true may be all that is necessary. Many reporters have ended up in libel court simply because they *thought* a statement was true but forgot that they needed to *prove* it true to successfully defend themselves against libel.

If you successfully prove that the statement is false, the second task is to prove that is was *published.* This is generally easy, since simply producing the news copy or a recording of the broadcast is all that is necessary. In libel law, the word "published" refers to both broadcast and print media. If something is "aired" on a radio or television station, it is considered "published."

Examining the published copy, you would next need to prove that it was *defamatory.* Are the words used actually harmful? If a person is called an "embezzler" or an "adulterer," there is little question that the words are defamatory. Such words, which are defamatory on their face value, are called libel *per se.* If the words are not libelous on their face value, but only in the context of other words, they are called libel *per quod.* For example, if a gossip column says that Mr. John Doe and Mrs. Jane Smith are going to make it legal and get married, it could imply that they have been living together or having an affair.

More difficult elements to prove are *negligence* or *malice,* which are closely related. Was the reporter careless in handling the story? Were there other safeguards that could have been taken? If these safeguards were thrown to the wind, does that imply malice? Some "negligence" cases are easier to prove than others. If a program director testifies that the news director arrives drunk on the job and doesn't pay much attention to his work, then the fact of his negligence may seem to be cut and dried. But even less flagrant behavior can be construed as negligent. For example, if the reporter could have checked other news sources but didn't, it can be construed as negligence. What if he had contacted one more person to verify the facts? What if he had made an extra effort to get both sides of the story? Would he then have written the same story? Questions like these can weigh heavily on the minds of a judge or jury. At the conclusion of this chapter, we'll read in the case of *Herbert* v. *Lando et al.* just how far a plaintiff can go in attempting to prove malice.

Finally, the plaintiff must be able to prove that he or she was *injured* by the publication of the defamatory material. And remember, libel damages have been awarded for nothing more than mental anguish. Being shunned by co-workers, even if a person keeps his or her job, can mean a decision in favor of the plaintiff.

defenses against libel

While an attorney has a major task in proving libel, the defense can have an equally difficult time proving innocence. Three primary defenses are used in libel cases, although it is not always necessary to prove all three.

The first defense is *truth*. In some states, proving that a published statement is true is an absolute defense against libel. But remember, the key word is "proving." Many a reporter has fallen victim to a rumor or unsubstantiated fact, only to find out after he has aired it that it was fictitious. *Saying* that someone is taking money from the retirement fund is one thing. *Proving* it *conclusively* in court is something else. Even criminal charges can lead a reporter astray. The word "alleged" does not always stand up as a defense if the local news media, by the extent and the tone of their coverage, are less than objective in reporting the arrest and trial of an accused. If the person is found innocent, biased reporting can spell a libel suit.

A second defense is *qualified privilege*. Certain forums permit immunity from libel actions. For example, if a witness in a murder case testifies that she saw the accused enter the widow's house just after the crime occurred, and her testimony is reported on a newscast, there would be little grounds for the accused to sue the witness after he was found innocent. Remarks made at official proceedings, such as Congressional hearings or other legislative sessions, are also immune from libel. However, it is well to keep in mind that irresponsible reporting can still mean trouble if the privilege is abused. If, for example, a news director can be shown to have aired particularly strong editorials against a candidate and to have then loaded a series of newscasts with attacks against that candidate made by his opponent at a legislative session, abuse of the qualified privilege may have occurred.

Still another primary defense against libel is *fair comment*. This is a somewhat gray area of the law, and each situation is different. The press is permitted a certain amount of freedom to criticize such people as elected officials or government administrators. Here the defense must prove that it was in the public interest for the comments to be made and that the public interest was paramount. Again, this privilege can be abused. A politician's official functions can be criticized, but if that politician is living with another man's wife, without endangering his ability to carry out his duties as an elected official, to openly expose his living arrangement may be grounds for libel under an invasion of privacy statute.

Consent can also be a defense, but again, consent must be proven. Let us assume that a radio journalist records an interview with a doctor and asks the doctor's permission to air a story about the police chief's speculation that he is distributing illegal drugs. The doctor consents. The story airs. The doctor sues for libel. If the reporter does not have the doctor's consent on tape or in writing, proving that the doctor actually consented to the story being aired could be a sticky problem.

In some states, *reply and retraction* of the allegedly libelous material can also be used as a defense against libel. Other states require that a personal apology be made by the media.

Libel law, like all law, is continually changing. In recent years, the courts, although still guaranteeing a free press, have looked more carefully at the press's responsibility in carrying out its functions. Moreover, when libel is proven, the damage awards can be staggering, even crippling. Television journalists are particularly vulnerable to libel, since libel can occur not only by word but by picture. Careless use of a file film or inappropriate use of an old slide from a previous story can provoke a libel suit. Even using the wrong lens, which distorts the picture, can be libelous. The key to avoiding libel is the use of responsible reporting practices. Accuracy should never be sacrificed, no matter how important the story, no matter how big the scoop, no matter how close the deadline.

Invasion of Privacy

Closely related to libel laws are invasion of privacy statutes. These statutes are generally divided into four categories: appropriation, intrusion, private information, and false information. *Appropriation* refers to the unauthorized use of a person's picture or likeness for some commercial purpose. *Intrusion* can become an issue if an overzealous electronic wizard decides to bug someone's room or office to gather information for a story. Although intrusion is rarely an issue in cases involving the press, the recent emphasis on investigative reporting and the miniaturization of electronic circuitry have increased the potential for abuse. Publishing *private information* about a person can result in an invasion of privacy suit. The difficulty lies in determining exactly what is private, and this difficulty is compounded when public officials are concerned. Publishing *false information* about a person's private life is closely related to libel law; in fact, the two often overlap. This situation is usually the product of sloppy reporting and can open up charges of negligence.

Privacy law is one of the more recent areas of developing judicial precedent. As we become more concerned about our privacy in an increasingly commercialized world, in which computers seemingly have the ability to store our most private secrets and investigative reporting continues to develop as a specialized field of journalism (albeit many times practiced by irresponsible and inexperienced reporters), more and more cases centering around invasion of privacy will find their way into the courts.

Search and Seizure

Although few newsrooms have ever been faced with a search warrant, the experience can be a chilling reminder of what police-state tactics mean and how vulnerable the First Amendment is to challenge. Such was the *Stanford Daily* case where the U.S. Supreme Court upheld a surprise search on the offices of the student newspaper at Stanford University.

zurcher v. stanford daily

The Stanford Daily case struck down most First Amendment protection that a news organization had against surprise searches of their premises. It gave police the right to search any premise upon showing that there was a reasonable chance that evidence of a crime could be found there. And the presence of a search warrant meant that the police could look anywhere for that evidence. Unlike a subpoena, which has a much better chance of being challenged in court, a search warrant is a much more immediate threat. Moreover, not every police officer will wait long enough for a local news outlet to call its attorney and wait until the warrant can be challenged or quashed. As an editorial in *Broadcasting* stated: "It will be a public-spirited cop indeed who chances upon evidence of a journalistic investigation of the local police and keeps the secret."[38]

kbci-tv, boise, idaho

In July of 1980, when inmates rioted at the Idaho State Prison in Boise, KBCI-TV, a CBS affiliate, entered the grounds of the prison and interviewed rioting prisoners on videotape. The Ada County prosecutor, who was not inside the prison with the television reporters, obtained a search warrant for the tapes. Police searched the newsroom of the station, going through files and desk drawers, and obtained two videotapes containing footage of the prison riot. While the station was being searched, two Ada County Sheriff's Deputies reportedly refused to allow one of the station's attorneys to leave his office in a nearby bank building. The Boise search-and-seizure incident was one of the first major searches of a newsroom to occur after the *Stanford* case. Idaho law did not provide for the issuance of a subpoena until a defendant had been named in a case, and, in the prison riot incident, no defendant had been named when the warrant was secured and served.

relief from search and seizure: privacy protection act

The results of the *Stanford Daily* decision, followed by the well-publicized Idaho incident (which included an interview with the prosecutor and the news director on ABC's "Nightline") caused politicians to call for federal protection against newsroom searches. Many attorneys were in favor of protection since the newsroom searches caused them to realize their offices were not immune from police intrusion.

Protection did arrive when President Jimmy Carter signed into law the Privacy Protection Act. At the ceremonies after the signing of the bill, White House counsel Lloyd Cutler paid tribute to Philip B. Heymann, head of the criminal division of the Department of Justice, who was credited with suggesting the legislation in the first place.

Taking effect in 1981, the Act made it "unlawful for a government officer or employee investigating or prosecuting a criminal offense to search for a work product possessed by someone reasonably believed to have a purpose to disseminate information to the public."[39] The key to the wording of the law is "work product," and a distinction is made between "work product" and "documentary materials." Specifically:

work product includes:
- reporter's, producer's and editor's notes and interviews, mental impressions, conclusions, opinions, theories,
- materials prepared, produced, authored or created in anticipation of their communication to the public, and
- materials possessed to be communicated to the public.[40]

documentary materials include:
- materials on which information is recorded, including but not limited to video and audio tapes, photographs, motion picture films, negatives, and other mechanically, magnetically or electronically recorded cards, tapes or discs, written or printed materials.[41]

Exceptions to the law do exist. If news personnel are believed to be in possession of material which directly relates to the commission of a crime or that seizing the material is necessary to prevent death or bodily injury, then police may still show up at the front door with a search warrant. As an example, if news personnel are in possession of stolen goods, then they would receive little protection under the law from being served with a search warrant.

Exceptions are also present when documentary material is considered as opposed to work product. For example, if law enforcement officials feel news personnel will destroy material when served by a subpoena, then they can argue for a search warrant. If a newsperson refuses to turn over material after being served by a subpoena (having failed to squash the subpoena) or if a delay typically caused by a subpoena should threaten the interests of justice, then law enforcement can argue for a search warrant.

Despite the Act, there are no guarantees search warrants will not be served in the future. If you are employed in a broadcast newsroom, it is a good idea to contact the station's attorney and familiarize yourself with the procedures to follow when served by a search warrant.

Right of Publicity

In one of the more unusual cases to come before the Supreme Court, a circus performer sued an Ohio television station after the station broadcast his human cannonball act in its entirety on the evening news. Hugo Zacchini was shot from a cannon some two hundred feet away, with each performance lasting about fifteen seconds. On a directive from his superior, a reporter from a local station filmed the act against the wishes of Zacchini. After the film aired, Zacchini brought suit, claiming that his act had been "showed and commercialized without his consent."[42] The issue at hand is commonly termed the "right of publicity." In the case of Zacchini, it was closely related to an invasion of privacy. In fact, the Ohio Supreme Court alluded to this fact when hearing the case, but nevertheless ruled in favor of the press, saying that the press must be given a wide latitude in determining how much of a story or incident it should include as part of the news.

The United States Supreme Court, in *Hugo Zacchini* v. *Scripps Howard Broadcasting Company,* however, took a much different view. The majority opinion, written by Justice White, stated:

> The broadcast of a film of petitioner's entire act poses a substantial threat to the economic value of that performance. As the Ohio court recognized, this act is the product of petitioner's own talents and energy, the end result of much time, effort and expense. Much of its economic value lies in the "right of exclusive control over the publicity given to his performance"; if the public can see the act for free on television, they will be less willing to pay to see it at the fair. The effect of a public broadcast of the performance is similar to preventing petitioner from charging an admission fee. "The rationale for [(protecting the right of publicity)] is the straight-forward one of preventing unjust enrichment by the theft of good will. No social purpose is served by having the defendant get for free some aspect of the plaintiff that would have market value and for which he would normally pay.". . .

> Moreover, the broadcast of petitioner's entire performance, unlike the unauthorized use of another's name for purposes of trade or the incidental use of a name or picture by the press, goes to the heart of petitioner's ability to earn a living as an entertainer. Thus in this case, Ohio has recognized what may be the strongest case for a "right of publicity"—involving not the appropriation of an entertainer's reputation to enhance the attractiveness of a commercial product, but the appropriation of the very activity by which the entertainer acquired his reputation in the first place. . . .

> There is no doubt that entertainment, as well as news, enjoys First Amendment protection. It is also true that entertainment itself can be important news. But it is important to note that neither the public nor respondent will be deprived of the benefit of petitioner's performance as long as his commercial stake in his act is appropriately recognized. Petitioner does not seek to enjoin the broadcast of his performance; he simply wants to be paid for it. . . .
> *Reversed*

More supportive of the press's position was the dissenting opinion of Justice Powell, with which Justice Brennan and Justice Marshall concurred:

> Although the Court would draw no distinction, . . . I do not view respondent's action as comparable to unauthorized commercial broadcasts of sporting events, theatrical performances, and the like where the broadcaster keeps the profits. There is no suggestion here that respondent made any such use of the film. Instead, it simply reported on what petitioner concedes to be a newsworthy event, in a way hardly surprising for a television station—by means of film coverage. The report was part of an ordinary daily news program, consuming a total of 15 seconds. It is a routine example of the press fulfilling the informing function so vital to our system.

The Court's holding that the station's ordinary news report may give rise to substantial liability has disturbing implications, for the decision could lead to a degree of media self-censorship. . . . Hereafter, whenever a television news editor is unsure whether certain film footage received from a camera crew might be held to portray an "entire act," he may decline coverage—even of clearly newsworthy events—or confine the broadcast to watered-down verbal reporting, perhaps with an occasional still picture. The public is then the loser. This is hardly the kind of news reportage that the First Amendment is mean to foster. . . .

In my view, the First Amendment commands a different analytical starting point from the one selected by the Court. Rather than begin with a quantitative analysis of the performer's behavior—is this or is this not his entire act?—we should direct initial attention to the actions of the news media: what use did the station make of the film footage? When a film is used, as here, for a routine portion of a regular news program, I would hold that the First Amendment protects the station from a "right of publicity" or "appropriation" suit, absent a strong showing by the plaintiff that the news broadcast was a subterfuge or cover for private or commercial exploitation.

Although the case was a very narrow one, it did open up new issues, whereby news coverage of the performing arts will be approached with caution. A sword swallower, a juggler, or even the climactic scene from a local play could fall under the umbrella of the Zacchini ruling if a zealous performer decides to bring suit.

summary

Although the Constitution is designed to assure a free press, certain safeguards in the form of laws and regulations have also been designed to assure a more responsible press. Many of these laws and regulations concern broadcast journalism.

Ever since the Lindbergh kidnapping trial, judges have been less than enthusiastic about cameras in the courtroom. Television joined the ranks of barred equipment from the courts after the trial of Texas financier Billie Sol Estes. More recently, however, some forward-thinking states have begun to permit both television cameras in the courts and the actual live coverage of judicial proceedings. Legislatures have also started opening up their proceedings to broadcast coverage, with both state and federal bodies experimenting with live coverage and videotaping of proceedings. Smaller television cameras and more compact recording equipment have aided the cause of the broadcast reporter.

Open meeting laws are helping to assure access to legislative proceedings on the state level. Although statutes differ from state to state, most laws guard against the press being barred from government and court proceedings. Some laws are more complete than others, providing for open legislatures, county boards, city councils, and establishing penalties for infractions.

Shield laws protect the confidentiality of a reporter's sources. Although most of them provide adequate protection, they do not guarantee protection against contempt citations for refusing to reveal those sources.

Judges trying to protect fair trials from being infringed upon by news media publicity will frequently issue gag orders, which prevent publication of court proceedings or facts surrounding a case. Although gag orders have not been upheld by the Supreme Court, they can have a stifling effect on the press, who must fight the legal battle to have such an order rescinded. Stronger precedent against pretrial publicity occurred in 1979, when the Supreme Court upheld the right to close such proceedings to the press when all parties involved agreed to the closing.

Two other controls faced by both the print and broadcast press are the libel and invasion of privacy laws. If a person is identified in a publication and defamed, that person may have grounds for a libel suit if he or she can prove that damages have occurred and that the reporter acted irresponsibly. Defending a libel suit can be difficult, and the defense must usually prove that the statement was true, that the person consented to having it published, or that it was privileged information, not subject to libel. An invasion of privacy suit can be brought if a person's likeness is used for commercial purposes without his or her permission, if a person's private life is intruded upon, or if false or defamatory information is published about an individual.

Search and seizure is another issue confronting the press. In the *Stanford Daily* ruling, police were given the Court's blessing to serve search warrants on premises occupied by news organizations and it was ruled that the organizations could not rely on First Amendment protection against such searches.

The ruling in the case of an Ohio performer who engaged in a "human cannonball" stunt has placed additional constraints on the press when it covers a live performance and it appears that such coverage may decrease the potential for paid admission to the event.

material for analysis

When Anthony Herbert accused his superior officers of covering up atrocities in the Vietnam war, he found himself the object of a CBS investigative report produced by Barry Lando and narrated by Mike Wallace. Herbert filed a libel suit, which eventually reached the Supreme Court. Important to the case of *Herbert* v. *Lando* is the issue of permitting a plaintiff to inquire about the "thoughts" a journalist may have had when making an editorial decision. Although the case did not change the precedents of libel law, for the student of broadcast law and regulation, it is a rich source for learning about the inner workings of a libel action in a broadcast setting while reviewing those precedents.

Herbert v. Lando

UNITED STATES SUPREME COURT, 1979

99 S.Ct.296, 441 U.S. 153

Mr. Justice White delivered the opinion of the Court.

By virtue of the First and Fourteenth Amendments, neither the Federal nor a State Government may make any law "abridging the freedom of speech, or of the press...." The question here is whether those Amendments should be construed to provide further protection for the press when sued for defamation than has hitherto been recognized. More specifically, we are urged to hold for the first time that when a member of the press is alleged to have circulated damaging falsehoods and is sued for injury to the plaintiff's reputation, the plaintiff is barred from inquiring into the editorial processes of those responsible for the publication, even though the inquiry would produce evidence material to the proof of a critical element of his cause of action.

I

Petitioner, Anthony Herbert, is a retired Army officer who had extended war-time service in Vietnam and who received widespread media attention in 1969–1970 when he accused his superior officers of covering up reports of atrocities and other war crimes. Three years later, on February 4, 1973, respondent Columbia Broadcasting System, Inc. (CBS), broadcast a report on petitioner and his accusations. The program was produced and edited by respondent Barry Lando and was narrated by respondent Mike Wallace. Lando later published a related article in Atlantic Monthly magazine. Herbert then sued Lando, Wallace, CBS, and *Atlantic Monthly* for defamation in Federal District Court, basing jurisdiction on diversity of citizenship. In his complaint, Herbert alleged that the program and article falsely and maliciously portrayed him as a liar and a person who had made war-crimes charges to explain his relief from command, and he requested substantial damages for injury to his reputation and to the literary value of a book he had just published recounting his experiences.

Although his cause of action arose under New York State defamation law, Herbert conceded that because he was a "public figure" the First and Fourteenth Amendments precluded recovery absent proof that respondents had published a damaging falsehood "with 'actual malice' —that is, with knowledge that it was false

or with reckless disregard of whether it was false or not." This was the holding of *New York Times* v. *Sullivan,* with respect to alleged libels of public officials, and extended to "public figures" by *Curtis Publishing Co.* v. *Butts.* Under this rule, absent knowing falsehood, liability requires proof of reckless disregard for truth, that is, that the defendant "in fact entertained serious doubts as to the truth of his publication." Such "subjective awareness of probable falsity," *Gertz* v. *Robert Welch, Inc.,* may be found if "there are obvious reasons to doubt the veracity of the informant or the accuracy of his reports."

In preparing to prove his case in light of these requirements, Herbert deposed Lando at length and sought an order to compel answers to a variety of questions to which response was refused on the ground that the First Amendment protected against inquiry into the state of mind of those who edit, produce or publish, and into the editorial process.[2] Applying the standard of Fed. Rule Civ. Proc. 26 (b), which permits discovery of any matter "relevant to the subject matter involved in the pending action" if it would either be admissible in evidence or "appears reasonably calculated to lead to the discovery of admissible evidence," the District Court ruled that because the defendant's state of mind was of "central importance" to the

---

[2]The Circuit Court summarized the inquiries to which Lando objected as follows: "1. Lando's conclusions during his research and investigation regarding people or leads to be pursued, or not to be pursued, in connection with the '60 Minutes' segment and the *Atlantic Monthly* article; "2. Lando's conclusions about facts imparted by interviewees and his state of mind with respect to the veracity of persons interviewed; "3. The basis for conclusions where Lando testified that he did reach a conclusion concerning the veracity of persons, information or events; "4. Conversations between Lando and Wallace about matter to be included or excluded from the broadcast publication; and, "5. Lando's intentions as manifested by his decision to include or exclude certain material."

issue of malice in the case, it was obvious that the questions were relevant and "entirely appropriate to Herbert's efforts to discover whether Lando had any reason to doubt the veracity of certain of his sources, or, equally significant, to prefer the veracity of one source over another."

The District Court rejected the claim of constitutional privilege because it found nothing in the First Amendment or the relevant cases to permit or require it to increase the weight of the injured plaintiff's already heavy burden of proof by in effect creating barriers "behind which malicious publication may go undetected and unpunished." The case was then certified for an interlocutory appeal under 28 U. S. C. § 1292 (b), and the Court of Appeals agreed to hear the case.[3]

A divided panel reversed the District Court. Two judges, writing separate but overlapping opinions, concluded that the First Amendment lent sufficient protection to the editorial processes to protect Lando from inquiry about his thoughts, opinions, and conclusions with respect to the material gathered by him and about his conversations with his editorial colleagues. The privilege not to answer was held to be absolute. We granted certiorari because of the importance of the issue involved. We have concluded that the Court of Appeals misconstrued the First and Fourteenth Amendments and accordingly reverse its judgment.

II

... *New York Times* and *Butts* effected major changes in the standards applicable to civil libel actions. Under these cases public officials and public figures who sue for

---

[3]Respondents' Petition for Leave to Appeal from an Interlocutory Order, which was granted, stated the issue on appeal as follows: "What effect should be given to the First Amendment protection of the press with respect to its exercise of editorial judgment in pretrial discovery in a libel ease governed by *New York Times Co.* v. *Sullivan.*

defamation must prove knowing or reckless falsehood in order to establish liability. Later, in *Gertz* v. *Robert Wlech, Inc., supra,* the Court held that nonpublic figures must demonstrate some fault on the defendant's part and, at least where knowing or reckless untruth is not shown, some proof of actual injury to the plaintiff before liability may be imposed and damages awarded.

These cases rested primarily on the conviction that the common law of libel gave insufficient protection to the First Amendment guarantees of freedom of speech and freedom of press and that to avoid self-censorship it was essential that liability for damages be conditioned on the specified showing of culpable conduct by those who publish damaging falsehood. Given the required proof, however, damages liability for defamation abridges neither freedom of speech nor freedom of the press.

Nor did these cases suggest any First Amendment restriction on the sources from which the plaintiff could obtain the necessary evidence to prove the critical elements of his cause of action. On the contrary, *New York Times* and its progeny made it essential to proving liability that plaintiffs focus on the conduct and state of mind of the defendant. To be liable, the alleged defamer of public officials or of public figures must know or have reason to suspect that his publication is false. In other cases proof of some kind of fault, negligence perhaps, is essential to recovery. Inevitably, unless liability is to be completely foreclosed, the thoughts and editorial processes of the alleged defamer would be open to examination.

It is also untenable to conclude from our cases that, although proof of the necessary state of mind could be in the form of objective circumstances from which the ultimate fact could be inferred, plaintiffs may not inquire directly from the defendants whether they knew or had reason to suspect that their damaging publication was in error. In *Butts,* for example, it is evident from the record that the editorial process had been subjected to close examination and that direct as well as indirect evidence was relied on to prove that the defendant magazine had acted with actual malice. The damages verdict was sustained without any suggestion that plaintiff's proof had trenched upon forbidden areas.

Reliance upon such state-of-mind evidence is by no means a recent development arising from *New York Times* and similar cases. Rather, it is deeply rooted in the common-law rule, predating the First Amendment, that a showing of malice on the part of the defendant permitted plaintiffs to recover punitive or enhanced damages. In *Butts,* the Court affirmed the substantial award of punitive damages which in Georgia were conditioned upon a showing of "wanton or reckless indifference or culpable negligence" or "ill will, spite, hatred and an intent to injure. . . ." Neither Mr. Justice Harlan, nor Chief Justice Warren, concurring, raised any question as to the propriety of having the award turn on such a showing or as to the propriety of the underlying evidence, which plainly included direct evidence going to the state of mind of the publisher and its responsible agents.

Furthermore, long before *New York Times* was decided, certain qualified privileges had developed to protect a publisher from liability for libel unless the publication was made with malice. Malice was defined in numerous ways, but in general depended upon a showing that the defendant acted with improper motive. This showing in turn hinged upon the intent or purpose with which the publication was made, the belief of the defendant in the truth of his statement, or upon the ill will which the defendant might have borne towards the defendant.[12]

Courts have traditionally admitted any direct or indirect evidence relevant to the state of mind of the defendant and necessary to defeat a conditional privilege or enhance damages. The rules are applicable to the press and to other defendants alike, and it is evident that the courts across the country have long been accepting evidence going to the editorial processes of the media without encountering constitutional objections.

In the face of this history, old and new, the Court of Appeals nevertheless declared that two of this Court's cases had announced unequivocal protection for the editorial process. In each of these cases, *Miami Herald Publishing Co.* v. *Tornillo,* and *Columbia Broadcasting System* v. *Democratic National Committee,* we invalidated governmental efforts to pre-empt editorial decision by requiring the publication of specified material. In *Columbia Broadcasting System,* it was the requirement that a television network air paid political advertisements and in *Tornillo,* a newspaper's obligation to print a political candidate's reply to press criticism. Insofar as the laws at issue in *Tornillo* and *Columbia Broadcasting System* sought to control in advance the content of the publication, they were

---

[12]See, *e. g.,* 50 Am. Jur. 2d § 455:

"The existence of actual malice may be shown in many ways. As a general rule, any competent evidence, either direct or circumstantial, can be resorted to, and all the relevant circumstances surrounding the transaction may be shown, provided they are not too remote, including threats, prior or subsequent defamations, subsequent statements of the defendant, circumstances indicating the existence of rivalry, ill will, or hostility between the parties, facts tending to show a reckless disregard of the plaintiff's rights, and, in an action against a newspaper, custom and usage with respect to the treatment of news items of the nature of the one under consideration. The plaintiff may show that the defendant had drawn a pistol at the time he uttered the words complained of; that defendant had tried to kiss and embrace plaintiff just prior to the defamatory publication; or that defendant had failed to make a proper investigation before publication of the statement in question. On cross-examination the defendant may be questioned as to his intent in making the publication." (Footnotes and citations omitted.)

deemed as invalid as were prior efforts to enjoin publication of specified materials. But holdings that neither a State nor the Federal Government may dictate what must or must not be printed neither expressly nor impliedly suggest that the editorial process is immune from any inquiry whatsoever.

It is incredible to believe that the Court in *Columbia Broadcasting System* or in *Tornillo* silently effected a substantial contraction of the rights preserved to defamation plaintiffs in *Sullivan, Butts,* and like cases. *Tornillo* and *Gertz* v. *Robert Welch, Inc.,* were announced on the same day; and although the Court's opinion in *Gertz* contained an overview of recent developments in the relationship between the First Amendment and the law of libel, there was no hint that a companion case had narrowed the evidence available to a defamation plaintiff. Quite the opposite inference is to be drawn from the *Gertz* opinion, since it, like prior First Amendment libel cases, recited without criticism the facts of record indicating that the state of mind of the editor had been placed at issue. Nor did the *Gertz* opinion, in requiring proof of some degree of fault on the part of the defendant editor and in forbidding punitive damages absent at least reckless disregard of truth or falsity, suggest that the First Amendment also foreclosed direct inquiry into these critical elements.

In sum, contrary to the views of the Court of Appeals, according an absolute privilege to the editorial process of a media defendant in a libel case is not required, authorized or presaged by our prior cases, and would substantially enhance the burden of proving actual malice, contrary to the expectations of *New York Times, Butts* and similar cases.

III

It is nevertheless urged by respondents that the balance struck in *New York Times* should now be modified to provide further protections for the press when sued for circulating erroneous information damaging to individual reputation. It is not uncommon or improper, of course, to suggest the abandonment, modification or refinement of existing constitutional interpretation, and notable developments in First Amendment jurisprudence have evolved from just such submissions. But in the 15 years since *New York Times,* the doctrine announced by that case, which represented a major development and which was widely perceived as essentially protective of press freedoms, has been repeatedly affirmed as the appropriate First Amendment standard applicable in libel actions brought by public officials and public figures. At the same time, however, the Court has reiterated its conviction—reflected in the laws of defamation of all of the States—that the individual's interest in his reputation is also a basic concern. *Time, Inc.* v. *Firestone, Gertz* v. *Robert Welch, Inc.*

We are thus being asked to modify firmly established constitutional doctrine by placing beyond the plaintiff's reach a range of direct evidence relevant to proving knowing or reckless falsehood by the publisher of an alleged libel, elements that are critical to plaintiffs such as Herbert. The case for making this modification is by no means clear and convincing, and we decline to accept it.

In the first place, it is plain enough that the suggested privilege for the editorial process would constitute a substantial interference with the ability of a defamation plaintiff to establish the ingredients of malice as required by *New York Times.* As respondents would have it, the defendant's reckless disregard of the truth, a critical element, could not be shown by direct evidence through inquiry into the thoughts, opinions and conclusions of the publisher but could be proved only by objective evidence from which the ultimate fact could be inferred. It may be that plaintiffs will rarely be successful in proving awareness of falsehood from the mouth of the defendant himself, but the relevance of answers to such inquiries, which the District Court recognized and the Court of Appeals did not deny, can hardly be doubted. To erect an impenetrable barrier to the plaintiff's use of such evidence on his side of the case is a matter of some substance, particularly when defendants themselves are prone to assert their good-faith belief in the truth of their publications, and libel plaintiffs are required to prove knowing or reckless falsehood with "convincing clarity." *New York Times* v. *Sullivan.*

Furthermore, the outer boundaries of the editorial privilege now urged are difficult to perceive. The opinions below did not state, and respondents do not explain, precisely when the editorial process begins and when it ends. Moreover, although we are told that respondent Lando was willing to testify as to what he "knew" and what he had "learned" from his interviews, as opposed to what he "believed," it is not at all clear why the suggested editorial privilege would not cover knowledge as well as belief about the veracity of published reports. It is worth noting here that the privilege as asserted by respondents would also immunize from inquiry the internal communications occurring during the editorial process and thus place beyond reach what the defendant participants learned or knew as the result of such collegiate conversations or exchanges. If damaging admissions to colleagues are to be barred from evidence, would a reporter's admissions made to third parties not participating in the editorial process also be immune from inquiry? We thus have little doubt that Herbert and other defamation plaintiffs have important interests at stake in opposing the creation of the asserted privilege.

Nevertheless, we are urged by respondents to override these important interests because requiring disclosure of editorial conversations and of a reporter's conclu-

sions about the veracity of the material he has gathered will have an intolerable chilling effect on the editorial process and editorial decisionmaking. But if the claimed inhibition flows from the fear of damages liability for publishing knowing or reckless falsehoods, those effects are precisely what *New York Times* and other cases have held to be consistent with the First Amendment. Spreading false information in and of itself carries no First Amendment credentials. "[T]here is no constitutional value in false statements of fact." *Gertz* v. *Robert Welch, Inc.*

Realistically, however, some error is inevitable; and the difficulties of separating fact from fiction convinced the Court in *New York Times, Butts, Gertz,* and similar cases to limit liability to instances where some degree of culpability is present in order to eliminate the risk of undue self-censorship and the suppression of truthful material. Those who publish defamatory falsehoods with the requisite culpability, however, are subject to liability, the aim being not only to compensate for injury but also to deter publication of unprotected material threatening injury to individual reputation. Permitting plaintiffs such as Herbert to prove their cases by direct as well as indirect evidence is consistent with the balance struck by our prior decisions. If such proof results in liability for damages which in turn discourages the publication of erroneous information known to be false or probably false, this is no more than what our cases contemplate and does not abridge either freedom of speech or of the press.

Of course, if inquiry into editorial conclusions threatens the suppression not only of information known or strongly suspected to be unrealiable but also of truthful information, the issue would be quite different. But as we have said, our cases necessarily contemplate examination of the editorial process to prove the necessary awareness of probable falsehood, and if indirect proof of this element does not stifle truthful publication and is consistent with the First Amendment, as respondents seem to concede, we do not understand how direct inquiry with respect to the ultimate issue would be substantially more suspect. Perhaps such examination will lead to liability that would not have been found without it, but this does not suggest that the determinations in these instances will be inaccurate and will lead to the suppression of protected information. On the contrary, direct inquiry from the actors, which affords the opportunity to refute inferences that might otherwise be drawn from circumstantial evidence, suggests that more accurate results will be obtained by placing all, rather than part, of the evidence before the decisionmaker. Suppose, for example, that a reporter has two contradictory reports about the plaintiff, one of which is false and damaging, and only the false one is published. In resolving the issue whether the publication was known or suspected to be false, it is only common sense to believe that inquiry from the author, with an opportunity to explain, will contribute to accuracy. If the publication is false but there is an exonerating explanation, the defendant will surely testify to this effect. Why should not the plaintiff be permitted to inquire before trial? On the other hand, if the publisher in fact had serious doubts about accuracy, but published nevertheless, no undue self-censorship will result from permitting the relevant inquiry. Only knowing or reckless error will be discouraged; and unless there is to be an absolute First Amendment privilege to inflict injury by knowing or reckless conduct, which respondents do not suggest, constitutional values will not be threatened.

It is also urged that frank discussion among reporters and editors will be dampened and sound editorial judgment endangered if such exchanges, oral or written, are subject to inquiry by defamation plaintiffs. We do not doubt the direct relationship between consultation and discussion on the one hand and sound decisions on the other; but whether or not there is liability for the injury, the press has an obvious interest in avoiding the infliction of harm by the publication of false information, and it is not unreasonable to expect the media to invoke whatever procedures that may be practicable and useful to that end. Moreover, given exposure to liability when there is knowing or reckless error, there is even more reason to resort to prepublication precautions, such as a frank interchange of fact and opinion. Accordingly, we find it difficult to believe that error-avoiding procedures will be terminated or stifled simply because there is liability for culpable error and because the editorial process will itself be examined in the tiny percentage of instances in which error is claimed and litigation ensues. Nor is there sound reason to believe that editorial exchanges and the editorial process are so subject to distortion and to such recurring misunderstanding that they should be immune from examination in order to avoid erroneous judgments in defamation suits. The evidentiary burden Herbert must carry to prove at least reckless disregard for the truth is substantial indeed, and we are unconvinced that his chances of winning an undeserved verdict are such that an inquiry into what Lando learned or said during editorial process must be foreclosed.

This is not to say that the editorial discussions or exchanges have no constitutional protection from casual inquiry. There is no law that subjects the editorial process to private or official examination merely to satisfy curiosity or to serve some general end such as the public interest; and if there were, it would not survive constitutional scrutiny as the First Amendment is presently construed. . . .

In years gone by, plaintiffs made out a prima facie case by proving the damaging publication. Truth and privilege were defenses. Intent, motive and malice were not necessarily involved except to counter qualified privilege or to prove exemplary damages. The plaintiff's burden is now considerably expanded. In every or almost every case, the plaintiff must focus on the editorial process and prove a false publication attended by some degree of culpability on the part of the publisher. If plaintiffs in consequence now resort to more discovery, it would not be surprising; and it would follow that the costs and other burdens of this kind of litigation have escalated and become much more troublesome for both plaintiffs and defendants. It is suggested that the press needs constitutional protection from these burdens if it is to perform its task, which is indispensable in a system such as ours.

Creating a constitutional privilege foreclosing direct inquiry into the editorial process, however, would not cure this problem for the press. Only complete immunity from liability from defamation would effect this result, and the Court has regularly found this to be an untenable construction of the First Amendment. . . .

The judgment of the Court of Appeals is reversed.

So ordered.

Mr. Justice Powell, concurring. . . .

Mr. Justice Brennan, dissenting in part.

Respondents are representatives of the news media. They are defendants in a libel action brought by petitioner. Lieutenant Colonel Anthony Herbert (U.S. Army, Ret.), who is concededly a public figure. The Court today rejects respondents' claim that an "editorial privilege" shields from discovery information that would reveal respondents' editorial processes. I agree with the Court that no such privilege insulates factual matters that may be sought during discovery, and that such a privilege should not shield respondents' "mental processes." I would hold, however, that the

First Amendment requires predecisional communication among editors to be protected by an editorial privilege, but that this privilege must yield if a public figure plaintiff is able to demonstrate to the prima facie satisfaction of a trial judge that the libel in question constitutes defamatory falsehood.

I

The Court of Appeals below stated that "the issue presented by this case is whether, and to what extent, inquiry into the editorial process, conducted during discovery in a *New York Times* v. *Sullivan* type libel action, impermissibly burdens the work of reporters and broadcasters." The Court grouped the discovery inquiries objected to by respondents into five categories:

"1. Lando's conclusions during his research and investigations regarding people or leads to be pursued, or not to be pursued, in connection with the '60 Minutes' segment and the *Atlantic Monthly* article;

2. Lando's conclusions about facts imparted by interviewees and his state of mind with respect to the veracity of persons interviewed;

3. The basis for conclusions where Lando testified that he did reach a conclusion concerning the veracity of persons, information or events;

4. Conversations between Lando and Wallace about matter to be included or excluded from the broadcast publication; and

5. Lando's intentions as manifested by his decision to include or exclude certain material." *Id.,* at 983.

The Court of Appeals concluded:

"If we were to allow selective disclosure of how a journalist formulated his judgments on what to print or not to print, we would be condoning judicial review of the editor's thought processes.

Such an inquiry, which on its face would be virtually boundless, endangers a constitutionally protected realm, and unquestionably puts a freeze on the free interchange of ideas within the newsrooms." *Id.,* at 980.

The Court of Appeals held that all five categories of information sought by petitioner were shielded by an editorial privilege.

The holding of the Court of Appeals presents a novel and difficult question of law. Rule 26 (b) (1) of the Federal Rules of Civil Procedure provides that "Parties may obtain discovery regarding any matter, *not privileged,* which is relevant to the subject matter involved in the pending action. . . ." (Emphasis supplied.) The instant case is brought under diversity jurisdiction, 28 U. S. C. § 1332 (a), and Rule 501 of the Federal Rules of Evidence states that "in civil actions and proceedings, with respect to an element of a claim or defense as to which State law supplies the rule of decision, the privilege of a witness [or] person . . . shall be determined in accordance with State law." Although *New York Times Co.* v. *Sullivan* placed constitutional limits on state libel claims, it did not itself create a federal cause of action for libel. The "rule of decision" in this case, therefore, is defined by state law. There is no contention, however, that applicable state law encompasses an editorial privilege. Thus if we were to create and apply such a privilege, it would have to be constitutionally grounded, as, for example, is executive privilege, or the privilege against self-incrimination. The existence of such a privilege has never before been urged before this Court. . . .

Although the various senses in which the First Amendment serves democratic values will in different contexts demand distinct emphasis and development, they share the common characteristic of being instrumental to the attainment of social

ends. It is a great mistake to understand this aspect of the First Amendment solely through the filter of individual rights. This is the meaning of our cases premitting a litigant to challenge the constitutionality of a statute as overbroad under the First Amendment if the statute "prohibits privileged exercises of First Amendment rights whether or not the record discloses that the petitioner has engaged in privileged conduct." Our reasoning is that First Amendment freedoms "are delicate and vulnerable, as well as supremely precious in our society," and that a litigant should therefore be given standing to assert this more general social interest in the "vindication of freedom of expression.". . .

In recognition of the social values served by the First Amendment, our decisions have referred to "the *right of the public* to receive suitable access to social, political, esthetic, moral, and other ideas and experiences." *Red Lion Broadcasting Co.* v. *FCC,* and to "the circulation of information *to which the public is entitled* in virtue of the constitutional guaranties" (emphasis supplied). . . . The guarantees of the First Amendment "are not for the benefit of the press so much as for the benefit of all of us. A broadly defined freedom of the press assures the maintenance of our political system and an open society."

The editorial privilege claimed by respondents must be carefully analyzed to determine whether its creation would significantly further these social values recognized by our prior decisions. In this analysis it is relevant to note that respondents are representatives of the communications media, and that the "press and broadcast media," *Gertz* v. *Robert Welch, Inc.,* have played a dominant and essential role in serving the "information function," *Branzburg* v. *Hayes,* protected by the First Amendment. "The press cases emphasize the special and constitutionally recognized role of that institution in informing and educating the public, offering criticism, and providing a forum for discussion and debate." "The newspapers, magazines and other journals of the country, it is safe to say, have shed and continue to shed, more light on the public and business affairs of the nation than any other instrumentality of publicity; and since informed public opinion is the most potent of all restraints upon misgovernment, the suppression or abridgement of the publicity afforded by a free press cannot be regarded otherwise than with grave concern." An editorial privilege would thus not be merely personal to respondents, but would shield the press in its function "as an agent of the public at large. . . . The press is the necessary representative of the public's interest in this context and the instrumentality which effects the public's right."

III

Miami Herald Publishing Co. v. *Tornillo* struck down as undue interference with the editorial process a Florida statute granting a political candidate a right to equal space to reply to criticisms of his record by a newspaper.

"Even if a newspaper would face no additional costs to comply with a compulsory access law and would not be forced to forgo publication of news or opinion by the inclusion of a reply, the Florida statute fails to clear the barriers of the First Amendment because of its intrusion into the function of editors. A newspaper is more than a passive receptacle or conduit for news, comment, and advertising. The choice of material to go into a newspaper, and the decisions made as to limitations on the size and content of the paper, and treatment of public issues and public officials— whether fair or unfair—constitute the exercise of editorial control and judgment. It has yet to be demonstrated how

governmental regulation of this crucial process can be exercised consistent with First Amendment guarantees of a free press as they have evolved to this time." *Id.*, at 258.

Through the editorial process expression is composed; to regulate the process is therefore to regulate the expression. The autonomy of the speaker is thereby compromised, whether that speaker is a large urban newspaper or an individual pamphleteer. The print and broadcast media, however, because of their large organizational structure, cannot exist without some form of editorial process. The protection of the editorial process of these institutions thus becomes a matter of particular First Amendment concern.

There is in this case, however, no direct government regulation of respondents' editorial process. But it is clear that disclosure of the editorial process of the press will increase the likelihood of large damage judgments in libel actions, and will thereby discourage participants in that editorial process." And, as *New York Times* stated: "What a State may not constitutionally bring about by means of a criminal statute is likewise beyond the reach of its civil law of libel. The fear of damage awards under a rule such as that invoked by the Alabama courts here may be markedly more inhibiting than the fear of prosecution under a criminal statute."

Of course *New York Times* set forth a substantive standard defining that speech unprotected by the First Amendment, and respondents' editorial process cannot be shielded merely so as to block judicial determination of whether respondents have in fact engaged in such speech. As the Court states: "[I]f the claimed inhibition flows from the fear of damages liability for publishing knowing or reckless falsehoods, those effects are precisely what *New York Times* and other cases have held to be consistent with the First Amendment." Maj. op., at 17. Our inquiry, therefore, becomes the independent First Amendment values served by the editorial process and the extent to which exposure of that process would impair these First Amendment values.

In *Tornillo* we defined the editorial process in a functional manner, as that process whereby the content and format of published material is selected. The Court of Appeals below identified two aspects of this process. The first concerns "the mental processes of the press regarding 'choice of material'. . . ." This aspect encompasses an editor's subjective "thought processes," his "thoughts, opinions and conclusions." The Court of Appeals concluded that if discovery were permitted concerning this aspect of the editorial process, journalists "would be chilled in the very process of thought."

I find this conclusion implausible. Since a journalist cannot work without such internal thought processes, the only way this aspect of the editorial process can be chilled is by a journalist ceasing to work altogether. Given the exceedingly generous standards of *New York Times,* this seems unlikely. Moreover, *New York Times* removed First Amendment protection from defamatory falsehood published with actual malice—in knowing or reckless disregard of the truth. Subsequent decisions have made clear that actual malice turns on a journalist's "subjective awareness of probable falsity." *Gertz* v. *Robert Welch, Inc.* It would be anomalous to turn substantive liability on a journalist's subjective attitude and at the same time to shield from disclosure the most direct evidence of that attitude. There will be, of course, journalists at the margin—those who have some awareness of the probable falsity of their work but not enough to constitute actual malice—who might be discouraged from publication. But this chill emanates chiefly from the substantive standard of *New York*

Times, not from the absence of an editorial privilege.

The second aspect of the editorial privilege identified by the Court of Appeals involves "the free interchange of ideas within the newsroom," "the relationship among editors." Judge Oakes concluded that "[i]deas expressed in conversations, memoranda, handwritten notes and the like, if discoverable, would in the future 'likely' lead to a more muted, less vigorous and creative give-and-take in the editorial room." Chief Judge Kaufman stated that "[a] reporter or editor, aware that his thoughts might have to be justified in a court of law, would often be discouraged and dissuaded from the creative verbal testing, probing, and discussion of hypotheses and alternatives which are the *sine qua non* of responsible journalism.". . .

The same rationale applies to respondents' proposed editorial privilege. Just as the possible political consequences of disclosure might undermine predecisional communication within the Executive Branch, so the possibility of future libel judgments might well dampen full and candid discussion among editors of proposed publications. Just as impaired communication "clearly" affects "the quality" of executive decisionmaking, so too muted discussion during the editorial process will affect the quality of resulting publications. Those editors who have doubts might remain silent; those who would prefer to follow other investigative leads might be restrained; those who would otherwise counsel caution might hold their tongues. In short, in the absence of such an editorial privilege the accuracy, thoroughness, profundity of consequent publications might well be diminished. . . .

Respondent is concededly a public figure; "[o]ur citizenry has a legitimate and substantial interest in the conduct of such persons, and freedom of the press to engage in uninhibited debate about their involvement in public issues and events is as crucial as it is in the case of 'public officials.'" *Curtis Publishing Co., v. Butts.* To the extent coverage of such figures becomes fearful and inhibited, to the extent the accuracy, effectiveness, and thoroughness of such coverage is undermined, the social values protected by the First Amendment suffer abridgment.

I find compelling these justifications for the existence of an editorial privilege. The values at issue are sufficiently important to justify some incidental sacrifice of evidentiary material.[14] The Court today concedes the accuracy of the underlying rationale for such a privilege, stating that "[w]e do not doubt the direct relationship between consultation and discussion on the one hand and sound decisions on the other...." The Court, however, contents itself with the curious observation that "given exposure to liability when there is knowing or reckless error, there is even more reason to resort to prepublication precautions, such as a frank interchange of fact and opinion." Because such "prepublication precautions" will often prove to be extraordinarily damaging evidence in libel actions, I cannot so blithely assume such "precautions" will be instituted, or that such "frank interchange" as now exists is not impaired by its potential exposure in such actions.

I fully concede that my reasoning is essentially paradoxical. For the sake of more accurate information, an editorial privilege would shield from disclosure the possible inaccuracies of the press; in the name of a more responsible press, the privilege would make more difficult of application the legal restraints by which the press is bound. The same paradox, however, inheres in the concept of an execution privilege: so as to enable the government more effectively to implement the will of the people, the people are kept in ignorance of the workings of their government. The paradox is unfortunately intrinsic to our social condition. Judgment is required

to evaluate and balance these competing perspectives.

Mr. Justice Stewart, dissenting.

It seems to me that both the Court of Appeals and this Court have addressed a question that is not presented by the case before us. As I understand the constitutional rule of *New York Times* v. *Sullivan,* inquiry into the broad "editorial process" is simply not relevant in a libel suit brought by a public figure against a publisher. And if such an inquiry is not relevant, it is not permissible.

Although I joined the Court's opinion in *New York Times,* I have come greatly to regret the use in that opinion of the phrase "actual malice." For the fact of the matter is that "malice" as used in the *New York Times* opinion simply does not mean malice as that word is commonly understood. In common understanding, malice means ill will or hostility, and the most relevant question in determining whether a person's action was motivated by actual malice is to ask "why." As part of the constitutional standard enunciated in the *New York Times* case, however, "actual malice" has nothing to do with hostility or ill will, and the question "why" is totally irrelevant.

Under the constitutional restrictions imposed by *New York Times* and its progeny, a plaintiff who is a public official or public figure can recover from a publisher for a defamatory statement upon convincingly clear proof of the following elements:

(1)   the statement was published by the defendant,

(2)   the statement defamed the plaintiff,

(3)   the defamation was untrue,

(4)   and the defendant knew the defamatory statement was untrue, or published it in reckless disregard of its truth or falsity....

The gravamen of such a lawsuit thus concerns that which was in fact published. What was *not* published has nothing to do with the case. And liability ultimately depends upon the publisher's state of knowledge of the falsity of what he published, not at all upon his motivation in publishing it—not at all, in other words, upon actual malice as those words are ordinarily understood.

This is not the first time that judges and lawyers have been led astray by the phrase "actual malice" in the *New York Times* opinion. In *Greenbelt Coop. Pub. Assn.* v. *Bresler,* another defamation suit brought by a public figure against a publisher, the trial judge instructed the jury that the plaintiff could recover if the defendant's publication had been made with malice, and that malice means "spite, hostility, or deliberate intention to harm." In reversing the judgment for the plaintiff, we said that this jury instruction constituted "error of constitutional magnitude."

In the present case, of course, neither the Court of Appeals nor this Court has overtly committed the egregious error manifested in *Bresler.* Both courts have carefully enunciated the correct *New York Times* test. But each has then followed a false trial, explainable only by an unstated misapprehension of the meaning of *New York Times* "actual malice," to arrive at the issue of "editorial process" privilege. This misapprehension is reflected by numerous phrases in the prevailing Court of Appeals opinions: "a journalist's exercise of editorial control and judgment," "how a journalist formulated his judgments," "the editorial selection process of the press," "the heart of the editorial process," "reasons for the inclusion or exclusion of certain material." Similar misapprehension is reflected in this Court's opinion by such phrases as "improper motive," "intent or purpose with which the publication is made," "ill will," and by lengthy footnote discussion about the spite or hostility required to constitute malice at common law.

Once our correct bearings are taken, however, and it is firmly recognized that a publisher's motivation in a case such as this is irrelevant, there is clearly no occasion for inquiry into the editorial process as conceptualized in this case. . . .

Like the Court of Appeals, I would remand this case to the District Court, but with directions to measure each of the proposed questions strictly against the constitutional criteria of *New York Times* and its progeny. Only then can it be determined whether invasion of the editorial process is truly threatened.

MR. JUSTICE MARSHALL, dissenting.

Although professing to maintain the accommodation of interests struck in *New York Times Co.* v. *Sullivan,* the Court today is unresponsive to the constitutional considerations underlying that opinion. Because I believe that some constraints on pretrial discovery are essential to ensure the "uninhibited [and] robust" debate on public issues which *Sullivan* contemplated, I respectfully dissent.

I

At issue in this case are competing interests of familiar dimension. States undeniably have an interest in affording individuals some measure of protection from unwarranted defamatory attacks. Libel actions serve that end, not only by assuring a forum in which reputations can be publicly vindicated and dignitary injuries compensated, but also by creating incentives for the press to exercise considered judgment before publishing material that compromises personal integrity.

Against these objectives must be balanced society's interest in promoting unfettered debate on matters of public importance. As this Court recognized in *Sullivan,* error is inevitable in such debate, and, if forced to guarantee the truth of all assertions, potential critics might suppress statements believed to be accurate "because of doubt whether [truthfulness] can be proved in court or fear of the expense of having to do so.". . .

To secure public exposure to the widest possible range of information and insights, some margin of error must be tolerated. Thus, absent knowing falsity or reckless disregard for the truth, the press is shielded from liability for defamatory statements regarding public figures.

Yet this standard of liability cannot of itself accomplish the ends for which it was conceived. Insulating the press from ultimate liability is unlikely to avert self-censorship so long as any plaintiff with a deep pocket and a facially sufficient complaint is afforded unconstrained discovery of the editorial process.

II

The potential for abuse of liberal discovery procedures is of particular concern in the defamation context. As members of the bench and bar have increasingly noted, rules designed to facilitate expeditious resolution of civil disputes have too often proved tools for harassment and delay.

The possibility of such abuse is enhanced in libel litigation, for many self-perceived victims of defamation are animated by something more than a rational calculus of their chances of recovery. Given the circumstances under which libel actions arise, plaintiffs' pretrial maneuvers may be fashioned more with an eye to deterrence or retaliation than to unearthing germane material.

Not only is the risk of *in terrorem* discovery more pronounced in the defamation context, but the societal consequences attending such abuse are of special magnitude. Rather than submit to the intrusiveness and expense of protracted discovery, even editors confident of their ability to prevail at trial or on a motion for summary judgment may find it prudent to "'steer far wid[e] of the unlawful zone' thereby keeping protected discussion from public cognizance." Faced with the pros-

pect of escalating attorney's fees, diversion of time from journalistic endeavors, and exposure of potentially sensitive information, editors may well make publication judgments that reflect less the risk of liability than the expense of vindication. . . .

III

The Court of Appeals extended a privilege subsuming essentially two kinds of discovery requests. The first included questions concerning the state of mind of an individual journalist, principally his conclusions and bases for conclusions as to the accuracy of information compiled during investigation. The second encompassed communications between journalists about matter to be included in the broadcast. Reasoning that discovery of both forms of material would be intrusive, that the intrusion would be inhibiting, and that such inhibition would be inconsistent with the editorial autonomy recognized in *Miami Herald Publishing Co.* v. *Tornillo,* and *Columbia Broadcasting System, Inc.* v. *Democratic National Committee, Inc.,* the Court of Appeals concluded that a privilege from disclosure was essential.

With respect to state-of-mind inquiry, that syllogism cannot withstand analysis. For although discovery may well be intrusive, it is unclear how journalists faced with the possibility of such questions can be "chilled in the very process of thought." Regardless of whether strictures are placed on discovery, reporters and editors must continue to think, and to form opinions and conclusions about the veracity of their sources and the accuracy of their information. At best, it can be argued only that failure to insulate the press from this form of disclosure will inhibit not the editing process but the final product—that the specter of questions concerning opinion and belief will induce journalists to refrain from publishing material thought to be accurate. But as my Brother BRENNAN notes, this inhibition would emanate principally from *Sullivan*'s substantive standard, not from the incremental effect of such discovery. So long as *Sullivan* makes state of mind dispositive, some inquiry as to the manner in which editorial decisions are made is inevitable. And it is simply implausible to suppose that asking a reporter why certain material was or was not included in a given publication will be more likely to stifle incisive journalism than compelling disclosure of other objective evidence regarding that decision.

I do not mean to suggest, as did the district court here, that *Tornillo* and *Columbia Broadcasting* have "nothing to do" with this case. To the contrary, the values of editorial autonomy given recognition in those decisions should inform district courts as they monitor the discovery phase of defamation cases. But assuming that a trial judge has discharged his obligation to prevent unduly protracted or inessential disclosure. I am unpersuaded that the impact of state-of-mind inquiry will of itself threaten journalistic endeavor beyond the threshold contemplated by *Sullivan*.

External evidence of editorial decision-making, however, stands on a different footing. For here the concern is not simply that the ultimate product may be inhibited, but that the process itself will be chilled. Journalists cannot stop forming tentative hypotheses, but they can cease articulating them openly. If prepublication dialogue is freely discoverable, editors and reporters may well prove reluctant to air their reservations or to explore other means of presenting information and comment. The threat of unchecked discovery may well stifle the collegial discussion essential to sound editorial dynamics....

Society's interest in enhancing the accuracy of coverage of public events is ill served by procedures tending to muffle expression of uncertainty. To preserve a climate of free interchange among journalists, the confidentiality of their conversation must be guaranteed.

It is not enough, I believe, to accord a discovery privilege that would yield before any plaintiff who can make a prima facie showing of falsity. Unless a journalist knows with some certitude that his misgivings will enjoy protection, they may remain unexpressed. If full disclosure is available whenever a plaintiff can establish that the press erred in some particular, editorial communication would not be demonstrably less inhibited than under the Court's approach. And by hypothesis, it is precisely those instances in which the risk of error is significant that frank discussion is most valuable.

Accordingly, I would foreclose discovery in defamation cases as to the substance of editorial conversation. Shielding this limited category of evidence from disclosure would be unlikely to preclude recovery by plaintiffs with valid defamation claims. For there are a variety of other means to establish deliberate or reckless disregard for the truth, such as absence of verification, inherent implausibility, obvious reasons to doubt the veracity or accuracy of information, and concessions or inconsistent statements by the defendant. To the extent that such a limited privilege might deny recovery in some marginal cases, it is, in my view, an acceptable price to pay for preserving a climate conducive to considered editorial judgment.

questions for discussion and further research ─────────

1. Stop and consider the free press vs. fair trial issue. Under what, if any, circumstances could one be justified in taking precedent over the other?

2. Justice William O. Douglas concluded: "TV and radio stand in the same protected position under the First Amendment as do newspapers and magazines." Although we

read about a great many comparisons between newspapers and the broadcast press, how should we consider magazines in this framework?

3. Based on a discussion posed by question #2, in what way should "magazine programs," such as CBS's "60 Minutes," be afforded the same press freedoms as printed magazines?

4. Are such programs news in the traditional sense of broadcast news, i.e. the "CBS Evening News"? If not, what legal differences could be posed by such distinctions?

5. If the press is guilty of unbalanced coverage favoring the executive branch of state governments, would permitting live radio and television coverage of legislature proceedings help correct this unbalance?

6. Could the definition and application of the terms "work product" and "documentary materials" be applied differently to the print versus the broadcast media? Will cases involving one medium be used as a precedent for another, such as deciding a newspaper case and applying it to radio, resulting in confusion about what can and cannot be classified "work product" and "documentary materials"?

7. Can you see difficulties with newspersons, law enforcement officials, or courts distinguishing between the Privacy Protection Act's definitions of "work product" and "documentary materials"?

8. In a typical newspaper office, information of an "editorial" nature is usually printed or written (stories, reporters' notes, pictures, negatives, etc.) and can be readily identified by the persons conducting the search. But what happens when the place to be searched is a broadcast newsroom? Video and audio tapes must be played to be "viewed." Could the police demand that tapes be played, so that they could determine what was applicable to the scope of the warrant?

9. Would the use of station equipment and personnel to play the tapes disrupt the operation of the broadcast newsroom even more than in the case of a newspaper office? If so, do the arguments for First Amendment protection become stronger for the broadcast newsroom than for the newspaper office?

10. Could difficulties exist in interpreting that section of the law which classifies a newsperson as someone "reasonably believed to have a purpose to disseminate information to the public"? How would the law treat a part-time student intern working intermittently in the newsroom of a local station?

11. The Privacy Protection Act exempts material from protection from search warrants if there is reason to believe the materials would be concealed, altered, or destroyed by issuing a subpoena. Will this argument be used by some law enforcement officials to try and circumvent the law?

12. In *Herbert* v. *Lando,* the Court raises the question of when the editorial process begins and when it ends. In arguing a libel case, this may prove to be important, since within such boundaries, malice could occur. Yet the process of defining such boundaries may pose some difficult questions. A number of examples can be posed. For example, could malice be involved and would it be within the bounds of the editorial process if a news director decided to lead with the story in question, as opposed to placing it later in a newscast? What if a news director chooses to use film or audio with a story, as opposed to just reading the story on the air? What if an assignment editor chooses to cover a story as opposed to disregarding it? What if the same editor made the decision to assign a live coverage ENG (electronic news gathering) crew to the story, as opposed to waiting to air the story on a regularly scheduled newscast?

13. In his dissenting opinion in *Herbert* v. *Lando,* Mr. JUSTICE BRENNAN, dissenting in part, strikes the paradox: "For the sake of more accurate information, as editorial privilege would shield from disclosure the possible inaccuracies of the press; in the name of a more responsible press, the privilege would make more difficult of application the legal restraints by which the press is bound." If such a paradox is, as Mr. JUSTICE BRENNAN notes, "intrinsic to our social condition," how should we then

"evaluate and balance these competing perspectives"?

14. Given that the media are the defendants in libel actions, are libel actions, as Mr. JUSTICE MARSHALL states in *Herbert* v. *Lando,* forums "in which reputations can be publicly vindicated . . ."?

15. In arguing the interpretation of the First Amendment in the broad social context, as opposed to that of individual rights, Mr. JUSTICE BRENNAN refers to the *Red Lion* case and the *right of the public* to receive suitable access to social, political, aesthetic, moral, and other ideas and experiences. Given that much of broadcast regulation rests on the concept of the limited resource of the electro-magnetic spectrum, should libel cases originating from the broadcast media take into consideration the guarantees of the Fairness Doctrine's personal attack rule permitting a legal basis for replying to such attacks?

16. Given that in a democracy, "the autonomy of each individual is accorded equal and incommensurate respect," (JUSTICE BRENNAN dissenting in part in *Herbert* v. *Lando,* footnote 1 and citing *Cohen* v. *California*) does approaching First Amendment guarantees from the broader "societal" context assure ample protection and redress from libel?

17. Should there exist a federal executive type of "editorial privilege," protecting the press from inquiry into thought processes and conversations during the editorial process?

additional resources

books

Adams, J. B., *State Open Meetings Laws: An Overview,* Columbia, Mo.: Freedom of Information Foundation, 1974.

Barron, J. A., *Freedom of the Press for Whom: The Rise of Access to Mass Media,* Bloomington: Indiana University Press, 1973.

Barron, J. A., and C. T. Dienes, *Handbook of Free Speech and Free Press,* Boston: Little, Brown, 1979.

Berger, F. R., *Freedom of Expression,* Belmont, Calif.: Wadsworth Publishing, 1980.

Blanchard, R. O., ed., *Congress and the News Media,* New York: Hastings House, 1974.

Bloustein, E. J., *Individual and Group Privacy,* New Brunswick, N.J.: Transaction Books, 1978.

Foley, J., R. C. Lobdell, and R. Trounson, eds., *The Southern California Conference on the Media and the Law,* Los Angeles: Times Mirror Press, 1978.

Kurland, P. B., ed., *Free Speech and Association: The Supreme Court and the First Amendment,* Chicago: University of Chicago Press, 1976.

Marnell, W. H., *The Right to Know: Media and the Common Good,* New York: Seabury Press, 1973.

Rohrer, D. M., *Mass Media, Freedom of Speech, and Advertising: A Study in Communication Law,* Dubuque, Iowa: Kendall/Hunt Publishing Co., 1979.

Ruckelshaus, W., and E. Abel, eds., *Freedom of the Press,* Washington, D.C., American Enterprise Institute for Public Policy Research, 1976.

Schmidt, B. C., Jr., *Freedom of the Press vs. Public Access,* New York: Praeger Special Studies, 1976.

Van Gerpen, M., *Privileged Communication and the Press: The Citizen's Right to Know versus the Law's Right to Confidential News Source Evidence,* Westport, Conn.: Greenwood Press, 1979.

articles

Adams, W. C., "Local Public Affairs Content of TV News," 55 *Journalism Quarterly* 690 (1978).

Ashdown, G. G., "Media Reporting and Privacy Claims: Decline in Constitutional Protection for the Press," 66 *Kentucky Law Journal* 759 (1977–78).

Balutis, A. P., "Congress, the President and the Press," 53 *Journalism Quarterly* 509 (1976).

Barron, J. H., "Warren and Brandeis, The Right to Privacy, 4 Harv. L. Rev. 193 (1890): Demystifying a Landmark Citation," 13 *Suffolk University Law Review* 875 (1979).

Bennett, R. W., "Broadcast Coverage of Administrative Proceedings," 67 *Northwestern University Law Review* 528 (1972).

Bertrand, C. J., "Press Councils around the World: Unravelling a Definitional Dilemna," 55 *Journalism Quarterly* 241 (1978).

Blanchard, M. A., "The Fifth-Amendment Privilege of Newsman George Burdick," 55 *Journalism Quarterly* 39 (1978).

Bollinger, L. C., Jr., "Freedom of the Press and Public Access: Toward a Theory of Partial Regulation of the Mass Media," 75 *Michigan Law Review* 1 (1976).

Boyd, J. A., Jr., "Cameras in Court: *Estes* v. *Texas* and Florida's One-Year Pilot Program," 32 *University of Miami Law Review* 815 (1978).

Broadfoot, J. W., "Defamation in Radio and Television—Past and Present," 15 *Mercer Law Review* 450 (1964).

Brough, J. C., "Defamation by Radio and Television," 4 *South Texas Law Journal* 253 (1959).

Butkus, C., "The Stanford Daily Rule: The Fourth Amendment and Less Drastic Means," 13 *Gonzaga Law Review* 522 (1978).

Craig, R. S., "Cameras in Courtrooms in Florida," 56 *Journalism Quarterly* 703 (1979).

Dennis, E. E., "Purloined Information As Property: A New First Amendment Challenge," 50 *Journalism Quarterly* 456 (1973).

Eichbaum, J., "The Antagonism between Freedom of Speech and Seditious Libel," 5 *Hastings Constitutional Law Quarterly* 445 (1978).

Emerson, T. I., "The Right of Privacy and Freedom of Press," 14 *Harvard Civil Rights–Civil Liberties Law Review* 329 (1979).

Felcher, P. L., and E. L. Rubin, "Privacy, Publicity, and the Portrayal of Real People by the Media," 88 *Yale Law Journal* 1577 (1979).

Fenner, G. M., and J. L. Koley, "The Rights of the Press and the Closed Court Criminal Proceeding," 57 *Nebraska Law Review* 442 (1978).

Garay, R., "Implementing Televised Coverage of Sessions of the U.S. Congress," 55 *Journalism Quarterly* 527 (1978).

Goldberger, D., "Skokie: The First Amendment under Attack by Its Friends," 29 *Mercer Law Review* 761 (1978).

Goldfluss, H. E., "*Herbert* v. *Lando:* No Cause for Alarm," 1 *Communications and the Law* 61 (1979).

Hale, D. F., "A Comparison of Coverage of Speech and Press Verdicts of the Supreme Court," 56 *Journalism Quarterly* 43 (1979).

Harum, A. E., "Broadcast Defamation: A Reformation of the Common Law Concepts," 21 *Federal Communications Bar Journal* 73 (1967).

Hollstein, M., "Government and the Press: The Question of Subsidies," 28 *Journal of Communication* 46 (1978).

Hoyt, J. L., "Courtroom Coverage: The Effects of Being Televised," *Journal of Broadcasting* 487 (1977).

Hudson, R. V., "FOI Crusade in Perspective: Three Victories for the Press," 50 *Journalism Quarterly* 118 (1973).

Hunter, H. O., "Editorial Privilege and the Scope of Discovery in Sullivan-Rule Libel Actions," 67 *Kentucky Law Journal* 789, (1978–79).

Ivacic, P., "The Flow of News: Tanjug, the Pool, and the National Agencies," 28 *Journal of Communication* 157 (1978).

Jensen, J. V., "Attempts to Televise Parliament," 16 *Journal of Broadcasting* 461 (1972).

Kamenshine, R. D., "The First Amendment's Implied Political Establishment Clause," 67 *California Law Review* 1104 (1979).

Kielbowicz, R. B., "The Freedom of Information Act and Government's Corporate Information Files," 55 *Journalism Quarterly* 481 (1978).

Killenberg, G. M., "Branzburg Revisited: The Struggle to Define Newsman's Privilege Goes On," 55 *Journalism Quarterly* 703 (1978).

Lashner, M. A., "Privacy and the Public's Right to Know," 53 *Journalism Quarterly* 679 (1976).

LeRoy, D. J., E. E. Wotring, and J. Lyle, "'Today in the Legislature': The Florida Story," 24 *Journal of Communication* 92 (1974).

Lively, D., "Affirmative Action and a Free Press: Policies and Problems in Promoting the First Amendment," 11 *Pacific Law Journal* 65 (1979).

McCarthy, W. O., "How State Courts Have Responded to *Gertz* in Setting Standards of Fault," 56 *Journalism Quarterly* 531 (1979).

McLean, D., "Justice White and the First Amendment," 56 *Journalism Quarterly* 305 (1979).

Monroe, W. B., Jr., "Free Press and a Fair Trial—A Symposium: A Radio and Television Newsman's View," 11 *Villanova Law Review* 687 (1966).

Moore, C. B., "Censorship of AFVN News in Vietnam," 15 *Journal of Broadcasting* 387 (1971).

Pequignot, M., "Criminal Procedure—Fair Trial—Constitution Does Not Grant an Affirmative Right to Access to a Pretrial Proceeding When All Participants Agree It Should Be Closed to Protect Defendant's Fair Trial Rights (*Gannett Co.* v. *DePasquale*, U.S. 1979)." 7 *Florida State University Law Review* 719 (1979).

Pinch, E. T., "The Flow of News: An Assessment of the Non-Aligned News Agencies Pool," 28 *Journal of Communication* 163 (1978).

Polelle, M. J., "The Unconstitutionality of the Qualified Truth Defense to Libel Actions," 11 *John Marshall Journal of Practice and Procedure* 259 (1977–78).

Posner, R. A., "Privacy, Secrecy, and Reputation," 28 *Buffalo Law Review* 1 (1979).

Posner, R. A., "The Right of Privacy," 12 *Georgia Law Review* 393 (1978).

Powe, L. A., Jr., " 'Or of the (Broadcast) Press'," 55 *Texas Law Review* 39 (1976).

Reed, O. L., "The Sunshine Society and the Legal Regulation of Business through Compulsory Disclosure," 16 *American Business Law Journal* 83 (1978).

Relyea, H. C., "The Freedom of Information Act: Its Evolution and Operational Status," 54 *Journalism Quarterly* 538 (1977).

Rendleman, D., "Free Press-Fair Trial: Restrictive Orders after Nebraska Press," 67 *Kentucky Law Journal* (1978–79).

Riley, S. G., "Pretrial Publicity: A Field Study," 50 *Journalism Quarterly* 17 (1973).

Rohde, S. F., "Real to Reel: The Hirsch Case and First Amendment Protection for Film-Makers' Confidential Sources of Information," 5 *Pepperdine Law Review* 351 (1978).

Rome, E. P., and W. H. Roberts, "Bellotti and the First Amendment: A New Era in Corporate Speech?" 3 *Corporation Law Review* 28 (1980).

Rose, L. M., "Interstate Libel and Choice of Law: Proposals for the Future," 30 *Hastings Law Journal* 1515 (1979).

Sadowski, R. P., "Defamation and Disclosure: Broadcast Precedent for State Shield Laws," 17 *Journal of Broadcasting* 437 (1973).

Schmidt, R. M. Jr., "The Gannett Decision: A Contradiction Wrapped in an Obfuscation inside an Enigma," 18 *Judges' Journal* 12 (1979).

Scott, C. F., "Trial by TV: The Recasting of Estes," 66 *Illinois Bar Journal* 560 (1978).

Siebert, F. S., "My Experiences with the First Amendment," 56 *Journalism Quarterly* 446 (1979).

Silber, J. S., "Broadcast Regulation and the First Amendment," No. 70 *Journalism Monographs* (1980).

Silver, I., "Libel, the 'Higher Truths' of Art, and the First Amendment," 126 *University of Pennsylvania Law Review* 1065 (1978).

Skinner, G. P., "Constitutional Aspects of Television in the Courtroom," 35 *University of Cincinnati Law Review* 48 (1966).

Sowle, K. D., "Defamation and the First Amendment: The Case of a Constitutional Privilege of Fair Report," 54 *New York University Law Review* 469 (1979).

Stanton, F., "Free Press v. Fair Trial: The Broadcaster's View," 41 *North Dakota Law Review* 7 (1964).

Stevens, G. E., "Media Tort Liability for Emotional Distress," 54 *Journalism Quarterly* 157 (1977).

Stonecipher, H. W., and R. Trager, "The Impact of *Gertz* on the Law of Libel," 53 *Journalism Quarterly* 609 (1976).

Swingle, M., "Constitutional Law—When Push Comes to Shove: The Newsman's Privilege versus the Criminal Defendant's Right to Compulsory Process," 44 *Missouri Law Review* 784 (1979).

Taillefer, F. J., E. H. Short, J. M. Greenwood, and R. G. Brady, "Video Support in the Criminal Courts," 24 *Journal of Communication* 112 (1974).

Tankard, J. W., Jr., K. Middleton, and T. Rimmer, "Compliance with American Bar Association Fair Trial–Press Guidelines," 56 *Journalism Quarterly* 464 (1979).

Trager, R., and H. W. Stonecipher, "Gag Orders: An Unresolved Dilemma," 55 *Journalism Quarterly* 231 (1978).

Watkins, J. J., "Newsgathering and the First Amendment," 53 *Journalism Quarterly* 406 (1976).

Wellington, H. H., "On Freedom of Expression," 88 *Yale Law Journal* 1105 (1979).

Wooddell, J., "Constitutional Law and the Criminal Trial: Exclusion of the Press from Voir Dire," 32 *Arkansas Law Review* 132 (1978).

Zuckman, H. L., "Censorship of Defamatory Political Broadcasts: The Port Huron Doctrine," 34 *New York University Law Review* 127 (1959).

cases: first amendment

Gitlow v. *People of State of New York*, 268 U.S. 652, 45 S.Ct. 625, 69 L.ed. 1138 (1925).

Near v. *Minnesota*, 283 U.S. 697, 51 S.Ct. 625, 75 L.ed. 1357, 1 Med.L.Rptr. 1001 (1931).

cases: source confidentiality

Branzburg v. *Hayes*, 408 U.S. 665, 92 S.Ct. 2646, 33 L.Ed.2d 626, 1 Med.L.Rptr. 2617 (1972).

cases: libel

Associated Press v. *Walker*, 388 U.S. 130, 87 S.Ct. 1975, 18 L.Ed.2d 1094 (1967).

City of Chicago v. *Tribune Co.*, 307 Ill. 595, 139 N.E. 86 (1923).

Cox Broadcasting Corp. v. *Cohn*, 420 U.S. 469, 95 S.Ct. 1029, 43 L.Ed.2d 328, 1 Med.L.Rptr. 1819 (1975).

Curtis Publishing Co. v. *Butts*, 398 U.S. 130, 87 S.Ct. 1975, 18 L.Ed.2d 1094, 1 Med.L.Rptr. 1568 (1967).

Gambuzza v. *Times, Inc.*, 18 A.D.2d 351, 239 N.Y.S.2d 466 (1963).

Garrison v. *Louisiana*, 379 U.S. 64, 85 S.Ct. 209, 13 L.Ed.2d 125, 1 Med.L.Rptr. 1548 (1964).

Gertz v. *Robert Welch, Inc.*, 418 U.S. 323, 94 S.Ct. 2997, 41 L.Ed.2d 789, 1 Med.L.Rptr. 1633 (1974).

Harwood Pharmacal Co. v. *National Broadcasting Co., Inc.*, 9 N.Y.2d 460, 214 N.Y.S.2d 725, 174 N.E.2d 602 (1961).

Herbert v. *Lando*, 99 S.Ct.296, 441 U.S. 153 (1979).

Kaplan v. *Greater Niles Township Pub. Corp.*, 2 Ill.App.3d 1090, 278 N.E.2d 437 (1971).

Karikan Pizza, Inc., v. *The Village Voice, Inc.*, 52 A.D.2d 553, 382 N.Y.S.2d 461 (1976).

Karrigan v. *Valentine*, 184 Kan. 783, 339 P.2d 52 (1959).

Kimmerle v. *New York Evening Journal*, 262 N.Y. 99, 186 N.E. 217 (1933).

Mabardi v. *Boston Herald-Traveler Corp.*, 347 Mass. 411, 198 N.E.2d 304 (1964).

Montandon v. *Triangle Publications, Inc.*, 45 Cal.App.3d 938, 120 Cal.Rptr. 186, certiorari denied (1975).

Nebraska Press Ass'n v. *Stuart*, 427 U.S. 539, 96 S.Ct. 279, 49 L.Ed.2d 683, 1 Med.L.Rptr. 1064 (1976).

New York Times Co. v. *Sullivan*, 376 U.S. 254, 84 S.Ct. 710, 11 L.Ed.2d 686, 1 Med.L.Rptr. 1527 (1964).

Phoenix Newspapers, Inc. v. *Church*, 24 Ariz.App. 287, 537 P.2d 1345 (1975).

Robert v. *Troy Record Co.*, 31 A.D.2d 574, 294 N.Y.S.2d 723 (1968).

Rosenbloom v. *Metromedia, Inc.*, 403 U.S. 29, 91 S.Ct. 1811, 29 L.Ed.2d 296, 1 Med.L.Rptr. 1597 (1971).

St. Amant v. *Thompson*, 390 U.S. 727, 88 S.Ct. 1323, 20 L.Ed.2d 262, 1 Med.L.Rptr 1586 (1968).

Time, Inc. v. *Firestone*, 424 U.S. 448, 96 S.Ct. 958, 47 L.Ed2d 154, 1 Med.L.Rptr. 1665 (1976).

Time, Inc. v. *Hill*, 385 U.S. 374, 87 S.Ct. 534, 17 L.Ed.2d 456, 1 Med.L.Rptr. 1791 (1967).

Time, Inc. v. *Pape*, 401 U.S. 279, 91 S.Ct. 633, 28 L.Ed.2d 45, 1 Med.L.Rptr. 1627 (1971).

cases: cameras in court/free press v. fair trial

Estes v. *State of Texas*, 381 U.S. 532, 85 S.Ct. 1628, 14 L.Ed.2d 543, 1 Med.L.Rptr. L187 (1965).

Irvin v. *Dowd*, 366 U.S. 717, 81 S.Ct. 1639, 6 L.Ed.2d 751, 1 Med.L.Rptr. 1178 (1961).

Rideau v. *Louisiana*, 373 U.S. 723, 1 Med.L.Rptr. 1183 (1963).

Sheppard v. *Maxwell*, 384 U.S. 333, 86 S.Ct. 1507, 16 L.Ed.2d 600, 1 Med.L.Rptr. 1220 (1966).

cases: access/newsgathering

Galella v. *Onassis*, 487 F.2d 986, 1 Med.L.Rptr. 2425 (C.A.N.Y. 1973).

Gannett Co. Inc. v. *DePasquale*, 99 S.Ct. 2898 (1979).

Houchins v. *KQED*, 438 U.S. 1, 98 S.Ct. 2588, 57 L.Ed.2d 553 (1978).

Pell v. *Procunier*, 417 U.S. 817, 94 S.Ct. 2800, 41 L.Ed.2d 495, 1 Med.L.Rptr. 2379 (1974).

Richmond Newspapers, Inc. v. *Commonwealth of Virginia*, 448 U.S.___, 6 Med.L.Rptr. 1833 (1980).

cases: search and seizure

Zurcher v. *Stanford Daily*, 436 U.S. 547, 98 S.Ct. 1970, 56 L.Ed. 2d 552 (1978).

cases: right of publicity

Hugo Zacchini v. *Scripps Howard Broadcasting Co.*, 433 U.S. 562, 97 S.Ct. 2849, 53 L.Ed.2d 965 (1977).

7

Regulating Commercial Programming

In the United States, broadcasting operates primarily as a commercial enterprise. Radio and television provide the public with information about everything from toys to tombstones. Even public broadcasting stations secure income from government and corporate donors to keep on the air. While commercial broadcasters must be concerned with the various regulations governing commercial programming, they must be equally aware of advertising's relationship to such issues as free speech and truthful presentations of commercials. Thus, to be fully versed in the field of commercial programming, we need to begin our discussion not in the station but in the courts, where we'll learn the framework for these "commercial" freedoms. In the pages that follow, we will first touch on the freedoms and restrictions applied to commercial speech in America and then narrow that focus to some of the specific regulations and statutes that govern the practice of advertising.

Historical Perspectives on Commercial Programming

Advertising as we know it today did not exist at the turn of the century. It was only when advertising "agents" began to remove product information out of the classified sections of local newspapers and into larger type that the concept began. As magazines became popular, these agents could experiment with still larger ad formats and creative copy. The world of Madison Avenue had arrived.

the beginnings of broadcast advertising: weaf

For radio, advertising arrived in the early 1920s, when WEAF, the AT&T station in New York City, began selling blocks of commercial time for what then was known as toll broadcasting. In August of 1922, New York City's Queensboro Corporation ushered in the era of commercial broadcasting with a set of five short programs to be aired over WEAF for a period of five days in order to sell real estate. For AT&T, the idea had considerable commercial merit and was a forward-thinking corporate strategy.

criticism of toll broadcasting

The scheme of toll broadcasting, however, had its critics. One of the first to criticize the concept was the trade publication *American Radio Journal.* The *Journal* suggested as an alternative that (1) cities undertake and pay for programs on an entertainment basis; (2) the government charge the public and collect revenues from a large number of "radio subscribers"; or (3) the government tax the manufacturers of radio equipment, the people who distribute it, and the people who sell it.

Hitting ever harder at the toll broadcasting concept was the well-known publication *Printer's Ink.* This trade journal of early advertising concluded that "any attempt to make the radio an advertising medium, in the accepted sense of the term, would, we think, prove positively offensive to a great number of people." *Printer's Ink* was wrong. Radio was not totally offensive when commercial matter was supplemented with entertainment and news programming, and people did listen.

the antitrust issue

Since WEAF was the only outlet for firms wishing to advertise on radio, it began to attract a sizable number of sponsors. Meanwhile, AT&T continued to pour money into its "experimental" station and even tried to prohibit other stations from doing remote broadcasts using telephone company lines and equipment. In addition, the company started charging license fees for the use of AT&T's long lines for long-distance relay of radio.

AT&T's action, while monopolistic, was part of the early unleashed competitive spirit of the 1920s. Without any real federal regulation to control them, stations and their parent corporations were playing havoc with the airwaves. It was the issue of the long lines, however, that brought the Federal Trade Commission into the broadcasting arena. The FTC stated that AT&T's exclusivity over the use of long lines and toll broadcasting was anticompetitive and in violation of the Clayton Act, the government's major piece of antitrust legislation. Before the whole FTC matter could boil over, AT&T stopped, took stock of the role that public opinion might play in its profits, and decided it would be better not to push the issue. In a complicated arrangement of assets, AT&T exited from traditional over-the-air broadcasting and sold WEAF. The foundation for regulating broadcast advertising was thus firmly established.

Regulation of Advertising: First Amendment Issues

In view of the billions of dollars that are spent on advertising, the thousands of stations in operation, and the fact that advertising is one of the most powerful forces in our democratic economy, it is little wonder that the courts and the media have taken a keen interest in attempts to control advertising. What First Amendment protections are available to advertisers? How much can a sponsor brag about a product without being in violation of the law? These are vital questions. To some extent, we have already touched on them in Chapter 3. We will also discuss them from a self-regulatory standpoint in Chapter 12. At this point, however, we need to examine the judicial precedent of advertising's restrictions and freedoms.

valentine v. chrestensen

One of the early cases that established precedent for quasi-government control over the *distribution* of advertising messages was brought to court in 1942. The matter started in 1940, when a Florida resident named Chrestensen bought a Navy surplus submarine, moored it to the State pier in the East River in New York, and began charging admission for people to tour the sub. He advertised by distributing handbills, which the police said violated a New York Sanitary Code prohibiting distribution of commercial and business advertising matter on the streets. However, the police did tell him he could distribute handbills devoted to "information or a public protest." Chrestensen found a printer, and on one side of the handbill printed a protest about the City Dock Department refusing him permission to dock his sub at the City Dock. On the other side of the handbill was the advertisement for tours of his sub, minus only a statement about the admission fee. The police again said "no." Chrestensen thought "yes" and proceeded to distribute the handbills anyway. The police again stepped in and stopped the distribution. Chrestensen sued, won in the District and Circuit Court of Appeals, but lost at the United States Supreme Court. In *Valentine v. Chrestensen,* Justice Roberts wrote:

> The question is not whether the legislative body may interfere with the harmless pursuit of lawful business, but whether it must permit such pursuit, by what it deems an undesirable invasion of, or interference with, the full and free use of highways by the people in fulfillment of the public use to which streets are dedicated. . . .
>
> If that evasion were successful, every merchant who desires to (distribute) advertising leaflets in the streets need only append a civic appeal, or a moral platitude, to achieve immunity from the law's command.

Although the Court did not rule on the *content* of the message, it did provide a municipality with the right to prohibit certain types of distribution. And while the *Chrestensen* decision might have dampened the history of free commercial speech if it had stood the test of time, other decisions gradually chipped away at it.

233

pittsburgh press v. pittsburgh commission on human relations

An interim case, although vague in its interpretation of the role the First Amendment might play in the content of advertising, was heard in Pittsburgh, Pennsylvania, when the Human Relations Commission sought to stop the *Pittsburgh Press* from using male and female categories in its help-wanted advertising. The Human Relations Commission injected a city ordinance prohibiting discrimination in hiring and won the favor of the United States Supreme Court. The Court avoided a discussion of the specific *content* of the ads, however, and although the *Press* legitimately argued that advertising was its lifeblood, and that interference with it could damage the newspaper, the Court did not see the threat as significant enough to inject the First Amendment argument into its opinion. The Court pointed out that when a practice itself is illegal, the First Amendment principle is absent. The *Pittsburgh Press* case was too similar in nature to *Chrestensen* to make any real headway for First Amendment protection of commercial speech.

bigelow v. virginia

The Supreme Court came a bit closer to the First Amendment issue in 1975, when it ruled in *Bigelow* v. *Virginia* that a Virginia newspaper editor had First Amendment protection in publishing an advertisement encouraging women to go outside Virginia to obtain abortions, which were prohibited within the state. Although clearly an issue of legality was involved, it was not a city ordinance that was being challenged, the readers were not going to violate a law in Virignia by going out of state, and the "distribution" of the advertisement was not at issue, as it had been in *Chrestensen*. For the real breakthrough, the media waited until 1976, when the Supreme Court ruled in the case of *Virginia Pharmacy Board* v. *Virginia Consumer Council.*

first amendment clarification: the virginia pharmacy board decision

Just how far the laws of the land could control the *content* of commercial speech was clarified in 1976, when a Virginia statute prohibiting licensed pharmacists to advertise the price of prescription drugs was challenged as being unconstitutional. The U.S. Supreme Court upheld the ruling of a lower appellate court and clarified many of the long-awaited issues regarding advertising and the First Amendment. In delivering the opinion of the Court, Justice Blackman wrote:

> It is clear, for example, that speech does not lose its First Amendment protection because money is spent to project it, as in a paid advertisement of one form or another. Speech likewise is protected even though it is carried in a form that is "sold" for profit, and even though it may involve a solicitation to purchase or otherwise pay or contribute money. If there is a kind of commercial speech that lacks all First Amendment protection, therefore, it must be distinguished by its content. Yet the speech whose content deprives it of protection cannot simply be speech on a commercial subject. . . . Nor can it be dispositive that a commercial advertisement is noneditorial, and merely reports a fact. Purely factual matters of public interest may claim protection. . . .

Advertising, however tasteless and excessive it sometimes may seem, is nonetheless dissemination of information as to who is producing and selling what product, for what reason, and at what price. So long as we preserve a predominantly free enterprise economy, the allocation of our resources in large measure will be made through numerous private economic decisions. It is a matter of public interest that those decisions, in the aggregate, be intelligent and well informed. To this end, the free flow of commercial information is indispensable. And if it is indispensable to the proper allocation of resources in a free enterprise system, it is also indispensable to the formation of intelligent opinions as to how that system ought to be regulated or altered. Therefore, even if the First Amendment were thought to be primarily an instrument to enlighten public decision-making in a democracy, we could not say that the free flow of information does not serve that goal.

In a concurring opinion, Justice Burger tempered the words of the majority opinion by noting:

I think it important to note also that the advertisement of professional services carries with it quite different risks from the advertisement of standard products. . . .

. . . even with respect to expression at the core of the First Amendment, the Constitution does not provide absolute protection for false factual statements that cause private injury. In *Gertz* v. *Robert Welch,* 418 U.S. 323, 340, the Court concluded that "there is no constitutional value in false statements of fact. . . ."

Since the factual claims contained in commercial price or product advertisements relate to tangible goods or services, they may be tested empirically and corrected to reflect the truth without in any manner jeopardizing the free dissemination of thought. Indeed, the elimination of false and deceptive claims serves to promote the one facet of commercial price and product advertising that warrants First Amendment protection—its contribution to the flow of accurate and reliable information relevant to public and private decision making.

regulatory pressures

In the *Virginia Pharmacy Board* decision, the Court clarified the important questions about the First Amendment and commercial speech but did not unleash uninhibited commercial expression. Nevertheless, we are now at a place in the development of First Amendment law that gives great latitude to advertisers to say almost anything they want through commercial speech, as long as it is truthful. Yet we should be aware of regulations which do monitor the content of certain commercial messages. For example, the Fairness Doctrine can cause a broadcaster to hesitate about accepting advertising whose content raises serious issues about the right of reply and the burden such a right would place on the station. Moreover, how does a small station, dealing with local merchants, really have any way of testing the legitimacy of every local product commercial that ends up on the air? And the Federal Trade Commission can still put the bite on advertisers who do not heed the Supreme Court's opinion that "there is no constitutional protection in false statements of fact."

We will now examine more closely the controls that exist over advertising, first with a general discussion of federal and state jurisdictions and then with specific FCC Rules.

Broadcast Advertising

Advertising provides the economic lifeblood for the American system of broadcasting, as opposed to the government-financed systems existing in many other parts of the world. But federal, state, and even municipal regulations can oversee this lifeblood. We will now concern ourselves primarily with state and federal jurisdiction over commercial radio and television.

state and federal jurisdiction

Although we tend to think of radio and television as being governed by federal law, as expressed in the Communications Act of 1934, state laws play an important part when advertising is involved. In the landmark case that applied state jurisdiction to broadcast advertising, a court upheld a New Mexico statute that prohibited a New Mexico radio station from accepting advertising from "across-the-border" Texas optometrists. The Texas advertising violated a New Mexico law regulating optometric advertising. In *Head* v. *New Mexico Board of Examiners in Optometry,* the U.S. Supreme Court upheld the New Mexico law and rejected the contention that the law interfered with interstate commerce and was thus preempted by federal law. In a concurring opinion, Justice Brennan said: "rather than mandate ouster of state regulations, several provisions of the Communications Act suggest a congressional design to leave standing various forms of state regulation, including the form embodied in the New Mexico statute."[1]

Robert Sadowski examined the subject of broadcasting and state statutes and found advertising to be second only to individual rights in the attention given it by state laws. Forty-three states have passed laws, which govern over thirty-one different areas of advertising affecting broadcasters.[2] The laws fall into two primary areas: (1) "general regulations, which govern fraudulent advertising, deceptive trade and consumer fraud practices," and (2) more specific regulations, covering "controls over foods, drugs, cosmetics, political advertising, and various other commodities such as insurance, loans, and real estate."[3] Eleven states have given protection to broadcasters who, in good faith, broadcast an advertisement that turns out to be deceptive. Although we do not hear much about prosecution, these state laws are more than just window dressing. In Mississippi, the Attorney General's office moved to stop an individual from advertising paintings which were supposedly painted by local "starving artists." The Attorney General's office concluded that the paintings were mass-produced in Asia, and that all the profits went to the promoter.[4]

Moving into the federal arena, we find that the two principal agencies affecting broadcast advertising are the Federal Communications Commission and the Federal Trade Commission. The FCC can call upon its blanket "public interest" clause to move in on an unscrupulous broadcaster involved in a deceptive advertising scheme. And move it does, right into a possible license revocation. We have already learned that the Commission is directly involved in political advertising through Section 315 of the Communications Act.

But the most pervasive agency in the control of advertising is the Federal

Trade Commission. Through its Bureau of Consumer Protection, the FTC keeps a watchful eye on advertising practices affecting both the broadcasting and the print media. The quickest way for an advertiser to get into trouble with the FTC is to violate one of its six "basic ground rules:"

1. *Tendency to deceive.* The Commission is empowered to act when representations have only a tendency to mislead or deceive. Proof of actual deception is not essential, although evidence of actual deception is apparently conclusive as to the deceptive quality of the advertisement in question.
2. *Immateriality of knowledge of falsity.* Since the purpose of the FTC Act is consumer protection, the Government does not have to prove knowledge of falsity on the part of the advertiser; the businessman acts at his own peril.
3. *Immateriality of intent.* The intent of the advertiser is also entirely immaterial. An advertiser may have a wholly innocent intent and still violate the law.
4. *General public's understanding of controls.* Since the purpose of the Act is to protect the consumers, and since some consumers are "ignorant, unthinking and credulous," nothing less than "the most literal truthfulness" is tolerated. As the Supreme Court has stated, "laws are made to protect the trusting as well as the suspicious." Thus it is immaterial that an expert reader might be able to decipher the advertisement in question so as to avoid being misled.
5. *Literal truth sometimes insufficient.* Advertisements are not intended to be carefully dissected with a dictionary at hand, but rather are intended to produce an overall impression on the ordinary purchaser. An advertiser cannot present one overall impression and yet protect himself by pointing to a contrary impression which appears in a small and inconspicuous portion of the advertisement. Even though every sentence considered separately is true, the advertisement as a whole may be misleading because the message is composed in such a way as to mislead.
6. *Ambiguous advertisements interpreted to effect purposes of the law.* Since the purpose of the FTC Act is the prohibition of advertising which has a tendency and capacity to mislead, an advertisement which can be read to have two meanings is illegal if one of them is false or misleading.[5]

One famous example of FTC action is the "Sandpaper Shave Case." A commercial for Rapid Shave shaving cream attempted to show the cream's merits by using it on a piece of heavy sandpaper.[6] An announcer spoke about the merits of the product, while Rapid Shave was being applied to what appeared to be sandpaper. The next thing you knew, a razor was shaving the sandpaper right before your eyes. As it turned out, the razor did not immediately shave the sandpaper, and what was supposed to be sandpaper was really a type of plexi-glass with sand affixed to it. After a series of decisions—including those of an FTC examiner, the FTC, and appeals to the Supreme Court—the Rapid Shave commercial was stopped. There were, however, convincing arguments that the public was not really harmed by the commercial and that Rapid Shave could in fact shave sandpaper after the sandpaper was soaked for a while. Although the Rapid Shave commercial was amended, the FTC action did not prohibit all artificial props from television commercials.

Corrective advertising is another area that is overseen by the FTC. The ITT Continental Baking Company, distributors of Profile Bread, ran corrective advertising to clarify earlier commercials which, the FTC alleged, misled people into thinking Profile Bread could help them lose weight. Firestone Tire and Rubber Co. agreed to pay $50,000 in penalties and $750,000 for a tire safety campaign to settle charges brought by an FTC order claiming that the company had aired misleading advertisements.[7] A substantial $550,000 of the settlement was appropriated for television commercials to air in major network news and sports programming. The FTC had pursued the company through the federal courts under provisions of the FTC Act. In another case, the J. B. Williams Co. of New York agreed to an out-of-court settlement in a suit brought by the FTC concerning ads for Geritol.[8] The FTC claimed the commercials violated an FTC order prohibiting statements that the products "helped relieve tiredness, loss of strength, run-down feeling, nervousness or irritability without also saying that these symptoms usually result from iron deficiency and that Geritol could not help in these cases."[9]

The most recent issue tackled by the FTC is children's advertising. In 1978, the FTC issued a series of guidelines designed to control not only the content of children's advertising on television but also the presence of such advertising. Prime targets were advertisements for sugar cereals and Saturday morning television. The latest proposals must survive hearings and lobbying efforts before becoming enforceable rules.[10] The proposals are certain to clash head on with the FCC, which may very well feel that regulations of the nature proposed by the FTC belong in the FCC's, not the FTC's, domain. Furthermore, regulating the *content* of broadcast advertising comes close to abridging the First Amendment as well as the no-censorship provisions of the Communications Act of 1934.[11]

sponsor identification

FCC rules require commercial sponsors to be identified on the air. Section 73.1212 of the FCC rules says:

> When a broadcast station transmits any matter for which money, service, or other valuable consideration is either directly or indirectly paid or promised to, or charged or accepted by such station, the station at the time of the broadcast, shall announce (i) that such matter is sponsored, paid for, or furnished, either in whole or in part, and (ii) by whom or on whose behalf such consideration was supplied. . . .

Not acceptable under the rules are indirect references to the business. For example, a commercial which ends with the announcement that "this commercial is sponsored by your neighborhood hardware man" would not be acceptable, even if the "neighborhood hardware man" was a slogan frequently used by a local hardware store.[12] Notice that money does not have to be the "consideration." If a record store gives a television station twenty-five albums under the implied agreement that a talk-show host will plug the record store, then the "plug" must be announced as being "sponsored, paid for, or furnished" by the record store.[13]

Certain logging rules also apply to commercial announcements made on television. The log must also contain the name of the sponsor, again making sure it is readily identifiable, and not just the "neighborhood hardware man."

special problem: the program-length commercial

One area of confusion among broadcasters has been the logging requirements for "program-length commercials" (PLC).[14] Program-length commercials
are actually programs into which so much commercial consideration is interwo-
ven that the entire program becomes a commercial. For example, a television station
may decide to conduct a remote broadcast from the local car dealer's showroom.
The fifteen-minute program includes five one-minute commercials for the car
dealer, together with interviews with the salespeople, who tell everyone about the
fine buys and great deals to be made. Since the interviews could be considered
commercial matter, as well as the five commercials, the entire program would be
a commercial in the FCC's eyes. Although the FCC is still hazy on how much PLC
programming it will approve, previous rulings suggest that about five minutes
would be on the safe side and that a fifteen-minute PLC would not be considered
to be in the public interest.

guarding against fraudulent billing

One of the most serious infractions in which a broadcaster can participate is
fraudulent billing, sometimes called "*double billing.*"[15] The FCC rules are definitive
in this area and warn in Section 73.1205 that:

> No licensee of a standard, FM, or television broadcast station shall knowingly issue or
> knowingly cause to be issued to any local, regional or national advertiser, advertising
> agency, station representative, manufacturer, distributor, jobber, or any other party,
> any bill, invoice, affidavit or other document which contains false information concern-
> ing the amount actually charged by the licensee for the broadcast advertising for which
> such bill, invoice, affidavit or other document is issued, or which misrepresents the
> nature or content of such advertising, or which misrepresents the quantity of advertis-
> ing actually broadcast (number or length of advertising messages) or which substan-
> tially and/or materially misrepresents the time of day at which it was broadcast, or
> which misrepresents the date on which it was broadcast.

Fraudulent billing can occur in a variety of situations, the most common
being "co-op advertising." In co-op advertising, the manufacturer or major distributor of a product pays part of the cost of the advertising. To understand this
concept, let's assume that the Ordinary Appliance Store sells a toaster manufactured by Tommy Toasters. Ordinary enters into an agreement with Tommy
Toasters to split the cost of 100 commercials from station WXXX, but instead of
mentioning Tommy Toasters, the Ordinary commercials talk about stoves and
refrigerators. The cost of the commercials is $500. WXXX sends a bill for $250
to Ordinary and another $250 bill to Tommy Toasters for co-op advertising.
The station is thus guilty of fraudulent billing practices and is in danger of
having its license revoked.

Another variation of fraudulent billing would be for WXXX to send a bill to
Tommy Toasters for more than the amount of the co-op advertising, such as
$500 instead of $250, in the hope that Tommy would pay the bill without realizing the overcharge. If Tommy recognizes it, WXXX could claim it expected
Tommy to pay only half the bill, since the remainder would be paid by Ordinary.

A more direct form of fraudulent billing would be charging an advertiser for commercials that did not air, or overbilling an ad agency to recoup the 15 percent discount normally given agency orders. A subtle fraudulent billing practice would take the Ordinary portion of the bill in trade-out, such as having Ordinary furnish WXXX's lunchroom with a new stove at wholesale prices. Since the stove would cost Ordinary less than $250, Tommy Toasters would be paying more than half of the bill.

combination sales agreements

Although not a common practice, some account executives are employed by more than one station. When this occurs, the FCC has some strict guidelines that guard against rate fixing or selling time on more than one station for a single rate.[15a] Although representing two stations is not illegal, selling time for two competing stations is. The definition of competing is any two stations whose signals overlap, regardless of which market they serve, Moreover, a radio and television station combining to offer a single rate is illegal, even if the two stations are jointly owned. Because other radio stations might not be able to team up with a television station, the FCC feels such arrangements are anticompetitive.

A single rate for an AM and FM station engaged in simulcasting is permissible. But if combination rates are offered for two stations commonly owned but not engaged in simulcasting, management must be careful not to use the combination rate to "carry along" the weaker of the two stations. And on stations not engaged in simulcasting, forcing an advertiser to buy a combination rate is illegal. If the advertiser wants to buy advertising on only one station, then that opportunity must be available to the advertiser.

network clipping

Network clipping is also considered fraudulent billing. Network clipping is the *practice of certifying to a network that a network commercial has been aired when in fact it has not.* Local affiliates provide networks with an accounting of all the network commercials that they air locally. Failing to air a commercial may cut the amount of compensation a station receives from the network. Nevertheless, when a station fails to air a commercial, either deliberately or inadvertently, the network is notified of that fact as part of the special certification report. Listing a network commercial as having been aired when it was not is considered a violation of FCC's Section 73.1205. The roster of commercial credits shown at the end of a game show is also considered commercial matter, and deleting this content without reporting that it was deleted is another violation. The FCC *does not prohibit* local stations from deleting network programming. What it prohibits is deleting the programming *without notifying* the network and thereby receiving compensation for services which were *not* rendered.

Fraudulent billing not only reflects directly on a broadcaster's character but also sheds negative light on the entire broadcasting industry. As a result, the FCC has shown few qualms about revoking a station's license over this issue.

political advertising and the fairness doctrine

We have already discussed political advertising and the Fairness Doctrine in Chapter 5. But let's briefly review the highlights of Section 315 and the Doctrine as they deal with programming regulations. Remember that political candidates receive the station's lowest unit charge when buying commercials, regardless of how many commercials they buy. And remember that *all* offices are affected, from city street cleaner to President of the United States. The candidates must also be given reasonable access to the station, which means opportunities to be heard that are equal to those of their opponents. In advertising, this includes comparable, though not identical, time periods. The rates apply only during the forty-five days preceding a primary election and sixty days preceding a general election.

Although the FCC, as part of assuring that broadcasters operate in the public interest, have guidelines governing the amount of commercials a station can carry in any hour, stations may exceed the normal number of commercial minutes by 10 percent at election time to give candidates access. Amendments to the Federal Election Campaign Act of 1976 seconded the requirement that political commercials must be clearly identified as such. The identification must be "clear and conspicuous" and must either tell who authorized the commercials, or, if they were not authorized, state this fact.[16]

We have also seen how commercials can trigger a Fairness Doctrine clamor, although stations are not necessarily required to provide equal time for all issues included in commercials. Stations can, however, refuse to air certain advertising. If a broadcaster legitimately suspects advertising to be fraudulent or objectionable, or that the credit rating of the sponsor is poor, then that broadcaster is on firm legal ground in refusing to air the commercials.[17]

special problems: alcohol, recording artists, subliminal advertising

Since few commercials for hard liquor appear on radio or television, we are normally left with the impression that these commercials are illegal. Not so. The restraint against commercials for hard liquor is found in the NAB Codes, not the FCC rules. For the FCC to prohibit advertising of hard liquor would be violating the anticensorship provisions of the Communications Act. Nevertheless, in adherence to the NAB Codes, broadcasters have kept most hard liquor advertising off the air. And without such voluntary restraint, Congress could very well pass a law prohibiting such advertising, as they did with cigarette advertising. Stations not adhering to the NAB Codes are free to advertise hard liquor. In doing so, however, the actual alcoholic content of the liquor or other alcoholic beverage cannot be stated. The Code of Federal Regulations, Department of the Treasury, and the Bureau of Alcohol, Tobacco, and Firearms prohibit advertising that includes "any statement of alocholic content, or any statement of the percentage and quantity of the original extract, or any numerals, letters, characters, or figures likely to be considered as designations of alcoholic content."[18]

Another area over which the FCC as well as the FTC has exercised its authority is the matter of commercials for record albums. It is a common practice for a lesser-known artist to imitate the style of or record a song made popular by a famous artist and take advantage of the publicity and popularity the original artist achieved. Look-alike record jackets and labeling add to the confusion. The broadcasters' role in this marketing scheme should be to lessen the confusion. The FTC requires record companies to make sure that their album covers and labels can be readily distinguished from each other. And radio and television commercials must orally state that: "This is not an original artist recording." Although the advertisers are held responsible by the FTC, the National Association of Broadcasters reminds stations that the FCC also holds them accountable for any programming and advertising that are knowingly in violation of an FTC rule.[19]

Still a third area of broadcast advertising embroiled in controversy is *subliminal advertising: advertising which uses techniques to convey information through messages which are below the threshold of normal awareness.* Here again, it is the NAB Television Code that restrains this practice among member stations, although the FCC considers subliminal advertising to be deceptive. A United Nations study sent shivers of alarm when it described subliminal advertising beamed directly into the home via satellite as the potential for the mass hypnotizing of millions.[20] Canada has even moved to make subliminal advertising illegal.[21] In the United States, the FCC does not consider subliminal advertising to be in the public interest.

Station-Conducted Contests

The station-conducted contest has become a successful marketing tool for many licensees, especially in highly competitive markets. The various types of contests would fill a book, varying from spotting station bumper stickers on cars to big-money giveaways. Such contests as "Dialing for Dollars" and "The Money Wheel" have become familiar to millions of viewers and listeners. Both radio and television stations conduct contests as a means of gaining audiences and commercial sponsorship. But with this "game" approach to programming, the FCC, charged with assuring the "public interest" factor in programming, has been careful to assure that the public is not duped into unscrupulous contests, which might not only cause personal displeasure but also reflect on the overall image of the broadcasting industry.

areas for possible violations and FCC safeguards

This concern over station-conducted contests manifested itself in an FCC Public Notice, which stated the practices the Commission felt would be irresponsible:

1. Disseminating false or misleading information regarding the amount or nature of prizes;
2. Failing to control the contest to assure a fair opportunity for contestants to win the announced prize;
3. Urging participation in a contest, or urging persons to stay tuned to the station in order to win, at times when it is not possible to win prizes;

4. Failing to award prizes, or failing to award them within a reasonable time;
5. Failing to set forth fully and accurately the rules and conditions for contests;
6. Changing the rules or conditions of a contest without advising the public or doing so promptly;
7. Using arbitrary or inconsistently applied standards in judging entries;
8. Providing secret assistance to contestants or predetermination of winners;
9. Stating that winners are chosen solely by chance, when in fact chance played little or no part;.
10. Broadcasting false clues in connection with a contest; and
11. Conducting contests without adequate supervision.[22]

The Commission has also put some teeth into its concern by adopting a new FCC rule covering station contests:

> A licensee that broadcasts or advertises information about a contest it conducts shall fully and accurately disclose the material terms of the contest, and shall conduct the contest substantially as announced or advertised. No contest description shall be false, misleading or deceptive with respect to any material term.[23]

The rule defines a contest as a "scheme in which a prize is offered or awarded, based upon chance, dilligence, knowledge or skill, to members of the public." The *material terms* cited in the rule include how to enter or participate, the restrictions on eligibility, deadlines for entry, whether prizes can be won, when they can be won, "the extent, nature and value of the prizes," the basis for evaluating the prizes, the "time and means of selection of winners," and the method of breaking ties. The station is responsible for disclosing the "material terms" when the audience is told for the first time how to enter and "periodically" thereafter. The station can also disclose material terms through nonbroadcast media, such as newspapers or direct mail. Exemptions to the rule include "licensee-conducted contests not broadcast or advertised to the general public...." The rule does not apply to commercials that mention a contest not sponsored by the licensee or conducted by some nonbroadcast division or company related to the licensee.

Responsibility in running contests is serious business, and lack of control over contest procedures can spell big trouble for broadcasters. Although alleged inappropriate considerations to political candidates was also an issue, the FCC denied renewal of the broadcast licenses of a group owner with stations in Indianapolis, Indiana; Omaha, Nebraska; and Vancouver, Washington primarily because of such lack of control.[24] In denying the renewals, the FCC said that although the political considerations were an issue, the "misconduct" in this area should "not be allowed to overshadow completely that fact that other misconduct has been proved which also has decisional significance."[25] The FCC scheduled the renewal of the Indianapolis stations for a hearing as the result of "contest improprieties" back in 1966, and notified the station that "its manner of conducting contests would be investigated in the hearing."[26] It further contended that the "safeguards to protect the public from fraud in contests continue to be inadequate...."[27] In its decision to deny renewal of the Star Stations, the FCC stated that: "During the period 1966–1968, [the] stations conducted four contests in which their practices were not adequate to insure that no abuse would occur, and in at least two of those contests, [a] $1,000 Mystery Melody Contest and [b] Black Box Contest, actual misconduct did take place."[28]

The FCC has been particularly cautious about contests directed toward children, and it admonished a Washington, D.C. station for conducting one that seemed to be misleading. An adult viewer apparently became upset when, although he saw the children's program host dial his number, his phone did not ring. The program was prerecorded. A local newspaper publicized the incident, and the station, responding to an FCC inquiry about the matter, said that it had started to run an aural announcement to accompany an already-running video announcement that the program was prerecorded. The children's program had also promoted a "bike-a-day" for the winners, but had actually given away bags of toys for part of the contest period. The FCC thus felt that the contest was potentially misleading on a number of counts. For one thing, the video-only notice would be of little value to preschool children who could not read. Second, the bike-a-day promotion might mislead a child to believe that every child who answered the host's question would receive a bicycle, which was not the case. And third, the promise of bicycles as prizes when toys were actually awarded was clearly misleading. As a result of the Washington experience, the FCC put broadcasters on notice that in broadcasting a children's contest, licencees should be "particularly careful" not to mislead the audience.

The FCC's new rule governing contests makes enforcement more effective and takes it beyond the license renewal process. Although stations continue to administer contests, the new rule has at least forewarned them that the FCC is ready to scrutinize station conduct in this area.

broadcasting lotteries and lottery information

One type of contest the Commission and the Federal courts do not condone, regardless of how "public" it may be, is the broadcast of a lottery. To be considered a lottery, three things must be present: (1) prize, (2) chance, and (3) consideration.

Just imagine that you are the general manager of a radio station and want to increase your ratings by conducting a contest. In the process, you also want to earn the station some money. You devise a scheme whereby listeners can purchase a gold star with a number on it. The gold stars cost $1.00 each and can be bought from local stores whose commercials run next to the promotional announcements for the contest. Each hour, you draw a number from a hat corresponding to a number on one of the gold stars. The person holding the winning number will receive a prize donated by the local stores. You are very careful to announce all of the "material terms" listed in our discussion of contests. Would you be in violation of the law?

Yes. You would be broadcasting a lottery under the definition punishable by law.[29] The three lottery factors were all present in your contest. You awarded a *prize* to each person with a lucky number on his or her gold star. Second, the selection of the winning number was by *chance,* drawn from a hat. Chance is also present in spinning a wheel of fortune, in roulette, in selecting names of persons randomly generated by a computer, or in taking guesses on something in which knowledge is not necessary.[30] The third element, *consideration,* was also present, since you charged $1.00 for a gold star to enter the contest. Variations of the three elements can still classify a contest as a lottery. If it is necessary to purchase a product before receiving a gold star, then consideration is present.[31] Keep in mind that a lottery must have *all three* conditions present—prize, chance, and consideration—to be defined as a lottery under law.

The statute under which violations are prosecuted is found in the United States Code, Title 18, the same law governing broadcast of obscene, indecent, or profane language. Section 1304 governing lotteries states:

> Whoever broadcasts by means of any radio station for which a license is required by any law of the United States, or whoever, operating any such station, knowingly permits the broadcasting of, any advertisement of or information concerning any lottery, gift enterprise, or similar scheme, offering prizes dependent in whole or in part upon lot or chance, or any list of the prizes drawn or awarded by means of any such lottery, gift enterprise, or scheme, whether said list contains any part or all of such prizes, shall be fined no more than $1,000 or imprisoned not more than one year, or both. Each day's broadcasting shall constitute a separate offense.[32]

The Communications Act also gives the FCC the authority to deny a construction permit, license, renewal of license, or any other authorization of a broadcasting station, when violations of the lottery rules are an issue.[33]

Notice also that Section 1304 prohibits a person from broadcasting " . . . any advertisement of or information concerning any lottery. . . ." This means that broadcasters are prohibited from running announcements that tell about anyone else's lottery, as well as their own. If a local car dealer decides to devise a contest which meets the three elements of a lottery, airing commercials publicizing his contest could jeopardize a broadcaster's license as much as if he ran the contest himself. Recent promotional contests involving banks and savings and loan institutions have put broadcasters on special alert.[34] When a person must first open a savings account in order to be eligible for a prize awarded in a free drawing, it is considered a lottery. And announcements do not have to be commercial to violate the law either. Simple community calendars or local bulletin boards announced as part of regular programming can trip up a broadcaster. Moreover, a commercial establishment does not even have to sponsor the event. The Ladies' Aid Society could get a station into as much trouble as the local bank.

enforcing lottery violations: FCC precedent and the wook decision

The FCC has not hesitated to enforce the lottery statutes. In *Ohio Quests, Inc.,* a licensee was found to have violated Section 1304 when an experienced operator made improper broadcasts without the knowledge or consent of the FCC.[35] In the case of *Laury Associates, Inc.,* the FCC determined that ignorance of the law was no excuse.[36] In the case of *University of Florida,* the FCC judged that even though a licensee may receive information in good faith for broadcast from an advertising agency, the licensee is still responsible for the content of the information being broadcast and accountable for violations of Section 1304.[37]

The FCC also denied license renewal to a station for broadcasting information construed to be a lottery. The license of WOOK in Washington, D.C. was revoked when, among other accumulated violations, it was found guilty of broadcasting a scheme whereby "ministers" enabled ". . . listeners to receive financial blessings, . . ." which turned out to be winning money in an illegal numbers game.[38] In the renewal hearing, a member of the Washington, D.C. police force testified that the illegal numbers game was prevalent in WOOK's listening area, and that people could place small bets on numbers determined by prices paid on horse races at a nearby track.

The Commission cited an "alleged testimonial," which had been read over the air:

> The first time I came to see you, I was blessed for $135 for a quarter, and the second time I came to see you I received $540 for a $1.00 investment. And the last time I was there I really hit the jackpot because I placed $10 where you told me to and the Lord blessed me with over $5,000.

The FCC noted that the ratio used for payoffs and referred to in the alleged testimonial "was the exact payoff for a winning number."

Many states have now adopted lotteries as a means of raising revenue. But there is a difference in broadcasting information about state lotteries and the type of information broadcast in the WOOK decision. Exempt are the numbers of winning tickets in state lotteries broadcast as part of a newscast. The ruling was evolved through the courts after a Wildwood, New Jersey broadcaster asked the Commission to rule on the legality of broadcasting the state's winning number.[39] The FCC said it was illegal, and the case went to the appeals court. The court said the FCC's position was in violation of the First Amendment and Section 326 of the Communications Act. The case was appealed to the Supreme Court, but Congress, meanwhile, had passed a law amending it to the Criminal Code exempting state-sponsored lotteries from the federal lottery statute. So now broadcasts, advertisements, and other promotional announcements for state lotteries are permitted on stations in states that hold state-sponsored lotteries. The Supreme Court, in view of the Congressional enactment, sent the case back to the Circuit Court, which affirmed its earlier ruling. There has yet to be a challenge on the constitutionality of broadcasting the winning number in a local lottery that is judged to be a legitimate news item in the community served by the station. All in all, broadcasters have found that adherence to the law is an easier route than a long court battle.

summary

Commercial programming on radio had its beginning in the 1920s, when the toll broadcasting concept was introduced by AT&T's station, WEAF, in New York City. Following WEAF's experiments and FTC involvement in the competitive practices of early commercial radio, broadcasting gradually established itself as a commercial enterprise, with commercial sponsorship becoming its prime source of income.

At the same time, both the broadcast and the print media had little precedent for what could or could not be placed on the air. First Amendment concerns over advertising did not appear to any great degree until 1942, with the case of *Valentine* v. *Chrestensen,* which placed limited controls over the distribution of advertising but not on advertising content. Not until 1976, in the case of the *Virginia Pharmacy Board* v. *Virginia Consumer Council* did the Supreme Court take a strong stand in favor of First Amendment rights for commercial speech.

Broadcast advertising can fall under both state and federal jurisdiction. On the state level, a landmark New Mexico case upheld the right of the state to prohibit a radio station from accepting advertising from optometrists in Texas. At the federal level, both the FCC and the FTC are involved in regulating advertising. Through its Bureau of Consumer Protection, the FTC watches over the content of advertising, occasionally ordering a company to air corrective advertising or imposing cease-and-desist orders against others. The FCC can control the content of advertising through its ability to enforce both the public interest standard of the Communications Act of 1934 and the Fairness Doctrine.

Violating FCC rules by conducting improper station contests can result in sizable fines or even license revocation. Some of the practices the FCC considers deceptive include failing to award prizes, disseminating false information about the nature and amount of prizes, and changing the rules of a contest without advising the public. Broadcasting lotteries is strictly prohibited by the FCC, although some provisions are made for broadcasting the results of state-supported lotteries. The three elements comprising a lottery are prize, chance, and consideration.

material for analysis

Ever since the "payola" scandals of the 1950s, when disc jockeys received special considerations for playing certain records, the FCC has been increasingly concerned about behind-the-scenes gratuities being provided employees of radio and television stations. Section 508 of the Communications Act spells out the law for disclosure of these gratuities. Figure 7-1 shows a typical certification form used by a television station to comply with the law. We will also examine specific FCC Rules which apply to Sec. 508, as well as FCC Rules covering the broadcast of lottery information and fraudulent billing practices.

The Communications Act of 1934 — Selected Provisions

EMPLOYEE'S ACCEPTING PAYMENTS FOR BROADCAST MATERIAL

sec. 508

(a) Subject to subsection (d), any employee of a radio station who accepts or agrees to accept from any person (other than such station), or any person (other than such station) who pays or agrees to pay such employee, any money, service or other valuable consideration for the broadcast of any matter over such station shall, in advance of such broadcast, disclose the fact of such acceptance or agreement to such station.

(b) Subject to subsection (d), any person who, in connection with the production or preparation of any program or program matter which is intended for broadcasting over any radio station, accepts or agrees to accept, or pays or agrees to pay, any money, service or other valu-

WTHR
Indianapolis 13
1401 NORTH MERIDIAN STREET

CERTIFICATION

The undersigned employee hereby acknowledges his agreement with the statement below and makes his adherence to it a condition of employment with WTHR-TV, with full knowledge that any violation of this policy may subject him to immediate dismissal.

I agree as follows that:

1. Other than normal gifts and reciprocal favors given or received in the normal course of business such as at Christmas time, I will not accept any outside compensation or other valuable consideration from record companies, or other persons advertising or promoting products or services or supplying programs to the station, which compensation or other valuable consideration is intended to influence or induce material broadcast or prepared for broadcast by me. If I should receive from any one of these people or companies any gift — regardless of the giver's intention — totalling in excess of $25 in any calendar year, it will be promptly reported to management or to its representative so that a decision may be made as to the disposition of the gift.

2. Unless the name of a commercial establishment or commercial enterprise is essential to a story, episode, or anecdote, I agree not to broadcast or cause to be broadcast, any mention of such commercial establishments or commercial enterprises or product.

3. I am familiar with Sections 317 and 508 of the Communications Act of 1934, as amended, and Section 73.1212 of the Commission's Rules and Regulations, and agree to abide by them.

4. I will not, without prior written approval from management or its representative, acquire any ownership interests in or any financial involvement with any business such as a record shop, a record distributorship or a record company, or any other business supplying program material to WTHR-TV.

I hereby certify that I have read, understand, and agree to the rules and the policies set forth in this statement.

_____
Signature

_____
Date

Figure 7-1

able consideration for the inclusion of any matter as a part of such program matter, shall, in advance of such broadcast, disclose the fact of such acceptance or payment or agreement to the payee's employer, or to the person for whom such program or program matter is being produced, or to the licensee of such station over which such program is broadcast.

(c) Subject to subsection (d), any person who supplies to any other person any program or program matter which is intended for broadcasting over any radio station shall, in advance of such broadcast, disclose to such other person any information of which he has knowledge, or which has been disclosed to him, as to any money, service or other valuable consideration which any person has paid or accepted, or has agreed to pay or accept, for the inclusion of any matter as a part of such program or program matter.

(d) The provisions of this section requiring the disclosure of information shall not apply in any case where, because of a waiver made by the Commission under section 317(d), an announcement is not required to be made under section 317.

(e) The inclusion in the program of the announcement required by section 317 shall constitute the disclosure required by this section.

(f) The term "service or other valuable consideration" as used in this section shall not include any service or property furnished without charge or at a nominal charge for use on, or in connection with, a broadcast, or for use on a program which is intended for broadcasting over any radio station, unless it is so furnished in consideration for an identification in such broadcast or in such program of any person, product, service, trademark, or brand name beyond an identification which is reasonably related to the use of such service or property in such broadcast or such program.

(g) Any person who violates any provision of this section shall, for each such violation, be fined not more than $10,000 or imprisoned not more than one year, or both.

FCC Rules Governing the Broadcast of Lottery Information

SEC. 73.1211

(a) No licensee of an AM, FM or television broadcast station, except as in paragraph (c) of this section, shall broadcast any advertisement of or information concerning any lottery, gift enterprise, or similar scheme, offering prizes dependent in whole or in part upon lot or chance, or any list of the prizes drawn or awarded by means of any such lottery, gift enterprise or scheme, whether said list contains any part or all of such prizes.(18 USC §1304, 62 Stat 763).

(b) The determination whether a particular program comes within the provisions of paragraph (a) of this section depends on the facts of each case. However, the Commission will in any event consider that a program comes within the provisions of paragraph (a) of this section if in connection with such program a prize consisting of money or thing of value is awarded, to any person whose selection is dependent in whole or in part upon lot or chance, if as a condition of winning or competing for such prize, such winner or winners, are required to furnish any money, or thing of value or are required to have in their possession any product sold, manufactured, furnished or distributed by a sponsor of a program broadcast on the station in question.

(c) The provisions of paragraphs (a) and (b) of this section shall not apply to an advertisement, list of prizes or other information concerning a lottery conducted by a state acting under authority of state law when such information is broadcast: (1) by a radio or television broadcast station licensed to a location in that state, or (2) by a radio or television broadcast station licensed to a location in an adjacent state which also conducts such a lottery.

(d) For the purposes of paragraph (c) of this section, "lottery" means the pooling of proceeds derived from the sale of tickets or chances and alotting those proceeds or parts thereof by chance to one or more chance takers or ticket purchasers. It does not include the placing or accepting of bets or wagers on sporting events or contests.

FCC Rules Governing Fraudulent Billing Practices

SEC. 73.1205

No licensee of a standard, FM, or television broadcast station shall knowingly issue or knowingly cause to be issued to any local, regional or national advertiser, advertising agency, station representative, manufacturer, distributor, jobber, or any other party, any bill, invoice, affidavit or other document which contains false information concerning the amount actually charged by the licensee for the broadcast advertising for which such bill, invoice, affidavit or other document is issued, or which misrepresents the nature or content of such advertising, or which misrepresents the quantity of advertising actually broadcast (number or length of advertising messages) or which substantially and/or materially misrepresents the time of day at which it was broadcast, or which misrepresents the date on which it was broadcast.

(b) Where a licensee and any program supplier have entered into a contract or other agreement obligating the licensee to supply any document providing specified information concerning the broadcast of the program or program matter supplied, including noncommercial matter, the licensee shall not knowingly issue such a document containing information required by the contract or agreement that is false.

(c) A licensee shall be deemed to have violated this section if it fails to exercise reasonable diligence to see that its agents and employees do not issue documents containing the false information specified in (a) and (b) above.

questions for discussion and further research

1. How might the regulation of broadcasting have been changed if the Supreme Court had ruled differently in *Virginia Pharmacy Board*? In *Valentine* v. *Chrestensen*?

2. Do the regulations administered by the FTC and the fact that products can be "tested" provide adequate safeguards against false advertising? Would any additional safeguards withstand a test of constitutionality?

3. While the FCC attempts to guard against

unscrupulous contests run by broadcasters, the Commission has no authority over, or, for that matter, knowledge of, contests constructed by other businesses that might buy commercial time to publicize such contests. And although a broadcaster is responsible for safeguarding against misleading advertising, many times management simply cannot police the contest of every company or organization buying commercials. In light of this situation, should more stringent FCC rules be enacted to prohibit broadcasters from publicizing on the air contests which the station does not conduct?

4. Would an alternative solution be to have the broadcaster investigate every contest publicized on the station to determine if it meets the criteria established by the FCC for contests conducted by broadcasters?

5. Should there be regulations prohibiting broadcast publicity for businesses or events where the broadcaster knows a lottery takes place, even though the lottery itself is not publicized on the air? (Examples might be local fraternal lodges, race tracks, picnics, etc.)

6. A station is located in a state where gambling is illegal. Yet the station broadcasts commercials for a casino in a neighboring state, where gambling *is* legal. Since the station is licensed to serve the community where the station is located, should the station be prohibited from publicizing an activity which is illegal in the community it serves?

7. Some citizens' groups and government agencies have argued for more controls over television advertising directed toward children. Some of these arguments center on a child's lack of ability to distinguish real from fictional televised situations and on the fact that children have not matured to the point where they are responsible consumers of persuasive campaigns. Contests, especially when tied into commercial campaigns, add yet another influence on a child's response to such campaigns. In view of these facts, should controls be placed on contests directed toward children—controls which go beyond current FCC guidelines?

8. What issues surface when we attempt to apply theories of First Amendment free speech to "commercial" communication?

9. Would it be wise to eliminate all controls on advertising and let the marketplace and the consumer be the ultimate judges of the validity of advertising claims?

10. In businesses other than broadcasting, it is not unusual for the stronger of two businesses under the same owner to carry along a weaker business which needs financial help or is operating at a loss. In broadcasting, however, if combination rates are employed by two stations under the same owner, and the stations are not simulcasting, why should the FCC frown on the stronger station "carrying" along the weaker one? What effect would this have on a station's ability to operate in the public interest?

11. Is there a type of double standard adhered to in self-regulation which permits the advertising of beer and wine but not hard liquor? Although the influence of self-regulatory organizations such as the NAB is widespread, not all broadcasters belong to the NAB or subscribe to the NAB Codes. In view of this fact, why hasn't Congress moved to ban all hard liquor advertising from the airways, as it did with cigarettes?

12. Noncommercial public broadcasting stations, although not permitted to sell commercials, can obtain grants. When a specific program is made possible by a grant, the donor can be announced at the beginning and the end of the program. The practice has elicited the ire of some commercial broadcasters, especially when public stations solicit funds from the same sources that commercial stations use to get advertising. The tension between commercial and public broadcasting gets even stronger when public stations heavily promote a program and include the name of the donor in such promotions.
   Questions: Should public broadcasting stations continue to be prohibited from selling advertising? Should such stations be even more restricted and be prohibited from announcing the names of donors at the beginning and end of programs? Are there other alternatives which would better serve both commercial and public broadcasting stations?

13. Is the requirement that certification forms be signed by all employees an effective way of controlling special considerations that might be provided by companies who have a special interest in radio or television programming decisions?

14. What additional safeguards could be taken against such abuses?

additional resources

books

Bloom, P. N., *Advertising, Competition, and Public Policy: A Simulation Study,* Cambridge, Mass.: Ballinger Publishing Co., 1976.

Hyman, A., and M. B. Johnson, eds., *Advertising and Free Speech,* Lexington, Mass.: Lexington Books/Heath, 1977.

Paletz, D. L., R. E. Pearson, and D. L. Willis, *Politics in Public Service Advertising on Television,* New York: Praeger Publishers, 1977.

articles

Blake, H. M., and J. A. Blum, "Network Television Rate Practices: A Case Study in the Failure of Social Control of Price Discrimination," 74 *Yale Law Journal* 1339 (1965).

Blalock, J., "Television and Advertising," 28 *Federal Bar Journal* 341 (1968).

Brennan, P., ed., "Federalism and the Control of Radio and TV Lotteries," 49 *Journal of Criminal Law and Criminology* 579 (1959).

Collins, T. A., "Counter-Advertising in the Broadcast Media: Bringing the Administrative Process to Bear upon a Theoretical Imperative," 15 *William and Mary Law Review* 799 (1974).

Conlon, S. B., "Comparative Advertising: Whatever Happened to 'Brand X'?" 67 *Trademark Reporter* 407 (1977).

Farber, D. A., "Commercial Speech and First Amendment Theory," 74 *Northwestern University Law Review* 372 (1979).

Haas, J. M., "*Warner-Lambert Co.* v. *FTC:* The Possibilities and Limitations of Corrective Advertising," 13 *New England Law Review* 348 (1977).

Hanneman, G. J., W. J. McEwen, and S. A. Coyne, "Public Service Advertising on Television," 17 *Journal of Broadcasting* 387 (1973).

Hogan, T. R., "The Legal Implications of the Use of Mock-Ups in Television Commercials," 26 *University of Pittsburgh Law Review* 857 (1965).

Jentz, G. A., "Federal Regulation of Advertising: False Representations of Composition, Character, or Source and Deceptive Television Demonstrations," 6 *American Business Law Journal* 409 (1968).

Johnson, N., and T. A. Westen, "Twentieth-Century Soapbox: The Right to Purchase Radio and Television Time," 57 *Virginia Law Review* 574 (1971).

Kozyris, Ph.J., "Advertising Intrusion: Assault on the Senses, Trespass on the Mind—A Remedy through Separation," 36 *Ohio State Law Journal* 299 (1975).

Loevinger, L., "Politics of Advertising," 15 *William and Mary Law Review* 1 (1973).

O'Donnell, W. J., and K. J. O'Donnell, "Update: Sex-Role Messages in TV Commercials," 28 *Journal of Communication* 156 (1978).

Powell, J. T., "Broadcast Advertising of Medical Products and Services: Its Regulation by Other Nations," 25 *Federal Communications Bar Journal* 144 (1972).

Powell, J. T., "Protection of Children in Broadcast Advertising: The Regulatory Guidelines of Nine Nations," 26 *Federal Communications Bar Journal* 61 (1973).

Putz, C. D., Jr., "Fairness and Commercial Advertising: A Review and a Proposal," 6 *University of San Francisco Law Review* 215 (1972).

Ramey, C. R., "The Federal Communications Commission and Broadcast Advertising: An Analytical Review," 20 *Federal Communications Bar Journal* 71 (1966).

Reed, O. L., Jr., "Psychological Impact of TV Advertising and the Need for FTC Regulation," 13 *American Business Law Journal* 171 (1975).

Riley, S. G., and J. Shandle, "Commercial Use without Consent: Privacy or Property?" 51 *Journalism Quarterly* 718 (1974).

Scharf, L., "State Regulation of Radio Lotteries," *Wisconsin Law Review* 177 (1952).

Silverstein, A. J., and R. Silverstein, "Portrayal of Women in Television Advertising," 27 *Federal Communications Bar Journal* 71 (1974).

Simmons, S. J., "Commercial Advertising and the Fairness Doctrine: The New F.C.C. Policy in Perspective," 75 *Columbia Law Review* 1083 (1975).

Stromberg, R. E., "Radio Broadcast Rate Regulation," 10 *Air Law Review* 325 (1939).

Tufts, J. D., III, "Attorney Advertisement Protected by First Amendment (*Bates* v. *State*

Bar of Arizona, U.S. 1977)," 24 *Loyola Law Review* 164 (1978).

Whitman, F., "Advertising by Professionals," 16 *American Business Law Journal* 39 (1978).

cases

Adult Film Ass'n of America v. *Times Mirror Co.,* 3 Med.L.Rptr. 2292, 3 Med.L.Rptr. 2292 (L.S.Cty.Sup.Ct. 1978).

Banzhaf v. *F.C.C.* 405 F.2d 1082, 132 U.S.App. D.C. 14, 1 Med.L.Rptr. 2037 (1968), certiorari denied.

Beneficial Corp. v. *F.T.C.,* 542 F.2d 611 (1976).

Bigelow v. *Virginia,* 421 U.S. 809, 1 Med.L.Rptr. 1919 (1975).

Capital Broadcasting Co. v. *Kleindienst,* 405 U.S. 1000 (1972).

Capital Broadcasting Co. v. *Mitchell,* 333 F.Supp. 582 (D.C.D.C. 1971); affirmed 92 S.Ct. 1289, 405 U.S. 1000, 31 L.Ed. 472.

Columbia Broadcasting System, Inc., v. *Democratic National Committee,* 412 U.S. 94, 93 S.Ct. 2080, 36 L.Ed.2d 772, 1 Med.L.Rptr. 1855 (1973).

F.T.C. v. *R.F. Keppel & Bro., Inc.,* 291 U.S. 304 (1934).

Person v. *New York Post,* 427 F.Supp. 1297, 3 Med.L.Rptr. 1784 (E.D.N.Y. 1977).

Pittsburgh Press v. *Pittsburgh Commission on Human Relations,* 413 U.S. 376, 93 S.Ct. 2553, 37 L.Ed.2d 669, 1 Med.L.Rptr. 1908 (1973).

Valentine v. *Chrestensen,* 316 U.S. 52, 1 Med.L. Rptr. 1907 (1942).

Virginia State Board of Pharmacy v. *Virginia Citizens' Consumer Council, Inc.,* 425 U.S. 748, 96 S.Ct. 1817, 48 L.Ed.2d 346, 1 Med.L.Rptr. 1930 (1976).

III

Broadcast and Cable Operations

8

The
Station

The daily business of promoting the station, keeping a public inspection file, administering equal employment opportunity, conducting television community needs and ascertainment surveys, and renewing licenses are all part of the station's responsibilities. Both starting a new station and transferring ownership of an existing one also come under FCC jurisdiction. In this chapter we will explore these daily requirements of station operations and in the next chapter examine how cable systems operate.

Promoting the Station

Regulatory agencies are as concerned about stations' promotional practices as they are about the content of broadcast commercials. Competing in the market place is fine, but such activities as misleading the public (about coverage area or leadership in audience ratings) or artificially inflating rating surveys can bring the wrath of the FTC, the FCC, and even the ratings services down on a broadcaster. Making a promotional announcement to the effect that "we're number one" when the station is actually third in the ratings, or calling oneself the "leading news station" when a recognized rating service can dispute that claim, are actions that are *not* what the FCC considers to be in the public interest. In fact, they might even provoke a cease-and-desist order, a fine, or court proceedings.[1]

hypoing and the ratings game

The most common complaint about stations' promotional activities is *hypoing*. Hypoing is described as "unusual advertising or other promotional efforts, designed to increase audiences only during the survey period."[2] The FTC, not the FCC, prosecutes hypoing violations. Although the FCC examines charges of hypoing at license renewal time and has issued short-term license renewals to stations involved in hypoing, it forwards these complaints to the FTC.

The most common type of hypoing is a major station contest conducted when the rating services are taking their surveys. Stations often have listeners log the amount of quarter-hours they listen to the station during this time and award them money based on the amount of listenership. These contests are closely aligned to the rating services' diary methods. The problem arises when the contests are conducted only at survey time and not during other times of the year.

If a station calls the attention of the audience to a survey in progress, the rating company can note this on the cover of its published rating book. Abusing an audience rating can also mean trouble with the FCC. The FCC cited a case in which a station employee received a diary and gave it to a station secretary, who promptly filled out the diary showing that her household had watched the station from sign-on until sign-off time. In another case, a licensee was accused of purchasing diaries from people who had received them from the rating companies. The Commission warned stations that such practices "raise questions as to whether a licensee that engages in them is qualified to remain a licensee."

The Federal Trade Commission guidelines covering station promotion and advertising go beyond hypoing.[3] They charge broadcasters with the responsibility of seeing that claims about the composition of their audiences are truthful, that survey data are interpreted accurately, and that surveys are cited as being only statistical estimates.

The FCC instituted a rulemaking proceeding in 1975 to inquire about specific ratings regulations.[4] The rules, which were not adopted, had proposed a ban on "unusual advertising, contest or promotional activities" within four weeks of a rating period if the promotions were not conducted regularly throughout the year. Other provisions would have penalized stations for using old ratings data and banned for three months before a rating period any promotion which rewards people for "stating that they listen to the licensee's station." The rule making was not adopted primarily because: (1) it was difficult to apply the rules to such factors as fall television promotions for new schedules, and (2) in larger markets, ratings are taken all the time. Thus, any change in a promotional activity could be construed as hypoing. Nevertheless, the proposed rulemaking did assure broadcasters that the Commission was serious and warned them that if the problem continued, the FCC might revoke a station's license.

The ratings services have also threatened serious reprisals against stations that abuse the ratings process or its results. Arbitron clamped down on stations in Arizona and in Colorado, which were conducting contests that could inflate diary responses.[5] Arbitron's sanctions could have included canceling the rating survey altogether, publishing a special supplement about the two stations, describing the inflationary contest in that supplement, and sending the supplement with an explanation to subscribing broadcasters, advertisers, and ad agencies as well as to the Advertising Research Foundation.[6]

Why are rating services so concerned about hypoing when they are paid by the station to conduct the survey? The rating services have learned that they can only be successful when the public and the industry have confidence in their products. Permitting stations to capriciously conduct hypoing and other questionable promotional activities can reflect poorly on both the rating services and their customers, the broadcasters.

representing coverage maps

Another area related to station promotion is the accurate representation of station coverage areas. The geographic area covered by a station translates into audience size and, consequently, into advertising dollars. Abuse can abound in this area as readily as it can with audience ratings. In a station's promotional and advertising literature, a coverage map *must* be an accurate representation of the station's ability to reach its listeners. Attorney Jim Popham lists some common inaccuracies associated with coverage maps:

(1) Overstating the population in the station's coverage area.
(2) Labeling the map as "coverage survey" without additional explanation.
(3) Failing to identify the communities on the map.
(4) Using contours based on measurements not taken in accordance with Commission requirements.
(5) Failing to label contours or other map features legibly, and . . .
(6) Failing to include a mileage scale in the legend.[7]

Misrepresenting a coverage map can reflect on the licensee in the same way as misuse of ratings data can. At license renewal time, the station is held accountable for all of its actions.

The Public Inspection File

As the trustee of the public domain, broadcasting stations are required by law to keep certain documents and information open for public inspection.[8] This means that members of the general public are entitled to inspect documents from the file. You can make a visit to a station at any time during normal business hours, and although the station has the right to ask for personal identification, you should not be "interrogated" about your motives for wanting to see the file. If you would like certain documents copied, then the station can charge you a reasonable fee to have the material reproduced.

What is contained in the public file varies somewhat among the different types of stations—AM, FM, and TV, as well as both noncommercial and commercial stations. So be sure that the station is required to keep a certain document before you request to see it. Your best route in this instance is to consult the

FCC rules. Our discussion of public inspection files will be a general one. And remember, it varies from station to station.

technical information

A public file contains technical information directly related to the construction and daily operation of the station. Construction permits, major changes in frequency, output power, or a change in the location of the station or the transmitters are typical inclusions. Do not expect to find minor technical information, such as pointers on the new antenna support wires, information about a new control board, or data about the new record racks. If a new construction permit has been granted, and if the FCC grants an extension of the permit, the extension is in the public file. The file will also include correspondence related to these changes. A copy of the station's coverage area (contour maps) should be in there, as should reports listing the ownership of the station and any FCC decisions arising from a hearing on the station's license renewal. A copy of the license renewal and the logs submitted as part of the license renewal should also be available.

political broadcasts

Politicians may be interested in examining the file's political documents. Most of what a station does in the way of political programming is an open book to the public, including candidates and their opponents. Requests for political time by legally qualified candidates, a record of what was done with those requests, and the rate charged for that time are kept for two years from the date of request. The spirit of the law behind the political file is to keep access to the airwaves open to any and every legally qualified candidate. This prevents an unscrupulous broadcaster or politician from claiming that a candidate has not talked with the station or bought any advertising—thus discouraging the opponent from buying time—when in fact the candidate has purchased and aired a series of political commercials.

Other information in the file includes the FCC procedural manual, *The Public and Broadcasting,* and copies of letters from the public (unless they are obscene, or the sender has specifically requested that they be kept confidential). Letters of little importance to the station, such as love letters to a movie star or fan mail for the local anchorperson, may also be absent.

Accessibility of Logs

Although not considered part of the public file per se, television and some radio program logs or copies of these logs are open for public inspection, beginning forty-five days after the date on the log. The requirements for viewing program logs are more strict than for other kinds of information. You'll need to make an appointment, identify yourself and tell who you represent, and state why you want to see the logs. If you are part of a large group of people who want to view the logs, the station may choose to limit the number of people. You can obtain copies of the logs, but, again, you will probably be asked to pay for the cost of reproduction. You'll have a reasonable time to inspect the logs, but if you want to come back again, the station may charge you for the time spent by its personnel in supervising your efforts. More specific guidelines on public inspection files are found in the FCC Rules.

Administering Equal Employment Opportunity Programs

The federal government's insistence that women and minorities be added to the work force has been implemented by the formation of the Equal Employment Opportunity Commission and the requirement that affirmative action measures be taken by business and industry throughout the United States. Although the Federal Communications Commission is not directly responsible for enforcing affirmative action programs, it has taken steps to assure that broadcasting stations do not fall behind in their commitments to affirmative action.[9] An extensive explanation of how a station administers its affirmative action program is required along with its license renewal. And when considering a license renewal, the FCC will evaluate the current affirmative action program in comparison with the one in the previous license renewal. By using the "public interest" clause of the Communications Act, the FCC is able to put some teeth into its requirements. Its power is based on the rationale that a "broadcaster who refuses to hire minority and women employees will face a difficult, if not insurmountable obstacle to the presentation of programming to meet the problems, needs and interests of minorities and women."

model affirmative action plan

The FCC has outlined a model affirmative action program for all stations.[10] Let's examine the steps that we could take to help assure a responsible affirmative action program. Keep in mind that our commitment would be communicated in writing to the FCC as part of the station's license renewal. (Our discussion here is a highly abbreviated version of the full FCC text.)

(1) Statement of General Policy.   The first part of our program would consist of a statement committing the station to affirmative action in all areas of station business, which would include not only hiring employees but also promoting, compensating, and terminating them. Take note of the word terminating—if we aren't going to discriminate in hiring, then we can't do so in firing. Overall, the program must be a positive effort, assuring equal opportunity without regard to sex, race, national origin, color, or religion.

an example of an equal employment opportunity statement, that was used by Jefferson-Pilot Broadcasting Company of Charlotte, North Carolina, can be seen in Figure 8–1.

(2) Responsibility for Implementation.   Our next responsibility would be to implement our commitment. We would want to appoint someone at the station as our affirmative action administrator. If we have delegated the responsibility

II. EQUAL EMPLOYMENT OPPORTUNITY

It is the policy of our Company not to discriminate in its employment and personnel practices because of a person's race, color, religion, sex, national origin or age. Discriminatory employment practices are specifically prohibited by Title VII of Civil Rights Act of 1964, the Federal Communications Commission, and the Equal Employment Opportunity Commission. It is, therefore, the responsibility of all management and supervisory personnel to assure compliance with the policies and procedures which follow in this section.

A. FAIR EMPLOYMENT PRACTICES POLICY

On August 12, 1969 the Board of Directors of Jefferson-Pilot Broadcasting Company adopted the Fair Employment Practices Policy set forth below.

"As in the past, equal opportunity in employment shall be afforded to all qualified persons, and no person shall be discriminated against in employment by the Jefferson-Pilot Broadcasting Company because of sex, race, color, religion or national origin.

In order to assure equal opportunity in every aspect of employment, the practices set forth below will be followed as part of our positive continuing program.

The Management Committee, which includes, among others, the Managing Director of each division, shall have the responsibility to insure a positive application and earnest enforcement of the Company's policy of equal opportunity, and to establish a procedure to review and control managerial and supervisory performance. The Committee shall make periodic oral and written reports to the President respecting the implementation of its aforesaid responsibility and the responsibilities set forth below.

It shall be the responsibility of the Committee to inform all current and future employees of the Company's positive equal employment policy and program and invite their cooperation in the implementation thereof.

It shall be the responsibility of the Committee to communicate the Company's equal employment opportunity policy and program and its employment needs to sources of qualified applicants without regard to sex, race, color, religion or national origin, and solicit their recruitment assistance on a continuing basis.

It shall be the responsibility of the Committee to conduct a continuing campaign to exclude every form of prejudice or discrimination based upon sex, race, color, religion or national origin from the station's personnel policies and practices and working conditions.

It shall be the responsibility of the Committee to conduct a continuing review of job structure and employment practices and to adopt positive recruitment, training, job design and other measures needed in order to insure genuine equality of opportunity to participate fully in all organizational units, occupations and levels of responsibility in the Company."

Figure 8-1

for firing and hiring to other administrators, such as a sales manager or news director, then we will want to make sure they also adhere to our commitment.

(3) Policy Dissemination. But it is not enough merely to have an affirmative action program. We need to publicize it through such means as posters, which tell applicants or employees where to write if they feel they have been discriminated against. The Department of Labor has posters available which contain such warnings. We could also put an affirmative action statement on the station's employment application.

(4) Recruitment. Hiring is usually the easiest task in an affirmative action program. What takes work is obtaining a pool of applicants from which to choose. We will need to recruit people by advertising our job openings. And in each ad, we will want to include a statement identifying our station as an equal opportunity employer. Potential women applicants can be reached via ads in newsletters such as *Matrix* of Women in Communication, Inc. (WICI) and *News and Views* of American Women in Radio and Television (AWRT). Minorities can be reached through similar publications. Employment agencies and the placement services at local colleges are two additional avenues. Keep in mind that we will need to provide the FCC with a list of the organizations we contacted and the number of applicants received from each one.

(5) Training. If our station is small, developing a full-scale minority training program may be difficult. On the other hand, an internship program initiated with a local college can at least show a good faith effort within our means. If we set up such a program, or if we are large enough to have a minority training program, we will want to describe these efforts to the FCC.

(6) Availability Survey. In order for the FCC to compare the success of our program with the work force in our local area, we will need to supply them with a recent availability survey. Such a survey discusses such factors as the percentages of women and minorities in the work force from which we can directly recruit—usually the metropolitan area in which the station is licensed or, in some cases, the county in which it is located.

(7) Current Employment Survey. In addition to the FCC's model EEO program, our station should also file an annual employment report. As part of the public file, this report details the number of women and members of minority groups who are employed by the station and notes how many are in top management positions. We may even want to supplement the employment report with a description of women and minority employees in all job classifications within the station. (For a more complete analysis, consult the Annual Employment Report at the end of this chapter.)

(8) Job Hires. Section 8 of our EEO program will note the number of women and minority employees hired in the past twelve months. If, in our opinion, not enough minority applicants are applying for positions, we will want to explain how we are going to beef up our recruiting practices in the future.

(9) Promotion. A responsible affirmative action program deals not only with hiring but also with promotion. When openings develop within our organization, we should always scan the current personnel to see who might be qualified for the jobs. If we find them, let's reward them. Visible opportunities for upward mobility increase station morale. Encourage women and minority em-

ployees to apply for advancement within the organization, and be sure to report the number of those affirmative action promotions to the FCC.

(10) Effectiveness of the Affirmative Action Plan. In reporting the results of our affirmative action program to the FCC, we will want to include an objective evaluation of our program's effectiveness.[11] As with the hiring data (#8), we will want to examine how the program can be improved if it is not meeting our expectations.[12]

fcc evaluation

What does the Commission look for when evaluating a station's affirmative action program? At the very least, the FCC suggests that it will see whether the station follows the ten-point program. The Commission will then examine the percentage of minority and female employees, both overall and in the top four job categories (see the Annual Employment Report at the end of the Chapter).

As a general rule, for most stations, the full-time minority and women employees must equal 50 percent of the work force availability overall in the upper four job categories. If not, the station could be headed for a review.[12]

Sexual Harassment

Broadcasters are becoming increasingly aware of the effects of sexual harassment both on individuals and the overall operation of broadcasting stations. Recent court rulings consider sexual harassment a form of sexual discrimination under Title VII of the 1964 Civil Rights Act. What exactly constitutes sexual harassment is something which must be determined by the circumstances surrounding each incident. Moreover, because such incidents often occur in private, the testimony of the plaintiff and the defendant without the benefit of other witnesses makes the sexual harassment area of discrimination law particularly difficult to determine.

Specifically, the Equal Employment Opportunity Commission considers unlawful sexual harassment to occur:

(1)   When submission to such sexual conduct is "explicitly or implicitly" a condition of an individual's employment;

(2)   When submission to or rejection of such sexual conduct becomes the basis of employment decisions "affecting" an employee; or

(3)   When such sexual conduct has the purpose or effect of substantially interfering with an individual's job performance or creating an intimidating, hostile or offensive working atmosphere.[13]

Because charges of sexual harassment can result in a potential violation of a station's affirmative action policy, communications attorneys advise stations to make an affirmative effort to make employees aware of what constitutes sexual harassment, penalties for those engaging in sexual harassment, and procedures for filing complaints of sexual harassment.

Ascertaining Community Needs

So that broadcasters can better serve their communities and meet the public interest standards of the FCC, the commission requires licensees to conduct regular assessments of the problems and needs affecting their individual communities. It then becomes the responsibility of the broadcaster to meet those needs through programming. These community needs and ascertainment surveys are another means of obtaining feedback from the broadcasters' communities. They can be quite involved, depending on the size of the station's market. Although requirements are more strict for television than radio, their importance cannot be overlooked, considering the fact that such surveys can be used as evidence in license challenges,[14] regardless of FCC requirements.

The guidelines that broadcasters follow in conducting the community needs and ascertainment surveys were first spelled out in the *Primer on Ascertainment of Community Problems,* which was issued by the FCC in 1971.[15] In further clarifying those guidelines in 1975, the FCC added noncommercial broadcasting stations to the list of those required to conduct the surveys.[16] Methodologies and reporting requirements differ among stations. When the FCC deregulated radio in 1981, non-commercial stations retained the ascertainment requirement.

demographic profile

For television stations and some non-commercial radio stations conducting detailed ascertainment, the process consists of three parts. The first is a *demographic profile.* Checking census data, the broadcaster determines the population of the community served by the station, the percentage of males and females in the population, the percentage of minorities, the percentage of older people (over sixty-five), and the percentage of youths (under seventeen). This demographic profile then shows the broadcaster what proportion of people will provide a good cross-section of information about the community's problems. For example, if the demographic profile shows that 30 percent of the residents are over sixty-five years of age, yet only 5 percent of the station's general public survey consists of older people, the broadcaster will need to conduct additional interviews with this population. Although the FCC has avoided requiring broadcasters to match their surveys precisely with the demographic profiles, the profiles do act as guides.

community leader interviews

The second part of the community needs and ascertainment survey consists of *community leader interviews.* Here the broadcaster interviews the leaders of different elements from which the community leaders can be drawn:

1. Agriculture
2. Business
3. Charities
4. Civic, neighborhood, and fraternal organizations
5. Consumer services

6. Culture
7. Education
8. Environment
9. Government (local, county, state, and federal)
10. Labor
11. Military
12. Minority and ethnic groups
13. Organizations of and for the elderly
14. Organizations of and for women
15. Organizations of and for youth (including children) and students
16. Professions
17. Public safety, health, and welfare
18. Recreation
19. Religion
20. Other

If we were interviewing people who represented our community's *educational* elements (#7), we might interview the local college president or administrators, and perhaps some professors. We might also interview local school board members, the principal of the local high school, the principals of the local elementary schools, and the teachers and officers in the local parent-teacher organizations. How many of these community leaders we interviewed would depend on the size of our community. A good rule of thumb would be the following combinations, suggested by the FCC:

population of city of license	number of consultations
10,001 to 25,000	60
25,001 to 50,000	100
50,001 to 200,000	140
200,001 to 500,000	180
Over 500,000	220

Although we would probably conduct even more community leader interviews, the FCC expects stations at least to fulfill these minimum requirements.[17] The community leaders must be contacted by station management or personnel under direct management supervision. And we would need to keep track of how many women and minority community leaders we contacted, the recommendation being that those interviews be conducted directly by management-level personnel.[18]

general public survey

The third phase of ascertainment would be to conduct a *general public survey.* Here we need to select a random sample of the community. We would interview each one in that sample, either in person, by telephone, or by mail.[19] Private firms may contract to do the surveys for some stations. Whatever method we choose, we would want not only to poll our audience on their opinions about the community but also to obtain their demographic characteristics. Again, the information in our demographic profile would be our guide, and we would want to match this as closely as possible to be sure we obtained a representative cross-section of the general public.

We would probably ask one of two types of questions—open-ended questions or close-ended questions.

Open-Ended Questions. Open-ended questions permit the greatest flexibility of answer. Consider the following: *What do you feel is the most important problem facing our community?* The person answering this open-ended question has a wide latitude of possibilities.

Close-Ended Questions. Now consider this close-ended question: *Is there a problem with public transportation in the community?* Yes_____ No_____. The only acceptable answer is either yes or no. The advantage of the open-ended question is its less restrictive nature. Its disadvantage is the difficulty in tabulating its various answers. Whatever questions we decide to ask, we would then conduct the survey and organize our results, ranking in importance those problems which were affecting our community.[20]

overlooking community elements

At first glance, it might appear that the procedures we have been discussing are quite thorough in locating community leaders. Such is not necessarily the case, and a station's general manager would need to at least consider getting feedback from leaders of smaller, more elusive groups. The FCC has suggested that broadcasters be aware of these groups, which might be overlooked in a traditional community leader survey. Researchers Orville G. Walker, Jr., and William Rudelius examined the procedures that are needed to reach this "voiceless" community.[21] They defined these "voiceless" groups as: "people with a common problem who were not formally organized and who had no widely recognized leaders or spokesperson in the community." The two researchers classified these groups into three categories.

The first category is the *Past-in, Future-out* groups. These people were once in the mainstream of society, but now watch from the sidelines. They include such people as the elderly, the mentally ill, and the deaf. The FCC ascertainment guidelines make provisions for the elderly. But Walker and Rudelius found that some people are equally concerned about improving medical facilities for the mentally ill or about arranging for captioned subtitles on television programs for the hard of hearing. These people had not voiced these concerns, however. No one had asked them.

The second category is the *Past-in, Future-in* groups. Here would be found such people as "runaway teenagers, unwed mothers, VD victims, and prisoners." This group has been in the mainstream in the past and intends to return in the future, once their physical or personal problems are overcome. Although the Minnesota researchers found that these people were not in need of considerable communication from broadcasters, the unwed mothers wished for information on special parental care, and the prisoners were receptive to educational programs.

The third group is the *Past-out, Future-out* people, those who are minorities through such factors as race or disabilities. They felt "more or less permanently removed from the mainstream of American life because of a lack of understanding or outright discrimination." The FCC ascertainment provides for reaching racial minorities and women, but ends there. The two researchers discovered that the primary desire for these groups was to have their story told, for broadcasters to communicate the negative misconceptions and stereotypes that had been attached to them in the past.

Walker and Rudelius also pointed out that, consistent with the Past-out, Future-out groups' "desire for a more realistic and truthful portrayal of their cultures and lifestyles, most of these groups expressed a very strong desire for greater influence over the creation and execution of television programs about themselves." In other words, these groups were less complacent about the type of messages being directed toward them. To these groups, media access was important. "Consequently, they see creative control and active participation—both in front of and behind the cameras—as the only guarantee that a television program or series would accurately reflect their viewpoint."

The Station License

Standard AM, FM, and TV stations are licensed by the FCC. Each license is valid for three years, although longer renewals of up to 5 years are frequently a topic of policy makers. The license, also called *station authorization* or *instrument of authorization* (Figure 8–2), specifies the authorized power of the station, its hours of operation, the brand name and model of the transmitter and the antenna, the location of the transmitter, the latitude and longitude of the antenna, and the name and address of the licensee. Television and AM licenses contain such additional information as directional antenna patterns or video transmission frequencies. The expiration date is coordinated to expire along with all of the other stations' licenses in the state.

A license is the single most important document that a station possesses. And every three years, the station must apply to renew that license and continue operating.

License Renewal

For a small number of stations, about 5 percent, the FCC requires a somewhat lengthy "audit" form to be used for license renewal.[22] On the longer forms, such things as programming goals and actual documents kept at the station and normally used only for FCC Field Office inspections are required to be sent to the FCC in Washington, D.C. with the license renewal. It permits the FCC to keep track of the effectiveness of the general committment to the public interest with a

FCC Form 352-A

United States of America
FEDERAL COMMUNICATIONS COMMISSION

File No. BRH-2019

Call Sign: W F Y N-FM

FM BROADCAST STATION LICENSE

Subject to the provisions of the Communications Act of 1934, as amended, treaties, and Commission Rules, and further subject to conditions set forth in this license,[1] the LICENSEE

FLORIDA KEYS BROADCASTING CORPORATION

is hereby authorized to use and operate the radio transmitting apparatus hereinafter described for the purpose of broadcasting for the term ending 3 a.m. Local Time: **FEBRUARY 1, 1979**

The licensee shall use and operate said apparatus only in accordance with the following terms:

1. Frequency (MHz) . . . . : 92.5
2. Transmitter output power . . . . . : 10 kilowatts
3. Effective radiated power . . . . . : 25 kilowatts (Horiz.) & 23.5 kilowatts (Vert.)
4. Antenna height above
   average terrain (feet) . . . . : 135' (Horiz.) & 130' (Vert.)
5. Hours of operation . . . . : Unlimited
6. Station location . . . . : Key West, Florida
7. Main studio location . . . . :
   **Fifth Avenue Stock Island
   Key West, Florida**
8. Remote Control point . . . . . . :

9. Antenna & supporting structure : North Latitude: 24° 34' 01"
   West Longitude: 81° 44' 54"
   ANTENNA: COLLINS, 37M-5/300-C-5, Five-sections (Horiz. & Vert.), FM antenna side-mounted near the top of the north tower of WKIZ(AM) directional array. Overall height above ground 155 feet.
10. Transmitter location . . . . . . :
    **Fifth Avenue Stock Island
    Key West, Florida**

11. Transmitter(s) . . . . : COLLINS, 830-F-1A

12. Obstruction markings specifications in accordance with the following paragraphs of FCC Form 715: 1, 3, 11 & 21.
13. Conditions:

The Commission reserves the right during said license period of terminating this license or making effective any changes or modification of this license which may be necessary to comply with any decision of the Commission rendered as a result of any hearing held under the rules of the Commission prior to the commencement of this license period or any decision rendered as a result of any such hearing which has been designated but not held, prior to the commencement of this license period.

This license is issued on the licensee's representation that the statements contained in licensee's application are true and that the undertakings therein contained so far as they are consistent herewith, will be carried out in good faith. The licensee shall, during the term of this license, render such broadcasting service as will serve public interest, convenience, or necessity to the full extent of the privileges herein conferred.

This license shall not vest in the licensee any right to operate the station nor any right in the use of the frequency designated in the license beyond the term hereof, nor in any other manner than authorized herein. Neither the license nor the right granted hereunder shall be assigned or otherwise transferred in violation of the Communications Act of 1934. This license is subject to the right of use or control by the Government of the United States conferred by section 606 of the Communications Act of 1934.

[1] This license consists of this page and pages --

Dated: **JANUARY 28, 1976**

FEDERAL
COMMUNICATIONS
COMMISSION

Figure 8-2 (FCC Broadcast Operators Handbook)

smaller sample of stations, as opposed to monitoring the total performance of every station.

The majority of stations complete license renewal using the FCC's "post card" renewal form that is seen in Figure 8-3. It requires the station to list the name of the applicant (commonly the corporation under which the station operated), the call letters of the station, and the address. In addition, the renewal forms ask if the Annual Employment Report and the Ownership Report are on file at the FCC. Both forms need some explanation here, since they are an important part of a station's operating procedure.

annual employment report

The Annual Employment Report lists the number of employees at the station who work in different job categories and the more detailed information on race and sex of the employees. The Annual Employment Report consists of four pages, the first of which contains basic statistical information about the station. The second page lists the address of the headquarters office (applicable to group owners) and the call letters and locations of the station(s). The third page (Figure 8-4) of the Annual Employment Report is the most detailed, with the upper half listing the various job categories for full-time employees, which include: "Officials and

Application for Renewal of License for Commercial and Non-Commercial AM, FM or TV Broadcast Station

1. Name of Applicant	Call Letters	Street Address	City	State	Zip Code

2. Are the following reports on file at the Commission:

(a) The three most recent Annual Employment Reports (FCC Form 395)
☐Yes ☐No
If No, attach as Exhibit No._____ an explanation.

(b) The applicant's Ownership report (FCC Form 323 or 323-E)
☐Yes ☐No
If No, give the following information:
Date last ownership report was filed.
Call letters of the renewal application with which it was filed.

THE APPLICANT hereby waives any claim to the use of any particular frequency or of the ether as against the regulatory power of the United States, because of the previous use of the same, whether by license or otherwise, and requests an authorization in accordance with this application. (See Section 304 of the Communications Act.)
THE APPLICANT acknowledges that all the statements mae in this application and attached exhibits are considered material representations and that all the exhibits are a material part hereof and are incorporated herein as set out in full in the application.

3. Is the applicant in compliance with the provisions of Section 310 of the Communications Act of 1934, as amended, relating to interests of aliens and foreign governments?

☐ Yes ☐ No   If No, attach as Exhibit No._____ an explanation.

CERTIFICATION

I certify that the statements in this application are true, complete and correct to the best of my knowledge and belief, and are made in good faith.

4. Since the filing of the applicant's last renewal for this station or other major application, has an adverse finding been made, a consent decree been entered, or final action been approved by any court or administrative body with respect to the applicant or parties to the application concerning any civil or criminal suit, action, or proceeding, brought under the provisions of any federal, state, territorial or local law relating to the following: any felony, lotteries, unlawful restraints or monopolies, unlawful combinations, contracts or agreements in restraint of trade; the use of unfair methods of competition; fraud; unfair labor practices; or discrimination?

☐ Yes ☐ No   If Yes, attach as Exhibit No. _____ a full description, including identification of the court or administrative body, proceeding by file number, the person and matters involved, and the disposition of the litigation.

Signed and dated this _____ day of _____ 19 _____

Name of Applicant_____

By Signature _____

Title _____

5. Has the applicant placed in its public inspection file at the appropriate times the documentation required by Section 73.3526 and 73.3527 of the Commission's rules?

☐ Yes ☐ No   If No, attach as Exhibit No. _____ a complete statement of explanation.

WILLFUL FALSE STATEMENTS MADE ON THIS FORM ARE PUNISHABLE BY FINE AND IMPRISONMENT, U.S. CODE, TITLE 18, SECTION 1001.

Figure 8-3 (Courtesy NAB and FCC)

FULL-TIME PAID EMPLOYEES JOB CATEGORIES 1	ALL EMPLOYEES2			MALE					FEMALE				
				MINORITY GROUP EMPLOYEES					MINORITY GROUP EMPLOYEES				
	Total (Col.2+3)	Male	Female	Black, not of Hispanic origin	Asian or Pacific Islander	American Indian or Alaskan Native	Hispanic	White, not of Hispanic origin	Black, not of Hispanic origin	Asian or Pacific Islander	American Indian or Alaskan Native	Hispanic	White not of Hispanic origin
	(1)	(2)	(3)	(4)	(5)	(6)	(7)	(8)	(9)	(10)	(11)	(12)	(13)
Officials and Managers													
Professionals													
Technicians													
Sales workers													
Office and Clerical													
Craftsmen (Skilled)													
Operatives (Semi-skilled)													
Laborers (Unskilled)													
Service Workers													
TOTAL													
Total employment from previous Report (if any)													

SECTION VI — (SECTION VI COLUMN TITLES SAME AS SECTION V)

PART-TIME PAID EMPLOYEES JOB CATEGORIES 1													
Officials and Managers													
Professionals													
Technicians													
Sales Workers													
Office and Clerical													
Craftsmen (Skilled)													
Operatives (Semi-Skilled)													
Laborers (Unskilled)													
Service Workers													
TOTAL													
Total employment from previous report (if any)													

1 Refer to Instructions for explanation of all title functions.
2 Include "Minority Group Employees" and others. See Instruction 7.

FCC Form 395 (page 3)
January 1981

Figure 8-4

Managers," "Professionals," "Technicians," "Sales Workers," "Office and Clerical Craftsmen (skilled)," "Operatives (semi-skilled)," "Laborers (unskilled)," and "Service Workers." The bottom half of the page lists the same information but for part-time paid employees.

Additional information requested on page 3 of the Annual Employment Report includes the sex of the employees along with requesting the number of employees in minority categories: "Black not of Hispanic origin," "Asian or Pacific Islander," "American Indian or Alaskan Native," and "Hispanic." in addition, the form requires the licensee to list the number of employees who are "White not of Hispanic origin." Page 4 of the Annual Employment Report lists the sum totals of the various categories requested on page 3.

The FCC pays particular attention to the number of females and minorities employed at the station and the number of females and minorities in the "top 4" job categories which include: "Officials and Managers," "Professionals," "Technicians," and "Sales Workers." If the number of female and minority employees drops significantly below a previous report or that reported at a previous license renewal, it can alert the FCC to consider the license renewal more closely.

ownership report

The Ownership Report tells the FCC who owns the station, the shareholders, how much stock the shareholders have in other media interests, and the voting privileges of shareholders. The Ownership Report is the FCC's way of monitoring whether there is a potential for one individual or company to become involved in a "media monopoly", or approach a violation of the FCC's crossownership rules. Our discussion of the Ownership Report is general and you should keep in mind there are many variations on what information must be filed with the Ownership Report and how often it must be filed.

In general, a station is required to file an Ownership Report at the time of the license renewal. However, a current and accurate Ownership Report must also be on file at all times. For example, nothing on the Ownership Report should become outdated more than 30 days. A *supplemental* Ownership Report must be filed if a change takes place in such things as officers or directors, the organization or capitalization (general fiscal arrangements), changes in ownership that may be direct or indirect, or voting rights of a licensee's stock. The same applies to the holder of a construction permit. Here the permittee is treated much like the licensee. The first Ownership Report must be filed within 30 days from the time the construction permit is granted.

In addition: "The identity of the owners of the licensee must be made plain. This is simple if an individual is the licensee. In the case of a partnership, each partner's name and percentage interest must be listed. In the case of a corporation, or any other legal entity (association, trust, estate, receivership, etc.), the *name, residence, citizenship,* and *stock held* of each (1) officer, (2) director, and (3) stockholder (or trustee, executor, administrator, receiver, or association member) must be listed."[23] Also, cross interests, such as directors who may be relatives, should be listed. Other information on the form includes the different classes of stocks, "whether each class is voting or non-voting, the par or stated value of shares and information concerning the number of *authorized, issued,* and *out-standing* on *unissued* shares."[24]

section 310

Section 310 of the Communications Act prohibits any license to be issued to any foreign government or representative thereof. The license renewal form asks if the applicant is in compliance with this provision. (See the text of SEc. 310 at the end of this chapter.)

legal action

The FCC wants to know if the applicant is involved in any legal action and specifically asks:

> Since the filing of the applicant's last renewal for this station or other major application, has an adverse finding been made, a consent decree been entered, or final action been approved by any court or administrative body with respect to the applicant or to the application concerning any civil or criminal suit, action, or proceeding, brought under the provisions of any federal, state, territorial or local law relating to the following: any felony, lotteries, unlawful restraints or monopolies, unlawful combinations, contracts or agreements in restraint of trade; the use of unfair methods of competition; fraud; unfair labor practices; or discrimination?

If the answer to the question is "yes," then the FCC requires the applicant to attach to the application a "full description, including identification of the court or administrative body, proceeding by file number, the person and matters involved, and the disposition of the litigation."

public inspection file

The renewal form also asks: "Has the applicant placed in its public inspection file at the appropriate times the documentation required . . . by the Commission's rules?"

For most stations the license renewal is routine, if still burdensome. Monitoring the accuracy of the information reported to the FCC falls primarily on the FCC Field Office.

Starting a New Station

Even though frequencies are getting harder and harder to find in many communities, enterprising entrepreneurs have not been deterred from seeking out locations for new stations. Let's briefly review the steps that one must go through to start a new station.

preliminary steps

The first step in starting a new station is to find an area where a frequency is available. For an AM radio station, the search will include not only consulting the engineering data of stations already in the market but also having a qualified engineer conduct a *frequency search*. The frequency search entails checking the exact broadcast contours of stations presently serving the area and determining what type of signal will not interfere with those currently operating. Thus, researching possible wattage, contour patterns, and available frequencies must all precede the application process.

Starting an FM radio or TV station is a bit different. An applicant for an FM radio license must select either an available frequency already assigned by the FCC to the area where the applicant wants to operate or a place within a specified radius where no FM frequency has been assigned. TV applicants must request a UHF or VHF channel, assigned either to the community or to a place where there is no channel assignment within fifteen miles of the community.

Once the frequency search has been completed, the next step is a community needs and ascertainment survey. We have already learned how to conduct such a survey.

construction permit to license

Once the community needs and ascertainment survey is completed, the applicant applies to the FCC for a *construction permit*. The applicant must also possess the financial ability to operate the station for at least one year after construction. Notice of the pending application must be made in the local newspaper, and a public inspection file must be kept in the locality where the station will be built. After the applicant has filed with the FCC, others have the opportunity to comment on the application or, in the case of competing applicants, file against it. If necessary, the FCC will schedule a hearing on the application. Following the hearing, the FCC Administrative Law Judge will issue a decision, which can be appealed.

If everything in the application is found satisfactory, and there are no objections, the FCC then issues the construction permit. Construction on the station must begin within sixty days from the date the construction permit is issued. Depending on the type of station, a period of up to eighteen months from the date the construction permit is issued is given to complete construction. If the applicant cannot build the station in the specified time allotted, then the applicant must apply for an extension in time.

After the station is constructed, the applicant then applies for the *license*. At this time, the applicant can also request authority to conduct program tests. These tests will usually be permitted if nothing has come to the attention of the FCC which would indicate that the operation of the station would be contrary to the public interest. When the license is issued, the station can go on the air and begin regular programming.

Although the procedure is somewhat systematic, putting the station on the air is anything but simple. The paperwork, dealing with engineers and communication attorneys, and securing the financing necessary not only to buy land and equipment but also to keep the station running for a year can all be difficult and time consuming obstacles to overcome. If objections or competing applications become an issue, the court costs involved can discourage an applicant from completing the application process. Still, for those who do succeed, the rewards can be substantial, both in personal satisfaction and the income to be earned.

Low Power TV (LPTV)

Along with standard broadcast stations, the FCC in 1980 initiated a procedure and issued a Notice of Proposed Rulemaking for the purpose of developing regulations and issuing licenses to a new class of television station providing low power broadcast service (LPTV) to areas which had previously been denied coverage or were under served by existing stations. When the new service becomes operable, stations operating with low power (1000 watt UHF and 100 watt VHF) will be permitted to operate much like larger stations but with a limited coverage area (Figure 8-5).

ILLUSTRATIVE LOW POWER
TELEVISION STATION COVERAGE

VHF (Channels 2 - 13)

Transmitter Power Output	Transmitting Antenna Gain	Effective Radiated Power*	Transmitting Antenna Height**	Approx. Useful Coverage Distance***
1 watt	5	5	100'	3.5
1 watt	5	5	500'	8.0
1 watt	5	5	1000'	11.0
10 watts	5	50	100'	6.2
10 watts	5	50	500'	14.0
10 watts	5	50	1000'	19.5

UHF (Channels 14 - 83)

10 watts	10	100	100'	2.9 mi.
10 watts	10	100	500'	6.5 mi.
10 watts	10	100	1000'	9.0 mi.
100 watts	15	1500	100'	6.5 mi.
100 watts	15	1500	500'	12.5 mi.
100 watts	15	1500	1000'	18.0 mi.
1000 watts	15	15000	100'	10.0 mi.
1000 watts	15	15000	500'	21.0 mi.
1000 watts	15	15000	1000'	26.5 mi.

* Technically, the loss in the cable between the transmitter and the transmitting antenna should be taken into account in calculating the ERP. The reduction in ERP that would occur has been approximated by using a lower than normal antenna gain.

** The "height above average terrain" which will coincide with the height above ground level only for flat terrain. Variation in terrain will cause variation in coverage.

*** Distance is to the "Grade B Contour"—At the extremes of this coverage distance, outside antennas will generally be necessary for adequate reception.

Figure 8-5

Low-power television stations are much like the numerous "translator" stations around the United States that rebroadcast the signals of other stations. The difference between a translator and a low-power station is that the LPTV station can originate programming. The application procedure is less complex than for a full-service station; specifically, in the areas of proposed programming and community needs and ascertainment surveys, which are not required to the full extent that they are for a full-service station. At the same time, however, a full service station is protected from interference, and should a full-service station decide to apply for the frequency used by a low-power station, the full-service station will be given priority consideration even if the LPTV station is already licensed and operating.

An applicant wanting to own and operate a LPTV station should consult the FCC's latest rules at the time of making the application and should be prepared to demonstrate that the applicant is legally qualified, financially able, and has made the necessary technical arrangements and engineering surveys to go on the air.

Crossownership

Although many broadcasting stations are profitable ventures, ownership is regulated by the FCC to avoid monopolies. The FCC rules include (1) the seven station rule; (2) the duopoly rule; (3) one-to-a-market rule; (4) regional concentration control rule, and (5) newspaper-broadcast ownership rule.

seven-station, duopoly, and one-to-a-market rules

One of the most inflexible rules is the seven station rule. It prohibits an owner from having more than seven stations of any one type—AM, FM, or TV. Thus, a total of twenty-one stations is permitted to the same owner. Only five of the TV stations can be VHF. The duopoly rule prohibits crossownership when two stations of the same type (such as two AMs) have certain overlapping contours. Directly related to the duopoly rule is the one-to-a-market rule, which prohibits a radio-TV crossownership whenever certain contours of the radio and television stations overlap. However an owner can operate an AM/FM combination in the same market.

regional concentration rule

Guarding against a monopoly of viewpoints over what the public receives in any given area, the FCC prohibits regional concentrations of ownership. To understand the regional concentration rule, imagine an owner with three stations in three different markets. By drawing a triangle representing the three markets, we discover that one side of the triangle is 100 miles long. If this distance is present, *and* if the primary contours of any of the stations overlap on any side of the triangle, the crossownership component is illegal. When the stations were purchased or started in the first place, however, the FCC would have prohibited such concentration, so finding an illegal crossownership is highly unlikely. The regional concentration rule is also applied when an owner wants to increase the power of one of the stations. Even though the owner may be within legal limits, operating the stations less than 100 miles apart, if increasing the power of one of the stations results in the contours overlapping on one side of the triangle, then the power increase would place the station in violation.

newspaper-broadcast crossownership rule

If the seven-station rule can be considered the most inflexible, then the newspaper–broadcast crossownership rule can be considered the most controversial. The controversy surfaced in 1977, when the U.S. Court of Appeals in Washington, D.C. came down hard on an FCC policy of not requiring long-standing newspaper–broadcast crossownerships to be dissolved, but prohibiting certain new ones from being formed. Brought to the court by the National Citizens' Committee for Broadcasting, the case placed hundreds of millions of dollars of crossownerships at stake, leaving an appeal to the U.S. Supreme Court the only alternative for over 150 newspaper–broadcast cross-ownerships. Except where there was a clear indication that the public interest would be harmed if the newspaper-broadcast crossownership continued to exist, the FCC permitted existing crossownerships to stand. The Appeals Court took an opposite view to the long-standing FCC policy. Refuting the rationale of leaving existing crossownerships alone, the Appeals Court said in part: "We believe precisely the opposite presumption is compelled, and that divesture is required except in those cases where the evidence clearly discloses the crossownership is in the public interest."

The Supreme Court's decision in the case in 1978, sent a muted sigh of relief throughout the industry. The Court, for the most part, upheld the FCC's interpretation of the crossownership rules and permitted already existing crossownerships to stand. It also affirmed the FCC's decision to break up crossownerships where there was clearly a media monopoly, consisting of a newspaper and broadcast crossownership arrangement in a small community with only one newspaper and few broadcasting stations.

Radio Deregulation: Operational Changes

When the FCC in 1981 deregulated commercial radio, it changed the operating procedure for most of the nation's AM and FM stations. Much of the paperwork was eliminated. Although stations are still responsible for serving the public interest and can have a license challenged on inadequate performance, the actual documentation and record keeping burden was to a large extent lifted from the operator's shoulders. The rulemaking proceeding on deregulating radio had begun at the FCC meeting of September 6, 1979. The following paragraphs highlight the primary areas of deregulation that went into effect in 1981. The proceeding itself resulted in the FCC receiving approximately 20,029 comments ranging from individuals to networks.

non-entertainment programming guideline

Prior to deregulation, a standard FCC guideline for non-entertainment programming (news, public affairs, and "all other") was 8 percent for AM stations and 6 percent for FM stations (Section 0.281 of the FCC Rules). Under commercial radio's deregulation the non-entertainment guidelines were removed. In other words, commercial radio stations are no longer required to propose the minimum percentages as a programming goal. This does not mean that commercial radio broadcasters can cast to the wind their responsibility to serve their community. It means the minimum percentages of non-entertainment programming as a means of accomplishing this goal are no longer in effect. Moreover, the Fairness Doctrine and such things as the equal-time provisions, which many times rely on such programming, remained in effect. In a nutshell, the commercial radio broadcaster gained more flexibility in the manner in which the issues of a community are addressed on the air. Programs meeting community issues can be produced locally, but are not required to be produced locally. Editorials, free-speech messages, community announcements, and religious programming are just some of the possibilities.

Especially meaningful at renewal time, the lack of the non-entertainment programming guidelines means that a commercial radio broadcaster's renewal application will not automatically be brought to the FCC's attention and possibly designated for a hearing simply because the proposed programming goals do not meet the minimum percentages levels.

The non-entertainment guidelines also provided some problems for broadcasters when petitions to deny arose. Under deregulation the FCC will not consider allegations based on percentages of non-entertainment programming in a petition to deny, at least not solely on the amount of non-entertainment programming a station offers. Specifically, the FCC's ruling stated:

> The focus of such an allegation should not be on the mere amount of programming. We do not wish to return to a "numbers game" whereby 6% non-entertainment programming is sufficient to warrant renewal whereas 5% will result in, at least, delay, and, perhaps, designation for hearing with the possibility of the loss of the license. A station with good programs addressing public issues and aired during high listership times but amounting to only 3% of its weekly programming may be doing a superior job to a station airing 6% non-entertainment programming little of which deals in a meaningful fashion with public issues or which is aired when the audience is small.[24]

Moreover, broadcasters can point to the service other stations in a market are providing as a reson for justifying the way issues are being addressed in the "marketplace,' as opposed to how they may be addressed on a single station.

community needs and ascertainment

Relaxed rules for ascertainment also went into effect with the deregulation of commercial radio. For example, the actual procedures used in community needs and ascertainment became more the individual choice of the commercial radio broadcaster, as opposed to the more specific guidelines we discussed earlier in this chapter and which apply to television and some non-commercial radio stations. Broadcasters cannot be unresponsive to their communities and they must still program to meet community needs. The FCC stated:

> We see no continuing reason to burden applicants, licensees or the Commission with detailed inquiries into which or how many community leaders were contacted, by whom, etc. This is not to say that the coverage of issues in a community would not be a relevant consideration in making such judgments. Rather, the methodological approach to those problems only obscures the issue of responsiveness and exhausts otherwise valuable resources in meaningless minutae.[25]

The action also meant that the actual procedures of a community needs and ascertainment survey would not be the primary grounds on which the outcome of a comparative hearing might be based.

program logs and public inspection files

With deregulation the requirement that commercial radio stations keep program logs was lifted. At the same time the retention requirement and public availability of logs was lifted. One of the reasons for the lifting of the logging requirement was a statistic by the General Accounting Office which said that compliance with the logging regulation for AM and FM stations meant spending 18,233,940 hours per year by the industry. At the same time, however, broadcasters realized the value of logs as a record-keeping device to verify commercials when were aired and to keep track of public service announcements and other types of programming. Deregulation, however, shifted responsibility from an FCC requirement to the chosen operating procedure of the local commercial radio broadcaster.

Public inspection files, although not requiring logs, were for the most part maintained by the new rules. Most important is the annual issues/programming list for each community. Specifically the FCC stated:

> Public inspection files will continue to be maintained by each licensee, and will provide considerable information of value to citizens making public interest programming inquiries of licensees. Items contained therein which have had and will continue to have great value include copies of the license application with all accompanying materials, and the political file. In addition, the most important programming document in the public inspection file will likely be the annual issues-programs list. There, each licensee will list five to ten of the important issues in its service area, examples of its public service programs aired over the past year which responded to those issues, and related information.[26]

commercial guidelines

Under the new rules promulgated by deregulation, commercial radio stations will no longer be required to meet maximum commercial guidelines. In other words, there are no restrictions on how much commercial time a station might air. The FCC felt the best way to regulate this is in the marketplace, and let the listeners determine how much is too much. In other words, if a station airs too much commercial matter the listenership might drop, which in turn would limit the amount of money that could be charged for commercials. At a certain point the licensee would determine an ideal profitable mix; the amount of commercial time with the most profit while still serving the public interest and retaining an audience. The FCC's position permitted the opportunity for certain experimental formats such as want-ad radio, where a large percentage of programming might be classified ads, each costing somewhat less than standard length commercials but being aired in much greater numbers.

Stations are still required to announce the sponsors of commercials or other commercial programming and are held responsible for any false or misleading advertising.

summary

A station's promotional activities are of as much concern to regulatory agencies as the content of its broadcast programming and advertising. One of the most common problems associated with station promotions is hypoing: i.e. artificially inflating such factors as the station's coverage area or the size of its audience. Hypoing can provoke the wrath of the FTC and earn a charge of false advertising. A visit from the FTC can also cause the FCC to consider whether or not the station may be operating in less than the public interest.

With the exception of logs, perhaps the most important part of a station's record-keeping procedure is its public inspection file. The content of this file varies somewhat among different types of stations, but all stations should have copies of their community's ten most important problems, letters from the broadcast audience, and basic technical information concerning the station. The public is entitled to examine a station's public inspection file during business hours, although there may be restrictions on the number of people who can view the file at one time, and the station may charge for duplicating material in its file.

The FCC has been in the forefront of federal agencies requiring proof of equal employment opportunity programs among the industries it regulates. Therefore, a station's EEO program should contain a statement of policy, responsibility for implementation, policy dissemination, recruitment, training, an availability survey, current employment survey, job hires, promotion, and effectiveness of an affirmative action plan. Community needs and ascertainment surveys are also important parts of a station's operations. The key is to make sure that such a survey is truly representative of the community and reflects the needs of its various social, political, and economic groups.

All stations must undergo license renewal every three years. The process of starting a new station or transferring ownership of an existing one must also conform to specific FCC requirements.

material for analysis

The heart of the FCC's licensing authority is found in the Communications Act. In the pages that follow, we will read Sections of the Act which give the FCC authority to issue licenses while voiding any actual "ownership" of a license. Notice how Sec. 304 requires the holder of the license to waive the right of any claim over the use of a particular frequency. This wording grew out of the chaos that developed when the Radio Act of 1912 could not handle all those who demanded to be assigned a frequency, regardless of how much interference those assignments might cause. When reading the Communications Act, notice also how the Commission is given the authority to judge a person's "character," "citizenship," and "technical" qualifications when considering applications for a license.

The Communications Act of 1934 — Selected Provisions

WAIVING THE RIGHT TO CLAIM A FREQUENCY

Sec. 304. No station license shall be granted by the Commission until the applicant therefor shall have signed a waiver of any claim to the use of any particular frequency or of the ether as against the regulatory power of the United States because of the previous use of the same, whether by license or otherwise. . . .

MAKING APPLICATION

Sec. 308. (a) The Commission may grant construction permits and station licenses, or modifications or renewals thereof, only upon written application therefor received by it: *Provided,* That (1) in cases of emergency found by the Commission involving danger to life or property or due to damage to equipment, or (2) during a national emergency proclaimed by the President or declared by the Congress and during the continuance of any war in which the United States is engaged and when such action is necessary for the national defense or security or otherwise in furtherance of the war effort, or (3) in cases of emergency where the Commission finds, in the nonbroadcast services, that it would not be feasible to secure renewal applications from existing licensees or otherwise to follow normal licensing procedure, the Commission may grant construction permits and station licenses, or modifications or renewals thereof, during the emergency so found by the Commis-

sion or during the continuance of any such national emergency or war, in such manner and upon such terms and conditions as the Commission shall by regulation prescribe, and without the filing of a formal application, but no authorization so granted shall continue in effect beyond the period of the emergency or war requiring it: *Provided further,* That the Commission may issue by cable, telegraph, or radio a permit for the operation of a station on a vessel of the United States at sea, effective in lieu of a license until said vessel shall return to a port of the continental United States.

(b) All applications for station licenses, or modifications or renewals thereof, shall set forth such facts as the Commission by regulation may prescribe as to the citizenship, character, and financial, technical, and other qualifications of the applicant to operate the station; the ownership and location of the proposed station and of the stations, if any, with which it is proposed to communicate; the frequencies and the power desired to be used; the hours of the day or other periods of time during which it is proposed to operate the station; the purposes for which the station is to be used; and such other information as it may require. The Commission, at any time after the filing of such original application and during the term of any such license, may require from an applicant or licensee further written statements of fact to enable it to determine whether such original application should be granted or denied or such license revoked. Such application and/or such statement of fact shall be signed by the applicant and/or licensee.

(c) The Commission in granting any license for a station intended or used for commercial communication between the United States or any Territory or possession, continental or insular, subject to the jurisdiction of the United States, and any foreign country, may impose any terms, conditions, or restrictions authorized to be imposed with respect to submarine-cable licenses by section 2 of an Act entitled "An Act relating to the landing and the operation of submarine cables in the United States," approved May 24, 1921.

HOLDING AND TRANSFER OF LICENSES

Sec. 310. (a) The station license required under this Act shall not be granted to or held by any foreign government or the representative thereof.

(b) No broadcast or common carrier or aeronautical en route or aeronautical fixed radio station license shall be granted to or held by—

(1) any alien or the representative of any alien;

(2) any corporation organized under the laws of any foreign government;

(3) any corporation of which any officer or director is an alien or of which more than one-fifth of the capital stock is owned of record or voted by aliens or their representatives or by a foreign government or representative thereof or by any corporation organized under the laws of a foreign country.

(4) any corporation directly or indirectly controlled by any other corporation of which any officer or more than one-fourth of the directors are aliens, or of which more than one-

fourth of the capital stock is owned of record or voted by aliens, their representatives, or by a foreign government or representative thereof, or by any corporation organized under the laws of a foreign country, if the Commission finds that the public interest will be served by the refusal or revocation of such license.

(c) In addition to amateur station licenses which the Commission may issue to aliens pursuant to this Act, the Commission may issue authorizations, under such conditions and terms as it may prescribe, to permit an alien licensed by his government as an amateur radio operator to operate his amateur radio station licensed by his government in the United States, its possessions, and the Commonwealth of Puerto Rico provided there is in effect a bilateral agreement between the United States and the alien's government for such operation on a reciprocal basis by United States amateur radio operators. Other provisions of this Act and of the Administrative Procedure Act shall not be applicable to any request or application for or modification, suspension, or cancellation of any such authorization.

(d) No construction permit or station license, or any rights thereunder, shall be transferred, assigned, or disposed of in any manner, voluntarily or involuntarily, directly or indirectly, or by transfer of control of any corporation holding such permit or license, to any person except upon application to the Commission and upon finding by the Commission that the public interest, convenience, and necessity will be served thereby. Any such application shall be disposed of as if the proposed transferee or assignee were making application under section 308 of this Act for the permit or license in question; but in acting thereon the Commission may not consider whether the public interest, convenience, and necessity might be served by the transfer, assignment, or disposal of the permit or license to a person other than the proposed transferee or assignee.

ADMINISTRATIVE SANCTIONS

Sec. 312. (a) The Commission may revoke any station license or construction permit—

(1) for false statements knowingly made either in the application or in any statement of fact which may be required pursuant to section 308;

(2) because of conditions coming to the attention of the Commission which would warrant it in refusing to grant a license or permit on an original application;

(3) for willful or repeated failure to operate substantially as set forth in the license;

(4) for willful or repeated violation of, or willful or repeated failure to observe any provision of this Act or any rule or regulation of the Commission authorized by this Act or by a treaty ratified by the United States;

(5) for violation of or failure to observe any final cease and desist order issued by the Commission under this section;

(6) for violation of section 1304, 1343, or 1464 of title 18 of the United States Code; or

(7) for willful or repeated failure to allow reasonable access to or to permit purchase of reasonable amounts of time for the use of a broadcasting station by a legally qualified candidate for Federal elective office on behalf of his candidacy.

(b) Where any person (1) has failed to operate substantially as set forth in a license, (2) has violated or failed to observe any of the provisions of this Act, or section 1304, 1343, or 1464 of title 18 of the United States Code, or (3) has violated or failed to observe any rule or regulation of the Commission authorized by this Act or by a treaty ratified by the United States, the Commission may order such person to cease and desist from such action.

(c) Before revoking a license or permit pursuant to subsection (a), or issuing a cease and desist order pursuant to subsection (b), the Commission shall serve upon the licensee, permittee, or person involved an order to show cause why an order of revocation or a cease and desist order should not be issued. Any such order to show cause shall contain a statement of the matters with respect to which the Commission is inquiring and shall call upon said licensee, permittee, or person to appear before the Commission at a time and place stated in the order, but in no event less than thirty days after the receipt of such order, and give evidence upon the matter specified therein; except that where safety of life or property is involved, the Commission may provide in the order for a shorter period. If after hearing, or a waiver thereof, the Commission determines that an order of revocation or a cease and desist order should issue, it shall issue such order, which shall include a statement of the findings of the Commission and the grounds and reasons therefor and specify the effective date of the order, and shall cause the same to be served on said licensee, permittee, or person.

(d) In any case where a hearing is conducted pursuant to the provisions of this section, both the burden of proceeding with the introduction of evidence and the burden of proof shall be upon the Commission.

(e) The provisions of section 9(b) of the Administrative Procedure Act which apply with respect to the institution of any proceeding for the revocation of a license or permit shall apply also with respect to the institution, under this section, of any proceeding for the issuance of a cease and desist order....

APPLYING FOR CONSTRUCTION PERMITS

Sec. 319. (a) No license shall be issued under the authority of this Act for the operation of any station the construction of which is begun or is continued after this Act takes effect, unless a permit for its construction has been granted by the Commission. The application for a construction permit shall set forth such facts as the Commission by regulation may prescribe as to the citizenship, character, and the financial, technical, and other ability of the applicant to construct and operate the station, the ownership and location of the proposed station and of the station or stations with which it is proposed to communicate, the frequencies desired to be used, the hours of the day or other periods of time during which it is proposed to operate the station, the purpose for which the station is to be used, the type of transmitting apparatus to be used, the power to be used, the date upon which the station is expected to be completed and in operation, and such other information as the Commission may require. Such application shall be signed by the applicant.

(b) Such permit for construction shall show specifically the earliest and latest dates between which the actual operation of such station is expected to begin, and shall provide that said permit will be automatically forfeited if the station is not ready for operation within the time specified or within such further time as the Commission may allow, unless prevented by causes not under the control of the grantee.

(c) Upon the completion of any station for the construction or continued construction of which a permit has been granted, and upon it being made to appear to the Commission that all the terms, conditions, and obligations set forth in the application and permit have been fully met, and that no cause or circumstance arising or first coming to the knowledge of the Commission since the granting of the permit would, in the judgment of the Commission, make the operation of such station against the public interest, the Commission shall issue a license to the lawful holder of said permit for the operation of said station. Said license shall conform generally to the terms of said permit. The provisions of section 309(a), (b), (c), (d), (e), (f), and (g) shall not apply with respect to any station license the issuance of which is provided for and governed by the provisions of this subsection.

(d) A permit for construction shall not be required for Government stations, amateur stations, or mobile stations. With respect to stations or classes of stations other than Government stations, amateur stations, mobile stations, and broadcasting stations, the Commission may waive the requirement of a permit for construction if it finds that the public interest, convenience, or necessity would be served thereby: *Provided, however,* That such waiver shall apply only to stations whose construction is begun subsequent to the effective date of the waiver. If the Commission finds that the public interest, convenience, and necessity would be served thereby, it may waive the requirement of a permit for construction of a station that is engaged solely in rebroadcasting television signals if such station was constructed on or before the date of enactment of this sentence. . . .

questions for discussion and further research ⸻⸻⸻⸻

1. Station promotion can become one of the most hotly contested areas of broadcast operations, expecially in highly competitive markets and during rating surveys. The

FCC rules governing station promotion are broad and fall under the umbrella of the "public interest" clause of the Communications Act. Should the FCC institute stricter rules governing station promotion, and, if so, what kind of rules might they be?

2. Although broadcasting is primarily governed by the FCC, the FTC can also become involved when a station promotion falls into the range of deceptive advertising. Even then, the matter is usually referred to the FCC for action. Since deceptive advertising is an issue quite common to FTC action and jurisdiction, should this agency take full responsibility for policing and instituting penalties for deception in broadcast promotion campaigns?

3. On the other hand, would it be more appropriate for the FTC to relinquish its authority to the FCC insofar as the matter of station promotion is concerned, while keeping within the FTC's jurisdiction the power to police deceptive advertising of actual goods and services advertised on the station?

4. A particularly sensitive time for station promotion is during rating surveys. The rating services take precautions to publicize in their rating reports any promotions or hypoing which seem to be scheduled and directed to an audience for the prime purpose of influencing a given survey. Should rules be instituted which give specific guidelines to broadcasters on what promotional material can and cannot be aired during a rating period, with appropriate penalties for violations of those rules?

5. Could such rules be enforced, and could they be flexible enough to apply to markets in which rating surveys occur almost continuously?

6. Arbitron and Nielsen are two of the more familiar rating survey companies. If we were to institute the rules discussed in questions 5 and 6, should the rules apply to surveys conducted by only the largest and most familiar firms? Would such distinctions hold up in court? If they did not hold up in court, would the rules be workable?

7. Most people who see a coverage map used in station promotional material are not privy to, or even familiar with, the coverage maps that are used for engineering, license renewal, and other "official" purposes. Would one way to guard against misrepresentation of coverage maps for promotional purposes be to include copies of "promotional" maps in the public file along with the "official" contour?

8. Many stations licensed by educational institutions find that their labor pool is made up almost entirely of students. This is especially true when the station pays minimum wages, offers small scholarships or grants-in-aid as forms of compensation for working at the station, or staffs the station primarily with volunteers. Based on the model affirmative action program, how should these stations meet the ten points of the model program?

9. Many broadcasters say that they have never had any member of the public ask to see the public inspection file. Others have complained about people wanting to see the file and not understanding its purpose or contents. Still others complain of members of the public making demands on management which go beyond the requirements associated with keeping and making the file accessible. In view of these criticisms, should the FCC continue to require stations to keep public files? (Keep in mind that if an issue concerning the station becomes serious enough to warrant court action, station documents can be subpoenaed.)

10. Community ascertainment is designed to make the licensee aware of the problems facing the community and to assure that its programming meets those needs. Consider that (1) a station's local news programming deals with issues facing the community; (2) a broadcaster can and is in fact encouraged to take editorial stands on local issues; (3) the Fairness Doctrine is designed to assure balanced coverage of controversial issues of public importance; and (4) in many larger markets, where broadcasters may not be in close touch with all aspects of the community, there are numerous stations to present a diversity of views. Given these conditions, is any form of ascertainment really necessary?

11. If ascertainment is necessary, should there be more closely standardized guidelines for conducting those surveys?

12. In what way could stations better assure representation of "Past-in-Future-out," "Past-in-Future-in," and "Past-out-Future-out" groups?

13. Later in the text, we'll discuss efforts to consider revision of the Communications Act of 1934. Based on what you have learned up to this point about broadcast regulation and license renewals, should the term of a station license be extended.

14. In larger markets, where more stations exist, the assumption is made that more communications channels are open to the public, which creates more opportunities for a diversity of views. Can we assume that this variety of stations permits less opportunity for control of public opinion than exists in smaller communities, where only one or two stations operate? If we can, can an argument be made for varying the license terms of stations, depending on the size of the markets they serve, and instituting longer license terms for stations in larger markets?

15. Could an argument be made for shorter license terms for stations in larger markets—where they can influence more people—and longer license terms in small markets—where the stations' audiences are smaller?

16. While group broadcasters are regulated in the number of broadcast properties they can own, group owners of newspapers, for the most part, face no such restrictions. Given the fact that there are more broadcasting stations than daily newspapers, what arguments can be made for removing the limitation on broadcast properties under the same owner or for limiting the number of newspapers under the same owner?

additional resources

books: general operations

Baer, W. S., H. Geller, and J. A. Grundfest, *Newspaper–Television Station Cross-Ownership: Options for Federal Action*, Santa Monica, Calif.: Rand Corp. Report R-1585-MF, 1974.

Baer, W. S., H. Geller, J. A. Grundfest, and K. B. Possner, *Concentration of Mass Media Ownership: Assessing the State of Current Knowledge*, Santa Monica, Calif.: Rand Corp. Report R-1584-NSF, 1974.

Citizens' Communications Center, *A Study of the Federal Communications Commission's Equal Employment Opportunity Regulation—An Agency in Search of a Standard*, Washington, D.C.: Citizens' Communications Center, 1976.

Corporation for Public Broadcasting, *Six Experiments in Ascertainment Methodology*, Washington, D.C.: Corporation for Public Broadcasting, 1977. (Contains articles and research by Robert Avery, Paige Birdsall, Antonio Rey, Alfred G. Smith, Patrick A. Nester, D. Lynn Pulford, James A. Anderson, Thomas A. McCain, C. Richard Hofstetter, Navita Cummings-James, James E. Hawkins, David LeRoy, Bernadette McGuire, Thomas M. Turner.)

Greenberg, B. S., T. F. Baldwin, B. Reeves, L. Thornton, and J. Wakshlag, *An Ascertainment Handbook for Public Broadcasting Facilities*, Washington, D.C.: Corporation for Public Broadcasting, 1976.

Jennings, R. M., *Television Station Employment Practices: The Status of Minorities and Women*, New York: Office of Communications, United Church of Christ, 1972.

Noll, R. G., M. J. Peck, and J. J. McGowan, *Economic Aspects of Television Regulation*, Washington, D.C.: Brookings Institution, 1973.

Smith, J. A., *Getting What You Bargained For: A Broadcaster's Guide to Contracts and Leases*, Washington, D.C.: National Association of Broadcasters, 1979.

books; station licensing

Corporations for Public Broadcasting, *The Low Power Television Guidebook*, Washington, D.C.: Corporation for Public Broadcasting, 1980.

Geller, H., *The Comparative Renewal Process in Television: Problems and Suggested Solutions.* Santa Monica, Calif.: Rand Corp., 1974.

Jennings, R. M., *Guide to Understanding Broadcast License Applications and Other FCC Forms,* New York: Office of Communications, United Church of Christ, 1972.

articles: general operations

Blankenburg, W. B., "Nixon vs. the Networks: Madison Avenue and Wall Street," 21 *Journal of Broadcasting* 163 (1977).

Blau, R. T., R. C. Johnson, and K. J. Ksobiech, "Determinants of TV Station Economic Value," 20 *Journal of Broadcasting* 197 (1976).

Collins, E. G. C., and T. B. Blodgett, "Sexual Harassment . . . Some See It . . . Some Won't," 59 *Harvard Business Review* 77 (1981).

Couric, J. M., "Small Market Radio Community Involvement," 14 *Journal of Broadcasting* 171 (1970).

David, M. M., "Financial Qualifications for the Purchase of a Radio Station," 5 *Performing Arts Review* 141 (1974).

Foley, J. M., "Ascertaining Ascertainment: Impact of the FCC Primer on TV Renewal Applications," 16 *Journal of Broadcasting* 387 (1972).

Geller, H., "Comparative Renewal Process in Television: Problems and Suggested Solutions," 61 *Virginia Law Review* 471 (1975).

Gordon, A. S., "Radio and Television Directors as Supervisors—Can They Vote for Union Representation?," 4 *Performing Arts Review* 3 (1973).

Heller, M. A., "Problems in Ascertainment Research," 21 *Journal of Broadcasting* 427 (1977).

Heller, M. A., "An Argument for Elimination of Ascertainment Requirements," 25 *Journal of Broadcasting* 71 (1981).

Hines, J. M., and S. Meyer, "Equal Employment Responsibilities of the Communications Industry," 24 *Federal Communications Bar Journal* 217 (1970–71).

Howard, H. H., "The Contemporary Status of Television Group Ownership," 53 *Journalism Quarterly* 399 (1976).

Howard, H. H., "Cox Broadcasting Corp.: A Group-Ownership Case Study," 20 *Journal of Broadcasting* 209 (1976).

Howard, H. H., "Cross-Media Ownership of Newspapers and TV Stations," 51 *Journalism Quarterly* 715 (1974).

Howard, H. H., "Multiple Broadcast Ownership: Regulatory History," 27 *Federal Communications Bar Journal* 1 (1974).

Hyde, R. H., "The Role of Competition and Monopoly in the Communications Industries," 13 *Antitrust Bulletin* 899 (1968).

Irion, H. G., "FCC Criteria for Evaluating Competing Applicants," 43 *Minnesota Law Review* 479 (1959).

Johnson, N., and J. M. Hoak, Jr., "Media Concentration: Some Observations on the United States' Experience," 56 *Iowa Law Review* 267 (1970).

Lago, A. M., "Price Effects of Joint Mass Communication Media Ownership," 16 *Antitrust Bulletin* 789 (1971).

LeRoy, D. J., and D. F. Ungurait, "Ascertainment Surveys: Problem Perception and Voluntary Station Contact," 19 *Journal of Broadcasting* 23 (1975). 23-30.

Levin, H. J., "Competition, Diversity, and the Television Group Ownership Rule," 70 *Columbia Law Review* 79 (1970).

Linton, J. A., "Tax Problems with Television Properties: Films, Copyrights and Property Rights," 26 *Journal of Taxation* 240 (1967).

Litman, B. R., "Is Network Ownership in the Public Interest?," 28 *Journal of Communication* 51 (1978). 51-59.

Mahaffie, C. D., Jr., "Mergers and Diversification in the Newspaper, Broadcasting and Information Industries," 13 *Antitrust Bulletin* 927 (1968).

Meeske, M. D., "Black Ownership of Broadcast Stations: An FCC Licensing Problem," 20 *Journal of Broadcasting* 261 (1976).

Minasian, J. R., "Television Pricing and the Theory of Public Goods," 7 *Journal of Law & Economics* 71 (1964).

Owen, B. M., "Newspaper and Television Station Joint Ownership," 18 *Antitrust Bulletin* 787 (1973).

Prisuta, R. H., "The Impact of Media Concentration and Economic Factors of Broadcast

Public Interest Programming," 21 *Journal of Broadcasting* 321 (1977).

Rowe, F. M., "Antitrust and Monopoly Policy in the Communications Industries," 13 *Antitrust Bulletin* 871 (1968).

Rubiner, A. J., "Primer for Purchase of a Radio Station," 53 *Michigan State Bar Journal* 398 (1974).

Schwartz, B., "Antitrust and the FCC: The Problem of Network Dominance," 107 *University of Pennsylvania Law Review* 753 (1959).

Smith, J. C., Jr., "The Broadcast Industry and Equal Employment Opportunity," 30 *Labor Law Journal* 659 (1979).

Smythe, D., "Facing Facts about the Broadcast Business," 20 *University of Chicago Law Review* 96 (1952).

Soley, L. C., "An Evaluation of FCC Policy on FM Ownership," 56 *Journalism Quarterly* 626 (1979).

Soley, L., and G. Hough, III, "Black Ownership of Commercial Radio Stations: An Economic Evaluation," 22 *Journal of Broadcasting* 455 (1978).

Solomon, K. I., "Tax Treatment of Pre-Opening Expenses," 47 *Taxes—The Tax Magazine* 521 (1968).

Surlin, S. H., "Ascertainment of Community Needs by Black-Oriented Radio Stations," 16 *Journal of Broadcasting* 421 (1972).

Surlin, S. H., and L. Bradley, "Ascertainment through Community Leaders," 18 *Journal of Broadcasting,* 97 (1973-74).

Walker, O. C., Jr., and W. Rudelius, "Ascertaining Programming Needs of 'Voiceless' Community Groups, 20 *Journal of Broadcasting* 89 (1976).

articles: station licensing

Baldwin, T. F., and S. H. Surlin, "A Study of Broadcast Station License Application Exhibits on Ascertainment of Community Needs," 14 *Journal of Broadcasting* 157 (1970).

Bell, D. S., "Impact of Quality Programming on FCC Licensing," 23 *Louisiana Law Review* 85 (1962).

Botein, M., "Comparative Broadcast Licensing Procedures and the Rule of Law: A Fuller

Investigation," 6 *Georgia Law Review* 743 (1972).

Brenner, D. L., "Toward a New Balance in License Renewals," 17 *Journal of Broadcasting* 77 (1972-73).

Fenton, B. S., "Federal Communications Commission and the License Renewal Process," 5 *Suffolk University Law Review* 380 (1971).

Ford, F. W., "Economic Considerations in Licensing of Radio Broadcast Stations," 17 *Federal Communications Bar Journal* 191 (1961).

Givens, R. A., "Refusal of Radio and Television Licenses on Economic Grounds," 46 *Virginia Law Review* 1391 (1960).

Grundfest, J., "Participation in FCC Licensing," 27 *Journal of Communication* 88 (1977).

Grunewald, D., "Should the Comparative Hearing Process Be Retained in Television Licensing?", 13 *American University Law Review* 164 (1964).

Holtkamp, J. A., "Suburban Community Issue: Rebutting the Presumption That a Suburban Applicant Intends to Serve the Central City," 27 *Federal Communications Bar Journal* 81 (1974).

Johnson, N., "Harnessing Revolution: The Role of Regulation and Competition for the Communications Industries of Tomorrow," 13 *Antitrust Bulletin* 881 (1968).

Jones, T., "Broadcast License Revocation for Deception and Illegal Transfer," 15 *George Washington Law Review* 475 (1947).

Kittross, J. M., "Fair and Equitable Service; or, A Modest Proposal to Restructure American Television to Have All the Advantages Claimed for Cable and UHF without Using Either," 29 *Federal Communications Bar Journal* 91 (1976).

Klein, H. S., "Legal Aspects of Radio Jamming," 4 *Performing Arts Review* 101 (1973).

Maher, D. W., "Purity versus Plugola: A Study of the Federal Communications Commission's Sponsorship Identification Rules," 23 *De Paul Law Review* 903 (1974).

Malin, M., "Administrative Rehearings and Judicial Review in Radio Station Licensing," 27 *Georgetown Law Journal* 783 (1939).

Meeks, J. E., "Economic Entry Controls in FCC

Licensing: The Carroll Case Re-appraised," 52 *Iowa Law Review* 236 (1966).

Metzger, S. D., and B. R. Burrus, "Radio Frequency Allocation in the Public Interest: Federal Government and Civilian Use," 4 *Duquesne University Law Review* 1 (1965).

Schement, J. R., F. F. Gutierrez, O. Gandy, T. Haight, and M. E. Soriano, "The Anatomy of a License Challenge," 27 *Journal of Communication*, 89 (1977).

Shelby, M. E., Jr., "Short-Term License Renewals: 1960-1972," 18 *Journal of Broadcasting* 277 (1974).

Sterling, C. H., "Second Service: Some Keys to the Development of FM Broadcasting," 15 *Journal of Broadcasting* 181 (1971).

Stull, M. A., and G. Alexander, "Passive Use of the Radio Spectrum for Scientific Purposes and the Frequency Allocation Process," 43 *Journal of Air Law and Commerce* 459 (1977).

Tansey, J. T. and F. L. Ruck, "Conditional Broadcasting Licenses: Defining the Legal Perimeters," 33 *George Washington Law Review* 764 (1965).

Wall, T. H., "Section 309 of the Communications Act—The Renewal Provision—A Need for Change," 25 *Administrative Law Review* 407 (1973).

Warner, H. P., "Transfers of Broadcasting Licenses under the Communications Act of 1934," 21 *Boston University Law Review* 585 (1941).

cases: licensing

Bilingual Bicultural Coalition v. *F.C.C.*, 3 Med.L.Rptr. 2233 (D.C. Cir. 1978).

Black Broadcasting Coalition of Richmond v. *F.C.C.*, 556 F.2d 59, 181 U.S.App.D.C. 182, 2 Med. L.Rptr. 1725 (1977).

Central Florida Enterprises v. *F.C.C.*, 4 Med.L.Rptr. 1502 (D.C.Cir. 1978).

Cosmopolitan Broadcasting Corp. v. *F.C.C.*, 581 F.2d 917, 4 Med.L.Rptr. 1003 (D.C.Cir. 1978).

Greater Boston Television Corp. v. *F.C.C.*, 444 F.2d 841, 143 U.S.App.D.C. 383, 1 Med.L.Rptr. 2003 (1970).

Las Vegas Valley Broadcasting v. *F.C.C.*, 4 Med.L.Rptr. 1727 (D.C.Cir. 1978).

Los Angeles Women's Coalition for Better Broadcasting v. *F.C.C.*, 584 F.2d 1089, 190 U.S.App.D.C. 108, 4 Med.L.Rptr. 1481 (1978).

National Ass'n for Better Broadcasting v. *F.C.C.*, 591 F.2d 812, 192 U.S.App.D.C. 203, 4 Med.L.Rptr. 1840 (D.C.Cir. 1978).

National Black Media Coalition v. *F.C.C.*, 4 Med.L.Rptr. 1685 (D.C.Cir. 1978).

National Organization for Women, New York City Chapter, v. *F.C.C.*, 555 F.2d 1002, 2 Med.L. Rptr. 1609 (D.C.Cir. 1977).

N.B.C. v. *United States,* decided with *C.B.S.* v. *United States,* 319 U.S. 190, 63 S.Ct. 997, 87 L.Ed. 1344, 1 Med.L.Rptr. 1965 (1943).

Pasadena Broadcasting v. *F.C.C.*, 2 Med.L.Rptr. 1856 (D.C.Cir. 1977).

cases: ownership

F.C.C. v. *National Citizens' Committee for Broadcasting,* 98 S.Ct. 2096, 436 U.S. 775, 56 L.Ed.2d 697 (1978).

National Citizens' Committee for Broadcasting v. *F.C.C.*, 567 F.2d 1095, 2 Med.L.Rptr. 1405 (D.C.Cir. 1977).

Syracuse Coalition v. *F.C.C.*, 4 Med.L.Rptr. 1623 (D.C.Cir. 1978).

United States v. *Storer Broadcasting Co.*, 76 S.Ct. 763, 351 U.S. 192, 100 L.Ed. 1081, 1 Med.L.Rptr. 1983 (1956).

WTAR v. *Virginia,* 2 Med.L.Rptr. 2194 (Va.Sup. Ct. 1977).

9

Cable

The twentieth century has brought us much more than basic radio and television. Today, live television coverage of events half way around the world is taken for granted. We sit down to an evening of prime-time television and watch a newscast switch live to correspondents in London, Paris, and Moscow. We watch continuous coverage of Olympic games—as clear as if they were being held around the corner. And we have many more choices of programs than we had in the past. In communities served by cable television, a different station can broadcast on every channel on the dial. We can watch programming that originates from our own communities or from hundreds, even thousands of miles away. All of this activity has set in motion a new set of regulations peculiar to the technologies and the societies affected by those technologies.

Cable: The Basic Concept

Oregon and Pennsylvania hold claim to the beginnings of cable television. In 1948, enterprising individuals in both states saw a way for communities located at long distances from television stations to get better reception by sharing an antenna located on top of an adjacent hilltop. From those small beginnings in 1948, cable systems have grown in size and number. Today there are approximately 4,400 cable systems operating in the United States, with subscribers numbering about 19 million. Pennsylvania tops the list with the most cable systems, about 300, while California has the most subscribers, estimated at 1.3 million.

The components of the cable system (Figure 9-1) consist of a *head-end, trunk cable, feeder cable* (also called subtrunk), *drop cables,* and *subscribers.* The *head-end* is the human and hardware combination responsible for originating, controlling, and processing signals over the cable system. An important part of the head-end is the receiving antenna, also called the master antenna. The receiving antenna receives the incoming signals from distant television stations. The *trunk cable* is the main cable leaving the head-end. Many times, the trunk cable follows the main arteries of a community, such as the main thoroughfares. Off the trunk cable run the *feeder cables* to smaller community units, such as individual streets. And from the feeder cable a *drop cable* brings the signal along the final leg, into the *subscriber's* home television set. Spaced intermittently along the routes of the trunk and feeder cables are amplifiers, which boost the incoming signal.

Recently, attention has turned to the capabilities of two-way cable systems. A variety of two-way systems are either operable or in the prototype stage. Al-

Basic Cable Television System

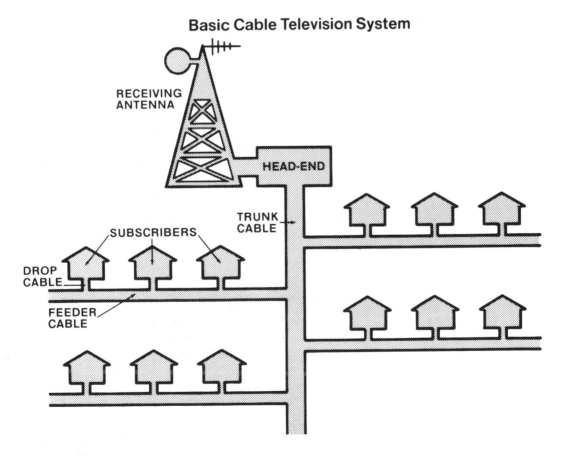

Figure 9-1 (NCTA)

though those in use have been used primarily in conjunction with a central computer and function as public opinion polling devices, other potential uses include remote reading of utility meters, interface between home and central computers, picture-phone processes, at-home banking and shopping, and monitoring of intensive care patients. When we consider that such systems can be interfaced with other systems and linked via satellite to systems anywhere in the world, the potential of a giant "wired city" concept becomes much closer to reality.

In our discussion of regulations, keep in mind that we are sitting on a threshold of new technology. Developments in fiber optics, thin strands of glass used to transmit thousands of channels, open up still new horizons in regulating the technology and developing policy which will meet the needs of users twenty-five years from now. And although we tend to discuss regulation of cable as a "what is" phenomenon, stretch your imagination and consider "what can be" the full potential of this relatively new medium.

United States v. Southwestern Cable Co.

The FCC began exercising its authority over cable in 1962. In 1965, the Commission established rules governing cable systems that received signals via microwave. A year later, the FCC added rules and regulations for cable systems not using microwave.

Knowing that a court case would soon test its jurisdiction to regulate cable, the FCC decided to prepare for the inevitable when it issued a decision limiting the ability of a San Diego, California cable system to import signals from Los Angeles. The test case came in *United States* v. *Southwestern Cable Co.,* in which the Supreme Court upheld the FCC's right to regulate cable as part of its mandate under the Communications Act to regulate "interstate commerce by wire or radio." By 1968, the FCC started an official rulemaking proceeding to develop comprehensive regulations for cable, which it finally issued in 1972.[1] In the midst of all of this activity, cable came under the framework not only of the federal government but of state and local governments as well. Recently, the FCC has been attempting to move away from federal regulation of cable and shift the burden of control to the local communities.

Our discussion of cable regulation will be general, rather than specific. The complex regulations affecting different communities and cable systems are a maze of legal and technical terminology. If you are interested in the regulations affecting a particular system, then you should obtain a copy of the cable TV ordinance for that community. Consult an attorney knowledgable in communication law and the local ordinance should you desire precise interpretation of a rule.

Local Regulatory Frameworks

The foundation of cable regulatory concepts is found at the local level. Unlike over-the-air broadcasting, cable can be regulated by its local community, which has the authority to place certain service and operational requirements upon it, to levy fees, and to determine community-access channels. The types of local control vary considerably. Professor Vernone Sparkes studied these different types and classified them into five agency organizations.[2] The first is an *administrative office,* where the local government establishes a regulatory agency much like the FCC. It might be found in the mayor's office or in the city planner's office. A second type is the *advisory committee,* which can be appointed by the mayor or the city council to "advise" city government on cable regulation. Closely related to the advisory committee is an *advisory committee with administrative office,* which "combines an appointed advisory committee with a full-time salaried executive office." Sparkes points out that the executive usually works independently from the advisory committee, with the latter advising the city council on policy matters. A fourth organization calls for the creation of an *independent regulatory commission,* which administrates and participates in rulemaking. A fifth plan provides for an *elected board* answering to the electorate on cable regulations, rather than to another elected body.

Recommended Franchise Standards

The franchise is the contractual agreement that exists between the local governmental unit and the cable company.

While the FCC has kept a regulatory distance between itself and local authorities governing cable systems, the Commission has adopted *recommended* standards, which local communities can follow in dealing with local cable systems. The FCC recommends that any cable franchise should contain the following provisions:

1. The franchising authority should approve a franchisee's qualifications only after a full public proceeding affording due process;
2. Neither the initial franchise period nor the renewal period should exceed 15 years, and any renewal should be granted only after a public proceeding affording due process;
3. The franchise should accomplish significant construction within one year after registering with the Commission and make service available to a substantial portion of the franchise area each following year, as determined by the franchising authority;
4. A franchise policy requiring less than complete wiring of the franchise area should be adopted only after a full public proceeding, preceded by specific notice of such policy; and
5. The franchise should specify that the franchisee and franchisor have adopted local procedures for investigating and resolving complaints.[3]

The FCC also recommends that local franchisees adopt a local complaint procedure, identify a local person to handle complaints, and specify how complaints can be reported and resolved. The FCC recommends that the franchisee identify, by title, the office or person who is responsible for the continuing administration of the franchise and the implementation of complaint procedures.

The Cable Television Ordinance

At the heart of the contractual relationship between the community and the cable system operator is the cable ordinance. The ordinance is the foundation and first step when a municipality or county decides to grant a franchise. Attorney Grainger R. Barrett of the Institute of Government at The University of North Carolina at Chapel Hill discusses in the following paragraphs what a good cable TV ordinance should contain:[4]

authority granted length of franchise

After defining certain key terms, the ordinance will deal with the *award and terms* of the franchise itself. It will grant authority to operate a cable TV system (including satellite transmission and interconnection) within the geographical area the franchise is to cover. The ordinance should state the length of the franchise term, whether renewals will be granted, and procedures for renewal. The FCC feels that renewals should not be granted automatically upon the operator's request, but should be a time to evaluate the operator's service. Although the FCC recommends a franchise term of no longer than 15 years, other groups have recommended a ten-year term, arguing that initial capital costs and investment can be recouped in that time.[5] It may also be wise to require reviews of the operator's service every three to five years and give the community a chance to renegotiate key items.

transfer of franchise

The ordinance should specify the circumstances under which the franchise may be transferred and whether a locality must consent before working control of the franchise changes hands. The right to transfer the franchise should be restricted to avoid trafficking in franchise awards. A good ordinance should provide that the franchise may not be transferred during the first two years of construction and thereafter only with the locality's consent—though perhaps the ordinance might also provide that consent will not be withheld unreasonably. The community should seek to retain the right to choose its franchisee throughout the entire term of the franchise. For this reason, the ordinance should also address involuntary transfers, such as bankruptcies or foreclosures by lenders.

If effective control of a cable TV franchise changes, the locality will find itself dealing with entirely new management. The ordinance should state what will constitute a change in control; for example, it might state that a change in control has occurred if more than 10 per cent of the stock of a corporation has been acquired by a person or persons acting in concert. To be fair to the operator, the ordinance can provide that a transfer is automatically approved if the governing board takes no action within 60 days of notice of transfer.

termination of franchise

The ordinance should state the grounds for terminating the franchise. Usually cable franchises can be terminated after notice and a public hearing if (1) the operator has failed to comply with or has violated in any material respect any provision of the ordinance; (2) the operator has knowingly made a materially false statement in its franchise application; (3) the operator, contrary to the public interest, is not providing subscribers with regular, adequate, and proper service; or (4) the installed cable system is unused for a continuous period of 12 months or more. A provision requiring an operator whose fanchise is terminated to continue to serve subscribers without interruption until the new operator takes over is helpful.

extension of service

The ordinance should set the community's guidelines for service coverage and extension. If cable is to be extended to less than all of the community, the operator should be required to offer service to areas that have at least a specified density of homes per street-mile (typically 40 or 50). The ordinance should require construction to begin within a certain time after the franchise is awarded and include a specific timetable for construction in the years that follow.

franchise fee and cable rates

The ordinance should contain provisions that establish the franchise fee and set initial rates. The fee should be based on gross subscriber revenues—which the FCC defines as including not only regular subscriber service revenue (as the FCC once defined gross revenues) but also all other revenues derived from operation of the cable system. The 3 per cent fee thus applies to basic monthly cable fees, installation fees, disconnect and reconnect fees, pay TV revenues, leased-channel revenues, advertising revenues, and any other revenue derived from operation of the system.

Some localities require a franchise fee even during the initial construction period when little revenue is coming in. Since the operator is already conducting business under the franchise, many of these localities call for a percentage fee or a lump sum, such as $500 per month, whichever is greater. If this lump sum exceeds 3 percent of gross subscriber revenues, this arrangement would seem to violate the FCC's fee rule unless it is approved by the FCC.

The locality should consider fixing initial rates until construction of the cable system is well under way. Most localities expect that at least half of the franchise territory should be covered within two or three years. After that time, the operator should be required to file proposed rate modifications with the governing board 30 or 60 days before they become effective. The municipality should be aware that if it decides not to regulate rates, it foregoes that power for the life of the franchise. A better practice is to retain the right to approve rate modifications and provide that if the municipality does not act within a 30- or 60-day period, the rate change is deemed approved.

channel capacity

The community must decide how many channels of cable capacity it wants. Without set top converters, cable TV has capacity for only twelve channels.

Twenty or more channels can be received with a relatively inexpensive converter; more sophisticated equipment can bring in over forty channels. The community should consider whether it wants access channels reserved for government, educational institutions, civic groups, and the general public and should provide for administering these channels—perhaps such as through an advisory committee or cable commission. Some ground rules should be set governing who has access and when and who pays what costs. Other regulations may also be needed, particularly in the area of political broadcasting.

construction standards, pole use, street work

Most ordinances go into some detail regarding construction standards, installation of poles and lines, conformance with zoning requirements, street and right-of-way excavation and restoration, and similar matters. The construction standards should incorporate national standards, such as the National Electrical Safety Code, by reference, in addition to local electrical and building codes. The town's permission should be required before tree-trimming, and the operator should be required to restore any sidewalks or pavements that are torn up.

The operator typically enters into an agreement separate from the ordinance or the franchise agreement to string cable on municipal or private utility poles. A cable TV ordinance should require that any pole-use agreements between a private utility and the operator be filed with the municipality. Most ordinances require the cable operator to use existing utility poles and permit it to install its own poles only where none now exist. Some localities require that cable lines be placed underground wherever telephone *or* power lines are underground, others require underground cable only if *both* telephone and power lines are buried, and still others do not specify any practice.

testing

The ordinance should require periodic testing of the system to insure that technical standards and quality are maintained. Results of system performance and tests, including measurements at the receiving antenna as well as various parts of the system, should be filed periodically with the municipality. The FCC has set technical standards in the Code of Federal Regulations,[6] but specific standards and descriptions of the system equipment performance can be included in the franchise agreement.

local business office

A good cable TV ordinance will require the operator to maintain and staff a local office, to adopt specific complaint procedures that include keeping a log of all complaints received, and to provide adequate maintenance crews within the community. The franchise agreement might also require that an adequate supply of spare parts be kept locally to avoid delay in making repairs.

purchase of system

The community should by ordinance reserve the right to buy the system's assets from the operator at fair value or through arbitration whenever the franchise is terminated. Or to ease the transition when the franchise ends, it can require an operator whose franchise is terminated—either for cause or by nonrenewal—to sell the system's assets to any successor franchisee.

bonds and indemnity

The ordinance should require the operator to hold the municipality harmless against all claims and actions arising from the franchisee's operation of the cable system. It should further require the operator to obtain liability insurance and to file those certificates with the municipality, sending the municipality copies of all policy changes. Typical coverage ranges from $100,000 to $500,000 per person for bodily injury; $500,000 to $1,000,000 per occurrence for bodily injury; and $300,000 to $500,000 per occurrence for property damage. The ordinance should also require a performance bond at least until all initial construction is finished. More and more, however, localities require a construction bond during that period and an additional performance bond for the duration of the franchise. This requirement will help to insure continuous satisfactory service and prevent financial loss to the locality if the operator should owe it money and should default.

financial records and reports

The ordinance should provide for the municipality to receive an annual certified audit of the system's finances 90 days or so after the fiscal year ends and for the governing board to have access to all cable system books and records. It should further require the operator to update annually its ownership information and list of major stockholders, which are on file with the municipality. The operator should also be required to send the governing board a copy of all of its communications to the FCC, the Securities and Exchange Commission, or other state and federal regulatory agencies.

Cable and Copyright: The Compulsory License

Under copyright law, cable systems are required to receive a *Compulsory License,* permitting them to carry over-the-air signals pursuant to FCC rules. This license should not be confused with the contracts or other agreements that are instituted by local or state agreements with cable systems, which govern the actual operation and fee schedule of the system.

structure of compulsory licensing

The copyright law views cable systems as commercial entities, involved in the "performance" of copyrighted works, and as such they must pay copyright fees under the compulsory licensing system. For example, under the new law and compulsory licensing, commercial broadcasters receive protection from infringement by cable systems, which might carry the cable system's programming but delete its commercials. As another example, assume a cable company carries Channel 2 television from Anytown, U.S.A. Channel 2 sells advertising to sponsors with the understanding that the station's signal reaches not only Anytown but also outlying communities via cable. The cable company, on the other hand, decides to delete Channel 2's commercials and insert either its own commercials or public service announcements. This action by the cable company could now be considered illegal. The law gives a television or radio station the right to take a cable company to court, not only to stop the practice of commercial substitution but also to receive damages.

obtaining and renewing the compulsory license

To obtain and keep its Compulsory License, a cable company must meet four requirements:

> **Initial Notice of Identity and Signal Carriage Complement.** The cable system obtains its compulsory license by filing an Initial Notice in the Copyright Office. The statute requires that the filing take place at least one month before the date when the cable system begins operations.
>
> **Notice of Change of Identity or Signal Carriage Complement.** If the owner of the cable system changes, or if there is a change in the list of television and radio stations that the system is carrying regularly, the system is required to send a notice of the change to the Copyright Office within thirty days.
>
> **Statement of Account for Secondary Transmissions by Cable Systems.** Every six months the cable system must send the Copyright Office a Statement of Account Form, depending on the amount of "gross receipts" [in the very simplest terms, think of "receipts" as income the cable system earns] for the accounting period.
>
> **Royalty Fee.** Each semiannual Statement of Account must be accompanied by the deposit of a royalty fee covering retransmissions during the preceding six months.[7]

Three different "Statement of Accounts" are employed by the Copyright Office: The *Short Form* is used for cable systems with gross receipts of $41,500 or less; those with gross receipts of more than $41,500 and less than $160,000 use the *Intermediate Form;* and the *Long Form* is for those with gross receipts in excess of $160,000.

figuring royalty fees

The Intermediate Form provides us with a good example of how royalty fees are computed. Figure 9-2 illustrates parts K (Gross Receipts) and L (Royalty Fee). Notice that the form further breaks down the gross receipts into "Block 1," gross receipts of $80,000 or less (but more than $41,500) and "Block 2," gross receipts of more than $80,000 (but less than $160,000). Notice also that the figure $80,000 appears in bold numerals under both Block 1 and Block 2. The $80,000 is the base amount used to determine all royalty fees for systems using the Intermediate Form.

Now examine Figure 9-3. Here we can see a step-by-step example of how two cable systems would figure their fees; one with gross receipts of $60,000, the other with gross receipts of $125,000. Keep in mind the fact that the fees listed have to be paid every six months. For larger systems, the semiannual fees can

Name	LEGAL NAME OF OWNER OF CABLE SYSTEM: (Give the name exactly as it appears in space B, line 1)

(K)

Gross Receipts

GROSS RECEIPTS

Instructions: The figure you give in this space determines the form you file and the amount you pay. Enter the total of all of the amounts ("gross receipts") paid to your cable system by subscribers for the system's "secondary transmission service" (the basic service of retransmitting television and radio broadcasts) during the accounting period. For a further explanation of how to compute this amount, see page (v) of the General Instructions.

- Gross receipts from subscribers for secondary transmission service
  during the accounting period ....

  $ _____
  (Amount of "gross receipts")

  NOTE: If the figure you give in this space is $41,500 or less, or $160,000, or more you should not use this Intermediate Form CS/SA-2. (See page (i) of the General Instructions.)

(L)

Copyright Royalty Fee

INSTRUCTIONS FOR COMPUTING ROYALTY FEE

To compute the royalty fee you owe:
- Complete either block 1 or block 2, not both;
- Use block 1 if the amount of "gross receipts" in space K is $80,000 or less, but more than $41,500.
- Use block 2 if the amount of "gross receipts" in Space K is more than $80,000 but less than $160,000.

See page (v) of the General Instructions for more information and examples.

BLOCK 1: "GROSS RECEIPTS" OF $80,000 OR LESS (but more than $41,500)

1. Base amount under statutory formula ....▶____**$80,000**

2. Enter amount of "gross receipts" from space K ....▶_____

3. Subtract line 2 from line 1 ....▶_____

4. Enter the amount of "gross receipts" from space K ....▶_____

5. Enter the amount from line 3 ....▶_____

6. Subtract line 5 from line 4 ....▶_____

7. Multiply line 6 by .005 (Enter figure here and in line 8) ....▶_____

8. **TOTAL ROYALTY FEE PAYABLE FOR ACCOUNTING PERIOD** ....▶ $ _____

BLOCK 2: "GROSS RECEIPTS" OF MORE THAN $80,000 (but less than $160,000)

1. Enter amount of "gross receipts" from space K ....▶ $_____

2. Base amount under statutory formula ....▶____**$80,000**

3. Subtract line 2 from line 1 ....▶_____

4. Multiply line 3 by .01 ....▶_____

5. Royalty due on the first $80,000 of gross receipts
   (under statutory formula) ....▶____**$400**

6. Add lines 4 and 5 (Enter figure here and in line 7) ....▶_____

7. **TOTAL ROYALTY FEE PAYABLE FOR ACCOUNTING PERIOD** ....▶ $ _____

IMPORTANT: When you file your Statement of Account on this form CS/SA-2, you must also enclose with it the royalty fee you have computed in block 1 or block 2, above. Your remittance must be in the form of a **certified check, cashier's check,** or **money order,** payable to: *Register of Copyrights.* Other forms of remittance, including personal or company checks, will be returned, and your Statement of Account will not be accepted until the correct form of remittance is received.

Figure 9-2

CALCULATING THE ROYALTY FEE		
Amount of "Gross Receipts"	**Statutory Formula**	**Examples**

$41,500-$80,000	**Step 1:** Subtract "gross receipts" (figure given in space K) from $80,000;	System's "gross receipts" for accounting period: .... $ 60,000
		 Step 1: $ 80,000
		      − 60,000
		      $ 20,000

	Step 2: Subtract the result of Step 1 from "gross receipts" (figure given in space K);	Step 2: $ 60,000
		      − 20,000
		      $ 40,000

	Step 3: Multiply the result of Step 2 by .005.	Step 3: $ 40,000 × .005 Royalty Fee $200.00

$80,000-$160,000	**Step 1:** Multiply the first $80,000 of "gross receipts" by .005 (the result of Step 1 is $400 in all cases);	System's "gross receipts" for accounting period: $125,000
		 Step 1: $ 80,000
		      × .005
		      $ 400.00

	Step 2: Multiply "gross receipts" over $80,000 by .01;	Step 2: $125,000
		      − 80,000
		      45,000
		      × .01
		      $ 450.00

	Step 3: Add the results of Steps 1 and 2.	Step 3: $ 400.00 + 450.00 Royalty Fee .... $ 850.00

Figure 9-3

easily run into the thousands of dollars. For cable systems with gross receipts of less than $41,500, the semiannual royalty fee was originally set at $15.00.

It is important to remember that all fees are subject to change.

primary and secondary transmission services

An important distinction made under the Compulsory License for copyright liability is between primary and secondary transmission services.

"Primary Transmission Service." This service includes *broadcasts by radio and television stations to the public* that are retransmitted by cable systems to their subscribers (Figure 9-4).

"Secondary Transmission Service." This is the *basic service of retransmitting television and radio broadcasts to subscribers* (Figure 9-5). Under the old law, as interpreted by the courts, secondary transmission services were free from copyright control. This is no longer true. The new statute requires all U.S. cable systems, regardless of how many subscribers they have or whether they are carrying any distant signals, to pay some copyright royalties. However, instead of obliging cable systems to bargain individually for each copyrighted program they retransmit, the law offers them the opportunity of obtaining a "compulsory license" for secondary transmissions.[8] The secondary transmission service *does not* include "transmission originated by a cable system (including local origina-

Name	LEGAL NAME OF OWNER OF CABLE SYSTEM: (Give the name exactly as it appears in space B, line 1)

(G)

Primary Transmitters: Television

INSTRUCTIONS:

General: In space G, identify every television station (including translator stations) carried by your cable system during the accounting period, **except:** (1) stations carried only on a part-time basis under FCC rules permitting the carriage of certain network programs [sections 76.59(d)(2) and (4), 76.61(e)(2) and (4) or 76.63 (referring to 76.61(e)(2) and (4))]; and (2) certain stations carried on a substitute program basis, as explained in the next paragraph.

Substitute Basis Stations: With respect to any distant stations carried by your cable system on a substitute program basis under certain FCC rules, regulations, or authorizations:

• Do **not** list the station here in space G—but **do** list it in space I (the Special Statement and Program Log)—if the station was carried **only** on a substitute basis.

• List the station here, and **also** in space I, if the station was carried both on a substitute basis and also on some other basis.

For further information concerning substitute basis stations, see page (iv) of the General Instructions.

Column 1: List each station's call sign.

Column 2: Give the number of the channel on which the station's broadcasts are carried in its own community. This may be different from the channel on which your cable system carried the station.

Column 3: Indicate in each case whether the station is a network station, an independent station, or a noncommercial educational station, by entering the letter "N" (for network), "I" (for independent) or "E" (for noncommercial educational). For the meaning of these terms, see page (iv) of the General Instructions.

Column 4: If the station is "distant," enter "Yes". If not, enter "No". For an explanation of what a "distant station" is, see page (iv) of the General Instructions.

Column 5: If you have entered "Yes" in column 4, you must complete column 5, stating the basis on which your cable system carried the distant station during the accounting period. Use the letters indicated below. If you carried the station on more than one basis, enter each appropriate letter.

A. **Part-time specialty programming:** enter the letter **"A"**.

B. **Late-night programming:** enter the letter **"B"**.

C. **Part-time carriage because of lack of activated channel capacity:** enter the letter **"C"**.

D. **Any basis of carriage other than those listed in "A," "B," and "C," above:** enter the letter **"D"**.

For an explanation of these categories, see page (iv) of the General Instructions.

Note: As explained above, distant stations carried only on a substitute basis during the accounting period should be listed in space I but not in space G. If the station was carried on both a substitute basis and some other basis, only the latter need be stated here in column 5.

Column 6: Give the location of each station. For U.S. stations, list the community to which the station is licensed by the FCC. For Mexican or Canadian stations, if any, give the name of the community with which the station is identified.

1. CALL SIGN	2. B'CAST CHANNEL NUMBER	3. TYPE OF STATION	4. DISTANT? (Yes or No)	5. BASIS OF CARRIAGE (If Distant)	6. LOCATION OF STATION

Figure 9-4

LEGAL NAME OF OWNER OF CABLE SYSTEM: (Give the name exactly as it appears in space B, line 1)

....

Name

SECONDARY TRANSMISSION SERVICE: SUBSCRIBERS AND RATES

In General: The information in space E should cover all categories of "secondary transmission service" of the cable system: that is, the retransmission of television and radio broadcasts by your system to subscribers. Give information about other services (including pay-cable) in space F, not here. All the facts you state must be those existing on the last day of the accounting period (June 30 or December 31, as the case may be).

Number of Subscribers: Both blocks in space E call for the number of subscribers to the cable system, broken down by categories of secondary transmission service. In general, you can compute the number of "subscribers" in each category by counting the number of billings in that category (the number of persons or organizations charged separately for the particular service at the rate indicated—not the number of sets receiving service).

Rate: Give the standard rate charged for each category of service. Include both the amount of the charge and the unit in which it is generally billed. (Example: "$6/mth"). Summarize any standard rate variations within a particular rate category, but do not include discounts allowed for advance payment.

Block 1: In the left-hand block in space E, the form lists the categories of secondary transmission service that cable systems most commonly provide to their subscribers. Give the number of subscribers and rate for each listed category that applies to your system. **Note:** Where an individual or organization is receiving service that falls under different categories, that person or entity should be counted as a "subscriber" in each applicable category. Example: a residential subscriber who pays extra for cable service to additional sets would be included in the count under "Service to First Set," and would be counted once again under "Service to Additional Set(s)."

Block 2: If your cable system has rate categories for secondary transmission service that are different from those printed in block 1, list them, together with the number of subscribers and rates, in the right-hand block. A two- or three-word description of the service is sufficient.

E

Secondary Transmission Service: Subscribers and Rates

BLOCK 1			BLOCK 2		
CATEGORY OF SERVICE	NO. OF SUBSCRIBERS	RATE	CATEGORY OF SERVICE	NO. OF SUBSCRIBERS	RATE
Residential:					
• Service to First Set					
• Service to Additional Set(s)					
• FM Radio (if different rate)					
Motel, Hotel					
Commercial					
Converter					
• Residential					
• Non-Residential					

SERVICES OTHER THAN SECONDARY TRANSMISSIONS: RATES

In General: Space F calls for rate (not subscriber) information with respect to all your cable system's services that were not covered in space E. There are two exceptions: you do not need to give rate information concerning: (1) services furnished at cost; and (2) services or facilities furnished to nonsubscribers. Rate information should include both the amount of the charge and the unit in which it is usually billed. If any rates are charged on a variable per-program basis, enter only the letters "PP" in the rate column.

Block 1: Give the standard rate charged by the cable system for each of the applicable services listed.

Block 2: List any services that your cable system furnished or offered during the accounting period that were not listed in block 1 and for which a separate charge was made or established. List these other services in the form of a brief (two- or three-word) description, and include the rate for each.

F

Services Other Than Secondary Transmissions: Rates

BLOCK 1				BLOCK 2	
CATEGORY OF SERVICE	RATE	CATEGORY OF SERVICE	RATE	CATEGORY OF SERVICE	RATE
Continuing Services:		**Installation: Non-Residential**			
• Pay Cable		• Motel, Hotel			
• Pay Cable—Add'l Channel		• Commercial			
• Fire Protection		• Pay Cable			
• Burglar Protection		• Pay Cable—Add'l Channel			
Installation: Residential		• Fire Protection			
• First Set		• Burglar Protection			
• Additional Set(s)		**Other Services:**			
• FM Radio (if different rate)		• Reconnect			
• Converter		• Disconnect			
		• Outlet Relocation			
		• Move to New Address			

Figure 9-5

tion cablecasting, pay-cable, background music services, and originations on leased or access channels)."[9]

restrictions of the compulsory license

While there are many benefits to the Compulsory License, such as not having to negotiate individual copyright licenses for retransmission of television and radio broadcasts, there are also certain things the License *does not* permit. For example, limitations of the License include:

Originations. To repeat: a cable system's compulsory license extends only to secondary transmission (retransmissions). It does not permit the system to make any originations of copyrighted material without a negotiated license covering that material.

Nonsimultaneous Retransmissions. In general, to be subject to compulsory licensing under the copyright law, a cable retransmission must be simultaneous with the broadcast being carried. As a rule, taping or other recording of the program is not permitted. Taping for delayed retransmission is permissible only for some (not all) cable systems located outside the 48 contiguous States; and, even in these exceptional cases, there are further limitations and conditions that the cable system must meet.

FCC Violations. The broadcast signals that a cable system can carry under a compulsory license are limited to those that it is permitted to carry under FCC rules, regulations, and authorizations. If signal carriage is in violation of FCC requirements, the cable system may be subject under the Copyright Act to a separate action for copyright infringement for each unauthorized retransmission.

Foreign Signals. In general, the copyright law does not permit a cable system to retransmit signals of foreign television and radio stations under a compulsory license. The only exceptions have to do with the signals of certain Mexican and Canadian stations. Unless foreign signals fall within these exceptions, their carriage would not be authorized under a compulsory license, even if permissible under FCC rules.

Program Alteration or Commercial Substitution. Cable systems are not permitted to alter the content of retransmitted programs, or to change, delete, or substitute commercials or station announcements in or adjacent to programs being carried. There is only one exception: under certain circumstances, substitutions involving "commercial advertising market research" may be permitted.[10]

forfeiture of the compulsory license

In somewhat the same way as a station license can be forfeited, the cable system can also lose its Compulsory License. For example, failure to file the required Initial Notice of Identity or Notices of Change can result in loss of the Compulsory License.[11] Other violations can include failing to file the Statements of Account or royalty fees; taping for delayed transmission; carrying signals in violation of FCC requirements; carrying certain foreign stations; and altering programs or substituting commercials."[12]

If a cable system goes so far as to disregard the copyright laws and not obtain a license, it can be sued by a copyright owner, and the owner can attempt to collect actual damages and profits, or statutory damages up to $50,000, in the case of willful infringement. Civil and criminal penalties as well as injunctions can be served on the cable system.[13]

special cases: syndicated programming and commercial establishments

The violation of certain syndicated programming rules by cable companies can also invite court action under copyright law. If a television station buys the exclusive carriage rights for a given market for a copyrighted program, the television station, along with the program copyright holder, is considered to own the copyright for the duration of the contract. And if a cable company violates FCC rules and imports the same program from a distant television station, the local station holding the rights to carry the program would have grounds for suit. The key is that the cable company must first violate FCC rules on syndicated program exclusivity before the local television station has grounds to go to court.

Use of broadcast signals, whether over-the-air or cable, in commercial establishments is another aspect of copyright law. The small restaurant owner who brings a radio to work and turns it on loud enough so that the customers can hear music might not need to worry about copyright violations. On the other hand, if a department store owner hooks his radio or the audio of an incoming cable channel up to a storewide sound system, with speakers on every floor, he could face copyright infringement charges. This area of the law is perhaps the grayest, and it will take a series of court decisions to determine the precise interpretation of the law.

State Regulation of Cable

State government also plays a major role in controlling cable.[14] However, state control is not widespread and varies in degree. State laws can be classified into three categories. First are *pre-empt* statutes. These are the strongest laws, and they take precedent over local regulations. With pre-empt statutes, cable falls under the jurisdiction of the Public Utility or Public Service Commission in some states. Pre-empt statutes give considerable clout to a state commission, permitting it to issue and enforce a separate set of state cable regulations. These rules can govern everything from the day-to-day operation of the cable system, to collecting fees on gross revenue, to demanding financial collateral before allowing construction. A second type of control falls under the *appellate* statutes. Here, local municipalities retain some control over franchising, but the state has the power to review local agreements and be the final arbiter of disputes. Everything works fine until the state and a municipality disagree, then the municipality stands a less than even chance against the state. A less powerful state statute is the *advisory* statute. This is more popular with cable systems and municipalities, since it does not have either the clout or the enforcement power of a state commission. Some serve as "general guidelines," which serve as a reference for local government.

Proponents of state control argue the need for consistency among cable systems within a state. Such arguments gain support when two municipalities cannot resolve their jurisdictional differences over a cable system or when significantly differing fee structures provoke public outcry. Control of cable can also be a political plum for legislators, since it means control of a communication system, and communication influences public opinion. Since cable commissions can have a significant effect on cable growth within a state, appointment to the commission can be a sweet political reward for someone in the party in power.

Arguments against state control are equally vociferous, asserting that it presents an unnecessary duplication of law. States are sometimes caught in the middle between local and federal control, and meeting the requirements of one can violate those of the other. Opponents claim that state control throws local interests into a political arena with representatives who are looking out for their own interests, not for those of the local community. The "Big Brother" argument also pops up as people argue that when a state becomes involved in direct programming, it will be oriented more toward propaganda than public interest.

Despite the existence of state statutes, local municipalities seem to continue to have fairly firm control over local cable systems. Moreover, with the tremendous diversity among the systems and the communities they serve, governance at the municipal level appears to have significant advantage over state control.

summary

This chapter deals with cable television, which evolved in the late 1940s, when operators in Pennsylvania and Oregon improved their television reception by having several communities share a single antenna located on a nearby hilltop or mountain. Today, cable systems serve some 10 million subscribers. The basic components of the system include the head-end, which consists of both hardware and human resources. At the heart of the head-end is the receiving antenna, used to pick up distant radio and television signals for distribution to subscribers. After leaving the head-end, the signal travels over trunk cables, feeder or subtrunk cables, and eventually reaches a subscriber's home via a drop cable and home terminal.

The FCC first won authority over cable in the *Southwestern* case. In addition to establishing controls for rates and carriage requirements, the Commission has tried to delegate regulatory responsibility over cable to states and local governments. Now communities wanting to construct cable systems need only follow basic guidelines, mostly dealing with system penetration, due process, and rate structures.

At the heart of the contractual relationship between the community and the cable operator is the local cable television ordinance. A good ordinance should provide for such things as the length of the franchise, provisions for transfer, termination of the franchise, extension of service, franchise fee and cable rates, channel capacity, construction standards, testing, local business office, purchase of the system, bonds and indemnity, and financial records and reports.

The U.S. Copyright Office became involved in cable with the passage of the 1976 copyright laws. Depending on their gross receipts, cable systems are required to file with the U.S. Copyright Office one of three forms, plus appropriate royalty fees. Royalty fees are computed by using a combination base amount formula, a percentage of gross receipts, or, in the case of small systems, a flat fee of $15.00. Royalty fees are paid, and Account Forms filed, semiannually.

While we tend to hear more about federal and local control of cable systems, some states also place control over cable. State statutes governing cable tend to fall into three categories: pre-empt statutes, which are the strongest and place the most control over cable and the municipalities controlling cable; appellate statutes, which give states the power to review municipal control of cable and arbitrate disputes; and advisory statutes, which are the weakest of the three and serve primarily to "guide" local governments in dealing with cable systems.

material for analysis

The definitions applied to cable television for the purposes of the Copyright Act provide a deeper understanding of how a cable system operates and how its function integrates with copyright law. Following the definitions is a succinct explanation of the provisions found in the Copyright Act as they apply to cable.

Definitions Applying to the Cable Television Provisions of the Copyright Act of 1976, Sec. 111(f)

PUBLIC LAW 94-553, 94TH CONGRESS

(f) DEFINITIONS

As used in this section, the following terms and their variant forms mean the following:

A "primary transmission" is a transmission made to the public by the transmitting facility whose signals are being received and further transmitted by the secondary transmission service, regardless of where or when the performance or display was first transmitted.

A "secondary transmission" is the further transmitting of a primary transmission simultaneously with the primary transmission, or nonsimultaneously with the primary transmission if by a "cable system" not located in whole or in part within the boundary of the forty-eight contiguous States, Hawaii, or Puerto Rico: *Provided, however,* That a nonsimultaneous further transmission by a cable system located in Hawaii of a primary transmission shall be deemed to be a secondary transmission if the carriage of the television broadcast signal comprising such further transmission is permissible under the rules, regulations, or authorizations of the Federal Communications Commission.

A "cable system" is a facility, located in any State, Territory, Trust Territory, or Possession, that in whole or in part receives signals transmitted or programs broadcast by one or more television broadcast stations licensed by the Federal Communications Commission, and makes secondary transmissions of such signals or programs by wires, cables, or other communications channels to subscribing members of the public who pay for such service. For purposes of determining the royalty fee under subsection (d)(2), two or more cable systems in contiguous communities under common ownership or control or operating from one head-end shall be considered as one system.

The "local service area of a primary transmitter," in the case of a television broadcast station, comprises the area in which such station is entitled to insist upon its signal being retransmitted by a cable system pursuant to the rules, regulations, and authorizations of the Federal Communications Commission in effect on April 15, 1976, or in the case of a television broadcast station licensed by an appropriate governmental authority of Canada or Mexico, the area in which it would be entitled to insist upon its signal being retransmitted if it were a television broadcast station subject to such rules, regulations, and authorizations. The "local service area of a primary transmitter," in the case of a radio broadcast station, comprises the primary service area of such station, pursuant to the rules and regulations of the Federal Communications Commission.

A "distant signal equivalent" is the value assigned to the secondary transmission of any nonnetwork television programming carried by a cable system in whole or in part beyond the local service area of the primary transmitter of such programming. It is computed by assigning a value of one to each independent station and a value of one-quarter to each network station and noncommercial educational station for the nonnetwork programing so carried pursuant to the rules, regulations, and authorizations of the Federal Communications Commission. The foregoing values for independent, network, and noncommercial educational stations are subject, however, to the following exceptions and limitations. Where the rules and regulations of the Federal Communications Commission require a cable system to omit the further transmission of a particular program and such rules and regulations also permit the substitution of another program embodying a performance or display of a work in place of the omitted transmission, or where such rules and regulations in effect on the date of enactment of this Act permit a cable system, at its election, to effect such deletion and substitution of a nonlive program or to carry additional programs not transmitted by primary transmitters within whose local service area the cable system is located, no value shall be assigned for the substituted or additional program; where the rules, regulations, or authorizations of the Federal Communications Commission in effect on the date of enactment of this Act permit a cable system, at its election, to omit the further transmission of a particular program and such rules, regulations, or authorizations also permit the substitution of another program embodying a performance or display of a work in place of the omitted transmission, the value assigned for the substituted or additional program shall be, in the case of a live program, the value of one full distant signal equivalent multiplied by a fraction that has as its numerator the number of days in the year in which such substitution occurs and as its denominator the number of days in the year. In the case of a station carried pursuant to the late-night or specialty programing rules of the Federal Communications Commission, or a station carried on a part-time basis where full-time carriage is not possible because the cable system lacks the activated channel capacity to retransmit on a full-time basis all signals which it is authorized to carry, the values for independent, network, and noncommercial educational stations set forth above, as the case may be, shall be multiplied by a fraction which is equal to the ratio of the broadcast hours of such station carried by the cable system to the total broadcast hours of the station.

A "network station" is a television broadcast station that is owned or operated by, or affiliated with, one or more of the television networks in the United States providing nationwide transmissions, and that transmits a substantial part of the programing supplied by such networks for a substantial part of that station's typical broadcast day.

An "independent station" is a commercial television broadcast station other than a network station.

A "noncommercial educational station" is a television station that is a noncommercial educational broadcast station as defined in section 397 of title 47.

questions for discussion and further research

1. The Copyright Act of 1976 views cable television as a commercial enterprise engaged in the "performance" of copyrighted works. Aside from the agreements, with music rights organizations, standard broadcast stations do not face the paperwork and accountability to the Copyright Office that cable systems do. Why is there such concern over cable's copyright liability?

2. The Copyright Act views cable systems as commercial enterprises engaged in the "performance" of copyrighted works. Could the same definition be applied to over-the-air commercial broadcasters?

3. One alternative to the Compulsory Licensing arrangement would be to have each cable system negotiate directly with the broadcast station or copyright owner about rebroadcasting their material. Would such an arrangement be workable, and would it be more or less satisfactory than the current Compulsory License?

4. Although the cable industry is regulated by the FCC, the industry also falls under the jurisdiction of various state and local authorities. On occasion, these different levels of jurisdiction conflict. Would it be wise for cable to be placed exclusively under the federal government, taking local and state authorities out of cable regulation altogether?

5. Could these conflicts be resolved if a *single* level of government (local, state, or federal) had jurisdiction over cable? If so, which level would be appropriate?

6. Professor Vernone Sparkes outlines the different regulatory frameworks under which cable television falls, ranging from administrative offices to elected boards. What are the advantages and disadvantages of each framework?

7. Many cable systems now possess two-way and data-processing capabilities. What new policy issues might arise as this technology becomes even more widespread?

8. Since local municipalities have the power to determine many of the conditions of a cable franchise, as well as to determine who gets the franchise, do the cable systems that originate their own news programming run a serious risk of repercussions if they criticize the local government? What safeguards and recourse are available to cable companies which feel they have been wronged by local officials because of criticism occurring on cable news programming?

9. It is becoming commonplace for cable systems to be linked together via satellite communication and for cable systems to originate as well as to distribute programming. The technology is available, and it will soon be economically practical for cable systems to be linked across continents. New regulatory issues are sure to arise which will integrate the policies affecting cable with those of satellite communication. Ask yourself: What are some of these issues and what role will international law play in the future development of worldwide cable systems?

10. For small cable systems, are the copyright forms more trouble than the $15 royalty fee is worth?

11. In addition to royalty fees, what additional costs might cable systems incur by the semiannual requirement to complete the Statement of Account forms?

12. Do you feel that the royalty fees are high enough? Too high?

13. Many nations, the United States among

them, are major producers and suppliers of international television programming. Many programs seen in the United States are seen in foreign countries, and, in some cases, programs from the major production centers of the United States are produced for direct export. In a world where multiple cable channels will increase the demand for diversified programming, what role will heavy producers and suppliers of programming play in the influencing of world opinion, as well as in international communication policy?

14. Will countries with high technology, regardless of their position in world affairs, be in a stronger position to influence international communication policy?

15. What role would the prestige or power of a given nation play in influencing international communication policy?

additional resources

books

Baer, W. S., *Cable Television: A Handbook for Decisionmaking,* Santa Monica, Cal.: Rand Corp., 1973.

Berman, P. J., *CATV Leased-Access Channels and the Federal Communications Commission: The Intractable Jurisdictional Question,* Cambridge, Mass.: Harvard Program on Information Technologies and Public Policy, 1975.

Berner, R. O., *Constraints in the Regulatory Process: A Case Study of Regulation of Cable Television,* Cambridge, Mass.: Harvard Program on Information Technologies and Public Policy, 1975.

Grundfest, J., and S. N. Brotman, *Teletext and Viewdata: The Issues of Policy, Service, and Technology,* New York: Aspen Institute for Humanistic Studies, 1979.

Johnson, L. L., and M. Botein, *Cable Television: The Process of Franchising,* Santa Monica, Calif.: Rand Corp., 1973.

Le Duc, D. R., *Cable Television and the FCC: A Crisis in Media Control,* Philadelphia: Temple University Press, 1973.

MacAvoy, P. W., ed. *Deregulation of Cable Television,* Washington, D.C.: American Enterprise Institute for Public Policy Research, 1977.

Ross, L., *Economic and Legal Foundations of Cable Television,* Beverly Hills, Calif.: Sage Publications, 1974.

Sola Pool, I. D., ed., *Talking Back: Citizen Feedback and Cable Technology,* Cambridge, Mass.: MIT Press, 1973.

Yin, R. K., *Cable Television: Citizen Participation in Planning,* Santa Monica, Calif.: Rand Corp., 1973.

articles

Angel, D., "Legal Protection for Titles in the Entertainment Industry," 52 *Southern California Law Review* 279 (1979).

Baldwin, T. F., M. O. Wirth, and J. Zenaty, "The Economics of Per-Program Pay Cable Television," 22 *Journal of Broadcasting* 143 (1978).

Barnett, S. R., "Cable Television and Media Concentration," 22 *Stanford Law Review* 221 (1970).

Barnett, S. R., "State, Federal, and Local Regulation of Cable Television," 47 *Notre Dame Lawyer* 685 (1972).

Barrow, R. L., "Program Regulation in Cable TV: Fostering Debate in a Cohesive Audience," 61 *Virginia Law Review* 515 (1975).

Beelar, D. C., "Cables in the Sky and the Struggle for Their Control," 21 *Federal Communications Bar Journal* 26 (1967).

Berman, P. J., "CATV Leased-Access Channels and the FCC: The Intractable Jurisdiction Question," 51 *Notre Dame Lawyer* 145 (1975).

Besen, S. M., "Economics of the Cable Television 'Consensus'," 17 *Journal of Law & Economics* 39 (1974).

Botein, M., "New Copyright Act and Cable Television—A Signal of Change," 24 *Bulletin of the Copyright Society of the U.S.A.* 1 (1976).

Brunner, R. D., and K. Chen, "Is Cable the Answer?," 28 *Journal of Broadcasting* 81 (1978).

Cox, K. A., "Competition in and among the Broadcasting, CATV, and Pay-TV Industries," 13 *Antitrust Bulletin* 911 (1968).

Davis, W. A., Jr., "Cable Television Franchising —The Role of Local Governments," 51 *Florida Bar Journal* 78 (1977).

Felsenthal, N. A., "Cherry-Picking, Cable and the FCC," 19 *Journal of Broadcasting* 43 (1975).

Gerlach, G. G., "Toward the Wired Society: Prospects, Problems, and Proposals for a National Policy on Cable Technology," 25 *Maine Law Review* 193 (1973).

Greene, S. C., "Cable Television Provisions of the Revised Copyright Act," 27 *Catholic University Law Review* 263 (1978).

Hagelin, T. M., "First Amendment Stake in New Technology: The Broadcast–Cable Controversy," 44 *University of Cincinnati Law Review* 427 (1975).

Jassem, H., "Selling of the Cable TV Compromise," 17 *Journal of Broadcasting* 427 (1973).

Jeffres, L., "Cable TV and Viewer Selectivity," 22 *Journal of Broadcasting* 167 (1978).

Johnson, R. C., and R. T. Blau, "Single versus Multiple-System Cable Television Markets," 18 *Journal of Broadcasting* 323 (1974). 323–46.

Kaplan, S. J., "The Impact of Cable Television Services on the Use of Competing Media," 22 *Journal of Broadcasting* 155 (1978).

Kay, P., "Policy Issues in Interactive Cable Television," 28 *Journal of Communication* 202 (1978).

Kohn, R. I., "Cable Television: To What Extent May the State Regulate?" 49 *Los Angeles Bar Bulletin* 513 (1974).

Lapierre, D. B., "Cable Television and the Promise of Programming Diversity," 42 *Fordham Law Review* 25 (1973).

Le Duc, D. R., "Cable TV Control in Canada: A Comparative Policy Study," 20 *Journal of Broadcasting* 435 (1976).

Le Duc, D. R., "Cable-TV Franchising and the Local Bar Association: A Tailor-Made Public Service Activity for the State's Local Bar Associations," 47 *Wisconsin Bar Bulletin* 38 (1974).

Lenny, D., "Copyright Infringement Problems of a Network/Home Cable Record Selection and Playing System," 5 *Rutgers Journal of Computers & the Law* 51 (1975).

Long, S., "Antitrust and the Television Networks: Restructuring via Cable TV," 6 *Antitrust Law & Economics Review* 99 (1973).

Lorenz, L., "Origins of Pan American Copyright Protection, 1889–1910," 49 *Journalism Quarterly* 717 (1972).

Marvin, C., "Computer Systems: Prospects for a Public Information Network," 28 *Journal of Communication* 172 (1978).

Meyer, G., "Feat of Houdini: or, How the New Act Disentangles the CATV-Copyright Knot," 22 *New York Law School Law Review* 545 (1977).

Ohls, J. C., "Marginal Cost Pricing, Investment Theory and CATV," 13 *Journal of Law & Economics* 439 (1970).

Pearson, D. B., "Cable: The Thread by Which Television Competition Hangs," 27 *Rutgers Law Review* 800 (1974).

Price, M., "The Illusions of Cable Television," 24 *Journal of Communications* 71 (1974).

Price, M. E., "Cable Television in Alaska: The Need for State Initiative," 2 *UCLA–Alaska Law Review* 135 (1973).

Reiner, R. F., "Home Videorecording: Fair Use or Infringement?" 52 *Southern California Law Review* 573 (1979).

Samuelson, P. A., "Public Goods and Subscription TV: Correction of the Record," 7 *Journal of Law & Economics* 81 (1964).

Schiller, H. I., "Computer Systems: Power for Whom and for What?" 28 *Journal of Communication* 184 (1978).

Smith, J. C., Jr., "Primer on the Regulatory Development of CATV (1950–72)," 18 *Howard Law Journal* 729 (1975).

Sparkes, V. M., "Local Regulatory Agencies for Cable Television," 19 *Journal of Broadcasting* 221 (1975).

Sparkes, V. M., "Community Cablecasting in the U.S. and Canada: Different Approaches to a Common Objective," 20 *Journal of Broadcasting* 451 (1976).

Synchef, R. M., "Municipal Ownership of Cable Television Systems," 12 *University of San Francisco Law Review* 205 (1978).

Taylor, R. H., Jr., "Case for State Regulation of CATV Distribution Systems," 23 *Federal Communications Bar Journal* 110 (1969).

Wallach, M. I., "Whose Intent? A Study of Administrative Preemption: State Regulation of Cable Television," 25 *Case Western Reserve Law Review* 258 (1975).

Wiley, R. E., "Procedural Accommodation of Federal and State Regulatory Interests in Cable Television," 25 *Administrative Law Review* 213 (1973).

Wittek, W. T., "Critical Look at Northern Illinois CATV Franchises," 26 *Federal Communications Bar Journal* 242 (1973).

cases

Big Valley Cablevision, Inc. v. *F.C.C.*, 529 F.2d 353, 174 U.S.App.D.C. 111 (1976).

Bucks County Cable TV, Inc. v. *United States*, 427 F.2d 438 (1970), certiorari denied.

Columbia Broadcasting System, Inc. v. *Teleprompter Corp.*, 476 F.2d 338, affirmed in part, reversed in part 94 S.Ct. 1129, 415 U.S. 394, 39 L.Ed.2d 415 (1973).

Home Box Office, Inc. v. *F.C.C.*, 567 F.2d 9,2 Med.L.Rptr.1561 (1977), certioari denied.

Midwest Television, Inc. v. *F.C.C.*, 426 F.2d 1222, 138 U.S.App.D.C. 228 (1970).

Midwest Video Corp. v. *F.C.C.*, 571 F.2d 1025,3 Med.L.Rptr.1817, certiorari granted 99 S.Ct. 77, affirmed 99 S.Ct. 1435 (1978).

National Ass'n of Regulatory Utility Com'rs. v. *F.C.C.*, 533 F.2d 601, 174 U.S.App.D.C. 374 (1976).

National Ass'n of Theatre Owners v. *F.C.C.*, 420 F.2d 194, 136 U.S.App.D.C. 352, 1 Med.L. Rptr.2257 (1969), certiorari denied.

National Cable Television Ass'n, Inc. v. *F.C.C.*, 554 F.2d 1094, 180 U.S.App.D.C. 235 (1976).

National Cable Television Ass'n, Inc. v. *United States*, 94 S.Ct. 1146, 415 U.S. 336, 39 L.Ed.2d 370 (1974).

Southwest Pennsylvania Cable TV, Inc. v. *F.C.C.*, 514 F.2d 1343, 169 U.S.App.D.C. 102 (1975).

Teleprompter Cable Systems, Inc. v. *F.C.C.*, 543 F.2d 1379, 178 U.S.App.D.C. 66 (1976).

TV Pix, Inc. V. *Taylor*, 304 F.Supp. 459, affirmed 90 S.Ct. 749, 396 U.S. 556, 24 L.Ed.2d 746 (1969).

United States v. *Midwest Video Corp.*, 92 S.Ct. 1860, 406 U.S. 649, 32 L.Ed.2d 390, rehearing denied 93 S.Ct. 95, 409 U.S. 898, 34 L.Ed.2d 157 (1972).

United States v. *Southwestern Cable Co.*, 88 S.Ct. 1994, 392 U.S. 157, 20 L.Ed.2d 1001, 1 Med.L.Rptr.2247 (1968).

IV

Citizens, Self-Regulation, and Legislation

10

The Citizens' Movement

While operating in the public interest has traditionally meant serving the mass audience, broadcasters are finding that they also must deal with the special interests of smaller segments of their mass audience. More and more public interest—or "citizens' groups," as they are called—have gained a sizable voice in both network and local station policy matters, operations, and programming.

The *United Church of Christ* Decision

The citizens' movement gained significant ground in the 1966 case of *United Church of Christ* v. *Federal Communications Commission,* which gave citizens' groups the authority to intervene and take an active part in proceedings involving broadcasters and the FCC.[1] For too long, many felt, had there been a closed association between the FCC and the industry it regulated. For too long had the FCC simply adhered to the status quo. The court pointed out that the traditional issues—electrical interference and economic injury—were no longer the only bases for citizen intervention. Circuit Judge Warren Burger, who became legendary as Chief Justice of the U.S. Supreme Court during a series of decisions on the rights of the press, said in the *United Church of Christ* decision: "After nearly five decades of operation, the broadcast industry does not seem to have grasped the simple fact that a broadcast licensee is a public trust subject to termination for

315

breach of duty."[2] Assessing the relationship of a regulatory agency such as the FCC, Burger wrote: "Taking advantage of this 'active interest' in the . . . quality of broadcasting rather than depending on governmental initiative is also desirable, in that it tends to cast governmental power, at least in the first instance, in the more detached role of arbiter rather than accuser."[3] Defending public participation, Burger wrote: "We cannot believe that the congressional mandate of public participation, which the Commission says it seeks to fulfill, was meant to be limited to writing letters to the Commission, to inspection of records, to the Commission's grace in considering listener claims, or to mere non-participating appearance at hearings."[4]

The encouragement that citizens' groups gained from the *United Church of Christ* case opened the participatory floodgate. Added to this encouragement was the mood of the times. It was the late 1960s, a time of antiestablishment protest over the United States' frustrating commitment to the Vietnam war. The civil rights movement was pushing ahead, calling for equality for blacks and other minorities. The resulting atmosphere confronted broadcasters with demands from a variety of individuals and organizations. Some took direct action, putting to use the statement of support from the *United Church of Christ (UCC)* decision. In fact, by 1971, there were some fifty petitions to deny license renewals.[5] Other groups wanted access to station programming and were granted it, even being allowed to produce on-air programming. Not every group was concerned about minorities, or license renewals, or even access. Some organizations, such as the Action for Children's Television (ACT), wanted to improve television programming for children and to make people more aware of the medium's potential and of how to responsibly consume television.

Most encounters between broadcasters and citizens' groups were productive. Broadcasters gained a new sensitivity to groups which had previously been virtually unknown and, consequently, unserved. Alerted to these elements in the community, some stations broadened their newsbeats to include issues facing these people. One example was in California, where Chicanos received more coverage consideration. Another in Texas provided coverage of and for blacks.

Some experiences brought confrontations, and broadcasters were quick to point out that certain groups, while labeling themselves with broad descriptive titles, represented only a handful of people. Many of these groups were temporary, lasting only as long as their enthusiasm or their money held out. But others with good organization and leadership became a major force in broadcast reform.

Characteristics of Citizens' Groups

To try to understand the characteristics of citizens' groups, we will examine some of the most influential, including Action for Children's Television (ACT), one of the largest and most visible groups; the National Citizens' Committee for Broadcasting (NCCB); the National Citizens' Communications Lobby (NCCL); the Citizens' Communications Center (CCC); and the Office of Communication of the United Church of Christ (UCC).

action for children's television (act)

One of the largest, most active, and best-organized citizens' groups currently participating in broadcast reform is Action for Children's Television. Started informally among parents and other interested professionals, ACT was incorporated as a nonprofit public organization in 1970.[6] The main direction of its early discussions and organizational meetings was to determine how to make children's television a constructive force by educating parents in the responsible use of the medium. It also set out to influence legislators and sponsors on the beneficial possibilities of television and on the regulatory and economic climate best suited to recognize and encourage those possibilities.

The power of this organization is reflected by the fact that when ACT first approached the FCC with its well-publicized petition to eliminate commercials on children's television, the FCC received 100,000 comments on the proposal. Leonard Gross, writing about citizens' groups for *TV Guide,* says that the petition and the national response put ACT on the political map.[7] Today, approximately 100 ACT contacts—individual representatives—operate within the United States, many serving as liaison between local groups and ACT headquarters in Newtonville, Massachusetts.

The organization puts out numerous publications, including a well-designed and highly professional newsletter titled *Action for Children's Television News.* A library guide titled *ACT Library News and Notes,* includes a reference list of articles about children's television. Additional information is disseminated through press releases and, when major issues arise, news conferences. Excerpts from the following ACT press release describing the results of a pre-Christmas television monitoring study conducted by Dr. F. Earle Barcus, of Boston University's School of Public Communication, is typical of ACT's punch:

> Toy commercials accounted for 84 percent of all children's advertising in the afterschool hours on a New York City independent TV station during the holiday season, and for 47.5 percent of all network children's ads, according to a study of "Pre-Christmas Advertising to Children" released today by Action for Children's Television (ACT). . . .
>
> Dr. Barcus found that "product descriptions seldom give more than very minimal product information. Although products are visually represented, it is often difficult for the child (or adult) to determine the materials, physical dimensions, operational procedures, or other necessary consumer information. . . . Warnings or cautions about the use of products are seldom given, even though the product itself may sometimes include such information."
>
> Although the ACT monitoring study did not find any evidence of selling by program hosts, a practice which has been banned by the NAB Code, Dr. Barcus did note that well-known personalities, celebrities, and cartoon, comic, or program characters are sometimes employed as integral parts of the commercials. . . .
>
> In his examination of commercial practices, the Boston University Professor found a frequent use of visual distortion and other special effects, which may be perceived literally by the child viewer and lead to unrealistic expectations of product performance. For example, in commercials for the "Six Million Dollar Man Doll" and "The Walton's Farmhouse Gift Set," the figures appeared to be walking without human help. . . .

In the advertising of cereals, premium offers are still a widespread promotional technique. . . . Although the Federal Trade Commission has considered issuing guidelines restricting the use of TV premiums on advertising directed to children for two years, the agency recently voted against the adoption of such regulations.

According to Peggy Charren, President of ACT, "the Pre-Christmas study proves that children's advertising is still misleading and unfair to young viewers." She emphasized the "necessity for regulatory action to compel the broadcasting and advertising industries to desist from practices that manipulate and confuse the members of the child audiences."[8]

ACT is also deeply involved in the policy areas of broadcasting. For example, ACT went so far as to seek an injunction against television advertisements for Spiderman vitamins. Part of ACT's criticism of the vitamin ads was the use of the comic character Spiderman as the spokesman and the promotion of the vitamins as chewable and candylike; which, according to ACT: "Creates a completely distorted notion of the medicinal contents of the bottle."[9]

Other actions have included filing appeals to FCC decisions. Not all of ACT's positions oppose those taken by the broadcasting industry, however. When the FCC's Family Viewing guidelines attempted to control fringe prime-time programming, ACT joined with the National Citizens' Committee for Broadcasting, another public interest group, and filed a "friend of the court" brief on the side of the Writers' Guild of American West. The brief claimed that Family Viewing violated "the public's paramount First Amendment right to maximum program diversity."[10]

Government hearings provide another active forum. Chief spokesperson at the hearings is ACT founder, Peggy Charren. Failure of the Federal Trade Commission to respond to ACT's petitions for restriction of advertising for foods, vitamins, and toys on children's programs has been a familiar topic.[11] Appearing at a hearing on FTC oversight, Charren testified: "We seek only to secure and protect the rights of our children to be safe and healthy, and their freedom to learn how to make responsible choices and decisions that are based on an unclouded presentation of information."[12] A four-day investigation by the House Subcommittee of Communications examining broadcast advertising to children heard Charren present evidence claiming the inadequacy of the NAB's Code and the need for FTC guidelines to govern advertising of heavily-sugared foods and harmful products directed to children from two to eleven years old. "ACT is concerned that the industry's self-regulatory agencies have advocated only reasonable advertising restrictions, for which there is substantial need and ample precedent," she testified.[13]

The respect for ACT among government agencies and in the industry appears to remain solid, and prospects for its continued influence are bright. It states that its current aims are:

To encourage and persuade broadcasters and advertisers to provide programming of the highest possible quality designed for children of different ages;

to encourage the development and enforcement of appropriate guidelines relating to children and the media;

to encourage research, experimentation and evaluation in the field of children's television.[14]

As more parents become responsible consumers of broadcast communication, and as we all begin to understand more about the real influence of television on children, organizations such as ACT may find even larger constituencies.

national citizens committee for broadcasting (NCCB)

Unlike ACT, which has children's television as its central theme, the NCCB's focus is broader in scope. But there is no mistaking the direction of that focus—regulatory reform and a close watch on legislation affecting the broadcasting public.

NCCB is heavily involved in legal actions involving broadcasters and frequently participates as a party in suits which challenge the status quo in broadcasting. For example, it joined with ACT and others in the fight against the Family Viewing Hour, and it has become involved in other cases affecting such issues as conglomerate ownership of broadcasting and pay cable. Cable rates and public service advertising are also part of its agenda.[15]

Striking at the heart of broadcasting, NCCB has conducted comparative rankings of television stations to determine which are the best and worst, based on programming and employment data. Such surveys, when well publicized, can spell serious trouble for broadcasters, especially at license renewal time.

Monitoring programming and supporting proposals for programming change have also been part of NCCB's activities. NCCB gathered endorsements from over a hundred national organizations and twenty-one members of Congress for a proposal which would require television stations to provide one hour per week of public affairs programming in prime time, when the highest audience levels exist.

On the issue of broadcast violence, NCCB has attacked the economic lifeblood of broadcasting by publicly linking specific advertisers with violent programs. Such public denouncements have caused some advertisers to guard against even inadvertent association with violent programming. Consider, for example, the case of Colgate-Palmolive, which sent the following statement to the chief executive officers of all its advertising agencies, as well as to the networks:

> So there is no doubt about our policy regarding violence in television programming, the Colgate-Palmolive Company is releasing this statement summarizing its policy and operating procedures on this subject for the guidance of television stations, television networks, and our advertising agencies.
>
> 1. The Colgate-Palmolive Company does not advertise its products in programs making gratuitous or excessive use of violence. This eliminates programs which include violence which is not necessary to the development of the program's characters or story line. It also eliminates those programs which, although some violence is an integral part of the story line, feature unnecessary violent deaths, brutality, or suffering.
> 2. The Colgate-Palmolive Company does not advertise its products in programs which it considers to be antisocial or in bad taste, or which could stimulate antisocial behavior through viewer imitation.
> 3. The Colgate-Palmolive Company has charged its advertising agencies with the

responsibility of prescreening any questionable program material and, if there is any doubt about a program's suitability, it is to be referred to Colgate for prescreening and decision.

Acknowledging the violence issue, Allegheny Airlines issued a similar statement:

Allegheny Airlines has announced that it will not place advertising on television programs which feature violence. Allegheny, whose "Big Airline" campaign is handled by J. Walter Thompson Company, becomes the first major airline to adopt the antiviolence advertising policy.

Harry Chandis, vice president of marketing for Allegheny, stated: "Allegheny believes that the public is becoming more and more offended by violence on television. We prefer to communicate to people when they are in a receptive frame of mind. Therefore, we will avoid advertising on television shows with a violent theme and seek placement of television time around news programs and sporting events."

A recent Gallup poll shows that over 70% of the U.S. public believes television contains too much violence. Of even greater concern to major advertisers are results of a study by J. Walter Thompson, which indicate that roughly 35% of television viewers avoid violent programs and 10% have considered not buying products advertised on these programs.

Some of the other companies issuing antiviolence statements were General Motors; Sears, Roebuck and Co.; and the Jos. Schlitz Brewing Company.

A NCCB publication titled *Access* carries news of general interest to citizens' groups, including citizen involvement in license renewals, changes of ownership, and citizen agreements with broadcasters. Foundations have helped support NCCB, but the organization has gained such a following to the point where membership dues are providing a higher and higher percentage of its operating budget.

citizens' communications center of the institute for public representation of the georgetown university law center

On January 1, 1981, the Citizens' Communications Center became affiliated with the Institute for Public Representation of the Georgetown University Law Center. To understand the work of the Center we need to trace its history prior to its 1981 affiliation with the Institute.

The Citizens' Communications Center has operated in Washington, D.C., since 1969.[16] Receiving early funding from such groups as the Rockefeller Brothers Fund and the Stern Family Fund, it matured with major support from the Ford Foundation and the Robert F. Kennedy Memorial.

The Center offered a variety of services, including legal help, a resource center, a legal education center, and a litigating firm. Cases accepted primarily on the basis of how the issue confronted would test the public-interest objectives of the Center. These issues ranged from a local station license dispute to a new direction in the policy of a federal agency's regulatory procedure. The Center did not accept cases, however, in which a party had a financial interest in the outcome.

Delivering testimony and serving as a resource center have been two additional functions of the Center. As a resource center, the organization has issued its own studies on such practices as employment policies at the FCC and in the broadcasting industry. Along with participating actively in FCC rulemaking and policy inquiries, the Center's staff has testified before Congressional committees, spoken at policy conferences, disseminated material and advice on the rights of the public, and submitted proposals for regulatory reform. Second- and third-year law students from many well-known universities benefited from the Center's internship programs. Through training at the legal education center, students could perform legal analysis, case strategy, client consultation, and negotiations and settlements.

The Center's direct involvement is perhaps best represented by the renewal hearing of the Alabama Educational Television Commission. Starting with a formal Petition to Deny to the FCC, the Center participated in this case for five years, with the result that the Alabama Educational Television Commission lost all eight of its public television licenses for alleged discrimination against the 30 percent black population of Alabama. The Alabama case was the FCC's first license renewal denial based on a citizens' group's Petition to Deny.

Radio station formats became the issue when the Center participated in legislation leading to the retention of unique radio formats for a New York City classical station and an ethnic station in Cannonsburg, Pennsylvania. The Center also participated in litigation leading to promises by the purchaser of a Washington, D.C. newspaper-broadcast combination to divest local media properties within three years, in order to comply with a new FCC policy of one newspaper or broadcast service in a market. Other provisions included helping women and members of minority groups obtain loans to acquire broadcast stations, televising of free-speech messages, and instituting other local program and employment reforms. Because of the Center's efforts, a Philadelphia cable television operator relinquished his franchise to avoid a court test over issues which centered around alleged trafficking in cable franchises and misrepresentations to the FCC.

The Center will continue its work under the Georgetown affiliation and with the resources and scope of the Institute.

office of communication of the united church of christ

One of the pioneer organizations in the public interest field is the Office of Communication of the Church of Christ. Constantly educating broadcast consumers about their rights, the Office has also become deeply involved in the broader issues of programming and regulatory reform. One of its most visible accomplishments began in 1964 when it petitioned the FCC to deny the license renewal of WLBT-TV in Jackson, Mississippi, charging the station with discrimination and censorship of programming. In the 1966 *United Church of Christ* case discussed earlier, the appeals court ordered the FCC to conduct a hearing in the case. After the hearing, the FCC again renewed the license, but the Office persisted with a second appeal. Three years later the court ruled the license must be vacated and called for the FCC to invite other applications. As noted earlier, the case opened the door for the citizens' movement. It was a precedent-setting example of how persistent attention by an organization against what were previously considered strong odds can pay off in improved service to the public.

One of the strongest charges issued by the Office came in 1977, when the General Synod of the United Church of Christ passed its Pronouncement on Exploitative Broadcast Practices. Coming down hard on excessive sex and violence in broadcasting, the Pronouncement stated the UCC:

> *Calls* upon Congress to impose the necessary oversight of the Federal Communications Commission to make that body fulfill its statutory requirement to have television and radio stations determine the needs, tastes and desires of their communities of license and to program to fulfill them.
>
> *Calls* upon the Federal Communications Commission to meet its responsibility to the public by regulating broadcasting to make station licensees responsive to the needs of their communities of license.
>
> *Calls* upon individual station licensees to fulfill the statutory requirement to be responsible for everything broadcast over their station by refusing to air network and syndicated entertainment programs until they have determined that such programs are in accord with the tastes and needs of their communities of license.
>
> *Calls* upon the United Church of Christ churches, conferences, and national agencies:
>
> > a. to initiate the development and sponsorship of programs that are true to life and that include the possibility of hope and healing for the problems of a broken world.
> >
> > b. to consult among members of the United Church of Christ and other religious bodies who are active in communications industries to share concern for the ethical standards of their industries.
>
> *Calls* upon the Office of Communication, the United Church Boards for World and Homeland Ministries and the Office of Church in Society:
>
> > a. to continue to foster the education of persons from developing countries and under-represented social groups—including the church itself—for careers in communication.
> >
> > b. to engage in a continuous study of constitutional rights, regulatory codes and procedures, and freedom of access by publics (U.S.A. and other nations) relating to the electronic spectrum.
>
> *Responsibility for Implementation*
>
> Implementation of this pronouncement shall be referred to the Office of Communication which will, in turn, involve such other UCC agencies and elements of other churches that have the resources to help implement it.

While the wording of the Pronouncement may seem strong, the Office of Communication has not been known for empty rhetoric. It backs up its stands with a staff of full-time personnel and a ready bank of consultants and lawyers. Its "Check Your Local Stations" program of community workshops trains local community leaders to work toward improving broadcast service and employment of minorities. In cooperation with other organizations, it cosponsors career training programs for high school students, specifically through the Career Recruitment in Telecommunications Industries, Inc. (CRTI). It monitors the annual broadcast employment forms that stations file with the FCC and keeps a running account of progress in minority hiring. The church's 1.8 million members can mount a sizable crusade toward an established goal, and the Office is generally respected among regulators and industry people.

local citizens' groups

While large, formal organizations work toward broadcast reform at the national level, many smaller, less visible groups are working at the local level to accomplish similar goals. Local groups of parents or community leaders in very small communities are even gathering financial support from foundations to conduct television awareness seminars, program monitoring, and negotiations with local stations. The size of these groups can range anywhere from a few concerned parents to hundreds of supporters. In some cases, the local groups align themselves with national ones, such as ACT. Others remain strictly independent.

Scope of Citizens' Group Activities

While focusing national attention on broadcasting issues is one function of citizens' groups, they may also become involved in more direct broadcasting activities. We will examine some of these activities, including filing Petitions to Deny renewal of licenses, seeking access to programming, monitoring programming, and encouraging responsible consumers.

petitions to deny

Except for attempting to block the sale of a station or set standards for who should buy one, Peititons to Deny license renewals are among the most complicated and expensive ventures in which citizens' groups take part. Although any individual has the right to respond to a proposed license renewal, filing a Petition to Deny a renewal is a serious undertaking. Citizens' groups which do file such petitions must have the advice of an attorney and the ability to pay for that advice, not only at the local level, but often also in Washington, D.C. Despite the complexity and expense, many citizens' groups are actively involved in license proceedings. If they are lucky, the stations end up paying the legal fees.

The types of issues involved in Petitions to Deny are varied. One of the most frequent is discrimination in employment. It is relatively easy, using employment reports, to determine the percentage of minority employees of a particular station and to determine whether or not it meets its quota, based on the percentage of minority group members in the population served by the station. Somewhat harder to prove are discrimination charges concerning particular individuals.

In one instance, citizens' groups presented twenty-five stations in Tennessee and Indiana with eight separate Petitions to Deny, charging that the stations had discriminated against blacks in both employment and programming services.[17] One of the petitions charged concentration of ownership of broadcasting and newspaper interests, while others zeroed in on employment and service to the black community.[18] The Indiana challenges charged a station with firing a black announcer and then changing the format of a jazz and black literature program that the announcer had created.[19]

Discrimination in employment was charged by the National Organization of Women (NOW) in petitions filed against two network-owned stations. When the FCC failed to act with sufficient speed on the peitions, the U.S. Court of Appeals stated that the lack of action amounted to rejection of the petition and commanded the FCC to act.[20] Other groups have used the courts to pressure the FCC into action. When the Feminists for Media Rights of Lancaster, Pennsylvania, had waited fourteen months for the FCC to act on a petition against a Lancaster TV station, they took the matter to the U.S. Court of Appeals. Charges in their petition included undue concentration of ownership in broadcasting and newspapers, as well as interests involving cable television.[21]

Fairness Doctrine violations are another favorite target of citizens' groups filing Petitions to Deny. The major charge is usually unbalanced coverage of issues, ranging fron nuclear power and environmental concerns to political coverage.

Despite the plethora of Petitions to Deny, success of citizens' groups in this area has been minimal. In many cases, broadcasters enter into contractual agreements with citizens' groups. In other cases, the money to fight a license challenge as well as the enthusiasm of the group's organizers runs out, and stations win by default. In still other cases, the petitions contain glaring errors, which detract from the overall credibility of the challenges. Courts have criticized petitions for generalities, and even for such basic mistakes as listing the wrong owner or even the wrong city served by a station. Nevertheless, petitions are something with which broadcasters must reckon. And the amateur efforts of the past are quickly being replaced by experienced groups, who are willing and able to give broadcasters a run for their money *and* for their station licenses.

access to programming

Other citizens' groups are working toward changing broadcast programming. The best way they can see to change it is either to have access to program producers, in order to tell them their views, or to have access to the actual airwaves, in order to produce their own programming. Making suggestions for a given type of programming to reach specialized audiences or replies to Fairness Doctrine issues are among the activities of citizens' groups.

Typical of such activity was a request to the FCC by four religious groups wanting more sustaining or continuous community-oriented public service programming. While the FCC looks favorably on public service programming, it has drifted away from strict requirements as to what type of public service programming stations should air—short public service announcements or longer block programming, for example. This issue arose in a petition requested by the Communication Committee of the United States Catholic Conference, the Communication Commission of the National Council of Churches of Christ in the U.S.A., the Office of Communication of the United Church of Christ, and the UNDA-USA, a national Catholic voluntary association of broadcasters.[22] The petition, which was also signed by seventy-nine individual church communicators, called for stations to meet public service obligations by providing sustaining programs in cooperation with government agencies and nonprofit organizations with significant membership in the stations' service area.[23]

Fairness Doctrine issues provide somewhat easier access, since the legal obligations of the station to provide balanced programming of controversial issues opens the door. As we learned earlier, when the Pacific Gas and electric Co. aired commercials for nuclear power in California, stations found themselves caught in a Fairness Doctrine issue. The California Public Media Center, among others, filed the Fairness Doctrine complaint, and the legal aspects were handled by another public interest organization, the Media Access Project in Washington, D.C. Ruling that some stations had not met their obligations under the Doctrine, the FCC required them to air statements counter to those of the Pacific Gas and Electric Co. The result? Broadcasters received a letter from Pacific Gas and Electric Co., stating: "One reason for our recent shift back to print advertising is that broadcast advertising . . . is vulnerable to counter-advertising, which, as you know, cuts deeply into our advertising effectiveness."[24] This time, the citizens' groups had been very effective.

Other organizations have been successful in placing their own programs on stations and even in helping in production. The Chinese Media Committee of San Francisco received foundation support of $30,000 for out-of-studio costs to produce a series of sixty-five half-hour, English-language instruction programs directed toward Cantonese-speaking Chinese, to be aired on a local station. In San Jose, California, representatives of the South Bay Community Coalition for Media Change worked in cooperation with a local station and gained access for programs dealing with the Chicano community. When broadcasters and citizens' groups cooperate, the result can be enlightening for both. But when communication breaks down, militancy by either party can create a stand-off, which ends up in arbitration before the FCC.

monitoring broadcast programming

An alternative action for citizens' groups is monitoring broadcast programming, especially sex and violence on television. The National Parent Teacher Association (PTA) launched a national awareness effort in 1977, to alert its 6.6 million members and the public both to the effects of violence on television and to the advertisers who supported violence with their ads. The PTA first held a series of hearings around the United States, at which experts and the public discussed the effects of violence on television. Then came the list of programs and sponsors. Sterling Drug Co. was named the "most offensive" advertiser, because it placed its ads in programs the PTA raters considered to be low in quality and high on violence.[25] Shows which showed up on the PTA's most violent list included the police series "Starsky and Hutch," the detective program "Charlie's Angels," and the adventure show "Wonder Woman." Some programs were also criticized for their "sexploitation." Programs praised as "most commendable" included the family-oriented "Little House on the Prairie" and "Disney's Wonderful World."[26]

The PTA also criticized commercials. Addressing advertisers sponsoring prime-time programming, the PTA said, "The type of commercial most offensive was the feminine hygiene product, frequently advertised during prime-time. Teenagers watching television with dates, in either a family setting or amid peers, were most disturbed and embarrassed. Even mature women found the ads distressing and felt that the market was not so competitive nor the purchasers so sparse that companies would suffer from limiting their advertising to appropriate print media."[27] The PTA also recognized advertisers which sponsored three or more of the "exemplary" shows and avoided low-quality shows. Avon, Campbell Soup Co., Consolidated Foods, Kellogg's, the Bell Telephone System, and Quaker Oats made the "positive" list.

On the issue of sex on radio, the Reverend Jesse Jackson came out against what was reported as "flagrant abuses of responsibility in the record industry where sex and violence is concerned."[28] Jackson saw a relationship between suggestive sexy lyrics and rhythms and responsibility among youths. A threatened boycott was used to attempt to change such lyrics and to alert the radio stations that might play such songs.

Television producers have also been the object of citizens' group criticism. When Norman Lear decided to drop John Amos, who played the father figure in the comedy series "Good Times," the National Black Media Coalition, based in Washington, D.C., said it would look into the possibility of boycotting products advertised on the show. A press release from the Coalition said black children need positive black male images, and that taking the father out of the show would eliminate TV's only positive black adult male character.[29] Lear claimed that the father figure in "The Jeffersons" and Fred Sanford in "Sanford and Sons" were positive black male images, but the coalition disagreed. The issue became somewhat moot when John Amos left the show to star in the highly acclaimed "Roots," a series about the emergence of a black family from their African heritage into the twentieth century.

encouraging responsible consumers

Part of the PTA's involvement in television included teaching interested members how to react to television at the local level, how to identify programming which contained excessive sex or violence, and how to communicate with government, the broadcasters, and advertisers. Other organizations have used similar measures to pressure for change by educating the public on what to watch for and how to react. Some citizens' groups have used as simple a method as posters. ACT, for example, makes available a flyer entitled "Treat TV with T.L.C.," which reads:

Talk about TV with your Child!

Talk about programs that delight your child.
Talk about programs that upset your child.
Talk about the differences between make believe and real life.
Talk about ways TV characters could solve problems without violence.
Talk about violence and how it hurts.
Talk about TV foods that can cause cavities.
Talk about TV toys that may break too soon.

Look at TV with your Child!

Look out for TV behavior your child might imitate.
Look for TV characters who care about others.
Look for women who are competent in a variety of jobs.

Look for people from a variety of cultural and ethnic groups.

Look for healthy snacks in kitchen instead of on TV.

Look for ideas for what to do when you switch off the set.

Read a book . . . draw a picture . . . play a game.

Choose TV programs with your Child!

Choose the number of programs you child can watch.

Choose to turn the set off when the program is over.

Choose to turn on public television.

Choose to improve children's TV by writing a letter to a local station . . . to a television network . . . to an advertiser . . . to Action for Children's Television.[30]

Similar content of placing the responsibility on the consumer is promoted by a San Francisco citizens' group, the Committee on Children's Television. Twelve questions are part of their "Guidelines for Selecting Television for Children." They ask:

1. Does the program appeal to the audience for whom it is intended? (A program for 12-year olds should be different from a program for 6-year olds.)
2. Does the program present racial groups positively and does it show them in situations that enhance the third world child's self image? (Who has the lead roles? Who is a professional leader and who is a villain?)
3. Does the program present gender roles and adult roles positively? (Are the men either super heroes or incompetents? Are the women flighty and disposed to chicanery? Are teenagers portrayed with adult characteristics?)
4. Does the program present social issues that are appropriate for the child viewer and perhaps are something a child can act on at a child's level? (Cleaning up litter vs. reducing atomic fallout, or caring for pets vs. saving wolves.)
5. Does the program encourage values, ideals, and beliefs that you consider worthwhile?
6. Does the program present conflict that a child can understand and does it demonstrate positive techniques for resolving conflict?
7. Does the program separate fact from fantasy? Does it separate advertisements from program content?
8. Does the program stimulate constructive activities and does it enhance the quality of a child's play?
9. Does the program present humor at a child's level? (Or is it adult sarcasm, ridicule, or an adult remembering what he thought was funny from his childhood?)
10. Does the program have a pace that allows the child to absorb and contemplate the material presented?
11. Does the program have artistic qualities?
12. Has your child seen an appropriate amount of television for the day? (Is it time to turn the set off?)[31]

The Christian Life Commission of the Southern Baptist Convention sponsors a campaign to help people be critical consumers of television programs. One sheet of a special packet makes the following recommendations: (1) study personal television viewing patterns and keep a record of programs watched to determine the amount of time spent with television; (2) plan television viewing and use the time responsibly by turning television on only for specific programs, thus controlling it instead of its controlling you; (3) parents should discuss commercials with children, guiding them against materialism; (4) families should watch television together and then discuss issues encountered in life; (5) write the National Association for Better Broadcasting, specifically to acquire its annual television guide; (6) don't let the television become a babysitter; (7) discuss with babysitters what programs the children may watch when parents are away; (8) decide the location of the television set in the home and place it where it doesn't dominate family life; (9) as a family, write letters expressing both negative and positive criticism for television programming; (10) as an alternative to television viewing, provide opportunities for good religious, social, and cultural experiences; (11) parents should be the ones to set an example as to how much and what types of television programs are watched; (12) older couples should seek ways to keep busy other than television.

The examples of these three citizens' groups' efforts provide a wide latitude for action. The groups are not directly involved in changing or even lobbying for broadcast regulation. Rather, they encourage the public to take the responsibility and consume with care. And the movement is growing. While many people feel that the bureaucracy of government or even of the networks prevents any opportunity for change, they can see the value of the individual and parental approach to controlling how television affects their daily lives.

Citizens' Group Agreements

Earlier we learned that the Petition to Deny is one of the most serious actions a citizens' groups can take when dealing with a local broadcaster. Although few groups actually take over control of a vacated license, the Petition does become a powerful bargaining agent, which, in some cases, results in a contractual agreement between the citizens' group and the broadcaster. Such agreements can be broad in nature and can include statements about operation "in the public interest" or "serving the community." Others are more specific and can deal with hiring quotas or specific types of programming.

the ktal agreement

One of the first citizens' group agreements occurred in 1969, when a group of citizens filed a Petition to Deny the renewal of license KTAL-TV in Texarkana, Texas.[32] By reading the KTAL agreement, we can see some of the typical issues that arise when citizens' groups and licensees arrive at contractual agreements on station performance as a condition upon the citizens' group's support for the stations' license renewal.

The KTAL Agreement

KCMC, Inc., licensee of KTAL-TV, and all parties to the petition to deny and to the reply filed with respect to KCMC, Inc.'s application for renewal of its television broadcast license, being hereinafter collectively referred to as "Petitioners," agree as follows:

1. KCMC, Inc., will broadcast on prime time, the statement of policy attached hereto. This agreement and this statement will also be filed with the Federal Communications Commission as an amendment to the pending renewal appli-

cation. Any material variance from said statement shall be deemed to be a failure to operate substantially as set forth in the license.

2. Simultaneously with the filing of said statement, petitioners will join and hereby join in requesting the Federal Communications Commission to give no further consideration to the pleadings filed by petitioners, or any of them, with respect to KTAL-TV. Petitioners also join in requesting the Federal Communications Commission to renew KTAL-TV's television broadcast license for a full term.

3. This agreement and the attached statement contain the complete agreement of the parties, and there are no other promises or undertakings, express or implied.

Statement of Policy

KTAL-TV, having in mind its duty to serve equally all segments of the public, makes the following statement of policy:

1. KTAL will continue to observe all laws and federal policies requiring equal employment practices and will take affirmative action to recruit and train a staff which is broadly representative of all groups in the community. As part of this policy, KTAL will employ a minimum of two full-time Negro reporters, one for Texarkana and one for Shreveport. These reporters will appear regularly on camera. In addition, KTAL will designate one person on its program staff to be responsible for developing local public affairs programs of the type described later in this statement and for obtaining syndicated or other programs to serve similar needs.

2. KTAL will continue to maintain and will publicize a toll-free telephone line from Texarkana to its studios in Shreveport. A person will be available in Shreveport to receive requests for news coverage and inquiries about public service announcements. KTAL will give adequate coverage to events in the State capitols of Texas and Arkansas, as well as those of Louisiana and Oklahoma.

3. KTAL recognizes its continuing obligation to maintain appropriate facilities in Texarkana, its city of assignment. To this end, it will assign to its main studios in Texarkana a color television camera.

4. KTAL recognizes its obligations to present regular programs for the discussion of controversial issues, including, of course, both black and white participants. The station will not avoid issues that may be controversial or divisive, but will encourage the airing of all sides of these issues.

5. Poverty is a primary problem in KTAL's service area. KTAL is obligated to try to help solve this problem by publicizing the rights of poor persons to obtain services and the methods by which they may do so. KTAL will also inform public opinion about the problem of poverty and the steps that are being taken to alleviate it. An aggregate of at least one-half hour of programming will be devoted to this subject each month.

6. KTAL religious programming should cover the entire range of religious thought. As part of its continuing effort to meet this obligation, KTAL will carry the religious programs presented by NBC representing the three primary American faiths. A discussion program will also be presented, to explore current religious issues, at least monthly. KTAL will regularly present ministers of all races on local religious programs. These ministers will be regularly rotated, in an effort to represent fairly all religious groups.

7. Network programs of particular interest to any substantial group in the service area will not be preempted without appropriate advance consultation with representatives of that group.

8. KTAL is obligated to discuss programming regularly with all segments of the public. In particular, a station employee with authority to act will meet once a month with a committee designated by the parties to the Petition to Deny KTAL's TV application for license renewal. Similar efforts will be made to consult with groups representing other segments of the public.

9. KTAL will regularly announce on the air that the station will consult with all substantial groups in the community regarding community taste and needs and will accept suggestions on how best to render this service. This announcement will be broadcast once a week, on a weekday, between 7 and 11 P.M.

10. KTAL reaffirms its existing policy to make no unessential reference to the race of a person. In cases where such references are made, the same practice shall be and will be followed for blacks as for whites. KTAL will continue to use courtesy titles for all women without regard for race.

11. KTAL will endeavor to develop and present at least monthly, in prime time, a regular local magazine-type program, including not only discussion, but also local talent, and seeking participation from the entire service area.

12. KTAL will solicit public service announcements from local groups and organizations. Sound on film will be used more extensively in covering local news. In covering demonstrations, picketing, and similar events, KTAL-TV will seek to present the diverse views which gave rise to the event.

13. KTAL-TV's undertakings are subject to all valid laws, rules and regulations of the Federal Communications Commission and to KTAL's primary obligation as a broadcast licensee to use its own good faith and judgment to serve all members of the viewing public. It is recognized that needs and circumstances change, that events may compel departure from these undertakings. However, KTAL-TV will not depart from these undertakings without advance consultation with the affected groups in the service area and advance notice to the Federal Communications Commission stating the reasons for the departure. In such instances, KTAL will seek to adhere to the objectives of this statement by alternative action.[33]

The KTAL agreement provides a good example of how citizens' groups can become involved in a station's programming and operation. Providing that sound on film be used more extensively in covering local news is a highly specific type of programming clause. At the same time, however, it should be pointed out that the citizens' group involved with the KTAL petition felt very strongly about the station's alleged lack of service to the community. When a KTAL type of agreement does emerge, it usually indicates that the station could have improved considerably in the programming or operational areas outlined in an agreement.

The Commission itself praised the agreement highly, stating: "Such cooperation at the community level should prove to be more effective in improving local service than would be the imposition of strict guidelines by the Commission."[34]

It was not long after the KTAL agreement that other citizens' agreements began to appear before the FCC. Citizens' groups suddenly realized that they had a very powerful weapon in the Petition to Deny. Most of them were not interested in taking over a broadcasting station, but they were interested in entering into contracts which supported their goals. Such activities also helped citizens' groups attract members and solicit contributions for active public-interest legal work.

The FCC continued to support the concept of citizens' groups agreements by lengthening the time between the filing deadline for license renewal and the license expiration date. It also changed from two to three months the cutoff date for filing a Petition to Deny.[35] By doing this, the FCC hoped to provide additional time for citizens' groups or any other interested party to: (a) examine a renewal application, (b) discuss any problems with licensees and determine if negotiation is desirable and possible, and (c) decide to file a timely Petition to Deny, not to file such a petition, or come with the licensee to the Commission and request an extension of time to continue negotiations.[36] This statement, filed as part of an FCC *Final Report and Order,* left no doubt that the Commission was still supportive of the station-community dialogue, which could very well result in a contractual agreement at license renewal time.

FCC policy statement on citizens' group agreements

Despite the Commission's enthusiasm for the citizens' group agreement concept, it was not long before it realized that some broadcasters were faced with signing agreements which delegated their public service responsibilities to a third party. When this began to happen, the FCC quickly disapproved some of the agreement language. In a 1975 policy statement on the subject of citizens' group agreements, the Commission provided examples of types of agreements which would not be accepted as part of a license renewal process. Specifically, these included:

1. An agreement with provisions which bind the licensee to broadcast a fixed amount of programming directed to a particular segment of the community or a particular number of citizen-initiated or issue-oriented messages at stated periods of time (i.e., an abdication of licensee responsibility by improper infringement upon the licensee's discretion in the matters of programming and program scheduling);
2. a provision requiring a licensee to hire an individual from a list of employment candidates supplied by a citizen group;
3. a provision conditioning a licensee's selection of a particular program host upon the approval by a citizen group;
4. an agreement provision expressly precluding the filing of a Petition to Deny by a citizen group.[37]

The Commission stated it would not peruse all citizens' group agreements, only those which were directly incorporated into a license renewal application or where a citizens' group expressly requested a Commission ruling.[38] The FCC continues to remind broadcasters that they have an affirmative responsibility for both programming and service to the community, and that this responsibility can in no way whatsoever be delegated.

the saving clause

In the agreements between citizens' groups and licensees, the responsibility for programming is in many cases proclaimed in the agreement's "saving clause." The saving clause is a disclaimer that states the affirmative responsibility the licensee holds for programming. Even the early KTAL agreement incorporated a form of saving clause: "KTAL-TV's undertakings are subject to all valid laws, rules and regulations of the Federal Communications Commission and to

KTAL's primary obligation as a broadcast licensee to use its own good faith and judgment to serve all members of the viewing public."[39] Professor Ronald Garay, writing in the *Journal of Broadcasting,* cites a similar saving clause between a Fresno, California station and a Mexican-American advisory committee. The clause states that the advisory committee "understands that communication law and the rules of the Federal Communications Commission require that the final responsibility for all program decisions must remain with station management, and nothing contained in this agreement shall be construed to be inconsistent with that requirement."[40]

What effect a saving clause has on the citizens' agreements nationwide is difficult to determine. But such clauses do relieve pressure in two areas: first of all, the station is provided with an "out," should it choose to enter into the agreement rather than fight the Petition to Deny; and, second, the FCC is more receptive to an agreement containing a saving clause. The clause itself is not free from criticism, however. For example, Garay has written that: "Now, plaudits are reserved not for accomplishments by citizens' groups in negotiation with a licensee nor for the spirit of public interest consciousness of an agreement, but for the 'Saving Clause' that virtually relieves the broadcaster of honoring any accompanying provisions of the agreement."[41]

Most citizens' agreements hinge on minority or special interest groups concerned with either programming or employment practices of a station. In a Washington, D.C. agreement, a public station adopted a goal of 25 percent black employment at all levels of station operation during the three-year license period. The agreement also called for the station to make "strenuous efforts to obtain additional funding for local programming and to increasing the number of blacks in all employment categories . . . [and to] endeavor to increase the number and/or percentage of locally produced shows that address the concerns of the black audience consistent with FCC standards."[42]

Also in the public broadcasting sector, a New York television station and a Puerto Rican action group entered into an agreement arising from a Petition to Deny. Under the agreement, the station made a commitment for a good-faith effort to increase the overall percentage of Lantinos in its work force to at least 5 percent of the total station employees. The station also agreed to place an increased emphasis on recruiting and hiring Latinos for positions with upward mobility potential and to include one or more Latinos in the FCC-classified "professional" employment category. Also forged out of the agreement came a bilingual intern and training program, as well as a $500 back pay settlement on a discrimination complaint.[43]

Still another agreement was made between a major Chicago independent radio and television station and a citizens' committee. In the agreement, the station committed itself to seeking out more women and minorities and placing them in upper-level positions in the station.[44]

Perspectives on the Future of the Citizens' Movement

The future of the citizens' movement and its effect on broadcast regulation and policy is tied to a number of important questions. Among them: Do citizens' groups really represent broad constituencies? Does even a very popular citizens' group with several thousand members speak on issues representative of an entire national population? Even if such groups do represent issues salient to larger populations, is the larger population that much *concerned,* and does it feel deeply enough about those issues to warrant changes in programming or policy? These questions become even more important when citizens' groups become involved in forging agreements with broadcasters as conditions for license renewal. Here, small groups can get down to very specific measures, designed to change the operation of programming of a station.

identifying the constituency

While some minority groups claim to represent all minorities, and political groups to represent large factions of a political movement, and even groups concerned just about programming to represent the general public, still little, if any, evidence exists to indicate that such groups have made distinct efforts to poll the public or their respective constituencies to determine what the broader public opinion might be toward the programming or operation they are trying to change. This is not necessarily any worse than the case of a congressman or senator who represents millions of people failing to poll his or her constituency. But congressmen and senators have to be reelected. Citizens' groups do not. And the question arises of whether or not the citizens' group is concerned primarily with raising money or with improving the quality of broadcast communication.

case example: lack of public concern

Based on what politicians and other vocal critics of television proclaim, few issues are of more widespread concern than the issue of violence on television. Yet when one group of researchers examined the broadcast audience to determine how many people were deeply concerned about television violence, the results showed very little concern among the general public.[45] When polling a group of Eugene, Oregon residents, the researchers found that people who were fans of current programming showed resentment for any kind of censorship that might be placed upon broadcasters. Approximately one-fifth of those interviewed were passive in their attitudes toward violence and did not care enough about programming even to exert their own personal domestic control over it. Even people who gave strong moral support to antiviolence factions preferred to control programming at home. Those who might be considered activists and expected to participate in attempts to change television programming objected mainly to programming *other* than violence. Moreover, those who stated they would become involved in attempting to change programming represented only about one-tenth of the sample. Although we must be extremely cautious about generalizing, this study did not unearth widespread support either for the widely publicized issue of stopping violence or for taking action to change the content of broadcast programming.

Examining the current status of citizens' group agreements raises further questions. For example, does the fact that a station hires some employees in a professional capacity make a difference in the kind of community service that station provides, especially when the majority of programming evolves from a national network? Does increasing the amount of sound on film used in newscasts make a difference in the quality of broadcast coverage of local and national issues? What is the broad public interest applicability of such measures?

criticism of the citizens' movement

A perceptive view of the future of the citizens' movement has been offered by professional researchers Anne W. Branscomb and Maria Savage, writing in the *Journal of Communication*.[46] Perhaps their most critical comment on the movement for broadcast reform is contained in the statement that media reformers are interested in promoting not a free marketplace of ideas, but a free marketplace where each one can merchandise his or her own "wares" to a "sophisticated consuming public, which, being discerning, will naturally agree with the proponent's conclusions."[47] They go on to state: "While the reform groups which are affiliated with an established institution seem strong enough to weather the storms of adversity, most of the ad hoc groups must ride the tides of popularity which bring in both volunteers and money."[48]

Researchers Branscomb and Savage predict that the future of broadcast reform will be determined in the legislative, not the judicial arena. In other words, the victories so far have been won in the courts, and attention must now be turned toward changing laws. They also see communication channels as having an effect. Specifically, the trend toward specialized media will tend to deflate arguments for the control of broadcasting as mass media. Satellite distribution, increased capacity of cable channels, corporate television networks, and new and diversified networks operated by small groups of people, may all play parts in changing the regulatory scene. The ability to reach small, specialized audiences on a regional scale will create many diversified production centers and distribution channels.

future of the public-interest law firm

Where will all of this activity place the public-interest lawyer who represents a citizens' group? Attorney Frank Lloyd offers some perspectives on the future of public-interest law as it will affect broadcast reform. In line with the position of Branscomb and Savage, Lloyd points out that most of the public-interest law firms are located in large cities—Boston, New York, Washington, Chicago, San Francisco, and Los Angeles. Few, if any, public-interest law resources exist in the interior of the country or in less densely populated areas to deal with broadcast policy and regulatory reform at the state or local level.[49] Lloyd mentions the difficulty of competing against opponents who may have significant financial resources at their disposal. He points out that this inequity can spawn "determined misuse of procedural opportunities for procrastination."[50] Lloyd offers two possible solutions to this problem. One would be to align public-interest law centers with private law firms. Unfortunately, this would require foundation funding, which would be hard to obtain if the public-interest sector were aligned with private profit-making institutions. Another solution would be for major professional associations like the American Bar Association to pledge a portion of their membership fees to a "Fund for Public-Interest Law."[51]

Accomplishments of the Citizens' Movement

As we conclude our discussion of the citizens' movement, we need to review its track record. The accomplishments of the broadcast reformers have been significant. Branscomb and Savage present a long list, including:

Establishment of the right of the public to participate in administrative proceedings at the FCC.

More vigorous enforcement of the Fairness Doctrine as watchdog groups and individuals exert their rights to hear conflicting views on issues of public importance.

Modification of the equal time requirements of the Communications Act to facilitate direct confrontation of presidential candidates Ford and Carter.

Opening up the processes of administrative agencies with "sunshine laws" and the invitation by the FCC to consumer groups to air their concerns in informal meetings.

Defeat of broadcasters' efforts to obtain five-year licenses and to avoid the danger of comparative hearings at renewal time.

Breaking up of media concentration and greater diversification of ownership. There have been numerous transfers of broadcast properties while proposed FCC rules were pending and in litigation, although the Supreme Court in *FCC* vs. *NCCB* (Docket no. 76-1471) affirmed the FCC's grandfathering of existing cross-owned media in large markets.

Increased minority employment . . . and increased female employment. . . . (Annual Employment Statistics prepared by OCC, released February 17, 1979).

Some progress in programs and policies related to minority station ownership, particularly in opening up supportive Federal Policies.

More female and minority faces on the media, particularly in major markets, among newscasters; substantial change in the use of ethnic and regional accents in commercials and in programming.

Improved network operating standards for news and public affairs, greater willingness to air corrections of errors, and increased responsiveness to letters of complaint about news distortion and error.

Many interactive radio talk shows showing a substantial increase in the access of a wide range of individuals and groups to public affairs programming.

Free speech messages in a number of markets, including the San Francisco Bay area, Pittsburgh, Twin Cities, Los Angeles, Denver, New Orleans, and the District of Columbia.

Innovations in news coverage such as interactive, in-depth reporting, or use of the simultaneous feedback format.

An expanded 90-minute local news format in some of the major markets.

In children's television since 1967, the establishment of a consortium of public agencies and private foundations; fewer commercials on children's programs; and a mounting awareness of and concern over the effect of television on children.

Withdrawal of ads by corporate advertisers concerned about the impact of violent episodes on viewers.

New entries of a cultural nature into the television diet.

The opening up of a national television debate on environmental problems, on nutrition and obesity, on many taboo subjects such as abortion and homosexuality, and on health habits as evidenced by the popularity of jogging, biking, health foods, etc.

Corporations' sponsorship of quality dramatic productions about current social issues.

Experimentation with the mini-series or docudrama format.

A number of new programs which are directed to the special concerns and interests of women viewers.

Inclusion of women along with minorities in annual employment reports of broadcasters to the FCC.

Inclusion of the "age" into the National Association of Broadcaster TV Code Special Program Standards (section 4, standard 7).[52]

The track record of the broadcast reformers, as we can see, is impressive. But the 1980s must bring changes if the movement is to exist in the 1990s. New technologies, smaller and smaller subgroups within the mass audience, changes in regulatory posture, and broadcaster skill in dealing with citizens' groups' challenges will all play significant roles in the movement's future.

New directions and new groups may also enter the citizen group arena. Some predict citizens' groups to move away from the content of broadcasting to opposition to ownership changes forming conglomerates. The National Citizens Committee for Broadcasting announced it might be one of the groups to move in this direction.[53] The conservative Moral Majority announced it would consider hiring a pollster to measure what the public felt were the most objectionable television shows and then mobilize a boycott against such programming.

summary

Citizens' groups gained clout with the 1966 *United Church of Christ* decision. Since that time, the citizens' movement has grown steadily, reaching all the way from major Washington lobby groups to small-town interest groups concerned with the quality of children's television. Our discussion examined a number of citizens' groups, expressing a variety of goals. Action for Children's Television is one of the most visible interest groups. Incorporated as a nonprofit organization in 1970, the original small group of concerned parents has grown into a major national organization, touching many smaller communities where "ACT contacts" operate to further local interest in programming. The National Citizens' Committee for Broadcasting is an example of a Washington lobby organization. It also joins with other citizens' groups in cases challenging broadcasting's status quo. An organization with broad-based goals and considerable institutional support is the Office of Communication of the United Church of Christ. Through its worldwide membership, through its consultants, and through the work of counsel, the Office is at the forefront of contemporary issues affecting radio and television.

The scope of citizens' group activities is as varied as the citizens' groups themselves. For example, Petitions to Deny licenses represent a major level in the activities of both local and national organizations. Trying to obtain access to programming is another activity that has met with considerable success in some larger cities. Monitoring the quality of broadcast programming has been a well-publicized activity of both Action for Children's Television and the National Parent Teacher Association.

When citizens' groups meet head-on with broadcasters, the result can be a citizens' group agreement. Such an agreement is a form of contract, wherein the broadcaster usually promises a certain type of programming or improvement in hiring policies. The FCC, however, makes it clear that such agreements cannot usurp the local management's responsibility for programming—responsibility which under FCC rules cannot be delegated to any individual or group.

If the citizens' movement is to continue as a strong voice in broadcast policy-making, it must identify closely its future constituency. Specialized media may begin to reflect changes in the policy framework of American broadcasting. Ad hoc groups, which in the past have ridden waves of popularity closely tied to short-lived issues, will need to establish long-range goals and support.

For the time being, let us reflect on the accomplishments of the citizens' movement. Major policy direction, changes in hiring practices, and new programming formats are just some of these accomplishments.

material for analysis

Office of Communication of the United Church of Christ v. Federal Communications Commission

UNITED STATES COURT OF APPEALS, DISTRICT OF COLUMBIA CIRCUIT, 1966
359 F.2d 994 (D.C. Cir.)

BURGER, *Circuit Judge:*

This is an appeal from a decision of the Federal Communications Commission granting to the Intervenor a one-year renewal of its license to operate television station WLBT in Jackson, Mississippi. Appellants filed with the Commission a timely petition to intervene to present evidence and arguments opposing the renewal application. The Commission dismissed Appelants' petition and, without a hearing, took the unusual step of granting a restricted and conditional renewal of the license. Instead of granting the usual three-year renewal, it limited the license to one year from June 1, 1965, and imposed what it characterizes here as "strict conditions" on WLBT's operations in that one-year probationary period.

The questions presented are (a)

whether Appellants, or any of them, have standing before the Federal Communications Commission as parties in interest under Section 309(d) of the Federal Communications Act[1] to contest the renewal of a broadcast license; and (b) whether the Commission was required by Section 309(e)[2] to conduct an evidentiary hearing on the claims of the Appellants prior to acting on renewal of the license.

Because the question whether representatives of the listening public have standing to intervene in a license renewal proceeding is one of first impression, we have given particularly close attention to the background of these issues and to the

---

[1]74 Stat. 890 (1960), 47 U.S.C. § 309(d) (1964).
[2]78 Stat. 193 (1964), 47 U.S.C. § 309(e) (1964).

Commission's reasons for denying standing to Appellants.

BACKGROUND

The complaints against Intervenor embrace charges of discrimination on racial and religious grounds and of excessive commercials. As the Commission's order indicates, the first complaints go back to 1955 when it was claimed that WLBT had deliberately cut off a network program about race relations problems on which the General Counsel of the NAACP was appearing and had flashed on the viewers' screens a "Sorry, Cable Trouble" sign. In 1957 another complaint was made to the Commission that WLBT had presented a program urging the maintenance of racial segregation and had refused requests for time to present the opposing viewpoint. Since then numerous other complaints have been made.

When WLBT sought a renewal of its license in 1958, the Commission at first deferred action because of complaints of this character but eventually granted the usual three-year renewal because it found that, while there had been failures to comply with the Fairness Doctrine, the failures were isolated instances of improper behavior and did not warrant denial of WLBT's renewal application.

Shortly after the outbreak of prolonged civil disturbances centering in large part around the University of Mississippi in Setpember 1962, the Commission again received complaints that various Mississippi radio and television stations, including WLBT, had presented programs concerning racial integration in which only one viewpoint was aired. In 1963, the Commission investigated and requested the stations to submit detailed factual reports on their programs dealing with racial issues. On March 3, 1964, while the Commission was considering WLBT's responses, WLBT filed the license renewal application presently under review.

To block license renewal, Appellants filed a petition in the Commission urging denial of WLBT's application and asking to intervene in their own behalf and as representatives of "all other television viewers in the State of Mississippi." The petition[3] stated that the Office of Communication of the United Church of Christ is an instrumentality of the United Church of Christ, a national denomination with substantial membership within WLBT's prime service area. It listed Appellants Henry and Smith as individual residents of Mississippi, and asserted that both owned television sets and that one lived within the prime service area of WLBT; both are described as leaders in Mississippi civic and civil rights groups. Dr. Henry is president of the Mississippi NAACP; both have been politically active. Each has had a number of controversies with WLBT over allotment of time to present views in opposition to those expressed by WLBT editorials and programs. Appellant United Church of Christ at Tougaloo is a congregation of the United Church of Christ within WLBT's area.

The petition claimed that WLBT failed to serve the general public because it provided a disproportionate amount of commercials and entertainment and did not give a fair and balanced presentation of controversial issues, especially those concerning Negroes, who comprise almost forty-five per cent of the total population within its prime service area;[4] it also claimed discrimination against local activities of the Catholic Church.

---

[3] By "petition," we refer to both the original petition and the reply to WLBT's opposition to the initial petition.

[4] The specific complaints of discrimination were that Negro individuals and institutions are given much less television exposure than others are given and that programs are generally disrespectful toward Negroes. The allegations were particularized and accompanied by a detailed presentation of the results of Appellants' monitoring of a typical week's programming.

Appellants claim standing before the Commission on the grounds that:

(1) They are individuals and organizations who were denied a reasonable opportunity to answer their critics, a violation of the Fairness Doctrine.

(2) These individuals and organizations represent the nearly one half of WLBT's potential listening audience who were denied an opportunity to have their side of controversial issues presented, equally a violation of the Fairness Doctrine, and who were more generally ignored and discriminated against in WLBT's programs.

(3) These individuals and organizations represent the total audience, not merely one part of it, and they assert the right of all listeners, regardless of race or religion, to hear and see balanced programming on significant public questions as required by the Fairness Doctrine[5] and also their broad interest that the station be operated in the public interest in all respects.

The Commission denied the petition to intervene on the ground that standing is predicated upon the invasion of a legally protected interest or an injury which is direct and substantial and that "peti-

tioners ... can assert no greater interest or claim of injury than members of the general public." The Commission stated in its denial, however, that as a general practice it "does consider the contentions advanced in circumstances such as these, irrespective of any questions of standing or related matters," and argues that it did so in this proceeding.

Upon considering Petitioners' claims and WLBT's answers to them on this basis, the Commission concluded that serious issues are presented whether the licensee's operations have fully met the public interest standard. Indeed, it is a close question whether to designate for hearing these applications for renewal of license.

Nevertheless, the Commission conducted no hearing but granted a license renewal, asserting a belief that renewal would be in the public interest since broadcast stations were in a position to make worthwhile contributions to the resolution of pressing racial problems, this contribution was "needed immediately" in the Jackson area, and WLBT, if operated properly,[6] could make such a contribution. Indeed the renewal period was explicitly made a test of WLBT's qualifications in this respect.

We are granting a renewal of license, so that the licensee can demonstrate and carry out its stated willingness to serve fully and fairly the needs and interests of its entire area—so that it can, in short, meet and resolve the questions raised.

The one-year renewal was on conditions which plainly put WLBT on notice that the renewal was in the nature of a probationary grant; the conditions were stated as follows:

(a) "That the licensee comply strictly with the established requirements of the fairness doctrine."

---

[5]In promulgating the Fairness Doctrine in 1949 the Commission emphasized the "right of the public to be informed, rather than any right on the part of the Government, any broadcast licensee or any individual member of the public to broadcast his own particular views on any matter ..." The Commission characterized this as "the foundation tone of the American system of broadcasting." *Editorializing by Broadcast Licensees,* 3 F.C.C. 1246, 1249 (1949). This policy received Congressional approval in the 1959 amendment of Section 315 which speaks in terms of "the obligation imposed upon [licensees] under this Act to operate in the public interest and to afford reasonable opportunity for the discussion of conflicting views on issues of public importance." 73 Stat. 557 (1959), 47 U.S.C. § 315(a) (1964).

[6]" ... we cannot stress too strongly that the licensee must operate in complete conformity with its representations and the conditions laid down."

(b) "... [T]hat the licensee observe strictly its representations to the Commission in this [fairness] area..."

(c) "That, in the light of the substantial questions raised by the United Church petition, the licensee immediately have discussions with community leaders, including those active in the civil rights movement (such as petitioners), as to whether its programming is fully meeting the needs and interests of its area."

(d) "That the licensee immediately cease discriminatory programming patterns."

(e) That "the licensee will be required to make a detailed report as to its efforts in the above four respects..."

Appellants contend that, against the background of complaints since 1955 and the Commission's conclusion that WLBT was in fact guilty of "discriminatory programming," the Commission could not properly renew the license even for one year without a hearing to resolve factual issues raised by their petition and vitally important to the public. The Commission argues, however, that it in effect accepted Petitioners' view of the facts, took all necessary steps to insure that the practices complained of would cease, and for this reason granted a short-term renewal as an exercise by the Commisssion of what it describes as a "'political' decision, 'in the higher sense of that abused term,' which is peculiarly entrusted to the agency."[7] The

Commission seems to have based its "political decision" on a blend of what the Appellants alleged, what its own investigation revealed, its hope that WLBT would improve, and its view that the station was needed.

STANDING OF APPELLANTS[8]

The Commission's denial of standing to Appellants was based on the theory that, absent a potential direct, substantial injury or adverse effect from the administrative action under consideration, a petitioner has no standing before the Commission and that the only types of effects sufficient to support standing are economic injury and electrical interference. It asserted its traditional position that members of the listening public do not suffer any injury peculiar to them and that allowing them standing would pose great administrative burdens.[9]

Up to this time, the courts have granted standing to intervene only to those alleging electrical interference, NBC v. FCC (KOA), 76 U.S. App. D.C. 238, 132 F.2d 545 (1942), aff'd, 319 U.S. 239, 63 S.Ct. 1035, 87 L.Ed. 1374 (1943), or alleging some economic injury, e.g., FCC v. Sanders Bros. Radio Station, 309 U.S. 470, 60 S.Ct. 693, 84 L.Ed. 869 (1940). It is interesting to note, however, that the Commission's

---

[7]Intervenor and the Commission depart from the record to argue that WLBT has fully complied with the conditions and that the Commission's hope that WLBT would make a valuable contribution to the problems of race relations is being fulfilled. Appellants respond that WLBT has not adequately corrected unbalanced programming. We do not consider these claims as to the alleged success of the Commission's effort to permit WLBT to purge itself of mis-

conduct relevant either to the question of standing or to the correctness of the grant of a renewal without a hearing. We confine ourselves to the record as made before the Commission.

[8]All parties seem to consider that the same standards are applicable to determining standing before the Commission and standing to appeal a Commission order to this court. See Philco Corp. v. FCC, 103 U.S. App. D.C. 278, 257 F. 2d 656 (1958), cert. denied, 358 U.S. 946, 79 S.Ct. 350, 3 L.Ed. 2d 352 (1959); Metropolitan Television Co. v. FCC, 95 U.S. App. D.C. 326, 221 F. 2d 879 (1955). We have, therefore, used the cases dealing with standing in the two tribunals interchangeably.

[9]See Northern Pacific Radio Corp., 23 P & F Rad. Reg. 186 (1962); Gordon Broadcasting of San Francisco, Inc., 22 P & F Rad. Reg. 236 (1962).

traditionally narrow view of standing initially led it to deny standing to the very categories it now asserts are the only ones entitled thereto. In *Sanders* the Commission argued that economic injury was not a basis for standing,[10] and in *KOA* that electrical interference was insufficient. This history indicates that neither administrative nor judicial concepts of standing have been static.

What the Commission apparently fails to see in the present case is that the courts have resolved questions of standing as they arose and have at no time manifested an intent to make economic interest and electrical interference the exclusive grounds for standing. *Sanders,* for instance, granted standing to those economically injured on the theory that such persons might well be the only ones sufficiently interested to contest a Commission action. 309 U.S. 470, 477, 60 S.Ct. 693. In *KOA* we noted the anomalous result that, if standing were restricted to those with an economic interest, educational and non-profit radio stations, a prime source of public-interest broadcasting, would be defaulted. Because such a rule would hardly promote the statutory goal of public-interest broadcasting, we concluded that non-profit stations must be heard without a showing of economic injury and held that all broadcast licensees could have standing by showing injury other than financial (there, electrical interference). Our statement that *Sanders* did not limit standing to those suffering direct economic injury was not disturbed by the Supreme Court when it affirmed *KOA.* 319 U.S. 239, 63 S.Ct. 1035 (1943).

It is important to remember that the cases allowing standing to those falling within either of the two established categories have emphasized that standing is accorded to persons not for the protection of their private interest but only to vindicate the public interest.

"The Communications Act of 1934 did not create new private rights. The purpose of the Act was to protect the public interest in communications. By § 402(b)(2), Congress gave the right of appeal to persons 'aggrieved or whose interests are adversely affected' by Commission action. . . . But *these private litigants have standing only as representatives of the public interest.* Federal Communications Commission v. Sanders Radio Station, 309 U.S. 470, 477, 642, 60 S.Ct. 693, 698, 84 L.Ed. 869, 1037." Associated Industries of New York State, Inc. v. Ickes, 134 F. 2d 694, 703 (2d Cir. 1943), vacated as moot, 320 U.S. 707, 64 S.Ct. 74, 88 L.Ed. 414 (1943), quoting Scripps-Howard Radio, Inc. v. FCC, 316 U.S. 4, 14, 62 S.Ct. 875, 86 L.Ed. 1229 (1942).

On the other hand, some Congressional reports have expressed apprehensions, possibly representing the views of both administrative agencies and broadcasters, that standing should not be accorded lightly so as to make possible intervention into proceedings "by a host of parties who have no legitimate interest but solely with the purpose of delaying license grants which properly should be made."[11] But the recurring theme in the legislative reports is not so much fear of a plethora of parties in interest as apprehension that standing might be abused by persons with no *legitimate* interest in the proceedings but with a desire only to delay the granting of a license for some private selfish reason.[12]

---

[10]It argued that, since economic injury was not a ground for refusing a license, it could not be a basis of standing. See generally Chicago Junction Case, 264 U.S. 258, 44 S.Ct. 317, 68 L.Ed. 667 (1924).

[11]S. Rep. No. 44, 82d Cong., 1st Sess. 8 (1951).

[12]See, *e.g., ibid.;* S. Rep. No. 1231, 84th Cong., 1st Sess. 1–3 (1955); H.R. Rep. No. 1051, 84th Cong., 1st Sess. 2–3 (1955); H.R. Rep. No. 1800, 86th Cong., 2d Sess. 9–10, U.S. Code Cong. & Admin. News 1960, p. 3516 (1960).

The Congressional Committee which voiced the apprehension of a "host of parties" seemingly was willing to allow standing to anyone who could show economic injury or electrical interference. Yet these criteria are no guarantee of the legitimacy of the claim sought to be advanced, for, as another Congressional Committee later lamented, "In many of these cases the protests are based on grounds which have little or no relationship to the public interest."[13]

We see no reason to believe, therefore, that Congress through its committees had any thought that electrical interference and economy injury were to be the exclusive grounds for standing or that it intended to limit participation of the listening public to writing letters to the Complaints Division of the Commission. Instead, the Congressional reports seem to recognize that the issue of standing was to be left to the courts.[14]

The Commission's rigid adherence to a requirement of direct economic injury in the commercial sense operates to give standing to an electronics manufacturer who competes with the owner of a radio-television station only in the sale of appliances,[15] while it denies standing to spokesmen for the listeners, who are most directly concerned with and intimately affected by the performance of a licensee. Since the concept of standing is a practical and functional one designed to insure that only those with a genuine and legitimate interest can participate in a proceeding, we can see no reason to exclude those with such an obvious and acute concern as the listening audience. This much seems essential to insure that the holders of broadcasting licenses be responsive to the needs of the audience, without which the broadcaster could not exist.

There is nothing unusual or novel in granting the consuming public standing to challenge administrative actions. In Associated Industries of New York State, Inc. v. Ickes, 134 F. 2d 694 (2d Cir. 1943), vacated as moot, 320 U.S. 707, 64 S.Ct. 74, 88 L.Ed. 414 (1943), coal consumers were found to have standing to review a minimum price order. In United States v. Public Utilities Commission, 80 U.S. App. D.C. 227, 151 F. 2d 609 (1945), we held that a consumer of electricity was affected by the rates charged and could appeal an order setting them. Similarly in Bebchick v. Public Utilities Commission, 109 U.S. App. D.C. 298, 287 F. 2d 337 (1961), we had no difficulty in concluding that a public transit rider had standing to appeal a rate increase. A direct economic injury, even if small as to each user, is involved in the rate cases, but standing has also been granted to a passenger to contest the legality of Interstate Commerce Commission rules allowing racial segregation in railroad dining cars. Henderson v. United States, 339 U.S. 816, 70 S.Ct. 843, 94 L.Ed. 1302 (1950). Moreover, in Reade v. Ewing, 205 F. 2d 630 (2d Cir. 1953), a consumer of oleomargarine was held to have standing to challenge orders affecting the ingredients thereof.[16]

These "consumer" cases were not decided under the Federal Communications Act, but all of them have in common with the case under review the interpretation of language granting standing to persons "af-

---

[13]H.R. Rep. No. 1051, 84th Cong., 1st Sess. 3 (1955).

[14]Perhaps the mention in these reports of economic and electrical injury arose out of preoccupation with problems surrounding initial licensing procedures, as distinguished from those involved in renewal proceedings. See . . . *infra.*

[15]Philco Corp. v. FCC, 103 U.S. App. D.C. 278, 257 F.2d 656 (1958); cert. denied, 358 U.S. 946, 79 S.Ct. 350, 3 L.Ed. 2d 35 (1959).

[16]In the most recent case on the subject, the Second Circuit, relying on cases under the Federal Communications Act, held that non-profit conservation associations have standing to protect the aesthetic, conservational, and recreational aspects of power development. Scenic Hudson Preservation Conference v. FPC, 354 F. 2d 608 (2d Cir. 1965).

fected" or "aggrieved." The Commission fails to suggest how we are to distinguish these cases from those involving standing of broadcast "consumers" to oppose license renewals in the Federal Communications Commission. The total number of potential individual suitors who are consumers of oleomargarine or public transit passengers would seem to be greater than the number of responsible representatives of the listening public who are potential intervenors in a proceeding affecting a single broadcast reception area. Furthermore, assuming we look only to the commercial economic aspects and ignore vital public interest, we cannot believe that the economic stake of the consumers of electricity or public transit riders is more significant than that of listeners who collectively have a huge aggregate investment in receiving equipment.[17]

The argument that a broadcaster is not a public utility is beside the point. True it is not a public utility in the same sense as strictly regulated common carriers or purveyors of power, but neither is it a purely private enterprise like a newspaper or an automobile agency. A broadcaster has much in common with a newspaper publisher, but he is not in the same category in terms of public obligations imposed by law. A broadcaster seeks and is granted the free and exclusive use of a limited and valuable part of the public domain; when he accepts that franchise it is burdened by enforceable public obligations. A newspaper can be operated at the whim or caprice of its owners; a broadcast station cannot. After nearly five decades of operation the broadcast industry does not seem to have

---

[17]According to Robert Sarnoff of NBC the total investment in television, by American viewers is 40 billion dollars, a figure perhaps twenty times as large as the total investment of broadcasters. FCC, *Television Network Program Procurement*, H.R. Rep. No. 281, 88th Cong., 1st Sess. 57 (1963). Forty billion dollars would seem to afford at least one substantial brick in a foundation for standing.

grasped the simple fact that a broadcast license is a public trust subject to termination for breach of duty.

Nor does the fact that the Commission itself is directed by Congress to protect the public interest constitute adequate reason to preclude the listening public from assisting in that task. *Cf.* UAW v. Scofield, 382 U.S. 205, 86 S.Ct. 335, 15 L.Ed. 2d 304 (1965). The Commission of course represents and indeed is the prime arbiter of the public interest, but its duties and jurisdiction are vast, and it acknowledges that it cannot begin to monitor or oversee the performance of every one of thousands of licensees. Moreover, the Commission has always viewed its regulatory duties as guided if not limited by our national tradition that public response is the most reliable test of ideas and performance in broadcasting as in most areas of life. The Commission view is that we have traditionally depended on this public reaction rather than on some form of governmental supervision or "censorship" mechanisms.

[I]t is the public in individual communities throughout the length and breadth of our country who must bear final responsibility for the quality and adequacy of television service—whether it be originated by local stations or by national networks. Under our system, the interests of the public are dominant. The commercial needs of licensed broadcasters and advertisers must be integrated into those of the public. *Hence, individual citizens and the communities they compose owe a duty to themselves and their peers to take an active interest in the scope and quality of the television service* which stations and networks provide and which, undoubtedly, has a *vast impact on their lives and the lives of their children.* Nor need the public feel that in taking a hand in broadcasting they are unduly interfering in the private business affairs of others. On the contrary, *their interest in television programming is direct* and their responsibilities important. *They are the owners* of the channels of television—indeed, of all broadcasting.

FCC, *Television Network Program Procurement,* H.R. Rep. No. 281, 88th Cong., 1st Sess. 20 (1963). (Emphasis added.)

Taking advantage of this "active interest in the . . . quality" of broadcasting rather than depending on governmental initiative is also desirable in that it tends to cast governmental power, at least in the first instance, in the more detached role of arbiter rather than accuser.

The theory that the Commission can always effectively represent the listener interests in a renewal proceeding without the aid and participation of legitimate listener representatives fulfilling the role of private attorneys general is one of those assumptions we collectively try to work with so long as they are reasonably adequate. When it becomes clear, as it does to us now, that it is no longer a valid assumption which stands up under the realities of actual experience, neither we nor the Commission can continue to rely on it. The gradual expansion and evolution of concepts of standing in administrative law attests that experience rather than logic or fixed rules has been accepted as the guide.

The Commission's attitude in this case is ambivalent in the precise sense of that term. While attracted by the potential contribution of widespread public interest and participation in improving the quality of broadcasting, the Commission rejects effective public participation by invoking the oft-expressed fear that a "host of parties" will descend upon it and render its dockets "clogged" and "unworkable." The Commission resolves this ambivalence for itself by contending that in this renewal proceeding the viewpoint of the public was adequately represented since it fully considered the claims presented by Appellants even though denying them standing. It also points to the general procedures for public participation that are already available, such as the filing of complaints with the Commission,[18] the practice of having local hearings,[19] and the ability of people who are not parties in interest to appear at hearings as witnesses.[20] In light of the Commission's procedure in this case and its stated willingness to hear witnesses having complaints, it is difficult to see how a grant of formal standing would pose undue or insoluble problems for the Commission.

We cannot believe that the Congressional mandate of public participation which the Commission says it seeks to fulfill[21] was meant to be limited to writing letters to the Commission, to inspection of records, to the Commission's grace in considering listener claims, or to mere non-participating appearance at hearings. We cannot fail to note that the long history of complaints against WLBT beginning in 1955 had left the Commission virtually unmoved in the subsequent renewal proceedings, and it seems not unlikely that the 1964 renewal application might well have been routinely granted except for the determined and sustained efforts of Appellants at no small expense to themselves.[22] Such beneficial contribution as these Appellants, or some of them, can make must not be left to the grace of the Commission.

Public participation is especially important in a renewal proceeding, since the public will have been exposed for at least three years to the licensee's performance,

---

[18]47 C.F.R. § 1.587 (1965).

[19]74 Stat. 892 (1960), 47 U.S.C. § 311 (1964).

[20]47 C.F.R. § 1.225 (1965).

[21]See 30 Fed. Reg. 4543 (1965).

[22]We recognize, of course, the existence of strong tides of public opinion and other forces at work outside the listening area of the Licensee which may not have been without some effect on the Commission.

as cannot be the case when the Commission considers an initial grant, unless the applicant has a prior record as a licensee. In a renewal proceeding, furthermore, public spokesmen, such as Appellants here, may be the only objectors. In a community served by only one outlet, the public interest focus is perhaps sharper and the need for airing complaints often greater than where, for example, several channels exist. Yet if there is only one outlet, there are no rivals at hand to assert the public interest, and reliance on opposing applicants to challenge the existing licensee for the channel would be fortuitous at best. Even when there are multiple competing stations in a locality, various factors may operate to inhibit the other broadcasters from opposing a renewal application. An imperfect rival may be thought a desirable rival, or there may be a "gentleman's agreement" of deference to a fellow broadcaster in the hope he will reciprocate on a propitious occasion.

Thus we are brought around by analogy to the Supreme Court's reasoning in *Sanders;* unless the listeners—the broadcast consumers—can be heard, there may be no one to bring programming deficiencies or offensive overcommercialization to the attention of the Commission in an effective manner. By process of elimination those "consumers" willing to shoulder the burdensome and costly processes of intervention in a Commission proceeding are likely to be the only ones "having a sufficient interest" to challenge a renewal application. The late Edmond Cahn addressed himself to this problem in its broadest aspects when he said, "Some consumers need bread; others need Shakespeare; others need their rightful place in the national society—what they all need is processors of law who will consider the people's needs more significant than administrative convenience." *Law in the Consumer Perspective,* 112 U.Pa.L.Rev. 1, 13 (1963).

Unless the Commission is to be given

staff and resources to perform the enormously complex and prohibitively expensive task of maintaining constant surveillance over every licensee, some mechanism must be developed so that the *legitimate* interests of listeners can be made a part of the record which the Commission evaluates. An initial applicant frequently floods the Commission with testimonials from a host of representative community groups as to the relative merit of their champion, and the Commission places considerable reliance on these vouchers; on a renewal application the "campaign pledges" of applicants must be open to comparison with "performance in office" aided by a limited number of responsible representatives of the listening public when such representatives seek participation.

We recognize the risks alluded to by Judge Madden in his cogent dissent in *Philco;*[23] regulatory agencies, the Federal Communications Commission in particular, would ill serve the public interest if the courts imposed such heavy burdens on them as to overtax their capacities. The competing consideration is that experience demonstrates consumers are generally among the best vindicators of the public interest. In order to safeguard the public interest in broadcasting, therefore, we hold that some "audience participation" must be allowed in license renewal proceedings. We recognize this will create problems for the Commission but it does not necessarily follow that "hosts" of protestors must be granted standing to challenge a renewal application or that the Commission need allow the administrative processes to be obstructed or overwhelmed by captious or purely obstructive protests. The Commission can avoid such results by developing appropriate regulations by statutory rule-making. Although it denied

---

[23]103 U.S. App. D.C. at 281, 257 F. 2d at 659 (1958), cert. denied, 358 U.S. 946, 79 S.Ct. 350, 3 L.Ed. 2d 352 (1959).

Appellants standing, it employed *ad hoc* criteria in determining that these Appellants were responsible spokesmen for representative groups having significant roots in the listening community. These criteria can afford a basis for developing formalized standards to regulate and limit public intervention to spokesmen who can be helpful. A petition for such intervention must "contain specific allegations of fact sufficient to show that the petitioner is a party in interest and that a grant of the application would be prima facie inconsistent" with the public interest. 74 Stat. 891 (1960), 47 U.S.C. 309(d) (1) (1964).

The responsible and representative groups eligible to intervene cannot here be enumerated or categorized specifically; such community organizations as civic associations, professional societies, unions, churches, and educational institutions or associations might well be helpful to the Commission. These groups are found in every community; they usually concern themselves with a wide range of community problems and tend to be representatives of broad as distinguished from narrow interests, public as distinguished from private or commercial interests.

The Commission should be accorded broad discretion in establishing and applying rules for such public participation, including rules for determining which community representatives are to be allowed to participate and how many are reasonably required to give the Commission the assistance it needs in vindicating the public interest.[24] The usefulness of any particular petitioner for intervention must be judged in relation to other petitioners and the nature of the claims it asserts as basis for standing. Moreover it is no novelty in the administrative process to require consolidation of petitions and briefs to avoid multiplicity of parties and duplication of effort.

The fears of regulatory agencies that their processes will be inundated by expansion of standing criteria are rarely borne out. Always a restraining factor is the expense of participation in the administrative process, an economic reality which will operate to limit the number of those who will seek participation; legal and related expenses of administrative proceedings are such that even those with large economic interests find the costs burdensome. Moreover, the listening public seeking intervention in a license renewal proceeding cannot attract lawyers to represent their cause by the prospect of lucrative contingent fees, as can be done, for example, in rate cases.

We are aware that there may be efforts to exploit the enlargement of intervention, including spurious petitions from private interests not concerned with the quality of broadcast programming, since such private interests may sometimes cloak themselves with a semblance of public interest advocates. But this problem, as we have noted, can be dealt with by the Commission under its inherent powers and by rulemaking.

In line with this analysis, we do not now hold that all of the Appellants have standing to challenge WLBT's renewal. We do not reach that question. As to these Appellants we limit ourselves to holding that the Commission must allow standing to one or more of them as responsible representatives to assert and prove the claims they have urged in their petition.

---

[24]Professor Jaffe concedes there are strong reasons to reject public or listener standing but he believes "it does have much to commend it" in certain areas if put in terms of "jurisdiction subject to judicial discretion to be exercised with due regard for the character of the interests and the issues involved in each case." Jaffe, *Standing to Secure Judicial Review: Private Actions,* 75 Harv. L. Rev. 255, 282 (1961). "There are many persons . . . who feel that neither the industry nor the FCC can be trusted to protect the listener interest. If this is so, the public action is appropriate. But a frank recognition that the action is a public action and not a private remedy would allow us to introduce the notion of discretion at both the administrative and judicial levels." *Id.* at 284.

It is difficult to anticipate the range of claims which may be raised or sought to be raised by future petitioners asserting representation of the public interest. It is neither possible nor desirable for us to try to chart the precise scope or patterns for the future. The need sought to be met is to provide a means for reflection of listener appraisal of a licensee's performance as the performance meets or fails to meet the licensee's statutory obligation to operate the facility in the public interest. The matter now before us is one in which the alleged conduct adverse to the public interest rests primarily on claims of racial discrimination, some elements of religious discrimination, oppressive overcommercialization by advertising announcements, and violation of the Fairness Doctrine. Future cases may involve other areas of conduct and programming adverse to the public interest; at this point we can only emphasize that intervention on behalf of the public is not allowed to press private interests but only to vindicate the broad public interest relating to a licensee's performance of the public trust inherent in every license.

HEARING

We hold further that in the circumstances shown by this record an evidentiary hearing was required in order to resolve the public interest issue. Under Section 309(e) the Commission must set a renewal application for hearing where "a substantial and material question of fact is presented *or* the Commission for any reason is unable to make the finding" that the public interest, convenience, and necessity will be served by the license renewal. (Emphasis supplied.)

The Commission argues in this Court that it accepted all Appellants' allegations of WLBT's misconduct and that for this reason no hearing was necessary.[25] Yet the Commission recognized that WLBT's past behavior, as described by Appellants, would preclude the statutory finding of public interest necessary for license renewal;[26] hence its grant of the one-year license on the policy ground that there was an urgent need at the time for a properly run station in Jackson must have been predicated on a belief that the need was so great as to warrant the risk that WLBT might continue its improper conduct.

We agree that a history of programming misconduct of the kind alleged would preclude, as a matter of law, the required finding that renewal of the license would serve the public interest. It is important to bear in mind, moreover, that although in granting an initial license the Commission must of necessity engage in some degree of forecasting future performance, in a renewal proceeding past performance is its best criterion. When past performance is in conflict with the public interest, a very heavy burden rests on the renewal applicant to show how a renewal can be reconciled with the public interest. Like public officials charged with a public trust, a renewal applicant, as we noted in our discussion of standing, must literally "run on his record."

The Commission in effect sought to justify its grant of the one-year license, in the face of accepted facts irreconcilable with a public interest finding, on the ground that as a matter of policy the immediate need warranted the risks involved, and that the "strict conditions" it imposed on the grant would improve *future* operations. However, the conditions which the Commission made explicit in the one-year license are implicit

---

[25] The Commission also argues that Appellants do not have standing in this Court as persons aggrieved or adversely affected under 66 Sta. 718 (1952), as amended, 47 U.S.C. § 402(b) (1964), because all their allegations were accepted as true. However, denial of the relief they sought rendered them persons aggrieved.

[26] In the 1959 renewal proceedings the Commission conceded that WLBT's misconduct then shown would preclude a grant except that there were only "isolated instances."

in every grant. The Commission's opinion reveals how it labored to justify the result it thought was dictated by the urgency of the situation.[27] The majority considered the question of setting the application for hearing a "close" one; Chairman Henry and Commissioner Cox would have granted a hearing to Appellants as a matter of right.

The Commission's "policy" decision is not a reflection of some long standing or accepted proposition but represents an *ad hoc* determination in the context of Jackson's contemporary problem. Granted the basis for a Commission "policy" recognizing the value of properly run broadcast facilities to the resolution of community problems, if indeed this truism rises to the level of a policy, it is a determination valid in the abstract but calling for explanation in its application.

Assuming *arguendo* that the Commission's acceptance of Appellants' allegations would satisfy one ground for dispensing with a hearing, *i.e.,* absence of a question of fact, Section 309(e) also commands that in order to avoid a hearing the Commission must make an affirmative finding that renewal will serve the public interest. Yet the only find on this crucial factor is a qualified statement that the public interest would be served, provided WLBT thereafter complied strictly with the specified conditions. Not surprisingly, having asserted that it accepted Petitioners' allegations, the Commission thus considered itself unable to make a categorical determination that on WLBT's record of performance it was an appropriate entity to receive the license. It found only that *if* WLBT changed its ways, something which the Commission did not and, of course, could not guarantee, the licensing would be proper. The statutory public interest finding cannot be inferred from a statement of the obvious truth that a properly operated station will serve the public interest.

We view as particularly significant the Commission's summary:

We are granting a renewal of license, so that the licensee can demonstrate and carry out its stated willingness to serve fully and fairly the needs and interests of its entire area—so that it can, in short, meet and resolve the questions raised.

The only "stated willingness to serve fully and fairly" which we can glean from the record is WLBT's protestation that it had always fully performed its public obligations. As we read it the Commission's statement is a strained and strange substitute for a public interest finding.

We recognize that the Commission was confronted with a difficult problem and difficult choices, but it would perhaps not go too far to say it elected to post the Wolf

---

[27]"24. The discussion in B and C, above, establishes that serious issues are presented whether the licensee's operations have fully met the public interest standard. Indeed, it is a close question whether to designate for hearing these applications for renewal of license. In making its judgment, the Commission has taken into account that this particular area is entering a critical period in race relations, and that the broadcast stations, such as here involved, can make a most worthwhile contribution to the resolution of problems arising in this respect. That contribution is needed now—and should not be put off for the future. We believe that the licensee, operating in strict accordance with the representations made and other conditions specified herein, can make that needed contribution, and thus that its renewal would be in the public interest.

25. But we cannot stress too strongly that the licensee must operate in complete conformity with its representations and the conditions laid down. In the last *two* renewal periods, questions have been raised whether the licensee has complied with the requirements of the fairness doctrine; in the last renewal period, substantial public interest questions have been raised by the petition filed by most responsible community leaders. We are granting a renewal of license, so that the licensee can demonstrate and carry out its stated willingness to serve fully and fairly the needs and interests of its entire area—so that it can, in short, meet and resolve the questions raised. Further, in line with the basic policy determination set out in par. 24, the licensee's efforts in this respect must be made now, and continue throughout the license period."

to guard the Sheep in the hope that the Wolf would mend his ways because some protection was needed at once and none but the Wolf was handy. This is not a case, however, where the Wolf had either promised or demonstrated any capacity and willingness to change, for WLBT had stoutly denied Appellants' charges of programming misconduct and violations.[28] In these circumstances a pious hope on the Commission's part for better things from WLBT is not a substitute for evidence and findings. *Cf.* Interstate Broadcasting Co. v. FCC, 116 U.S. App. D.C. 327, 323 F. 2d 797 (1963).

Even if the embodiment of the Commission's hope be conceded *arguendo* to be a finding, there was not sufficient evidence in the record to justify a "policy determination" that the need for a properly run station in Jackson was so pressing as to justify the risk that WLBT might well continue with an inadequate performance. The issues which should have been considered could be resolved only in an evidentiary hearing in which all aspects of its qualifications and performance could be explored.

It is open to question whether the public interest would not be as well, if not better served with one TV outlet acutely conscious that adherence to the Fairness Doctrine is a *sine qua non* of every licensee. Even putting aside the salutary warning effect of a license denial, there are other reasons why one station in Jackson might be better than two for an interim period. For instance, in a letter to the Commission, Appellant Smith alleged that the other television station in Jackson had agreed to sell him time only if WLBT did so.[29] It is

arguable that the pressures on the other station might be reduced if WLBT were in other hands—or off the air. The need which the Commission thought urgent might well be satisfied by refusing to renew the license of WLBT and opening the channel to new applicants under the special temporary authorization procedures available to the Commission on the theory that another, and better suited, operator could be found to broadcast on the channel with brief, if any, interruption of service. The Commission's opinion reflects no consideration of these or other alternatives.

We hold that the grant of a renewal of WLBT's license for one year was erroneous. The Commission is directed to conduct hearings on WLBT's renewal application, allowing public intervention pursuant to this holding. Since the Commission has already decided that Appellants are responsible representatives of the listening public of the Jackson area, we see no obstacle to a prompt determination granting standing to Appellants or some of them. Whether WLBT should be able to benefit from a showing of good performance, if such is the case, since June 1965 we do not undertake to decide. The Commission has had no occasion to pass on this issue and we therefore refrain from doing so.[30]

The record is remanded to the Commission for further proceedings consistent with this opinion; jurisdiction is retained in this court.

Reversed and remanded.

---

[28]The Commission should have discretion to experiment and even to take calculated risks on renewals where a licensee confesses the error of its ways; this is not such a case.

[29]Letter to Commission from Rev. Robert L. T. Smith, received Jan. 17, 1962, Record, p. 1.

[30] In light of our holding, the special form of license granted here is not unlike a special temporary authorization. Under the Commission's position in Community Broadcasting Co., Inc. v. FCC, 107 U.S. App. D.C. 95, 174 F. 2d 753 (1960), it may be that the Commission will conclude that good performance under this conditional or probationary license should not weigh in favor of WLBT.

questions for discussion and further research

1. Do you feel that Frank Lloyd's proposal that professional associations, such as the American Bar Association, fund public-interest law activities has merit?
2. If so, would professional associations or their members agree to such an arrangement?
3. If public-interest law became part of the private sector, how could it be financed?
4. Would the very fact that it is part of the private sector create an immediate conflict of interest for law firms involved with communication clients?
5. If public-interest law became part of the private sector, would law firms specializing in communication matters shy away from such involvement for fear of turning away larger, more industry-oriented clients?
6. Some people have suggested that the control of broadcast programming belongs in the home, and that the best way to reform the broadcast movement is to shut off the television set or just not watch distasteful programming. Is this a substantive argument, and is it practical in the system of competitive commercial programming that exists in the United States?
7. Does the "saving clause" that is found in many citizen-broadcaster agreements in effect neutralize the agreement and make it ineffective or weighted in the broadcaster's favor?
8. Should there be separate controls over certain specific types of television entertainment programming, such as that directed to the child audience?
9. Controversy still exists over whether or not broadcasters should reimburse citizens' groups for legal fees incurred as a result of challenging the license of a broadcaster. Should the FCC institute formal rules, whereby a broadcaster would pay such a fee only if the citizens' group's charges proved to be justified, or if the license renewal were denied, or if an agreement materialized from the dialogue with the citizens' group?
10. What would stop abusive practice and price gouging if such a rule were instituted?
11. As a general rule, the FCC will examine a broadcast-citizen agreement only if it is a contractual or intricate part of a license renewal application. Does the public interest warrant closer scrutiny of these agreements, as in having the FCC approve any agreement before it in any way affects a station's operation or programming?
12. How can a broadcaster be certain that a citizens' group's claim that it represents a broad segment of the population is valid and not merely an attempt to cover up the self-centered interests of a very small group of people?
13. How will the citizens' movement change— economically, socially, and politically—if the arena for broadcast reform moves out of the judiciary and into the legislative area?
14. Would the role of citizens' groups be strengthened if station license renewals within each state were staggered instead of occurring all at the same time?

additional resources

books

Bennett, R. W., *A Lawyer's Sourcebook: Representing the Audience in Broadcast Proceedings,* New York: United Church of Christ, 1974.

Grundfest, J. A., *Citizen Participation in FCC Decision Making,* Santa Monica, Calif.: Rand Corp., 1976.

articles

Branscomb, A. W., and M. Savage, "The Broadcast Reform Movement: At the Crossroads," 28 *Journal of Communication* 25 (1978).

Garay, R., "Access: Evolution of the Citizen Agreement," 22 *Journal of Broadcasting* 95 (1978).

Gross, L. Schafer, and R. Patricia Walsh, "Factors Affecting Parental Control Over Children's Television Viewing: A Pilot Study," 24 *Journal of Broadcasting* 411 (1980).

Nielsen, R. P., "Court Ruling Gives Edge to Nonprofit Broadcasters," 54 *Journalism Quarterly* 385 (1977).

Nord, D. P., "The FCC, Educational Broadcasting, and Political Interest Group Activity," 22 *Journal of Broadcasting* 321 (1978).

Rada, S. E., "KIPC-FM Pueblo Indian Radio: Case Study of a Failure," 56 *Journalism Quarterly* 97 (1979).

Stanley, N. E., "Federal Communications Law and Women's Rights: Women in the Wasteland Fight Back," 23 *Hastings Law Journal* 15 (1971).

Volner, I. D., "Games Consumers Play," 25 *Federal Communications Bar Journal* 121 (1972).

Yasser, R. L., "*Federal Communications Commission* v. *National Citizens' Committee for Broadcasting:* The Ultimate Media Hype," 67 *Kentucky Law Journal* 903 (1978–79).

cases

Illinois Citizens' Committee for Broadcasting v. *F.C.C.,* 515 F.2d 397, 169 U.S.App.D.C. 166 (1975).

Office of Communication of United Church of Christ v. *F.C.C.,* 359 F.2d 994, 123 U.S.App.D.C. 328, appeal after remand 425 F.2d 543, 138 U.S. App. D.C. 112, 1 Med. L. Rptr. 1992 (1966).

Office of Communication of United Church of Christ v. *F.C.C.,* 425 F.2d 543, 138 U.S.App. D.C. 112 (1969).

Office of Communication of United Church of Christ v. *F.C.C.,* 465 F.2d 519, 150 U.S.App.D.C. 339 (1972).

More about the role of citizens' groups in communication can be found by perusing the cases listed with other chapters.

11

Self-Regulation
and
Ethics

Today, self-regulation and codes of ethics are found to exist throughout business and industry, with varying degrees of success. Some consider them to be buffers against legislative and judicial controls. Others view them as role models for their own behavior. Still others, more critical of the concept, look at them as whitewash or sham—something that businesses can hide behind while all the time operating without constraint and consideration of right or wrong.

In broadcasting, self-regulation is perhaps best exemplified in the National Association of Broadcasters' Radio and Television Codes. Other allied organizations, from advertising agencies to press associations, also have codes of ethics. Essentially, they all encourage ethical conduct among their members. In this chapter, we will examine the forms of self-regulation and codes of ethics that directly affect the flow of information through the media of radio and television.

Our indoctrination into this material needs to be supplemented by an understanding of what broadcasting really is and how its codes fit into the operation of the industry. Specifically, we need to ask ourselves whether or not broadcasting is really a "profession." If we feel that it is, and if we argue our case before other "professions," such as law or medicine, we may find ourselves standing on shaky ground. If a doctor is found guilty of violating the "ethics" of his profession, he or she could lose a license to practice. If a lawyer violates the canons of the bar, the same loss might result. But what happens if a broadcaster violates a code of ethics? Very little. Although a station might lose its membership (paid for by monthly dues) in the NAB Code, there is no enforcement power to put a station out of business unless an FCC Rule or a law is violated. Does the fact that these codes are "unenforceable" rob broadcasting of its "professional" category? Probably not. But you should read this chapter with this question in mind. And keep in mind, too, that there are members of every profession, regardless of how enforceable the codes, who need no enforcement provisions to make them adhere to good business practices.

National Association of Broadcasters (NAB)

Of all the organizations involved in broadcast self-regulation, perhaps none is more active nor receives more publicity than the National Association of Broadcasters (NAB). Although there are other groups representing special interests, such as the broadcast-journalism-oriented Radio/Television News Directors' Association and the National Radio Broadcasters' Association, the NAB remains one of the most powerful lobbying forces in Washington. Its Radio and Television Codes are the major guidelines for self-regulation in the broadcasting industry.

early history of the nab

The origins of the National Association of Broadcasters go back almost to the origins of radio. The scenario was one of declining sales of phonograph records and sheet music, for which radio found itself taking much of the blame. At the heart of the consternation was the American Society of Composers, Authors, and Publishers (ASCAP), who decided that the broadcasting of music over radio stations was an infringement of copyright law. ASCAP's attorneys continued to push the copyright issue until they forced a meeting in September, 1922 between the Society and the broadcasters. Under the threats of copyright suits if the broadcasters did not attend, the meeting only further antagonized the two groups. In the following year, a handful of broadcasters met in Chicago to discuss their mutual concerns over copyright.[1] By April of 1923, an organization of fifty-four people had hired an executive director, Paul B. Klugh, and had chosen New York City as its headquarters. The NAB was officially launched.[2]

With the common foe of ASCAP at hand, the NAB held its first convention in October, 1923 in New York.[3] Its purpose was twofold: (1) to begin a major lobbying effort, and (2) to bring ASCAP under control. To compete head on with ASCAP, the NAB formed its own "music bureau," which solicited directly from writers and publishers. With a goal of influencing legislation that would overhaul the copyright laws, the organization publicized its plight to the public and raised $4,500 in contributions.

But instead of things getting better, they got worse. By the late 1920s, not only was the music licensing organization still on the backs of the broadcasters but baseball associations were now objecting to the broadcasting of baseball games, on the basis that it hurt attendance. Moreover, by the early 1930s, the Interstate Commerce Commission was talking about regulating broadcast advertising rates. The Federal Radio Commission, in the meantime, was having problems with legal challenges from the industry as well as a lack of funds for its own operations. ASCAP leveled another blow in 1932 by increasing its copyright fees 300 percent. The broadcasters countered by launching a Radio Program Foundation, with $150,000 designated to encourage new creativity among music composers.[4]

A short burst of joy occurred in 1934, when the government filed an antitrust suit against ASCAP. Jubilance quickly met reality, however, when, in an effort to keep securing ASCAP songs, some of the larger broadcasters went ahead and signed ASCAP's agreements. The action split the broadcasters' unity and cast doubt on the future effectiveness of the NAB.

Undaunted, the NAB bounced back. In 1940, broadcasters unified again with over 1½ million dollars' worth of stock sold or pledged for a new broadcast-oriented licensing organization, Broadcast Music, Incorporated (BMI).[5] BMI has since become a separate entity, with no direct relationship to the NAB.

After the formation of BMI, the direction of the NAB's primary role moved more strongly toward lobbying, where it has remained. The NAB also works closely with programming executives and the FCC to develop a regulatory atmosphere in which a broadcaster can try not to restrict creativity while keeping sensitive to the government's charge that radio and television operate in the public interest.

Today, the NAB considers its own accomplishments to be in such areas as:

Instituting voluntary codes for radio and television which provide broadcasters with guideposts in determining acceptable programming and advertising practices.
Upholding the American system of broadcasting, free from government censorship.
Combatting discriminatory legislative proposals.
Obtaining more liberal acceptance of radio and television coverage of public proceedings.
Improving the industry's relationship with public service groups.
Achieving fair labor relations laws and wage-hour regulations.

The Association also has enabled broadcasters to operate more effectively by:

Gaining authorization by the Federal Communications Commission for remote control for radio and TV stations.
Drafting engineering and recording standards universally accepted by the broadcasting industry.
Introducing simplified program and engineering logs meeting FCC requirements.[6]

A more general statement of the purposes and goals of the NAB is found in Article 2 of its bylaws, which states that:

The object of this Association shall be to foster and promote the development of the arts of aural and visual broadcasting in all its forms; to protect its members in every lawful and proper manner from injustices and unjust exactions; to do all things necessary and proper to encourage and promote customs and practices which will strengthen and maintain the broadcasting industry to the end that it may best serve the public.[7]

While the organization's lobbying efforts provide a buffer against excessive government regulation, perhaps nowhere is the self-regulatory stance of the broadcasting industry manifested more clearly than in the NAB Codes.

nab radio code

The first efforts toward providing an industrywide Radio and Television Code were made in 1937. The NAB conducted a major revision and review of the document in 1945. Since then, it has made revisions whenever necessary.

Let us briefly review the outline of the Radio Code and its various provisions concerning programming and advertising.

Dealing with *news sources,* the Radio Code encourages broadcast journalists to use professional care in the selection of these sources, since they are directly tied to the reputation of radio as a well-balanced news medium. The Code calls for *news reporting* to be in good taste and to be factual, fair, and without bias. Discouraged are sensationalism or the use of alarming details not essential to factual reporting. Broadcast techniques creating panic or unnecessary alarm are to be avoided, and care is called for in selecting editors and reporters directly involved in a station's broadcast reporting functions. The Code calls for *commentary and analyses* to be clearly labeled apart from the other news programming and sets the same requirements for *editorializing.* High ethical standards in the *coverage of news and public events* are stressed, as is care in the *placement of advertising,* to keep such commercial messages distinguishable from news programming.

A charge of community responsibility calls upon broadcasters to acquaint themselves with the needs and characteristics of the community and to carefully review any group or organization requesting time for public service messages. Broadcasters are called upon to clearly label political broadcasts and to refrain from restrictive interference in political messages. Criteria for religious programming, responsibilities to children, and the responsible presentation of dramatic programming are all part of the Radio Code's programming standards.

Indicative of the actual language of the Radio Code is that section dealing with broadcasters' responsibilities toward children:

Broadcasters have a special responsibility to children. Programming which might reasonably be expected to hold the attention of children should be presented with due regard for its effect on children.

1. Programming should be based upon sound social concepts and should include positive sets of values which will allow children to become responsible adults, capable of coping with the challenges of maturity.
2. Programming should convey a reasonable range of the realities which exist in the world to help children make the transition to adulthood.
3. Programming should contribute to the healthy development of personality and character.

4. Programming should afford opportunities for cultural growth as well as for wholesome entertainment.

5. Programming should be consistent with integrity of realistic production, but should avoid material of extreme nature which might create undesirable emotional reaction in children.

6. Programming should avoid appeals urging children to purchase the product specifically for the purpose of keeping the program on the air or which, for any reason, encourage children to enter inappropriate places.

7. Programming should present such subjects as violence and sex without undue emphasis and only as required by plot development or character delineation.

> Violence, physical or psychological, should only be projected in responsibly handled contexts, not used to excess or exploitatively. Programs involving violence should present the consequences of it to its victims and perpetrators.

> The depiction of conflict, and of material reflective of sexual considerations, when presented in programs designed primarily for children should be handled with sensitivity.

8. The treatment of criminal activities should always convey their social and human effects.

Equally detailed are the advertising standards of the Code. Broadcasters are called upon to avoid presenting false, misleading, or deceptive advertising. In addition, the Radio Code states:

> Advertising is the principal source of revenue of the free, competitive American system of radio broadcasting. It makes possible the presentation to all American people of the finest programs of entertainment, education, and information.

> Since the great strength of American radio broadcasting derives from the public respect for and the public approval of its programs, it must be the purpose of each broadcaster to establish and maintain high standards of performance, not only in the selection and production of all programs, but also in the presentation of advertising.

> This Code establishes basic standards for all radio broadcasting. The principles of acceptability and good taste within the Program Standards section govern the presentation of advertising where applicable. In addition, the Code establishes in this section special standards which apply to radio advertising.

A. General Advertising Standards

1. Commercial radio broadcasters make their facilities available for the advertising of products and services and accept commercial presentations for such advertising. However, they shall, in recognition of the responsibility to the public, refuse the facilities of their stations to an advertiser where they have

good reason to doubt the integrity of the advertiser, the truth of the advertising representations, or the compliance of the advertiser with the spirit and purpose of all applicable legal requirements.

2. In consideration of the customs and attitudes of the communities served, each radio broadcaster should refuse his/her facilities to the advertisement of products and services, or the use of advertising scripts, which the station has good reason to believe would be objectionable to a substantial and responsible segment of the community. These standards should be applied with judgment and flexiblity, taking into consideration the characteristics of the medium, its home and family audience, and the form and content of the particular presentation.

B. Presentation of Advertising

1. The advancing techniques of the broadcast art have shown that the quality and proper integration of advertising copy are just as important as measurement in time. The measure of a station's service to its audience is determined by its overall performance.

2. The final measurement of any commercial broadcast service is quality. To this, every broadcaster shall dedicate his/her best effort.

3. Great care shall be exercised by the broadcaster to prevent the presentation of false, misleading or deceptive advertising. While it is entirely appropriate to present a product in a favorable light and atmosphere, the presentation must not, by copy or demonstration, involve a material deception as to the characteristics or performance of a product.

4. The broadcaster and the advertiser should exercise special caution with the content and presentation of commercials placed in or near programs designed for children. Exploitation of children should be avoided. Commercials directed to children should in no way mislead as to the product's performance and usefulness. Appeals involving matters of health which should be determined by physicians should be avoided.

5. Reference to the results of research, surveys or tests relating to the product to be advertised shall not be presented in a manner so as to create an impression of fact beyond that established by the study. Surveys, tests or other research results upon which claims are based must be conducted under recognized research techniques and standards.

C. Acceptability of Advertisers and Products

In general, because radio broadcasting is designed for the home and the entire family, the following principles shall govern the business classifications:

1. The advertising of hard liquor shall not be accepted.

2. The advertising of beer and wines is acceptable when presented in the best of good taste and discretion.

3. The advertising of fortune-telling, occultism, astrology, phrenology, palm-reading, numerology, mind-reading, character-reading, or subjects of a like nature, is not acceptable.

4. Because the advertising of all products and services of a personal nature

raises special problems, such advertising, when accepted, should be treated with emphasis on ethics and the canons of good taste, and presented in a restrained and inoffensive manner.

5. The advertising of tip sheets and other publications seeking to advertise for the purpose of giving odds or promoting betting is unacceptable.

The lawful advertising of government organizations which conduct legalized lotteries and the advertising of private or governmental organizations which conduct legalized betting on sporting contests are acceptable provided such advertising does not unduly exhort the public to bet.

6. An advertiser who markets more than one product shall not be permitted to use advertising copy devoted to an acceptable product for purposes of publicizing the brand name or other identification of a product which is not acceptable.

7. Care should be taken to avoid presentation of "bait-switch" advertising whereby goods or services which the advertiser has no intention of selling are offered merely to lure the customer into purchasing higher-priced substitutes.

8. Advertising should offer a product or service on its positive merits and refrain from discrediting, disparaging or unfairly attacking competitiors, competing products, other industries, professions or institutions.

Any identification or comparison of a competitive product or service, by name, or other means, should be confined to specific facts rather than generalized statements or conclusions, unless such statements or conclusions are not derogatory in nature.

9. Advertising testimonials should be genuine, and reflect an honest appraisal of personal experience.

10. Advertising by institutions or enterprises offering instruction with exaggerated claims for opportunities awaiting those who enroll, is unacceptable.

11. The advertising of firearms/ammunition is acceptable provided it promotes the product only as sporting equipment and conforms to recognized standards of safety as well as all applicable laws and regulations. Advertisements of firearms/ammunition by mail order are unacceptable.

D. Advertising of Medical Products

Because advertising for over-the-counter products involving health considerations is of intimate and far-reaching importance to the consumer, the following principles should apply to such advertising:

1. When dramatized advertising material involves statements by doctors, dentists. nurses or other professional people, the material should be presented by members of such profession reciting actual experience, or it should be made apparent from the presentation itself that the portrayal is dramatized.

2. Because of the personal nature of the advertising of medical products, the indiscriminate use of such words as "safe," "without risk," "harmless," or other terms of similar meaning, either direct or implied, should not be expressed in the advertising of medical products.

3. Advertising material which offensively describes or dramatizes distress or morbid situations involving ailments is not acceptable.

E. Time Standards for Advertising Copy

1. As a general rule, up to 18 minutes of advertising time within any clock hour are acceptable. However, for good cause and when in the public interest, broadcasters may depart from this standard in order to fulfill their responsibilities to the communities they serve.

2. Any reference to another's products or services under any trade name, or language sufficiently descriptive to identify it, shall, except for normal guest identification, be considered as advertising copy.

F. Contests

1. Contests shall be conducted with fairness to all entrants, and shall comply with all pertinent laws and regulations.

2. All contest details, including rules, eligibility requirements, opening and termination dates, should be clearly and completely announced or easily accessible to the listening public; and the winners' names should be released as soon as possible after the close of the contest.

3. When advertising is accepted which requests contestants to submit items of product identification or other evidence of purchase of products, reasonable facsimiles thereof should be made acceptable. However, when the award is based upon skill and not upon chance, evidence of purchase may be required.

4. All copy pertaining to any contest (except that which is required by law) associated with the exploitation or sale of the sponsor's product or service, and all references to prizes or gifts offered in such connection should be considered a part of and included in the total time limitations heretofore provided. (*See Time Standards for Advertising Copy.*)

G. Premiums and Offers

1. The broadcaster should require that full details of proposed offers be submitted for investigation and approval before the first announcement of the offer is made to the public.

2. A final date for the termination of an offer should be announced as far in advance as possible.

3. If a consideration is required, the advertiser should agree to honor complaints indicating dissatisfaction with the premium by returning the consideration.

4. There should be no misleading descriptions or comparisons of any premiums or gifts which will distort or enlarge their value in the minds of the listeners.

administering the radio code

The NAB Codes are administered by a Radio Code Board and a Television Code Board, the members of which are appointed by the president of the NAB, subject to confirmation by the NAB Radio and Television Board of Directors.

Nine of the eleven Radio Code Board members are selected by the management of individual radio stations or group operations subscribing to the Radio Code. The two remaining members are chosen from one of the four networks subscribing to the Code. Each Code Board member serves two years, after which the station representatives can be reappointed to a second consecutive two-year term; whereas Network representatives can serve only one two-year term.

television code

Similar in many ways to the Radio Code is the Television Code. Under programming standards are provisions covering responsibility toward children, community responsibility, special program standards, treatment of news and public events, controversial public issues, political telecasts, and religious programs. A section dealing with advertising standards covers such things as the presentation of advertising, advertising claims, advertising of medical products and services, contests, premiums and offers, time standards for network affiliated stations, and time standards for independent stations.

An example of the specific language of the Television Code is seen in its provisions covering community responsibility:

1. Television broadcasters and their staffs occupy positions of unique responsibility in their communities and should conscientiously endeavor to be acquainted fully with the community's needs and characteristics in order better to serve the welfare of its citizens.

2. Requests for time for the placement of public service announcements or programs should be carefully reviewed with respect to the character and reputation of the group, campaign involved, the public interest content of the message, and the manner of its presentation.

Special Program Standards

1. Violence; conflict. A. Violence, physical or psychological, may only be projected in responsibly handled contexts, not used exploitatively. Programs involving violence should present the consequences of it to its victims and perpetrators.

Presentation of the details of violence should avoid the excessive, the gratuitous and the instructional.

The use of violence for its own sake and the detailed dwelling upon brutality or physical agony, by sight or by sound, are not permissible.

B. Conflict and children. The depiction of conflict, when presented in programs designed primarily for children, should be handled with sensitivity.

2. Anti-social behavior; crime. The treatment of criminal activities should always convey their social and human effects.

The presentation of techniques of crime in such detail as to be instructional or invite imitation shall be avoided.

3. Self-destructive behavior: drugs; gambling; alcohol. A. Narcotic addiction shall not be presented except as a destructive habit. The use of illegal drugs or the abuse of legal drugs shall not be encouraged or shown as socially acceptable.

B. The use of gambling devices or scenes necessary to the development of plot or as appropriate background is acceptable only when presented with discretion and in moderation, and in a manner which would not excite interest in, or foster, betting nor be instructional in nature.

C. The use of liquor and the depiction of smoking in program content shall be deemphasized. When shown, they should be consistent with plot and character development.

4. Sports programs. Telecasts of actual sports programs at which on-the-scene betting is permitted by law shall be presented in a manner in keeping with federal, state and local laws, and should concentrate on the subject as a public sporting event.

5. Mental/physical disadvantages. Special precautions must be taken to avoid demeaning or ridiculing members of the audience who suffer from physical or mental afflictions or deformities.

6. Human relationships; sex; costume. The presentation of marriage, the family and similarly important human relationships, and material with sexual connotations, shall not be treated exploitatively or irresponsibly, but with sensitivity. Costuming and movements of all performers shall be handled in a similar fashion.

7. Pluralism; minorities. Special sensitivity is necessary in the use of material relating to sex, race, color, age, creed, religious functionaries or rites, or national or ethnic derivation.

8. Obscenity; profanity. Subscribers shall not broadcast any material which they determine to be obscene, profane or indecent.

Above and beyond the requirements of law, broadcasters must consider the family atmosphere in which many of their programs are viewed.

There shall be no graphic portrayal of sexual acts by sight or sound. The portrayal of implied sexual acts must be essential to the plot and presented in a responsible and tasteful manner.

Subscribers are obligated to bring positive responsibility and reasoned judgment to bear upon all those involved in the development, production, and selection of programs.

9. Hypnosis. The creation of a state of hypnosis by act or detailed demonstration on camera is prohibited, and hypnosis as a form of "parlor game" antics to create humorous situations within a comedy setting is forbidden.

10. Superstition; pseudo-sciences. Program material pertaining to fortune-telling, occultism, astrology, phrenology, palm-reading, numerology, mind-reading, character-reading, and the like is unacceptable if it encourages people to regard such fields as providing commonly accepted appraisals of life.

11. Professional advice/diagnosis/treatment. Professional advice, diagnosis and treatment will be presented in conformity with law and recognized professional standards.

12. Subliminal perception. Any technique whereby an attempt is made to convey information to the viewer by transmitting messages below the threshold of normal awareness is not permitted.

13. Animals. The use of animals, consistent with plot and character delineation, shall be in conformity with accepted standards of humane treatment.

14. Game programs; contests. A. Quiz and similar programs that are presented as contests of knowledge, information, skill or luck must, in fact, be genuine contests; and the results must not be controlled by collusion with or between contestants, or by any other action which will favor one contestant against any other.

B. Contests may not constitute a lottery.

15. Prizes: credits, acknowledgements. The broadcaster shall be constantly alert to prevent inclusion of elements within a program dictated by factors other than the requirements of the program itself. The acceptance of cash payments or other considerations in return for including scenic properties, the choice and identificiation of prizes, the selection of music and other creative program elements and inclusion of any identification of commercial products or services, their trade names or advertising slogan within the program are prohibited except in accordance with Sections 317 and 508 of the Communications Act.

16. Misrepresentation; deception. A. No program shall be presented in a manner which through artifice or simulation would mislead the audience as to any material fact. Each broadcaster must exercise reasonable judgment to determine whether a particular method of presentation would constitute a material deception, or would be accepted by the audience as normal theatrical illusion.

B. A television broadcaster should not present fictional events or other non-news material as authentic news telecasts or announcements, nor permit dramatizations in any program which would give the false impression that the dramatized material constitutes news.

17. Applicability of Code standards. The standards of this Code covering program content are also understood to include, wherever applicable, the standards contained in the advertising section of the Code.

The Network representations are then replaced by representatives from a different network, thus permitting all four national radio networks to share the two network positions. Representation on the Radio Code Board is balanced as to market size, location, network affiliation, and AM or FM affiliations.[8]

administering the television code

Membership on the Television Code Board is similar to that of the Radio Board, although the Television Board is composed of nine members appointed by the president and subject to confirmation by the Television Board of Directors. Six of the members are from the management of individual stations or group operations who are Television Code subscribers. The three remaining members represent each of the subscribing commercial television networks. Television Code Board members are appointed for three years, and station or group representatives on the Board are eligible for a second consecutive two-year reappointment. "Network Code Board members may be re-appointed to an indeterminate number of additional two-year terms."[9] As with the Radio Code Board, market size, location, and group and network affiliation (or independent status) are taken into consideration when appointing Code Board members.

enforcement of the code

Any Code is only as strong as the willingness of the members to support it and the ability of the sponsoring organization to enforce it. Of the various codes of ethics centered around self-regulation in broadcasting, the NAB is one of the few codes to be monitored and enforced. A "continuing, willful or gross violation of any of the provisions . . ."[10] of the Codes can result in revocation of a station's membership in the Code. Prior to this revocation, however, the Code Authority and the subscriber can follow administrative procedures to examine and respond to the issues before them. If appropriate, they may have counsel present.

the nab code news

The NAB constantly reviews and updates both the Radio and the Television Codes. The changing needs of the industry, the regulatory atmosphere, and the public are all taken into consideration when the Codes are changed or reinterpreted.

The actions of the Code Authority and the Code Boards are communicated to subscribers in a monthly publication put out by the NAB, called *Code News*. Customarily a four-page document, the *Code News* carries short articles of interest to subscribers, important new interpretations of the Code, and such regular features as toy or motion picture ads which have been approved or reviewed by the Code. *Code News* offers advice on advertisements for everything from self-defense devices to health and beauty salons.[11]

Motion picture ads can be particularly troublesome for broadcasters. Thus, when appropriate, the *Code News* carries a list and an explanation of motion picture advertisements which have been reviewed by the Code Authority. Typical of how the *Code News* reviews commercials for motion pictures and reports to broadcasters are the following listings:[12]

"Carrie" (R)	1–60 sec.	All trailers raise questions of appropriate scheduling under Television Code IV–1 (psychological violence). Recommend that they be shown away from programs designed primarily for children under Television Code Section II (Responsibility toward children).
"The Enforcer" (R)	5–30 sec.	All trailers raise questions of appropriate scheduling under Television Code IV–1 (psychological violence). Recommend that they be shown away from programs designed primarily for children under Televi-

sion Code Section II (Responsibility toward children).

"King Kong"   4–30 sec.   All trailers raise questions of appropriate
(PG)   scheduling under Television Code IV–1
                                        (psychological violence). Recommend that
                                        they be shown away from programs de-
                                        signed primarily for children under Televi-
                                        sion Code Section II (Responsibility toward
                                        children).

The *Code News* also publishes toy ads which have been approved by the Code Authority. Because of the sensitivity of issues centering around television and children, some toy manufacturers are relying more heavily on the Code's approval before disseminating commercials to agencies, networks, and local television stations.

Other regular features of *Code News* include additions and deletions of Code member stations. A subscriber status report is also included, noting the monthly total number of Code subscribers.

criticism and court challenge of the nab codes

Among dedicated and large group members of the National Association of Broadcasters there is considerable support for the Radio and Television Codes. Other individuals and groups are more critical of these Codes. The influence of the networks and the number of Code subscribers, especially in radio, are two common complaints leveled against the NAB's self-regulatory efforts. For example, although individual television stations are Code subscribers, they still must secure most of their programming from the networks. Thus, although the networks are Code subscribers, the individual stations have little control over programming and, consequently, over meeting the Code standards. Among the radio stations in the United States, less than 50 percent are subscribers to the Radio Code. This does not mean that the others are irresponsible broadcasters. It does mean, however, that when the NAB lobbies for radio's interests, the effect of its efforts can be weakened by the lack of membership. Some small radio broadcasters argue that the Code has little effect on overall programming and that it does not take into consideration the economic difficulties of turning away ads for hard liquor or other products prohibited under Code sponsorship.

Some of the strongest criticism of the Code comes from commercial broadcasters. Donald H. McGannon, former president of the Westinghouse Broadcasting Company, which dropped Code subscribership, called the Code too permissive.[13] He felt that the Code "has not been tough enough in dealing with crime and violence on TV...."[14] The use of thirty-second commercials instead of sixty-second ones virtually doubles the commercial content of any given time period. McGannon criticizes the Code for falling short in its responsibility "to maintain a reasonable level of commercialization."[15] Professor Joe Persky, writing in the *Journal of Communication*, is equally critical of the Code and finds little merit in the claim by some that self-regulation is a dynamic and successful means of supervising broadcasting.[16] In a research study examining the first and eighteenth editions of the Television Code, he found large portions of the advertising and program sections of the Code to be more than two decades old.[17] Specifically, he found no significant change in such areas as "program standards," the "treatment of news and public events," "controversial public issues," "political telecasts," and "religious telecasts." Conversely, others argue that this steadfastness is positive, not negative, indicating that the Code does not leap after every passing issue.

Ironically, one of the strongest attacks on the NAB's Codes came not from its critics but from the United States Justice Department, which took the NAB to court in 1979, claiming its Television Code violated antitrust practices. The target of the Justice Department action was the advertising time standards of the Television Code. The suit was significant. Here was one federal agency attacking a nongovernment organization, when the organization's code of good practice supported the "public interest" foundation upon which another federal agency's whole theory of operation was based. The Television Code restricts stations to nine and one-half minutes of nonprogrammed time per hour during prime time, with an additional thirty seconds per hour for promotional announcements when the station deems them necessary. A time limit of nine and one-half minutes per hour also exists for children's programming on weekends, and twelve minutes per hour for children's programming on other days. The Code sets up a sixteen-minute per hour limit for other broadcasting times. All of these time limits are for network affiliated stations. Independent stations have a seven and one-half minute per hour limit during prime time and eight minutes per half hour for other times. The Justice Department claimed that such standards created an anticompetitive effect and that broadcasters should be free to let the marketplace determine how many commercials they aired and what percentage of their programming was devoted to advertising.

The NAB reacted quickly to the Justice Department's suit. In a statement by NAB president Vincent T. Wasilewski, the NAB stated: "We have always believed that industry-imposed limitations on the amount of advertising in regular and children's television programming are in the public interest. These Code actions have been taken after consultation with counsel and have always been a matter of public record. The Justice Department's action is ironic, yet flies in the face of overwhelming support from the public, the Congress, the courts, and the regulatory agencies for the concept of the broadcast industry regulating itself in lieu of government controls."[18] Other NAB officials were afraid that if the Justice Department should win this suit and no standards existed, the logical result would be for the Federal Trade Commission and the Federal Communications Commission to move in and "fill the vacuum."[19] Losing the suit in 1982, the NAB stopped enforcing the codes' advertising provisions.

Is self-regulation effective? What is its primary goal? Can it stave off government regulation? In an age of information processing and new technology in society, will self-regulation in the form of the NAB Codes continue to be viable, or will the multiple channels of communication open to the public place more responsibility on the individual, rather than on the institution? Finding answers to these questions is a primary goal of self-regulation in the 1980s.

Advertising: Self-Regulation and Codes of Ethics

In addition to the NAB, with its guidelines on broadcast advertising, other organizations are also actively involved in the self-regulation of advertising. Most of them accomplish this through their codes of ethics, which help to assure professional conduct in the preparation and dissemination of advertising messages.

the business and professional advertising association (b/paa)

A number of professional advertising associations take part in the self-regulatory effort. The Business and Professional Advertising Association's (B/PAA) Code of Ethics, for example, focuses on guarding against misleading statements in advertising. Provisions of the B/PAA Code of Ethics include such statements as: "claims made must be capable of substantiation." It furthermore stresses that: "no form of advertising should be prepared or knowingly accepted that contains or suggests false, exaggerated, or misleading statements, claims, or implications." The B/PAA Code also discourages advertising that unfairly disparages products or any that "plays on superstitions and fears of others for the purpose of exploitation. . . ." Other provisions ban vulgar and offensive advertising, advertising that would harm users, or advertising that distorts the meanings of quotations or other statements attributable to speakers or authors.

american advertising federation (aaf)

Similar to the B/PAA Code of Ethics is the Advertising Code subscribed to by the American Advertising Federation. This nine-point, succinctly worded Code of Ethics, which has been in effect since 1965, states:

1. *Truth*—Advertising shall tell the truth, and shall reveal significant facts, the concealment of which would mislead the public.
2. *Responsibility*—Advertising agencies and advertisers shall be willing to provide substantiation of claims made.
3. *Taste and Decency*—Advertising shall be free of statements, illustrations, or implications which are offensive to good taste or public decency.
4. *Disparagement*—Advertising shall offer merchandise or service on its merits, and refrain from attacking competitors unfairly or disparaging their products, services or methods of doing business.
5. *Bait Advertising*—Advertising shall offer only merchandise or services which are readily available for purchase at the advertised price.
6. *Guarantees and Warranties*—Advertising of guarantees and warranties shall be explicit. Advertising of any guarantee or warranty shall clearly and conspicuously disclose its nature and extent, the manner in which the guarantor or warrantor will perform and the identity of the guarantor or warrantor.
7. *Price Claims*—Advertising shall avoid price or savings claims which are false or misleading, or which do not offer provable bargains or savings.

8. *Unprovable Claims*—Advertising shall avoid the use of exaggerated or unprovable claims.

9. *Testimonials*—Advertising containing testimonials shall be limited to those of competent witnesses who are reflecting a real and honest choice.[20]

Notice how the Federation's Code parallels that of the Business and Professional Advertising Association. Especially important to both Codes is the method of dealing with competitiors' products. Look at point 4 in the Federation's Code, on *Disparagement.* Echoing point 4, the B/PAA Code states: "No form of advertising shall be prepared or knowingly accepted that unfairly disparages products, services, or the reputation of another company. . . ." The B/PAA statement continues with: "comparative advertising which makes a clear and factual product or service comparison under similar conditions shall not be deemed to be disparaging." Notice that neither statement prohibits comparative advertising; they both stress instead that such advertising must not unfairly belittle competitive products.

Yet these very clauses became the object of a Federal Trade Commission investigation into advertising self-regulation in 1976. Concluding its investigation in 1979, the FTC said it would challenge industry advertising codes that in any way restrained comparative advertising.[21] The FTC pointed out that language in many of the codes of ethics could be interpreted as discouraging comparative advertising, and it warned that "restrictive use of anti-disparagement rules" would be subject to FTC attack.[22] The government investigated twenty-three different organizations, including the American Advertising Federation, the American Association of Advertising Agencies, the NAB, the three major commercial networks, the Counsel for Better Business Bureaus, and such specific product organizations as the Cosmetic Toiletries & Fragrances Association, the American Petroleum Institute, the Wine Conference of America, the Soap & Detergent Association, and the Pharmaceutical Manufacturers' Association.

Many trade organizations, such as those listed above, have their own codes of ethics or guidelines for advertising. One example is the Financial Advertising Committee on Ethics (FACE), a group formed in 1975 to assist self-regulatory efforts in bank advertising. Its guidelines deal with those areas most susceptible to misrepresentation, such as free banking services, free checking accounts, savings claims, package services, premiums and giveaways, deposit insurance, and information related to interest rate computations.[23] FACE states that: "free service (other than free checking) may be advertised only if the service is an unconditional gift and does not require another tie-in service; free checking accounts may be advertised, provided there is no charge for other parts of the service such as monthly statements, checks, or other instruments."[24]

As with the NAB Code, the code of ethics of any association is only as effective as the commitment from its members to support such a code. And enforcement is a continual problem. The ability to control the activities of a large membership in the highly competitive field of advertising is a difficult challenge. As new technology opens up more channels of communication, and as the mass audience grows more specialized, will the multiplicity of channels available to the consumer lessen or strengthen the need for codes and guidelines?

economic and political pressure for self-regulation

In our chapter on the citizens' movement, we learned how companies limited their sponsorship of programs showing gratuitous sex and violence because of pressure from citizens' groups to do so. Such actions are a form of economic pressure for self-regulation and are becoming more and more frequent in the broadcasting industry. Religious groups and consumer organizations have been especially active in applying such pressure to advertisers.

One of the most prominent examples of economic pressure for self-regulation occurred when ABC television launched its comedy series, "SOAP." A soap opera spoof with a much more sexually-oriented theme than that of the somewhat controversial "Mary Hartman, Mary Hartman," "SOAP" was launched amidst criticism from the Christian Life Commission of the Southern Baptist Convention; dissatisfaction from smaller religious groups, such as the Roman Catholic Bishops Office in Providence, R.I.; and even industry criticism, echoed by Donald H. McGannon, Chairman and President of Westinghouse Broadcasting Co.[25] While the show has managed to remain profitable and on the air, its early start was clouded by an uproar over sexual inferences. And although many advertisers remain with the series, Vlasic Foods and Jovan, Inc., were among those who dropped their sponsorship. Dennis Sullivan, serving as President of Vlasic Foods, declared that his company had decided to drop the series because the program was not consistent with Vlasic's media strategy and family-oriented commercials. He also said he had received numerous negative letters from religious groups.[26] Some stations were consequently shy about carrying the series, and Westinghouse's McGannon wrote ABC Television President, Fred Pierce, notifying the network of Westinghouse's dissatisfaction with the first two episodes of "SOAP." McGannon pointed out that clearance for the program would be predicated on a review of each show.[27]

While the FCC prods many broadcasters into self-restraint, state government is also stepping up its self-regulation efforts. The New York State Assembly, for example, recently reacted to a report on the food commercials that are carried on children's television.[28] Although the report was criticized for its methodology, the Assembly nevertheless focused on its main conclusion: the commercials needed to be counteracted. The report charged that "long-range effects of eating patterns encouraged by advertising include obesity, diabetes, heart disease, numerous other conditions, and possibly cancer."[29] Based on these and other recommendations of the report, the assembly called for broadcasters in New York state to "pledge in their license renewal applications to carry educational and informative food and nutritional and public service announcements during time periods when children make up a significant part of the audience and when food commercials are being carried."[30] The report also called for the state to develop a means of intervention in FCC proceedings and called on the state's Consumer Protection Board to represent the public before the FCC.

So far, the pressure on broadcasters from state government has been minimal. The clearly established precedence for exclusive jurisdiction of the FCC in these areas restrains state governments from becoming overly involved. Nevertheless, with the influx of cable systems and municipal jurisdiction over such

368

systems, the future may see government pressure coming even from the local level.

the national advertising division and the national advertising review board

The emphasis on self-regulation of broadcast advertising first manifested itself in 1971, when the industry set up a mechanism to curtail deceptive advertising. The two-part system functions as (1) the National Advertising Division (NAD) of the Council of Better Business Bureaus (CBBB) and (2) the National Advertising Review Board (NARB) (Figure 11-1).

The system can trace its roots back to 1930, when review committees of advertising professionals were created to monitor deceptive advertising. Even more concern arose during the Great Depression, when stronger amendments to the Federal Trade Commission Act were passed in 1938. The prosperity of the 1950s seemed to lull self-regulation proponents, however, and uptrends in the economy lessened both public criticism and government intervention. The consumer era of the 1960s saw government once again stepping in with truth-in-packaging legislation and with public safety acts centered around motor vehicles and cigarette smoking. Renewed efforts at self-regulation materialized in the early 1970s, after a 1969 report by the American Bar Association criticized the Federal Trade Commission for being acquiescent to broadcasting practices. Enter the NAD and the NARB.

How does the NAD operate? First, the Division evaluates the complaint or question that has been filed. It can either dismiss the complaint or contact the advertiser for additional documents to substantiate or refute the complaint. If the NAD is not satisfied with the advertiser's substantiation, it can ask the advertiser to change or discontinue the advertising message. If the advertiser agrees, then the NAD dismisses the complaint. But if the advertiser disagrees, the complaint can be appealed to the NARB.

At the NARB, the chairperson appoints a review panel, which evaluates the complaint and either dismisses it or again asks the advertiser to change or discontinue the message. If the advertiser agrees, as with the NAD, the panel can dismiss the complaint. If the advertiser refuses, the matter is then referred to a government agency for further action.

Cases reaching the final review stage of the NARB have dealt with everything from oil companies to electric razors. One panel dismissed a complaint against an oil company when it found the company had substantially documented its survey data, ruling that country singer Johnny Cash did not deliver a deceptive testimonial. Another complaint was dismissed against a vitamin manufacturer when the panel ruled that the value of iron supplements for women of child-bearing age had been established. Yet the NARB ruled that an electric shaver manufacturer's advertising claims were false, especially in comparison with competing shavers.

It is also not unusual for either the NAD or the NARB to become embroiled in a legal dispute, not necessarily as a major litigant, but as a result of a civil suit being filed against an advertiser during the sometimes lengthly review process. When this happens, the final opinion of the NARB can clearly have an impact on

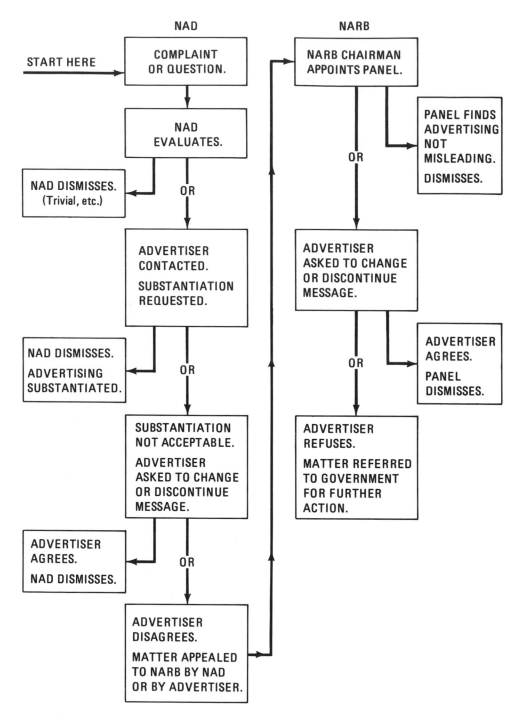

Figure 11-1 (William Ewen, The National Advertising Review Board 1971–1975: A Four Year Review and Perspective on Advertising Industry Self Regulation, pamphlet published by the National Advertising Review Board, 1975, p. 12. As described in: Eric J. Zanot, "The National Advertising Review Board, 1971–1976," *Journalism Monographs,* #59 (February, 1979), p. 10.)

the outcome of the case. While not having any legal or formal authority per se, the NARB's policy of turning unresolved disputes over to federal agencies has given it enough clout to be taken very seriously by many members of the advertising industry.

The Broadcast Press: Self-Regulation and Codes of Ethics

The First Amendment guarantees a free press. Yet government has not hesitated to regulate certain aspects of broadcast news. The Fairness Doctrine, which assures a balance in overall programming, makes no attempt to exclude broadcast news as one area of that balanced programming. Legislatures and the courts have not hesitated to limit access of broadcast reporters who want to take television cameras or tape recorders into a judicial chamber. Even the number of broadcast "outlets" is limited when we consider that the allocation of broadcast stations is based on the government's desire to eliminate overcrowding on the electromagnetic spectrum and interference on the airwaves. Although new technologies have increased the number of channels available, cable being one example, the government has not hurried to deregulate electronic communication. Even such lobbying groups as the Radio/Television News Directors' Association have had a tough time breaking through legislative and judicial barriers. The printed press may fall under the same restraints in the future as its technologies, especially the new teletext systems, begin to interact with home television.[31]

code of the society of professional journalists–sigma delta chi

In 1909, a group of student reporters on a small university campus in the Midwest formed a journalism organization called Sigma Delta Chi, later to be called the Society of Professional Journalists–Sigma Delta Chi. The accounts of that first meeting indicate that the real purpose was to form a group more resembling a typical college fraternity than an organization with professional direction.[32] The constitution of the new "secret fraternity" read:

> In Order to associate college journalists of TALENT, TRUTH and ENERGY into a more intimately organized unity of good fellowship, with the element of mysticism as a binding force in order to assist the members in acquiring the noblest principles of journalism and to cooperate with them in this field ... In Order to advance the standard of the press by fostering an ethical code, thus increasing its value as a social uplifting agency, we do hereby establish and ordain this Constitution of the Sigma Delta Chi fraternity.[33]

At its national convention in 1973, the Society adopted its first Code of Ethics. Although historically the organization has been primarily directed toward print journalism, many broadcast journalists are members. Some of the Society's Code provisions include:

Freedom of the Press:

Freedom of the press is to be guarded as an inalienable right of people in a free society. It carries with it the freedom and the responsibility to discuss, question and challenge actions and utterances of our government and of our public and private institutions. Journalists uphold the right to speak unpopular opinions and the privelege to agree with the majority.

Ethics:

Journalists must be free of obligation to any interest other than the public's right to know.

1. Gifts, favors, free travel, special treatment or privileges can compromise the integrity of journalists and their employers. Nothing of value should be accepted.
2. Secondary employment, political involvement, holding public office, and service in community organizations should be avoided if it comprises the integrity of journalists and their employers. Journalists and their employers should conduct their personal lives in a manner which protects them from conflict of interest, real or apparent. Their responsibilities to the public are paramount. That is the nature of their profession.
3. So-called news communications from private sources should not be published or broadcast without substantiation of their claims to news value.
4. Journalists will seek news that serves the public interest, despite the obstacles. They will make constant efforts to assure that the public's business is conducted in public and that public records are open to public inspection.
5. Journalists acknowledge the newsman's ethic of protecting confidential sources of information. . . .

Fair Play:

Journalists at all times will show respect for the dignity, privacy, rights, and well-being of people encountered in the course of gathering and presenting the news.

1. The news media should not communicate unofficial charges affecting reputation or moral character without giving the accused a chance to reply.
2. The news media must guard against invading a person's right to privacy.
3. The media should not pander to morbid curiosity about details of vice and crime.
4. It is the duty of news media to make prompt and complete correction of their errors.
5. Journalists should be accountable to the public for their reports and the public should be encouraged to voice its grievances against the media. Open dialogue with our readers, viewers, and listeners should be fostered. . . .

Today, the Society of Professional Journalists-Sigma Delta Chi, has about 35,000 members. Its monthly magazine, *The Quill,* deals with current topics of interest to both print and broadcast journalists.

rtnda code of broadcast news ethics

Founded in 1946 as the National Association of Radio News Directors, the Radio/Television News Directors' Association (RTNDA) today represents broadcast news directors and journalists in legislative and professional endeavors. It publishes a newsletter, the *RTNDA Communicator.* In many ways like the Society of Professional Journalists, Sigma Delta Chi, the RTNDA keeps keenly aware of issues affecting the broadcast press, championing the causes of broadcast news.

The RTNDA is more exclusively an organization for broadcast journalists and thus tailors its Code of Broadcast News Ethics to the broadcast medium. The complete text of the RTNDA Code is found at the end of this chapter.

broadcasting public proceedings: nab standards of conduct

Earlier in this chapter, we discussed the NAB Radio and Television Codes. But we should also be aware that the Freedom of Information Committee and the Board of Directors of the NAB have adopted a *Standards of Conduct for Broadcasting Public Proceedings*. Concerned with both legislative and judicial reporting, the *Standards* have taken on new significance in recent years, as broadcast journalists have been permitted access into formerly closed sessions of legislatures and courtrooms. Like the other Codes discussed in this chapter, the *Standards* provide a general statement of purpose, followed by more specific guidelines for "public hearings and meetings" and coverage "in the courtroom."

> Broadcast newsmen are devoted guardians of our priceless heritage of freedom. They are particularly concerned with safeguarding freedom of speech and freedom of communications. They believe that the surest way to preserve these freedoms is to exercise them with vigor. They recognize that the vigorous exercise of freedom must be carried forward with a decent respect for the rights and opinions of others and for the established procedures of public agencies, judicial, legislative, and executive.

Public Hearings and Meetings

> In keeping with these principles, broadcast newsmen, special events broadcasters, film cameramen and technical personnel who work with them will conduct themselves at public hearings in accordance with the following standards:
>
> - They will conform to the established procedures, customs, and decorum of the legislative halls, hearings rooms, and other public places where they provide broadcast coverage of public business.
> - At all public hearings they will respect the authority of the presiding officer to make appropriate rules of order and conduct.
> - Coverage arrangements will make maximum use of modern techniques for unobtrusive installation and operation of broadcasting equipment. Coverage will be pooled where necessary. Call letters should not be displayed in cases of multiple coverage.
>
> In those many instances where commercial sponsorship of news coverage of public proceedings is desirable on economic grounds, commercials will be in good taste and will be clearly separated from the news content of the program. Broadcasters, of course, will honor to the letter any agreements with the presiding official regarding sponsorship.
>
> Newsmen will present summaries of the proceedings, and will conduct interviews, or broadcast commentaries only during recesses, or outside the hearing room, or during appropriate portions of other proceedings in a manner that will assure that the broadcast does not distract from the public business.

In the Courtroom

> The sanctity of public trial and the rights of the defendant and all parties require that special care be exercised to assure that broadcast coverage will in no way interfere with

the dignity and decorum and the proper and fair conduct of such proceedings. In recognition of the paramount objective of justice inherent in all trials, broadcast newsmen will observe the following standards:

- They will abide by all rules of the court.
- The presiding judge is, of course, recognized as the appropriate authority, and broadcast newsmen will address their applications for admission to him and will conform to his rulings. The right to appeal to higher jurisdiction is reserved.
- Broadcast equipment will be installed in a manner acceptable to the court and will be unobtrusively located and operated so as not to be disturbing or distracting to the court or participants.
- Broadcast newsmen will not move about while court is in session in such a way as to interfere with the orderly proceedings. Their equipment will remain stationary.
- Commentaries on the trial will not be broadcast from the courtroom while the trial is in session.
- Broadcasting of trials will be presented to the community as a public service, and there will be no commercial sponsorship of such trials.
- Broadcast personnel will dress in accordance with courtroom custom.

While the *Standards of Conduct* are not part of the NAB Code per se, they indicate the broadcast journalists' respect for responsible coverage of judicial proceedings and suggest guidelines for judges and courts on allowing sound and video recording of courtroom procedures. As a practical matter, the *Standards* represent concern over the American Bar Association's Code of Judicial Conduct, which, in Canon 3A(7), still restricts "broadcasting, television, recording, or taking photographs in the courtroom." The NAB also offers technical suggestions for operating equipment in courtrooms and legislative proceedings. Among others are suggestions for a precoverage survey of the locations, including checking out power and circuit capacity, the length of cables for power and microphones, the types of connectors to be employed, and the location of the cables to assure minimum obstruction and maximum safety.[34]

Allied Professional and Educational Associations

The National Association of Broadcasters, the Society of Professional Journalists–Sigma Delta Chi, and the Radio/Television News Directors' Association are actively involved in improving professionalism in the broadcasting industry. Other professional associations are also committed to this goal. Among them are two organizations concerned with the role of women in communication: the American Women in Radio and Television (AWRT) and Women in Communications, Inc. (WICI). Do not let their names confuse you, however. Both organizations admit men to their membership.

american women in radio and television (awrt)

Founded in 1951, AWRT includes among its goals job advancement for qualified women and improving the quality of broadcasting. An awards program also promotes a positive image for women. More than sixty local chapters operate in metropolitan areas throughout the United States, and student chapters of "College Students in Broadcasting" operate on approximately thirty campuses. The 2,600-member association publishes *News and Views,* which has a circulation of about 3,500.[35]

women in communications, inc. (wici)

Women in Communications, Inc. (WICI) was founded in 1909 by seven female journalism students at the University of Washington, who christened it Theta Sigma Phi. The name of the organization was changed in 1972, and its objective was described then as being to "unite women engaged in news, advertising, public relations and other fields of communication and to recognize distinguished achievements of such women."[36] Other activities of the organization include job and salary surveys of its members, lobbying for First Amendment legislation, and opposition to court decisions unfavorable to journalists.[37] Both campus and professional members belong to the organization, which lists its strength at 9,000. WICI publishes *Matrix,* a quarterly publication.

press associations: ap and upi

Both wire services also have organizations which serve broadcasters. The Associated Press Broadcasters (APB) began in 1951 as a committee to assist AP executives with the radio news report. Today, the organization holds an annual convention, and regional and state organizations meet regularly with award programs and publications. Subscribers to the Associated Press Broadcast Services are eligible for membership, and a newsletter is published eight times a year, with a circulation of about 4,000.[38]

The United Press International Broadcasters operate primarily at the state level. The group is made up of UPI broadcast service affiliates and offers extensive award programs to boost state and regional winners into national recognition. Funding and membership in the various state UPI organizations vary, and the consistency and organization of the individual state groups often depend on the strength and number of UPI affiliates.

educational associations

Other broadcast organizations operate in the field of education. The Broadcast Education Association (BEA), for example, is an arm of the NAB, founded in 1955 to improve broadcast education. It offers both individual and institutional memberships. The NAB keeps its hand in the organization by appointing five of the eleven members of its Board of Directors. The BEA publishes the *Journal of Broadcasting,* a quarterly journal with a circulation of about 1,500.[39]

Another educational organization concerned with broadcasting is the Association for Education in Journalism (AEJ). Founded in 1912 as the American Association of Teachers of Journalism, AEJ has become a national organization of college and secondary journalism teachers, administrators, and practitioners. Working toward the improvement of journalism education, it also operates through its cofounding affiliates—the American Association of Schools and Departments of Journalism (AASDJ) and the American Society of Journalism School Administrators (ASJSA). Along with publishing the *Journalism Quarterly*, the organization holds an annual convention, handles a placement service, and sponsors scholarships.[40] The 1,700-member organization receives partial support for its operations from foundations.[41]

We have only skimmed the surface of the many organizations directly or peripherally concerned with the broadcasting industry. From advertising agencies to public relations agents to sports writers, all are involved in various ways in influencing policy and legislation over the electromagnetic spectrum.

Press Councils

Press Councils are organizations that are designed to perform a "watchdog" function over both the print and broadcast press.

national news council (nnc)

Envision the following scenario: professional organizations are wrestling with codes of ethics; the Congress and the state governments are wrestling with the issue of protecting the confidentiality of reporter sources and whether to write such protections into law; the networks are recoiling under criticism that they are too powerful and monopolistic. The date is 1973. The Twentieth Century Fund commissions a fifteen-month study into such wrestlings and criticisms. The result is the formation of the National News Council (NNC).

The fifteen-member NNC is designed to promote accurate and fair reporting while defending the free press. A year after its inception, the Council began accepting complaints from any citizen in the United States who wanted to file a charge of unfair news reporting. Although the Council received considerable publicity in academic journalism circles, some larger organizations initially refused to support its activities. Such major institutions as the *New York Times*, the Associated Press, NBC, and ABC refused cooperation.[42] Despite this resistance, however, the Council has continued to function and to process complaints from a wide variety of organizations. Its activities are published in a yearly summary, titled, *In the Public Interest*, and in 1977, the *Columbia Journalism Review* started to carry reports of its activities.[43] The NNC also sponsors fellowships for first-year law students and graduate journalism students at the Council's headquarters in New York. Private organizations and other institutions have funded the NNC; the organization does not accept any government assistance. Even though the NNC continues to function, the data are scant on how effective it is in fostering a more responsible press. The NNC has no formal power over any medium and relies on publicity for its clout. Under those conditions, some might feel that its impact is, in reality, negligible.

state press councils: the minnesota example

What many consider to be the role model for the NNC is the Minnesota Press Council (MPC), organized in 1971 as the only statewide press council in the

United States. Like the NNC, the MPC has no formal power, and it, too, relies on publicity for its impact. Original support for the Council came from the Minnesota Newspaper Association, but the Association severed its relationship when the Council's first official act was to declare itself independent from the newspaper trade organization.[44] The early years of the Council saw a small budget, no staff or office, and meetings conducted on volunteered time by its members. Although beginning as a newspaper organization, the Council brought the broadcast press under its fold in 1977 by adding three broadcast members to its twenty-four-member group. Membership is divided equally between the journalistic community and the public, with the chairman of the Council being a jurist from the Minnesota Supreme Court. Some attribute the success of the Council to the fact that numerous complaints are settled among the parties involved before the Council itself has to act.

Although primarily print-oriented, similar press councils have sprung up all over the country. Foundation support from the Mellett Fund financed experimental press councils in Bend, Oregon and Redwood City, California.[45] Other Mellett Fund grants established councils in Cairo and Sparta, Illinois; Littleton, Colorado; and Honolulu, Hawaii. The Cairo council dealt primarily with the issue of media coverage of race relations. Similar race-relation-oriented councils were developed with Mellett Fund support in Seattle and St. Louis. Because of lack of support, the St. Louis council lasted for only five meetings, and the Cairo group survived just ten months of operation. With varying amounts of success, Peoria, Illinois; Hilo, Hawaii; and Eagle Valley, Colorado have also operated municipal press councils.[46] As with the Minnesota and the National News Councils, these municipal councils have been primarily void of power to force change on any medium.

Although press councils are a commendable idea, their widespread effect has been at best unassessed and at worst minimal. As noted earlier, data do not exist on the influence they exert on either the local or the national press, and the indifference of many media or the lack of proper emphasis has hindered these evaluative efforts.[47] Professor Emeritus J. Edward Gerald of the University of Minnesota succinctly critiques the press council concept when he states: "A press council is only one of the remedies indicated by modern times by which newspapers and broadcasting stations can proceed to improve community understanding and media credibility. The press council remedy is quite narrow in terms of the whole problem."[48]

summary

Self-regulation continues to be an important buffer between government regulation of broadcasting and the free speech guarantees of a democratic society. In Chapter 11, we have examined a number of organizations concerned with self-regulation. Perhaps the most visible is the National Association of Broadcasters (NAB). Formed in 1923 to squash copyright fees, the NAB today is primarily a lobbying organization. Through its well-known Radio and Television Codes, it establishes programming and commercial standards for Code subscribers to adhere to and nonsubscribers to support. Administered by a Code Authority, the NAB Codes deal with such areas as news programming, political broadcasting, responsibility toward children, and advertising standards. The NAB's *Code News* alerts subscribers to specific interpretations of the Codes. The NAB Codes are not free from criticism, however, especially concerning the influence that networks exert on programming and the total number of Code subscribers.

Although the NAB Codes deal with advertising, a number of allied professional organizations also promote ethical advertising standards. The Business and Professional Advertising Association (B/PAA) and the American Advertising Federation (AAF) both have codes of ethics. The AAF Code focuses on nine areas: truth, responsibility, taste and decency, disparagement, bait advertising, guarantees and warranties, price claims, unprovable claims, and testimonials.

While some economic and political pressures are placed on advertisers, important mediators encouraging self-restraint are the National Advertising Division (NAD) and the National Advertising Review Board (NARB). Complaints can be resolved in the NAD/NARB review process as an alternative to judicial or agency review.

Two organizations concerned with news reporting standards are the Society of Professional Journalists–Sigma Delta Chi and the Radio/Television News Directors' Association (RTNDA). Both have codes of ethics. The Society of Professional Journalists–Sigma Delta Chi's Code treats such issues as responsibility of the press, accepting gifts and favors, accuracy and objectivity, and fair play. The ten-article RTNDA Code deals with personal conduct and the coverage of court proceedings, among other issues.

Allied professional and educational organizations also foster responsibility and scholarship in broadcast journalism and related fields. Among these are the American Women in Radio and Television (AWRT); Women in Communications, Inc. (WICI); the Broadcast Education Association (BEA); and the Association for Education in Journalism (AEJ).

Designed to perform a "watchdog" function over both the print and broadcast press are press councils operating at the national, state, and local levels.

material for analysis

Radio Television News Directors Association

CODE OF BROADCAST NEWS ETHICS

The members of the Radio Television News Directors Association agree that their prime responsibility as newsmen—and that of the broadcasting industry as the collective sponsor of news broadcasting—is to provide to the public they serve a news service as accurate, full and prompt as human integrity and devotion can devise. To that end, they declare their acceptance of the standards of practice here set forth, and their solemn intent to honor them to the limits of their ability.

ARTICLE ONE

The primary purpose of broadcast newsmen—to inform the public of events of importance and appropriate interest in a manner that is accurate and comprehensive —shall override all other purposes.

ARTICLE TWO

Broadcast news presentations shall be designed not only to offer timely and accurate information, but also to present it in the light of relevant circumstances that give it meaning and perspective.

This standard means that news will be selected on the criteria of significance, community and regional relevance, appropriate human interest, service to defined audiences. It excludes sensationalism or misleading emphasis in any form; subservience to external or "interested" efforts to influence news selection and presentation, whether from within the broadcasting industry or from without. It requires that such terms as "bulletin" and "flash" be used only when the character of the news justifies them; that bombastic or misleading descriptions of newsroom facilities and personnel be rejected, along with undue use of sound and visual effects; and that promotional or publicity material be sharply scrutinized before use and identified by source or otherwise when broadcast.

ARTICLE THREE

Broadcast newsmen shall seek to select material for newscast solely on their evaluation of its merits as news.

This standard means that news reports, when clarity demands it, will be laid against pertinent factual background; that factors such as race, creed, nationality or prior status will be reported only when they are relevant; that comment or subjective content will be properly identified; and that errors in fact will be promptly acknowledged and corrected.

ARTICLE FOUR

Broadcast newsmen shall at all times display humane respect for the dignity, privacy and the well-being of persons with whom the news deals.

ARTICLE FIVE

Broadcast newsmen shall govern their personal lives and such nonprofessional associations as may impinge on their professional activities in a manner that will protect them from conflict of interest, real or apparent.

ARTICLE SIX

Broadcast newsmen shall seek actively to present all news the knowledge of which will serve the public interest, no matter what selfish, uninformed or corrupt efforts attempt to color it, withhold it or prevent its presentation. They shall make constant effort to open doors closed to the reporting of public proceedings with tools appropriate to broadcasting (including cameras and recorders), consistent with the public interest. They acknowledge the newsman's ethic of protection of confidential information and sources, and urge unswerving observation of it except in instances in which it would clearly and unmistakably defy the public interest.

ARTICLE SEVEN

Broadcast newsmen recognize the responsibility borne by broadcasting for informed analysis, comment and editorial opinion on public events and issues. They accept the obligation of broadcasters, for the presentation of such matters by individuals whose competence, experience and judgment qualify them for it.

ARTICLE EIGHT

In court, broadcast newsmen shall conduct themselves with dignity, whether the court is in or out of session. They shall keep broadcast equipment as unobtrusive and silent as possible. Where court facilities are inadequate, pool broadcasts should be arranged.

ARTICLE NINE

In reporting matters that are or may be litigated, the newsman shall avoid practices which would tend to interfere with the right of an individual to a fair trial.

ARTICLE TEN

Broadcast newsmen shall actively censure and seek to prevent violations of these standards, and shall actively encourage their observance by all newsmen, whether of the Radio Television News Directors Association or not.

questions for discussion and further research

1. Trying to balance the forces of government and industry is a delicate task. Codes of ethics and other self-regulatory measures are constantly running up against the practicalities of what industry demands and what the government will allow. Consider the provisions of the NAB Radio and Television Codes. Are there portions of the Codes you feel could be changed? What areas might contain more restrictive language? What areas might contain less restrictive language?

2. Hard liquor is advertised through many media which reach the home and children of all ages. Major news magazines, newspapers, and even some broadcast stations not adhering to NAB Code standards advertise alcoholic beverages other than beer. In view of these advertising practices, is the NAB Code restriction against accepting advertising for hard liquor too restrictive?

3. With the U.S. Constitution guaranteeing freedom of the press, is a code of ethics such as that subscribed to by RTNDA really necessary?

4. If it is, what purpose does it serve?

5. Is the NAB's periodic monitoring satisfactory as an enforcement procedure to make sure stations are programming within the guidelines of the Codes?

6. Should the standards of the NAB Codes be applied to all radio and television stations and be enforced by the FCC?

7. With the major network providing such a large part of the average television station's programming schedule, does the NAB Code really serve any real purpose for these local affiliates?

8. As new technologies, such as fiber optics and satellite communication, open up many more channels of communication to the average consumer, will industry self-regulation be more or less important?

9. If enough new channels of communication become operable through the technological advances of cable and satellite communication, could the government completely deregulate radio and television, letting self-regulation guide the future of the industry?

10. If it develops that less government regulation *is* possible, what areas of broadcast operations or programming would self-regulation *not* be able to control effectively?

additional resources

articles

Mills, E. C., and N. Miller, "The ASCAP-NAB Controversy—The Issues," 11 *Air Law Review* 394 (1940).

Persky, J., "Self-Regulation of Broadcasting— Does It Exist?," 27 *Journal of Communication* 202 (1977).

12

Reexamining the Communications Act

While throughout this text we have discussed the application of the Communications Act of 1934 to the operation of broadcast stations and the Act's impact on broadcast policy, we should remember that laws are many times dynamic, not static. When something is as filled with rapid change as broadcasting is, it is expected that the attention of policy makers will focus on changes in communications legislation. Recently, considerable attention has been paid to completely overhauling the Communications Act and in some ways restructuring the broadcasting industry in the United States. At times, this discussion reaches no farther than a legislative cloakroom. On other occasions it becomes heated debate preceding a key vote in Congress.

This chapter surveys recent attention paid to the reconsideration of the Communications Act of 1934; not the frequently appended rules and regulations but the very heart of the Act itself. The Act, as we have learned is what the American system of broadcasting is based upon and what forms and controls what the public eventually sees and hears.

Early Impetus: the "Bell Bill"

The impetus for a major revision of the Communications Act of 1934 came out of congressional hearings held in 1976 on the proposed Consumer Communications Reform Act, which would have overhauled telephone regulation. Commonly called the "Bell Bill," the proposed legislation went into hearings before the U.S. House of Representatives' Communications Subcommittee, under the chairmanship of Lionel Van Deerlin (later defeated for re-election). Cable Television also received close scrutiny by Van Deerlin during that year. And in October of 1976, Van Deerlin announced a full-scale inquiry into the possibility of rewriting communications legislation, after concluding during the hearings that the 1934 legislation was no longer effective in regulating the new technology that had been developed since its passage—technology which included satellites, microwave, cable, fiber optics, citizens' band radio, radar, land mobile communication, and light wave or laser beam communication. The House Commerce Committee stamped its approval on such a review by doubling Van Deerlin's committee's budget appropriations.

a review begins

The Subcommittee's review announcement prompted industry professionals, government bureaucrats, academicians, and citizens' groups to turn out in support of or in opposition to the rewrite. Not wanting to be left behind, the U.S. Senate announced that a special Senate hearing, conducted by Senator Ernest Hollings, a South Carolina Democrat, would review the Communications Act and everything associated with telecommunication policy.

The number of possible changes and approaches that could be taken to rewriting the Act were almost as numerous as the voices that clamored to be heard. Early reaction was limited to cautious rhetoric. No one knew exactly what a rewrite meant or how it might benefit or hurt any one particular cause. Cable and standard broadcast interests lined up to be heard, supported or at least observed by their various professional organizations, such as the National Association of Broadcasters and the National Cable Television Association. Those who were watchful of the First Amendment also made known their concern. The Radio/Television News Directors Association's legal counsel, Larry Scharff, prepared a position paper, which said in essence that the best way to revise the law would be to make sure that broadcast journalists received the same First Amendment rights as print journalists.

forums for issues

The rewrite became the topic of numerous symposia, and the divisions began to grow between its supporters and those who felt that a radical change in the Act would not be in their best interests. The first major forum was the February, 1977 meeting of the National Association of Television Program Executives (NATPE).[1] All the players were present, including Congressman Van Deerlin. Supporting the rewrite was Donald H. McGannon, chairman and president of Westinghouse Broadcasting Company. McGannon suggested a cabinet-level Department of Communication, bringing under one roof all of the agencies now controlling use of the electromagnetic spectrum. Also supporting the rewrite was Russel Karp, president of Teleprompter, who felt that cable should be given more independent regulatory status. On the other side of the fence was Bill Leonard, a vice president of CBS. He characterized the American system of communication as the finest on earth and, in reference to the fact that the 1934 Act was enacted before advances in technology, said that the U.S. Constitution did not mention anything about railroads, cars, telephones, or a number of other forms of modern technology.

The next rewrite forum took place at the March, 1977 meeting of the National Association of Broadcasters, in Washington, D.C. There, Congressman Van Deerlin stated the position that the "broadcaster should be entitled to the same First Amendment protection afforded newspapers." He also came out in favor of repealing the Fairness Doctrine. For those favoring more competition, he asked whether there were "advantages to augmenting existing radio service with short-range broadcasting service provided by low power, narrow band width radio stations." He told the broadcasters present: "I am told that we could have the capability for up to 450 channels, which could be reused at relatively short geographic spacing. If all 450 channels were licensed for use in Washington, D.C., they could be licensed for use in Baltimore. In other words, we could address the problems of diversity consistent with our concern for localism."

the option papers: visible target

But even before industry could react to Van Deerlin's comments, he suddenly gave rewrite opponents a visible target. Less than three weeks after the NAB Convention, the Van Deerlin staff released the "option papers" for rewriting the Communications Act of 1934. The staff members working on the document had been divided into eight groups: spectrum management, FCC procedural reform, broadcasting, cable television, common carrier, international common carrier, safety, and special services and privacy. Coordinating the broadcasting inquiry was subcommittee counsel Harry M. Shooshan. Staff assistant Karen Possner coordinated the cable inquiry. Although the final documents were not statements of policy or absolute legislative direction, the option papers opened up vigorous discussion over the possible consequences of a major rewrite.

Options and Questions: Broadcasting

For example, in writing the broadcasting section, Shooshan offered the option of scrapping the current system of license renewals for a *lease option* system.[2] In a lease option system, the broadcaster would lease the frequency from the government for a fixed term, say five to seven years, after which time the frequency would be auctioned off to the highest bidder or perhaps offered in a lottery. Another alternative is the *license option,* changing the current license renewal system from staggered renewals on a national scale to staggered renewals on a local scale. All renewals currently expire in the same state at the same time. The license option would be a plus for local citizens' groups, relieving their burden of evaluating the performance of *all* the stations in a given community or state at one time. Another option, the *access or quasi-common-carrier option,* suggested the possibility of regulating broadcasting like a common carrier, such as the telephone, for a portion of the broadcasting day. Such status would allow access to the medium to virtually everyone, not just to a select few, as is now the case. Under this option, access to the media would be on a fee basis, much like that for the telephone. Still a fourth option, the *public utility option,* would regulate broadcasting like a public utility. Traditionally, public utilities operate on regulated profits. For broadcasting, this would mean having its profits controlled by government or utility commissions, much like power and light companies. A built-in incentive in this option would be to have broadcasters use their excess profits to increase local news and public affairs programming or to upgrade minority training programs.

A controversial section of the option papers was the treatment of localism—the theory that the purpose of stations is to serve the public interest of their *local* communities. In radio, for example, even though each station is licensed to a local community, it is still true that some stations, because of their power and frequency, are more reflective of a regional or national audience than are their smaller counterparts. The smaller stations were allocated later in broadcasting's development, after many of the larger stations had already been assigned frequencies and the authority to operate at a higher power. This same "localism" posture is retained in television, setting priority for local stations serving local communities as opposed to regional or national service. The ideal envisioned by the FCC after lifting the 1948 television freeze was to allocate 2,000 stations to serve approximately 1,300 communities. Each community of moderate size was to have at least one television station. The option papers suggested, however, that perhaps the localism idea has not panned out the way it was planned, that as a regulatory philosophy it remains largely unchallenged, and that it is time to investigate the concept seriously.

The broadcasting section of the option papers divides these localism questions into three broad categories: (1) industry structure (2) programming, and (3) program content.

industry structure:
1. Is localism a desirable goal for structuring the broadcast industry?
2. If so, does the 1934 Act adequately reflect this goal? For instance, should local ownership be given statutory preference over absentee ownership? Is localism advanced or impaired by a ban on ownership of broadcast stations by local newspapers? Is localism impaired by the FCC's current multiple ownership rules, which allow a single entity to own up to 14 radio stations and 7 television stations?
3. If localism is retained as a goal, what can be done to provide additional local outlets? Options include legislation (to require VHF/UHF parity other than simply on the tuner), and spectrum management (VHF drop-ins, a shift of all television service to UHF, allocating additional spectrum for radio outlets in large markets, eliminating clear channel stations, extending hours of daytime broadcasting, etc.).
4. If increasing the number of local outlets threatens the viability of existing broadcast stations, should Congress limit competition or, alternatively, provide direct support to insure that additional broadcasting will survive (increased funding for public broadcasting, government loans, etc.)?
5. In order to provide local service to areas which cannot support a commercial broadcast station, should restraints on broadcasters' use of other technology be removed (the ban on broadcast/cable cross-ownership, restrictions on program origination by translators, etc.)?

6. Failing such "marketplace" solutions, should specific regulatory requirements be placed on licensees to require them to act as local outlets (for example, requiring New York City television stations to allocate fixed percentages of time for serving various New Jersey cities reached by their signals, or requiring clear channel radio stations to make similar allocations for areas covered by their signals)?

Questions about localism in relation to broadcast programming service included:

programming:
1. Is localism (obligatory service to the community of license) a desirable goal? If most viewers are satisfied with local stations as "conduits for national programming," and if local programs fare so poorly, should "localism" continue to be promoted? If local service *is* desirable, could it be supplied by sources other than local broadcast stations? If the responsibility to provide local programs were eliminated, would there be any basis for regulation of broadcasters (other than for technical compliance and to prevent fraudulent practices, etc.)?
2. If the promotion of localism is to be continued, is the 1934 Act specific enough to provide guidance to the FCC? Are current FCC policies adequate, or are explicit statutory provisions required?
3. Is the concentration of control over programming selection currently evidenced by network practices contrary to the promotion of localism?
4. If so, should the creation of new VHF stations and the enhancement of UHF reception be adopted as policy goals? Or, should all television service be shifted to UHF in order to provide outlets for new networks, thereby expanding the range of choice for local licensees and the potential service to the viewer?
5. Is it necessary to require divestiture of the networks' owned and operated stations in order to deal with concentration of control? Or should the content of network-affiliate agreements be subject to more specific restrictions (such as limiting the amount of programming which could be supplied from a single source, either on an overall basis or broken down by period)?
6. Should the licensee be compelled to provide certain types of programming through direct regulation? If so, are present FCC policies adequate to accomplish the desired program goals? In relation to programming, should Congress provide a more specific standard than "public interest, convenience and necessity?" Are quantitive standards (program percentages) required? Should the prime-time access rule be modified to require locally produced programming? Can present FCC standards, such as "superior performance" or "substantial service," be applied with any degree of predictability?

Regarding program content, Shooshan's option paper asked:

program content:
1. How extensive is the broadcaster's right to free speech? Should broadcasters be afforded the same First Amendment right as newspapers? If not, why not? Should different degrees of protection be afforded broadcasters as journalists as opposed to broadcasters as suppliers of entertainment programming? Do vague regulatory standards and general guidelines tend to have a "chilling effect" on a broadcaster's programming decisions (or do they have any impact at all)?
2. Can or should government attempt to control or eliminate the program content control that results from commercial sponsorship of individual programs? What would be the effect of prohibiting the purchase of advertising time on specific programs and substituting a system in which commercials were rotated randomly (or

systematically) among all program offerings? (Such an approach could not only eliminate content control by program sponsors but could also begin to reduce the broadcaster's reliance on ratings as the arbiters of public tastes and desires.)

3. How is the public's right to free speech affected by broadcasting? What *First Amendment* (as opposed to "public interest") obligations does the broadcaster have to the public? Does the concept of the broadcaster as a custodian of the airwaves on behalf of the public (public trustee or fiduciary) necessarily imply a right of the public to be heard or to be presented with "vigorous debate of controversial issues?" Does the theory of *Red Lion* make sense? Can Congress abrogate the rights of the public set out in *Red Lion*?

4. Are the public's rights enhanced or frustrated by a general regulatory standard ("public interest") and broad guidelines (the Fairness Doctrine)?

5. If such rights exist, and are to be protected and promoted, should more specific guarantees be afforded (access, free speech messages, voters' time)?

The First Amendment questions were opposed to statements made earlier by Van Deerlin at the NAB convention, but the option papers did not try to hide the obvious reference to a First Amendment confrontation. Instead, they placed the burden of this confrontation on the fact that broadcasters had not "traditionally recognized, nor sought to achieve, absolute First Amendment rights." This statement was backed up by numerous examples, including that of President Eisenhower and Secretary of State Dulles reviewing films of press conferences and ordering cuts as a precondition for television coverage.

Options and Questions: Cable

The cable section of the option papers, prepared by Karen B. Possner, first examined the nature of cable stating: "Instead of being introduced into the marketplace and allowed to develop in response to consumer demand, some basic assumptions were made about the probable effects of cable on competing technologies, and regulatory restraints were imposed to neutralize those predicted effects."[3] Possner went on to suggest that there was no evidence that the public would be adversely affected if cable were free from federal regulation. She said: "In fact, if the FCC were truly dedicated to reaping the benefits of this developing communications technology, it would allow cable to offer all the services it is technically capable of providing, and would wait for consumer response before concluding which products could be offered to its subscribers, based on harm to other competing services and media."

Another part of the cable papers discussed the role that telephone companies may play in cable's future. Possner noted that: "If cable is ever to serve a significant portion of the nation, then vast sums of money will be necessary to increase cable capacity. Between AT&T and approximately 1,600 independent telephone companies, at least 95 percent of all U.S. homes have telephone service. With developing technologies, such as fiber optics, telephone companies might be induced to install increased capacity if they knew that that capacity could be put to some revenue-producing use beyond standard telephone service." In discussing the division of authority over cable, the cable papers said: "If common carrier status were applied to cable, and if the distributional facility were owned by the local telephone company, then the forum currently available in the form of state public service and public utility commissions might obviate the need for a separate state regulatory entity, for their goals would be analogous."

Industry Response to Rewrite Options

Some of the first reactions to the options papers came, understandably, from the National Association of Broadcasters, in a document titled "NAB Initial Comments, House Communications Subcommittee Staff's Options Papers," released May 4, 1977.[4] Among other arguments, the NAB contended that "presumption in favor of radical change is unjustified. . . . Americans today have the best broadcast service of any nation in the world," and that "this system is a model of free enterprise working with government to give service free of any direct charge to virtually every citizen. . . . It makes little sense to consider radical revision of the basic law that has served the public well and continues to do so. . . ."

lease option

Critical of the "lease option" portion of the broadcast paper, the NAB said the Subcommittee failed to point out the drawbacks to such a system. Nowhere, the NAB pointed out, ". . . is it mentioned that the leasing alternative is likely to produce results that would contravene the public interest. For example, would leases be awarded to the highest bidder? And if so, doesn't this guarantee that only the wealthy will be in the broadcast business? Will broadcast experience and expertise play any part in such a system? What effect would such a system have on financing of broadcast facilities? Wouldn't successful bidders be increasingly interested in maximizing profits as the lease expires? Wouldn't the public responsiveness be greatly lessened?"

localism

Becoming a bit more direct in their reaction to the "localism" portion of the option paper, the NAB stated: "We reject the staff conclusion that localism has failed. Localism cannot be judged merely by noting the percentage of programming that is locally produced. We would suggest the staff has failed to consult with the people of this nation, and the community leaders of this nation, about the service provided by local broadcasters." As to the inference that broadcasters had been less than diligent on behalf of their First Amendment rights, the NAB said: "We believe strongly that this statement does not reflect the industry's continuing commitment to full First Amendment rights and our determination to let no one dictate programming decisions to broadcasters."

reactions from cable

Although the option papers did not meet with much enthusiasm from the broadcasters, the cable interests were more receptive. Representing major interests of the cable industry and presenting a response to the cable option paper was the National Cable Television Association (NCTA).[5] In a letter from NCTA president Robert L. Schmidt to Van Deerlin, Schmidt said: "We reiterate our support of the Subcommittee's rewrite of the Communications Act of 1934."[6] The response of NCTA especially supported relieving cable of regulatory constraints. NCTA strongly supported "Total deregulation of the FCC's programming restrictions," saying: "No empirical data exist demonstrating adverse impact on a television broadcaster's service to the public justifying continuance of cable's restrictions. These program restrictions . . . have been a severe deterrent to cable systems' growth in many markets. . . ."

Less enthusiastic, however, were NCTA's comments on a possible relationship with the telephone company. It stated: "The issue the Congress faces is whether it desires to grant a monopoly of all of this country's wire communications services into homes and businesses to AT&T and the other major telephone companies. Numerous government and public interest groups have opposed an expanded telephone monopoly into all voice, data and video communications services." NCTA further deplored: "The long history of protracted FCC proceedings involving AT&T rates and practices . . . demonstrates that accountants and economists cannot sanitize the unfair tactics of the telephone companies."

Van Deerlin's Subcommittee continued hearings on the proposed rewrite. Representatives of the industry, its professional organizations, citizens' groups, foundations, academicians, and others all voiced their opinions. Their arguments seemed to repeat those voiced earlier on the subject.[7] While NBC Vice Chairman David Adams described network programming as that most preferred by local audiences, Reverend Everett Parker of the United Church of Christ said that viewers had never really had an alternative choice. Minorities called for more opportunities, both regulatory and financial, to become substantially involved in broadcast ownership. Commercial broadcasters argued for more nighttime authorization of daytime-licensed stations and for clearing some of the clear channel frequencies for more local programming services. The broadcasting option paper's suggestion of leasing frequencies and auctioning them to the highest bidder met with almost unanimous opposition. It was criticized on grounds that broadcasters, feeling the threat of losing their licenses, would maximize profits, not public service, and that there would be little opportunity for blacks and minorities without large financial backing to secure licenses. Both the Subcommittee's staff and those testifying did agree on First Amendment issues, with Van Deerlin himself supporting the concept at the NAB meeting.

Legislative Proposals for Rewriting the Communications Act

On the foundations of numerous congressional hearings, with testimony from industry and from citizens' groups, various legislative proposals for rewriting the Communications Act have been introduced in both houses of Congress.

Below are some of the different proposals which at one time or another were discussed as possible rewrite legislation.[8] Some of the measures were quite similar in certain areas; other measures saw widely varying proposals. Our dicussion will concentrate on general proposals, rather than the strength or weakness of any particular measure.

changing the FCC

Although most legislation left the FCC as broadcasting's main regulator, other measures proposed abolishing the FCC and substituting a Communications Regulatory Commission. Instead of the seven commissioners now on the FCC, the Regulatory Commission would have five members appointed by the President, by and with the advice and consent of the Senate. The President would also appoint the commission's chairperson. Each member would serve for a ten-year term and could not be reappointed unless the initial appointment was for less than five years. Not more than four commissioners could be from the same political party.

Much like the FCC, the Communications Regulatory Commission would, among other things, classify radio stations, assign frequencies, establish rules, assign call letters, and oversee standards for radio and television transmitting and receiving equipment. A special consumer assistance office would provide liaison with the public and work with citizens' groups.

Still other proposals dealt with the funding of the FCC. Some suggestions were made to create license fees and tax the users of the electromagnetic spectrum—those using the airwaves. Included were fees to also be charged to anyone who provided a telecommunication service; thus, telephone and other common carrier industries would help fund the agency. The FCC took on a bill collector status and would have the power to charge penalties for those industries or stations who were past due in fee payments. The FCC would have the power to determine how much the fees would be and specific industries would pay what amounts toward a proportion of the overall costs of running the commission. As an impetus for deregulation, one measure called for the FCC to annually report to Congress a review of all regulations and eliminate those regulations which were unnecessary. Other proposed bills would give Congress the power to veto FCC decisions and make it easier for a court review of those decisions.

executive branch involvement

The executive branch of government would still be active in telecommunications policy. The National Telecommunications and Information Administration, now in the Department of Commerce, would be replaced by the National Telecommunications Agency. The new agency would also be part of the executive branch, but would be separate from the Commerce Department. A perusal of the responsibilities assigned to the new agency finds considerable similarity to the NTIA, as well as to its predecessors, the former Office of Telecommunications Policy (OTP) in the executive office of the President and the former Office of Telecommunications (OT) in the Department of Commerce.

licensing

A variety of legislative options dealt with station licensing. Legislation proposed changing license terms, including (1) giving radio indefinite terms, and (2) extending the terms of television stations to two five-year terms and then making the terms indefinite after the tenth year. Other proposals included lengthening television to five-year terms and making radio indefinite, but having a regulatory commission spot-check 5 percent of the licenses every year. Still other proposals broke down markets by size and based license terms on such breakdowns. For instance, legislation would have lengthened the terms of television licenses in markets 26 through 100 to four years and television stations beyond the top 100 markets to five years. In the top 25 markets, the license term would remain three years.

Other proposals suggested changing the actual renewal process. New frequency assignments would require a lottery, and minorities would have two chances to win. Licenses already in existence would come up for renewal as usual, but comparative hearings from challengers would be eliminated. If a license was not renewed, its frequency would be open to lottery. One legislative option proposed keeping comparative renewals. Other legislation proposed giving the regulatory commission power to renew a license automatically, but differed on the degree of commitment to "public interest" a licensee would have to display to be awarded automatic renewal.

public interest participation

The question of whether citizens' groups have the right to be reimbursed for participation in comparative hearings or to challenge licenses and be reimbursed with government funds has long been a topic of debate. Probably reflecting the amount of time that citizens' groups had to participate in the drafting of the legislation proposals contained provisions to reimburse citizens' groups for their participation in commission rulemaking.

Other legislation made no provision for citizen participation.

the electromagnetic spectrum

One of the ongoing discussions of broadcast regulation has been the way in which frequencies have been allocated. Rewrite proposals kept the discussion alive. Some legislation went so far as to propose actual changes in spectrum allocation, such as making assignments based on each community served and guaranteeing full-time AM service to every community. Other issues included the continued protection of high-powered clear channel stations operating on protected frequencies. A single agency devoted to studying allocations was also proposed.

proposals for deregulating broadcasting

While the proposals for changing the regulatory structure of broadcasting were popular with many groups, they encountered a wave of negative public sentiment against overregulation by government. Thus, it was not surprising that significant attempts at deregulation were also proposed. Some of the proposals offered were designed to eliminate controls on news and public affairs programming, local programming standards, community needs and ascertainment surveys, the Fairness Doctrine, and certain logging requirements. More controversial were proposals to eliminate equal-opportunity enforcement and program format regulations. Deregulation did occur for radio, although not specifically tied to a rewrite.

cable

Although not favored by the cable interests, who feared a developing monopoly, some of the legislation proposed permitting telephone companies unlimited ownership of cable systems. Restrictions would be placed on the telephone companies if they ventured into pay TV, requiring them to make their facilities available to anyone else who wanted into pay TV. More moderate proposals would have permitted cable ownership by telephone companies, but prohibited cable from controlling program content. Also concerned with the cable-programming relationship were proposals to prohibit close corporate ties between cable systems and production companies. Legislative planners saw the potential for monopoly over both functions on the part of companies who controlled large cable systems and effectively prohibited any programs except those their own companies produced from airing on the system. Some proposals removed restrictions on broadcast-cable crossownerships, even in the same communities. Other proposals turned the matter over to the Justice Department to administrate. Under one measure, the National Copyright Office would be removed from cable regulation, and cable would deal directly with broadcasters and program suppliers.

public broadcasting

The structure of public broadcasting would be changed. In part, these would provide for certain basic criteria to be met by public broadcasting stations before being awarded licenses. Specifically, legislation proposed that licenses be assigned to private nonprofit corporations, foundations, or associations organized primarily for educational or cultural purposes. Although the criteria were not substantially different from those that characterized most current public broadcasting licensees, the legislation took a hard look at the corporations that owned groups of public stations. Most controversial were proposals permitting advertising on public stations. Other measures called for public stations to have community advisory boards.

As with any proposed legislation, and especially legislation as sweeping and as controversial as the Communications Act rewrite, the final product becomes the result of many forces and opposing interests. The measures that become public enough to hit a responsive chord in the electorate will almost surely be incorporated into final drafts. At the same time, broadcasting is an industry most legislators take very seriously. After all, elected officials have a stake in radio and television, since they are among their chief means of communicating with their constituencies. Measures such as the Fairness Doctrine, political advertising, and news programming do not originate from a vacuum of vested interests. Industry organizations, such as the National Association of Broadcasters, and the National Cable Television Association, have acquired considerable clout in influencing policy. Citizens' groups, representing an elitist segment of the population actively involved in the political process, have clout as well, but in many cases need liaison with industry representatives to attain their full impact. Within this atmosphere of give and take, of dialogue, rests the future of broadcast regulation.

Future Prospects for a Communications Act Overhaul

Throughout the late 1970s and into the early 1980s, broadcasters, the cable industry, and common carrier interests experienced a series of highs and lows as forces at work on revising the Communications Act jumped from one position to another and from one Congressional committee to another. While broadcasters heralded the rewrite issue as being dead, other lobby groups promised to carry the rewrite banner.

Such issues as teletext, 9 kHz spacing, deregulation of cable, direct satellite-to-home broadcasting, and others facing the FCC and Congress provide ample arenas in which to reexamine existing legislation. Whether the efforts will result in piecemeal change through FCC rules or major policy shifts in a Communications Act rewrite depends on how successful Congress will be in grabbing hold of an issue long enough to see it through passage.

summary

The idea for rewriting the Communications Act of 1934 grew out of hearings on the "Bell Bill," conducted by Representative Lionel Van Deerlin of California. This rewrite immediately became the topic of discussions in Congress, as well as in the broadcasting industry. The two professional organizations most concerned with the rewrite are the National Association of Broadcasters and the National Cable Television Association. Each took positions on the rewrite proposals and later issued specific statements of reaction to a set of option papers authored by members of Van Deerlin's staff. Some of the options proposed included lease option, license option, access or quasi-common-carrier option, and public utility option. Especially important were questions as to how broadcasters should better serve their local communities if the current concept of localism proved to be ineffective.

Some of these proposals introduced as bills included replacing the Federal Communications Commission with a Communications Regulatory Commission, which would include an Office of Consumer Affairs. The National Telecommunications and Information Administration would be replaced by a National Telecommunications Agency. License terms would be changed. Some measures proposed extending television license terms to five years and, after two renewals, deregulating television altogether. Other measures suggested immediate deregulation of radio. Other deregulatory efforts centered around eliminating such things as community needs and ascertainment surveys, certain restrictions on news and public affairs programming, and equal-opportunity enforcement. Cable was deregulated in many ways, although some measures permitted telephone companies more latitude to own cable systems, as long as programming and system control were divorced from each other.

Public broadcasting received some restructuring under measures originally proposed by Congressman Van Deerlin, measures which proposed creating community advisory boards and closely restricting the types of entities and associations which could be awarded public licenses.

An attempt in 1980 to change the common carrier sections of the Act failed after being effectively stopped by a political maneuver in a congressional sub-committee.

questions for discussion and further research

1. New developments in technology, as well as in the application of those developments, are expanding at an ever-increasing place. What will guarantee that new communication legislation will not be out of date almost as soon as it becomes law? What will assure that new legislation, constantly requiring amendments, will be any more beneficial to the public than current laws, as amended?

2. If a lottery system were placed in effect, how would a regulatory commission make sure that licenses would be awarded to the applicants *most qualified* to meet the needs of the public?

3. Would total deregulation of broadcasting create such a glut of stations in the marketplace that the whole system would eventually be controlled by the giant conglomerates that proved best able to command the necessary technology and capital? What would prevent the virtual monopoly of the media marketplace by such conglomerates?

4. To prevent or to break up such monopolies, would we find that new legislation was necessary—legislation which might closely resemble the guards against monopoly that already exist in current broadcast regulation?

5. Given that the 1927 law went through years of court challenge before it achieved the foundation upon which the 1934 legislation was built, what would prevent similar legal quagmires from developing as any new laws took effect?

6. Although it could be argued that the foundation upon which the 1934 Act was built would also be the basis upon which new legislation would rest, how can we answer the criticism that the level of technological development that existed when the 1934 Act was passed was almost infantile compared to current technology?

7. Will Congress expend more energy in passing amendments to patch up holes in new legislation than it would by simply amending current legislation to reflect changing technology and the marketplace?

8. What is the justification for and the rationale behind a measure permitting minority applicants to have two chances to win a frequency-allocation lottery?

9. Would a community-based frequency allocation plan, permitting maximum service by AM radio stations, withstand a court test, or would such a provision in effect discriminate against other technologies, such as FM radio?

10. Some measures have proposed permitting the executive branch of government to retain its involvement in broadcasting through a separate telecommunications agency. What would prevent the abuses of power the executive branch might wield through the use of such an agency?

11. What is the rationale behind scrapping the FCC and replacing it with a Communications Regulatory Commission? Would any real purpose be served by such a change? Would reducing the number of commissioners from seven to five and lengthening their terms from seven to ten years solve any inequities?

12. Are the deregulation of radio and television and a continuation of the public interest standard compatible?

13. Would community advisory boards be a more effective means of assuring that a broadcaster is sensitized to local community problems than the community needs and ascertainment surveys?

14. Community advisory boards have been proposed for public broadcasting. Does the idea have merit for commercial broadcasters as well? What vested interests might

broadcasters take into consideration if they were given the power to select members of their community advisory boards?

15. The general public rarely becomes aware of legislative measures affecting large segments of the population unless significant media attention is focused on such measures. Although broadcasting affects all of us, rewriting the Communications Act has not been one of the issues to receive widespread attention by the popular press, at least not in comparison to other issues, such as civil rights or energy shortages. Yet any legislation that concerns broadcasting can have a profound impact on literally an entire national population. Given the importance of such legislation, are there any effective ways for members of Congress to educate their constituencies and to receive feedback from those constituencies before voting on communications legislation?

16. Business leaders, as well as representatives of professional associations, have called on the public to rise above "economic illiteracy," to learn more about and understand the importance of our economy and how it affects our society. Are most people "communication illiterates" when it comes to understanding such things as the way broadcasting is structured and regulated? What would society demand if its members were more knowledgable about the assets and liabilities of our expanding technology?

additional resources

Possner, K. B., "Options for Cable Television," Memorandum to the Subcommittee on Communications, U.S. House of Representatives, 1977.

Shooshan, H. M., "Options for Broadcasting," Memorandum to the Subcommittee on Communications, U.S. House of Representatives, 1977.

National Cable Television Association, "Response to Option Papers on Cable Television," Washingtin, D.C., 1977.

National Association of Broadcasters, "Initial Comments: House Subcommittee Staff's Option Papers," Washington, D.C., 1977.

V

The
Legal System
and
Legal Research

13

Understanding the Legal System and Legal Research

by Colleen Kristl Pauwels
Director, Law School Library, Indiana University, Bloomington[1]

Every facet of our society has felt the increasing influence of the law. In the field of communications, this is strikingly apparent, with the growing body of statutes, regulations, and administrative and judicial decisions that direct the actions of every radio and television station, every journalist and broadcaster. To be properly informed and to stay abreast of the changes are the responsibilities of everyone in this field.

Legal research is different from most other types of research, and students attempting it for the first time may be intimidated by the enormity of their task. Actually, legal research should not be feared, as it can be mastered by those who are willing to devote some time and enthusiasm. Understanding the legal system and the materials it generates will help dispel the mystique.

It may be useful first to read through these pages without trying to master the material. This reading will identify the range of sources available. Every source may not be necessary for each research project; the issues that are covered and the strategy that is chosen will dictate the appropriate material.

Some sources discussed here may not be available in a general academic library. Law school libraries offer the most complete set of materials. If you are not near a law school, and if your college library does not contain the needed material, try the court library at your county seat. If you are near the state capitol, there is usually a large legal collection available at the state library or the appellate court library. Depository libraries for U.S. government publications are likely to have much of the material, and there are at least two such libraries in

397

each Congressional district. As a last resort, try to obtain the material through interlibrary loan, although a clear idea of what you need is necessary for this method. When in doubt, ask a reference librarian for assistance.

The Legal System

If you wish to research any aspect of the law effectively, it is important to understand the structure of the legal system. There are three branches of government: the legislative, the executive, and the judicial, and each branch plays a part in the development of the law. The legislature enacts the law, the executive agencies administer the law, and the courts rule on the interpretation, applicability, and constitutionality of the law, as well as providing rulings in other special areas.

Under our federal constitution, each state is sovereign, and each one has jurisdiction over all legal matters governed by its own constitution and statutes. Federal courts have jurisdiction over matters involving the U.S. Constitution and laws enacted by Congress; treaties and disputes involving ambassadors, public ministers, and consuls; laws relating to navigable waters; and controversies between the U.S. and individuals, between two states, or between individuals from different states.

The federal court system (Figure 13-1) calls its trial courts District Courts. Its appeals courts, divided into ten regional circuits and the District of Columbia circuit, are called the Courts of Appeals. The court of last resort is the U.S. Supreme Court. In most states, the court system has the same three-tiered structure. The courts vary a little in name, but ultimately they function in the same way. The American court system operates in accord with the doctrine of "stare decisis," a principle of law that means that as the courts interpret the law, each case holds as a precedent for similar cases in that jurisdiction in the future. It is not only essential, then, to know the statute or regulation that is to be followed but also to locate prior cases that have interpreted the law and therefore have set the precedent for future rulings. For this reason, various forms of legal materials must be consulted for effective research.

A Legal Research Strategy

In developing a strategy for legal research, it is important to understand that law materials can be divided into three broad categories. The first category is *secondary materials,* including books and journal articles that discuss the laws and the related issues. The second category consists of *primary materials,* which are the actual forms of the law, such as constitutions, statutes, regulations, and administrative agency and court decisions. The third group includes the various *finding aids* and *indexes* that are used to locate the primary materials.

Choosing the proper strategy at the outset will save valuable time and make more effective use of the materials available. The first step is to get a clear idea of what it is you want to know. This can be done by consulting a variety of second-

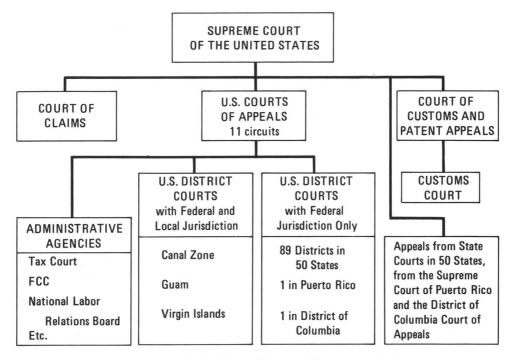

THE UNITED STATES COURT SYSTEM

Figure 13-1   (Committee on the Judiciary, House of Representatives)

ary sources in order to provide the background to help define your issue. The use of these materials alone, however, does not constitute legal research. Once you have refined the question and pinpointed the issue or issues involved, you must identify and retrieve all the primary materials. It is important here to be both comprehensive and up to date in your search. One decision can change a whole body of previous law, so careful attention must be paid to *all* the material.

Secondary Materials

annotated law reports

There are several types of secondary materials that can be consulted.

American Law Reports, or *ALR,* selects state and federal cases and includes with each opinion an analytical essay on the subject of the decision. These annotations analyze the issues of the case and discuss its impact. One of the assets of each annotation is that it brings into perspective the current standing of case law in other jurisdictions. This is a valuable source to use at the outset of your research to develop your background information or narrow your topic.

journals and periodicals

Reviewing the periodical literature is another excellent way to develop background knowledge. There are many specialized journals and periodicals that discuss legal issues in communications and media law. Some of the more familiar are:

Advertising Age
Published weekly; contains news of the advertising business.

Access Reports
Biweekly newsletter on freedom of information and privacy. Includes reports on federal and state government activities concerning laws.

Broadcast Daily
Published for delegates at major broadcasting conventions.

Broadcast Engineering
A technology publication of the broadcast/communications industry.

Broadcast Management/Engineering
Contains articles of interest to broadcast management and engineering personnel.

Broadcasting
Weekly business news of the television and radio profession. Reports of interest to advertisers as well as to programmers, journalists, engineers, and others. Includes reports on the Federal Communications Commission's decisions, hearings, and procedures.

Broadcasting and the Law (Perry's)
A biweekly newsletter which reports and interprets current court and FCC rulings affecting broadcasting.

Bulletin of the Copyright Society of the USA
Contains articles concerning legal issues related to copyright. Also includes recent legislation, administrative activities, and treaties, conventions, and proclamations.

Cable News
A weekly magazine covering cable television matters.

Cablecasting
Covers engineering and technical aspects of cable television.

Cablevision
Directed toward those in the cable television industry responsible for managing, constructing, and operating CATV systems.

CATV
A weekly trade publication on cable television.

Comm/Ent: Journal of Communication and Entertainment Law
Quarterly law journal, covering issues in entertainment law.

Communications News
Summarizes recent developments in all areas of broadcasting and telecommunication.

Communications and the Law
Law journal, covering all areas of communication law.

Copyright Bulletin
Published by UNESCO. Contains documents and reports on proceedings of copyright conventions and other material on international copyright law.

CPB Report
Newsletter of the Corporation for Public Broadcasting.

Educational & Instructional Television
Contains articles and notes on recent developments and uses of television in both industry and education.

Educational Broadcasting
Contains both scholarly and general articles on ETV.

Feedback
Articles on broadcast education.

FOI Digest
Newsletter covering federal and state activities concerning freedom of information.

Federal Communications Law Journal (formerly *Federal Communications Bar Journal*)
Includes articles relating to the activities of the FCC.

Journal of Broadcasting
Devoted to all aspects of broadcasting.

Journal of College Radio
Contains general articles of interest to management and staff of college radio stations.

Journal of Communication
On the study of communication theory, practice, and policy. Articles on such topics as television violence, censorship in broadcasting, and radio programming.

Journalism Quarterly
Covers all areas of journalism and mass communication.

Mass Comm Review
Devoted to the study of mass communication, including broadcasting.

NAB Highlights
Affiliate newsletter of the National Association of Broadcasters.

News Media and the Law
Contains articles on legal issues as they pertain to journalists, broadcasters, and photographers.

PEAL: Publishing, Entertainment, Advertising and Allied Fields Law Quarterly
Law journal covering all aspects of the communications, advertising, and entertainment fields.

Public Telecommunications Review
A journal of articles on public television.

The Quill
Publication of the Society of Professional Journalists–Sigma Delta Chi. Contains articles of interest to both print and broadcast journalists.

RTNDA Communicator
Newsletter of the Radio/Television News Directors' Association.

Satellite Communications
For users, systems designers, common carriers, and manufacturers in the international satellite communications industry.

Student Press Law Center Report
Newsletter concerned with legal issues relating to student journalists.

Television/Radio Age
Similar in some ways to *Broadcasting,* but with longer, more substantial articles.

TV Communications
Devoted to cable television, it deals with topics on management systems design, finance, engineering, pay-cable, and others.

TV Guide
Local program listings and articles about radio and television.

In addition, law journals that are not solely concerned with media law often contain important articles discussing the developments in this field. Law journals are of particular importance, because some of the finest legal scholars contribute to them. These journals can also provide analyses of court decisions more rapidly than books can. Law journals are published by law schools, legal associations, and commercial houses.

periodical indexes

Articles in general periodicals, as well as those in the law journals, can be found through periodical indexes. *Readers' Guide to Periodical Literature* indexes general and media journals. *Public Affairs Information Service Bulletin,* or *P.A.I.S.,* indexes a selection of law and media journals and other magazines concerned with public-affairs issues. This index can be found in most academic libraries. There are several legal periodical indexes. *Index to Legal Periodicals* and *Current Law Index* are two of the most comprehensive. Although some academic libraries may subscribe to one of these legal periodical indexes, they are more often found in law school libraries.

Other frequently used indexes include:

Business Periodicals Index, 1958 to date
  An index to over 100 journals on various aspects of business.
Education Index
  An index to over 200 periodicals relating to education.
Humanities Index
  Formerly part of the *Social Sciences and Humanities Index,* an index to over 260 journals in the humanities.
New York Times
  The index of the *New York Times.* Check your library for available indexes of other newspapers.
Social Sciences Index
  Formerly part of the *Social Sciences and Humanities Index,* an index to over 260 journals in the social sciences.
Social Sciences and Humanities Index 1965–1972 (formerly *International Index 1920–1965*)
  An index of over 200 journals, which in 1973 was divided into two indexing services: *Humanities Index* and *Social Sciences Index.*
Topicator
  An article guide to broadcasting, advertising, communication, and marketing.

books

A great number of books have been written on media law topics. Some will be available in your library and can be found through the subject index of the card catalog. To make sure the material is as current as possible, it is still best to consult the primary sources whenever possible.

law dictionaries

While reading, you may come across words or phrases that you do not understand. There are several legal dictionaries that will define the terms for you.

Black's Law Dictionary is the most common and is often found in academic libraries.

Primary Materials

After defining your topic, your search should focus on primary materials. But before using such materials, it is important to understand legal citation form.

legal citations

Legal citations to statutes, regulations, decisions, and most other law materials follow a uniform method of citation that is much different from the citations you ordinarily see in books and periodicals in other fields. The standard method for legal materials consists of giving the volume of the work, an abbreviation of the title of the work, and the first page of the case decision or periodical noted. Therefore, you might see cited 88 Colum.L.R. 156. This is the citation for an article in volume 88 of the *Columbia Law Review* that begins on page 156.

For citations to court decisions from the U.S. Supreme Court, you will often see the following:

New York Times v. *United States,* 403 U.S. 713, 91 S.Ct. 2140, 29 L.Ed.2d 822 (1971).

What has been given here is the name of the case (*New York Times* v. *United States*) and three citations for different reporters or sets of volumes where you can find the same case. These are called parallel citations—three places to find the same case. (The date in parentheses indicates the year the case was decided.)

There are two major exceptions to the basic legal citation form. Some looseleaf services cite to paragraph numbers as well as or instead of page numbers. For example, Pike & Fischer *Radio Regulation,* a looseleaf service that pulls together statutes, cases, and administrative agency materials, uses page numbers for cases (e.g., 37 RR 2d 744) but paragraph numbers for the other materials (e.g., RR ¶ 69.58). In the *U.S. Code* or other statute volumes, the proper citation is to section numbers (e.g., 5 U.S.C. §315). A sign is usually but not always used for paragraph (¶) and section (§).

Here are some abbreviations of the legal materials that you are most likely to encounter. For a more detailed list of abbreviations, look in the back of *Black's Law Dictionary.*

A.B.A.J.	*American Bar Association Journal*
A.L.R.	*American Law Reports*
A.L.R. 2d	*American Law Reports* (2d series)
A.L.R. 3d	*American Law Reports* (3rd series)
A.L.R. Fed	*American Law Reports,* Federal cases
Am.Jur.2d	*American Jurisprudence,* Second (edition)
Atl.	*Atlantic Reporter*
Cal.Rptr.	*California Reporter*
C.F.R.	*Code of Federal Regulations*
C.J.S.	*Corpus Juris Secundum*
Colum.L.R.	*Columbia Law Review*

F.	*Federal Reporter*
F.2d	*Federal Reporter,* 2d series
F.C.C.	*Federal Communications Commission Reports*
F.C.C.2d	*Federal Communications Commission Reports,* 2d series
F.R.	*Federal Register*
F.Supp.	*Federal Supplement*
Harv.L.R.	*Harvard Law Review*
L.Ed.	*U.S. Supreme Court Reports, Lawyers' Edition*
L.Ed.2d	*U.S. Supreme Court Reports, Lawyers' Edition,* 2d series
LW	*U.S. Law Week*
Med.L. Rptr.	*Media Law Reporter*
N.E.	*Northeastern Reporter*
N.W.	*Northwestern Reporter*
N.Y.Supp.	*New York Supplement*
P.& F. Radio Reg.	Pike and Fischer *Radio Regulation* (unofficial cite)
Pac.	*Pacific Reporter*
RR	Pike and Fischer *Radio Regulation* (unofficial cite)
RR 2d	Pike and Fischer *Radio Regulation,* 2d series (unofficial cite)
Rad. Regs. (P&F)	Pike and Fischer *Radio Regulation* (official cite)
Rad. Regs.2d (P&F)	Pike and Fischer *Radio Regulation,* 2d series (official cite)
S.Ct.	*Supreme Court Reporter*
S.E.	*Southeastern Reporter*
So.	*Southern Reporter*
Stan.L.R.	*Stanford Law Review*
S.W.	*Southwestern Reporter*
U.Chi.L.R.	*University of Chicago Law Review*
U.S.C.	*U.S. Code*
U.S.C.A.	*U.S. Code Annotated*
U.S.	*U.S. Reports*
Yale L.J.	*Yale Law Journal*

Some case citations will provide—in addition to the volume, reporter system, and first page of the case—the year the decision was released and, in some instances, the jurisdication of the court.

For example: *United States* v. *Hunter,* 459 F.2d (4th Cir. 1972).

This citation tells you that the U.S. Court of Appeals for the 4th Circuit handed down this case in 1972.

constitutions and statutes

A constitution, whether for a state or the federal government, is the framework for that government. It delegates power and responsibilities to the government and defines the rights and liberties of its citizens. It is the supreme law of the jurisdiction and supersedes all other forms of law.

Statutes are the forms of law enacted by the legislative body. The Congress and most state legislatures are bicameral, or two-house, systems. The legislation must proceed through both houses and be signed by the chief executive before it is enacted into law.

Constitutions and statutes are available in several sources. As statutes or public laws are passed, they are compiled in chronological order. Federal laws can be found in the *Statutes at Large.* State laws are called session laws and are issued under a variety of titles, such as *Acts of Indiana* or *Laws of Minnesota.*

More workable forms of statutes are codes. Codes, available for both federal and state statutes, are subject arrangements of the laws in force. The authorized or official code for federal statutes is called the *U.S. Code.* Some states also have official codes, with varying titles. These official codes contain only the texts of the statutes and the constitutions. There are, however, annotated codes, published commercially, that include the legislative background along with each section of the law, as well as a summary of each court case that has interpreted the law. The two annotated codes for federal laws are the *United States Code Annotated* and *United States Code Service.* There is also an annotated code for each state. A pamphlet insert, called a pocket part, in the back of each volume contains the most current amendments and cases.

Indexes provide access by subject, popular name, or law number. A version of the code and session laws for the U.S. and your home state are available in most academic libraries. A collection of all state codes is usually available only in law school libraries.

Other sources of the federal statutes in the communications area are two looseleaf services, Pike and Fischer *Radio Regulation* and Commerce Clearing House *Trade Regulation Reporter.* These services compile the statutes and other primary materials relevant to many communications issues involving broadcasting and advertising. They are updated regularly, but these sources cannot be relied on for their comprehensiveness, and the codes should be consulted for verification as well as for citing purposes. These services are ordinarily available only in large academic or law school libraries.

"Legislative history" is the term used for the publications generated during the passage of each bill. These materials often shed light on the legislative intent of a particular statute and are sometimes used by the courts for clarification. Legislative history is rarely available for state laws, but can readily be found for federal legislation. Material published in the *Congressional Record,* House and Senate reports, and Congressional hearings are all parts of the legislative history. This material can be found through a variety of indexes available in many academic libraries. Your reference librarian can help you locate the material you need.

regulations

Regulations are the product of agencies. Under authority delegated by the legislature, agencies such as the Federal Communications Commission and the Federal Trade Commission may adopt rules which set policy or establish procedures to be followed for compliance with a statute. Regulations have the force of law and are enforced by the executive agency.

Federal regulations are published as they are issued in a daily publication called the *Federal Register.* They are then compiled annually in the *Code of Federal Regulations.* Its index provides access through subject or agency or authorizing statute, but this index is not particularly thorough, and assistance from a librarian might save time. Because of the somewhat complex updating system, finding the most current material is difficult in this source. Currency is essential, and care must be taken to find all the material. Both the daily and the annual sources can be found in many academic libraries.

The two looseleaf services in communications, Pike and Fischer *Radio Regulation* and Commerce Clearing House *Trade Regulation Reporter,* do include regulations specific to the issues they cover. Like any looseleaf service, however, they cannot be relied upon for comprehensive coverage, and you should verify your finding in the official source. These looseleaf services are not routinely found in academic libraries, but are available in many law school libraries.

State agency regulations are becoming available in a growing number of states, but often are available only through the issuing agency. A reference librarian can assist you in finding these regulations.

administrative agency decisions

Administrative decisions are the quasi-judicial decisions of the executive agencies. As part of their enforcement responsibilities, agencies hold hearings and may hand down opinions, orders, or decisions clarifying issues or mandating action. The FCC and FTC are the two primary agencies concerned with communications issues.

Federal administrative decisions are published by the individual agencies. Decisions related to communication law can be found in the *Federal Communications Commission Reports* and the *Federal Trade Commission Reports.* Each of these sets of reports includes the full texts of all opinions, as well as orders and decrees of the agency. Although these agencies publish preliminary pamphlets, called advance sheets, containing current decisions, even these may be delayed several months before publication.

For this reason, commercially published looseleaf services are used for the most current agency decisions. Again, those that include communications law issues are Pike and Fischer *Radio Regulation* and Commerce Clearing House *Trade Regulation Reporter.* Although they are not comprehensive sources, most of the important decisions are included in them. These services are not usually held by academic libraries, but are available in many law school libraries. The official version of the decision reports are more likely to be found in academic libraries, particularly those that are depositories for U.S. government publications.

Most states do not routinely distribute the decisions of their administrative agencies. Although some are available for the largest states, most must be obtained directly from the agency.

court decisions

Court decisions are the rulings of the various units of the court system. The decision or judgment of the court is always accompanied by an opinion at the appellate level, but an opinion is only occasionally included with trial-level decisions. At the appellate level, where there is more than one judge, the opinion, if it has the support of the majority of the court, is called the opinion of the court and is offered to clarify the reasoning behind the decision. These opinions provide the courts with the precedents used in subsequent cases. If there is a disagreement on the court regarding the reasons offered to justify the judgment, or even regarding the judgment itself, concurring and/or dissenting opinions are written and signed by the judges who wrote them.

Because of the principle of stare decisis, court decisions form the largest body of legal research materials. Publications called court "Reporters" contain the decisions and opinions of the judges for cases in various jurisdictions. There are thousands of cases reported in these sets each year. However, many cases, although decided, are not reported. The overwhelming majority of cases at the trial level have little or no consequence for anyone beyond the parties involved, therefore there is no value or justification for the expense of publishing them. It is important to remember that although some cases are discussed by the news media at the trial level, since they pertain to a new or budding point of law, it is the rare trial-level case that is available through the standard reporters. Ordinarily, transcripts of these cases can be obtained only from the clerk of the local court where the case was tried.

The court decisions may be published by the state or federal government or by a commercial publishing company. The reporters authorized by the government for publication are called "official" reporters. These reporters, although often preferred for citing purposes, are not different in any substantive way from the commercial or "unofficial" reporters. In actuality, the commercial reporters are often more easily obtained and therefore more commonly held by libraries.

It is important to reiterate here that a court decision is only valid as precedent within the jurisdiction of that court. That is, an Indiana case cannot be used as a precedent for a subsequent New Jersey case; what is ruled in the Second Federal Circuit is not precedent in the Fifth. Cases in other jurisdictions can be used by the courts as a persuasive authority, but they do not control the ruling of courts in other jurisdictions. Finding the appropriate case in the correct jurisdiction is essential to your research.

a short-cut to finding decisions

The field of communications is especially lucky to have several looseleaf services that bring together court cases from all jurisdictions. The service most commonly found in academic libraries is the Bureau of National Affairs' *Media Law Reporter*. It includes the full text of opinions from all U.S. Supreme Court cases dealing with these issues and from most important cases from other jurisdictions. It has an easy-to-use index, as well as a summary or digest of each case included. Its weekly updates include a news section, which discusses new cases in the field, and it also mentions periodical articles on related issues. It is not a totally comprehensive source, but it does include the most important cases in media law. Many academic libraries that cannot afford the great expense of the individual reporters may subscribe to this service.

There are other services that also include statutes, regulations, and some administrative agency decisions. Pike and Fischer *Radio Regulation* and Commerce Clearing House *Trade Regulation Reporter* are the sets that are concerned with issues related to communications. These provide the same access to decisions, but they are often available only in law school libraries.

court reporters—the supreme court

U.S. Supreme Court decisions are published officially in a series called *U.S. Reports.* In addition, two commercial versions are published. The *Supreme Court Reporter,* a publication of West Publishing Company, and the *U.S. Supreme Court Reports, Lawyers' Edition* (commonly called *Lawyers' Edition*) is published by Lawyers' Cooperative Publishing Company. All of these reporters include every U.S. Supreme Court decision. The commercial versions vary only in the kind of supplementary material they include in addition to the opinions.

Prior to the publication of the bound volumes, each of the Supreme Court reporters publishes paperback pamphlets called advance sheets. These advance sheets are issued regularly to provide quick access to recent decisions. The advance sheets have the same pagination that will appear in the final bound volume and can be used and cited in the same way.

Loose-leaf services, such as the Bureau of National Affairs' *U.S. Law Week* and Commerce Clearing House *Supreme Court Bulletin,* also contain the full text of these opinions, sometimes within two weeks of the decision. Academic libraries often subscribe to one of these sources if the reporters are not available.

court reporters—lower federal courts

Decisions of the federal Courts of Appeals and District Courts are available only through commercial court reporters. The most comprehensive of these reporters are published by West. The Court of Appeals decisions are available in the *Federal Reporter.* As part of its jurisdiction, this court hears appeals from the administrative agencies. These appeals are usually, but not always, heard in the District of Columbia circuit.

The District Court, or trial-level, cases can be found in the West's *Federal Supplement,* but it reports only a fraction of the total number of District Court cases. Other sources, such as looseleaf services or computer systems, may contain some cases not available in the West reporters, but there are many that go unreported in any source.

court reporters—the state courts

Most states publish an official reporter for both the Court of Appeals and the Supreme Court. Advance sheets are not ordinarily published, and there is often a considerable delay before the bound volumes are available. For these reasons, the commercial reporters provide the primary access to state court decisions.

The National Reporter System, published by West, is the most inclusive of the reporters. The series includes a group of regional reporters incorporating all the reported cases in the state courts. There are seven regional reporters: Atlantic, Pacific, Southern, Southwestern, Southeastern, Northwestern and Northeastern. The *New York Supplement* and the *California Reporter* have been added to supplement the reporters for the two states with the most active courts. Remember that although the National Reporter System includes all reported cases, this does not mean it includes every state case. There are no trial court cases included, and only a selection of appellate cases. Advance sheets are available for each segment of the National Reporter System, providing current reporting of state cases.

finding decisions by computer

There are a number of computer systems currently available that provide access to legal materials. Two of the most common are *LEXIS* and *WESTLAW*. Both of these systems provide full text searching of court opinions from all jurisdictions for recent years. Some types of searches are better suited than others to computerized searching. Locating opinions written by a certain judge on a particular topic or finding cases on an extremely narrow point of law both lend themselves to this type of research.

The popularity of these systems is growing rapidly, and one or the other is available at most law school libraries. You will do the actual searching, and training is available through simulated programs and video tapes. Restrictions on use will vary, but if a terminal is available, you might ask a librarian if your research should be approached in this way.

Finding Aids

The digest is the most comprehensive subject approach to court decisions. By identifying each of the legal issues discussed in the opinion, the case is summarized or digested, together with others concerned with the same issue. There are a number of digests, ranging from those including all reported cases to those concerned with an individual state. The most important thing to remember when using any digest is to select the digest most appropriate for your needs. Do not use the most comprehensive one when a selective digest will do. A librarian can help you determine the right digest for your research.

Legal encyclopedias are another basic legal research source. They combine a summary of the current case law on an issue with a case finding facet. There are two general legal encyclopedias and one for each state.

Because there are so many cases decided each month, it is difficult to be sure that a particular case is still valid today. It may have been overruled or modified by a later decision. There may also have been cases with similar issues that have altered the interpretation in some way. *Shepard's Citations* provides the judicial history and further court interpretation for all published decisions. There is a series of volumes for each reporter, both official and unofficial, which enables you to (1) locate further appeals or parallel citation of your case; (2) verify the current status of your case by finding out if it has been overruled or upheld by subsequent cases; (3) locate other cases on the same or similar points of law. Ask a librarian how to use it. This source can be found in all law school libraries, but rarely in academic libraries.

The most important thing to remember is that legal research should be approached with confidence. Even though it may seem complex at first, after working with the sources for a while, you will begin to feel more comfortable. Digging into the legal implications of any area takes time, but it can be an interesting, even an exciting, task.

summary

The growing influence of the law has made legal research an essential skill for members of the communications field. Understanding the legal system is the first step toward mastery of this skill.

The legislative, executive, and judicial branches all play a part in the development of the law. The various forms of law—the constitution, statutes, regulations, and administrative and judicial decisions—make up the primary sources to be consulted when determining the law on a specific issue.

The proper strategy is essential for effective legal research, however. By first consulting background material to gain insight on the issues involved, you will get a clear idea of the way to approach your research. Periodical articles and books provide valuable assistance in this task.

The primary sources must then be consulted. Locating the appropriate statutes, the implementing regulations, and the judicial or administrative interpretations are all steps toward a comprehensive search of the law. Many different sources can be consulted along the way, and there are various indexes and finding aids to assist you. Looseleaf services, such as the BNA *Media Law Reporter* or Pike and Fischer *Radio Regulations,* provide short-cuts in your research by compiling primary material such as statutes, regulations and decisions on communication law issues.

additional resources

books: the legal system

Cataldo, B., *Introduction to the Law and the Legal Process,* 2d ed., New York: John Wiley & Sons, 1973.

Franklin, M. A., *The Dynamics of American Law; Courts, the Legal Process and Freedom of Expression,* Mineola, N.Y.: Foundation Press, 1968.

Grilliot, H. J., *Introduction to Law and the Legal System,* 2d ed., Boston: Houghton Mifflin, 1979.

Jewell, M., and S. C. Patterson, *The Legislative Process in the United States,* New York: Random House, 1977.

Keefe, W. J., and M. S. Ogul, *The American Legislative Process; Congress and the States,* 4th ed., Englewood Cliffs, N.J.: Prentice-Hall, 1977.

Murphy, C. F., Jr., *Cases and Materials on Introduction to Law, Legal Process and Procedure,* St. Paul, Minn.: West Publishing Co., 1977.

Reinbar, C., *The Law of the Land; The Evolution of Our Legal System,* New York: Simon & Schuster, 1980.

books: legal research

Cohen, M. L., *How to Find the Law.* 7th ed., St. Paul, Minn.: West Publishing Co., 1976.

Cohen, M. L., *Legal Research in a Nutshell,* 3d ed., St. Paul, Minn.: West Publishing Co., 1978.

Goehlert, R., *Congress and Law Making: Researching the Legislative Process,* Santa Barbara, Calif.: Clio Books, 1979.

Honigsberg, P. J., *Cluing Into Legal Research,* Berkeley, Calif.: Golden Rain Press, 1979.

Jacobstein, J. M., and R. M. Mersky, *Fundamentals of Legal Research,* Mineola, N.Y.: Foundation Press, 1977.

Jacobstein, J. M., and R. M. Mersky, *Legal Research Illustrated,* Mineola, N.Y.: Foundation Press, 1977.

Price, M. O., and H. Bittner, *Effective Legal Research,* 4th ed., Boston: Little, Brown, 1979.

Research Group, Inc., *Basic Legal Research Techniques,* San Mateo, Calif.: American Law Publishing Service, 1975.

Statsky, W., *Legislative Analysis: How to Use Statutes and Regulations,* St. Paul, Minn.: West Publishing Co., 1975.

Introduction

1. Harold L. Nelson and Dwight L. Teeter, Jr., *Law of Mass Communications* (Mineola, N.Y.: Foundation Press, 1973), p. 1.

2. Lee Loevinger, "The Role of Law in Broadcasting," *Journal of Broadcasting* 8 (Spring 1964): 115-117.

3. Ibid.

4. V. Blasi, "The Newsman's Privilege: An Empirical Study," *Michigan Law Review* 70 (December 1971): 233.

5. Loevinger, "Role of Law," pp. 115-17.

1 history and development

1. The Wireless Ship Act of 1910, Public Law 262, 61st Congress, June 24, 1910.

2. The Radio Act of 1912, Public Law 264, 62d Congress, August 13, 1912. Sec. 1.

3. See: Edward F. Sarno, Jr., "The National Radio Conferences," *Journal of Broadcasting* 13 (Spring 1969): 189-202.

4. Ibid. For a summary of the role of the Department of Commerce during this period see: Marvin R. Bensman, "Regulation of Broadcasting by the Department of Commerce, 1921-1927," in Lawrence W. Lichty and Malachi C. Topping, eds., *American Broadcasting: A Source Book on the History of Radio and Television* (New York: Hastings House, 1975), pp. 544-55; see also: Carl H. Butman, "Better Radio Service," *Radio News* 6 (December 1924).

5. *Hoover* v. *Intercity Radio Co., Inc.,* 286 F. 1003 (D.C. Cir), February 25, 1923.

6. *United States* v. *Zenith Radio Corporation* et al., 12 F. 2d 614 (N.D. Ill.), April 16, 1926.

7. Eric Barnouw, *A Tower in Babel: A History of Broadcasting in the United States* (New York: Oxford University Press, 1966), p. 175.

8. Attorney General's Opinion, 35 Ops. Att'y Gen. 126, July 8, 1926.

9. H. Doc. 483, 69th Congress, 2d Session, December 7, 1926.

10. The Radio Act of 1927, Public Law 632, 69th Congress, February 23, 1927, sec. 3.

11. Don R. Le Duc and Thomas A. McCain, "The Federal Radio Commission in Federal Court: Origins of Broadcast Regulatory Doctrines," *Journal of Broadcasting* 14 (Fall 1970), 393-410.

12. Ibid., p. 395.

13. *Technical Radio Laboratory* v. *FRC,* 36 F. 2d 111 (1929). Although not all of the cases challenging the FRC are found in the main body of this text, Le Duc and McCain cite forty-one key cases setting legal precedent for FRC authority. The student or teacher who wishes to engage in detailed research centering on these cases should see the Le Duc and McCain article cited in footnote 11, specifically pages 407-10, or the cases listed in the "Additional Resources" section of Chapter 1.

14. *Carrell* v. *FRC,* 36 F. 2d 117 (1929), as cited in Le Duc and McCain, "The FRC in Federal Court," pp. 396 and 407.

15. *FRC* v. *Nelson Brothers Bond and Mortgage Co. (Station WIBO),* 289 U.S. 266 (1933), as cited in Le Duc and McCain, pp. 396-97 and 409.

16. *Pote (Station WLOE)* v. *FRC,* 67 F. 2d 509 (1933), as cited in Le Duc and McCain, pp. 397 and 410.

17. *Whitehurst* v. *Grimes, Chief of Police,* et al., 21 F. 2d 787 (1927), as cited in Le Duc and McCain, pp. 389 and 407.

18. *United States* v. *Gregg* et al., 5 F. Supp. 848 (1933), as cited in Le Duc and McCain, pp. 398 and 410.

19. Le Duc and McCain, p. 398.

20. *Westinghouse Electric and Manufacturing Co.* v. *FRC,* 47 F. 2d 415 (1931), as cited in Le Duc and McCain, pp. 399 and 408.

21. Le Duc and McCain, p. 399.

22. *Richmond Development* v. *FRC,* 35 F. 2d 883 (1930), as cited in Le Duc and McCain, pp. 400 and 407.

23. *Reading Broadcasting* v. *FRC,* 48 F. 2d 458 (1931), and *Journal Co.* v. *FRC,* 48 F. 2d 461 (1931), as cited in Le Duc and McCain, pp. 401 and 408.

24. *KFKB Broadcasting* v. *Federal Radio Commission,* 47 F. 2d 670 (1931).

25. Ibid.

26. Ibid.

27. *Trinity Methodist Church, South* v. *Federal Radio Commission,* 62 F. 2d 850 (1932).

28. Ibid.

29. Le Duc and McCain, "The FRC in Federal Court," p. 402.

30. Act of July 1, 1930 (4658 at 844).

31. S. Doc. 144, 73d Congress, 2d Session, February 26, 1934—President Franklin D. Roosevelt's message to Congress, suggesting the formation of the Federal Communications Commission.

32. Section 326.

2 the federal communications commission

1. A more general description of the FCC's charge is:

    1. The orderly development and operation of broadcast services and the providing of rapid, efficient nationwide and worldwide telephone and telegraph service at reasonable rates.

    2. The promoting of safety of life and property through radio, and the use of radio and television facilities to strengthen national defense.

    3. Consultation with other Government agencies and departments on national and international matters involving wire and radio communications, and with State regulatory commissions on telephone and telegraph matters.

    4. Regulation of all broadcast services—commercial and educational AM, FM, and TV. This includes approval of all applications for construction permits and licenses for these services, assignment of frequencies, establishment of operating power, designation of call signs, and inspection and regulation of the use of transmitting equipment.

    5. Review of station performance to assure that promises made when a license is issued have been carried out.

    6. Evaluation of stations' performance in meeting the requirement that they operate in the public interest, convenience, and necessity.

    7. Approval of changes in ownership and major technical alterations.

    8. Regulation of cable television through issuance of certificates of compliance before cable systems may begin operation.

    9. Action on requests for mergers and on applications for construction of facilities and changes in service.

    10. The prescribing and reviewing of accounting practices.

    11. Issuance of licenses to, and regulation of, all forms of two-way radio, including ship and aviation communications, a wide range of public safety and business services, and amateur and citizens' radio services.

    12. Responsibility for domestic administration of the telecommunications provisions of treaties and international agreements. Under the auspices of the State Department, the Commission takes part in international communications conferences.

    13. Supervision of the Emergency Broadcast System (EBS), which is designed to alert and instruct the public in matters of national and civil defense. [Source: *FCC Annual Report,* 1974, pp. 2–3]

2. Based on: "The FCC and Broadcasting," FCC Broadcast Bureau Publication #8310-100.

3. "Staged" news events are not considered to be operating in the public interest, however.

4. "The FCC and Broadcasting."

5. A report of the Commission's first open meeting is chronicled in: "Like a Day with the Sunshine at the FCC," *Broadcasting,* 46 (March 28, 1977), 29. Procedural policy was announced in "FCC in the Sunshine," NAB *Highlights,* 3 (March 7, 1977), 2.

6. Nicholas Johnson and John Dystel, "A Day in the Life: The Federal Communications Commission," *Yale Law Journal,* 82 (July 1973), 1575–1634.

7. Ibid.

8. Nicholas Johnson and John Dystel (ibid.) are critical of the rule permitting a maximum of seven

AM, FM, or TV stations to be owned by the same company. What was intended as a "per se maximum" has been converted into a "presumptively permissible number."

9. Ibid.

10. Ibid.

11. See: Lawrence W. Lichty, "Members of the Federal Radio Commission and the Federal Communications Commission 1927–1961," *Journal of Broadcasting* 6 (Winter 1961–1962), 23–24; Lawrence W. Lichty, "The Impact of FRC and FCC Commissioners' Background on the Regulation of Broadcasting," *Journal of Broadcasting* 6 (Spring 1962), 97–110.

12. Wenmouth Williams, Jr., "Impact of Commissioner Background on FCC Decisions: 1962–1975," *Journal of Broadcasting* 20 (Spring 1976), 239–60.

13. As discussed in FCC publications, *FCC Annual Reports, Broadcasting Yearbook,* and "How the FCC Is Organized into Offices and Bureaus," *Communication News* 14 (January 1977), 46–48. "FCC Makes over Broadcast Bureau," *Broadcasting* 45 (April 5, 1976), 53.

14. "FCC Lab Tests Radios for Rule Compliance," *Communications News* 14 (January 1977), 50.

15. *FCC Annual Report,* 1974.

16. The Policy and Rules Division was formed in 1976, as a consolidation of the Rules and Standards Division and the Research and Education Division.

17. The importance of cable as a "developing" medium is evidenced by the presence of two divisions directed toward future growth issues: the Research Division and the Policy Review and Development Division.

18. *FCC Annual Report,* 1974, p. 78.

19. See, for example: Donald M. Gillmor and Jerome A. Barron, *Mass Communication Law* (St. Paul, Minn.: West Publishing Company, 1974), p. 889. Citing: *Richard Sneed, 15 P. & F. Radio Reg. 158 (1967).*

20. As reported in *Broadcasting* 46 (June 20, 1977), 68.

21. *FCC Annual Report,* 1974, pp. 37–38.

22. See: Charles Clift, III, Fredric A. Weiss, and John D. Abel, "Ten Years of Forfeitures by the Federal Communications Commission," *Journal of Broadcasting* 15 (Fall 1971), 379–85.

23. Ibid. Categories are as defined in the Communications Act. The period covered was 1961 through June 1971.

24. Authority granted by the same statute that permits forfeitures.

25. *FCC Annual Report,* 1974, p. 37.

26. Maurice E. Shelby, Jr., "Short-Term License Renewals: 1960–1972," *Journal of Broadcasting* 18 (Summer 1974), 277–88.

27. Ibid., 282.

27a. Originally prepared for the Virginia Association of Broadcasters and released as an NAB *Counsel* memorandum.

28. Johnson and Dystel, "A Day in The Life," 1575–1634.

29. Ibid.

30. Erwin G. Krasnow and Lawrence D. Longley, *The Politics of Broadcast Regulation* (New York: St. Martin's Press, 1973), p. 25.

31. Ibid.

32. Marc C. Franklin, *The First Amendment and the Fourth Estate* (Mineola, N.Y.: Foundation Press, 1977), pp. 465–66.

33. Ibid., p. 466. It is interesting to note that, although not adhering to "regional" assignments of frequencies on a domestic scale, international agreements on frequency management are regional. This points out the peculiar nature of the electromagnetic spectrum as a resource. When the overall territory (the world) is big enough, regional allocations are practical. Moreover, the political realities of trying to localize spectrum management on a world scale makes the task almost prohibitive.

34. *A Study of the Federal Communications Commission's Equal Employment Opportunity Regulation—An Agency in Search of a Standard* (Washington, D.C.: Citizens' Communications Center, 1976).

35. *Window Dressing on the Set: Women and Minorities in Television* (Washington, D.C.: United States Commission on Civil Rights, 1977).

36. Joseph A. Grundfest, *Citizen Participation in FCC Decision Making* (Santa Monica, Calif.: Rand Corp., 1976).

37. Erwin G. Krasnow and Lawrence D. Longley, *The Politics of Broadcast Regulation,* p. 24.

38. Robert R. Smith and Paul T. Prince, "WHDH: The Unconscionable Delay," *Journal of Broadcasting* 18 (Winter 1973–74), 85–86.

39. See also: Sterling Quinlan, *The Hundred Million Dollar Lunch* (Chicago: J. Philip O'Hara, 1974), p. 4.

40. "FCC Berated for Policy on Stockholdings of the Employees," *Broadcasting* 46 (May 30, 1977), 8, 30.

41. Johnson and Dystel, "A Day in The Life," 1575–1634.

3 allied agencies

1. *Your FTC: What It Is and What It Does* (Washington, D.C.: Federal Trade Commission, 1977).

2. Ibid., p. 19.

3. Ibid., p. 17.

4. Ibid., p. 16.

5. Ibid., pp. 13–15.

6. Ibid., pp. 14–15.

7. Ibid., p. 25.

8. Ibid., p. 26.

9. "The FTC Advertising Review Process," *Advertising Age* 48 (July 11, 1977), 142.

10. *Your FTC,* p. 26.

11. *Telecommunication,* without the "s," commonly refers to the "process" of information transfer. The term *telecommunications* refers not only to the process but also to the industries and to the components of those industries that are in some way related to the process.

12. Executive Order #11556, Reorganization Plan No. 1 of 1970, September 4, 1970, Richard M. Nixon, President of the United States (section 2).

13. Ibid. (section 13).

14. Ibid. (section 14).

15. Remarks of Clay T. Whitehead, Director, Office of Telecommunications Policy, Executive Office of the President, Meeting of the Indianapolis Chapter of the Society of Professional Journalists-Sigma Delta Chi, December 18, 1972 (copy of the address provided by the OTP).

16. Office of Telecommunications Policy, *Activities and Programs 1975–1976,* p. 5.

17. Office of Telecommunications: U.S. Department of Commerce, *Progress Report 1976,* p. 22.

18. Ibid., p. 5.

19. Ibid., p. 9.

20. Ibid., pp. 11–12.

21. The initials correspond to the French identification of the organizations.

22. *Progress Report 1976,* pp. 13–14.

23. Ibid., pp. 20–28.

24. Most helpful in the preparation of material on the U.S. Department of Justice was attorney Kenneth Robinson of the Department. His efforts on the author's behalf in providing information are gratefully acknowledged. In addition, Linda Cobb-Reiley's paper, "The Department of Justice and the Federal Communications Commission: Interactions and Conflicts in the Formulation of a Newspaper-Television Station Cross-Ownership Policy," presented at the 1978 annual meeting of the Association for Education in Journalism, proved very helpful and is quoted extensively in this chapter.

25. Congress passed the McFarland Act in 1952, 47 U.S.C. 310b (1953), assuring that transferees would be considered as if they were the sole applicants. Thus, the Act minimizes scrutiny of the buyer's media holdings.

26. Donald I. Baker, "The Antitrust Division, Department of Justice: The Role of Competition in Regulated Industries," *Boston College Industrial and Commercial Law Review* (1970), pp. 571–93. Also see American Broadcasting Company, 7 F.C.C. 2d 245 (1966), and American Broadcasting Company, 9 F.C.C. 2d 546, 699 (1967).

27. Baker, "The Antitrust Division," pp. 579–80.

28. 1968 BNA Antitrust and Trade Regulation Reports No. 357, A-12; Beaumont Broadcasting Corp., 13 F.C.C. 2d 989 (1968).

29. Frontier Broadcasting Company, 21 F.C.C. 2d 570 (1968).

30. Baker, "The Antitrust Division," p. 579, note 57; 1968 Trade Cases, Sec. 72, 644 (January 6, 1969).

31. U.S. Federal Communications Commission, *Further Notice of Proposed Rulemaking*, 22 F.C.C. 2d 339 (1970).

32. *Broadcasting*, March 11, 1974, p. 42.

33. The cities were Des Moines, St. Louis, Minneapolis, Topeka, Salt Lake City, Fresno, and Spokane. See 1974 BNA Antitrust and Trade Regulation Report No. 645, A-14; 1974 BNA Antitrust and Trade Regulation Report No. 662, A-11.

34. Walter S. Baer, Henry Geller, Joseph A. Grundfest, and Karen Possner, *Concentration of Mass Media Ownership: Assessing the State of Current Knowledge* (Santa Monica, Calif.: Rand Corp., No. R-1584-NSF, 1974), p. 26.

35. See testimony of Attorney General William Saxbe, Deputy Attorney General Laurence H. Silberman, and Assistant Attorney General Thomas E. Kauper, U.S. Senate, Committee on Appropriations, *State, Justice, Commerce, the Judiciary, and Related Agencies Appropriations, Part 1*. 93d Cong., 2d sess., 1974, pp. 177–80, 279–81. Also see Statement of Deputy Assistant Attorney General Bruce B. Wilson, U.S. Senate, *Broadcast License Renewal Act, Hearings before the Subcommittee on Communications of the Committee on Commerce, Part 1*. 93d Cong., 2d sess., 1974, pp. 131–34.

36. Ibid.

37. Testimony of Assistant Attorney General Thomas E. Kauper, *State, Justice, Commerce, the Judiciary, and Related Agencies Appropriations*, p. 279.

38. Richard E. Cohen, "Justice Report/Antitrust Division Emerges as a Major Regulatory Watchdog," *National Journal*, June 15, 1974, p. 878.

39. Ibid., p. 879.

40. Ibid.

41. *OTA Priorities 1979*, Washington, D.C.: *Office of Technology Assessment*, p. i.

42. Ibid., p. 15.

43. Ibid., p. 19.

44. Ibid.

45. "DCA is the Key Link in Military Communications Systems," *Communications News* 15 (July 1978), 52–55.

46. Ibid., p. 52.

47. Ibid., p. 54.

48. Discussions of the history, organization, function, and issues facing ITU can be found in: David M. Leive, *International Telecommunications and International Law: The Regulation of the Radio Spectrum* (Dobbs Ferry, N.Y.: A. W. Sijthoff, Leyden, and Oceana Publications, 1971); John and Mary R. Markle Foundation and the Twentieth Century Fund, eds., *Global Communications in the Space Age: Toward a New ITU* (New York: John and Mary R. Markle Foundation and the Twentieth Century Fund, 1972).

49. Harold K. Jacobson, "The International Telecommunication Union: ITU's Structures and Functions," in John and Mary R. Markle Foundation and the Twentieth Century Fund, eds., *Global Communications in the Space Age: Toward a New ITU* (New York: John and Mary R. Markle Foundation and the Twentieth Century Fund, 1972), p. 40.

50. Final Protocol, Documents of the Berlin Preliminary Conference (1903), pp. 83–85, as cited in Leive, *International Telecommunications*. The thrust of the protocol agreement is carried throughout contemporary broadcast regulation.

51. International Telecommunication Convention (Montreux, 1965). See also: Jacobson, "The ITU," pp. 40–41.

52. *United Nations Yearbook* 27 (1973), 955.

53. As discussed in Leive, *International Communications*, pp. 32–40; and *Global Communications*, pp. 6–7.

54. *Global Communications*, pp. 8–9.

1. For the early development of legal precedent in the area of regulating obscene, indecent, and profane programming, see: James Walter Wesolowski, "Obscene, Indecent, or Profane Broadcast Language as Construed by the Federal Courts," *Journal of Broadcasting* 13 (Spring 1969), 203–19.

2. Title 18, United States Code (Codified June 25, 1948, Ch. 645, 62 Stat. 769).

3. *Regina* v. *Hicklin*, L.R. 3 QB. 360 (1868). For a discussion of the *Hicklin* case, see: Donald M. Gillmor and Jerome A. Barron, *Mass Communication Law* (St. Paul, Minn.: West Publishing Co., 1974), pp. 329–30.

4. In particular: Ex parte *Jackson*, 96 U.S. 727 (1878): *United States* v. *Bennett*, 24 Fed. Cas. 1093 (N.Y.S.D. 1879); *United States* v. *Harmon*, 45 F. 414 (D.C. Kan, 1891) rev'd 50 F. 921 (C.C.); *People* v. *Friede*, 133 Misc. 611, 233 N.Y.S. 565 (1929).

5. Weakening of the *Hicklin* decision is seen in: *United States* v. *Kennerley*, 209 F. 119 (S.D.N.Y. 1913); *Halsey* v. *New York Society for the Suppression of Vice*, 191 App. Div. 245, 180 N.Y.S. 836 (1920); *United States* v. *Dennett*, 39 F. 2d 564 (2d Cir. 1930).

6. *Duncan* v. *United States*, 48 F. 2d 128 (1931).

7. 48 F. 2d 128, 132, as cited in Wesolowski, "Obscene, Indecent, or Profane Broadcast Language."

8. Ibid.

9. *United States* v. *Levine*, 83 F. 2d 156 (2d Cir. 1936), as cited in Gillmor and Barron, *Mass Communication Law*, p. 330.

10. *Roth* v. *United States*, 354 U.S. 476, 77 S.Ct. 1304, 1 L.Ed. 2d 1498 (1957). Decided at the same time was *Alberts* v. *State of California*.

11. *Ginsberg* v. *State of New York*, 390 U.S. 629, 634, 88 S.Ct. 1274, 1277 (1968).

12. In re *Palmetto Broadcasting Company (WDKD)*.

13. *Robinson* v. *F.C.C.*, 334 F. 2d 584 (1964).

14. In re *WHUY–FM Eastern Educational Radio*, 24 F.C.C. 2d 408 (1970).

15. Sonderling Broadcasting Corporation, WGLD-FM, 27 Radio Reg. 2d 285 (F.C.C., 1973). The appeals case affirming the FCC ruling is: *Illinois Citizens' Committee for Broadcasting* v. *Federal Communications Commission*, 515 F. 2d 397 (D.C. Cir. 1975). The *Ginzburg* ruling cited in the text is *Ginzburg* v. *United States*, 383 U.S. 463, 86 S. Ct. 942, 16 L.Ed. 2d 31 (1966). See also: Charles Feldman and Stanley Tickton, "Obscene/Indecent Programming: Regulation of Ambiguity," *Journal of Broadcasting* 20 (Spring 1976), 273–82.

16. *Pacifica Foundation*, 56 F.C.C. 2d 94 (1975).

17. Ibid.

18. *Pacifica Foundation* v. *Federal Communications Commission*, U.S. Court of Appeals, District of Columbia, CA, No. 75-1391, March 16, 1977. Also see footnote 7 of the decision and Amicus's Brief, quoting statement of John A. Schneider before the House Subcommittee on Communications, July 15, 1975, p. 9.

19. Ibid., footnote 19 of the *Pacifica* decision.

20. *Miller* v. *State of California* is widely used in arguing the applicability of local community ordinances to everything from magazine stands to movies.

21. "Programming of Violent, Indecent and Obscene Material," *Broadcast Management/Engineering* 11 (June 1975), pp. 22, 24, 25.

22. "Origins of the Format Change Controversy," *Broadcasting* 45 (August 2, 1976), 21. *Citizens' Committee to save WEFM* v. *FCC*, 506 F. 2d 246 (D.C. Cir. 1974); *Citizens' Committee to Preserve the Voice of the Arts in Atlanta* v. *F.C.C.*, 436 F. 2d 263 (D.C. Cir. 1970).

23. "FCC Defends Licensee Right to Choose Radio Formats," *Broadcasting* 45 (August 2, 1976), 21.

24. "FCC Urged to Take Another Look at Its Format Ruling," *Broadcasting* 45 (September 6, 1976), 42.

25. FCC, Docket No. 19743, Inquiry into Subscription Agreements between Radio Broadcast Stations and Musical Format Service Companies. Adopted: November 4, 1975; released November 7, 1975, p. 8.

26. *Third Report and Order* in Docket No. 19622, FCC 75-542, May 13, 1975. The different times result from different network feed times to affiliates in the various time zones. For two perspectives on the sports antiblackout issue, see: Ira Horowitz, "Sports Telecasts: Rights and Regulations,"

Journal of Communication 27 (Summer 1977), 160–68; and John J. Siegfried and C. Elton Hinshaw, "Professional Football and the Anti-Blackout Law," *Journal of Communication* 27 (Summer 1977), 169–74.

27. *National Association of Independent Television Producers and Distributors* et al. v. *F.C.C.*, CA No. 75-4021, April 21, 1975.

28. A commercial should be registered as a copyrighted work, however.

29. Except for cable radio retransmission, the disc jockey's program would typically be copyrighted if it were placed in syndication.

30. Most publishing contracts and other copyright agreements do provide for monies received from the sale (performance) of the work to go to the beneficiaries of the deceased automatically.

31. Copies can also be made for security purposes.

32. Archibald Cox, in a speech delivered to the Anti-Defamation League of B'nai B'rith, New York, December 7, 1976.

33. As in the case of Gerald Ford on a tax-cut issue: Source: Associated Press, October 7, 1975.

34. Section 73.120 of the Communications Act of 1934. Two publications have updated rules and regulations and have provided guidelines to broadcasters in interpreting Section 315. These are: "Uses of Broadcast and Cablecast Facilities by Candidates for Public Office," Fed. Reg. 5796; and "Licensee Responsibility under Amendments to the Communications Act of 1971," FCC *Public Notice,* June 5, 1974, 47 FCC 516 (1974).

35. *Farmers' Educational and Cooperative Union of America, North Dakota Division,* v. *WDAY,* 89 N. W. 2d 102, 109 (N.D. 1958).

36. *Farmers' Educational and Cooperative Union of America* v. *WDAY, Inc.,* 360 U.S. 525, 79 S.Ct. 1302, 3 L.Ed. 2d 1407 (1959).

37. "RTNDA files Amicus Brief in Connecticut Broadcast Case," *RTNDA Communicator* 31 (May 1977).

38. "Reinterpretation of Equal Time Passes First Court Challenge," *Broadcasting* 45 (April 19, 1976), 26–27.

39. For example, exempting Kennedy and Nixon in 1960. 74 Sta. 554 (1960).

40. Associated Press, April 27, 1976.

41. "NAB Supports Your Right to Delay Political Broadcasts," *NAB Highlights,* 3 (March 28, 1977), 1.

42. "RTNDA Says Coverage of Political Debates Should Not Be Limited," *RTNDA Communicator,* 31 (April 1977), 6. The brief was in the case of *United Church of Christ* v. *F.C.C.*

43. *McCarthy* v. *Federal Communications Commission,* 390 f. 2d 471 (D.C. Cir. 1968).

44. *Political Broadcast Catechism,* 8th ed. (Washington, D.C.: National Association of Broadcasters, 1976), p. 7.

45. "Hooks Wants FCC off the Fence on Section 315," *Broadcasting,* 31 (May 16, 1977), 36–38.

46. Associated Press, May 6, 1977. "Political Candidates Set Back by F.C.C. on Broadcast Time," *New York Times* (May 7, 1977), p. 28 (italics added).

47. Ibid.

48. "Use of Broadcast and Cablecast Facilities by Candidates for Public Office," FCC *Public Notice,* March 16, 1972; 37 *Fed. Reg.* 5804 (March 21, 1972).

48a. "FCC Overturned on Lowest Units for Politicians," *Broadcasting* 49 (October 27, 1980), 46.

48b. "Double Jeopardy for Networks in C-M Decision," *Broadcasting* 49 (March 17, 1980), 29–30.

49. "FCC says Public Stations Must Give 'Reasonable' Amount of Access to Candidates," *Broadcasting,* 45 (November 1, 1976), 53–54.

50. "Use of Broadcast and Cablecast Facilities by Candidates for Public Office." FCC *Public Notice,* March 16, 1972; 37 *Fed. Reg.* 5805 (March 21, 1972).

5 the fairness doctrine

1. *In the Matter of Editorializing by Broadcast Licensees,* 13 FCC 1246, June 1, 1949.

2. *Great Lakes Broadcasting Co.,* 3 FRC Ann. Rep. 32 (1929), modified on other grounds, 37, F. 2d 993 (D.C. Cir.) certiorari dismissed, 281 U.S. 706 (1930); as cited in Franklin, p. 601.

3. *In the Matter of the Mayflower Broadcasting Corporation and the Yankee Network, Inc. (WAAB),* 8 FCC 333, 338, January 16, 1941.

4. Ibid.

5. Ibid.

6. In re *United Broadcasting Co. (WHKC),* 10 FCC 515 June 26, 1945.

7. In re *Petition of Robert Harold Scott for Revocation of Licenses of Radio Stations KOW, KPO and KFRC,* 11 FCC 372, July 19, 1946.

8. *In the Matter of Editorializing by Broadcast Licensees,* 13 FCC 1246, June 1, 1949.

9. "Applicability of the Fairness Doctrine in the Handling of Controversial Issues of Public Importance," 29 *Fed. Reg.* 10416 (July 25, 1964).

10. Ibid.

11. Ibid.

12. *Red Lion Broadcasting Co.* v. *Federal Communications Commission,* 127 U.S. App. D.C. 129, 381 F. 2d 908 (1967). *Red Lion Broadcasting Co., Inc.* v. *Federal Communications Commission; United States* v. *Radio-Television News Directors' Association,* 395 U.S. 367, 89 S.Ct. 1794, 23 L.Ed. 2d 371 (1969). The cases are well documented in numerous legal texts. The reader is referred to the latest edition of Gillmor and Barron, *Mass Communication Law,* for a detailed discussion—as well as an informative one—of pertinent questions surrounding the decision. (Further citations of the case in this book are listed as *Red Lion*).

13. *Radio-Television News Directors' Association* v. *United States,* 400 F. 2d 1002 (7th Cir. 1968).

14. *Red Lion.*

15. "Broadcast Licensees Advised concerning Stations' Responsibilities under the Fairness Doctrine as to Controversial Issue Programming," FCC 63-734, July 25, 1963.

16. FCC Rules: 73.123 (AM); 73.300 (FM); 73.598 (Noncommercial Educational FM); and 73.679 (TV). All carry the same wording.

17. "FCC Extends Rule on Personal Attacks," *Broadcasting* 45 (August 9, 1976), 39.

18. *FCC Annual Report,* 1974, p. 18.

19. "Fairness Case Goes against Eight California Radio Stations," *Broadcasting,* 45 (May 24, 1976), 40, 42. A discussion of the legal aspects of editorial advertising is found in Milan D. Meeske, "Editorial Advertising and the First Amendment," *Journal of Broadcasting* 17 (Fall 1973), 417–26.

20. Associated Press, March 22, 1976.

21. *FCC Annual Report,* 1974, p. 19.

22. Ibid.

23. Frederick W. Ford and Lee G. Lovett, "Fairness Doctrine: 1974 Part II," *Broadcast Management/Engineering* 10 (November 1974), 20, footnote 2. Also, *FCC Annual Report,* 1974, p. 19.

24. Gillmor and Barron, *Mass Communication Law,* p. 834.

25. *Brandywine–Mainline Radio, Inc.* v. *Federal Communications Commission,* 473 F. 2d 16 (D.C. Cir. 1972). The case is also studied as an example of group defamation under the Fairness Doctrine (Gillmor and Barron, *Mass Communication Law,* p. 846).

26. Gillmor and Barron, *Mass Communication Law,* p. 846.

27. *Brandywine–Mainline Radio, Inc.* v. *Federal Communications Commission.* Also cited in the FCC's 1974 "Fairness Report."

28. *In the Matter of the Handling of Public Issues under the Fairness Doctrine and the Public Interest Standards of the Communications Act,* 30 FCC 2d 26 (1971).

29. *In the Matter of the Handling of Public Issues under the Fairness Doctrine and the Public Interest Standards of the Communications Act,* 48 FCC 2d 1 30 R.R. 2d 1261; "Fairness Doctrine and Public."

30. *Healey* v. *F.C.C.,* 148 vs. App. D.C. 409 (1972).

31. *Memorandum Opinion and Order on Reconsideration of Fairness Doctrine,* 36 R.R. 2d 1021 (1976).

32. Julian Goodman, "Freedom the First Priority," speech delivered to the Anti-Defamation League Dinner in Atlanta, Georgia, December 6, 1975.

33. Joseph L. Brechner, "A Statement on the 'Fairness Doctrine'," *Journal of Broadcasting* 9 (Spring 1965), 109. In the *Journal* article, Brechner's quote is in italics.

34. Herbert W. Hobler, "The Fair Less Doctrine," speech delivered to the New Jersey Broadcasters' Association's annual convention, Wildwood Crest, New Jersey, June 25, 1975.

35. Recommendations of the Communications Law Committee, Section on Science and Technology, American Bar Association, "Electronic Journalism and First Amendment Problems," *Federal Communications Bar Journal* 29 (November 1, 1976), 10.

36. Ibid., p. 9. *Miami Herald Publishing Co.* v. *Tornilla,* 418 U.S. 241, 258 (1974).

37. Recommendations of the Communications Law Committee.

38. Ibid., p. 15.

6 the broadcast press

1. *Gitlow* v. *New York,* 268 U.S. 652, 666 (1925). The reference was a "casual statement not necessary to the decision." Source: Donald M. Gillmor and Jerome A. Barron, *Mass Communication Law* (St. Paul, Minn.: West Publishing Co., 1974), p. 1. Readers interested in in-depth treatment of the broad field of journalism and law can consult: Gillmor and Barron, *Mass Communication Law* (St. Paul: West Publishing Co., 1979); Marc A. Franklin. *The First Amendment and the Fourth Estate* (Mineola, N.Y.: Foundation Press, 1977); Harold L. Nelson and Dwight L. Teeter, Jr., *Law of Mass Communications* (Mineola, N.Y.: Foundation Press, 1978).

2. Eric Sevareid, in a speech delivered at the "First Amendment Confrontation," during the 55th Annual Convention of the National Association of Broadcasters, March 28, 1977.

3. Paley's remark was quoted by Archibald Cox during a speech by Cox to the Anti-Defamation League of B'nai B'rith, on the occasion of Paley's receiving the First Amendment Freedoms Award, December 7, 1976, in New York City.

4. *CBS* v. *the Democratic National Committee,* 412 U.S. 94 (1973); William Small, "The First Amendment/Radio and Television: Treated Like Distant Cousins," *The Quill* (September 1976), p. 32.

5. "State Court Holds Free-Press Rights Are Applicable to Broadcasting," *Broadcasting* 45 (April 12, 1976), 59.

6. Ibid., p. 59.

7. The Communications Act of 1934, Public Law 416, 73d Congress, June 19, 1934, amended. Additional perspectives on the First Amendment's relationship to the Communications Act are found in: "Electronic Journalism and First Amendment Problems: Recommendations of Communications Law Committee, Section on Science and Technology, American Bar Association," *Federal Communications Bar Journal* 29 (1976), 1–62.

8. *Rideau* v. *Louisiana,* 373 U.S. 723, 10 L.Ed. 2d 663, 83 S. Ct. 1417 (1963).

9. *Estes* v. *State of Texas,* 381 U.S. 532, 85 S.Ct. 1628, 14 L.Ed. 2d 543 (1965). The reader wishing a good current discussion of issues surrounding cameras in court can consult the Florida Guidelines: *In re Petition of Post-Newsweek Stations,* 5 Med. L. Rptr. 1047.

10. "Cameras in the Courtroom," *The Quill* 63 (April, 1975), 25.

11. "Georgia Supreme Court Lets Cameras In," *Broadcasting* 46 (September 26, 1977), 51.

12. Ibid.

13. Ibid.

14. Depending on a particular state's "degree of openness."

15. "Law Poll: Lawyers Aren't Convinced that TV Belongs in Courtrooms," *American Bar Association Journal* 65 (September 1979), 1306, 1308.

16. *Congressional Record,* 62 (1922) 3130. As cited in Ronald Garay, "Implementing Televised Coverage of Sessions of the U.S. Congress," *Journalism Quarterly* 55 (Autumn 1978), 527. Garay's article is an excellent historical review of the development of live radio and television coverage of the U.S. House of Representatives.

17. *Congressional Record,* 119 (1974) 42724, as cited in Garay, "Implementing Televised Coverage," p. 529.

18. U.S. Congress, *Broadcasting House and Senate Proceedings.* Interim Report of the Joint Committee on Congressional Operations on Congress and Mass Communications, 93rd Congress, 2d Session, 1974 (Sen. Rept. No. 93-1275), p. 20, as cited in Garay, "Implementing Televised Coverage," p. 530.

19. Ibid., p. 19. Garay, "Implementing Televised Coverage," p. 530.

20. "The House Will Let Cameras In," *Broadcasting* 46 (October 31, 1977), 25.

21. Ibid.

22. Ibid.

23. "House Blacks Out Votes as Coverage by Cameras Begins," *Broadcasting* 45 (March 26, 1976), 100–02.

24. Ibid.

25. "In-House Television," *Broadcasting* 48 (September 24, 1979), 61.

26. Ibid.

27. Illinois Commerce Commission, Release #IL.C.C. . . . 064-77, August 24, 1977.

28. John B. Adams, *State Open Meeting Laws: An Overview* (Columbia, Mo.: Freedom of Information Foundation), 1974.

29. Ibid.

30. Ibid., pp. 24–29.

31. Section 1. IC 1971, 34-3-5-1, 1973. See also: John R. Bittner, "Politics and Information Flow: The Oregon Shield Law," *Western Speech* 39 (Winter 1975), 51–59; *Shield Laws: A Report on Freedom of the Press, Protection of News Sources and the Obligation to Testify,* Lexington Council of State Governments, Kentucky: 1973; D. Eshelman and A. Barbour, "Legal References on Newsmen and Compulsory Disclosure," *Journal of Broadcasting* 17 (Winter 1972–73), 37–50; V. Blasi, "The Newsman's Privilege: An Empirical Study," *Michigan Law Review* 70 (December 1971), 229–35, 284. Recent cases which dealt with the confidentiality include *State* v. *Bachanan,* 250 Oregon 244, 436 p. 2d 729, cert. denied, 392 U.S. 905, 88 S.Ct. 2055, 20 L.Ed. 2d 1363 (1968), which involved the editor of a student newspaper; and *Branzburg* v. *Hayes in the Matter of Pappas and United States* v. *Caldwell,* 408 U.S. 665, 92 S.Ct. 2646, 33 L.Ed. 2d 626 (1972), concerning a reporter who authored a story about a chemical process changing marijuana into hashish.

32. Roger M. Grace "The Courts v. the News Media: Is the Conflict Necessary?" *Case and Comment* 79 (March–April 1974), 3–10; Tom Petersen, "Gag Orders in Iowa Reversed through Media Pressure," *RTNDA Communicator* 30 (July 1976), 6; Stan Crock, "A Flurry of Gag Rules," *The Quill* 62 (March 1974), 21–23; Lyle Denniston, "What Next for Burger's Nebraska Loophole?" *The Quill* 65 (May 1977), 24–25.

33. *Gannett Company, Inc.* v. *DePasquale,* United States Supreme Court, 1979. State courts were quick to jump on the bandwagon, citing the case as a precedent.

34. "High Court Rules Defendant Rights Supersede Those of Press, Public," *Broadcasting* 48 (July 9, 1979), 46.

35. Ibid.

36. Ibid.

37. Ibid.

38. "Nothing Sacred," *Broadcasting* 47 (June 12, 1978), 82.

39. Privacy Protection Act, 1980. Especially helpful in the preparation of the section on Search and Seizure was NAB Counsel, L-029 available to the author in the final stages of this manuscript's preparation.

40. Ibid.

41. Ibid.

42. *Hugo Zacchini* v. *Scripps-Howard Broadcasting Company,* United States Supreme Court, 1977, 2 Med. L. Rptr. 2089.

7 regulating commercial programming

1. *Head* v. *New Mexico Board of Examiners in Optometry,* 374 U.S. 424 (1963). As cited in: Robert P. Sadowski, "Broadcasting and State Statutory Laws," *Journal of Broadcasting* 18 (Fall 1974), 435.

2. Ibid.

3. Ibid.

4. *NAB Highlights* 3 (May 9, 1977), 4. Station liability for deceptive advertising is discussed in: Leon C. Smith, "Local Station Liability for Deceptive Advertising," *Journal of Broadcasting* 25 (Winter 1970–71), 107–12.

5. Earl W. Kinter, *Michigan Law Review* 64 (May 1966), 1280–81 (reprinted by permission).

6. *Federal Trade Commission* v. *Colgate-Palmolive Co.,* 380 U.S. 374, 85 S.Ct. 1035 (1965). See also: Harold L. Nelson and Dwight L. Teeter, Jr., *Law of Mass Communications* (Mineola, N.Y.: Foundation Press, 1973), pp. 537–40.

7. "Firestone Agrees to Pay for Remedial Ads," *Broadcasting* 45 (February 23, 1976), 73.

8. "Williams Settles with FTC over Geritol Ads," *Broadcasting* 45 (January 19, 1976), 45.

9. Ibid.

10. Such hearings and lobbying can be substantial, and can include efforts on behalf of broadcasters, advertising agencies, food companies, and even the FCC concerning jurisdictional questions.

11. The FTC is still optimistic, pointing to the decision of Congress to ban cigarette advertising on television and radio.

12. Enforcement of every commercial on the air is difficult, however, especially when program-length commercials are involved.

13. The FCC's latest statement on sponsorship identification is found in: "Applicability of Sponsorship Identification Rules," dated May 6, 1963 (40 FCC 141), as modified by *Public Notice,* dated April 21, 1975 (FCC 75-418).

14. "Remote Broadcasts—Avoiding Program-Length Commercials," *NAB Counsel* L-615 (December 1976), 2.

15. See: "Applicability of Fraudulent Billing Rule," (FCC 70-513), 35 FR 7906, May 18, 1970.

15a. See: B. Fox, "Points of Law," *Radioactive,* 3 (April 1977), 6–7.

16. Federal Election Campaign Act of 1971, amended May 11, 1976. Public Law 94-283, Section 323.

17. *McIntire* v. *Wm. Penn Broadcasting Co.,* 151 F. 2d 597. A discussion on refusal rights of broadcasters can be found in: John Summers, "Saying 'No' Legally," *Radioactive* 2 (May 1976), 6–7.

18. Title 27, Section 7.54 (c). A good discussion of the Code and legal issues surrounding advertising of hard liquor is found in *Perry's Broadcasting and the Law* 6 (September 15, 1976), 1–2.

19. "New Rules for Advertising 'Sound Alike' Recordings," *Memorandum:* NAB Legal Department, L-605 (June 1976), pp. 1–2.

20. United Press International, November 11, 1974.

21. Correspondence of January 10, 1975, between Ian Connerty, research assistant to Lloyd Francis, M.P., and Professor Wilson Brian Key, of the University of Western Ontario. House of Commons, Ottawa, Ontario, January 10, 1975.

22. FCC *Public Notice,* March 1974, as cited in NAB Legal Memorandum, "License-conducted Contests," October 1976 (L-612).

23. Section 73.1216, effective October 26, 1976.

24. FCC 75-127, 29849. In re Applications of Star Stations of Indiana, Inc., for Renewal of Licenses of WIFE and WIFE-FM, Indianapolis, Indiana (Docket No. 19122); Indianapolis Broadcasting, Inc., for a Construction Permit for a Standard Broadcast Station, Indianapolis, Indiana (Docket No. 19123); Central States Broadcasting, Inc., for Renewal of Licenses of KOIL and KOIL-FM, Omaha, Nebraska (Docket No. 19124); Star Broadcasting, Inc., for Renewal of License of KISN, Vancouver, Washington (Docket No. 19125).

25. Ibid., p. 18.

26. Ibid.

27. Ibid.

28. Ibid.

29. FCC Rules, Section 73.112 (AM), 73.292 (FM), 73.656 (TV).

30. A discussion of lottery regulations up to 1974 is found in: *Broadcasting and the Federal Lottery Laws* (Washington, D.C.: National Association of Broadcasters, 1974).

31. FCC Rept. #14492. A case example of the concept is found in "Lotteries," *Perry's Broadcasting and the Law* 6 (October 15, 1976), 3–4.

32. Title 18, United States Code, Section 1304.

33. FCC Rules, Section 73.112 (AM), 73.292 (FM), 73.656 (TV).

34. "Promotions for Savings Accounts May Be Illegal," *Broadcasting* 46 (March 28, 1977), 75.

35. *Ohio Quests, Inc.,* 8 FCC 2d 859 (1967).

36. *Laury Associates, Inc.,* 27 FCC 2d 870 (1971).

37. *University of Florida,* 40 FCC 2d 188 (1973).

38. FCC 75-1018 (36929). In re Applications of United Television Company, Inc. (WFAN-TV) Washington, D.C., for Renewal of License (Docket No. 18559), United Television Company, Inc. (WFAN-TV) Washington, D.C. (Docket No. 18561), for Construction Permit (Docket No. 18561); United Broadcasting Company, Inc. (WOOK) Washington, D.C., for Renewal of License (Docket No. 18562); Washington Community Broadcasting Co., Washington, D.C., for Construction Permit for New Standard Broadcast Station (Docket No. 18563). Adopted September 9, 1975; Released September 12, 1975.

39. *New Jersey State Lottery Commission* v. *U.S.,* 29 RR 2d 157 (CA 3d, 1974). The development of the revised lottery statute is discussed in: Frederick W. Ford and Lee G. Lovett, "Lottery Information Broadcasts," *Broadcast Management/Engineering* 11 (October 1975), 22, 24.

8 the station

1. A Cedar Rapids, Iowa, station came under criticism from two competitors for calling itself "Eastern Iowa's Leading News Station." The station claimed that one rating service had verified its claim, while the competitors claimed that two other surveys refuted it. A complaint against the station was filed with the FCC by the competitors. (Source: Correspondence to the FCC from Edgar F. Czarra, of the law firm of Covington and Burling, Washington, D.C., representing the station, September 9, 1976).

2. Based on FTC's 1965 guidelines, cited in *Report and Order,* in Docket No. 20501, FCC 76-226, March 10, 1976.

3. Ibid.

4. Notice of Proposed Rulemaking in Docket No. 20501, FCC-643, adopted May 29, 1975.

5. J. P. Fordan, "Arbitron Blows Whistle on Station Games," *Advertising Age,* 48 (May 2, 1977), 12.

6. Ibid.

7. Jim Popham, "Charting a Straight Course at the FCC," *Radioactive* 2 (November 1976), 6.

8. FCC Rules 1.526.

9. Docket No. 20550, FCC 76-426, adopted June 22, 1976; released July 26, 1976. Additional sources which discuss the EEO requirements include: Frederick W. Ford and Lee G. Lovett, "New EEO Rules," *Broadcast Management/Engineering* 12 (October 1976), 24, 26, 28; Brenda Fox, "EEO Reporting Simplified," *Radioactive* 2 (August 1976), 6; Erwin Krasnow, "Affirmative Action Means Affirmative Action," *Radioactive* 3 (July 1977), 6; "FCC Ties Up Loose Ends in Its EEO Package," *Broadcasting* 45 (July 28, 1976), 34, 36–37; Docket 20419; FCC 76-868, adopted September 15, 1976, released September 20, 1976.

10. A concise explanation is found in: Ford and Lovett, "New EEO Rules," 24.

11. "Objective" honesty is important, even if the program is deficient.

12. Can work toward improving self-imposed or FCC standards.

13. EEOC Sexual Harassment Guidelines. Additional perspectives on sexual harassment in the workplace can be found in: K. A. Thurston, "Sexual Harassment: An Organizational Perspective," *Personnel Administrator* (December 1980), 59-64; C. R. Klasoon, D. E. Thompson, and G. L. Luben, "How Defensible is Your Performance Appraisal System?," *Personnel Administrator,* (December 1980), 77-83. A summary advisory and procedural statement is NAB Counsel L-026 authored by communications attorney Wade H. Hargrove of the firm of Tharrington, Smith & Hargrove, Raleigh, North Carolina.

14. Thomas F. Baldwin and Stuart H. Surlin, "A Study of Broadcast Station License Application Exhibits on Ascertainment of Community Needs," *Journal of Broadcasting* 14 (Spring 1970), 157–70. A further perspective on the ascertainment process is found in: Stuart H. Surlin and Less Bradley, "Ascertainment through Community Leaders," *Journal of Broadcasting* 18 (Winter 1973–74), 97–107; Joseph M. Foley, "Ascertaining Ascertainment: Impact of the FCC Primer on TV Renewal Applications," *Journal of Broadcasting* 16 (Fall 1972), 387–406; Stuart H. Surlin, "Ascertainment of Community Needs by Black-Oriented Radio Stations," *Journal of Broadcasting* 16 (Fall 1972), 421–29; and Kenneth W. Hirsch and John C. Hwang, "Community Problems Measurement and Policy Setting," Department of Communication Studies, California State University, Sacramento.

15. "In the Matter of Primer on Ascertainment of Community Problems by Broadcast Applicants," *Federal Register* 36 (March 3, 1971). Three different terms tend to be used interchangeably when

ascertainment is discussed: "problems," "issues," and "needs." All three are concerned with finding out what is wrong with a community and how the broadcaster can help to correct it.

16. "Ascertainment of Community Problems by Broadcast Renewal Applicants Primer," *Federal Register* 41 (January 7, 1976), adopted in 1975; "Ascertainment of Community Problems by Noncommercial Educational Broadcast Applicants, Permittees, and Licensees," *Federal Register* 41 (March 25, 1976).

17. "Ascertainment . . . Primer," 1382.

18. The object, from management's perspective, is not only to learn what the needs of the community are but also to show that more than adequate measures have been taken to assure that these groups are represented in the survey and to avoid any question about procedure, should a license challenge develop. Also see: Frederick W. Ford and Lee G. Lovett, "New Community Ascertainment Guidelines for Broadcast Renewals," *Broadcast Management/Engineering* 12 (March 1976), 24, 28, 32, 34. Note, also, that 50 percent of community leader interviews can be conducted by nonmanagement personnel under management supervision.

19. Herschel Shosteck, "Dangers of Mail Surveys in Ascertainment Proceedings," *Journal of Broadcasting* 16 (Fall 1972), 431–39. Also: David J. LeRoy and Donald F. Ungurait, "Ascertainment Surveys: Problem Perception and Voluntary Station Contact," *Journal of Broadcasting* 19 (Winter 1975), 23–30.

20. Along with the *FCC Primer,* several other sources are available to assist broadcasters in conducting the various surveys used in ascertainment. These include: Bradley S. Greenberg, Thomas F. Baldwin, Lee Thornton, and Jack Wakshlag, *An Ascertainment Handbook for Public Broadcasting Facilities* (Washington, D.C.: Corporation for Public Broadcasting, 1975), prepared under a grant to the Departments of Communication and Telecommunication at Michigan State University. Material from the Greenberg et al. report is included in a report of the same title, copyrighted by CPB in 1976. Also, NAB stations received an NAB Legal *Memorandum,* RE: the Subject "Ascertainment of Community Needs," In June 1976.

21. Orville C. Walker, Jr., and William Rudelius, "Ascertaining Programming Needs of 'Voiceless' Community Groups," *Journal of Broadcasting* 20 (Winter 1976), 89–99.

22. The procedure for the "post-card" renewal form went into effect in 1981. Prior to that time all stations completed the longer renewal forms. Although the information and procedures did not radically change (with the exception of relaxed rules from the deregulation of radio in the same year), the FCC Field Offices as opposed to the FCC's Washington office took up much of the responsibility. It is interesting to note that at the time this increased responsibility was placed on the FCC Field Offices, the Reagan administration was actively considering trimming the budgets and role of the Field Offices of the Federal Trade Commission.

23. Frederick W. Ford and Le. G. Lovett, "Ownership Report: FCC Form 323," Broadcast Management/Engineering, 13 (December 1977), 94, 96–97. (Source: p. 96.)

24. *Ibid.*

25. 46 F.R. 13896-97 (February 24, 1981). *In the matter of Deregulation of Radio,* BC Docket No. 79-219, RM 3099, RM 3273.

26. 46 F.R. 13899 (February 24, 1981).

27. 46 F.R. 13904 (February 24, 1981).

9 cable

1. A discussion of the compromise made in the 1972 rules and an example of the issues that can confront a local change of service can be found, respectively, in: Harvey Jassem, "The Selling of the Cable TV Compromise," *Journal of Broadcasting* 17 (Fall 1973), 427–36; and Norman Felsenthal, "Cherry-Picking, Cable, and the FCC," *Journal of Broadcasting* 19 (Winter 1975), 43–53. The full citation of the *Southwestern* case is: *United States* v. *Southwestern Cable Co.,* 392 U.S. 157 (1968). The 1972 rules were issued in: *Cable Television Report and Order,* 36 FCC 2d 143 (1972). Discussion of specific cable rules can be found in: *Regulatory Developments in Cable Television* (Washington, D.C.: Federal Communications Commission, May 1977), definitions cited on pages 7–8; see also the most recent editions of the *Cable Sourcebook,* and *FCC Information Bulletin* #13632, "Cable Television," March 1979.

2. Vernone Sparkes, "Local Regulatory Agencies for Cable Television," *Journal of Broadcasting* 19 (Spring 1975), 228–29.

3. *Regulatory Developments in Cable Television* (also discussed in the *FCC Bulletin #13632*).

4. Grainger R. Barrett, "Franchising Cable TV Today," *Popular Government* (Winter 1980), 1–5, 18.

5. Center for the Analysis of Public Issues, *Crossed Wires* (Princeton, New Jersey: The Center, 1971), p. 56; Sloan Commission on Cable Communications, *On the Cable: the Television of Abundance,* Report of the Sloan Commission on Cable Communications (New York: McGraw-Hill Book Company, 1971), p. 149.

6. 47 C.F.R. 601 *et seq.*

7. Adapted from: *Statement of Account for Secondary Transmission by Cable Systems,* Forms CS/SA-1 thru 3. Licensing Division, United States Copyright Office, Washington, D.C., p. ii.

8. Ibid., p. i (italics added).

9. Ibid.

10. Ibid., p. ii.

11. *Statement of Account,* Short Form (CS/SA-1), p. iii.

12. Ibid.

13. Ibid.

14. Frederick W. Ford and Lee G. Lovett, "State Regulation of Cable Television, Part I: Current Statutes," *Broadcast Management/Engineering* 10 (June 1974), 18, 21, 50; Frederick W. Ford and Lee G. Lovett, "State Regulation of Cable TV, Part II: States with No CATV Statutes: Short-Term and Long-Term Trends," *Broadcast Management/Engineering* 30 (June 1974) 20, 21, 22.

10 the citizens' movement

1. *Office of Communication of the United Church of Christ* v. *Federal Communication Commission,* 359 F.2d 944 (D.C. Cir.), 1966.

2. Ibid.

3. Ibid.

4. Ibid.

5. "The Struggle over Broadcast Access," *Broadcasting* 40 (September 27, 1971), 24.

6. The information on the history and operation of ACT is taken from: *Actfacts,* Newtonville, Mass.: Action for Children's Television, n.d.

7. Leonard Gross, "Television under Pressure," *TV Guide* 23 (February 22, 1975), 4–7.

8. "ACT Survey of Pre-Xmas Children's TV Finds Ad Time Up, Toy Prices High," press release from ACT, September 7, 1976.

9. "ACT Seeks Injunction against Hudson TV Ads for Spiderman Vitamins," *Action for Children's Television News* 5 (Winter 1976), 1, 13.

10. "ACT Joins with NCCB vs. the Family Hour," *Action for Children's Television News* 5 (Summer 1976), 8.

11. "House Subcommittee Hears ACT Testimony and FTC's Silences," *Action for Children's Television News* 5 (Spring 1976), 8.

12. "ACT Prods the FTC for Response to 'Buried' Petitions," *Action for Children's Television News* 4 (Spring/Summer 1974), 8.

13. "Midsummer advertising hearings don't convince Rep. McDonald that self-regulation can work." *Action for Children's Television News* 5 (Fall 1975), 1, 12.

14. *Actfacts,* p. 4.

15. NCCB Progress Report (1976), p. 2.

16. The author is grateful to the Citizens' Communications Center for providing the information used in preparing this section of the chapter. Other helpful material included: "Washington's Citizens' Communications Center: Tower of Strength in Media Reform," *Access* 42 (October 1, 1976), 6–12; and Donald L. Guimary, *Citizens' Groups in Broadcasting* (New York: Praeger, 1975), pp. 133–39.

17. "Blacks Continue Renewal Pressures in Tenn., and Ind.," *Broadcasting* (July 12, 1976), 28.

18. Ibid.

19. Ibid.

20. "Yardsticks Discriminate Too?" *WICI National Newsletter* (April 1975), p. 3.

21. "Too Much Time?" *Broadcasting* 45 (October 4, 1976), 48.

22. "Religious Groups Make Plea for Community Service," *Broadcasting* 45 (May 31, 1976), 50.

23. Ibid.

24. "How Effective Is PMC?" *Public Media Center Newsletter* (1976), p. 2.

25. Nancy F. Millman, "PTA Raps Advertisers Linked to Low Quality Shows," *Advertising Age* 50 (February 19, 1979), 10.

26. Ibid.

27. Ibid.

28. "Sex and Violence in Rock Meets Resistance," *Broadcast Management/Engineering* 13 (January 1977), 6.

29. "Boycott Threatened against Lear Show," *Broadcasting* 45 (June 14, 1976), 50.

30. "Tender Loving Care" poster, Action for Children's Television, Newtonville, Mass.

31. "Guidelines for Selecting Television Programs for Children," Committee on Children's Television, 1976.

32. *KCMC, Inc.,* 19 FCC 2d 109 (1969). (KCMC, Inc., was the licensee of KTAL-TV.)

33. Ibid. (provided through the courtesy of the Office of Communication of the United Church of Christ).

34. *Bob Jones University, Inc.,* et al., 32 FCC 2d 781 (1971). Also cited in Ronald Garay, "Assess: Evolution of the Citizen Agreement," *Journal of Broadcasting* 22 (Winter 1978), 95–106.

35. Garay, "Access" p. 98.

36. Ibid. p. 99, citing: *Final Report and Order in the Matter of Formulation of Rules and Policies Relating to the Renewal of Broadcast Licenses,* 43 FCC 2d 1 (1973).

37. *Proposed Policy Statement and Notice of Proposed Rulemaking,* Re: *Agreements between Broadcast Licensees and the Public.* Docket No. 20495, FCC 75-633, 40 *Fed. Reg.* 25689 (May 29, 1975). Also cited in Frederick W. Ford and Lee G. Lovett, *Broadcast Management/Engineering* 12 (February 1976), 24, 28, 32.

38. Ibid.

39. KTAL agreement (*KCMC, Inc.,* 19 FCC 2d 109–1969).

40. Garay, "Access," p. 102.

41. Garay, "Access," p. 104.

42. "Joint Licensee in Washington, D.C., Forges Agreement with Community Group, Submits Affirmative-Action Plan to FCC," *CPB Report* 6 (October 6, 1975), 2.

43. "WNET Makes a Deal with Puerto Rican Group," *Broadcasting* 45 (June 28, 1976), 50.

44. "Chicago Stations, Citizen Group Come to Terms," *Access* 44 (November 1, 1976), 22.

45. Deanna Campbell-Robinson, Jerry F. Medler, and B. K. L. Genova, "A Consumer Model for TV Audiences: The Case of TV Violence," unpublished paper, Department of Speech, University of Oregon, 1978.

46. Anne W. Branscomb and Maria Savage, "The Broadcast Reform Movement: At the Crossroads," *Journal of Communication* 28 (Autumn 1978), 25–34.

47. Ibid., p. 34.

48. Ibid.

49. Theodore J. Schneyer and Frank Lloyd, *The Public-Interest Media Reform Movement: A Look at the Mandate and a New Agenda,* Washington, D.C., Aspen Institute for Humanistic Studies, 1977.

50. Ibid., p. 26.

51. Ibid., p. 27.

52. Branscomb and Savage, pp. 30–31.

53. "No Man," *Broadcasting,* 49 (November 10, 1980), p. 7.

11 self regulation and ethics

1. An early account of NAB's history is found in: David R. Mackey, "The Development of the National Association of Broadcasters," *Journal of Broadcasting* 1 (Fall 1957), 305–25.

2. Ibid., p. 309.

3. Ibid., p. 310.

4. Ibid., p. 315.

5. Ibid., p. 317.

6. "History of the National Association of Broadcasters" (National Association of Broadcasters, Washington, D.C., 1975), p. 2.

7. NAB By-Laws, Article 2.

8. "A Look at the Codes' Governing Boards: Individuals Who Tackle the Issues That Face the Industry," *Code News* 12 (March 1979), 1.

9. Ibid., p. 3.

10. *Radio Code* (1978), p. 23. Note also: *The Radio Code/The Television Code,* published by the Code Authority of the National Association of Broadcasters, Twenty-Second/Twenty-First Edition.

11. "Health Salon Ads Should Make It Clear Diet, Exercise Are Needed to Reduce," *Code News* 9 (August 1976), 1-2.

12. "Motion Picture Ads Reviewed by Code," *Code News* 10 (December 12, 1976), 3.

13. Donald H. McGannon, "Is the TV Code a Fraud?" *TV Guide* 25 (January 22, 1977), 11-13.

14. Ibid., p. 12.

15. Ibid., p. 13.

16. Joel Persky, "Self-Regulation of Broadcasting—Does It Exist?" *Journal of Communication* 27 (Spring 1977), 202-10.

17. Ibid., p. 208.

18. "Justice Department Brings Suit against NAB," *Code News* 12 (August 1979), 3.

19. "Another Hand of Government Strikes at NAB TV Codes," *Broadcasting* 96 (June 18, 1979), 27.

20. Code of Ethics of the American Advertising Federation, from "Professional Paper No. 6," Women in Communications, Inc., July 1976.

21. "FTC Ends Self-Regulation Probe," *Advertising Age* 50 (July 9, 1979), 8.

22. Ibid.

23. "Banks Adopt Ethics Code and Guidelines for Advertising," *Broadcasting* 45 (September 13, 1976), 35.

24. Ibid.

25. "Advertisers Feel Pressure on 'SOAP'," *Broadcasting* 46 (August 29, 1977), 22.

26. "ABC Strong in Net Survival Test; Stragglers Face Early Extinction," *Advertising Age* 48 (September 26, 1977), 2.

27. "Advertisers Feel Pressure on 'SOAP'."

28. "N.Y. State Report Urges Reforms in Ads Aimed at Children," *Broadcasting* 46 (May 9, 1977), 80-81.

29. Ibid., p. 81.

30. Ibid.

31. See, for example: John R. Bittner, "The Day the First Amendment Died," *Vital Speeches* 44 (October 15, 1977), 24-28.

32. William M. Glenn, *The Sigma Delta Chi Story* (Coral Gables, Fla.: Glade House, 1979).

33. Ibid.

34. *Broadcasting Public Proceedings* (Washington, D.C.: National Association of Broadcasters, 1972).

35. Information on AWRT is from: Warren K. Agee, "The Journalism Organization," *The Quill* 66 (November 1978), 24-25.

36. Ibid., p. 25.

37. Ibid., p. 25.

38. Ibid., p. 24.

39. Ibid., p. 28.

40. Ibid., p. 27.

41. Ibid., p. 27.

42. W. Robert Nowell, *Press Councils in the United States and Abroad* (Bloomington, Ind.: Center for New Communications, School of Journalism, Indiana University, 1979): pp. 8-9.

43. Ibid.

44. Fred Johnson, "The Minnesota Press Council: A Study of Its Effectiveness," *Mass Communications Review* (Winter 1976/77), pp. 13–18.

45. Nowell, "Press Councils," p. 8.

46. Ibid.

47. Ibid.

48. Johnson, "The Minnesota Press Council," p. 19.

12 reexamining the communications act

1. "Van Deerlin Rewrite Project Gets Kibitzed at the NATPE," *Broadcasting* 46 (February 21, 1977), 57–60.

2. Harry M. Shooshan, "Memorandum to Members of the Subcommittee on Communications," U.S. House of Representatives, 1977.

3. Karen B. Possner, "Memorandum to Subcommittee on Communications," U.S. House of Representatives, 1977.

4. National Association of Broadcasters, *NAB Initial Comments, House Communications Subcommittee Staff's Options Papers* (Washington, D.C.: NAB, May 4, 1977).

5. National Cable Television Association, *Response to Option Papers on Cable Television* (Washington, D.C.: NCTA, July 31, 1977).

6. Letter from Robert L. Schmidt to the Honorable Lionel Van Deerlin, July 13, 1977.

7. "Broadcasting's Turn in Barrel before Communications Act Review," *Broadcasting* 46 (August 1, 1977), 34–36.

8. The earliest came in June 1978, when Congressman Van Deerlin introduced House Bill #13015, which became known as the Communications Act of 1978. A revised version (H.R.3333), plus other pieces of proposed legislation, came from numerous hearings on the measure. In addition to Congressman Van Deerlin, additional sponsors of legislation have included, among others, Senator Barry Goldwater (S.622) and Ernest Hollings (S.611 and S.2827). Some felt that Van Deerlin had been upstaged by his Senate colleagues, and some felt that the bills introduced by Goldwater and Hollings were designed to head off the rewrite entirely by bogging it down in the legislative machinery. In any case, the early bills placed some powerful senators in a position to deal with industry interests. More recent bills introduced issues which were more piecemeal than a complete Communications Act overhaul. Some of these included bills by Senator Goldwater (S.601), Representative James Collins (H.R.1298), Senator Robert Packwood (S.281), and Representative James Broyhill (H.R.1801). Others active in the rewrite issue have included Representative Timothy Wirth, Senator Harrison Schmitt, Representative Al Swift, Representative George Danielson (performer royalty bill), Representative Robert Kastenmeier (copyright), Senator Harrison Williams and Representative Frank Guarini (both from New Jersey and introducing legislation to provide at least one VHF station in each state), Representative Joseph Addabbo (radio sets capable of receiving both AM and FM bands), and Senator William Proxmire (repeal of the Fairness Doctrine).

13 understanding the legal system and legal research

1. © 1980 Colleen Kristl Pauwels. Reprinted by permission of Colleen Kristl Pauwels.

Index to Cases and Legal Citations

Index to Names and Subjects